Something Abides

*Discovering the Civil War
in Today's Vermont*

Something Abides

*Discovering the Civil War
in Today's Vermont*

COUNTRYMAN PRESS

Photography by Bob Eddy,
done on behalf of the farmers who own
Cabot Creamery

Book design and composition by
Faith Hague Book Design

Front cover design by Bob Eddy, First Light
Studios

Published by The Countryman Press,
P.O. Box 748, Woodstock, VT 05091

Distributed by W. W. Norton &
Company, Inc., 500 Fifth Avenue,
New York, NY 10110

Library of Congress Cataloging-in-
Publication Data have been applied for.

Something Abides
978-0-88150-981-6

Printed in the United States of America
10 9 8 7 6 5 4 3 2 1

Dedicated to my wife, Susan Coffin,
who was ever helpful in completing this book,
and to the Civil War–era women of Vermont,
without whom Vermont could not have
done its full duty, 1861–1865.

In great deeds, something abides. On great fields, something stays. Forms change and pass; bodies disappear; but spirits linger, to consecrate ground for the vision-place of souls. And reverent men and women from afar, and generations that know us not and that we know not of, heart-drawn to see where and by whom great things were suffered and done for them, shall come to this deathless field, to ponder and dream; and lo! the shadow of a mighty presence shall wrap them in its bosom, and the power of the vision pass into their hands.

—Joshua Lawrence Chamberlain, former commander of the 20th Maine Regiment, speaking October 3, 1888, at the dedication of the Maine monuments at Gettysburg

Contents

Julian Scott's The Mounted Sentry, *in the Cedar Creek Room of the Vermont State House.*

Foreword

By Peter Shumlin, Governor of Vermont

There's no better place than Vermont, where we care so deeply about our land and its history, to still see the America of the Civil War era. And now, as we mark the war's 150th anniversary, this remarkable book, *Something Abides,* appears, identifying more than 2,500 Vermont sites associated with that terrible conflict. I don't know of any book like it, anywhere.

In his three previous books Howard Coffin rediscovered Vermont's Civil War history by describing its outsized contribution to Union victory. More than 34,000 men went to war from an 1860s population of just 315,000. Vermonters were key to Union victories at Gettysburg and at Cedar Creek, made a heroic stand at the Wilderness, and led the attack at Petersburg that finally broke Robert E. Lee's lines.

But Vermont's Civil War story is far more complex. Its war effort was sustained by a quietly determined people here at home who sent an unending supply of necessary items to soldiers and hospitals and kept homes, farms, and factories going despite the absence of many able-bodied men.

The story that emerges in *Something Abides* is full of discoveries and surprises. I had no idea, for instance, that in a Cavendish building that still stands the abolitionist John Brown once spoke, or that in a well-preserved building in West Fairlee, a woman ran a knitting business that provided much-needed income for local women.

This book reveals in great depth the complete Vermont Civil War experience. Identified here are places where families learned of the death of loved ones and welcomed home the broken and emaciated bodies of their boys from battlefields and prisons. The houses where women made goods for the war effort and the halls where abolitionists spoke and war meetings took place are all given their place in the landscape. Also included are buildings associated with the Underground Railroad, fields and streets where troops drilled, churches where antislavery societies met and where soldier funerals were held.

Anyone who takes this book with him in search of Civil War sites or just takes the time to read it cannot help but be touched by the sadness, the glory, and the incredible resolve of those four momentous years. Though Vermont was 500 miles from the battlefields (save for the day in 1864 when Confederates raided St. Albans), we learn here that the state was nonetheless in the thick of the war. Perhaps that was destined to be from the time Vermont adopted the first American constitution outlawing slavery and chose as our motto the words *Freedom and Unity.*

I hope that people everywhere with even a mild curiosity about the past will explore Vermont history with this book. Seeking out our Civil War places will, I assure you, be an intriguing journey through a truly beautiful landscape. These sites are in our hill and valley villages, in our cities, on our farms, and in our fields and woods; along the Green Mountains and the Champlain Valley—they are everywhere. Even our State House is a Civil War site, displaying treasures that include one of the greatest of all Civil War paintings and a highly important bust of Abraham Lincoln.

So I invite you to seek out Vermont's Civil War past as we honor the conflict's sesquicentennial. All you need is a Vermont state road map and a copy of *Something Abides: Discovering the Civil War in Today's Vermont.* I think you will be amazed.

Foreword

By James M. McPherson, Civil War historian,
winner of the Pulitzer Prize for *Battle Cry of Freedom*

Vermont's contribution to the Union cause in the Civil War was greater, in proportion to its population, than that of almost any other Northern state. The first Vermont Brigade had more men killed and mortally wounded in action than any other Union brigade. Vermont was at or near the top among Northern states in the percentage of its men who served and the percentage of men of military age who lost their lives. Three of the eighteen elite sharpshooter companies in the Army of the Potomac were from Vermont. At a factory in Windsor, Vermont, that is today the American Precision Museum, some fifty thousand rifles were manufactured during the war, but even more important, about half of all rifles and revolvers for Union armies were turned out by machine tools produced in this factory.

Today we can visit many of the battlefields in the South where Vermont soldiers fought. At Crampon's Gap in Maryland, at the Wilderness, Spotsylvania, Cold Harbor, Winchester, Cedar Creek, and Petersburg in Virginia, and at Gettysburg in Pennsylvania, we can see where Vermonters played key roles in achieving victory or preventing defeat for Union armies. Many battlefield guidebooks and maps help us to understand those battles. But until now there was no guidebook to take us to sites in Vermont itself associated with the Civil War. Howard Coffin has remedied that deficiency with this stunning volume. Nothing like *Something Abides* exists for any other state. It offers a cornucopia of historical riches for history tourists. It takes us to buildings where recruiting meetings were held, town squares where recruits were mustered, factories where war materiel was manufactured, hospitals and hospital sites where wounded soldiers convalesced, homes and home sites where soldiers of all ranks lived and some came home to die, cemeteries where thousands of Vermont veterans are buried, and much else.

In recent years a great deal of scholarship on the Civil War has focused on the home front—in the North as well as in the South. The impact of the war on families and communities, and the roles that the 90 percent of the population who were civilians played in the war effort is finally receiving its due from historians. But as with the stories of military campaigns and battles, merely reading about them is not enough. You have to go *where* they happened to understand and appreciate fully *how* and *why* they happened. In his writing Howard Coffin has taken us to Gettysburg and the Wilderness and Cedar Creek and Petersburg and other fields where Vermonters fought and died. And now he takes us to hundreds of places in Vermont where these soldiers came from and where their families and friends worked to support them and hoped, often in vain, that they would return home safely.

Something Abides took six years and 150,000 miles of travel to compile. The result is commensurate with the effort. It is a *tour de force*.

Preface

On a bright winter morning in 2006, I drove into Windsor, Vermont, to begin research on what would become *Something Abides*. I passed the Constitution House where Vermont had adopted the first American constitution that outlawed slavery and proceeded along Main Street to the American Precision Museum, located in a factory that produced fifty thousand rifle-muskets for the Union cause. Later, I would learn that the making of about half the Union armies' rifle-muskets and pistols could, in some way, be traced to that building. Six years later, I drove into the farm town of Bakersfield, its woods and fields all early spring green against a backdrop of the Green Mountains, pure white from a late snowstorm, rising into a blue Vermont sky. Bakersfield was the last of all the Vermont towns I visited to research this book. And there I found a house in which a Vermont captain, who was shot while leading his men at Gettysburg, had died a long and painful death.

Through six years of travels throughout Vermont, seeking Civil War sites, I received help from hundreds of people. Their interest made each morning of setting off to still another town a moment of pleasure and high anticipation. Of course, there were days of sleet and snow that turned me back, and I soon learned that seeking Vermont Civil War sites is a spring, summer, and fall job. Winters were for research, for libraries and other repositories. Then, when work on a town seemed complete, the phone would ring,

and someone in Belvidere, or Vernon, or Cambridge, had found another site. So back I would go again, sometimes again and again.

But in the end, I found hundreds and hundreds of Vermont sites, though I know there are many more that await discovery. After all, more Vermonters are becoming interested in the Civil War, delving into town and family history. Yet, as I ended research on this book, I knew full well that I had done it just in time. So many Vermonters who care deeply about history are getting older, as is the author. Too often on arriving at a town clerk's office, I was informed that the person I needed to see, the one who really knew the town's history, had, sadly, just passed away. But here is what I found. It's a book about sites, not a book of town histories. A site had to be identified for its history to be included. I am sure there are mistakes and omissions in the book, particularly because the project was far more massive than I had anticipated, and I had to deal with daunting amounts of material. Research files and folders filled a room and more of my home. The task became so enormous that, to everyone who reads this, I ask they contact me with corrections, and suggestions, for future editions. I am in the Montpelier phone book and online with a Web site.

I think this book may have been needed for several reasons. Principal among them was, as I have indicated, a desire to find these places while they are still findable, while people still exist who know where to look. But the primary benefit of all this might be for the young. Young people need to be interested in history. Our nation needs a sense of history for our democracy to function effectively. As has been so often been said, those who do not understand history are destined to repeat its mistakes. The Civil War was all about correcting great American mistakes. It saved a nation that said it was dedicated to freedom and attempted to make real its founding premise that all men are created equal. From what I have observed, no subject interests young people in history like the Civil War. And that interest may best be piqued by associating events with sites.

Also, since I believe the Civil War was the great event in the nation's, and Vermont's, history, it is important to preserve the sites associated with it. I hope that this book will serve as a preservation tool. Think more than twice about demolishing that house where a soldier lived, that hall where a war meeting took place, that building where a fugitive slave was given refuge, that place where women met to make items for the war effort.

Preservation was very much in my mind when, twenty years ago, I decided to write a book about Vermont in the Civil War and took that idea to Countryman Press in my hometown of Woodstock. That resulted in a lunch with Peter Jennison, who was to become my editor and dear friend. I told Peter that I had in mind a book on Civil War sites in Vermont, through which I would tell the state's Civil War story. Peter heard me out and said, "What you really want to do is to write a history of Vermont in the Civil War. We'll publish *that*." I did, and they did. Several years later, Peter presented me, at Christmas, with a copy of his latest edition of *Vermont: An Explorer's Guide*. The inscription:

For Howard Coffin,
Who doesn't need it.

Well, I now have written that book Peter rejected. And I wish he were here to receive a copy. Sadly, he went to his reward some time ago. But after six years of visiting every town, city, and gore in the state, traveling some 150,000 miles, and going through three cars, I rather think his inscription now really rings true. And, once again, his beloved Countryman Press is publishing a Howard Coffin book.

In it, the reader will note that monuments may be found throughout our state commemorating Vermont's outsized contribution to Union victory. Among them, markers stand at the birthplaces of two of our great Civil War heroes. In Georgia, a big granite stone honors George Stannard who, at Gettysburg, may well have changed the course of world history when he ordered his 2nd Vermont Brigade to attack the right flank of Pickett's Charge. In the hills of Bethel Gilead, a more modest stone honors Stephen Thomas, whose 1864 heroics had something important to do with seizing the vitally important Shenandoah Valley and its golden abundance from

Robert E. Lee's hungry men at Petersburg. They are important Civil War sites as is the house facing the Townshend green where lived Clarina Howard Nichols, who fought hard as any Vermonter, with words and deeds, against slavery.

Throughout the state survive halls where war meetings were held and abolitionists spoke, fields where soldiers drilled, houses where women gathered after a long day's work to make items for the soldiers. Also identified here are hundreds of homes from which Vermonters went to war, some to become heroes, some to die, some to come home and rise on their war records in public life. But also there are many houses from which men went to war, served, then came home to resume previously quiet lives.

Those mainly very young men had gone off into an existence totally foreign to them, far beyond the familiar hills and fields, where they got yelled at, were pushed and shoved, and were sometimes forced to live at their very limits. Off there in the war zone far to the south, they lugged impossibly heavy loads on too long marches, endured freezing and sweltering camps, ate disgusting food, then found themselves amid the din and gore of desperate battle. Then, hopefully, they came home and got on with things, stoic as Vermonters of the time were supposed to be.

But back in their so longed-for homes, deep in the night, or in the quiet of an afternoon break from the hayfield, surely their thoughts often went back to those years when they, and all they knew, were touched by war. Surely at such times, many softly and privately shed a tear for those old times and comrades lost. Then rising and stretching aging muscles, did they not glance with a wink through a lace-curtained window at the familiar fields of home?

In such settings that can be associated with the state of Vermont's remarkable Civil War history, something remains. Visiting them, on many occasions, I was reminded of the words Joshua Lawrence Chamberlain spoke at Gettysburg in 1886—in dedicating the Maine monuments: "In great deeds, something abides," Chamberlain said. "On great fields, something stays. Forms change and pass, bodies disappear, but spirits linger, to consecrate the ground for the vision-place of souls. And reverent men and women from afar, and generations that know us not and that we know not of, heart drawn to see where and by whom great things were suffered and done my them, shall come to this deathless field, to ponder and dream, and lo! The shadow of a mighty presence shall wrap them in its bosom, and the power of the vision pass into their souls."

Using This Book

Before going in search of Vermont Civil War sites, please read the brief Vermont Civil War history at the book's beginning. Having done so, most of what the people identified in the book did during the war should become clear.

Take with you an "Official Vermont Road Map," one of the best maps in all the fifty states. And it's free. By looking carefully, and with the book's help, sites can be found. Be aware that hills and mountains often separate apparently nearby places and driving times can be surprisingly long.

Vermont's Civil War sites are everywhere, on back roads, at the ends of roads, by busy downtowns, at crossroads, in store blocks, on islands, in remote woods, in fields, in churches and cemeteries, and on college campuses and school grounds. As you go in search of them, be ever respectful of private property. Most sites can be adequately seen without leaving one's vehicle. Please observe no-trespassing signs, and treat any property on which they are located as land treasured by others.

Seek them in spring, summer, and fall.

I found that hunting for Civil War sites in winter is virtually impossible. It is too dangerous an undertaking, with icy roads and sudden storms. Also, too much is hidden by snow.

When on the search and frustrated at possibly confusing directions, I generally found Vermonters friendly and most willing to give advice. Town clerks are also great sources of information who welcome visitors.

Drive carefully! Driving and looking for things can be a dangerous combination. Many of the sites are on very narrow, steep, and winding roads. Beware.

Above all, enjoy. And if you find things I missed, let me know. I hope you will emerge from your quest as amazed as I at the scope of the Civil War's impact on this state and at the remarkable extent of Vermont's participation. You will find, in traveling the highways and byways of this state, that it is larger than it looks. So was Vermont's contribution to Union victory in the war to defeat the evil of slavery and preserve the Union.

chapter one

Vermont Civil War History

Cows still graze the high Vermont field, with its view far along the Green Mountains, where, more than two centuries ago, a man of peace had a mystical experience that foretold the Civil War. Quaker minister Joseph Hoag, not long before he died in 1846, wrote a memoir in which he recalled a late summer day in 1806. While alone in the fields, he remembered that the sun shone clear but that suddenly "a mist eclipsed the brightness of its shining." He wrote, "And I heard a voice from heaven say, 'This that thou seest, which dims the brightness of the sun, is a sign of the present and coming times. I took the forefathers of this country from a land of oppression; I planted them here among the people of the forest. I sustained them . . . and they became a numerous people; but they have now become proud and lifted up, and have forgotten Me."

And the voice said, "I have taken qui-etude from the land and suffered a dividing spirit to come among them." That spirit 'broke out like a volcano' and 'set the country in an uproar.'" An "abundance of blood" was shed in the course of a conflict, and that the southern states lost their power, and slavery "was annihilated from their borders."

Overlooking the field in which Hoag's vision occurred is the farmhouse where the Quaker preacher and his wife, Huldah, gave shelter to fugitive slaves. And in a far corner of the field is a Quaker graveyard where the Hoags are buried, close by two Quaker men who went against their peace-loving faith and fought in the Civil War. The field is one of hundreds on hundreds of sites associated with the Civil War that remain in Vermont, a state that has long held a high regard for human freedom and for preservation. Vermont was born with freedom words, just over a quarter century before Hoag's experience. It officially came into being the better part of a century before more than 34,000 Vermonters donned Union uniforms and went south to fight for a "new birth of freedom" and the beloved Union. Surely by the time the war ended four years later, every Vermonter, every Vermont farm, home, and field, had been in some way touched by the Civil War.

But now go back to a mighty day in 1777 and the words: "All men are born free and independent and have natural and inalienable rights." That statement was adopted by delegates from the land between New York and the Connecticut River who convened in a Windsor tavern in July of that year to form an independent state called Vermont. There they wrote a document that became the Vermont Constitution, the first in America to outlaw slavery. It only freed men eighteen and older and women over twenty-one, but still it was a significant step forward on mankind's long road to human freedom.

Fourteen years after the Windsor convention, Vermont became the United States of America's fourteenth state, and in subsequent years, its reputation as a freedom bastion was steadily enhanced.

The state's attitude toward slavery was eloquently expressed by Judge Theophilus Harrington, who told a New York man,

seeking the return to his ownership of a woman slave spirited away to Vermont, that he would accept nothing less as of her ownership than "a bill of sale from God almighty."

To Bennington in 1828 came William Lloyd Garrison where for five months he published an antislavery newspaper, the *Journal of the Times.* The Vermont Anti-Slavery Society was founded in 1834, one year after the American Anti-Slavery Society came into being in Philadelphia. The first local antislavery society organized in Jamaica in 1833, and soon, there were ninety such organizations throughout the state.

Garrison and fellow abolitionists Frederick Douglass, Wendell Phillips, Samuel May, and others decried the evils of slavery, speaking in many towns, though not always receiving warm welcomes. All the while, the Underground Railroad was active in Vermont, helping escapees from servitude make their way to freedom in Canada, as the state rebelled against the fugitive slave laws that required officials in all states to assist in returning slaves to their masters.

As Congress debated slavery's expansion into the western territories, the Vermont legislature and individual citizens sent petition after petition to the state's congressional delegation opposing such measures as the Kansas Nebraska Act and Missouri Compromise. In the U.S. House of Representatives, Vermont's William Slade spoke in defiance of the so-called gag rule that barred the discussion of slavery-related matters. Risking censorship, Slade declared that "the right to hold men as goods and chattel . . . should cease and be discontinued instantly and forever."

Clearly, as Vermonters were well aware, the possibility that the nation could go to war within itself over the great issue of slavery was looming ever larger as the nineteenth century passed its midpoint. Then in 1860, when Abraham Lincoln faced Brandon native Stephen Douglas in the presidential election, the matter of slavery's expansion was, in effect, put to a national referendum. Green Mountain State voters went for the Illinois Republican, over the native son candidate of a fractured Democrat Party, by a margin of almost six to one.

Yet with the nation at war's brink, like most northern states, Vermont was poorly prepared militarily. In the summer of 1860, when the governor ordered a militia muster at Montpelier, only nine hundred men appeared. State records listed just 957 aged muskets, six cannons, and 503 old Colt pistols as its military property.

Lincoln took office as the nation's sixteenth president in March 1861, and southern states began seceding to form the Confederate States of America. War erupted April 12, and Vermont governor Erastus Fairbanks summoned the state legislature into an extra session on April 23. Speaking in the House of Representatives, Fairbanks asked legislators to appropriate a half million dollars to begin the war effort. After brief deliberations, a war fund of one million dollars was approved.

Primarily to protect Washington, Lincoln called on the country for 75,000 soldiers. In response, Vermont sent south the 782-man 1st Vermont Regiment. It served just ninety days and fought in the war's first battle, Big Bethel, a small, confused affair in which Woodstock's Colonel Peter Washburn led 500 Vermonters into action.

The 2nd Vermont Regiment was soon in the war zone, enlisted for three years as part of the Army of the Potomac, the Union's largest army. On July 21, the 2nd engaged in the Civil War's first major battle, fought along a Virginia stream called Bull Run. The Vermonters were briefly in action, on the exposed right of the Union line. Private Urban Woodbury (a future governor) was among the sixty-six Vermont casualties, becoming the first Vermonter in the war to lose a limb.

Soon joining the Army of the Potomac, commanded by George Brinton McClellan, were the 3rd, 4th, 5th, and 6th Vermont regiments and the 1st Vermont Cavalry. The four new infantry regiments, along with the 2nd Vermont, were formed into the 1st Vermont Brigade, a favor granted against War Department policy by General McClellan to his friend William Farrar Smith, brigade commander. The Old Brigade, as it became known, was the only Union brigade composed entirely of regiments from one state to serve throughout the war, and it became part of the Army of the Potomac's 6th Corps.

One brigade member, 3rd Vermont private William Scott of Groton, soon became the most famous private in the Union armies when he was sentenced to death for sleeping at his sentry post near Washington. The "Sleeping Sentinel" was spared a firing squad at the last minute, with Abraham Lincoln's consent.

The Vermont Brigade spent the war's first winter at Camp Griffin, across the Potomac River from Washington, part of a vast Union encampment. Vermonters there took sick en masse, with hundreds dying from smallpox, typhus, and other contagious diseases.

Winter finally ended, and in April 1862, McClellan moved his 100,000-man army by ship to the Peninsula of Virginia, in a move against the Confederate capital of Richmond. The Vermont Brigade suffered its first heavy casualties in a skirmish at Lee's Mill on April 16. McClellan ordered the Vermonters to wade the dammed Warwick River and attack Rebel fortifications on the far side. The Vermonters captured some earthworks but, unsupported and with enemy reinforcements arriving, were forced to retreat. "The water fairly boiled around us with bullets," a Vermont soldier wrote, as 44 members of the brigade were killed and 148 wounded. Among the slain was the Sleeping Sentinel. Musician Julian Scott (later to become a famed Civil War artist), sixteen, who entered the water to bring back wounded was later awarded a Medal of Honor.

McClellan's army moved slowly to the outskirts of Richmond, where the Confederates struck. On June 29, with the Army of the Potomac in retreat, at Savage's Station the 5th Vermont took the heaviest losses of any Vermont regiment in a single day, moving across a field against Rebel infantry with artillery support. The Equinox Guards, a Manchester company, was decimated, and among the dead were four brothers of the Cummings family, a brother-in-law, and a cousin. Another brother died years later, apparently as the result of a wound sustained that same day. Probably no other family North or South suffered such a loss.

Vermonters fought well at White Oak Swamp, protecting the Union withdrawal. Meanwhile back home, Frederick Holbrook of Brattleboro had taken office as Vermont's second Civil War governor. He asked the War Department for permission to open soldier hospitals in Vermont, believing that the sick and wounded would recuperate best back home. After months of discussions, Holbrook was authorized to create medical facilities at the Brattleboro drill field, where many regiments assembled, and on a hilltop overlooking Montpelier. He was also allowed to expand the federal hospital at Burlington. Later in the war, all three facilities were filled to capacity.

Also at home, the legislature elected Peter Washburn, veteran of Big Bethel, as adjutant general. Washburn established the office in his hometown, making Woodstock the administrative center of Vermont's war effort—in effect, the Pentagon of Vermont.

Though Vermont generally retained a look of peace, the war was having an increasing impact on the people at home. Soldier funerals were becoming frequent occurrences, and trains from the war zone carried more and more sick and wounded soldiers back into the state. Women organized in most towns to make items for loved ones at war and for the hospitals. As the holidays approached, large boxes containing turkeys, maple sugar, and other treats were shipped south. Woolen mills produced blankets, uniform cloth, and other items for the army. A factory in Windsor manufactured thousands of rifle-muskets, using a pioneering precision manufacturing process. Indeed, by war's end, half the rifle-muskets and pistols made for the Union armies could, in some way, be traced to the Windsor facility. With so many able-bodied men at war, women, young people, and the elderly operated the state's thirty thousand farms. Some women worked in factories. "Vermont women enlisted for the duration," a Vermont historian later wrote.

As Washington asked for more and more troops, Governor Holbrook soon ordered the 7th, 8th, 9th, 10th, and 11th regiments formed. The 7th and 8th made long sea voyages around the tip of Florida to join Benjamin Butler's forces, which had captured New Orleans. At his headquarters near that city, Colonel John Phelps insisted that black men be allowed to enlist, saying, "They might become a beneficent element of government power." Butler refused to back Phelps, who resigned in disgust. The 8th Vermont, commanded by Stephen Thomas of West Fairlee, had several skirmishes with Rebels in the bayou country of Louisiana. In one, Thomas steadied his men saying, "Stand firm. Old Vermont is looking at you." The regiment soon joined the Union assault on Port Hudson, a fortification overlooking the Mississippi south of Vicksburg.

The 9th Vermont, under George Stannard, was forced to surrender in total on September 15, 1862, at Harpers Ferry, just before the Battle of Antietam. The 9th spent the winter in a Union prison camp near Chicago, until an exchange was negotiated for a like number of Confederate prisoners, and the regiment returned to service. The Vermont Brigade fought at South Mountain on September 14, 1862, helping clear the way for the Army of the Potomac to converge on Lee's army, occupying high ground above Antietam Creek near Sharpsburg, Maryland. On September 17, the bloodiest single day of the war, the brigade fought only briefly in the Battle of Antietam. That indecisive Union victory, which stopped Robert E. Lee's first invasion of the North, prompted Lincoln to issue his Preliminary Emancipation Proclamation. It declared that all slaves in states still then rebellious would be freed as of January 1, 1863.

The 10th Vermont Regiment, like the Vermont Brigade, became part of the Potomac Army's 6th Corps. The 1,500-man 11th Vermont, largest regiment the state sent to war, became an artillery unit when assigned to Washington's defenses, manning forts north of the city.

The 1st Vermont Cavalry saw extensive action early in the war, battling cavalry attached to Stonewall Jackson in the Shenandoah Valley. Then it fought guerrillas under John Singleton Mosby south and west of Washington.

Fighting in 1862 ended with the bloody repulse at Fredericksburg, Virginia, along the Rappahannock River. The Vermont Brigade missed the suicidal daylong attacks ordered by Ambrose Burnside against Marye's Heights and the Sunken Roads but still sustained 150 casualties, fighting south of the city. The battered

Army of the Potomac then went into winter camp at Falmouth, across the Rappahannock from Fredericksburg, with pickets often in plain sight of Rebel outposts on the river's south bank.

In the summer of 1862, with the war going poorly for the Union, President Lincoln called on the states to furnish his armies with 300,000 soldiers to serve for just nine months. Vermont's quota was 4,898 to fill the new 12th, 13th, 14th, 15th, and 16th Vermont regiments. Those five units constituted the 2nd Vermont Brigade, commanded by dashing and careless Edwin Stoughton of Bellows Falls, the Union's youngest brigadier general. The brigade went south in October and spent the winter patrolling the farm country of northern Virginia. Their generally quiet winter was interrupted the night of March 8, 1863, when Confederate cavalry, in Union uniforms, rode into Fairfax Courthouse, where Stoughton had his headquarters well away from his brigade's main lines. John Mosby, the famed guerrilla fighter, entered Stoughton's bedroom and spirited the sleepy young general into the night, a prisoner of war. Lincoln said in disgust, "I can always make another brigadier general, but I sure hate to lose all those horses." To the 2nd Brigade as commander came quiet, competent George Stannard, formerly of the 9th Vermont.

Fighting in the spring of 1863 commenced at Chancellorsville, Virginia, when new commander Joseph Hooker marched the Army of the Potomac up the Rappahannock River, intent on outmaneuvering Robert E. Lee. In the resulting fierce fighting, Lee and Stonewall Jackson routed the Union army and sent it in retreat across the river. The Vermont Brigade made a heroic stand to protect the retreat of the 6th Corps. Lee promptly put his victorious army on the march north, all the way into southern Pennsylvania. The Army of the Potomac, now led by George Meade, moved north, keeping between the Rebels and Washington.

The inevitable collision came on July 1 at a Pennsylvania college town where many roads met—Gettysburg. At the end of that day's fighting, the Army of the Potomac was forced back to the high ground south and east of town. The 2nd Vermont Brigade, now part of the army's 1st Corps, reached the field the evening of July 1, after a six-day march of 120 miles. Near Gettysburg, two of the Brigade's five regiments were ordered to guard wagon trains, thus depriving Stannard of two-fifths of his fighting force.

On July 2, the Confederates attacked from the south, along the Emmitsburg Road. The presence of Rebel troops menacing the southern end of the fishhook-shaped Union line had been detected before the assault by Union sharpshooters, including Vermonters. The Green Mountain State sent three sharpshooter companies to the union armies, having more marksmen in the federal ranks per capita than any other state. When the fighting began in late afternoon, the Vermont long riflemen helped to slow the initial onslaught.

Fighting erupted at Devil's Den, Little Round Top, the Wheat Field, and the Peach Orchard. At evening, the Confederates made a final try at breaking the

Union line, and Stannard's undermanned brigade was called into action atop Cemetery Ridge. The Vermonters quickly recaptured a Union battery, then Company A of the 13th Vermont advanced to seize eighty Confederates firing from a house along the Emmitsburg Road.

July 3 became the most famous day of the Civil War. At 3 PM, Lee attacked the Union center, aiming for a breakthrough at the now-famous Clump of Trees on Cemetery Ridge. After a two-hour artillery duel, some twelve thousand Rebel infantrymen moved across the mile-wide valley from Seminary Ridge in what history would know as Pickett's Charge. As the assault neared Cemetery Ridge, its southern end bore directly toward the 2nd Vermont Brigade's three regiments. As the Vermonters rose to fire, the attack suddenly swung north, crossing the Vermonters' front. In minutes, the Confederates were converging on the Clump of Trees. Recognizing a golden opportunity, and leaving his 14th Regiment in place, Stannard ordered the 13th and 16th regiments to attack the Rebel assault. Obeying his order to "change front forward on first company," the two regiments' nine hundred men swung out from Cemetery Ridge to face the exposed Rebel right flank. The Vermonters unleashed a dozen heavy volleys, inflicting severe losses as they moved ever closer to their nearly defenseless foes. The flank of Pickett's Charge crumpled. As his men rounded up prisoners, 16th Vermont commander Wheelock Veazey noticed a second Confederate attack advancing toward the 14th Vermont. Realigning his regiment, Veazey then pivoted it 180 degrees to face south, and struck the 1,500 Confederates in the flank. The second attack was routed, and by 4 PM, Lee's final try for victory at Gettysburg had ended in a bloody repulse.

Near Round Top after the repulse of Pickett's Charge, Brigadier General Judson Kilpatrick ordered a cavalry attack on the southern end of the Confederate line. Despite protests from subordinates that the venture was suicidal, it went forward with Major William Wells of Waterbury one of its leaders. Some three hundred members of the 1st Vermont Cavalry were among the blue-clad horsemen, who briefly broke through Rebel lines. The Vermonters lost sixty men, and the attack accomplished nothing.

The 2nd Vermont Brigade, its nine months' enlistments having expired days after the battle, returned to Vermont and a heroes' welcome. Also present at Gettysburg was the 1st Vermont Brigade, having arrived at evening of the second day. The brigade led the 6th Corps' march from northern Virginia to Gettysburg, covering more than 30 miles on the final day in high southern Pennsylvania heat. Hastening his men toward the battlefield, corps commander John Sedgwick gave his famous command, "Put the Vermonters in the lead and keep the column well closed." On the field, the brigade protected the Union line's southern end but did no fighting.

In the aftermath of the war's most costly battle, more than twenty thousand wounded Union and Confederate soldiers lay on the bloody Gettysburg field. Assigned to supervise their care was Major

Henry Janes of Waterbury, an experienced army surgeon. Janes ably handled the most challenging assignment ever given an American surgeon. On November 17, 1863, when Abraham Lincoln dedicated the Gettysburg National Cemetery, Janes was honored with a seat on the speakers' platform with the president.

On the Fourth of July 1863, a day after Gettysburg, along the Mississippi River another major Union triumph was achieved as Confederates manning fortified Vicksburg surrendered to Ulysses Grant. Then on July 7, the last major Rebel stronghold along the big river was forced to surrender. The 8th Vermont had been part of the besieging army that finally forced Port Hudson's capitulation. Hearing that the Mississippi bastions had fallen, Abraham Lincoln said, "The father of waters once again flows unvexed to the sea."

The Army of the Potomac camped during the winter of 1863–1864 at Brandy Station, along the upper Rappahannock, in northern Virginia. While that army rested, far to the south, in Florida, a vicious little battle took place on February 20 near the railroad town of Olustee. One of the regiments involved was the famed 54th Massachusetts, a "colored" outfit organized by Robert Gould Shaw. Vermont blacks were in the 54th's ranks at Olustee, as the regiment fought well in protecting the Union retreat after a Confederate victory. Not until 1863, after Congress had authorized the use of black troops, were black regiments formed. Eventually, 200,000 African American men served in the Union forces. In his book on Vermont African Americans in

the Civil War, James Fuller states that 113 black Vermonters wore Union blue, out of a statewide population of 709. Thus, a higher percentage of black men served the Union from Vermont than white men.

In March 1864, Ulysses Grant arrived at Brandy Station, having been appointed by Lincoln to command all the Union armies. Grant decided to make his headquarters with the Army of the Potomac, led by Gettysburg victor George Meade. That army's spring offensive began in the darkness of May 3 and 4, as the army moved south against Lee's Army of Northern Virginia.

The clash came south of the Rapidan River, as Lee struck the long federal columns in a dense second-growth forest known as the Wilderness. At midday on May 5, Grant and Meade learned that the vital intersection of the Orange Plank Road and the Brock Road was undefended. To prevent the army from being cut in two, George Washington Getty's 6th Corps division, including the 2,800 men of the Old Brigade, was rushed to the point of danger. Getty's men arrived just in time, stopping a Confederate advance within yards of the intersection. At 4 PM, orders came for Getty to advance. The Vermont Brigade moved west on the south side of the Plank Road, entering the thick greenery of the Wilderness. Within moments, a massive volley exploded from a hidden Rebel line that, according to Vermont Brigade commander Lewis Addison Grant, felled hundreds of his men. The fighting went on into darkness, with the Vermonters losing 1,000 men, either killed, wounded, or captured. Next morning, the Vermonters were part of a heavy

Union attack that drove the Confederates nearly a mile. The Vermonters held an advanced position until they saw Rebels moving toward their rear, the result of a surprise flank attack launched by James Longstreet. The Vermonters withdrew to entrenchments along the Brock Road, where they helped fight off repeated assaults. By the time the two battered armies moved south on May 7, the Old Brigade had suffered 1,234 casualties at the Battle of the Wilderness. But the Potomac army was intact.

The fighting moved south to Spotsylvania Courthouse, a crossroads village on the road to Richmond, where Grant faced Confederate entrenchments. The Vermont Brigade was part of the four-thousand-man Upton's Attack on May 10 that briefly penetrated the Confederate lines. Based on its success, Grant launched a massive assault May 12 on a vulnerable portion of the Rebel works known as the Mule Shoe Salient. The result was a twenty-four-hour battle, in a steady rain, with the two armies at the Bloody Angle separated only by an earthwork. Some Vermont soldiers briefly fired from atop those fortifications down into the Confederate ranks. The brutal, indecisive fighting at Spotsylvania cost Vermont 350 casualties.

Joining the Vermont Brigade at Spotsylvania in mid-May were the 1,500 men of the 11th Vermont. That regiment had served in the Washington forts, until Ulysses Grant turned it and many other artillery regiments into infantry units. The addition of the big 11th nearly made up for the Old Brigade's losses thus far in the Overland Campaign.

From the Wilderness and Spotsylvania, Grant sent his wagon trains filled with wounded into the battered town of Fredericksburg, already the scene of two major battles. There, virtually every building became a Union hospital. On learning that one thousand wounded Vermonters were at Fredericksburg, Vermont governor John Gregory Smith rounded up fifteen Vermont doctors and arrived within days. Smith and Vermont congressman Portus Baxter worked as nurses alongside the physicians who, a Vermonter soldier said, "came like angels of mercy."

Word of the Overland Campaign's heavy casualties reached Vermont by mid-May, and front pages of the state's newspapers were filled with the names of dead and wounded Vermonters. Trains bearing wounded soon were coming north, to fill the state's military hospitals.

The relentless calls from Washington for more troops caused Vermont towns to offer bounty payments to meet enlistment quotas, some reaching $1,000. More and more war meetings were held, patriotic gatherings with speeches and music, often staged in town halls. Prominent Vermont soldiers, home from the war or on leave, spoke to encourage the men to sign up.

At the front, the Overland Campaign moved on, to the North Anna River, then to the country crossroads of Cold Harbor half a dozen miles from Richmond. Ulysses Grant launched a preliminary attack there on June 1, to position his army. On June 3, he sent forward a massive assault along a 6-mile front, the result being a bloody repulse before carefully prepared Confederate defenses. Some seven thousand Union soldiers fell in minutes. After nearly two weeks of trench warfare, Grant suddenly moved south, stealing a march on Lee. Crossing the James River by boat and pontoon bridge, Grant brought his army in on the vital railroad center of Petersburg, 25 miles south of Richmond. But Grant failed to break the Petersburg lines, beginning a siege that would last nine months.

Back home in Vermont, more and more families were caring for sick and wounded men. Despite the rising toll, in Rutland, thousands turned out in the rain to greet the famous entertainer Tom Thumb and his bride. Fair time was nearing, and though Vermont had sent hundreds of mounts to the armies, the horses on display at the Windsor County Fair were judged the finest ever seen there.

On June 23, Grant ordered the 6th Corps to strike one of the railroad lines supplying Petersburg. Lee met the attack in strength, and along the Weldon Railroad, 1,600 Union soldiers were cut off. Among them were 401 Vermonters, most of whom ended up in the infamous Rebel prison at Andersonville, Georgia, where more than half of them were dead within six months.

On July 30, Grant tried a direct assault on the Petersburg lines, as Pennsylvania soldiers tunneled under the Rebel works and exploded a massive gunpowder charge. An assault directed at the gaping crater in the enemy lines failed after heavy fighting. The newest, smallest, and last Vermont regiment to join the Army of the Potomac, the 17th Vermont, was the only Vermont unit in the Battle of the Crater taking heavy casualties.

To relieve the pressure on his Petersburg lines, Lee sent 15,000 men under Jubal Early west into the Shenandoah Valley. From there, Early moved down the valley in an attempt to invade Washington. He was met on July 9 along the Monocacy River near Frederick, Maryland, by six thousand hastily assembled federal troops, including James Ricketts's Division of the 6th Corps. The 10th Vermont Regiment fought bravely in the Battle of the Monocacy. A detachment of 10th Vermont skirmishers led by Captain George Davis fought for several hours on the Rebel side of the river, finally running under fire across a high railroad bridge to Union lines. Later, a Vermont soldier described the final victorious Rebel assault: "The long swaying lines of grey in perfect cadence with glistening guns and brasses." Early was victorious, but the battle delayed his progress toward Washington a key full day.

As Early resumed his advance, the bulk of the 6th Corps, including the Old Brigade, took ships to Washington. Abraham Lincoln was at the Potomac River docks when the Vermonters arrived, and an officer apologized because no high-ranking officer was present to greet him. Lincoln responded, "I did not come to see generals. I came to see the Vermont Brigade." In a brisk fight at Fort Stevens, within sight of the capitol dome, Early was turned away. Also sent to defend Washington was the 19th Corps, just arrived from Louisiana, including the 8th Vermont. The 6th and 19th Corps were made part of a 35,000-man army, led by Philip Sheridan, and were assigned the task of defeating Early's army in the

Shenandoah Valley, the famed Bread Basket of the Confederacy.

While Union and Confederate troops battled in the heat of a southern summer, to Manchester in southwestern Vermont in 1863 and 1864 came the nation's first lady to vacation in the cooler mountains. Mary Todd Lincoln rented accommodations for several days at the Equinox House; her son Robert, a Harvard student, accompanied her. Before returning to the White House in 1864, Mrs. Lincoln made a reservation for both herself and the president.

In the war zone, the first major fight of Sheridan's Valley Campaign came at Winchester on September 19, 1864. After an hours-long stalemate, the right of the Union battle line began to drive the Confederates, after 8th Vermont commander Stephen Thomas personally led an attack. "Remember Ethan Allen and we'll drive them to hell," Thomas told his men. "Come on old Vermont." As the infantry advanced, Union cavalry, including the 1st Vermont, swept down from the north, and the battle known as Third Winchester became a resounding Union victory. Three days later, Sheridan again defeated Early at Fisher's Hill, employing a surprise flank attack that spared the Vermonters heavy casualties, as they joined in a frontal assault. The victorious federals pushed Early 50 miles up the Shenandoah Valley. On returning, Sheridan's army burned the valley's farms, crops, and mills, finally coming to rest on high ground north of Cedar Creek.

Jubal Early, though twice defeated, was soon reinforced by Lee and, in the predawn of October 19, 1864, quietly crossed Cedar Creek to strike Sheridan's army a surprise blow. Sheridan was in Winchester, 12 miles north, returning from a meeting in Washington, when the assault hit. By 9 AM, his army had been driven back 3 miles, its retreat finally ending when the Vermont Brigade led a heroic stand on a ridge just outside the village of Middletown. There, three Confederate assaults were repulsed before the defenders withdrew to join the rest of the battered army on high ground still farther north. Sheridan reached the field in late morning after a 12-mile ride, rounding up retreating soldiers along the way. Realigning his army, he launched a counterattack at 3 PM, with the Vermont Brigade advancing near the left flank of his line. The 8th Vermont, which had suffered severe losses in attempting to slow the early morning attack, that afternoon became the first unit to break Early's line. When Confederate resistance stiffened, George Custer's cavalry, including the Vermont regiment, swept down from the northwest to rout Early's forces. Cedar Creek was turned from a Rebel victory into a Union triumph. The vital Shenandoah Valley had been wrenched from Confederate control, and three weeks later Abraham Lincoln was reelected.

On the day of that important battle, 600 miles away in Vermont, the northernmost land action of the war took place. In the week preceding October 19, some twenty Confederate soldiers wearing civilian clothes, escapees from northern military prisons, quietly arrived in the busy railroad town of St. Albans, taking rooms at three hotels. Their leader, Kentuckian Bennett Young, passed himself off as a theology student, reading the Bible and taking rides in the country. On the afternoon of October 19, as Sheridan readied his forces for the counterattack at Cedar Creek, Young's men emerged on St. Albans's Main Street, declaring themselves to be Confederates. Entering the town's three banks with pistols drawn, they stole $208,000 and galloped out of town on stolen horses in a hail of gunfire. The raiders made it into Canada, pursued by a St. Albans posse, which seized several raiders next morning in the territory of the British Empire. But Canadian authorities took custody, and after a legal proceeding in Montreal, a judged refused to extradite the raiders to the United States, where they likely faced hanging.

The Petersburg siege dragged on through the winter, with Lee's and Grant's lines lengthening. Several tries by Grant to breach the thinning Rebel lines failed, with heavy casualties, and one sudden stroke by Lee against Union fortifications ended in a bloody repulse. On April 1, with the Vermont cavalry in the assault, Sheridan smashed the western end of Lee's lines at Five Forks. In the dark early morning hours of April 2, 1865, Grant massed the 6th Corps just west of Petersburg. The Vermont Brigade was placed at the front of a wedge-shaped attack formation, and just before dawn, twelve thousand men rolled forward. The first Union soldier over the works was Captain Charles Gould, of Windham, who was promptly bayoneted in the face and back. But Gould survived to be known ever after as the man who broke the Petersburg lines, after a nearly ten-month siege. Soon, Lee's defenses were overwhelmed, and the Con-

federate commander ordered his army to retreat west.

Petersburg's abandonment meant that Richmond could no longer be defended. On April 3, Union troops entered the Confederate capital, with the 9th Vermont Regiment in the vanguard and its former commander, Edward Hastings Ripley of Rutland, near the front of the column. Lee moved west, hoping to link his army with a Confederate force under Joseph Johnston, moving up from the Carolinas. On April 6, Lee lost more than eight thousand men in a brisk fight along Sayler's Creek. In that battle, the Old Brigade fired its last shots of the war. Two days later, Custer's cavalry, including the Vermont regiment, blocked Lee's escape route. Lee met Grant at Appomattox Courthouse the afternoon of Palm Sunday, April 9, and surrendered the Army of Northern Virginia.

On April 12, the Confederate port city of Mobile, Alabama, surrendered. The fall of the vital Spanish Fort was key to the victory, and the 7th Vermont Regiment fought there. The 7th had spent most of the war along the Florida coast but finally got in on an important action as the war closed. Then, the regiment was assigned to duty along the Rio Grande River, coming home a year after all other Vermont regiments.

The night of April 14, Abraham Lincoln was mortally wounded by a Confederate sympathizer, the noted actor John Wilkes Booth, while attending a play in Washington's Ford's Theatre. Word reached the Vermont Brigade in Danville, Virginia, where they had marched after the Appomattox surrender. In Vermont, "funerals" for the slain president were held in many churches, with a Manchester service concluding with the singing of "America."

Soon, most of the Vermont troops came home to resume civilian lives, mainly as farmers but some as store clerks, railroad men, and factory workers. Many went west to seek new adventures. Wilbur Fisk wrote on his return to Tunbridge, "We have seen home so often like a fairy vision in our imaginings and dreams . . . that now the ideal is realized it almost seems as if we were dreaming it still . . . A lifetime of experience has been crowded into this fierce term of war. If I was asked 'how it seemed' to be a free citizen once more, I should say it seemed as if I had been through a long dark tunnel, and had just got into daylight once more." When final statistics were tallied, it was determined that 34,238 Vermonters had served in the Civil War. Of them, the official statistics set the death toll at 5,224. The actual total was considerably higher, particularly since many men who died of war-related causes after returning home were not counted.

As the years passed, veterans organized local chapters of the Grand Army of the Republic, the GAR, which became a major force in state and national politics. In 1876, the legislature contracted with Julian Scott, a former hero of Lee's Mill, to create for the Vermont State House a huge painting of the Battle of Cedar Creek. The well-known artist finished his major work four years later, a painting that has long been regarded as one of the best the war inspired. In 1889, many veterans were present for the dedication of Vermont monuments where the 2nd Brigade had fought at Gettysburg. State monuments were also placed at Cedar Creek, Winchester, Antietam, and, years later, at the Wilderness. Many Vermont communities also erected monuments, usually on the village green and often topped by the statue of a soldier.

The last surviving Vermont veteran of the Civil War, Gilbert Lucier of the Canadian border town of Jay, died in Newport's Orleans County Memorial Hospital on September 22, 1944, at ninety-seven. By that time, the Second World War was in its last year. Today, the astonishing numbers of those who served in the Civil War, and those who died, can perhaps best be seen in the old cemeteries that lie throughout the hills and valleys of Vermont. As Memorial Day approaches each year, bright new flags flap in spring's fresh breezes by the graves of the mostly young men who fought in Abraham Lincoln's forces. With them lie the people who remained on the home front and helped make possible Vermont's remarkable war effort.

Perhaps the state's contribution to Union victory in the Civil War was most appropriately marked on March 9, 1865, exactly one month after Lee surrendered to Grant at Appomattox Courthouse. Meeting in an extra session at the State House, the Vermont General Assembly ratified the Thirteenth Amendment to the U.S. Constitution, which banished slavery from the United States of America. The vote was 207 to none, fulfilling a promise in effect written down in 1777, when Vermont adopted the first American constitution that outlawed slavery.

chapter two

Addison County

On a December morning in 1859, with a fresh coat of snow covering the Champlain Valley, John Brown's body arrived at the Vergennes railroad station three days after his hanging at Charles Town, Virginia. Brown had died trying to end American slavery, and it now seems fitting that to Addison County came his remains, a place where antislavery feeling was once very prevalent. In Middlebury's Congregational Church, the Vermont Anti-Slavery Society was formed. The Quaker Robinson family welcomed fugitive slaves at Rokeby, the Robinson home in Ferrisburg, and paid them to work on the family farm. Frederick Douglass and William Lloyd Garrison were guests there. The home of William Slade still stands in Cornwall. As a congressman, he spoke forceful words in the U.S. House on behalf of Vermonters against slavery and its westward expansion.

....

ADDISON

 Snake Mountain rises 1,000 feet above Addison Four Corners, at the intersection of Routes 22A and 17. On July 7, 1862, Lucy Ann Rose wrote a letter from an Addison farm that said:

"Last Friday the 4th we had a Snake Mt. Excursion estimated there were 2,000 people there, canon and martial music. Pa was one of the musicians. A recruiting officer was there trying to get volunteers for the army. Cousin Myron Clark says he would like to go. Aunt Harriet (his mother) does not like to hear him talk about it. Brother Albert says he would like to but I hope he NEVER will. I don't know but it would kill Pa & Ma if he should."

Brother Albert, Lucy's brother Albert Stickle, did not enlist, remaining at home on the farm. But her cousin Myron did, joining the 14th Vermont. He kept a diary and late in the long march to Gettysburg, he wrote, "I'll fall out tomorrow for I cannot stand it." But he made it to the battlefield and early on July 2 wrote, "Picket skirmishing this AM." The next entry is in another hand. "July 3, 1863—Early in the morning, about 4 o'clock, the batteries commenced firing & CLARK WAS KILLED at nearly the first fire by a solid 12 lb. shot taking off all the back part of his head, killing him instantly. He was a good boy and soldier. The whole Co. mourns his loss & Especially his Capt. Such are the fortunes of war." The shot that killed Clark blew up a caisson, an event that convinced 2nd Vermont Brigade commander George Stannard to move his men forward, making the Vermonters the most advanced command along the main Union line on Cemetery Ridge. From that position, part of the brigade swung out to strike Pickett's Charge, with the 14th holding position to battle a supporting attack. Clark's body never came home, and no stone marks his resting place in the Gettysburg National Cemetery, where he likely lies as an unknown.

Snake Mountain has long been a popular picnic spot, with roads once reaching its summit from both the Addison and Weybridge sides. The views take in much of Lake Champlain. Below, at Addison Four Corners, is the 1816 Baptist Church whose membership on April 1, 1846, adopted a resolution stating: "Whereas slavery is contrary to the letter and spirit of the Gospel and consequently a sin against God, Therefore Resolved—we will not hold in Church fellowship slaveholding churches, or any brother or sister who is a member of such church until they have given evidence of reformation."

The 1922 Addison war memorial, by the church, lists ninety-one men who served in the Civil War. Stars by fifteen names denote those killed. Among them is Private James Dallison, a member of Private Clark's company, likely a victim of the same explosion that killed Clark. Another name with a star is that of Private Walter Hurd, 2nd Vermont, killed at Funkstown, Maryland, July 10, 1863, a week after Gettysburg. To find Hurd's home, drive south along Route 22A for 3 miles and turn right on Town Line Road. In 2.5 miles, note the prominent old white house on a knoll to the right, the home from which Hurd went to war. Continue along Town Line Road to Town Line Cemetery, actually in the town of Bridport. Hurd's stone notes his death "in a skirmish" near Hagerstown, Maryland.

Myron Clark lived in a farmhouse 0.2 mile north of Addison Four Corners on Route 22A. A modern house has been built on the old house's foundation.

The Addison town offices, in a modern building to the rear of the Baptist Church, preserve the selectmen's enlistment records from early 1863 until the war's end. The first entry, dated February 25, 1863, lists men of the town deemed unfit for service and the reasons:

Samuel Benedict, 44, Bright's disease of the kidney.
Seneca Prevost, 37, Imperfect use and Anchylosis of Elbow joint.
Edward Gorham, 34, Tuberculosis.
Charles Merrill, 38, Tuberculosis.

Dennis Norton, 23, Inability to stand and
walk long.
George Sheldon, 27, Weakness knee joint
Partial dislocation of knee.
Ezra Smith, 39, Imperfect vision Blown
right eye.
Orville Whitford, 39, Painful disease of
testicle.
Judson Day, 24, Chronic Cutaneous disease.

SOURCES
ADDISON BAPTIST CHURCH RECORDS.
ADDISON TOWN RECORDS.
CLARK, MYRON. DIARY. OWNED BY IRWIN AND
   JANET CLARK.
WITH THANKS TO IRWIN AND JANET CLARK
   AND JANE GRACE.

....

BRIDPORT

A place that knew the sadness of the Civil War, the Bridport Congregational church parsonage stands midway along the west side of the Bridport Common, just west of Route 22A. In 1867, two years after the Civil War, Reverend Warren Winchester, with wife, Mary, came to Bridport to serve as pastor of the Congregational church. The church he served does not survive, but the present-day church, on the north side of the green, is built within the old building's foundation. Mary grew up on a Middlebury farm, and in 1848 married Warren. Soon thereafter, Warren became a minister, and when the war began, he became an army chaplain and was assigned to a military hospital in Washington. Mary and their four young children, three daughters and a son, hastened south to be with him. She wrote home to Middlebury that she was "full of life & hope and joyous at the prospect of being again united with the dear Husband and Father."

The four children were fine singers, and two weeks after reaching Washington, the family went to Warren's hospital so the children could sing to the soldiers. Mary wrote, "Their little voices all blended with the rest . . . and many a brave Soldier had to wipe his eyes—as he was so forcibly reminded of his own little ones at home."

Soon after the concert, four-year-old Nellie complained of an earache and sore throat. As she became more ill, a doctor diagnosed diphtheria, which often brought death from suffocation. Nellie was dead within days. Soon daughter Mary was ill, dying an agonizing death, after giving her treasured possessions to her brother and sister. Then daughter Minnie, seven, was gone, and then six-year-old Willie was ill. He seemed to be the sickest of all the children but recovered after a long struggle.

In a letter to her parents in Middlebury, Mary wrote of the Washington spring. "The grass is tall & green, but there is a strange sadness about it all to me. The Band plays gaily in the shady grove just below our dwelling . . . but it fills my heart with sorrow rather than joy."

Warren was pastor in Bridport for fourteen years, during which time his wife taught Sunday school and served as president of the Bridport Women's Christian Temperance Union. Mary bore twelve children, but only one, a son named Benjamin, lived to adulthood.

The Bridport Ladies Sewing Circle, organized in 1856 within the Congregational Church to make items for the soldiers, surely met often in the parsonage.

Bridport sent some 130 men to war, and many are interred in the cemetery behind the Congregational Church. One building north of the church is the town hearse house, one of few such structures that survive in Vermont from the Civil War era. Surely, the hearse was used in the funerals of several Bridport Civil War soldiers, likely including the rites for Lieutenant Albert Crane, killed at the Wilderness on May 5, 1864. The *Rutland Herald* on May 31, 1864, said: "The funeral of the late Lieut, A. A. Crane, Company A, Sixth Vermont regiment, will be held at the Congregational Church in Bridport on Sunday, June 12th. Funeral sermon by Rev. Dr. Labaree, of Middlebury College. We learn that Lieut. Crane was not killed instantly, as at first reported, but died in an ambulance while being moved to hospital, about an hour after receiving his death wound."

From the Bridport Green, go north on Route 22A, and quickly turn right on Route 125 at the Bridport Grange Hall. In 1.3 miles, turn north on East Street, and in 3 miles is the large white farmhouse on the left from which Albert Crane went to war. Soon, turn right on Mountain Road, and the first building on the left is the Crane School, which Albert attended. Return to Bridport, go south past the Bridport Green, and in a 0.1 mile, note the large old white house set back from the highway on the right where Edgar Harkness Gray was born on March 9, 1865. Gray, pastor of E Street Baptist Church in Washington, D.C., was elected chaplain of

the U.S. Senate on March 9, 1865. He was one of four ministers who presided at the funeral, held at the Capitol, for Abraham Lincoln. Gray delivered the final prayer.

SOURCES

ALBERS, JAN. "PAST TIMES: STORIES FROM THE SHELDON MUSEUM; 'MARY WINCHESTER'S WAR.'" *ADDISON COUNTY INDEPENDENT* (MIDDLEBURY), MAY 2008.

PAYNE, WALLACE L. *THERE'S ONLY ONE BRIDPORT IN THE USA*. EDITED BY RAYMOND H. LOUNSBURY. BRIDPORT, VT: BRIDPORT HISTORICAL SOCIETY, 1876.

WINCHESTER, MARY SEVERANCE. MEMOIR. HENRY SHELDON MUSEUM OF VERMONT HISTORY, MIDDLEBURY.

WITH THANKS TO ELAINE NAYLOR AND MARGARET SUNDERLAND.

BRISTOL

Approach Bristol from the west, along Route 17, and soon after crossing Route 116, Evergreen Cemetery is on the left. Take the second entrance, and quickly, on the right, an obelisk marks the grave of Captain Riley Bird, commander of the 6th Vermont's Company A. Bird fell in the heavy fusillade that greeted the Vermont Brigade as it advanced on May 5, 1864, at the Wilderness. Words on his stone note that he died at twenty-eight and lists the battles in which he fought, from Lee's Mill to the Wilderness. At the end of the list are the words, "These are his epitaph."

Continue on Route 17 into the village of Bristol, and note the large park on the left. In it, Company G, 14th Vermont, made up of men from Bristol and surrounding Addison County towns, drilled before departing for war and Gettysburg. In the 1819 Baptist Church facing the green, on August 27, 1862, a war meeting was held to encourage enlistments in the 14th Vermont. According to the *Middlebury Register,* a cannon was fired several times to "bring in people," and "a guarantee was read," saying that each volunteer would receive $100.

At the park's southeast corner, Bristol's Civil War memorial lists the names of 101 men who served. The 1862 cannon beside it is a 6.4-inch Parrott rifled weapon manufactured at the West Point Foundry in Cold Springs, New York. It fired a 100-pound shell that, propelled by a 10-pound black powder charge, could travel nearly 7,000 yards. A photo owned by the historical society shows several aged Civil War veterans, members of the local Walter C. Dunton GAR Post, posed by the big gun.

In the parking lot across Fitch Avenue once stood the Bristol House, the village's primary hostelry. The *Middlebury Register* on May 15, 1861, reported on a meeting that began with "a procession led by 25 ladies carrying the National Standard" and "men and boys as they could tramp followed suit." The procession marched to martial music and "adjourned to the hall in the hotel" for a meeting. Four days later, the *Register* recorded another procession making its way through the village to the front of the hotel. Here, three cheers were given for the Union, three for the Stars and Stripes, and three for Major Robert Anderson, who had commanded Fort Sumter.

At the intersection of Fitch Avenue and North Street is the large old frame house from which Riley Bird went to war. Sharing the Bird home early in Riley's life was his grandfather, Joseph Bird, a veteran of both the Revolutionary War and the War of 1812.

Return along North Street to Route 17 and turn left. Note on the right several connected wooden stores. The last and tallest was owned by Noble Dunshee, who, after the war, operated a store in this building, living until ninety. Captain Dunshee commanded the 14th Vermont's local Company G, which faced Pickett's Charge and a supporting attack at Gettysburg. Later in the war, Dunshee undertook the dangerous duty of serving as a recruiter in Union-occupied portions of the South.

SOURCES
CIVIL WAR FILES. BRISTOL HISTORICAL SOCIETY.
WITH THANKS TO GERALD HEFFERNAN AND JOHN REYNOLDS.

....

CORNWALL

In 1841, members of the 1803 Congregational Church, on Route 30 by the Cornwall green, 4 miles west of Middlebury, divided over slavery. New minister Jacob Scales once owned slaves, but had set them free, and gave assurances that he was now an opponent of slavery. But some members doubted that Scales would work for abolition, and twenty-seven church members left, intent on forming a new church. They went to West Cornwall.

On September 10, 1862, the *Middlebury Register* reported on a funeral for

Sergeant Linus Everts, 5th Vermont, held at the Congregational Church. "Friends have abandoned the lingering hope that he might still be alive," the paper said, and noted the "strong probability that he had been killed at Savage's Station." The *Register* also said, "It is noticeable that three young men, Everts, Baxter, and Potter have, within the year, died from the same regiment, and all from a district within a radius of 500 paces."

The other two soldiers mentioned, who were privates in Company F, 5th Vermont, were Nelson Baxter, eighteen when he died of sickness in June 1862, and Adams Potter, eighteen when he succumbed to disease on November 11, 1861, two months after enlisting.

From the Congregational Church, go north 0.4 mile on Route 30, and turn right on Morse Road. In 0.5 mile is a large farm on the left, once the home of Nelson Baxter.

Return to the Cornwall green by the Congregational Church. When Abraham Lincoln issued his first call for troops after Fort Sumter fell, forty-four Cornwall men drilled on the green under the direction of Edwin Stowell, a Norwich University graduate. The Cornwall Civil War monument, on the green, lists seventeen Cornwall men who died. Among them are Baxter, Everts, and Potter, and James Fenton "hung by guerillas."

At March town meeting in 1866, Cornwall authorized money for a Civil War monument. Rochester had already ordered a monument but on delivery rejected it. Cornwall bought it and hauled it over the Green Mountains with ox and

horse teams. The Rochester lettering was erased and replaced by tributes to Cornwall's war dead. At the November 24, 1868, dedication, Edwin Stowell spoke, as did Wheelock Veazey, former commander of the 16th Vermont.

From the monument, go south on Route 30, and soon note a huge farmhouse and barns on the ridge to the right. Edwin Stowell lived there, going to war leading the 5th Vermont's Company F. Later promoted to major, he became lieutenant colonel of the 9th Vermont under George Stannard.

Continue south 0.25 mile on Route 30, and the house on the right, with small columned porch, was William Slade's home. Slade graduated from Middlebury College in 1807, became a successful lawyer, and was elected to the U.S. Congress in 1831. There, he became a close ally of John Quincy Adams, particularly in opposing a House of Representatives gag rule prohibiting discussion of slavery. More than one fiery Slade speech caused Southerners to leave the House chamber. "I cannot stand here as a freeman and the Representative of freemen without declaring in the face of this House," he said in one speech, "and of the World, that the right to hold men as goods and chattels . . . should cease and be discontinued instantly and forever." From 1844 to 1846, Slade served as Vermont governor.

From the Slade house, continue south 1.5 miles on Route 30, and go right on Park Hill Road. At the southwest corner of the intersection once stood a house in which Solomon Foot was born, later to serve in the U.S. Senate during the Civil War (see Rutland).

Continue on Park Hill Road to a Y, go right, and on reaching Route 74 in West Cornwall, the old Cornwall Baptist Church is directly ahead. When those twenty-seven abolitionists broke away from the Congregational Church, they formed the Free Congregational Church and held services in this building. They also used the Methodist Church, which once stood across the road. The Free Congregationalists were addressed in West Cornwall by William Lloyd Garrison and Wendell Phillips, likely in the Baptist Church.

On July 3, 1864, a funeral for Corporal Charles Stearns, of the 5th Vermont's Company F, was held in the Baptist Church. Stearns was killed at Cold Harbor, and shortly before his death, according to the *Middlebury Register,* he wrote home, "For my part I do believe it my duty to stay here and see this rebellion put down."

On February 22, 1865, an oyster supper was held at the Baptist Church to raise money for the soldiers.

SOURCES

GREEN, MARY PEET. *CORNWALL PEOPLE AND THEIR TIMES.* NEW HAVEN, VT: ANTIOCH PRESS, 1993.
MATTHEWS, REV. LYMAN. *HISTORY OF THE TOWN OF CORNWALL, VERMONT.* MIDDLEBURY, VT: MEAD AND FULLER, 1862.
SANFORD, BEULAH M. *TWO CENTURIES OF CORNWALL LIFE.* RUTLAND, VT: SHARP PRINTING, 1962.
WITH THANKS TO MARY PEET GREEN AND SUSAN JOHNSON.

FERRISBURGH

North of Ferrisburgh Center, overlooking Route 7 from a ridgetop just east of the road, stands Rokeby, now a museum, once a stop on the Underground Railroad. In the 1830s and 1840s, Quakers Rowland and Rachel Gilpin Robinson, early and strong supporters of William Lloyd Garrison, here gave shelter to fugitive slaves. Though countless houses make claim to having been Underground Railroad sites, Rokeby's authenticity is well documented in the Robinson family papers. Not only were the fugitives given lodging, sometimes for extended periods of time, they were paid for their labors on the Robinsons' 1,000-acre sheep farm. Among them was Aaron Freeman, who became a Ferrisburgh resident and served in the 54th Massachusetts Regiment. While soldiering in Florida, he wrote to the Ferrisburgh town clerk in February 1864, seeking help: "I have work all night and then had to drill all day they make them that hav got no boats go out in thair bair feet in the thistl and drill then they set on thair horses and laf at us that aint right I hant had but one shirt for more than a month . . . I want to get home as soon as I can far I don't get fair play here they don't treat this rigment as they do the others regmint."

Rokeby today owns ninety of the farm's original acres, and trails lead throughout the grounds. Stroll to the foundation of the Brick Academy, once a two-story brick building with cupola, a school founded by Rowland Robinson in 1839, where black and white children were educated, together. On March 11, 1836, the Ferrisburgh Anti-Slavery Society was founded here, with Roland Robinson elected secretary. The society's constitution began: "Whereas, it has pleased the all wise Creator to make of one blood all nations of men to dwell upon the face of the earth; to create them free and equal, and to endow them with certain unalienable rights."

On a Rokeby wall is the framed photo of a young man in uniform, William Stevens, a nephew of the Robinsons, who went to war against the wishes of his Quaker family (see East Montpelier). Also displayed is a poster advertising an appearance in Ferrisburgh by Fredrick Douglas in July 1843. Douglas, at the time of that speech, was a guest at Rokeby, as was William Lloyd Garrison, when he spoke in Ferrisburgh in 1865.

Go south from Rokeby 1 mile on Route 7, and the Ferrisburgh Park is on the left. There, a historic marker notes that Frederick Douglass spoke at the town hall in July 1843. That building no longer stands, but the 1840 Union Society Meeting House, which stood beside it, survives. Douglass's appearance was one of one hundred conventions planned by the American Anti-Slavery Society, and the famed abolitionist had previously appeared at conventions in Randolph and Middlebury. Given a harsh welcome in Middlebury, the *Vergennes Vermonter* reported on "an attempt wantonly and cruely to insult to his face a man, because God had given 'a skin not colored like his own.'" The article continued, "A fool might as well attempt to blot the face of the sun by throwing filth at it, as try to insult Frederick Douglass."

Civil War Ferrisburgh town meetings were usually held in the town hall, though the larger meetinghouse was used when necessary. In 1860, Ferrisburgh voters went for Lincoln here, 129 to 8. In December 1863, they approved $300 bounty payments on a vote of 99 to 15, "after much debate." The following July, bounties of $500 were voted, and soon the selectmen were given the power to decide the amounts. The grove of maples in front of the meetinghouse is said to have been planted in honor of Ferrisburgh soldiers.

Return north on Route 7 past Rokeby 2.75 miles, and in North Ferrisburg, go right on Hollow Road. The frame house at the corner, on the right, was once the Martin home. The Martins owned a large store and post office directly across Hollow Road. Remembering his childhood in North Ferrisburgh before the Civil War, William Wallace Higbee wrote, "About those days, the slavery question was the prominent feature in politics, and a newspaper called the *National Era,* published *Uncle Tom's Cabin,* by Harriet Beecher Stowe in weekly installments. I remember as a boy being sent . . . to Martin's when the *Era* was due, and we never went to bed after the paper came until every word of *Uncle Tom* was read to us."

Just beyond the Martin house is the North Ferrisburgh Methodist Church, whose membership was once divided over slavery. Continue past the church, go left on Mount Philo Road, and the second house on the left was the Sorrell home. Private Joseph Sorrell, 17th Vermont, was nineteen when killed at the Wilderness on May 6, 1864. Exactly a week later, twenty-one-year-old Private Abraham Sorrell, 5th Vermont, was killed at Spotsylvania.

Return to Hollow Road, and in 0.2 mile, just past the old cement block fire station on the left, a small sign marks the site of Mud Church. When the local Methodists split in 1843, strongly antislavery members built a church of bricks and clay here. It stood until 1900, and on September 29, 1865, William Lloyd Garrison spoke here while a guest of the Robinsons. The *Burlington Free Press* said that the church was crowded, and many former members of the local antislavery society were present. At one point, Garrison raised a Bible, saying, "The Bible is becoming a new book to many expositors,—without any new translation or new revision, it is being transformed from a pro-slavery Bible into an anti-slavery bible, simply because its readers are becoming more in love with the Truth it has all along proclaimed."

Continue on Hollow Road across Lewis Creek, and abruptly on the right is an old store once owned by the Mallory family. Loren Mallory, a 5th Vermont private, survived a wound at Spotsylvania's Bloody Angle but was captured near Petersburg ten weeks later. He died in the prison at Salisbury, North Carolina, at twenty-one.

Return as you came on Hollow Road to Route 7 and cross it onto Stage Road. Go to the road's end, and directly ahead is a large frame house with a stone foundation, the postwar home of Henry Phelps. He joined the 6th Vermont in the fall of 1861 and served eighteen months before he became ill. His parents dispatched a friend to Virginia to bring him here,

where it took him three years to recover. He lived until 1924.

SOURCES

DOUGLASS, FREDERICK. *LIFE AND TIMES OF FREDERICK DOUGLASS: HIS EARLY LIFE AS A SLAVE, HIS ESCAPE FROM BONDAGE, AND HIS COMPLETE HISTORY.* NEW YORK: COLLIER BOOKS, 1892.

FERRISBURGH TOWN RECORDS.

HIGBEE, WILLIAM WALLACE. *AROUND THE MOUNTAINS: HISTORICAL ESSAYS ABOUT CHARLOTTE, FERRISBURGH AND MONKTON.* CHARLOTTE, VT: CHARLOTTE VERMONT HISTORICAL SOCIETY, 1991.

ROKEBY ARCHIVES.

WITH THANKS TO BOB MITCHELL AND JANE WILLIAMSON.

GOSHEN

On Route 73 in the mountains between Brandon and Rochester, look for a sign for Goshen, and there turn to the north onto Town Hill Road. In 0.6 mile, go left on Carlisle Hill Road to the Goshen town hall, in whose basement meeting room Civil War–era town meetings were held. On July 29, 1862, with three local boys already dead in battle, a meeting was held here that town records called a war convention. The three lads— Volney Salls, Heman Hooker, and Louis Dutton, all privates in Company H, 5th Vermont—had been killed at Savage's Station a month before. The first business was to elect Lucius Allen president of the meeting, and he promptly appointed a committee of six to present resolutions. They read:

"Whereas—In this day of the nation's trouble, caused by the attempts of the South to destroy our Country—thereby rendering a

Republican form of government a byword and reproach among all nations; And whereas we have been called upon by the Government we love to sustain it, with our friends to fight against the unholy rebellion, which we responded to with such ready zeal that those in authority cried ENOUGH— And whereas, by our recent reverses before Richmond that authority now calls upon us again for more men, therefore

"Resolved—That from this time forward we will use all honorable means in our power to furnish such supplies, believing it to be the duty of every patriot to furnish the Government with such means to crush Jeff Davis and his minions in such manner that there will not be sufficient brass or brains to create another rebellion for the next three thousand years, to say the least. Therefore, resolved that from this time forward we will act.

"Resolved—It has been our duty to mourn for the Soldiers who have fallen in battle; and we deeply sympathize with the afflicted, and while the falling tear pulses away, the mind rallies again with the hope that our Nation will extricate itself from the foul rebellion forced upon us by traitors, and once more become a country as formerly, with the best government the sun ever shone upon; and that we may live under the protection of the Stars and Stripes, and that they may float over succeeding generations, as long as wood shall grow and water run.

"Resolved—That as citizens of Goshen we are ever ready to furnish our quota of men and money to wrest from the hands of traitors our country which they have so basely endeavored to destroy.

"Resolved—That enough men to make out the quota from this town, who shall leave their homes and their businesses and enlist in response to the call of the President for three hundred thousand men, shall be compensated by those who do not go, so that they shall receive in addition to the amount of the United States and State of Vermont pay, enough to make the sum of one dollar per day."

That dollar-a-day pay was approved on a vote of 38 to 9.

In the 1886 *History of Addison County*, edited by H. P. Smith, the observation was made that "there are two things, at least . . . of which the people of Goshen are proud. One is, that three presidents, Lincoln, Grant, and Hayes, received the unanimous vote of the town. The other is that, during the late rebellion, the quota of the town was more than filled. No higher eulogy can be passed upon the past of the town, and no higher praise bestowed on those who fought in the Civil War."

All had not always been unity in Goshen, however. In a brief history of Goshen, published in 1931, it was noted that the Methodist Episcopalians of the town in 1848 built "the present commodious house of worship," that is, the addition set atop the town hall. In 1844, some members of the church had broken away because of a dispute over slavery. The more ardent antislavery members built a smaller church nearby.

Goshen's war record is remembered on the 1901 Civil War memorial by the town hall. The names of four men are listed as killed in action, one who died of wounds and ten who "died in service and after."

Just across the brook from the town hall is the Goshen Cemetery. The breakaway Methodists built their church beside it, on the near side, the site now in woods. Several Goshen soldiers are buried here.

From the cemetery, return to Route 73 and turn left, going east. In 1.75 miles, turn right on South Hill Road. Cross a bridge, and in the first house on the right lived Dan Brown, who fought at Gettysburg as a private with the 14th Vermont.

Return to Route 73 and cross it onto Hathaway Road. James Washburn, also a private in the 14th and a veteran of Gettysburg, lived in the first house on the right. In the second house on the right lived Andrew Brown, who procured a substitute and did not serve.

SOURCES

GOSHEN TOWN RECORDS.
SMITH, H. P. *HISTORY OF ADDISON COUNTY.* SYRACUSE, NY: D. MASON AND CO., 1886. WITH THANKS TO BILL POWERS.

....

GRANVILLE

The 1838 Granville Methodist Church fronts the west side of Route 100 in Lower Granville, once the site of Granville town meetings. Here, voters wrestled with the challenges of meeting draft quotas, and on September 2, 1862, they "chose Joseph Lamb a committee to investigate the matter and see if we can have credit for the whole number of soldiers who have enlisted from this town and given their residence as being in other towns." The strategy didn't work. In July 1863, Granville approved bounties of $100, and the following November, bounties of $200 were approved, along with a tax of 200 cents on each dollar of the grand list to fund them. In February 1864, to meet a quota of six soldiers, six bounties of $250 each were voted. In November 1864, voters approved a payment of $140.20 to the selectmen "for recruiting services" and voted a whopping tax of 450 cents on each grand list dollar to meet war expenses.

Among the soldiers who enlisted at the meetinghouse was Albert Clarke, son of Jedediah and Mary (Woodbury) Clarke. Though the family lived just over the town line on a hill farm in Rochester, they considered Granville their hometown. Albert had just joined a Montpelier law firm when he joined Company I, 13th Vermont, in the summer of 1862. A lieutenant at Gettysburg, Clarke took command of the company on July 2, when its captain was mortally wounded as the company moved from Cemetery Ridge to recapture a battery. Though wounded in an ankle, Clarke was able to fight the next day in the attack on Pickett's Charge. According to fellow soldier George Scott, at the end of the attack, "as the air was thick with hissing shot, Lieutenant Clarke ordered the prisoners to lie down, which they were glad to do. One of our men said to him, 'You are treating the enemy better than you treat us,' to which he replied, 'that is true, but we are at work and their work is over.'" After the war, Clarke became a wealthy Massachusetts businessman and was prominent in Vermont veterans' affairs, organizing 13th Vermont reunions and seeing to it that monuments honored the regiment's service.

Driving down the narrow upper White River Valley today through Granville, with its modern population of some three hundred, it's hard to imagine that this town sent eighty men to war. Among them was Arba Ford, who joined the 4th Vermont in December 1863. Ford was killed at Cold Harbor on June 8, 1864, probably by a sharpshooter. He is buried in the national cemetery at Cold Harbor. Ford attended school in Granville's District One School, built in 1857, which is now attached to the meetinghouse.

Go south from the meetinghouse 0.1 mile, and the next to the last house on the left, a sizeable frame house, was once the Eastman family home. From here, Willard Eastman went to war, a corporal in the 17th Vermont. Wounded at the Wilderness and again on April 2, 1865, in breaking the Confederate lines at Petersburg, he came home and recovered, living until 1912.

Continue south 0.8 mile on Route 100 and turn left on Buffalo Farm Road. In just under 1.5 miles, the old District Two schoolhouse is on the left, where James Ford, Eugene Harvey, and Albert Vinton were pupils. Enlisting late in the war, Ford was never assigned to a regiment and died of sickness on January 30, 1864, probably in camp at Brattleboro. Harvey joined the 4th Vermont in the fall of 1861 and served three years, fighting in most of the major battles in the east. Vinton paid a $300 commutation fee and did not serve.

The Granville town office on Route 100 preserves a letter written by a Granville woman named Jane on May 24, 1864, to her soldier brother. The identity of the two is unclear, but the letter reveals something of the experience of those at home. Jane wrote:

"When you write again, tell us all about the boys from this town and Rochester for their folks always ask us if you spoke about them . . . If you know where Charlie is tell us so his mother can write him . . . Since beginning this Mrs. Church went by and called here . . . She said her boys are well. Take care of yourself. Be a brave and faithful soldier and kill one hundred old Rebs. O, won't it be a glorious day when you come marching home! But if you never come you may have the thought that you will always be remembered, never forgotten. I think of you the first thing in the morn and the last thing at night, but I am going to try to believe that you will come again. Clara dreamed one night that you was wounded in your hip before we got your letter . . . Give my love to Gen. Grant. Tell him to lift old Jeff when he get into Richmond enough so that I can see him over these mountains . . . Just write every chance you can. Keep a letter written all the time to send to us."

SOURCES
GRANVILLE TOWN AND SCHOOL RECORDS.
WITH THANKS TO KATHY WERNER.

HANCOCK

Hancock village, located where Route 125 joins Route 100, would be instantly recognizable today to a Hancock Civil War soldier. Go south from that intersection, and after passing the old Methodist Church, now the town hall, one soon comes to the village school, also on the left. Town meetings were held here, in this former District One School, during the Civil War. On July 29, 1862, a war matter first came on the agenda as the town voted to "raise 25 cents on a dollar on the Grand List to be paid to the first four volunteers (including Joseph Sargent who has this day enlisted) in the town of Hancock who shall volunteer in the 10th Regiment." A further motion was passed to the effect that no money would be paid until "they shall have passed a final army inspection."

On December 12, 1863, Hancock voters meeting here approved bounties of $300. On March 1, 1864, the town voted to "raise 95 cents on the dollar of the Grand List for payment of bounties to volunteers." At that meeting, a $300 payment for four volunteers was voted. In January 1865, the town elected Ehud Darling agent of the town "for the purpose of procuring men to fill the quota of Hancock under the past call of the President of the United States [for] 300,000 men." With men increasingly hard to find, voters that day agreed to "raise money on the Grand List of 1864 sufficient to pay bounties to all men" needed to fill the latest quota and to instruct selectmen "to make out a tax bill on said list to pay said bounties." The war sent Hancock well into debt, and a year after it ended, voters were approving a tax to defray "the liabilities of the town."

The Hancock town history states: "In 1850, a boy's wages were 37 cents a day and a man still worked 10 hours for 50 cents; but the war of 1861 brought it up to one dollar per day . . . During the war . . . prices went up but so did the cost of things. A cow brought 50 dollars but men's boots cost 6 dollars, and his pants 4 dollars. The 'special war tax' took a big chunk out of the farmer's income, one farmer paying 74 dollars in 1864."

Go back to the intersection of Routes 100 and 125, and note the old store building at the southwest corner. It is believed that the Flint family lived on its second floor at the time of the war and that eighteen-year-old Charles Flint went to war from here. Flint, a private in the 4th Vermont, was captured at Weldon Railroad and died in Andersonville four months later. He is buried at Andersonville. Ehud Darling, the man elected to head Hancock's recruiting, owned the store that still operates just to the west along Route 125.

Just west on Route 125 and across the street is a flat-roofed house in which an old soldier, Azro George, lived his last years. George went to war at age thirty-four in August 1863, as a substitute for a Rochester man who did not want to serve, enlisting as a private in the 3rd Vermont. He kept a diary that included the following entries from 1864:

June 2: "Stayed on skirmish line till afternoon then marched to the rite. Arrived at Cold Harbor yesterday."

June 3: "Formed line at daylight to charge on the rebel works. I was wounded in the thigh 7 o'clock a.m. Hard fighting all day."

June 4: "Arrived at White House Landing at 3 o'clock a.m. and lay in wagon until after noon 2 men in wagon lost a leg each. Took boat here at 5 p.m. to Washington."

After his wounding in the big attack at Cold Harbor, George was taken by boat to a Washington hospital. By January 1, 1865, he had been transferred to the hospital at Burlington, where he continued to keep a diary. Most of the entries concern the weather, which was very cold that winter, and his doing light duty and guard duty. He frequently took walks down to the Lake Champlain shore. Spring came and the following entries were made:

April 3: "Some excitement in afternoon in coming of news of the fall of Richmond."

April 4: "Fired a salute of 100 guns for the fall of Richmond, flags flying all day."

April 10: "200 guns fired in honor of Gen. Grant's victory over Lee."

April 15: "Pleasant and warm. Reported to quarters 7 1/2 a.m. News arrived of the death of President Lincoln."

April 16: "Snowed most all day. Fired one gun every half hour in honor of the President."

George died in 1909. During his last years, he was cared for in his home by William and Lucretia (Rhodes) Goodyear. Lucretia was the daughter of Lyman Rhodes, who left a Hancock farm to enlist at Rochester in the 11th Vermont. He served the last nine months of the war, fighting at Winchester and Cedar Creek.

The second house west of the George house is believed to have been the home of Hiram Perry, a private in the 14th Vermont, who was wounded at Gettysburg on the day of Pickett's Charge.

Return to Route 100 and turn north. In 0.8 mile is an old farmhouse above the road on the left. David Eaton lived here, who, before the Civil War, according to the Hancock town history, "in the Kansas struggle of 1856–1857, . . . subscribed to the cause of freedom and willingly aided in fitting two sons and two neighbors for the army of emigrants. Later he went himself."

If you go south from Hancock along Route 100 toward Rochester, you will be traveling the route of many Hancock residents on nights during the war, bound for Rochester and the nightly readings of war news at the town hall.

SOURCES
THE STORY OF HANCOCK, VERMONT: 1780–1964; WITH SUPPLEMENT TO 1969. HANCOCK, VT: HISTORICAL COMMITTEE OF HANCOCK, 1969.
WITH THANKS TO EULA BANNISTER.

LEICESTER

Leicester Four Corners lies along Route 7, with the little town center just west of the road. During the Civil War, town meetings were held upstairs in the white frame building that faces the small green. The building's lower floor was, at the time, a school. Beside the town hall is the 1829 Leicester Meeting House, a Congregational Church at the time of the war. The *Middlebury Register* reported in the winter of 1862 that "weekly lyceums" were held at the church to fund repairs to the church." The paper also stated, "We have not had a wedding in town this winter, something rather strange though easily accounted for by saying, 'The young men have all gone to war.'"

William Flint of Leicester was a private in the 1st Vermont. He wrote in his diary on April 19, 1861, "Enlisted for three months in the first Vt. regt in co. with Chancey Stanley . . . I went up to Leicester, Vt. there was a meeting last night held in the town hall for the purpose of enlisting men to answer a call for 75,000 from President Lincoln. I should have been one of the first to enlist but my father was with me and objected but after talking the matter over during the night, he withdrew his objections and I promptly reported for enlistment I will say that while my father was in sympathy with the Union cause and in favor of the call for troops he did not think I was old enough . . . The Co. commenced drilling at once both forenoon, afternoon and evening. The town is filled with people wearing badges and talking of the firing on Fort Sumter." On April 28 he wrote, "Sunday Whole Co. went to Cong. church."

Flint came home unscathed after three months and found work building the Brandon town hall. But he soon reenlisted as a corporal in the 2nd Vermont Light Artillery Battery. The battery participated in the siege of Port Hudson, and he wrote on May 27, 1863: "Our battery was in the fight but in the rear of the infantry so we did not feel the awful effects of lead and iron hurled at the troops in front though several shots passed through our guns." He wrote the next day, "Flag of truce to bury dead left on the field."

On November 7, 1865, Flint wrote, "Arrived Albany early this morning went to Troy and took Troy and Boston train for Rutland and arrived Brandon Vt. 2:30—took train for Leicester to my home after absence 4 years three months 10 days in service of the U.S. Army."

To find the Flint home, go north on Route 7 from Leicester Four Corners, and in 1 mile, bear right at the Y. In 0.3 mile, where Shackett Road comes in on the right, the Flint home is the cape across the road on the left.

Return south on Route 7, and note the last house on the left before the corners. Charles Horton, a private in the 5th Vermont who enlisted in Rutland, lived out his last years here. He lost an arm at Cedar Creek. The two-story house in the southwest quadrant of the corners was once the Jenney family shoe shop. George Jenney and Silas Jenney both were privates in the 5th Vermont. Silas was wounded at Spotsylvania's Bloody Angle, dying three weeks later. George was wounded April 2, 1865, at the Breakthrough at Petersburg but survived.

From the corners, go west on the Leicester/Whiting Road 2 miles: the farm on the right with a large barn was the home of Private William Powers, a member of both the 12th and 17th Vermont Regiments, who came home unscathed.

Continue on the Leicester/Whiting Road, and soon cross railroad tracks. Here at Leicester Junction, known also as Whiting Junction, Private Flint and other Leicester soldiers arrived home.

SOURCES
FLINT, WILLIAM. DIARY. COURTESY OF DOROTHY STEWART.
RUTLAND HERALD, 1862–1864. VERMONT STATE LIBRARY.
WITH THANKS TO PEG OLIVER.

LINCOLN

Go east of Bristol on Route 116, and quickly, after crossing the New Haven River, take the Lincoln Road to the south. In 3.5 miles, enter the village of Lincoln and see a small veterans monument on the left, on a triangular patch of grass. No Vermont town was more fortunately named during the Civil War, bearing the name of the nation's president. Indeed, towering along the east side of the town is the highest continuous stretch of the Green Mountains, the Lincoln Massif. The dominant peak is Mount Abraham, also called Potato Hill; just north of it is Lincoln Peak, Vermont's third highest summit, and nearby is Nancy Hanks Peak. Lincoln Peak got its name long before anyone here heard of the sixteenth president, named for Benjamin Lincoln, a general of the Revolutionary War. But Abraham was apparently named in Abraham Lincoln's honor. The president's mother was Nancy Hanks, and the Hankses lived in Lincoln long before the Civil War, some up on the side of Mount Abraham.

The Civil War monument lists the names of 104 Lincoln men who served Abraham Lincoln. According to the *Middlebury Register,* in the presidential election of 1864, Lincoln voters cast 209 votes for President Lincoln and none for George McClellan.

Turn north here on Quaker Street, and soon on the right is the Starksboro Historical Society, which contains a poignant reminder of the price paid by one Lincoln man for his service in Mr. Lincoln's armies. Charles Green crossed Lake Champlain to enlist, serving as a private in a New York regiment that fought at Gettysburg. There he was wounded, with lead pellets entering a thigh, but he recovered and returned home to Lincoln. He then reenlisted, this time in the 8th Vermont, just before Christmas 1863, but he served only a month, as his wound plagued him, and soon was discharged. As time passed,

his leg worsened, and he was finally forced to make use of a wheelchair. He died in 1896. The three-wheeled wheelchair, with caned seat, is preserved in the museum.

Continue on Quaker Street past the museum and soon come to Maple Cemetery. Charles Green is among the many Lincoln soldiers buried here. Also here is Frank Baslow, a private in the 17th Vermont, who was captured on September 30 at Poplar Springs Church, near Petersburg. A prisoner for six months, he was paroled on the day he died. His stone notes that he expired at age "19 years, five months, and 15 days" and that "He died for his country." Also in the cemetery is Private Michael Delphy, who joined the 2nd Vermont in the summer of 1863 and served until the war ended. Delphy was a substitute for another man who paid commutation, and he lied about his age to do so, claiming he was forty-five. Delphy was, in fact, fifty-six. At Cedar Creek, he was shot in a shoulder, and after coming home, he was never able to do much work on his farm. His gravestone faces the high hills to the west where he lived.

Continue on Quaker Street along which much of Lincoln's sizeable Quaker community once lived. A mile beyond the cemetery, on the left, is a farmhouse with a small barn behind, where Sewell Sargent lived. A sergeant in the 2nd Vermont, Sargent was wounded at the Wilderness on May 5.

Just over 2 miles beyond the Sargent house, Zeno Road bears right. Just beyond it on the right, on Quaker Street, is the trace of a clearing, and past it, in the trees, is a large foundation. This was the Whittier family home. James and Edwin Whittier both enlisted in the 6th Vermont's Company A in the fall of 1861. Both privates, they served nearly four years, and both were wounded May 5 at the Wilderness. James was also shot at Lee's Mill. Both came home safely. Another Whittier lad, Washington, was a private in the 17th Vermont the last year of the war. The Starksboro town line lies just beyond the Whittier site.

Return on Quaker Street to Lincoln's veterans' monument, and turn left, south, on East River Road. Quickly, pass the Old Hotel; the second house beyond it, with a porch across the front, was the Cushman family home. Adolphus and Elijah Cushman each served three years in the 6th Vermont and came home safely. Just beyond, a narrow road goes left and uphill to an old barn foundation. On this farm lived Lester Bryant, a private in the 12th Vermont.

Continue on East River Road for 2.5 miles and turn right on Grimes Road. In 0.2 mile, take Cobb Hill Road, and in 0.5 mile, see an old farmhouse on the right, once the home of Luther Kent. A private in the 14th Vermont, the twenty-one-year-old was wounded at Gettysburg on July 3.

Return to Grimes Road, turn left, and in just under 0.5 mile, come to broad fields on the left, once part of the Caldwell farm. Private James Caldwell, 10th Vermont, was wounded at Spotsylvania's Bloody Angle on May 12, 1864. He came home and lived until 1912.

Continue on Grimes Road, go left at the T, and then right up West Hill Road, which soon commands long views of Mounts Abraham and Lincoln. In 1.5

miles, Browns Road turns right. Look down it to an old farm amid broad fields, once one of several Gove family homes in this area. Aaron and Ira Gove were privates in the 6th Vermont. Edwin was wounded at Lee's Mill, while Ira was mortally wounded at Cold Harbor. George Gove served the last year of the war in the 17th Vermont. William Gove was a private in the 14th Vermont..

Continue on West Hill Road and go right on Gove Road, back into Lincoln village.

SOURCES

LINCOLN BICENTENNIAL COMMITTEE. *LINCOLN, VERMONT HISTORY, 1780–2007.* LINCOLN, VT: LINCOLN HISTORICAL SOCIETY, 2007.
WITH THANKS TO BEVERLY BROWN, ELEANOR MENZER, AND JOHN REYNOLDS.

··

MIDDLEBURY

On entering Middlebury along Route 7, the tall spire of the Middlebury Congregational Church dominates the skyline. The church was the scene of Middlebury College commencements during the Civil War, including the 1862 event. Class of 1862 valedictorian Aldace Walker had just joined the 11th Vermont and shortly before graduation had been elected a lieutenant of the company. (He would rise to the rank of lieutenant colonel serving with distinction throughout the war and write the book *Vermont Brigade in the Shenandoah Valley.*) A classmate, Ezra Brainerd, wrote of the 1862 commencement:

"The exercises proceeded till his name

was reached at the close of the program, but he had not appeared. As I remember it, another piece of music was called for, which was long drawn out. Anxiety was visible on the faces of all from the President to the girls in the gallery. Suddenly Walker appeared at the entrance of the audience room. The music abruptly ended; Walker's name was announced by President Benjamin Labaree; and in blue uniform, with glittering epaulets, Lieutenant Walker marched with stately strides to the stage. The applause that broke forth in the dignified old church was intense and prolonged. The speaker was frequently interrupted, and many sentences were only half heard. He soon gave up the attempt to follow his poorly committed manuscript. But he spoke with enthusiasm; his presence was impressive; it was the voice of the newly honored soldier hastening to war; and doubtless the applause would have been as fervid, had he spoken in an unknown tongue."

In that church in August of 1861, at the previous year's commencement, the speaker had been Edward Everett. The former Harvard president and Massachusetts governor was destined to deliver the main address at the Gettysburg national cemetery dedication on November 19, 1863, just before Abraham Lincoln spoke his Gettysburg Address. On May 1, 1834, eighty-six Vermonters had gathered in the church to found the Vermont Anti-Slavery Society, among them were the Robinsons of Ferrisburgh. The meeting agreed that the only remedy for slavery was immediate emancipation. On February 18, 1836, the society again gathered here after an all-day meeting to hear an address by the abolitionist Oliver Johnson. At the conclusion, everyone sang a hymn written by Johnson that included these words:

Long, too long, have we been dreaming,
O'er our country's sin and shame;
Let us now the time redeeming,
Press the helpless captive's claim,
Till exalting.
He shall cast away his chain.

Earlier that day, the society had been read a letter from William Lloyd Garrison, which said, in part: "Almost my first efforts in the universal emancipation . . . were made in Vermont . . . It was a suitable place, of all others the best chosen, to plant the standard of liberty upon the summit of her Green Mountains and blow the trumpet of liberty through all her valleys."

The Congregational Church was a center of life in Middlebury during the war years. On October 16, 1861, ladies of the town met there to form a group to assist the war effort. Across Route 7 from the church is the Middlebury Inn, known as the Addison House during the Civil War. Many meetings of the Women's Relief Corps were held here, as well as in the church. The *Middlebury Register* reported that a "social gathering" in the form of "a tableau party" was held at the Addison House on October 31, 1862, and the proceeds were used "to purchase hospital supplies." At a room in the hotel, the young recruit George Plumb, of Bennington, killed on a train south of Middlebury, died of his injury (see Salisbury).

Back at the church, the abolitionist

Wendell Phillips lectured here on March 9, 1864, and according to the local paper, the place was "well filled despite foul weather making travel other than by rail almost impossible." Phillips's topic was reconstruction, and he said that the time had come to "give the finishing touches to the southern aristocracy."

The large brick house just north of the inn, now the inn annex, was the home of the Warner family. From that house, James Meech Warner, a Middlebury student who boarded at home, went to join the army, serving first in the west under John Sedgwick, who later led the army of the Potomac's 6th Corps. In 1862, at Sedgwick's request, Warner was named commander of the largest Vermont regiment, the 11th. Colonel Warner led the regiment during its service as an artillery unit in the forts around Washington. Then when the 11th was made an infantry unit and a part of the 1st Vermont Brigade, Warner led it to Spotsylvania Courthouse, for its first combat. In an attack against well-prepared Confederate positions on May 18, Warner was severely wounded, though he stayed on the field until the fighting ended late that day. The *Middlebury Register* of May 25, 1864, reported that Warner "reached his home . . . on Monday evening, having received a wound which, though not dangerous, will disable him for weeks. A sharpshooter ball passed in at the back of the neck and came out below the right ear." Warner returned to the 11th but was soon promoted to command a brigade in the 6th Corps and was brevetted a brigadier general.

Middlebury sent some 350 men to the Civil War. Their service is memorialized by the massive Civil War monument across the green from the church. Dedicated in 1885, figures on the four corners honor the army, navy, cavalry, and marines.

Among those honored was Sergeant Frederick Swift, 6th Vermont, who died of disease in July 1862 at the close of the Peninsula Campaign. Just west of the Congregational Church stands the Swift home, a large and stately yellow house. Frederick's sister, Mary Ann Swift, kept a diary, and her entries from that early summer are filled with comments concerning anxious reports on Frederick's health being received from the front. Though she usually made a daily entry, she wrote on August 17: "It is more than two weeks since I made any record, yet that period has been one of the most eventful of my life. In that time a dashing brother has passed away from earth and all that is mortal has been brought from the camp at Harrison's Landing, Va. and laid to rest among the other dear sleepers in the little enclosure at the cemetery."

On the green just downhill from the Congregational Church is St. Stephens Church. The *Register* reported in May 1861 that "public prayers for our country are offered daily in St. Stephens church." The pastor, Reverend Henry Frost, joined the 7th Vermont as its chaplain in January 1862, but after going south to Louisiana with the regiment, he became ill and returned to Middlebury.

Between the Congregational Church and the Swift home, Seymour Street leads north. Follow it through its left-right jog, and 0.3 mile beyond, on the left, several houses before the covered bridge, is 101 Seymour Street. Once a farmhouse, it was the postwar home of Corporal William Cady, 14th Vermont, who fought at Gettysburg. Cady was so exhausted after the long march to the battlefield and the fight that he was left for dead behind a fence on the field. But he recovered to rejoin the 14th just before it headed home for Vermont.

Proceed west on Route 30 through the village of Middlebury and to the Middlebury College campus. At the campus's center, three stone buildings, known as the Old Stone Row, survive from the Civil War era. Facing the row, the building on the left is Starr Hall, in the center is the Old Chapel, and on the right is Painter Hall. Some two hundred men who attended Middlebury went to war. By using college catalogs from the era, it is possible to determine where many of them roomed during their time at the college. A sample:

Lt. John Converse, class of 1862, who survived Gettysburg, but was killed at the Battle of the Crater at Petersburg, lived in room 2 of Painter Hall.

Pvt. Henry Eaton, class of 1862, wounded at Gettysburg as a captain in the 16th Vermont and who was killed at the Crater as a lieutenant colonel in the 17th, lived in room 1 of Painter Hall.

Lt. Albert Crane, class of 1863, 6th Vermont, killed May 5, 1864 in the Wilderness, room 11 Painter Hall.

Lt. Charles Newton, class of 1865, 10th Vermont, killed at Cold Harbor, room 17 Starr Hall.

Capt. Lyman Knapp, class of 1862, 16th Vermont, wounded at Gettysburg, room 32 Painter Hall.

The *Middlebury Register* reported on December 28, 1864, on a fire that destroyed Starr Hall. "On Sunday evening . . . the new college building was discovered to be on fire, and before any effective aid could be rendered, the flames had made such progress as to make all attempts to suppress them futile. In two or three hours nothing was left of the building, but the gaping walls." Starr Hall was rebuilt within a year.

When the war began, the Middlebury student body responded enthusiastically. D. K. Simonds, class of 1862, recalled in 1898 for *The Undergraduate,* "It was a poor time for study, but the professors were lenient, as they were as greatly interested as were the students. A military company was quickly formed with almost all the students as members, of which Prof. Seeley was Captain. Recreation hours were mostly spent in drill. A glee club sang nothing but patriotic airs and frequently attended war meetings in Middlebury and neighboring towns to encourage enlistments. A large number of students left before graduation to join the army and never returned to college; in fact, after the commencement of 1863 the college was almost deserted."

On April 12, 1865, the *Register* said: "Never before has the sober village of Middlebury betrayed such a capacity for enthusiasm as on the reception of the glorious news on Monday morning that Lee's army had surrendered. Everybody met everybody with a beaming face and a hearty shake of the hand; all the bells rang out an irrepressible clangor . . . the morning trains came to and left the village with a prolonged scream and multitudes came in from all the country around to see what was the matter. Later in the day the demonstrations became more coherent; a procession formed at the depot, composed of 50 or 60 horsemen of the State Militia, armed and equipped, and the fire company in full uniform, gallant young men put the livery stables in requisition, and loads of fair women and brave men brought up the rear of the triumphal procession which traversed the streets with banners flying. Before the Addison House the procession and assembled citizens listened to a few brief speeches, interspersed with songs and volleys from the military, and went on their way rejoicing."

Three days later, Mary Ann Swift wrote, "The land mourneth! The great victories overshadowed by calamity! Scarcely does the echo of rejoicing die away when a wail of sorrow breaks upon the ear! Abraham Lincoln President of the United States was shot by an assassin last night, in the theater at Washington."

She wrote April 16, the next day, "The Congregational Church was draped in mourning and Mr. Hyde preached a discourse appropriate to the occasion from Psalms 19:9. 'The judgments of the Lord are true and righteous altogether': a passage quoted by Mr. Lincoln in his last inaugural address."

April 19, she wrote, "Today is the funeral of President Lincoln at 12 o'clock a.m. services were held in the Congregational and Episcopal churches. All the bells tolled from one to two o'clock." The *Reg-*

ister reported that the college students attended the services at the Congregational Church "wearing crape on the left arm."

SOURCES

BAIN, DAVID HAWARD. *THE COLLEGE ON THE HILL: A BROWSER'S HISTORY FOR THE BICENTENNIAL.* MIDDLEBURY, VT: MIDDLEBURY COLLEGE PRESS, 1999.

DOUGLASS, FREDERICK. *THE LIFE AND TIMES OF FREDERICK DOUGLASS, FROM 1870 TO 1882, WRITTEN BY HIMSELF.* EDITED BY JOHN LOBB. LONDON: CHRISTIAN AGE OFFICE, 1882.

MIDDLEBURY COLLEGE CATALOGS, 1858–1865. SPECIAL COLLECTIONS, MIDDLEBURY COLLEGE.

MIDDLEBURY REGISTER, 1860–1865. HENRY SHELDON MUSEUM OF VERMONT HISTORY, MIDDLEBURY.

SHAMESHKIN, DAVID. *THE TOWN'S COLLEGE: MIDDLEBURY COLLEGE, 1800–1915.* MIDDLEBURY, VT: MIDDLEBURY COLLEGE PRESS, 1985.

SWIFT, MARY ANN. DIARIES, 1861–1865. HENRY SHELDON MUSEUM OF VERMONT HISTORY, MIDDLEBURY.

SWIFT, SAMUEL. *HISTORY OF THE TOWN OF MIDDLEBURY IN THE COUNTY OF ADDISON, VERMONT.* RUTLAND, VT: CHARLES E. TUTTLE, 1971.

WITH THANKS TO SPECIAL COLLECTIONS, MIDDLEBURY COLLEGE, AND THE HENRY SHELDON MUSEUM AND STAFF MEMBERS ELLEN ZERN, SUSAN PEDEN, AND JAN ALBERS.

MONKTON

The Monkton town office, on the west side of the main road through Monkton Ridge, housed town meetings in the 1860s. Voters here, on December 10, 1863, authorized the selectmen "to pay a bounty not to exceed $300 to each volunteer who shall be enlisted in the United States service before Jan. 6, 1864, and applied on the quota of this town to be raised under the last call of the President of the United States for volunteers." The selectmen were also authorized to pay an additional $50 to each volunteer "contingent on the full quota of volunteers being raised." The selectmen were also allowed to borrow $5,000 to support all that. On January 19, 1865, at a special meeting here, voters approved bounties of $500 to recruit soldiers "under the call of the president for 300,000 more." On March 5, 1865, at the annual town meeting, Monkton people were informed that the town debt amounted to $13,620.

From Monkton Ridge go north, in 0.2 mile bear left on Davis Road, and then quickly go left on Rotax Road. In 2 miles, go right on Roscoe Road and take a swift left on Cemetery Road. Down this narrow road 0.25 mile, see a rough lane that leads to an old Quaker Cemetery. On entering the lane, look left to where an old cedar tree stands amid bushes. There once stood a Quaker meetinghouse. Proceed into the cemetery, and at the far end, find the crude slate gravestones of Joseph Hoag and his wife Huldah Case Hoag. The two came to this area from Duchess County, New York, in the 1780s and established a farm that encompassed this cemetery. The cemetery and the southern part of the field are in Monkton, while the house the Hoags built in 1834 is in Charlotte. A Quaker minister, Hoag held services in the adjacent church. He was known locally as a good farmer and an expert on fruit growing and gardening. Hoag traveled along the East Coast preaching, sometimes visiting the southern states. He was an outspoken opponent of slavery, and he sometimes gave shelter to fugitive slaves in his home, the house visible far across the field to the northwest. But beyond that, he was famed as a man who saw visions.

Shortly before he died in 1846, Hoag wrote a book about his life. In it, he recalled an event that happened on this farm more than two score years before. "In the year 1803, probably in the eighth or ninth month," he wrote, "I was one day alone in the fields, and observed that the sun shone clear, but that a mist eclipsed the brightness of its shining . . . And I heard a voice from heaven say, 'This that thou seest, which dims the brightness of the sun, is a sign of the present and coming times. I took the forefathers of this country from a land of oppression; I planted them here among the people of the forest. I sustained them, and, while they were humble, I blessed them and fed them, and they became a numerous people; but they have now become proud and lifted up, and have forgotten Me, who nourished and protected them in the wilderness, and are running into every abomination and evil practice of which the old countries are guilty, and I have taken quietude from the land, and suffered a dividing spirit to come among them. Lift up thine eyes and behold.'"

The voice went on to say that the dividing spirit "broke out in appearance like a volcano, in as much as it set the country in an uproar for a time." And then Hoag heard, "it entered politics throughout the United States, and did not stop until it produced a civil war, and an abundance of blood was shed in the course of the combat. The Southern States lost their power, and slavery was annihilated from their borders." This vision of the Civil War happened more than a decade and a half before the guns opened on Fort Sumter. The voice was heard from above this high field, in which the cemetery is located, which commands a long view to the south, across the fields and ridges of Monkton and along the high main ridge of the Green Mountains, toward the distant fields of battle.

In the Quaker cemetery are two Civil War gravestones. Charles L. Ransom served in a New York regiment. John Noonan, who lived on a farm that could be seen from the cemetery, was a private in the Vermont Cavalry. He enlisted in the fall of 1861, got sick, and died ten months later.

Return as you came to Monkton Ridge and go past the old town hall, going due south on Bristol Road just under 3 miles. In the farmhouse on the left, with barn beside it, lived Augustus Cox, a corporal in the 6th Vermont. Enlisting in 1861 when the regiment was formed, Cox was wounded and taken prisoner at Savage's Station. Soon paroled, he reenlisted and was again wounded at the Wilderness on May 5. Recovering and promoted sergeant, he was wounded a third time at Cedar Creek. He died of those wounds three days after the battle.

Continue south on Bristol Road and soon turn right on Hardscrabble Road. Go 0.5 mile to an intersection, turn left to stay on Hardscrabble, and in 0.5 mile come to another intersection. Look right here to the old Kaolin School, where it is believed that John Horan attended school. Horan enlisted in the 11th Vermont in

July 1863 and a year later was captured at Weldon Railroad. Confined at Andersonville, he was released the following February but died at a hospital in Annapolis, Maryland, in June 1865. He was not quite eighteen.

Go straight at the intersection, and just beyond the school, on the right, is a frame house with a porch across the near section. Henry Barnum went from here to enlist as a private in Company F of the 1st U.S. Sharpshooters in August 1862. Wounded at Petersburg soon after the siege began, likely by another sharpshooter, he died at twenty-two on July 14, 1864.

Return via Hardscrabble Road to Bristol Road and turn right, going south. In 0.25 mile, go left on Church Road to the Morgan Cemetery. Walk to the high point of the cemetery to the gravestone of Watson Morgan, who joined Company F of the sharpshooters in August 1862. Taken prisoner at Weldon Railroad on June 23, 1865, he ended up in Andersonville. Like young Horan, he died on the way home, at Annapolis, on March 1, 1865. He was twenty. His stone notes that he was the son of George and E. A. Morgan and says, on the back, "Prisoner at Andersonville." The Morgans lived in the farmhouse just south of the cemetery, and the parents obviously could see the gravestone from their house. Private Morgan's funeral was held at the family home on March 22, 1865, and the sermon was preached by Reverend Charles Morgan, apparently an uncle. "War has its artillery, swords, shells, bayonets, and its prisons," he said, "yes, alas, its prisons. These latter and direful evils have always sprung into active existence wherever and whenever the wild tocsins of war has rung out its exciting tones." The reverend then said that young Morgan's death had been unnecessary. "Most of their prisons are in the interior of the country," he said, "far from the seat of war, and where the prisoners might be fed, if the disposition to feed them existed. Any one knows that if a camp of five or ten thousand prisoners was located here in Vermont, small as our state is, and rocky as our soil is, we could feed them. Georgia is several times as large, with mellow soil, and sunny months, and slaves to work; still our captured patriots are denied bread enough to keep the skin upon their bones."

From the cemetery, go north of Mountain Road 3.5 miles and cross State Prison Road, going straight onto Turkey Lane. In 0.2 mile, look for the trace of a shallow cellar hold dug into the bank on the left. After the war, Michael Furlong lived here. A native of Ireland, as a private in the 14th Vermont he received a shell wound in the head at Gettysburg on the day of Pickett's Charge. A year later, he went completely blind but lived until 1890.

Return to Mountain Road, go south, take State Prison Hollow Road right, and return to Monkton Ridge.

SOURCES
BUSHEY, LEON V., JESSIE THOMAS, AND HOWARD M. FRENCH, EDS. *HISTORY OF MONKTON, VERMONT, 1734–1961.* MONKTON, VT: MONKTON MUSEUM AND HISTORICAL SOCIETY, 1961.
CARLISLE, LILIAN BAKER, ED. *LOOK AROUND CHITTENDEN COUNTY, VERMONT.* BURLINGTON, VT: CHITTENDEN COUNTY HISTORICAL SOCIETY, 1976.
FURLONG, MICHAEL. PENSION HISTORY AND SERVICE RECORD. COURTESY OF GERALD HEFFERNAN AND BRISTOL HISTORICAL SOCIETY.
HOAG, JOSEPH. *JOURNAL OF THE LIFE OF JOSEPH HOAG: CONTAINING HIS REMARKABLE VISION.* LONDON: A. W. BENNETT, 1862.
MONKTON MUSEUM AND HISTORICAL SOCIETY. *CIVIL WAR SOLDIERS OF MONKTON, 1861–1865.* MONKTON, VT: MONKTON MUSEUM AND HISTORICAL SOCIETY, 2008.
MORGAN, REV. CHARLES P. "A SERMON PREACHED ON THE OCCASION OF THE DEATH OF WATSON P. MORGAN." MARCH 22, 1865. COURTESY OF HOPE BURRITT.
WITH THANKS TO GILL COATES, JOHN REYNOLDS, AND HOPE BURRITT.

NEW HAVEN

New Haven's village green lies along the south side of Route 17, between New Haven Junction and Bristol. Opposite the green's northwest corner is New Haven's memorial to the veterans of modern wars, and a flagpole. By them, the footprints of the Congregational Church and the town hall are still visible, both long ago lost to fires. Meeting in the town hall, New Haven voters approved bounties that began at $75 in August 1862 and rose to $600 within two years. Those payments drove the town into an indebtedness that exceeded $11,000 by town meeting 1864.

In the Congregational Church, New Haven women met to make items for sick and wounded soldiers. On the first Sunday in October 1862, funeral services were held there for Captain M. P. S. Cadwell, an 1859 Middlebury College graduate who enlisted in the 22nd New York and was killed at Second Bull Run. From 1836 to 1846, James Meacham was pastor. Later, as a member of Congress, he was an outspoken opponent of slavery. Speaking in the

House of Representatives on February 15, 1854, against the further expansion of slavery in the western territories, he said:

"Pass these bills, and you will arouse a stronger and more-bitter anti-slavery feeling that has ever before existed in this nation . . . If any man representing Missouri believes that slavery will not go to Kansas on the passage of this bill, I now invite him to say so . . . Pass that bill, and the spawn will be cast along all the streams, and the larva will be deposited in all the soils, from which is hereafter to spring a race of bondmen—of slaves."

Then he added, "If the Missouri compromise is repealed, I honestly believe that it is the last compromise that will ever be made between the clashing interests of different sections in this Republic."

From the green, go north on North Street and quickly see the New Haven town hall on the right. The house directly across the street was once the town post office where Henry Roscoe was postmaster. He fought at Gettysburg with Company G of the 14th Vermont. Indeed, nine New Haven men served in that company. Continue along North Street 1.75 miles, cross Plank Road, and the first farm beyond, on the right, belonged to the King family. From the graceful Greek Revival house, Peter King went to war as a private in the 5th Vermont, dying on May 12, 1863, eight days after he was wounded protecting the retreat of the 6th Corps at Banks Ford, near Fredericksburg.

Return to the green and turn west, right, on Route 17, passing through fertile farm fields. The *Middlebury Register* noted on May 26, 1861, that nearly every farmer in New Haven "has a large field of beans intending to raise enough to feed a regiment." On reaching Route 7, turn north and quickly stop at the brick depot, built about 1850. Here, Company G, 14th Vermont, recruited at Bristol, departed for war. Private Abel Peck, a Ferrisburgh lad, wrote in his diary on October 6, 1862: "I started for Brattleboro went to New haven Depoe + thair I met the rest of the company left the station at half pass 9 got to Brattleboro at half pass 5."

Go south 1.75 miles on Route 7 and note the large and handsome house on the hilltop to the right, once the home of Alice Doud. She noted in her diary on April 14, 1861, "Washed. Heard Fort Sumter taken and Anderson with men prisoners of war."

Continue south 1 mile and turn right on Dog Team Road. In 1.2 miles, enter the hamlet of Brooksville and see its 1854 Advent Church on the right. On March 11, 1861, people gathered here heard a reading of Abraham Lincoln's first inaugural address, which included the words: "The mystic chords of memory, stretching from every battlefield, and patriot grave, to every living heart and hearthstone, all over this broad land, will yet swell the chorus of Union, when again touched, as surely they will be, by the better angels of our nature."

According to diarist Dowd, a gun known as the thunderer was then taken to the top of the hill, accompanied by the cheers and hurrahs of boys, and fired. Surely, the hill referred to was the little eminence across the road from the church.

Continue on Dog Team Road to Route

7 and turn right, then quickly left on River Road. In 1 mile, cross Nash Bridge, once a covered bridge, over the New Haven River and look to the big Nash house on the left. Edward Nash, sergeant major of the 14th Vermont, went to war from here to fight at Gettysburg. Continue on River Road 3 miles, enter New Haven Mills, and look to the tall and elegant Victorian masterpiece, the Lampson School, built in 1868. The school is a celebration of the end of war, built by New Haven as it emerged from the war period.

SOURCES

FARNSWORTH, HAROLD, AND ROBERT H. RODGERS. *NEW HAVEN IN VERMONT, 1761–1983*. NEW HAVEN, VT: TOWN OF NEW HAVEN, 1984.

MEACHAM, JAMES. SPEECH IN THE HOUSE OF REPRESENTATIVES. FEBRUARY 15, 1854. VERMONT HISTORICAL SOCIETY.

MIDDLEBURY REGISTER, 1864. HENRY SHELDON MUSEUM OF VERMONT HISTORY, MIDDLEBURY.

WITH THANKS TO BETTY BELL.

··

ORWELL

Orwell's Congregational and Methodist churches, side by side, face the village green, located just east of Route 22A, along Route 73. During the Civil War, Orwell town meetings took place in the Methodist building. On July 29, 1862, at what town records show to have been a war meeting, voters gathered to consider whether to tax the grand list to pay soldier bounties. But after considerable discussion, such a tax was deemed to "have no lawful right," and instead, $1,700 was raised by subscription. In January 1863, Orwell voted 107 to 84 against

a tax to pay bounties. But the town soon changed its mind. By war's end, Orwell had, according to its records, spent a total of $21,586 on bounties. The town sent 110 men to war, of whom 90 enlisted in Orwell. A total of 14 Orwell men avoided serving by providing substitutes, while 5 men paid $300 commutation fees.

In the Methodist Church, Orwell cast 144 votes for Lincoln, 15 for Stephen Douglas, and 4 for John Breckinridge in 1860. Four years later, Orwell went for Lincoln over George McClellan, 189 to 28.

A women's organization had been formed within the Congregational Church before the present building was erected in 1843. When the war began, that group adopted the name the Soldiers' Aid Society and met throughout the conflict to make items for the troops, sometimes gathering in the church.

In 1865, a new tracker organ, built by Hook Brothers of Boston, was installed by the Congregationalists, at a cost of $1,500. A history of the church states that "the organ's swelling harmonies filled the church when the men came home at the end of the Civil War."

In May 1889, Orwell veterans formed the John A. Logan Post of the GAR and met in a hall in the village that no longer stands. By 1891, the post had twenty-eight members and had become the only mounted GAR post in the nation. That year, the post was invited to participate in the August 19 dedication of the Bennington Battle Monument. The men assembled on the green the morning of August 18 and rode north to the depot in North Orwell, where at 9 AM they boarded a southbound train, loading the horses in two boxcars. They reached Bennington at 2 PM, and next morning, the post escorted President Benjamin Harrison to the Old Soldiers Home. According to the Orwell history, "at 9:15 a.m. the Troops moved out by fours, followed by the President's carriage drawn by four white horses, 28 mounted men and six carriages, five miles in 30 minutes over country roads. Promptly at 9:45 o'clock the boys landed the President at the Home, with every horse steaming and nobody hurt."

To follow the route of the post horsemen from the village to the depot, go to the east end of the long green and proceed north on North Orwell Road. In 2.5 miles, look closely for the old railroad bed at the depot site.

Turn around and come back on North Orwell Road 0.8 mile and go left on Royce Hill Road. In 1.3 miles, see the small house on the left, which was once a part of the Baptist church complex (perhaps the parsonage) that once stood here. Church members had many disagreements concerning slavery, and one resulted in the expulsion of the pastor, who had been hired in 1837, the prominent and fiery abolitionist Orson Murray (see Brandon).

Turn around and soon go left on Beauvais Road. In 1 mile, turn left on Hibbard Hill Road, and in 0.3 mile on the right is the Hibbard farmhouse. At eighteen, Henry Hibbard enlisted as a private in Company D of the 14th Vermont, fought at Gettysburg, and returned here safely.

One-third mile past the Hibbard Farm, go right on Fisher Road, and in just over 1 mile, go left, east, on Route 73. In 1 mile, come to Abel's Corner, where the roads form a triangle on the left. From a farm here, Charles Abel joined the 5th Vermont as a sergeant in the fall of 1861, returning home four months later, discharged for disability. But he recovered and joined Company D of the 14th Vermont and served at Gettysburg.

Return west on Route 73 to Orwell village, and go north 1 mile on Route 22A. The Royce farm is on the right, home of Sergeant Darwin Royce, who served at Gettysburg with Company D of the 14th. Look west from here, across the fields, to a complex of buildings, once the Spaulding Farm. Sergeant Charles Spaulding, of the same company, also fought at Gettysburg.

Continue north 0.1 mile on 22A and go right on Brown Lane. In 0.6 mile is the old Brown farmhouse, from which twenty-five-year-old David Brown enlisted with the 14th Vermont. Wounded at Gettysburg, Private Brown came home to live until 1912.

Return to 22A and go south 1.8 miles; pass the turn to Orwell village en route and go right on Cook Road. In 0.5 mile, go left on Old Stage Road, and in 0.8 mile, go right on Brock Lane. The road ends at the old Brock farm. John Brock, forty-five, and his son, John Jr., both joined the 11th Vermont as privates in December 1863. The son died on June 24, 1864, of sickness, at the close of the Overland Campaign. The father came home at war's end in poor health.

SOURCES
BISHOP, DORIS S. *A HISTORY OF THE TOWN OF ORWELL*. ORWELL, VT: TOWN OF ORWELL, 1963.

CROCKER, REV. HENRY. *HISTORY OF THE BAPTISTS IN VERMONT*. BELLOWS FALLS, VT: P. H. GOBIE PRESS, 1913.

"A CHURCH IS BORN . . . AND LIVES ON FOR TWO HUNDRED YEARS." FIRST CONGREGATIONAL CHURCH OF VERMONT, ORWELL. PAMPHLET, 1989.

WITH THANKS TO SUSAN ARNEBOLD, BETTY WALKER, GLORIA JAMES, AND STEVE BUXTON.

....

PANTON

The little procession that bore John Brown's body passed through Panton on December 6, 1859, on its way to his mountain home at North Elba, New York. To follow its route, from Vergennes, cross the Otter Creek Bridge and go south on Route 22A for 0.2 mile, then turn right on Panton Road. In just over 4 miles, on reaching the ridgetop village of Panton Corners, turn right on Jersey Street, then take a quick right on Adams Ferry Road. A local boy with the last name of Kent witnessed the passing and years later said that about sixty people were gathered in Panton Corners for the event. He said that the wagon paused briefly so that people might pay their respects. He also said that the coffin, or box containing it, had been badly cut up by souvenir hunters carving out pieces. The 1854 Baptist Church witnessed the event, as did the old blacksmith shop across the road, a wagon shop in 1859, and the house just beyond it at the top of the hill, the Kent home.

From Panton Corners, continue on Adams Ferry Road, with the high peaks of the Adirondacks, where Brown lived, growing more prominent to the west, covered with fresh snow that morning. In 1 mile, cross Arnold's Bay Road and proceed past the water treatment plant down to the lake shore at Arnold's Bay, where ferryman Daniel Adams transported the body to the New York shore. The next day, Reverend Joshua Young, of Burlington's Unitarian Church, arrived at Arnold's Bay, accompanied by fellow Burlington abolitionist Lucius Bigelow. Young wrote years later, "When we arrived at Vergennes, the threatening storm (it had been drizzling all day) had begun. It was pouring hard, with every prospect of a 'North-Easter.' To our inquiries, the answer came that the funeral procession had crossed the lake the evening before and must now be near its destination. Confident that we could overtake it before it reached North Elba, or at any rate get there in season for the funeral services, we lost no time in hiring a driver to take us to the ferry in the township of Panton, 6 miles distant. We at once made known to the ferryman our object, and our great desire to be landed as soon as possible, on the further shore, Baber's Point. He shook his head at our request and at once gave us to understand that his license as ferryman did not require him to cross the lake at so late and hour and in such a storm; and, moreover, that in his opinion, John Brown deserved the fate which had befallen him . . . Our hearts sank like lead . . . One hour went by, and two and three and yet there was no softening of that rock, no relenting. Suddenly there was a brightness outside the window of the dimly-lighted room; and on going to the door, lo! the wind had veered to the West, the clouds had broken up, and all around the darkness was disappearing . . . God's full-orbed moon had thrown a bridge of silver across the lake."

Young arrived at North Elba in time to participate in the funeral, which closed with the lowering of John Brown's body into its grave. Young recalled, "Then it was that there came to my lips the triumphant words . . . 'I have fought a good fight, I have finished my course, I have kept the faith. Henceforth there is laid up for me a crown of righteousness which the righteous judge shall give me at that day, and not to me only, but until all them also that love his appearing.'"

From the time of Brown's raid on Harpers Ferry, the Civil War may well have been inevitable. To see one of its consequences, on leaving the lake return to Arnold's Bay Road and turn left, stopping at the cemetery just beyond the farm. Just in from the main entrance is the grave of Panton's John Converse, twenty-one and a lieutenant in the 17th Vermont when he was killed in the Battle of the Crater at Petersburg. Converse also fought at Gettysburg with the 14th Vermont.

Return along Adams Ferry Road to Panton Corners and turn right on Jersey Street. From the house on the corner to the right, Gerard Holcomb went to war, also fighting at Gettysburg with the 14th Vermont. Just beyond is the old stone school, referred to in Panton town records as "the schoolhouse near the meeting house," for its proximity to the 1852 Methodist Church, now the Panton town hall. In the 1860s, Panton town meetings were held in schoolhouses. Meeting in this schoolhouse

in March 1863, Panton residents approved a $995.65 tax on the grand list to pay soldier bounties. The following November, a bounty of $200 was approved.

Continue south on Jersey Street 0.5 mile and bear left at the intersection to stay on Jersey Street. In another mile, just beyond Spaulding Road, is another stone schoolhouse referred to in Panton records as "the schoolhouse near John Spaulding's." Meeting here on August 25, 1862, Panton voted its first bounties, $50 for each of seven men.

From the school, continue south on Jersey Street 0.5 mile and turn right on Allen Road. In the first farmhouse on the right lived Jesse Converse, a 2nd Vermont private who was discharged for disability after the long march to Gettysburg. A local man, Russell Kent, wrote years later, "Jesse was a boy of sixteen at the battle of Gettysburg and one day when he was coming home from celebrating the battle, having a few drinks aboard, he fell in a bumble bee's nest. When I came by, he said, 'Russell, those bees sound just like the minie balls at Gettysburg.'"

Return to Panton Corners, and go due north past the store on Jersey Street. In just over 0.5 mile is a large farm where lived Isaac Hatch, a private in the 2nd Vermont who was wounded at the Wilderness. Continue north another 0.5 mile to another large farm, the Allen farm. Private John Allen, 8th Vermont, had served only two months when he died of disease, just before the war's end, on April 14, 1865, the day Lincoln was shot. Captain Solomon Allen led Company I, of the 14th, at Gettysburg. From a population of 390 in 1860, Panton sent some 40 men to war. Take Jersey Street north to Panton Road, turn right, and soon come to Route 22A.

SOURCES

KENT, ALBERTA, AND WILLIAM KENT. *PANTON PAST AND PRESENT: CONDENSED HISTORY OF THE TOWN OF PANTON, VERMONT*. PANTON, VT: PANTON BICENTENNIAL COMMITTEE, 1961.

KENT, RUSSELL L. "PANTON CORNERS." PAMPHLET, UNDATED. VERMONT HISTORICAL SOCIETY.

MIDDLEBURY COLLEGE CATALOG, 1860. SPECIAL COLLECTIONS, MIDDLEBURY COLLEGE.

YOUNG, REV. JOSHUA. "THE FUNERAL OF JOHN BROWN." *NEW ENGLAND MAGAZINE*, APRIL 1904.

RIPTON

Go east from East Middlebury on Route 125 and on reaching the top of the hill and the village of Ripton, a store is on the right. Just past it, a steep-sided knoll called the Pinnacle rises. Continue past the store, and quickly, on the left, are three old buildings, the last being the 1864 Methodist Church. The July 17, 1861, *Middlebury Register* reported that on that Fourth of July, three hundred people formed a procession in this area and marched to the Grove "a little westerly of the Pinnacle." The flag was raised, the Declaration of Independence was read, and "The Star Spangled Banner" sung, followed by patriotic speeches.

It appears that some Civil War–era town meetings were held in the Methodist Church. Ripton voters were tight fisted, according to town records, refusing to approve any bounty payments to soldiers until January 1865, leaving the amount to the discretion of the selectmen.

After the war, George King lived in the first house on the left, past the church. At eighteen, he enlisted in the 5th Vermont as a private and served nearly three years. The second building beyond, a tiny house also on the left, was once the rear portion of a store owned by Josiah Chandler, who served with King in the 5th's Company B and was wounded at the Wilderness.

Cross the bridge and turn left on National Turnpike, then quickly right on Peddler's Brook Road. Herman Damon, a musician in the 7th Vermont, lived in the first house on the right after the war. Private Damon served four years, being sent with his regiment, after the war ended, for duty along the Rio Grande.

In under 0.25 mile, turn right on Maiden Lane and in .75 mile turn left, east, on Route 125. In 0.75 mile, on the right, is the Robert Frost Trail parking lot. Just beyond, on the left, is the Robert Frost Wayside Area. The poet made Ripton his primary residence the last few years of his life. Frost wrote only one poem about the Civil War, "The Black Cottage," concerning an abandoned house where the widow of a Civil War soldier lived. The lengthy poem includes the lines:

> He fell at Gettysburg or Fredericksburg,
> I ought to know—it makes a difference which:
> Fredericksburg wasn't Gettysburg, of course.

Just beyond the wayside area is a small cemetery shaded by maple and cedar, certainly familiar to Frost, with several Civil War graves. Eugene Farr lies here, a private in the 6th Vermont for nearly three years, until mortally wounded at Cold Harbor at twenty-one. Lieutenant Henry Downer, of the 1st Vermont Battery, was twenty-six when, according to his stone, he drowned at Carrolton, Louisiana, on August 7, 1862.

Continue 0.3 mile on Route 125 and go left on Stream Mill Road. In 0.6 mile on the left is the house from which brothers James and Samuel Kirby enlisted as privates in Company A, 6th Vermont, on October 15, 1861. Samuel, twenty-seven, was discharged for disability a year later and died three months after returning home. James lost an arm and was discharged about the same time. He lived until 1919, making a living as a woodchopper, one of the best in town.

Continue past the Kirby house, following a National Forest road in the shadow of Breadloaf Mountain. In 4 miles, bear left at an intersection and continue through another intersection until coming to a small schoolhouse on the right, now a hunting camp. Once Ripton's District Seven School, several lads studied here who became Civil War soldiers. Among them was Wallace Newton, a 5th Vermont private, wounded at twenty-three at Savage's Station.

Continue past the school 1.5 miles, pass through an intersection, and in 0.25 mile come to Cooke Cemetery. Samuel Kirby is buried here, as is Joseph Hale, who enlisted at forty as a private in the 14th Vermont and fought at Gettysburg. He reenlisted in the 5th Vermont's Company F and was killed at Spotsylvania's Bloody Angle. His son George, also a private in Company F, was wounded at the Wilderness and at the April 2, 1865, Breakthrough at Petersburg. He died in 1913.

Also buried here is Frederick Deattrich, who, his stone says, was a drummer boy with the British army at Waterloo. He died during the Civil War, in Ripton, on February 20, 1864, at age sixty-four.

SOURCES

FROST, ROBERT. *COLLECTED POEMS OF ROBERT FROST*. NEW YORK: HENRY HOLT, 1930.
JOHNSON, CURTIS B., ED. *HISTORIC ARCHITECTURE OF ADDISON COUNTY: INCLUDING A LISTING OF THE VERMONT STATE REGISTER OF HISTORIC PLACES*. MONTPELIER, VT: STATE OF VERMONT DIVISION FOR HISTORIC PRESERVATION, 1992.
RIPTON TOWN RECORDS.
WITH THANKS TO JOHN REYNOLDS.

SALISBURY

Some 8 miles south of Middlebury on Route 7, turn east on West Salisbury Road and soon come to a triangle of grass with a small monument. Placed there by the Salisbury Ladies' Aid Society in 1920, it lists the names of the fifteen Salisbury men who died in the Civil War.

Continue straight past the monument and quickly, on the left, is the Salisbury Congregational Church. Among the soldier funerals held here was that of Private Charles A. Walker, killed on May 12, 1864, at Spotsylvania's Bloody Angle. A local woman, a Mrs. Bump, noted in her diary on May 21, "Martha carried Sarah Walker home to the village. Mrs. Walker just heard of her husband's death on the battlefield. Oh, how sad it makes us feel to have the glory of our country slain by merciless traitors. How many hearts are made sad? Oh, who but feels the weight of this awful rebellion, when will it cease?"

Continue into Salisbury village and turn left on Smead Road. In 0.25 mile, the first large house on the right, just outside the village, was the home of the owner of a woolen mill that stood along the Leicester River, just behind it. That mill made cloth for uniforms during the war.

Return to the village and to Route 7 as you came, cross the road to continue on West Salisbury Road, and in just under 1 mile on the right is a large farmhouse. Captain Eugene Hamilton lived here, who helped organize Company F of the 5th Vermont, which contained fifteen Salisbury men. After fighting at the Wilderness and Spotsylvania's Bloody Angle, Hamilton wrote home, "I have just four men left in my company this morning. I have been in command of our regiment for two days for all the officers above me have been killed or wounded. Tongues can't describe what we have been through for the past 10 days." A hired man on the Hamilton farm, Private Lester Hack, served in Hamilton's company. Hack was wounded at the Wilderness but recovered and served on until the war's end. On April 2, 1865, he was in the forefront of the 6th Corps attack at Petersburg. One of the few enlisted men from Vermont to win a Medal of Honor, Hack, according to historian G. G. Benedict, "seized a Confederate flag, knocked down the color bearer, though surrounded by a squad of his com-

rades, and secured the flag." Hack came home to Salisbury and lived a troubled life, sometimes getting into fights.

One-third mile beyond the Hamilton place, Kelley Road turns north. Just beyond the intersection, on the right, is a huge old farmhouse, the postwar home of Captain Samuel Kelley, who served in both the 1st and 9th Vermont regiments. Kelly hosted several 9th Vermont reunions here, the men sleeping in tents set up around the house. The gatherings were military in nature—bugle calls waking the veterans for reveille and taps ending the day.

Continue on West Salisbury Road 0.5 mile, and note stone foundations on the right around a driveway turning to the right. This area of Salisbury was peopled by Canadian immigrants. Just downhill on the right is a cellar hole in the field, all that remains of a house where Sifroi Maheu lived after the war. Called John by the neighbors, Maheu fought at Gettysburg as a private in the 14th Vermont.

Continue on West Salisbury Road to the intersection of Leland Road, and turn left to the West Side Cemetery, where many veterans lie. On Memorial Day 1877, a grand observance was held here, organized by Captain Kelley. Speakers included Oliver Otis Howard and Edward Hastings Ripley.

Continue on West Salisbury Road 0.5 mile to a Y, and go right on Creek Road. Just ahead is the railroad track where the old West Salisbury depot stood. On the morning of June 7, 1861, a train carrying recruits for the 2nd Vermont Regiment, gathering in Burlington, passed here. People here at the depot saw one young soldier standing atop a car. The train had originated in Bennington, and as it rolled north, eighteen-year-old George Plumb, a member of Company A from Bennington, climbed to the roof of a car. Some 2 miles north of the depot was a covered railroad bridge, according to one account known as the Oxbow Bridge. According to the *Rutland Herald*'s Middlebury correspondent:

"A son of Mr. Wainwright was near the bridge when the unfortunate Plumb met his sad fate, who informs me that as the train approached the bridge, he saw a man standing on the top of the car riding backwards, and appeared to be looking at something in the rear of the cars,—he was in that position when the train entered the bridge, as his head came in contact with the bridge he fell on his face with both arms extended . . . He was seen on top of the cars at the West Salisbury station."

When the train reached Middlebury, the unconscious young man was taken to the Addison House (Middlebury Inn), where, according to a doctor "there was a deep depression on the back side of the head, the bones of the back of the head were separated, and probably an extensive fracture at the base of the brain." Despite two operations aimed at easing pressure on the brain, Plumb never regained consciousness. "He soon after had three slight spasms, after which he sank rapidly, and died at 15 minutes to 9 p.m."

In Bennington, Plumb's funeral, one of the largest ever held in that town, took place at the Congregational Church. He was, apparently, the first member of the 2nd Vermont to perish.

SOURCES
PETERSEN, MAX P. *SALISBURY: FROM BIRTH TO BICENTENNIAL*. SALISBURY, VT: DUNMORE HOUSE, 1991.
SALISBURY TOWN RECORDS.
WITH THANKS TO MAX PETERSEN AND JAMES PETERSEN.

SHOREHAM

The Shoreham village green is along Route 74, just west of where it leaves Route 22A in the apple country of Addison County. The Shoreham Congregational Church is on the green's west side and south of it is the Shoreham Civil War memorial, with the names of twenty Shoreham men who perished. The names include: Private Robert E. Hitchcock, twenty-one, a Marine, killed at First Bull Run; Sergeant Edward Dorsey, twenty-four, 5th Vermont, killed at Savage's Station; Private William Higgins, twenty-four, 2nd Vermont, killed at Banks Ford; Sergeant John Kalaher, twenty-nine, 2nd Vermont, dead at Spotsylvania's Bloody Angle; Private Moses Keefe, thirty-one, 5th Vermont, killed at Cold Harbor; Private Alfred Mosby, twenty-four, a cavalryman dead at Andersonville; Private Luscius Northrup, eighteen, 4th Vermont, dead at Andersonville; Private Peter LaDam, 5th Vermont, eighteen, killed at Charles Town, Virginia; Private John Woodward, twenty-three, 11th Vermont, killed at Cedar Creek; and Corporal Lewis Young, twenty-two, 5th Vermont, killed at the April 2, 1865, Petersburg Breakthrough.

Near the monument, a tall flagpole flies the Stars and Stripes. The *Middlebury Register* of May 12, 1861, reported that a flagpole, 75 feet high, was raised there and "went up as a cannon fired," amid loud cheering and celebration. Shoreham people have kept a flagpole there since.

On September 16, 1862, a war meeting was held in the Congregational Church, and according to the *Register,* "Capt. Abel's company was in the gallery." Captain Charles Abel, of Orwell, commanded Company D of the 14th Vermont, made up of Addison County men. That day, the company was soon to leave for Brattleboro to join the 2nd Vermont Brigade. According to the paper, the Reverend Byron Sunderland, of Washington, D. C., gave "a report on the war." Sunderland concluded, "We have a destiny before us . . . we are to work out the will of God." Sunderland was an avowed abolitionist, who, as pastor of Washington, D.C.'s First Presbyterian Church, had begun preaching against slavery, in that largely pro-slavery city, in 1857. To bid farewell to Company D, Sunderland had come back to the town where he was born on November 22, 1819. From 1861 to 1864, he served as chaplain of the U.S. Senate. After the war, he was for two years president of Howard University, the all-black college founded in Washington by Oliver Otis Howard (see Burlington).

Shoreham people gathered in the Congregational Church throughout the war on the fourth Sabbath evening of every month to pray for the country.

Where Route 74 joins 22A, the house in the northeast corner of the intersection, just north of a service station, was the home of Private Lucius Northrup, 4th U.S. Infantry, who died at Andersonville.

The large house in the northwest quadrant of the 22A/74 intersection was the home of George Catlin, who gave Shoreham the big flagpole erected in 1861. A much later owner of the house discovered that its fireplace mantels had once been painted black. That seemed to verify a local legend that Shoreham people blackened their mantels on hearing of Lincoln's death.

Across Route 74, the first house past the Shoreham post office was the home of Robert Hitchcock, one of the first Marines killed in the Civil War and one of the first Vermonters to die by hostile fire, when he fell at First Bull Run on July 21, 1861. Farther west, the last house on the left before the Platt Memorial Library was, after the war, the home of William Anderson. The son of a slave, Anderson is said to have come to Vermont at war's end with a Vermont regiment. He prospered in Shoreham, owning an orchard.

SOURCES
SHOREHAM HISTORICAL SOCIETY. *SHOREHAM, THE TOWN AND ITS PEOPLE.* SHOREHAM, VT: SHOREHAM HISTORICAL SOCIETY, 1988.
SHOREHAM TOWN RECORDS.
WITH THANKS TO SUSAN MCINTYRE AND JOHN REYNOLDS.

STARKSBORO

The 1838 Starksboro Village Meeting House, beside the town office on Route 116 in the village of Starksboro, was built as a Methodist Church. But its basement meeting room has been the site of Starksboro town meetings since 1840. The *Middlebury Register* of June 19, 1862, reported that a "military meeting" was held there "last Friday at 1 p.m. during which the [Middlebury] College Glee Club sang patriotic songs, followed by a series of speeches." The topics were "enducements for young men to enlist," "struggles of our forefathers," and "progress of the war."

On August 26, 1862, voters here resolved "that the town of Starksboro hereby votes to raise a tax on the Grand List of said town for 1862, to pay volunteers to fill out the quota for said town of forty men, on the two last calls of the President of the United States, for six hundred thousand men; a bounty of one hundred dollars each." On December 19, 1863, $400 bounties were voted, and a month later, $600 payments were approved.

Nineteen men enlisted here at the meetinghouse to serve in Company G of the 14th Vermont, the Bristol Company. All fought at Gettysburg. Among them was Private Charles Ross (see Hinesburg), killed at Gettysburg, and Private Hoyt Sales, who joined at sixteen, survived Gettysburg, and then signed on with the 5th Vermont, dying of wounds suffered at the Wilderness. When word of a soldier death was received in Starksboro, the meetinghouse bell was tolled at 9 AM, as it was for all deaths in town.

Another soldier who enlisted at the meetinghouse was Andrew Brown, who at twenty-three joined the 5th Vermont in December 1863. Brown survived a wound suffered at the April 2, 1865, breakthrough at Petersburg. After the war, Brown joined a Quaker church at Monkton Ridge but refused to accept its pacifist ways. They let him remain a member.

From the Starksboro Meeting House, go 5 miles south on Route 116, then turn west on Route 17 and climb into the Green Mountains. In just under 7 miles, go left on Gore Road, which leads toward Buell's Gore. In 0.5 mile, on the left, is a one-room schoolhouse, which some of Lawrence Swinyer's children attended. Swinyer, a veteran of the War of 1812, had eight sons serve in the Civil War. Twins Alepheus and Alfred were privates in the 7th Vermont. Twins Truman and William joined the 5th Vermont. Truman was wounded at Savage's Station while William was wounded at Weldon Railroad. Son John fought at Gettysburg with the 13th Vermont, then joined the 9th Vermont. Stephen, who enlisted in the 17th Illinois, was wounded at Shiloh. Father Lawrence Swinyer is buried in the Buell's Gore Cemetery, not far beyond the school.

SOURCES
MIDDLEBURY REGISTER, 1861–1862.
    VERMONT STATE LIBRARY.
STARKSBORO TOWN RECORDS.
WITH THANKS TO ELSA GILBERTSON AND
    JOHN REYNOLDS.

VERGENNES

From Route 7 take Route 22A into Vergennes and, passing beneath the railway underpass, look closely within the industrial area on the left for the little Vergennes railway station. At 8 AM on December 6, 1859, with a fresh fall of light snow down on the Champlain Valley, a train bearing the body of abolitionist John Brown arrived at this station. The casket was accompanied by Brown's widow, Mary Ann Brown, and the abolitionist Wendell Phillips. The *Vergennes Citizen* reported that the remains were deposited in an "open cutter" and taken to the Stevens Hotel "in front of which it remained for some time." The paper said, "As the news spread through the place a large crowd assembled to get a glimpse of the coffin, and many offered to pay for a sight of the remains—which idea, of course, could not be entertained. Pieces of the box containing the coffin were broken off by spectators to be retained as keepsakes. A procession numbering about 60 persons escorted the body and those having charge of it, a short distance west of the bridge which crosses Otter Creek, near the center of town. The cutter containing the body and the covered sleigh in which were the widow and friends, proceeded to Adams Ferry on their way to North Elba. Mr. Brown is remembered by several of our citizens—he was detained here a day or two by bad weather about a year ago."

Brown had been hanged in Charles Town, Virginia, on December 2. His widow and Phillips were taking the body to the Brown home in the Adirondacks at North Elba, passing through Vergennes since no railway line as yet led up the New York side of the lake.

From the railway station, continue south on Route 22A, which becomes Main Street. At the intersection of Main and Green streets, note the building at the corner that has the look of an old hotel. This was the Stevens House where Mrs. Brown stopped, perhaps for breakfast, before moving on to the lake and the Adams Ferry at Panton. Returning from Brown's funeral, Phillips stopped at the Stevens House, as the *Vergennes Citizen* noted, "a week after the death of John Brown." The paper said that the hotel quickly became crowded with "the curious and those who felt desirous of learning all the incidents connected with Brown's last moments and his burial." Phillips quickly agreed to give a speech at the town hall (which no longer stands), where the paper reported that he "has the appearance of a plain quakerish looking gentleman of about 50, with an air of thought and earnestness which comports well with his feverish but unimpassioned style of oratory." In the crowded hall, the paper said that Phillips, "Placed him [Brown] as a spotless offering on the altar of slavery."

Many years later a Vergennes man, Christopher Yattaw, recalled the arrival of Brown's body. Yattaw said that he was, at the time, a young man working as a handyman at the Stevens House. One of his jobs was to give rides to people arriving at, or going to, the station. Yattaw said that he had given rides to Brown in the past. Indeed, several accounts state that Brown, on several occasions, came to Vergennes to procure supplies for his family and for the community of free blacks that he lived with at North Elba, New York. Yattaw told a reporter for the Massachusetts' *Springfield Union* that he had previously met Brown and that "the next time I heard of John Brown was when a casket bearing his body was brought into the Stevens hotel." Yattaw said he drove the casket to the ferry on Lake Champlain.

Continue along Main Street and note

the block of stores built with stone on the left, where Brown is said to have shopped. Quickly turn right on Macdonough Street, but as you do, notice the first house on the left just ahead, with a large glassed-in porch added, once the home of Christopher Yattaw. Four years after Yattaw drove the conveyance bearing Brown's body, he enlisted in the 14th Vermont and was wounded during Pickett's Charge.

Proceed along Macdonough Street, and in 0.5 mile, the old stone federal arsenal building is on the left. On May 31, 1861, the *Vergennes Citizen* reported that a company was enlisted here, choosing Solon Eaton, of Addison, as captain, and Amasa Tracy, of Middlebury, as first lieutenant. The company would become Company K of the 2nd Vermont and serve throughout the war. Tracy would write one of Vermont's distinguished war records, rise to the rank of colonel, and win a Medal of Honor at Cedar Creek.

More than three years later, on learning of the October 19, 1864, Confederate raid on St. Albans, a Vergennes man, Charles Parker, reacted. Parker, who had served as a captain in the 7th Seventh Vermont, gathered 40 young men, ages fourteen to eighteen, into an informal company. Marching them to the arsenal, he issued arms and then divided his command, placing men at posts along the approaches to Vergennes, including roads to the lake. The city was most relieved to learn, next day, that the raiders had fled into Canada.

Return to Main Street, pass directly across it onto South Water Street, and the redbrick 1834 Congregational Church is soon on the right. The *Vermonter*, another Vergennes paper, reported on a concert given here on April 14, 1863. "The Battle Cry of Freedom fitly closed the entertainment," the paper said. "This is one of the best patriotic songs which the times have given birth to, and quartette with chorus—it warmed up the hearts with patriotic fervor." Julia Ward Howe had written the hymn little more than a year previous.

Return to Main Street and turn right, again passing the Stevens House. Note the small brick building across the green from the old hotel, on Park Street, which was once the law office of Frederick E. Woodbridge, longtime mayor of Vergennes. Woodbridge was elected to Congress in 1863. He hastened to Fredericksburg after the Wilderness battle in the spring of 1864 to help treat the wounded. Turn right on Green Street, keeping straight past the jog where New Haven Road bears left. The third house past the corner on the right, now much changed, was the home of the Tucker family. Philip Tucker, a lawyer who represented Vergennes in the legislature, was a Democrat who took a dim view of the approaching war. Tucker had watched John Brown's body pass through town and in a letter to his sister observed, "Poor John's remains went through here on their way to North Elba with a procession, tolling of the bells of the churches, & Wendell Phillips's personal attendance. I of course stood at the door, or on the piazza of my office, & despised and frowned upon the attempted respect to the remains of a murderer." Tucker died in 1860, but his wife lived to keep a diary through the war years.

SOURCES

BROWN, JOHN. FILE. BIXBY MEMORIAL
LIBRARY, VERGENNES.

DEGREE, KENNETH A. VERGENNES IN 1870:
A VERMONT CITY IN THE VICTORIAN AGE.
PRIVATELY PRINTED, UNDATED.

TUCKER, MARY. DIARY, 1861–1865. SPECIAL
COLLECTIONS, BAILEY/HOWE LIBRARY,
UNIVERSITY OF VERMONT, BURLINGTON.

VERGENNES CITIZEN. CIVIL WAR ERA. BIXBY
MEMORIAL LIBRARY, VERGENNES.

VERMONTER. CIVIL WAR ERA. BIXBY
MEMORIAL LIBRARY, VERGENNES.

WITH THANKS TO JOHN REYNOLD AND THE
BIXBY MEMORIAL LIBRARY STAFF.

WALTHAM

Little 9-square-mile Waltham sent 20 soldiers to war from a population of about 250. At least three died. H. P. Smith's *History of Addison County, Vermont,* published in 1886, says of the town: "Her quota of men to be raised under the several calls of the president in the War of the Rebellion was promptly furnished, submitting to the draft on one occasion, when two citizens of her town paid a commutation of $300 each."

Go south from Vergennes on Maple Street and in 2.5 miles on the left is the Waltham town hall, attached to Waltham's old District Two schoolhouse, which now houses the town office. During the Civil War, Waltham did not yet have a town hall, so town meetings were held in its three schoolhouses. Some of the decisions made by Waltham voters on bounties and taxes were made in this building. And surely some Waltham men enlisted here.

Proceed south on Maple Street, and quickly come to the first farm on the right, once owned by the Jackman family.

From here, John W. Jackman, twenty, went to war, joining Company F, 1st U.S. Sharpshooters in August 1862. Jackman served only until January 10, 1863, when he was discharged for disability. Still, he saw action along the Potomac River in a skirmish with the rear of Lee's army retreating from Antietam.

Continue south on Maple for 0.7 mile to Sunset View Cemetery on the left, commanding a remarkable view across the fertile farm fields of Addison County to the High Peaks of the Adirondacks. From Waltham, Artemus Cassius Cross enlisted with young Jackman as a private in Company F, 1st U.S. Sharpshooters. Cross, known to his family as Cassius, was mortally wounded at the Wilderness, according to the inscription on his stone, on May 5. That day, his company was fighting very close to the embattled 1st Vermont Brigade, protecting the vital intersection of the Brock and Plank roads.

Cross is buried in the national cemetery at Fredericksburg, but his family erected a cenotaph in his memory in the family plot, located in the upper left corner of Sunset View. The stone says that Cassius Cross died "in the Wilderness in front of Hancock's Corps" and that he was "18 years and 11 months" old. The brief epitaph is hard to read but says, in part, "Noble boy Having died for others. Rest in Him."

SOURCES

SMITH, H. P. HISTORY OF ADDISON COUNTY.
SYRACUSE, NY: D. MASON AND CO., 1886.

WALTHAM TOWN RECORDS.

WITH THANKS TO MARY KINSTON.

WEYBRIDGE

Go north from Middlebury on Route 123, and in 2.5 miles on the left is the Weybridge Congregational Church where Weybridge held town meetings during the Civil War. Just past the church, bear right on Quaker Village Road, and in just over 1.5 miles on the left is the present-day Weybridge town hall, built in 1847 as the Wesleyan Methodist Church. The church was organized in 1843 because of slavery. In 1843, some Methodists congregations in New York state left the Methodist Episcopal Church over the slavery question. Some Vermont Methodists in the Champlain Valley joined the revolt. In Weybridge, the avidly antislavery Methodists chose Reverend John Croker as their minister and built themselves this church. In 1893, that building was sold to the town as a town hall, well after the Weybridge Methodists reunited.

Continue on Quaker Village Road, and quickly take the turnoff on the right, by the power dam, just before crossing Otter Creek. Stop by the power station and look to the large old house ahead. Once some ten Sturtevant families lived along Otter Creek in this area. But twentieth-century construction of a power dam flooded the area known as Sturtevant Bow. Only this Sturtevant house survives. The family is one of Weybridge's oldest, and indeed, a monument near where the Lemon Fair River joins Otter Creek marks the site where British raiders in 1778 captured Justus Sturtevant and spirited him to Canada as a captive. A grandson of Justus, Wesley Sturtevant, who lived in one of the houses along the Creek in this area, served as a corporal in the 14th Vermont. His cousin, Ralph Sturtevant, of the 13th Vermont, wrote a history of his regiment (see Swanton). Ralph and Wesley grew up together in this area, and years later they had a battlefield conversation, on Cemetery Ridge at Gettysburg, just before Pickett's Charge. Ralph wrote in his history: "Corporal Wesley C. Sturtevant, my cousin and playmate from birth to early manhood came from his regiment only a few rods to the left to see me and this is part of what he said, 'I shall never see home and dear friends again, something tells me I shall be slain in this battle, and I cannot drive away the awful thought. I have come to tell you and request that you tell father and mother, brothers and sisters and dear friends for me and say good-by; that I would like to be buried in Weybridge, my native town."

Ralph Sturtevant wrote that Wesley's mother had been "impressed with the idea that there was some mysterious connection unexplainable between natural and immortal life that revealed to the living premonitions of the future." He said that he tried, there on the battlefield, to convince his cousin not to be greatly concerned. But, he said, "My efforts were all in vain."

After Pickett's Charge, according to Ralph, "I wondered now if his premonitions of death had proven a reality. I could not wait and hastened to the 14th to ascertain if dead or alive. Just before reaching his company I met some of his tent mates that were then on their way to find me. They took me only a few steps further and there on the ground as he fell was the mangled body of my cousin W. C. Sturtevant having been shot through the breast by a solid shot or shell. His comrades told me that he fell just as the regiment rose to take part in the advance against General Pickett's charge, being instantly killed."

A brother of Ralph, John Sturtevant, who also grew up in the area, served as a private in the 1st Vermont Regiment, then as a corporal in the 5th Vermont. He was mortally wounded at Spotsylvania's Bloody Angle.

Continue north on Quaker Village Road, cross the bridge by the dam, turn right on Field Days Road, and in 0.25 mile a road comes in from the right. In the southeast corner of the intersection once stood the Methodist Church, which was divided by the slavery issue. The house to the north, across the intersecting road, was its parsonage. Just north of the intersection, on the left, is the old Methodist Cemetery and to its rear is an obelisk, Wesley Sturtevant's memorial. The inscription says that he was killed at Gettysburg "while gallantly charging upon the rebels," that he was twenty-four, and that "I have fallen for my country." Also in the cemetery is Frank Grenville's stone, which says that he also served in the 14th Vermont, died at nineteen at Wolf Run Shoals, Virginia, and "gave his life for his country." Nearby is a small government-issue stone for Private William T. Cole, 2nd Vermont, who died of disease after serving only five weeks.

The population of Weybridge when the war began was 667. One count puts the number of men who served at 51, of whom 7 died.

SOURCES

STURTEVANT, LEVI WALTER. *STURTEVANT FAMILY GENEALOGY.* MIDDLEBURY, VT: S.N., 1968. COURTESY OF HENRY SHELDON MUSEUM.

STURTEVANT, RALPH ORSON, AND CARMI LATHROP MARSH. *PICTORIAL HISTORY OF THE 13TH REGIMENT VERMONT VOLUNTEERS, WAR OF 1861–1865.* PRIVATELY PRINTED BY THE REGIMENT, 1910.

WASHINGTON, IDA H. *HISTORY OF WEYBRIDGE, VERMONT.* WEYBRIDGE, VT: WEYBRIDGE BICENTENNIAL COMMITTEE, 1991.

WITH THANKS TO PHYLLIS WEST AND IDA WASHINGTON.

WHITING

South of Cornwall and north of Sudbury, the village of Whiting lies along Route 30. At the crossroads of Route 30 and the Leicester/Whiting Road is the 1811 meetinghouse, in whose basement Civil War–era town meetings were held. In 1863, town voters approved bonuses for all men who served. A year later, bounties of $400 were voted, and selectmen were authorized to borrow $3,600 to pay them. A tax of $1.31 for each dollar on the grand list was voted in 1865 to meet war expenses.

Whiting sent forty-two men to war, among them Franklin Hubbard, who enlisted at twenty-three as a musician in the 2nd Vermont Light Artillery. Hubbard was captured August 3, 1864, in a skirmish at Jackson, Louisiana. A fellow Whiting soldier serving with Hubbard, Sergeant Major Perry Baker, wrote Hubbard's father Asahel on August 4, 1863:

"Sunday morning Lieut C. H. Dyer and 28 men started out, (with two pieces and Caissons) with a party of Caverly, & Infantry, on a scout that is the last I saw of Frank. This morning about 3 o'clock eleven of the men come back, bringing with them 5 horses. They report that they met with the rebels at Jackson, La. Which were to many for them but the rebs made the attack, surrounded, and took all of our boys, & guns, etc. Frank was taken prisoner at the first charge. The rebs took all of his arms & bugle, horse etc. and in the next fight Frank made his escape and was seen after the firing had ceased All right and said if the rebs got him again that they would do well, we look for him every minute."

Hubbard was recaptured and eventually confined at Andersonville. A Whiting history states that Hubbard and others escaped but that Hubbard was recaptured when he returned for his bugle. Hubbard died at Andersonville on June 19, 1864, and is buried there. His cenotaph is located in the cemetery behind the meetinghouse with this verse:

Sleep on sleep on no more in rain,
He'll long to see his home in vain.
Safe in the mansions of the blest,
The soldier finds his home and rest.

From the meetinghouse, go north 0.25 mile on Route 30 to a large frame house on the right. It is believed that Perry Baker went to war from here as sergeant major of the 2nd Vermont Light Battery, later commissioned a lieutenant. Earlier, he was a private in the 1st Vermont.

Continue north 1.5 miles on Route 30, and go right on Gibeault Road, which dead-ends at an old farm, once the Asahel Hubbard farm, where Franklin Hubbard grew up.

Return south on Route 30 to the crossroads by the meetinghouse, and go left on the Leicester/Whiting Road. In 0.75 mile, Crosby Road goes left to a farm with huge barns. Bowman Crosby operated an extensive stockyard here and reportedly sent mules to the Union armies.

Continue on the Leicester/Whiting Road 1.75 miles, pass Stove Pipe Road on the left, and the second house past it on the right, with two chimneys, was once the Bryant family home. George Bryant joined the Vermont Cavalry in late 1861 but was soon discharged for disability. He recovered and reenlisted in the 5th Vermont a year later and was wounded at the Wilderness.

SOURCES

JOHNSON, CURTIS B., ED. *THE HISTORIC ARCHITECTURE OF ADDISON COUNTY: INCLUDING A LISTING OF THE VERMONT STATE REGISTER OF HISTORIC PLACES.* MONTPELIER, VT: STATE OF VERMONT DIVISION FOR HISTORIC PRESERVATION, 1992.
WEBSTER, HAROLD. *THE OLD ADDISON RAILROAD: THE LITTLE RAILROAD THAT CAME AND WENT.* WHITING, VT: PRIVATELY PRINTED, 1986.
WEBSTER, HAROLD, AND ELIZABETH WEBSTER. *OUR WHITING: THE HISTORY OF THE TOWN OF WHITING, VERMONT.* WHITING, VT: TOWN OF WHITING, 1976.
WITH THANKS TO GRACE SIMONDS.

chapter three

Bennington County

In the quiet cemetery behind Vermont Veterans Home, the headstones of Vermont Civil War soldiers stand rank on rank. Many bear the treasured symbol of the Army of the Potomac's 6th Corps, in which the 1st Vermont Brigade served. With the corps, those men fought at the Wilderness, Spotsylvania Courthouse, Cold Harbor, and Cedar Creek. A cannon has long guarded their resting places. In Manchester is the home of Edmund Cummings, one of seven members of the Cummings clan who perished as a result of the brief but bloody battle at Savage's Station. Not far away is Hildene, the home Abraham Lincoln's son Robert built so that he might spend summers in Vermont. He had discovered Manchester while vacationing at the local hotel with his mother, Mary Todd Lincoln. In Readsboro is the house from which Newton Stone went to war and to which his body returned after he was shot dead at the Wilderness. Throngs turned out for his services in Bennington and Readsboro. In his hometown, while his family looked on, the colonel's warhorse was brought out to prance along the street in response to the crowd's demand. In Arlington, on a December day in 1859, a woman who hated slavery instructed her grandson to ring long the bell in the stone church on the day John Brown was hanged. It tolled all the day, the sound long remembered in the Valley of Vermont.

ARLINGTON

Along the Valley of Vermont, in Arlington, just south of where Route 313 turns west from Route 7A to follow the winding Battenkill River, is St. James Church. Just across the street is the Arlington Community House. Built in 1829, the house was written about, in 1859, by Robert Willis Allen in his book *Marching On: John Brown's Ghost from the Civil War to Civil Rights*. Allen said that on December 2, 1859: "In Arlington, Vermont, Almera Hawley Canfield woke her grandson early in the morning. 'Get up, Jim,' she told him. 'This is the day John Brown is to be hanged. And I want you to go over and toll the bell for him. Jim tolled the bell very slowly as was the custom for a death until relieved two hours later by his cousin." All day long the two boys alternated the task, and the tolling never stopped until nightfall. Meanwhile, across the street in her home, Mrs. Canfield sat "in a straight rocking chair holding a Bible in her lap from which she read aloud caustic passages from the Old Testament about God's plans for the evil-doers . . . Townspeople well understood Mrs. Canfield's outspoken views on the abolition of slavery." Allen continued, "Ever after that day, Jim Canfield said that he could still hear in the early morning the 'heart-shaking, Day of Wrath knell, solemnly filling with its deep resonance our corner of the Vermont valley.'" Bells were rung that day in many towns in the North, Allen wrote, noting, "This was the last time for six years that so many bells would be rung across America for a single death. A majority of these bells were taken down and used to make rifles, bullets, and cannons during the conflict which John Brown had predicted 'would purge the land with blood.' And after the conflict,

those same rifles and cannons would be turned into bells again."

From the Canfield house, go south 2.5 miles along Route 7A and turn left on Depot Lane. From the big old farmhouse on the knoll to the right, Nathan Andrew went to war, joining the 14th Vermont and fighting at Gettysburg. He was one of 133 Arlington men who served in the Civil War.

Return north on 7A, and on reentering the village, note the town hall on the right, just south of the Canfield house. Here, Arlington voters met to pass on matters related to the war, and after the war, the local Dudley Post of the GAR often met here. Indeed, a photo taken of the old veterans assembled in front of the hall includes an aged, bearded Nathan Andrew. On three nights in late March 1876, the post staged in the town hall a fundraiser that posters advertised as a "Thrilling War Drama: The Loyal Mountaineers, or the Guerilla's Doom."

Among the twenty-one local soldiers who died in the war were two Blowers lads who, it seems, were never cut out to be soldiers. The Blowers family apparently took up residence in western Arlington, along the New York border, sometime in the late 1700s. Not much is known of them, except that at one time some of them were members of the Baptist church. The building that once housed that church still stands in West Arlington. To get there, go 4 miles on Route 313 west from 7A toward the New York line and turn left, crossing the 1852 covered bridge. The first building on the right, now a Grange hall, was once the Baptist Church. Surely the bridge and the church, set amid the high Taconics, were well known to George and William Blowers. The brothers entered the 2nd Vermont in the summer of 1862. Private George Blowers deserted on July 1, 1863, apparently on the march to Gettysburg, returned the following October, and on December 18, 1863, was executed by a firing squad on the orders of a court-martial. Also shot that day was another 2nd Vermont deserter, Private John Tague, of Rouses Point, New York. Private Wilbur Fisk wrote:

"The band discoursed a dirge-like piece of music, when the prisoners were conducted to their coffins, on which they kneeled, and the guard filed around and took position in front of them, scarcely half a dozen yards distant . . . The prisoners were not blindfolded, but looked straight into the muzzles of the guns that shot them to death . . . Blowers had been sick, his head slightly drooped as if oppressed with a terrible sense of the fate he was about to meet. He had requested that he might see his brother in Co. A, but his brother was not there. He had no heart to see the execution, and had been excused from coming. Tague was firm and erect till the last moment, and when the order was given to fire, he fell like a dead weight, his face rested on the ground, and his feet still remaining on the coffin." Apparently, the firing squad was not quite as effective with Blowers. Fisk wrote that he exclaimed, "Oh dear me!," struggled for a moment, and was dead." A soldier from Brownington, Pvt. Daniel Skinner, 3rd Vermont, said that Blowers lived "until . . . the Dr. cut his jugular vain in the throat."

Brother William Blowers remained with the 2nd and was wounded at Cold Harbor. But at the Battle of Winchester, September 19, 1864, he deserted. Apparently, he never came home.

SOURCES
ALLEN, ROBERT WILLIS. *MARCHING ON!: JOHN BROWN'S GHOST FROM THE CIVIL WAR TO CIVIL RIGHTS.* NORTHFIELD, VT: NORTHFIELD NEWS AND PRINTERY, 2000.
ANDREW, NATHAN LUTHER. CIVIL WAR DIARY. RUSSELL COLLECTION, MARTHA CANFIELD LIBRARY, ARLINGTON.
BLOWERS FAMILY FILE. RUSSELL COLLECTION, MARTHA CANFIELD LIBRARY, ARLINGTON.

BENNINGTON

The Bennington Battle Monument dominates the Bennington landscape, commemorating a nearby battle fought four score and four years before the Civil War. The monument's dedication, on August 19, 1891, resulted in a reunion of Vermont Civil War veterans. Participating in the parade that preceded ceremonies were 625 members of the Grand Army of the Republic, and no doubt many more veterans were in the crowd of 30,000. Among the Civil War luminaries in attendance were Wheelock Veazey, Oliver Otis Howard, Redfield Proctor, William Wells, Samuel Pingree, Roswell Farnham, William Ripley, Urban Woodbury, and Thomas Seaver.

Ceremonies took place on a stage erected along the south side of the 306-foot monument. Veazey, then a member of the Interstate Commerce Commission, was master of ceremonies. While most speeches focused on the August 16, 1777,

Revolutionary War Battle of Bennington, several references honored the Civil War veterans. President Benjamin Harrison said: "The participation of this state in the War of the Rebellion was magnificent. Her troops took to the fields of the South that high consecration to liberty which had characterized their fathers in the Revolutionary struggle. They did not forget on the green savannas of the South, the green tops of these hills, ever in their vision, lifting up their hearts in faith that God would again bring the good cause of freedom to a just issue."

From the monument, take Monument Avenue to the Old First Church, going against the route of the 1891 parade. The *Bennington Banner* of May 16, 1861, reported that a flag was presented at the church "to the company departing for Rutland." That company was to become Company A of the 2nd Vermont, commanded by Captain James Walbridge, of Bennington.

Just south of the church is a small green with stone marker. It stands near the site of a building where, from October 1828 to March 1829, a young William Lloyd Garrison published the *Journal of the Times,* a campaign publication supporting the reelection of President John Quincy Adams. But Garrison crammed into the paper much criticism of slavery, though at the time he was a supporter of the American Colonization Society, dedicated to purchasing slaves and returning them to Africa. During his brief Vermont stay, Garrison sent a petition with 2,352 Vermont signatures to Congress asking for an end to slavery in the District of Columbia. He left Vermont gladly, having formed a rather low opinion of Vermonters. But he would be back, speaking for abolition, and his opinion of Vermonters would improve, markedly.

In the old graveyard beside the church lie soldiers who fought for the British at Bennington in 1777 and many Civil War graves. Among them is a broken column symbolizing a life too soon ended at the grave of Colonel Newton Stone, who died at the Wilderness leading the 2nd Vermont (see Readsboro). He had come to Bennington to study law before the war, and when Company A of the 2nd Vermont formed, he was elected second lieutenant. Not far from Stone lies Hiland Hall, who, among other things, participated in the 1861 peace conference that tried to head off the war.

From the church and cemetery, take Main Street (Route 9) downhill, and the Bennington Museum is on the right. The Bennington Civil War monument is by the entrance, a bas-relief that depicts four prominent Civil War Vermonters—George Stannard, Wheelock Veazey, Edward Hastings Ripley, and Bennington's James Walbridge—watching Vermont troops march to war. Surrounding the scene are leaves bearing the names of the 337 Bennington men who served. Stars are by the names of those who died.

Also by the museum entrance is a sculpture of Abraham Lincoln, the work of Clyde du Vernet Hunt. Known as the *Lincoln Trilogy*, it depicts the president with two young people and is believed to have been inspired by the words of the Second Inaugural "with malice toward none and charity for all." It was given to the museum in 1949. The Bennington Museum displays many Civil War items.

Continue on Main Street to Bennington's main intersection, where Routes 9 and 7 meet. At the southwest corner is a large old brick hotel, and some portions may date to, or near to, the Civil War. In the summer of 1862, sharpshooter trials were held here, certainly somewhere behind the building.

Go straight through the intersection, continuing on Main Street, and the Methodist Church is on the left. The rear portion, the stone sanctuary, predates the Civil War. The *Bennington Banner* of December 15, 1864, reported on the funeral of Henry Wadsworth, a private in the 4th Vermont, who died of wounds on July 4, 1864, the victim of a sharpshooter in the Petersburg trenches. The paper said, "He died in the hospital last July, but the present was the most favorable opportunity for bringing his body home, which was done by Mr. Henry Baker, with whom the deceased had lived a number of years."

Beyond the Methodist Church, on the right, is the Baptist Church, built on the site of the Civil War–era church. A funeral for Captain Frank Roy, who led the Vermont Cavalry's Company G, was held here on a November day in 1864. Roy died at Tom's Brook, in the Shenandoah Valley. The *Banner* reported that "his death was made more saddening from the fact that he had received papers which authorized his mustering out on the next Wednesday." The funeral procession, including many soldiers, formed on Main Street to take his body to the cemetery by Old First Church.

Look far ahead along Main Street to an area that was rocked by a gigantic early morning blast on February 2, 1864. More than one hundred barrels of gunpowder exploded at the Bennington Gunpowder Company, on the east edge of town. The *Banner* said, "The streets were soon filled with a hurrying, awe-stricken crowd, all hastening toward the scene of the disaster. . . ." The blast was so powerful it was heard in Troy, New York. Miraculously, no one was killed. The factory made gunpowder for the Union armies.

Return to the main intersection, and go north on Route 7 to the Vermont Veterans Home. Once called the Vermont Soldiers Home, it opened on April 1, 1887, for Vermont Civil War veterans who needed care, particularly those who remained disabled from wounds and wartime sickness. The first man admitted was George Wood, of Randolph, who, as a captain in the 6th Vermont, was wounded and taken prisoner at Savage's Station. Within six months, 50 veterans filled the place to capacity and the trustees voted to expand. It still operates, caring for some 200 Vermont veterans, male and female. A portion of the original building remains, a graceful old mansion with a wide porch. Indeed, photos exist of Civil War veterans seated on the porch, taking the air, no doubt occasionally turning their conversations to Antietam, Gettysburg, the Wilderness, and other faraway battlefields.

Today, photos are still to be found on the walls of early trustees, including William Wells, Amasa Tracy, Redfield Proctor, and other Vermont heroes. Behind the main building is the cemetery, where lie row on row of veterans. They include members of every Vermont Civil War regiment, all protected by a brass cannon cast for the Union armies in 1864. The 6th Corps Cross is on many stones, the emblem of the corps in which the Old Brigade served.

The evening of the Bennington Monument dedication, a dinner attended by five thousand people took place in two giant tents in front of the home. President Harrison attended, and a guest of honor was Alexander Webb, who commanded a brigade at Gettysburg. Oliver Otis Howard gave one of several speeches: "Comrades of the Rebellion," he said, "my mind and heart are full of reminiscences connected with Vermont men. Lately, I was reminded at Gettysburg . . . of your work there, and was glad to see that your General Stannard had the loftiest monument . . . The Second Vermont formed a part of my first brigade, and went with me into our first battle, that of Bull Run."

From the Vermont Veterans Home, go north on Route 7 and soon bear left on Route 67A, for North Bennington. In just under 0.5 mile, an old concrete block factory is close by the road on the left. Just across the road, a frame house with huge old trees on the lawn was the home of James Walbridge, who led the Bennington Company to war with the 2nd Vermont.

Continue into North Bennington and watch for signs for the Park-McCullough House. President Benjamin Harrison was a guest here for the battle monument dedication. The Orwell-mounted GAR company (see Orwell) came here to escort him

to the ceremonies, the president riding in a carriage pulled by four white horses.

Go past the house on Park Street to the white frame house behind it, once the home of Hiland Hall. Elected governor in 1858 and 1859, he spoke out strongly against slavery in both inaugural addresses. In 1860, he headed the Vermont delegation to the Virginia peace conference that attempted to head off war. When the war began, Hall provided financial help to area families with sons at war, recruited for local regiments, and traveled throughout New England, speaking in support of the war effort.

SOURCES
BENNINGTON BANNER, 1861–1865.
    BENNINGTON MUSEUM.
KOSCHE, EUGENE. "BENNINGTON'S CIVIL WAR
    MONUMENT." BENNINGTON BANNER, JUNE
    16, 1983.
RESCH, TYLER. THE METICULOUS ADVOCATE:
    HILAND HALL OF VERMONT; A BIOGRAPHY.
    2009. COURTESY OF THE AUTHOR.
WITH THANKS TO JOE HALL AND TYLER
    RESCH.

DORSET

Approach Dorset from the south along Route 30, from Manchester Center, and a prominent rounded summit commands attention ahead and slightly to the east. Owl's Head is a mountain made of marble, and on it are three quarries once worked by the Norcross West Company. One of those quarries has long been known as the Gettysburg Quarry, and local legend holds that marble for the grave markers in the Gettysburg National Cemetery came from it. Nearing Dorset, note the old quarry on the right with a historic marker that labels it the oldest quarry in the United States, begun in 1785. Just beyond the quarry is Kelly Road, and turning right from it is Black Rock Road. From well up that road, trails lead to the Gettysburg Quarry, a hike of about a half hour. To obtain directions, inquire at the Dorset Historical Society, farther north on Route 30.

Some 145 men from Dorset served in the Civil War, and the town's death toll was high, with 28 perishing. Dorset contributed men to the doomed Company E of the 5th Vermont Regiment, decimated at Savage's Station (see Manchester). The Wilderness cost the town 2 men, 1 was killed at Gettysburg, 1 at Spotsylvania's Bloody Angle, and 1 at the April 2, 1865, Breakthrough at Petersburg.

Continue north on Route 30 from the quarry, and in 1.2 miles on the right, come to the north entrance of the Maple Hill Cemetery. About 50 yards in, note a family plot on the right with a prominent obelisk marking the grave of Reverend William Jackson, once pastor of the Dorset Congregational Church. To the front and left of that stone is a memorial stone for Private William Jackson Fuller, Vermont Cavalry, captured near Richmond on June 29, 1864. Fuller died less than two months later at Andersonville, age twenty-two. His fading epitaph says, in part:

Faithful, firm,
Kind in spirit, calm in danger,
Brave in Battle, Honored & loved,
Dying in prison with 13 thousand
Loyal men—a victim to treason
And barbarity—a martyr for Freedom.

Fuller, born in New York state on the day Reverend Jackson died and named for him, lost his mother at an early age. He ended up living in Dorset with Charles and Susanna Baldwin, the daughter of Reverend Jackson. He enlisted at age nineteen. His stone is a cenotaph as he is buried at Andersonville.

Continue north on Route 30 and quickly note, set back on a rise on the right, a large white house, now an inn. Once the Congregational church parsonage, Reverend Jackson once lived here, and the Baldwins raised William Fuller here.

Continue north and look to the left, noting the second building south of the Dorset post office. Another man who endured Andersonville was William McWayne, a private in the 96th Illinois Regiment. McWayne, a native Vermonter, came to Dorset after the war and lived his later years in this house, even as a very old man coming out to watch the Memorial Day parade march past to the cemetery. Captured along Missionary Ridge near Chattanooga just after the Battle of Chickamauga, McWayne told the *Rutland Herald* in 1920:

"I remember three days at a time when we got nothing to eat at all. My first meal in Andersonville was a little cup of corn meal, ground coarse (cobs and all, the boys said). I had a two-quart pail to put it in, without salt, and mix it stiff with a little swamp water. Then I put it on a board, set it in a trench in the ground, and made a little fire in front of it to bake it. That was what we had to eat. Do you wonder that they carried out 25 or 30 men daily?"

Continue north and quickly see the

Dorset Historical Society on the right. The first two buildings beyond it on the right were once Alanson Gray's home and store. Gray's son John went south before the war, to North Carolina, and opened a marble business. There he was drafted, against his will, into the Confederate army. Relatives eventually located him in a northern prison camp and set him free.

Just north of the Gray buildings is a large house close by the road. Set behind it is an older house, once the home of Warren Dunton, who formed a small militia unit in Dorset when the war began. The unit went to Manchester and became part of the Equinox Guards, which later became Company E, 5th Vermont. Dunton, a sergeant, survived Savage's Station, where he was commended for bravery. He was wounded on December 13, 1862, at Fredericksburg and discharged the following May for disability. Dunton regularly attended reunions of the Equinox Guards and was eulogized by his comrades when he died in 1905.

SOURCES

GILBERT, A. W. SR. "THREE EASY WALKS IN DORSET TO HISTORIC MARBLE QUARRY SITES ON MTS. AEOLUS AND DORSET." PAMPHLET, 2005. DORSET HISTORICAL SOCIETY.

KNIGHT, BRIAN L. *NO BRAVER DEEDS: THE STORY OF THE EQUINOX GUARDS.* MANCHESTER, VT: FRIENDS OF HILDENE, 2004.

RESCH, TYLER. *DORSET: IN THE SHADOW OF THE MARBLE MOUNTAIN.* DORSET HISTORICAL SOCIETY. WEST KENNEBUNK, ME: PHOENIX PUBLISHING, 1989.

WITH THANKS TO ARTHUR GILBERT AND BRIAN KNIGHT.

GLASTENBURY

Today Glastenbury, a mountain town, has but a handful of people. The 1860 population was forty-seven, and figures vary on the number of men who served from the town, from a half dozen to twelve. Most of the inhabitants made their living as loggers.

One way to reach the town is by taking Route 9 east from Bennington's main intersection and soon turn left, or north, on Park Street. Pass the rear side of the Old Soldiers Home on the left and the high school on the right, and Park Street soon becomes East Road. The road roughly follows Route 7 along the base of the Green Mountains, and in about 8 miles, turn right on Glastenbury Road. In 0.75 mile, pass under Route 7, and you are now in Glastenbury. Quickly see an old house on the left surrounded by trees. In this house at the time of the Civil War lived the McDonald family, and at least two sons were of draft age. Elisha McDonald paid $300 in commutation and did not serve. Property McDonald entered the 8th Vermont in March 1865 and came home less than three months later when the war ended. He marched into Richmond with his regiment.

SOURCES

LEVIN, RUTH. *ORDINARY HEROES: THE STORY OF SHAFTSBURY.* EDITED BY TYLER RESCH. SHAFTSBURY, VT: SHAFTSBURY HISTORICAL SOCIETY, 1978.

RESCH, TYLER. *GLASTENBURY: A HISTORY OF A VERMONT GHOST TOWN.* CHARLESTON, SC: HISTORY PRESS, 2008.

LANDGROVE

Go west from Londonderry on Route 11 up along the Green Mountains just over 2 miles, turn right on Ridge Road, and stop. Once, in this little valley, a village called Landgrove Hollow thrived. From here, William Harrison Benson, twenty-two, Abel Patterson, twenty-one, and Cornelius Warner, nineteen, qualified with their marksmanship for Company H of the 2nd U.S. Sharpshooters when it formed in 1861. Benson, son of the local physician, was wounded at the bloody Cornfield at Antietam and died three weeks later. Patterson, a mechanic in civilian life who stood just 5 feet tall, served two years until discharged for disability. Warner's family owned a store in Landgrove Hollow. He was a musician in his company, served two years, then reenlisted. On September 25, 1862, he wrote home from Keedysville, Maryland, soon after Antietam: "My dear parents, You have heard of the awful battle that was fought near here last week. I happened to escape but many of my regiment was killed. Harrison was wounded in the right leg just below the knee."

Proceed on Ridge Road 1.25 miles to a frame house with a prominent stone chimney on the left, slightly below the road. From here, Daniel Eddy, at forty-one, went to join the 1st Vermont Cavalry in August 1864, served until the war ended, and was in the grand cavalry charges at Third Winchester and Cedar Creek.

Continue past the Eddy house and soon enter the village, noting a tennis court on the right. In the small frame house directly across the road, Mary Jane Coolidge lived out her years. Before the Civil War, she married Dr. Joseph Shaw and bore him four children. One, George Shaw, a private in the 2nd Vermont, survived a wound at the Wilderness. The doctor died in 1858, and Mary Jane again remarried, to Gilbert Hilliard. Just after New Year's Day 1862, Hilliard, forty, enlisted in the 8th Vermont. He died nine months later, apparently of disease. By him, his wife had triplets to go with her other four sons. She never remarried.

Continue past the house out of the village, cross a bridge, and bear right up steep Cody Road. Look back through the trees at the first house on the right. The front section was once a school in which Civil War–era town meetings took place. In this building in November 1860, Landgrove went for Lincoln over Douglas, 66 to 3. Four years later, the town favored Lincoln, this time 77 to 5 over McClellan. Here on August 23, 1862, Landgrove voted to pay $50 bounties, plus $7 per month extra pay, to men who would sign up for the 2nd Vermont Brigade. Six Landgrove men fought at Gettysburg with the 16th Vermont. On January 21, 1865, Landgrove approved $500 bounties with the caveat "not to pay soldiers that have been enlisted any more bounties."

Return down Cody Road and bear right, soon coming to the 1850s Methodist Church on the right. Certainly, this building heard much discussion of slavery. In the 1840s, Landgrove Methodists deserted this Methodist Church for the Wesleyan Methodist Church, because its stand against slavery was stronger. When the old church strengthened its antislavery position, the local faithful came back into the fold.

SOURCES

MARTIN, FONTAINE. THE LANDGROVE MEETINGHOUSE: A CROSS SECTION OF LANDGROVE, VERMONT, HISTORY. LANDGROVE, VT: PRIVATELY PRINTED, 1981.

WARNER, CORNELIUS. CIVIL WAR LETTERS. LANDGROVE HISTORICAL SOCIETY.

WITH THANKS TO PRISCILLA GRAYSON.

MANCHESTER

Abraham Lincoln never visited Vermont, but he planned to. His wife, Mary, on concluding her visit to Manchester in the summer of 1864, made reservations for the following summer at the Equinox House for both herself and her husband. Of course, John Wilkes Booth intervened. Still, Manchester today houses the most powerful Lincoln presence in the state, at Hildene, the home of Robert Todd Lincoln, the president's son. And one of the treasures of that grand estate is an oval mirror from the White House into which, the son said, his father looked before heading to Ford's Theater the night of his assassination.

A visit to Civil War Manchester must start with Hildene, whose entrance is located just south of Manchester village on Route 7. Robert Lincoln had visited Manchester with his mother, who vacationed in Manchester in the summers of 1863 and 1864 to escape the oppressive heat of Washington, D.C. On graduating from Harvard in 1864, Robert was determined to enlist. Partly to assuage his mother's fears, his father had Robert assigned to Ulysses Grant's staff, where Mary rightly believed he would be safe. Young Lincoln was present at Grant's headquarters in the last weeks of the war and was at Appomattox Court House when Lee surrendered his Army of Northern Virginia.

After the war, like his father, Robert became a successful lawyer. Appointed secretary of war by President Garfield, he also served as minister to Great Britain under President Benjamin Harrison. Later, he became president and board chair of the Pullman Company, makers of railway cars. He became a wealthy man, and in 1902, at the height of his career, he built Hildene, making it his summer home until his death there in 1926. One of New England's loveliest homes, with formal gardens and great lawns, hilltop Hildene commands sweeping views of the Valley of Vermont. The Friends of Hildene lovingly maintain the estate. Among its treasures are the oval mirror, a top hat owned by Lincoln, a book of Lord Byron's poetry given by Abraham Lincoln to his law partner William Herndon, and copies of the biographies of Declaration of Independence signers that Lincoln used to prepare his famed Cooper Union speech. Also at Hildene are chairs from the White House used by the president's sons, Willie and Tad, Mary Lincoln's embroidery, and books owned and signed by the first lady.

Manchester's Civil War history centers on the Equinox Guards, the local militia company named for Equinox Mountain, the highest peak in the Taconic Range, which looms over the village. Made up of

87 local lads, mostly from Manchester and Dorset, the Guards assembled in Manchester on September 9, 1862, and took the train to St. Albans, where they became Company E of the 5th Vermont Regiment. On June 29, 1862, the 5th Vermont fought in the Peninsula Campaign's Battle of Savage's Station. Advancing against Confederates supported by artillery fire, the regiment sustained the highest losses suffered by any Vermont regiment in the entire war. The Equinox Guards entered the battle with 59 men and only 7 were fit for duty when the firing ceased. The *Manchester Journal* editorialized, "If ever there was a sad and gloomy hour in this valley, it was that which brought us the first terrible tidings of those most near and dear to us who were engaged in the recent battles before Richmond. In more than one of our homes there was a grief and agony no words can depict."

From the entrance to Hildene, proceed 2 miles south on Route 7 and take Muddy Lane. Drive to the end of the road and look to the left at the large columned house. From here, Private Cyrus Hard went to war with Company E of the 5th Vermont. The unit's most prolific letter writer, Hard died of disease in an army hospital at Yorktown, Virginia, more than a month before Savage's Station. His father, Cyrus, traveled to Virginia, found his body, and brought it home to Manchester.

Return to Route 7 and go back north. Just past the entrance to Hildene, enter Dellwood Cemetery on the right. Within it are buried Jesse Lincoln Randolph, granddaughter of Abraham Lincoln, and Lincoln Isham, great grandson of Lincoln. In the first section by the road are several members of the Equinox Guards, including Captain Charles Dudley, Private Willard Bennett, and Private Hard. Also buried here is Reverend James Anderson, who held a reception for the Equinox Guards in the garden of his Manchester home on the eve of their departure. A large stone marks the grave of Manchester native Brigadier General Benjamin Roberts, a West Point graduate and career army soldier. Robert served mainly in the far West but also commanded Major General John Pope's cavalry during the Second Manassas campaign.

Continue north of Route 7 into Manchester, soon coming to the grand old Equinox House, where Mary Lincoln and her son stayed. Ulysses Grant also slept there, after the war. Across Route 7 from the hotel, at the southeast corner of Main and Union streets, stands an old two-story wooden building, which housed, on its second floor, a Civil War recruiting office. The Equinox Guards drilled in the square here and sometimes slept in the Bennington County Court House, which once stood on the site of the present-day building. They also boarded across the street in Vanderlip's Hotel, portions of which survive in the northern, recessed part of the Equinox. It should be noted that, after the war, the surviving veterans of the local company sometimes met at the present courthouse for reunions. The Civil War memorial in front of the building was dedicated in 1897.

On September 9, 1861, the Equinox Guards assembled in the square, then marched to the railway station at Manchester Depot. The local coronet band led the way, as the men, followed by many local people, tramped along a familiar route of march, many for the last time. To follow the route, go east on Union Street at the old recruiting office, pass the Equinox Country Club, and turn left on Richville Road, then right on Depot Street and to the depot area. The guards took the train to St. Albans, where they became Company E of the 5th Vermont Regiment.

Proceed north on Route 7 and quickly come to a Y. Turn left there on Manchester West Road, and the third building on the left was the home of Jonas and Anna Bennett. Son George, a private in the 14th Vermont, fought at Gettysburg. Son Harrison served in the navy, aboard the U.S.S. *Connecticut.* Son Willard died an agonizing death hours after being wounded at Savage's Station. A fellow soldier from Manchester, Private Henry Styles, wrote to his mother: "Towards the close of the fight I passed to the right to find my Regt. pausing a moment amid a shower of bullets, I heard some one speak and I knew it was Willard's voice. I asked him if he was hurt and he said he was fatally wounded in the center of the bowels. I then went to him to help him from the field but he wished me to leave him for he said it was no use—I cannot live."

Return to Route 7 and the Y, continue north on Route 5, and the fourth house on the right, with a barn in back, was the Dudley home. Charles Dudley, a veteran of the 1st Vermont Regiment, was elected captain of Company E and led it to war.

Surviving Savage's Station, he served with distinction into the Overland Campaign of 1864. At Spotsylvania Courthouse, though ill, he lead the 5th Vermont in the late afternoon assault known as Upton's Attack. Dudley received a wound in the arm; his wife hastened south to care for him and was at his side when he died, in a hospital in Fredericksburg. His body came home to Manchester for a funeral in the crowded Congregational church, which no longer stands.

Continue north on Route 7, pass the crossroads where Routes 30, 7, and 11 meet, and soon go right on Barnumville Road. In 2 miles, turn left on Johnny Cake Street, and in just under 0.5 mile, note the cape and small barn on the left. This was the home of Henry Cummings, a member of a family that probably suffered the greatest loss sustained by any family, North or South, in the Civil War, all as a result of the Battle of Savage's Station. Brothers Henry, Edwin, Hiram, Silas, and William Cummings, cousin W. H. H Cummings, and brother-in-law Horace Clayton were all members of the Equinox Guards. At Savage's Station, brothers Silas, Edmund, and Hiram were wounded and captured, dying of their wounds as prisoners. William was shot and taken to a Union hospital, where his leg was amputated. He soon died. Cousin W. H. H. Cummings's leg was shattered on the battlefield, and he died in prison. Brother-in-law Horace Clayton was killed on the battlefield. Henry, shot in a thigh, came home to his wife, Mary Jane, and lived in this house. But he never fully recovered and died here at sixty-seven, in

1885. The brothers' parents were spared all that agony, having died before the war.

SOURCES

HILDENE ARCHIVE.

KNIGHT, BRIAN L. *NO BRAVER DEEDS: THE STORY OF THE EQUINOX GUARDS.* MANCHESTER, VT: FRIENDS OF HILDENE, 2004.

MANCHESTER JOURNAL, 1861–1862. MARK SKINNER LIBRARY, MANCHESTER.

MANCHESTER TOWN RECORDS.

··

PERU

Approach the little village of Peru from the west, along Route 11, and Pierce Road enters from the north. Albert Smith went from the first house beyond it, on the right, to enlist as a private in the 9th Vermont at eighteen and served the last year and a half of the war, marching into Richmond. His daughter, Mabel, served as Peru town clerk, 1910 to 1962.

Soon bear left on Old Route 11, now Peru's Main Street, and the first house on the left, a large frame building, was the home of Everett Edward Adams. Joining the 2nd Vermont at twenty-four in 1861, Adams deserted a year later. Soon returning, he was discharged for disability, but he recovered to join the 9th Vermont and serve out the war.

Continue on Main Street, pass the Village Cemetery, and quickly come to the hamlet's main intersection. The old village store is on the right. During the Civil War, the Hapgood family owned the store, and the foundation of their home is beside the building. In the spring of 1864, fourteen-year-old Marshall Hapgood wrote in his diary here, "Charley was wounded today,

in the head." He was referring to his brother Charles, 2nd Vermont private, who was hit at the Wilderness and, a week later, at Spotsylvania's Bloody Angle. On June 15, Marshall wrote, "Work on road all day go home and while washing me who should stand before me but Charley. Lord my prayers has been answered."

Across the street is the 1840s Peru Congregational Church. The *Bennington Banner* reported that a war meeting was held on May 14, 1861, and "the church was full of anxious listeners." A funeral was held here at that year's end for William Weymouth, the first Peru casualty. Weymouth joined the 2nd Vermont in October 1861 but died two months later of sickness in Washington, D.C. He was forty-four. A neighbor, Ira Bacheldor, recalled that "slowly and sadly was he carried to his grave [in the Village Cemetery] to the music of the drums and fifes, accompanied by his family and a large number of friends and citizens."

Turn left at the church onto Hapgood Road, and in 0.3 mile, Private Weymouth's house, a cape, sits well below the road. His body came here from Washington.

Return to the church, and at the intersection, see the stone foundation of what once was Howards Hall. Civil War–era town meetings took place here, and voters approved bounties that peaked in late 1864 at $450. Here, Peru went for Lincoln over McClellan, 82 to 17.

By the foundation, go left on Main Street, and in 0.1 mile is a long frame house, on the right, once the Bryant family home, from which three brothers went to serve. Private Calvin Bryant spent the war's last year as a member of the 9th Vermont. Private Clark Bryant was for three years a member of the 2nd Vermont. Warren, after three years in the 4th Vermont, was court marshaled in December 1864 and discharged for cowardice. He was one of fifty-one men credited to Peru.

SOURCES
PERU TOWN RECORDS.
STEVENS, JONATHAN W. "THE FREDERICK HOLTON PLACE." UNPUBLISHED ESSAY ON PERU HISTORY, UNDATED. COURTESY OF THE AUTHOR.
WITH THANKS TO JONATHAN STEVENS.

....

POWNAL

From Route 7 going south, on reaching the Pownal fire station, turn right on North Pownal Road, then take a quick left on Center Street into Pownal Center. The 1849 church, on the left, once called the Union Meeting House, was the center of town life during the Civil War. A drill field was located behind the building, though Route 7 now slashes through it. Town meetings were held in the meetinghouse basement. The April 24, 1861, *Bennington Banner* reported that a "spirited" war meeting was held here and that a 112-foot flagstaff was raised outside. The *Banner* carried an account of another event here in August 1864. "There was a rousing war meeting at Pownal on Saturday evening last, to rouse up patriots in the town to the importance of raising her quota in the demand from the war powers for 300,000 men. The best spirit prevailed, and a determination was manifested to raise the number of men which she has been called upon to furnish, immediately. Patriotic speeches were made by Rev. Mr. Heath, the pastor of the Methodist Church," and others.

Pownal sent some 142 men to war and 22 died. Here in the meetinghouse, the town voted for Lincoln in 1860 117 to 10 over Douglas and in 1864 voted 198 to 98 over McClellan. A vote in 1862 approved paying 34 men bounties of $300 each.

Return to North Pownal Road and go left, west. In 2.75 miles of winding road, enter the village of North Pownal. Just before coming to the junction of Route 346, note a large old barn on the left, once part of the Whipple farm. Future president Chester A. Arthur (see Fairfield) sometimes spent the night on the Whipple farm when he taught school here in North Pownal. Go south on Route 346 and quickly, on the left, is a historic marker by the Congregational Church. The church stands on the location of an 1859 Congregational house of worship, in whose basement North Pownal Academy was located.

As the marker notes, two young men who would become American presidents taught here at the beginning of their careers. In 1881, just after graduating from Union College in Albany, New York, Arthur was here. It is likely that his students heard considerable talk about slavery, since the teacher was committed to the antislavery cause. Later, James A. Garfield also taught at the academy, while a student at nearby Williams College. In 1881, Vice President Arthur became president after the assassination of President Garfield. Both men played roles in the

Civil War. Arthur, as a New York lawyer, defended the rights of blacks in the city. When the war began, he became inspector general, then quartermaster general, of New York state and served admirably in keeping the state's troops supplied.

Early in the Civil War, Garfield led the 42nd Ohio Regiment. Soon a brigade commander, he won a small victory at Pound Gap in January 1862 and was present at Shiloh and Corinth, though playing no important role. He later was chief of staff of the Army of the Cumberland and after the war used his war record to good advantage in his rise to highest office.

Go south 3 miles on Route 346 to the village of Pownal, and where the road turns sharp right, the Methodist Church is straight ahead. Area people packed the predecessor of the present building in late November 1864 for the funeral of Sergeant Packer Hall, of the Vermont Cavalry, son of Walton Hall, of Pownal. Sergeant Hall, briefly a Rebel prisoner before he fought at Gettysburg, died of sickness in Washington, D.C.'s Douglas Hospital on November 13, 1864. The *Bennington Banner* said "the services throughout were conducted with military honors, there being some 40 mounted men as escort."

By the church, turn right on Main Street and soon cross the Hoosick River. From the bridge, look left for traces of the foundation of a mill that once stood on the near bank. It is said to have manufactured cloth for the Union war effort.

Return to Route 346 and go south to Route 7. Turn left, north, and soon go right on Ladd Road. In 0.3 mile on the right, at the corner of Pratt Road, is a small house with extension added. Here, Merritt Barber, Pownal's best-known local Civil War soldier, spent summer vacations during his latter years. Barber, born in 1838, graduated from North Pownal Academy and Williams College. Enlisting in the 10th Vermont in August 1862, as a private, Barber rose through the ranks to become a major. Wounded at Monocacy and Fisher's Hill, he was said to have distinguished himself for gallantry in every battle from the Wilderness through Cedar Creek. He stayed in the army after the war, reached the rank of brigadier general, and retired in 1901.

SOURCES
BENNINGTON BANNER, 1862–1864. VERMONT STATE LIBRARY.
PARKS, JOSEPH. *POWNAL: A TOWN'S TWO HUNDRED YEARS AND MORE*. POWNAL, VT: POWNAL BICENTENNIAL COMMITTEE, 1977.
POWNAL TOWN RECORDS.
WITH THANKS TO WENDY HOPKINS, KEN HELD, AND JOYCE HELD.

READSBORO

In the center of Readsboro, the 1840 Methodist Church stands on the north side of Route 100, where the abolitionist Reverend Ambrose Stone became pastor in 1855. When the Civil War began, the reverend saw four sons go to war, two in Massachusetts regiments and two in the 2nd Vermont. Son Newton Stone, also an avowed abolitionist, in 1859 had gone to Bennington to study the law and was admitted to the Bennington County Bar just before he went south as captain of Company A. He rose to command of the regiment, and on May 5, 1864, he was shot in a leg as the Vermont Brigade advanced into the Wilderness. Going to the rear for medical attention, he was soon back with his men, but a bullet through the lungs killed him. It was said that many of his men wept at the death of the popular colonel, just twenty-seven. His brother, Lieutenant Pratt Stone, a member of Ulysses Grant's staff, brought the body home to Readsboro. Pratt returned to war and was wounded at Cedar Creek.

A funeral for the colonel was held in the Stone home, which still stands two houses east of the church, a frame house with a large triangular window high on its front. Then a memorial service was held so that the public could attend, and the town hall was packed. A Reverend Lamb, from Whitingham, presided and preached a sermon based on a ninetieth Psalm verse: "Satisfy us early with thy mercy that we may rejoice and be glad all our days."

Colonel Stone's warhorse, a chestnut, had come home with his body, and after the service, he was brought out in front of the town hall. The body was then taken to Bennington for another memorial service and burial.

The old town hall has long been gone where in 1864 Readsboro voters went for Lincoln, 117 to 53. But on its site is the town soldier memorial, across the street from the Stone home. The names of fifty-eight Readsboro men are listed as having served in the Civil War.

From the village, go west 5 miles on Route 100 to where Routes 8 and 100 join, just past the Heartwellville Cemetery. Go right on Route 8, and on the right is an eighteenth-century tavern. In the house just past it lived Franklin Bellows, who left here at forty-two to join the 8th Vermont in December 1863. He died the following July of disease in Natchez, Mississippi, but his body came home to be buried in the nearby cemetery.

From the intersection, go east on Routes 100 and 8, and quickly, on the right, is County Lane. Marcena Reed, a stonemason, lived in the house at the corner. In December 1863, at age fifty-seven, Reed, like his neighbor Bellows, enlisted in the 8th. He served a year, then came home to live until age ninety-four.

Heartwellville was once a village large as Readsboro. Little is now left. Continue past the Reed house, and the first house on the left is believed to have been the home of Joseph Jillson. He joined the 6th Vermont at forty-one as a private when it formed. Captured at Savage's Station, he was imprisoned at Belle Isle, in Richmond. He died two months later, just after being paroled, in a military hospital near Fortress Monroe. His widow continued to live here.

Just past the house is the Heartwellville Church where Marcena Reed's funeral was held in 1900, with many fellow members of the GAR attending.

SOURCES

ROSS, FRANK SETH. DOWN THROUGH THE YEARS AT READSBORO, VERMONT, 1786–1936. WILLIAMSTOWN, MA: MCCLELLAND PRESS, 1936.
WITH THANKS TO TOM BOUDREAU.

RUPERT

Along Rupert's main street, which is Route 315, is the 1786 Rupert Congregational Church, believed to be the oldest continuously operating house of worship in Vermont. In 1859, the sanctuary was jacked up, and a meeting hall created under it, which immediately became the center of town activities.

Town historian George Hibbard wrote in 1899 that "this town supported heartily the war for preservation of the Union, and the nobler, though less understood, purpose of freeing an enslaved race. I think less than a dozen voters were hostile to the policy of the administration, in its main features, though, naturally, there were sharp and angry criticisms as to management. The first public meeting to consider the state of the country, was held in the 'basement' in the month of February, 1861 . . . When the call for troops came, and often repeated, came town meetings, to comply with the demands of the government. These meetings, which were held very often, especially in 1862 and '63, sometimes two and three a week, were called 'war meetings,' and will be so remembered by the people of that period."

Upstairs, the pastor of the Congregational Church during the Civil War was Reverend Josiah Clark, an opponent of slavery. His son, Waldo Clark, joined the Vermont Cavalry in 1862 and served two years. Captured in May 1862 in the Shenandoah Valley, he was soon exchanged. A year later, Clark was wounded in a fight with John Mosby's guerrillas. He came home safely a year later, then went west and became a miner in the Rocky Mountains.

Adjacent to the church is the Rupert Street Cemetery, which has several Civil War graves. Serving in Company C of the 14th Vermont, organized in Manchester, were twenty-four Rupert men, among them Miner Kinne, a private who died at twenty-four of sickness in February 1863. His stone says:

His life a sacrifice he gave
His country's flag to save.

South of the cemetery on Route 315, look to the right, near the Grange Hall, for the Rupert railroad depot, now a residence. It stands along the bed of the old Delaware and Hudson line, and was opened the day before the first train came through in 1852. Hibbard's history says, "On three occasions troops passed through here by rail for the seat of war: May 9, '61, the 1st [Vermont] Infantry; Dec. 14, '61 six companies of the [Vermont] cavalry; March 10, 1862, the 7th [Vermont] Infantry. On these occasions the people gathered at the R. R. station to greet, cheer and God speed the daring troops."

Not all Rupert war meetings were held in the church basement. On July 31, 1862, a meeting took place in the Grove, a local picnic spot believed to have been located by the depot. Bounties of $100 were approved and six men promptly enlisted in the 10th Vermont, at T. S. Bisbee's Store, which stood south of the depot.

Continue 1.5 miles south on Route 315 to West Rupert, and note the store on the right at the intersection. Rupert slavery opponents met in a meeting hall on the second floor. On March 8, a group of abolitionists in Boston wrote to the Rupert Anti-Slavery Society asking that its members support publication of William Lloyd Garrison's abolitionist newspaper *The Liberator.* At a cost of $2 each a year, Rupert slavery opponents were urged to purchase at least fifty-two subscriptions, because each could lead to "the conversion of at least two minds to the cause of truth and humanity." How the Rupert Society responded is not known. In 1868, a celebration was held in the field behind the store—when word arrived that Ulysses Grant was elected president. During the festivities, a cannon exploded, blowing both hands off a local boy, Wayne Bailey.

In the second house beyond the store, a young student from Union Theological Seminary in Schenectady, New York, lived while doing some apprentice preaching in the local Disciples Church. James Garfield's Civil War record would be important in his political rise to the White House. The church he preached in is the small redbrick church at the corner of East Street, which goes east from Route 315. Take East Street and soon come to a large open area on the right, where a Baptist church once stood. The house beyond was the Baptist parsonage, where Reverend L. B. Ames, lived. He became pastor in 1862. A year later, Ames was drafted into military service. Lacking the $300 necessary to pay commutation, his parishioners raised the money..

Continue on East Street just under 1 mile to the intersection of Sandgate Road.

The cape house set below the road on the right was the home of Private Augustus Wright, who joined the 5th Vermont on September 16, 1861, but took sick at Camp Griffin in Virginia and died on November 5.

Return to Rupert and the Congregational Church and go north to the junction of Route 315. In 1.3 miles on Route 315, note a frame house above the road on the right. From a house that stood on this site, John Gookins enlisted as a private in the Vermont Cavalry in the summer of 1864. He died three months later of sickness. His body came home to the Rupert depot and a grave in the Rupert Street Cemetery. He was twenty-one, and his stone says, "He was our only son we miss him." The barn behind the house dates to his time.

Return to the village and go right on Route 155. In 1.75 miles is a large house set below the road on the left. Albert Sheldon joined Company C of the 14th Vermont as a private, fought at Gettysburg, and came home here. In 1.3 miles, go right on Perkins Road. Quickly on the left is a one-room school; a large frame house, in two sections, is just beyond. Miner and William Kinne attended the school and lived in the house. They joined the 14th as privates. Miner died of disease, as his stone in the Rupert Street Cemetery notes. William came home safely after Gettysburg.

By one count, 56 Rupert men served in Vermont units, and at least 4 in New York regiments. At least 10 died.

SOURCES
HIEL, HOLLISTER. *PAWLET FOR ONE HUNDRED YEARS.* PAWLET, VT: PAWLET HISTORICAL SOCIETY, 1976.

Letter from Massachusetts Anti-Slavery Society to Rupert Anti-Slavery Society. Courtesy of Rupert Historical Society. With thanks to Eugene Higgins.

....

SANDGATE

From Route 7A at Arlington, go west to West Arlington and take the Sandgate Road 3.3 miles north. Above the road, on the right, is the Sandgate town office, on the site of the Sandgate town hall, long ago destroyed by fire. In the old hall, Sandgate voters approved war expenditures totaling $18,198.95. Of that, $17,925 went for bounties, with Sandgate sending sixty men to war. The December 24, 1863, *Bennington Banner* reported on a war meeting here at which Francis Voltaire Randall, commander of the 13th Vermont, spoke. Randall, though a Braintree native, had relatives in Sandgate. To drum up recruits, he talked about the 2nd Vermont Brigade's performance at Gettysburg.

From the town hall, go north on Sandgate Road, and soon the District Two School is on the left. Among the pupils were John Snow, a private in the 14th Vermont who fought at Gettysburg; Ira Monroe, briefly a private in the Vermont Cavalry; and Reuben Hurd, 10th Vermont. Continue past the school, pass Hamilton Hollow Road on the right, and the first house on the left, above the road, was Private Hurd's home.

Reuben Hurd, eighteen, enlisted in Sandgate for the 10th Vermont in January 1864, with several other local boys. They went to Brattleboro, then on to Brandy

Station, Virginia, where they joined the regiment in winter camp. Hurd first saw combat at the Wilderness. "On the first day of the fight," he recalled years later, "our regiment was marching to a position when a cannon shot smashed through the trees ahead of the column. A mounted staff officer shouted to our colonel to march the regiment to the right. The officer had no more than given this command when a second shot cut his horse in two, close behind the saddle. The rider leaped clear as the horse went down, then he drew his pistol and quickly ended the poor beast's sufferings. We Vermont farm boys were not used to seeing such things happen to horses and I never forgot the incident."

And Hurd said, "As a rule nobody who fought in the war could see any enemy individuals to shoot at . . . with the clouds of smoke from the black powder covering everything, such a thing was impossible." Yet at Cold Harbor he remembered, "My company was stationed in a hollow. We saw through the dusk several rebels on a hill above us, apparently not knowing that we were there within range. Without orders, I foolishly fired at the distant figures. The smoke from my gun prevented my seeing the result of my shot but one of my comrades exclaimed, 'You got him, Hurd! I saw him fall.' I had to take his word for it. I didn't see anything."

Hurd remembered being close to Appomattox Court House when word came that Lee surrendered to Grant. "The air was full of hats," he recalled. Hurd went west after the Civil War, as did many Sandgate men, as the town's population fell.

Continue past the Hurd house 0.75

mile, and on the right is a cape with two prominent chimneys. George Tomb, twenty-five, left this house to enlist in the 10th Vermont in January 1864. Six months later, near Petersburg, he was wounded and died five days later.

SOURCES
RENNER, IRMA E. *THE STORY OF SANDGATE, VERMONT, 1761–1961.* SHAFTSBURY, VT: FARNHAM & FARNHAM, 1961.
SANDGATE TOWN RECORDS.

SEARSBURG

The town office in the small mountain town of Searsburg, which is credited with sending twenty-four men to war, is located where Route 8 goes south from Route 9. Few old buildings remain in town, including the schoolhouse where Searsburg voters favored Lincoln, 26 to 10, in 1860 over Stephen Douglas. But just south of the intersection, a narrow lane leads left to the oldest cemetery in town. Here lie four Searsburg men who went to war, including Private George Shippee, 2nd Vermont, wounded at Fredericksburg's Marye's Heights, and Private Nathan Mann, who enlisted in the 4th Vermont at forty-three. Captured at Weldon Railroad, he died three weeks after his release from Andersonville.

From the cemetery, go south 2.5 miles on Route 8 to another cemetery, on the left. Foster Grousbeck is buried here, who joined the 2nd Vermont at twenty-seven as a private. He was wounded twice, at Mine Run and Cold Harbor. The second wound sent him home to live the rest of his life on a farm that included this ceme-

tery. The house once stood directly across the road. Also buried here is William O'Brien, a 2nd Vermont private, who was shot at Marye's Heights and at Charles Town. But he served until war's end, was discharged a sergeant, and came home to serve Searsburg in the legislature. He died in 1881, as the result of a fistfight along a Bennington roadway.

SOURCES
SEARSBURG TOWN RECORDS.
WITH THANKS TO MARLELE RODERICK.

SHAFTSBURY

Go south on Route 7A from Arlington, and on entering the hilltop village of Shaftsbury Center, the 1846 Baptist Church is on the left, now the Shaftsbury Historical Center. On the lawn is a historic marker for Jacob Merritt Howard, noting that he was born nearby and that he wrote the resolutions on which the Republican Party was founded. He also authored the Thirteenth Amendment outlawing slavery. The marker was unveiled in July 1954 with great ceremony with Leonard Hall, Republican Party national chair, the featured speaker. Also present was Howard's grandniece, Ruth Howard Matteson, ninety-seven. Before his talk, Hall chatted with Matteson about Republican matters, assuming her to be a faithful member of the GOP. Displaying something of her ancestor's rebellious spirit, she told Hall, "I've been a lifelong Democrat, and I'm afraid I'm a little too old to change my ways."

Just south of the marker is the 1847

Shaftsbury town hall where Civil War–era town meetings took place. Here in 1860, Shaftsbury went for Lincoln over Douglas, 156 to 77. On November 27, 1863, the town selectmen were authorized "to borrow any sum of money not in the treasury" to pay necessary bounties. Shaftsbury bounty payments reached $500 by the fall of 1864, and by war's end, the town was more than $25,000 in debt. Lincoln's popularity had dropped by 1864 when he defeated McClellan only by 157 to 142. The town sent 162 men to war.

Continue 1.5 miles on Route 7A, pass a motel on the left, and the next house beyond has a large Palladian window. The wife of Lieutenant Abel Parsons, 4th Vermont, was living here with her mother-in-law when a telegram arrived with the news that Parsons had been killed in the assault on June 3, 1864, at Cold Harbor. The body came home here.

Continue south, and soon turn left on Airport Road, which becomes Trumbull Road. In 2.5 miles, come to a hilltop horse farm with large brick house, where Jacob Merritt Howard was born July 10, 1810. Known as Merritt, Howard schooled in Brattleboro and Bennington, then at Williams College. He became a lawyer and soon moved to Michigan, where he was elected to Congress in 1840. As a Whig representative, he was a staunch opponent of slavery. In 1854, Howard attended the convention in Jackson, Michigan, where the Republican Party was founded. Howard was key in writing a series of antislavery resolutions adopted by the convention . Elected to the Senate in 1861, he worked closely with

Lincoln in drafting and passing the 13th Amendment. Howard also served on the Joint Committee on Reconstruction.

Return to Route 7A and continue south; quickly go right on Route 67, and soon come to an 1850s stone factory close beside the road. Here at the Henry Burden and Sons factory, carpenters' squares were made from locally mined iron. Burden and Sons also sent iron from their Shaftsbury furnaces to their factories in Troy, New York, where they made horseshoes for the Union armies. Four houses south of the factory is a frame house with gingerbread trimming, owned by the Burden family.

Return to Route 7A, go south; quickly turn left on Buck Hill Road and follow it to its end on East Road. Turn left, and in 0.75 mile, on the right, is a frame house with an L, once the home of Jonas and Elizabeth Galusha. Here, they bid farewells to their son, Jonas, departing to enlist in the 24th New York Battery. Captured in December 1864 in battle at Plymouth, North Carolina, he was confined in Andersonville until released the following spring. He died on the way home, at a military hospital at Annapolis, Maryland. According to the *Bennington Banner* his funeral was held in this house on April 25, 1865. Continue on East Road, and soon go right on Waite Cemetery Road. Jonas's stone is at the high point of the cemetery, the end of his long journey from Andersonville.

SOURCES

LEVIN, RUTH. *ORDINARY HEROES: THE STORY OF SHAFTSBURY.* EDITED BY TYLER RESCH. SHAFTSBURY, VT: SHAFTSBURY HISTORICAL SOCIETY, 1978.

ROLANDO, VICTOR R. *200 YEARS OF SOOT AND SWEAT: THE HISTORY AND ARCHEOLOGY OF VERMONT'S IRON, CHARCOAL, AND LIME INDUSTRIES.* BURLINGTON, VT: VERMONT ARCHAEOLOGICAL SOCIETY, 1992.

SHAFTSBURY TOWN REPUBLICAN CENTENNIAL COMMITTEE. *THE STORY OF SHAFTSBURY, VERMONT: WITH AN ACCOUNT OF JACOB MERRITT HOWARD WHO WROTE THE RESOLUTIONS ON WHICH THE REPUBLICAN PARTY WAS FOUND.* SHAFTSBURY, VT: SHAFTSBURY TOWN REPUBLICAN CENTENNIAL COMMITTEE, 1954.

BENNINGTON BANNER, JUNE 9, 1864.

BENNINGTON MUSEUM.

WITH THANKS TO JOE HALL AND JOE MESKUN.

....

STAMFORD

From Readsboro, where Routes 100 and 8 meet, go south on the conjoined roads 3 miles and turn left on Bushika Road. Quickly, Rondeau Road turns east, and from the intersection, look uphill to the small frame house that is the only house on the road. From here, J. H. Richardson saw two sons go to war. George, a medical student, at twenty-three enlisted in the 4th Vermont in January 1862. He died three months later of typhoid fever. Henry was eighteen when he joined in the 2nd Vermont as a private in August 1862. He was killed at the Wilderness on May 5, 1862.

Continue south on Routes 100/8 for nearly 3 miles, and turn left on Clough Road. The frame house on the right, just before the road turns sharp right, was once the Stamford District One School. Wartime town meetings took place here, and in 1861, voters went 71 to 69 for Stephen Douglas over Lincoln. Four years later, in this building, Lincoln carried the town, 65 to 59. With nearby Massachusetts towns competing for Stamford's young men, filling quotas was sometimes difficult. In July 1864, voters authorized selectmen to pay "what they deem necessary" in bounties. In January 1865, a $600 ceiling was set on such payments. In March 1865, voters approved a tax of 400 cents on each grand list dollar to help the town meet its war debt. Some sixty-eight men are credited to Stamford.

The man responsible for many local men being in uniform was J. O. Sanford, town recruiting officer. Continue to the end of Clough Road, go south on Routes 100/8 and in 0.5 mile, his large frame house, with barn behind, is on the right. The men who Sanford persuaded to enlist must have liked him, for the Stamford Historical Society owns several friendly letters sent him here by local soldiers. Eighteen-year-old Henry Seegar was convinced to enlist one August day in 1862 while mowing on his father's upland farm. After listening to Sanford for but a few minutes, Seegar dropped his scythe and went off to sign on as a 2nd Vermont private. Nearly three years later, Seegar was wounded at the Petersburg Breakthrough but came home to live until 1923.

Just south of the Sanford house is the Baptist Church, where in early December 1861 a funeral was held for the first Stamford soldier to die. John Clough Jr. was an only son, and typhoid fever killed him less than two months after joining the 2nd Vermont. Friends of the eighteen-year-old in Company A passed the hat to fund shipment of his body home. At the service, a Reverend Kirkam preached from Job "If a man died, shall he live again?"

In early March 1863, a funeral took place here for Private Milo Johnson, a private in the 14th Vermont. He died in his regiment's camp in northern Virginia, of small pox, at eighteen.

From the church, go south 0.2 miles to a long frame house on the left, with a prominent chimney and attached barn. Patrick Morrissey at twenty-four joined the Vermont Cavalry as 1863 began. Morrissey said that he served for a time as an orderly for fellow Irishman Thomas Meagher, who once commanded the Irish Brigade.

SOURCES
LAWRENCE, MARION B. AN EARLY VERMONT SAMPLER. PRIVATELY PRINTED, 1979.
STAMFORD TOWN RECORDS.
WITH THANKS TO NANCY BUSHIKA.

....

SUNDERLAND

Sunderland sent sixty men to war, and at least three died. A certain Bentley boy was not among them. Driving south on Route 7A from Manchester, one comes upon a crossroads, just north of a house where both Ethan and Ira Allen once lived. Here, Bentley Hill Road bears right and Hill Farm Road goes left. Turn right, and 0.5 mile up, on the right, is a large old farmhouse where the Bentley family once lived. Family tradition holds that on a day during the Civil War, some men came to the house seeking to take a young Bentley son to war. The family hid the lad in the wood box, covering him with kindling. The house was searched, but the wood box was never examined.

And thus the lad, who, the family says, was too badly needed on the farm, did not go to war.

Return to Route 7A, cross it onto Hill Farm Road, and in 0.5 mile, turn right on Sand Hill Road. In just over 1 mile, the road drops into a ravine where the narrow Chiselville covered bridge crosses Roaring Branch. In the Russell Collection at the Martha Canfield Library in Arlington, an 1840s broadside is preserved advertising a reward for the return of twelve-year-old Elijah Welch to Walter Matteson, of Shaftsbury, to whom the black lad was apprenticed. Local historian Shirley Letiecq says that Elijah ran away from Matteson, after serving him eleven months, and set out in the winter to join his parents, who had moved somewhere many miles to the north. Letiecq wrote:

"Plodding as fast as he could through the snowdrifts, he arrived just before daybreak at the Chiselville Bridge. A barn loomed in the adjacent meadow. Shivering with cold and exhaustion, the boy crept inside. There he found a basin of milk that had been left for the cats, and this he drank ravenously. Then wriggling himself into the haymow, he found heavenly respite in its soft warmth from his long night's battle with the zero cold and wind. But not for long." According to Letiecq, the lad was awakened by the light of a lantern and, fearing capture, fled the barn and took refuge among the timbers supporting the covered bridge. There he was found by sympathetic local people, who arranged for him to be transferred to the care of a kind local family, for whom he worked in a sawmill.

The present Chiselville Bridge long ago replaced the historic bridge, which stood a couple of hundred yards upstream. Returning out of the hollow that holds the bridge, note the farm and small house on the left. The barn is believed to have been the one in which young Welch took refuge.

Return along Sand Hill Road and pass the intersection of Hill Farm Road. Continue on Sand Hill Road for 0.75 mile, turn right on Burrough Road, and enter Sunderland Burrough. It is believed that young Welch lived and worked here, after gaining his freedom. Sunderland Burrough was one of several small communities that once existed in Sunderland, and it retains the look of the Civil War era. People living here surely experienced the financial difficulties visited on many small Vermont towns by the war. For example, in January 1864, Sunderland selectmen sent a letter to Brig. Gen. Thomas Gamble Pitcher, a War Department official who from 1863 until war's end was assigned to Vermont, with an office in Brattleboro, as State Provost Marshall General. The selectmen were concerned about $1,500 of Sunderland money that Pitcher had apparently seized from the Windham County Bank. The selectmen wanted it back and their letter included the following lengthy sentence that summed up Sunderland's financial plight:

"The small town of Sunderland with a grand list of less than $1,500 voted to raise the sum of $500 bounty to be paid to each volunteer under the call for 300,000 troops, other towns in the county with a list varying from three to ten times that of Sunderland having held town meetings and offered at that time the sum of $300 only—the town of Sunderland having not only responded to former calls but having been drained of her able bodied men by inducements offered by more able towns on former calls which by an unjust and unequal application in our opinion were accredited to the towns offering the largest inducements, thereby not only exhausting the numbers of the smaller towns but subjecting them to the support of widows and orphan children compelled us to raise the bounties offered."

A list compiled by the Sunderland selectmen shows that the little town paid more than $20,000 in bounties to meet its quotas. A list of 1864 bounties shows payments to some soldiers of $800 and more. A town official who wrote the list gave the name of each recipient and the amount paid, with one exception. A portion of the list:

David Wyman	*$725*
Walter Nichols	*$725*
Michael Ryan	*$700*
Herbert Jenkins	*$500*
Nigger	*$400.85*
August Eckel	*$825*

SOURCES
LETIECQ, SHIRLEY L. "HISTORY OF SUNDERLAND." UNPUBLISHED MANUSCRIPT, UNDATED. COURTESY OF THE AUTHOR.
SUNDERLAND CIVIL WAR SOLDIER LIST. RUSSELL COLLECTION, MARTHA CANFIELD LIBRARY, ARLINGTON.
WITH THANKS TO SHIRLEY LETIECQ.

WINHALL

⭐ The town of Winhall is set between the prominent summits of Bromley and Stratton mountains. Enter its village of Bondville, from the north along Route 30, and just before the bridge, on the left, is an old hotel. Once called the Lincoln Maples Inn, the hotel name commemorates the fact that on the day word of Lincoln's assassination reached Winhall, Bondville people planted a row of maples in his honor. The row stretched across the front of the inn northward. Two or three of those maples, or their offspring, in 2010 still stood in front of the large old house, just across the little street to the north of the inn.

The Overland Campaign of 1864 exacted a considerable toll from Winhall. Among the soldiers credited to the town who died at the Wilderness were Private Edwin Butterfield, 2nd Vermont, and Privates Dana Kidder, George Lyon, and Horace Taft, all of the 5th Vermont. All, of course, served in the 1st Vermont Brigade, the Old Brigade, commanded at that time by its longest-serving commander, Brigadier General Lewis Addison Grant, a Winhall native.

From the center of Bondville, go 7 miles north on Route 30, and on reaching Route 11, turn east. In 3.5 miles, having entered the town of Peru, bypass Peru village and turn right, or south, on South Road, soon reentering Winhall. Go 2.75 miles along South Road and turn right on Read Road; the first house on the right, much altered and added to, is Grant's birthplace. Born here on January 17, 1828, the son of James and Elizabeth (Wyman) Grant, Lewis attended a district school in Townshend, then the academy in Chester. He taught school for several years, including a stint in Chester, during which time he read law. In 1855, he opened a law practice in Bellows Falls.

Grant, who had become a friend of the influential Stoughton family of Bellows Falls, joined the 5th Vermont as a major and soon commanded the regiment. Wounded at First Fredericksburg, he recovered to be appointed commander of the Old Brigade in February 1863. He led it until the close of the war. Grant, apparently an able commander, was given the nickname Aunt Lydia by his soldiers. It appears to have come from a facial resemblance to a female figure pictured on boxes of a popular product of the time known as Aunt Lydia's Carpet and Button Thread. Grant was also known to be a bit fussy, a stickler for military detail.

One of Grant's finest moments came late in the war when, while scouting west of Petersburg, he detected a weak point in the Confederate lines. Grant's recommendation of an attack at that point was accepted, and his Old Brigade led the April 2, 1865, 6th Corps assault that, after ten months of siege, broke the Rebel lines at Petersburg. Lee surrendered his army a week later. The Vermont Brigade fought valiantly under him in many battles, including the Wilderness and Spotsylvania.

After the war, "the other Grant," as he was known, moved west to Illinois, Iowa, and finally to Minnesota, where he fathered a son, Ulysses Sherman Grant.

Lewis Grant served, during the Benjamin Harrison administration, as assistant secretary of war. He returned to Vermont several times, speaking on one occasion at dedication ceremonies for the Brandon Civil War memorial (see Brandon). On November 15, 1876, the 13th annual gathering of the Reunion Society of Vermont was held at the State House in Montpelier. That evening, at a banquet, Grant was called on to address his fellow veterans. His remarks concluded, "While I live, let me live in the regard of my comrades, and in the enjoyment of the civil liberties secured by our arms; and when I die, it will be enough, if they wrap me in the old flag, and write on my gravestone: "He once commanded the First Vermont Brigade." Grant died in Minneapolis on March 20, 1918, age ninety.

SOURCES

SUNDERLAND CIVIL WAR FILE. RUSSELL COLLECTION, MARTHA CANFIELD LIBRARY, ARLINGTON.
WITH THANKS TO BRIAN KNIGHT.

....

WOODFORD

From Bennington, go east on Route 9 and soon cross the town line into the mountain town of Woodford. A mile along, above the road, is the Woodford Hollow School. Part of it was built in 1809, and here, Civil War–era town meetings were held. Woodford voters twice voted against Lincoln for president. In 1860, they gave Stephen Douglas 25 votes, Lincoln 24, and Breckenridge 3. Four years later, Woodford went for McClellan, 44 to 37. Bounties of $300 were approved in August 1863, and a year later, the town voted to send $1,000 to the state treasury to fund a search for recruits in the South to meet local quotas. That year in this building, Charles Bliss was elected first selectman. From 1855 to 1858, Charles C. Dunn was a pupil in the Woodford Hollow School, a member of a local family decimated by war.

Continue east on Route 9, pass the town office and church on the left, and 3.75 miles beyond, on the left by a store, is the Woodford Cemetery. Charles C. Dunn Sr.'s name is atop the family stone, and the inscription says that he "fell in Kilpatrick's Raid" and died at forty-seven on March 1, 1864, in a Richmond prison. Below are the names of three sons, who with their father joined Company G of the cavalry as privates at the end 1863. The father and his three sons all went on the failed raid against Richmond led by Judson Kilpatrick in 1864. Charles C. Dunn Jr. died in the Brattleboro Hospital of sickness in October 1864. George E. Dunn and William Dunn were captured during the raid and died in Andersonville, where both are buried. Another son, Albert, fought at Gettysburg as a private with the 14th Vermont and came safely home.

Continue east on Route 9, and the first house past the store, on the left, was once the District Three School. Among its pupils in 1856 was Stephen Gleason, who served the last eighteen months of the war as a private in the 11th Vermont, surviving the Overland Campaign and the Petersburg siege.

The first house on the right past the old school, a cape with dormers, was the home of selectman Charles Bliss, who may have been the first Vermonter to enlist for the Civil War. According to historian G. G. Benedict, "Charles M. Bliss, then of Woodford, claims to have been the first volunteer to have put his name on an agreement to serve for the war. On the 19th of April, 1861, upon learning of President Lincoln's first call for troops, Mr. Bliss drew up a paper which he signed and offered to others to sign, pledging his services as a soldier for the war. Mr. Bliss enlisted in the 2nd Vermont, and served till discharged after the Peninsula campaign, on account of disability resulting from Chickahominy fever."

SOURCES

BENNINGTON BANNER, 1862. VERMONT STATE LIBRARY.

HEMENWAY, ED. *THE VERMONT HISTORICAL GAZETTEER*.

WOODFORD TOWN RECORDS.

WITH THANKS TO RON HIGGINS.

Lee farm in Waterford

chapter four

Caledonia County

The abolitionist Oliver Johnson rang the Peacham Congregational Church bell the day John Brown was hanged. In subsequent years, it would toll many times for Peacham's war dead. The church and the bell survive. A mile away is the house where Thaddeus Stevens lived while attending Peacham Academy. He became one of the most powerful members of Congress during the Civil War, an unflinching champion of human freedom. A granite marker stands on the foundations of the Scott family home outside Groton. One son, William, was perhaps the Union army's most famous private soldier. Known as the Sleeping Sentinel, he was spared death by firing squad only to die seven months later at Lee's Mill. The marker does not say that two of his brothers also died in the war. Look closely for the marker where Route 5 passes under Interstate 93, just south of St. Johnsbury. Here, on the old St. Johnsbury fairgrounds, William Scott was one of a thousand soldiers of the 3rd Vermont who drilled here before going south. At the main intersection on the hill in St. Johnsbury, a casket symbolizing the Confederacy was buried during a celebration of Union victory in the Civil War. It's probably still there. Drive west on Route 2 from St. Johnsbury to Danville, and you follow the route taken by Danville people escorting home the body of Colonel Addison Preston. A Rebel bullet had slain him near Cold Harbor. His wife wanted nothing military about his funeral, the largest held in Caledonia County up to that time.

BARNET

McIndoes Academy, built in 1853, is on the east side of Route 5 in McIndoe Falls, in the town of Barnet. This handsome building, with columned portico, counted among its alumni, according to the town history, thirty-one men who served the Union. The best known was Samuel Pingree (see Hartford). Five former academy students died in the war, and the town history states that James Kent, class of 1857, was killed at Gettysburg.

Another former student, Corporal William H. Johnston, got sick and died in camp late in January 1863. Johnson was a member of Company F, 15th Vermont, which formed at McIndoe Falls the autumn of 1862, made up of Barnet, Peacham, Ryegate, and Groton men. Some twenty-two Barnet men served in the regiment. Danville's *North Star* noted on September 20, 1862, that the company was commanded by Captain Xerxes Stevens, of Barnet, and that it was "quartered in McIndoe Falls and drilling daily." It is believed that many of the men were housed in the academy building. In the late summer of 1862, Company A of the 10th Vermont, formed at St. Johnsbury, paraded in McIndoe Falls, just before departing for war.

Go north on Route 5, paralleling the Connecticut River 2.25 miles, and on nearing the village of Barnet, bear right on Main Street and soon look to the right at the old Barnet depot area at the end of Creamery Lane. Barnet men going to and from war boarded trains there. The Reverend Oliver Johnson (see Topsham) and fellow abolitionist William Lloyd Garrison took a train here in 1859, bound for White River Junction. The two were quickly recognized by some fellow travelers, who began insulting Garrison for his antislavery views. Peace was made by a local doctor.

Pass Creamery Lane and bear left, uphill, noting the falls of Stevens Brook, which once powered two mills that made woolen cloth for Union uniforms. At the hilltop, look across Route 5 to the large store, built on the foundation of one of the mills. Turn right on Route 5, and in 0.1 mile, go right through Pleasant View Cemetery's narrow entrance. Proceed on the cemetery road to the rear right section and watch along the right for the gravestones of William Cade and Robert White. Cade, a private in the 10th Vermont, died of wounds received at Mine Run in November 1863. According to a newspaper account reprinted in the *Addison Independent* in late November 1863, "He was the first body buried in the new cemetery . . . On the next day the body of Robert White was buried in the same beautiful cemetery." The article noted that White, like many Barnet people, was a native of Scotland and was a veteran of the War of 1812. The account continued, "Thus our new cemetery has been dedicated to its holy purpose by resigning into its bosom the bodies of two soldiers who served their country in defense of their liberties and rights."

Just beyond those markers, on the left, are the three identical stones with carved hands pointing skyward. Brothers Seth, Hiram, and Warner Somers, sons of Alexander and Sarah Jane Eames Somers, lie here. Neither parent saw their sons off to war, for the father died in 1847 and his wife three years later. The youngest of the orphans, Hiram Somers, left Barnet and a young wife at age eighteen, in 1861, to enlist in the 2nd Vermont. The following February, he died of typhoid at the Vermont Brigade's winter encampment at White Oak Church, Virginia. Brother Warren, unmarried and a farmer, joined the 3rd Vermont in the summer of 1862 and served until typhus claimed him at Brandy Station, Virginia, in February 1864. Seth, also a bachelor, was nineteen when he joined the 2nd Vermont. Shot at Savage's Station and left on the field, he was captured and taken to Richmond. He returned to Barnet a sick man and died in January 1863. The boys' sister Clara married a local blacksmith, Edwin Dewey, who enlisted in the 11th Vermont at age twenty-nine. Wounded at Cold Harbor, he was sent to a Washington, D.C., hospital, where a leg was amputated. He died August 7 of gangrene after suffering excruciating pain.

From the cemetery, return south on Route 5 and turn right at the Barnet store into Monument Square where the town's Civil War memorial lists the names of 183 Barnet men who served. Dedicated on Memorial Day, 1915, it became the centerpiece of Memorial Day activities. Veterans from Monroe, New Hampshire, joined the annual commemorations, which alternately involved decorating veterans' graves in Barnet's Pleasant View Cemetery and in the Monroe cemetery. The day always began with services in the 1854 Barnet Congregational Church, just west of the monument, and ended with a Memorial Day address there.

From Monument Square, take Church Street past the Congregational Church to the Barnet town hall, used during the war. Voters here in December 1863 approved $350 bounty payments. The following August, payments of $800 were voted.

Pass the church and the second house on the left, a large frame structure, is believed to have been the home of Miss Laura Moore, who worked tirelessly providing items for the soldiers. The Barnet history notes that women met in each village in the town "preparing warm garments for the men in the field and delicacies for the sick and wounded." It also states, "There were those who drove from farm to farm collecting such articles as could be spared, which were sent to the front."

Continue on Church Street to West Barnet Road, and in 2 miles, turn right and go uphill to the 1854 Barnet Center Presbyterian Church. A service was held here in January 1863 for Private Thomas W. Gibson, 15th Vermont, who died at Fairfax Courthouse, Virginia, of sickness the last day of 1862. The service marked the first time that a body was allowed in the sanctuary during a funeral.

Return to West Barnet Road, go right, and in 2.5 miles, reach West Barnet and the West Barnet Presbyterian Church, on the left. The *Caledonian Record* reported in late July 1864 that the Reverend William Reed, pastor, held a reception at his home for recently returned soldiers and that "three cheers and a Stars and Stripes" were given at the end of his speech.

Continue past the church, and soon bear left on Harvey Mountain Road. In 1.75 miles, go right on Mosquitoville Road, and in just under 0.5 mile, note a farmhouse on the right, with barn across the road. From this farm, Private Peter Abbott went to war in Company K of the 3rd Vermont. He wrote home on February 28, 1863, from winter camp near Falmouth, Virginia, about a massive snowball fight involving the 3rd and 5th Vermont regiments and others, resulting "in a good many bludy noses and black Eyes." And he wrote, "Walter Harvey has received $75 to send Hirams body home but he has not concluded what it is best to do yet." Hiram Somers body was sent home, to lie in Pleasant View Cemetery.

Return to Barnet village, go north on Route 5 just over 6 miles to Passumpsic, and go right on Bridge Street. Pass the Baptist Church, and on the left, back from the road, is a small, shingled building. After the war, Andrew and James Smith operated a blacksmith shop here. Andrew served in the 17th Vermont and James in the 8th New Hampshire Infantry. At First Bull Run, brother Ezra Smith was killed fighting beside James. Brother George Smith, of the 2nd New Hampshire Infantry, was captured at Second Bull Run but survived a Confederate prison to return home. Another brother, William Smith, who also enlisted in New Hampshire, died of typhoid fever in New Orleans in 1862. Brother Charles Smith, a private in the 11th Vermont, was captured on June 14, 1864, near Petersburg and died at Andersonville. All the Smith boys grew up in Barnet.

SOURCES

BARNET TOWN RECORDS.

GIBSON, ALEXANDER DUNNETT. *HISTORY OF MCINDOES ACADEMY*. MCINDOE FALLS, VT: ACADEMY ALUMNI ASSOCIATION, 1953.

MARSHALL, JEFFREY D., ED. *A WAR OF THE PEOPLE: VERMONT CIVIL WAR LETTERS*. LEBANON, NH: UNIVERSITY PRESS OF NEW ENGLAND, 1999.

RAFFO, STEVEN M. *A BIOGRAPHY OF OLIVER JOHNSON, ABOLITIONIST AND REFORMER, 1809–1889*. LEWISTON, ME: EDWIN MELLEN PRESS, 2002.

WELLS, FREDERIC PALMER. *HISTORY OF BARNET, VERMONT: FROM THE OUTBREAK OF THE FRENCH AND INDIAN WAR TO THE PRESENT TIME*. BURLINGTON, VT: FREE PRESS PRINTING, 1923.

WITH THANKS TO DAVE WARDEN.

BURKE

Go north from Lyndonville on Route 5 and into the town of Burke, soon coming to the village of West Burke. In the village center, Route 5A branches west, and the first building along it, on the right, is an old store. Beside once stood the Burke GAR Hall, long ago torn down. A photograph taken in the early 1900s shows a score of gray and bearded Civil War veterans, many in uniform, assembled along the sidewalk in front of their hall.

Continue north on Route 5, quickly cross a bridge, and make a quick right on Burke Hollow Road. In just over 2 miles, enter Burke Hollow and turn sharp right on Bugbee Road. About 100 yards along on the right is a large frame house with barn across the road. The level area around the house was once the Burke militia drill field, used before and during the Civil War.

Return to Burke Hollow Road, and soon come to Schoolhouse Road on the left. Just up the hill on the right is the Burke Hollow Schoolhouse, built in 1912. Across the road stood an older school, which this building replaced, the site of town meetings in the 1860s. Burke voters approved their first soldier bounties in 1863, $325 each. In 1864, a bounty of $600 was voted for men who voluntarily enlisted, with only $300 going to those drafted. Later that year, a tax of $2.25 on each dollar of the grand list was voted to cover expenses. Burke historian Phyllis Burbank wrote, "This tax was five to 10 times higher than any previous tax raised."

Return to Burke Hollow Road and pass Union Meeting House. In 2.5 miles, on reaching Route 114, go left, or north. The handsome building with cupola is the Burke Mountain Club, which contains the town library. The club was the gift to Burke of the Darling family, who had made a fortune through the ownership of a Fifth Avenue hotel. Within the building is a bronze plaque, originally placed in the Burke town hall in West Burke, with the names of 103 Burke men who served in the Civil War. Proceed north along Route 114, and the West Burke Congregational Church is on the left. Albert Darling, raised in Burke and destined for Fifth Avenue, was a member and generous supporter of the church. On April 13, 1865, Abraham Lincoln wrote a pass for Darling that read: "Allow the bearer, A. B. Darling, to pass, and visit Mobile, if, and when that City shall be in our possession. A. Lincoln."

The next night, Lincoln was shot by John Wilkes Booth at Ford's Theater, and he died the next morning. The pass, certainly one of the last things the president wrote, is preserved at the Vermont Historical Society.

The Walter family were longtime faithful members of the West Burke Congregational Church. True Walter enlisted as a fifer in the 15th Vermont Regiment but became ill in the regiment's winter encampment. A newspaper account of January 31, 1863 stated:

"Died Jan. 2, in the hospital near Fairfax Courthouse, Virginia, True B. Walter, son of Porter and Charlotte Walter of Burke, aged 21 . . . A correspondent who sends us the above adds: He had an impression for some time before he died that he should have but a short time, and accordingly packed and arranged his things to be sent home—sought and found the Savior. Just before he died, he said that he was willing and ready to die . . . His body was embalmed and sent home . . . The funeral exercises were at West Burke, on Thurs. Jan 15. The text, Job 19:21, for the occasion, was selected by his afflicted mother. There was as large a congregation as ever met on a funeral occasion in Burke." The account stated that fifty members of the local military company gave an escort "to his last resting place."

Continue past the church, traveling the route of Private Walter's procession to the cemetery and quickly note Mountain Road on the right. Go past it and remain on Route 114, which quickly bears left, and note the house at the top of the rise on the left. This is believed to have been the home of the Reverend Charles W.

Wells, an 11th Vermont private captured at the Weldon Railroad, who was sent to Andersonville. Wells kept a diary that is preserved at St. Johnsbury's Fairbanks Museum. He wrote August 17, "Oh Lord how long must we stay in this dreadful place?" September 12, he wrote: "Sick all day. Got orders to go. Expect to go tomorrow . . . Hope soon to leave. About half have gone . . . Very warm. Sick yet expect very soon to go away." A friend wrote in the diary on September 17, "Mr. Wells died this a.m. he passed this life easy without a groan or struggle and died happy in the Lord."

Beyond the Wells house is the cemetery to which Private Walter's body was taken. Also buried there are the Darlings, around a massive stone. The cemetery also contains the grave of Private Enos Thurber, 5th Vermont.

Return along Route 114 and turn left on Mountain Road. Ascending along Dish Mill Brook, the road rises toward the Burke Mountain ski area, into high old fields where the Eggleston family once owned several farms. In just under 2 miles, turn left on rough Pinkham Road, and in 0.3 mile come to an old schoolhouse the Egglestons attended. Private Charles Eggleston, 3rd Vermont, was twenty-one when he died of sickness in April 1862. Private Harley Eggleston joined the 17th Vermont, at eighteen, in August 1864, serving until the war ended. Private Henry Eggleston died less than a year after coming home at war's end, having served a year in the 9th Vermont. Joseph Eggleston served three years in the 3rd Vermont as a private and came home safely. Private Myron Eggleston, 3rd Vermont, was wounded, at twenty-four, at the Wilderness, but survived. Private Royal Eggleston safely served the war's last year in the 9th Vermont. Private William Eggleston enlisted for the war's last ten months in the 11th Vermont and came home. The men were all cousins.

Continue past the school just under 1 mile, and the farmhouse on the right, facing Burke Mountain, was the John Thurber home. Danville's *North Star* reported November 11, 1862: "Enus W. Thurber, son of John Thurber, died on the mail train, last week Saturday, at Newbury. He was a member of Co. D, 5th Vermont regiment, had been sick for some time, but was considered better and was on his way home, and was but two hours ride there from, when death overtook him."

Go just over 2 miles past the Thurber house to Route 114 and turn right, then in 0.2 mile, go left on Schoolhouse Road. In 0.5 mile, go right on Newland Road, and the first house on the left, the brick cape, was True Walter's home. Return to Route 114 and follow it south to Route 5 and Lyndonville.

Burke town historian Phyllis Burbank also noted in her book, "After the war, many men with their families headed for the west. When Burke had its Bicentennial, the Historical Society had letters from all over the United States."

SOURCES
Burbank, Phyllis. *Burke: More Than Just a Mountain*. Burke, VT: Burke Mountain Club, 1989.

BURKE CHURCH RECORDS. BURKE MOUNTAIN
CLUB, BURKE.
NORTH STAR (DANVILLE), 1861–1865.
VERMONT STATE LIBRARY.
WELLS, C. R. CIVIL WAR DIARY. FAIRBANKS
MUSEUM.
WITH THANKS TO PHYLLIS BURBANK.

DANVILLE

Danville lies 10 miles west of St. Johnsbury, along Route 2, its hilltop village centered on a large green that commands views of New Hampshire's White Mountains. On June 9, 1864, a procession of saddened Danville folks arrived in the village escorting the body of Colonel Addison Preston, commander of the 1st Vermont Cavalry. Preston had been killed in a skirmish near Cold Harbor on June 3, and according to a cavalryman from St. Johnsbury, George Custer knelt by Preston's body and said, "There lies the body of the best colonel in the cavalry corps." Danville's *North Star* reported, "Last week Thursday, the remains of colonel P. arrived at St. Johnsbury, about half past five p.m., and were received at the depot by the relatives of the deceased, and a large number of sympathizing friends from Danville. The County Court (then in session) adjourned for the occasion, and the Judges . . . joined the procession, and with muffled drum, amid the tolling bells, escorted the Danville procession from the depot to the main road leading to our village . . . and on arriving here, the bells were again tolled."

Preston, born in Burke, as a child came with his parents to live in Danville. He attended Brown University, then took to the sea at the suggestion of a physician to improve his health. After briefly living in Australia, he returned to Danville and went into business. When the war began, he recruited for the cavalry and was elected captain of the 1st Vermont Cavalry's Company D. Preston, a popular officer who seemed without fear, rose through the ranks to lead the regiment.

The North Danville Road goes north from the Danville green. Just after turning onto it, look to the left for the large white Congregational Church. It stands on the site of the big church in which Preston's funeral was held, said to be the largest funeral ever held in Caledonia County, as people packed the church and stood outside. The St. Johnsbury diarist Henry Herrick wrote that Preston's widow would not allow a military funeral. Continue past the church and see the grand old house on the right, at the top of the rise, where Preston lived. Preston came home in the winter of 1862–1863 and scoured the countryside for cavalry horses, purchasing many from Northeast Kingdom farmers.

Continue on the North Danville Road 3.3 miles, and turn left on McDowell Road, following signs for the Old North Church. In 1.75 miles, at the corner of Stannard Mountain Road, is the Stanton School House. Mary Willard, the mother of Frances Willard, once taught school here. Frances was born later in New York state and became a founder and, in 1874, national president of the Women's Christian Temperance Union. The fight against alcohol abstinence burned as hot as the slavery issue at the time of the Civil War, and Mary Willard was a key figure in the cause.

Continue on the North Danville Road 0.75 mile, and on the left is a large and much remodeled Italianate house that was, at the time of the war, the Kelsey family home. The *North Star* reported in the winter of 1864: "Robert Kelsey Esq., of North Danville, has just learned of the death of his son, Alvah Kelsey. He was a resident of the South, and was engaged in the rebel service. He was killed at the battle of Corinth, which was fought a year or two since. Mr. Kelsey has two more sons now serving in the federal army, and he is himself a most thorough Union man."

Continue into North Danville and follow signs to the North Danville Church. On February 7, 1863, the *North Star* said that Danville's Captain John Drew was to give a lecture here on his experiences in a southern prison: admission 10 cents to defray expenses.

Return south to the village of Danville. The town's Civil War memorial stands on the west side of the green, and Colonel Preston's name is the first of two hundred names. Charles Brainerd wrote in 1879:

"The record that the town of Danville made in the War of the Rebellion was one that her citizens have reason to be proud of. Two hundred forty-five men furnished under the different calls, five more than her share, thirty six thousands paid by her taxpayers in little over two years, to raise men for the army, was certainly a task to try her patriotism to a great extent; and should the patriotism of the town ever again in the future be called upon, I hope that her sons of that time will be found, as they were at this, not wanting."

Danville's voters met time and again during the war in the town hall, which stood on the site of the present town hall, which faces the green from the north. A marker honoring Thaddeus Stevens stands in front of it.

In October 1833, an antislavery meeting was held at the Baptist Church, the brick building that still stands along the east side of the Danville green, and at the end, a collection was taken to support the New England Anti-Slavery Society. A year later, the Danville Anti-Slavery Society advertised its first meeting at the Congregational Church. Two weeks after the firing on Fort Sumter, a rally was held in a packed Baptist Church, during which patriotic speeches were heard and several resolutions passed. One called on the legislature to prepare the state to respond to whatever might be the military demands made by the federal government. A contemporary account said that flags waved throughout the village that day, while bands played military music.

Go south from the Baptist Church on Brainerd Street and one soon comes to the home of Charles Brainerd, his white frame house now headquarters of the national dowsers' organization. Brainerd, a lieutenant in the 15th Vermont, reenlisted in the 17th Vermont. Wounded at the Wilderness, he recovered and was brevetted a captain for his heroic service during the April 2, 1865, attack at Petersburg. Continue past the Brainerd house to the Danville Cemetery, go in the first entrance, and Preston's stone is about 75 yards in on the right. Buried beside him are his wife and a son who died in 1865.

Return to the village and turn right, east, on Route 2. In 1 mile, turn right on Penny Lane (Town Road 61). Follow it for 1.5 miles, dropping into a wooded valley. In a cabin believed to have been in this area, Thaddeus Stevens was born on April 4, 1792. A crippled child with clubbed feet and the son of an alcoholic father who deserted the family, Stevens was raised by his devoted hardworking mother, Sarah Stevens. Thanks to the mother he called Sally, Stevens graduated from Peacham Academy, then from Dartmouth College in 1814. He soon moved to Pennsylvania, where he practiced law in Lancaster, then in Gettysburg, and became involved in the iron industry. He also became a defender of fugitive slaves. Rising to prominence as a member of the Anti-Mason Party, Stevens became a power in Pennsylvania politics. Elected to the state legislature, he championed the cause of public education. Elected to the U.S. House of Representatives, he vigorously opposed the fugitive slave law and the expansion of slavery. There he became perhaps the most powerful of all Civil War–era congressmen, a hater of slavery who championed emancipation and black suffrage. As chair of the Way and Means Committee, Stevens worked diligently to fund the war. Stevens was instrumental in the passage of the Thirteenth and Fourteenth Amendments and was a prime mover in President Andrew Johnson's impeachment. Ever mindful of his humble beginnings, he became known as the Great Commoner.

On his death, he insisted on being buried in a cemetery where blacks were also interred.

Return to Danville village, and turn left again on Brainerd Street. Pass a cemetery and soon bear right on Greenbank Hollow Road. In just under 2 miles, cross a narrow covered bridge and make a quick right. A historic marker stands among the ruins of the Greenbank woolen mill that was once the center of a thriving little community. The day of the Baptist Church war rally, the ladies of this village raised a flag here, and that night it was saluted with the firing of guns. The woolen mill, built in 1849, once employed forty-five people and produced up to 700 yards of cloth a day. It received a large order from the federal government in 1861 for blue uniform cloth. Sally Stevens brought her family of four sons to this village when Thaddeus was seven years old. They lived here for several years, then moved to Peacham, likely taking what is now called the Thaddeus Stevens Road that leads uphill from the covered bridge.

SOURCES
DANVILLE TOWN RECORDS.
NORTH STAR (DANVILLE). VERMONT STATE
    LIBRARY.
WITH THANKS TO MARY PRIOR.

GROTON

Groton's Civil War Memorial erected in 1919, "in memory of the brave soldiers from the town of Groton who served during the Civil War 1861–1865," stands by the Groton town office on the north side of Route 302. Listed are 82 men who served, and a history of the town states that 3 died in battle and 9 of illness, while 10 were wounded. The town building occupies the site of Welch's store. A Groton man recalled after the war, "Every evening except Sunday a large portion of the male population would gather at the store of Hosea Welch II to await the arrival of the daily stage from Wells River, bringing in the mail and one copy of the daily newspaper. After the mail was sorted and distributed, Mr. Welch, the storekeeper and postmaster, would take a vantage position, adjust the kerosene lamp, and read from the Boston Journal the news of the day to a most eager and attentive audience. Sometimes it was 'All Quiet along the Potomac'; at other times it told of carnage at Bull Run, Cedar Creek, Gettysburg, or the Wilderness. It made men wonder whether any Groton boy was killed or injured in the fight, or taken prisoner, as rarely were individuals mentioned."

Across Route 302 and two houses before the Methodist Church is the postwar home of Dr. Seth Eastman, who as a Topsham lad enlisted in the 6th Vermont. After the war, he became a doctor and practiced in Groton for almost forty years. In 1907, in this house, he assembled his Civil War letters into a booklet. One said of the Overland Campaign:

"I never expected to see Vermont again. We called Vermont 'God's Country,' then, and it has always seemed that it was my 'God's Country' ever since. I like it now just the same. I could not see any way that a fellow would live much longer amid such strife as I was in most every day. The comrades were falling one-by-one, and most of them were either killed or wounded since the campaign began. I could not see when it was to end, so I gave up all hope of ever seeing home and friends again."

The tall 1837 Methodist Church was remodeled in 1863. Methodists meeting here in 1839 adopted three resolutions favoring temperance and three opposing slavery. The first of the latter said that "slavery as it exists in the United States of America is, under all circumstances, a sin against God & contrary to the rights of our fellow men enslaved." A memorial window in the church honors Private Thomas Burnham, 4th Vermont, killed at Cedar Creek.

Across Route 302 is the Groton library. The eastern part of the building was, during the Civil War, a hall sometimes rented for town meetings. Groton voters approved bounties that exceeded $600 late in the war and in 1865 voted a tax of $4 on every grand list dollar to pay the town's war debt.

Past the library and across the road is an old store (in 2012 a restaurant) built in 1927 to house Burton Brown's Meat and Groceries. Eighty years later, ninety-year-old Dale Brown remembered being in his father's store and seeing very old Civil War veterans gathered around the woodstove. Among them, he said, was Marshall Darling, a West Groton farmer, who served a short time in the Vermont Cavalry. Brown said the old soldiers never talked about the war.

Three buildings past the store is the

1840 Peter Paul House, home of the Groton Historical Society. It is believed that soldiers were once quartered in the upper story, when Groton had a militia company, which existed for more than a decade until disbanding in 1855. Some of the company's training served Groton soldiers well in the Civil War.

Continue east on 302, and in just under 1 mile is a brick house on the left, the home of Robert Taisey, a private in the 3rd Vermont for three years. Turn around and pass through the village on Route 302, and in 1.5 miles, where Route 232 branches right, the house at the intersection was the home of William Annis. A private in the 3rd Vermont, Annis deserted and was discharged from service by a court-martial.

In another 2.5 miles is the monument that honors William Scott of Groton, nicknamed the Sleeping Sentinel, perhaps the most famous of all Civil War privates. It stands on the site of the farmhouse in which Thomas and Mary Scott raised seven sons and a daughter. Indeed, look over the bank behind the monument and see the house's foundation stones. An army friend of Scott's said, "William always worked at home . . . His father always had his wages. His father was in very reduced circumstances." Apparently, it was hard to pull a living from the boulder-strewn land of this upland farm. Still, when the war began, the five boys old enough to serve, Daniel, George, John, Joseph, and William, enlisted.

William joined the 3rd Vermont, drilling at St. Johnsbury, a big, awkward, country lad who had trouble marching but was popular with fellow soldiers. In late summer 1862, the 3rd was camped on Georgetown Heights, near Washington, D.C., overlooking Chain Bridge, which spanned the Potomac River. On the night of August 30, 1862, Scott took the place of a friend on picket duty, though the Groton lad had been on duty the previous night. Sometime after midnight, an officer found Scott and his fellow pickets sleeping. Scott was arrested and charged with the capital offense of sleeping at his post. A court-martial of 12 officers, including Vermonters Wheelock Veazey and George Stannard, sentenced Scott to die by firing squad. Scott's fellow soldiers protested with 191 officers and men signing a petition asking that he be pardoned. Newspapers far and wide ran stories, and Scott's dilemma became something of a cause célèbre. But not everyone wanted mercy, including the *New York Times*. Still, Abraham Lincoln got involved, apparently appealing to General George McClellan that Scott be spared.

The morning of September 9, the 3rd Vermont was assembled to witness an execution. Scott was led, trembling, from a tent, but when the execution order was read, it turned out to be a pardon, issued at McClellan's directive. The ranks erupted in cheers. Later, Veazey said he came to understand that the whole thing had been staged in an effort to encourage discipline, and there never had been any real intent of shooting Scott. Had the fatal shots been fired, the Groton boy would have been the first Union soldier executed in the Civil War.

Scott soldiered on through the winter.

Then on April 16, at Lee's Mill, when a portion of the Vermont Brigade was ordered to wade through a millpond and attack Confederate entrenchments, Scott was hit as he reached the Rebel side of the pond. A friend wrote, "Willie Scoot was killed on making the charge he had five bullets in his body. I see where he was buried. He was buried in a peach grove the trees was blossomed out." Years later Carl Sandburg wrote that Scott "among the fresh growths and blooms of Virginia springtime at Lee's Mill took the burning message of six bullets into his body . . . All he could give Lincoln, or his county, or his God was now given." Scott's body never came home. It rests in the federal cemetery at Yorktown, not far from Lee's Mill, Virginia, with two thousand other Union soldiers.

From the Scott memorial, cross the road and walk a bit east, to the small cemetery just above the road. At the right rear is the grave of Private Joseph Scott, 6th Vermont, who died soon after returning from the war. Two other Scott boys never came home. George and Daniel, both of the 6th Vermont, died of disease. Local legend holds that Thomas Scott visited the White House and met with Lincoln, who handed him a $10 bill. The loss of four sons to the war may have been too much for Thomas and Mary Scott, and they soon left Groton.

SOURCES
EASTMAN, SETH N. *THE CIVIL WAR (AS RECOLLECTED BY AN ORDINARY SOLDIER).* GROTON, VT: GROTON HISTORICAL SOCIETY, 1909.
GLOVER, WADE F. *MISTER GLOVER'S GROTON: THE CHRONICLE OF GROTON, VERMONT*

FROM 1789 TO 1978. GROTON HISTORICAL SOCIETY. CANAAN, NH: PHOENIX PUBLISHING, 1978.
WITH THANKS TO RICHARD BROOKS, DALE BROWN, AND MARILYN RUITER.

HARDWICK

Hardwick's Memorial Building was dedicated on March 7, 1912, with ceremonies at the nearby Opera House. Governor John A. Mead, a veteran of the 12th Vermont, spoke: "What a beautiful thing you have done here, through your own effort and your own granite, produced and manufactured in your own town." Judge W. H. Taylor told the crowd, "In thinking of the sacrifices of those who went to the front, we should not forget the sacrifices of those who stayed behind in the homes. In many ways theirs was a harder lot and a greater sacrifice. They were called upon to give up husbands and fathers and sons, often the only defense of their homes against abject want. In spite of this, even with breaking hearts, they bade their loved ones Godspeed."

The *Hardwick Gazette* said that at the time of the dedication, 25 Hardwick veterans were still alive, 5 living in town. After the Opera House ceremonies, a reception was held at the Memorial Building. That handsome granite edifice now houses the Hardwick town offices. In a room off the front hallway, the names of 167 Hardwick soldiers of the Civil War, and men of other wars, are displayed on white marble plaques. Upstairs are large rooms where the Ellsworth Post of the

GAR and the local chapter of the Women's Relief Corps once met.

Routes 15 and 14 meet in the center of Hardwick. Go north from their intersection and quickly bear right on North Main Street. The Memorial Building is on the right, at the corner of Main and Church streets. Turn right on Church and on the left, at the corner of Depot Street, is the Hardwick Town House, built in 1860, where the dedication ceremonies were held. Hardwick voters met here during the war, including a gathering on August 21, 1862, when a bounty of $50 was voted for the local men answering President Lincoln's call for ninety-day volunteers. In 1864, at another town meeting, bounties of $400 were approved. That November 6, in the hall, Hardwick cast 254 votes for Lincoln and 37 for George McClellan. The building was remodeled in 1898 and became an opera house.

Behind the town house is the old depot area, along the bed of the now long-defunct St. Johnsbury and Lamoille County Railway. From here, men boarded trains to go to war. On July 28, 1913, five former soldiers, including Daniel Bridgeman, boarded a special train here bound for the fiftieth anniversary commemoration at Gettysburg.

Return to North Main, turn right, and at the northeast corner of Main and Wakefield streets stands the house built by Daniel Bridgman, once of the 2nd Vermont, who once commanded the local GAR post. He and his wife were given a housewarming here in 1905 and presented with a set of china dishes by local GAR and WRC members. A dollar left over from the gift's purchase was presented to the Bridgmans, a silver dollar, and they donated it as the first dollar raised to build the Memorial Building. That dollar was returned to them at the building's dedication seven years later.

Continue north of Main, which soon becomes Bridgman Hill Road. One-half mile along, look to the fields on the left for the foundations of buildings that were once part of the large Bridgeman farm, begun in 1796. Dorman Bridgman became owner of the farm about 1820, and he became involved in Underground Railroad activities, sheltering and shuttling fugitive slaves. Fire destroyed the farm in 1943. From the farm, his son Daniel Bridgman went to war, as a sergeant in the 2nd Vermont. Wounded at the Wilderness, he came home to live here forty-one years before building the house in town.

Return south onto North Main, and back in the village, turn left on Route 15. In just over 2 miles, turn north on Route 16, and in 3 miles, go left on Cedar Street. Proceed 1 mile and turn left, cross the bridge, and bear right on Church Street. The Reverend Charles Wright (see Montpelier), an abolitionist who helped transport fugitive slaves, was pastor of the Congregational Church on the left. Continue on Church Street 1.25 miles and the Revolutionary War–era Bayley-Hazen Military Road enters on the right. Just past its intersection, on the left, is a small white house, once the home of the Reverend Kiah Bailey and his wife, Abigail. Kiah was cofounder, with Reverend Wright, of the

Caledonia County Anti-Slavery Society. He once wrote, "I assist the poor fugitive, as my conscience requires, and am persecuted . . . the Fugitive Slave Law prohibits the free exercise of charity to the poor by pains and penalties."

Beyond the Bailey house, also on the left, is a rambling old tavern known as the Stage House. It was here that Reverend Bailey hid fugitives, often receiving them from Reverend Wright or Dorman Bridgman.

SOURCES
HARDWICK GAZETTE, 1860–65, 1913.
VERMONT STATE LIBRARY.
HARDWICK TOWN RECORDS.
WITH THANKS TO SUSAN COFFIN, LORRAINE HUSSEY, DEANNA FRENCH, AND DIANN PERRY ROSS.

....

KIRBY

Along the Moose River on Route 2, 1.3 miles east of East St. Johnsbury, the southern tip of the town of Kirby touches the road, and here stands a large frame house with big barn across the way. Grouts founded this farm in 1792, and Josiah Grout and his brother William, though born in Canada, grew up here. Josiah enlisted in the Vermont Cavalry in the fall of 1861 and was elected a lieutenant, being promoted to captain a year later. Grout saw action in seventeen engagements, the last being April 1, 1863. That day, he encountered John Mosby's raiders at a farm along Broad Run in northern Virginia. Caught in a tight spot, Grout and a group of men rushed the Confederates, Grout on his warhorse Lit-

tle Sorrel. Grout found himself in the midst of a dozen rebels, one of whom slashed his head with a saber, while another shot him in the side. Grout remembered, "We had fourteen killed and wounded. The enemy had three killed, and some that rode away were badly wounded; how many I never knew . . . I found seven bullet holes in my clothes, one in my body, and knew that Little Sorrel arrested three of that morning's busy messengers . . . It was close, sharp, spiteful work, and best described by an old lady who lived at the road corner where we left the pike. She said the firing sounded like popping corn."

Grout soon returned to Kirby, discharged because of wounds, He studied law with his brother, William, and was elected to the legislature. He then moved to Illinois to practice law but returned to Vermont and was elected Speaker of the house, then served in the state senate. In 1896, he was elected Vermont governor, and in that capacity led Vermont delegations to William McKinley's inauguration and to the dedication of Grant's Tomb in New York City.

Josiah's brother William also compiled a distinguished Civil War record (see Barton) and later lived in this house, much enlarging and "Victorianizing" the old homestead. From the Grout house, continue east on Route 2, soon entering the town of Concord, and in 0.75 mile, turn left on Kirby Mountain Road. In 1 mile, cross the town line back into Kirby, and the first farm in Kirby, with house and barn on the right, was purchased by Edson Ranney after the Civil War. Look to the large hillside farm behind this farm, the place where Ranney grew up and from which he left to enlist at twenty-one as a private in the 15th Vermont. A year later, he reenlisted in the 17th Vermont. Ranney lost an eye fighting at Spotsylvania Courthouse on May 12, 1864, but served until the war's end. He came home to farm here the rest of his life.

Continue past the Ranney farm to the crossroads schoolhouse, on the site of the school that Ranney attended. Watson Bean also attended the old school. He enlisted in the 11th Vermont at forty-two and served as a private the last two years of the war. Bean is buried in the cemetery just beyond the school.

Continue on Kirby Mountain Road 3 miles and look left, below the road, to a pond. Along the left side of the road here once stood the Kirby Town House, where Civil War–era town meetings were held. On November 25, Kirby voters authorized selectmen to borrow not more than $2,100 to pay seven men a bounty for their service in the 15th Vermont. On February 12, 1864, facing a new draft call, bounties of $300 were authorized for three men, on the motion of Josiah Grout, home wounded from the war. Bounties of $500 were approved in January 1864, with an additional payment of $100 quickly added. By March of 1865, bounties of $600, with an additional payment of $100, were approved.

Continue 1.5 miles on Kirby Mountain Road and turn right on Brookside Road. From the farmhouse above the road on the right in 0.3 mile, Homer Young joined the 3rd Vermont as a private in September 1862, at eighteen. In August 1864, he deserted, during the long marches of the early Shenandoah Valley campaign. But he returned in January, was soon promoted corporal, and served until the war ended.

Return to Kirby Mountain Road and cross it onto North Kirby Road. In just over 0.5 mile, go right on a road that soon ends at a farm with a striking view of the mountain valley that holds Lake Willoughby. From this farm, Henry Brown enlisted in the 10th Vermont in late 1862. He served as a private until he died in April 1865 of sickness, at twenty-three.

Kirby, from a population of 425, saw 47 men go to war, with 3 enlisting in other towns. At least 7 died. Ephriam Harrington, credited to Kirby, as a sergeant won a Medal of Honor at Second Fredericksburg, in the assault on Lee's Hill. He soon became an officer and was awarded a battlefield promotion to major for bravery in the 6th Corps assault that broke the Confederate lines at Petersburg April 2, 1865.

SOURCES
KIRBY TOWN RECORDS.
WITH THANKS TO ALBERT TAYLOR AND
    WANDA GRANT.

LYNDON

Going north from St. Johnsbury on Interstate 91, take exit 23 and turn right, south, on Route 5. Entering the village of Lyndon Corner, turn right on York Street. The first house on the left, set above the road, was the home of Lyndon's best-known Civil War soldier, David Duhigg. A native of County Limerick, Ireland, Duhigg was instrumental in recruiting the 15th Vermont's Company G, and indeed, Lyndon citizens presented him with a Colt revolver for "saving the town from a draft." Duhigg served as 15th Vermont sergeant major under Colonel Redfield Proctor. On Christmas eve, 1862, he wrote from camp at Fairfax Courthouse, Virginia, to his sister, Mary, of how much he liked soldier life. Mentioning his small cabin and a tent roof, he noted a "general atmosphere as you have in September—and you are hundreds of miles way amidst the snow-clad hills of a free Vermont." Back in Lyndon in July 1863, Duhigg reenlisted, becoming a lieutenant in Company M, 11th Vermont. With him went Marshall Wilmarth, husband of Duhigg's sister, Honora. Wilmarth was also a lieutenant.

In the fall of 1864, the 11th was in the Shenandoah Valley as part of the Vermont Brigade. At Winchester on September 19, Duhigg was shot in the heart, and comrades heard him say, "My last prayer is offered. I die happy." According to Duhigg family tradition, Duhigg's fiancée died several weeks after learning of his death.

A month after Winchester, the 11th was in action at Cedar Creek. Brother-in-law Marshall Wilmarth was shot, dying a few days later, having told a hospital steward, "Tell my wife that although we are never to meet again in this world I hope we shall meet in another."

Honora once said of her brother, David Duhigg, "If he had lived, he'd have been another George Washington."

Go past the Duhigg house and to the First Congregational Church, where the Wilmarth funeral was held. Honora Wilmarth's father was pastor of the church.

Continue past the church to the Y, and bear left, staying on York Street. The first house on the right, with barn, was the longtime home of the widow Honora Wilmarth, who never remarried.

Return on York Street to Route 5 and turn left, north. In 1.5 miles, on entering the village of Lyndonville, Center Street turns left. Just beyond it two bronze lions guard the entrance to a bank, a gift to his hometown from Luther B. Harris, who made a fortune in the banking business. They were procured by Harris from Italy, with the help of sculptor Larkin Mead (see Brattleboro).

Take Center Street just under 0.5 mile into Lyndon Center, and on crossing the bridge, note the small green on the left with Civil War cannon. The bronze statue of a wild boar beside it was also a Harris gift to the town. In 1861, Harris enlisted in the 4th Vermont and served until captured at Weldon Railroad. Taken to Andersonville, he was paroled in late February and survived. Harris wrote a book about his wartime experience twenty years later. He said of Andersonville, "The bones had little covering of flesh. Scurvy made the skin unhealthy, therefore when one was compelled to lay on the ground, sores soon came on the exposed joints of the body, shoulders, hips, knees, and ankles. The very earth seemed poisoned with the many thousands that never moved from where they lay and had no care. Taking into account the time of year and the terrible heat, it is wonderful that the air was not so poisoned that one breath would kill. The stench was something indescribable."

Harris wrote that he escaped by fashioning a crude rope from bits of cloth and leather but that hounds soon tracked him down. Of his release, he wrote, "It seemed as if the dead were looking on in dismay at our going, as though we were deserting them."

After making his fortune, Harris became a world traveler, and while in Florence, Italy, he admired a Renaissance sculpture of a wild boar. Harris had a bronze replica made and, like the lions, presented it to his hometown. Knowing that Harris survived Andersonville, the boar can easily be seen as a vision of plenty, as such a pig would have provided a great deal of meat to starving prisoners. In the summer, water runs from the animal's mouth. The statue is a fountain, and for years the locals have called it the puking pig. Continue past the little green on Center Street, and the first house on the left, the brick structure, was Harris's home. He had a good view of his gift.

Continue on Center Street, and soon come to the old Lyndon town hall on the left. In this area, Dennis Duhigg and his fellow recruits for the 15th Vermont drilled. As the war began, a mass meeting was held in the town hall, and the May 5, 1861, *Caledonian Record* reported that sixty-three men volunteered. The paper on June 14 reported that the "ladies of this village met at the town hall yesterday in large numbers . . . It was an unusual sight, that of 75 ladies and 11 sewing machines in that large hall making . . . shirts, sick gowns, sheets, pillow cases, etc." Here, Lyndon voters authorized selectmen to borrow up to $20,000 to meet war costs. The newspaper stated that in January 1865, a tax of 451 cents on each grand list dollar was approved to raise almost $30,000 to pay the town debt.

Lyndon's Civil War veterans organized a GAR post in 1890, named for Orrin Farnsworth, a 4th Vermont private who died of wounds at Second Fredericksburg. In 1891, a Women's Relief Corps auxiliary was organized. Both groups met in a GAR hall in this area, which has long since disappeared.

Many of Lyndon's Civil War dead lie in the large cemetery behind the old town hall. Enter by the stone tomb, and about 100 yards in, on the right, is an obelisk in the Duhigg family plot with the names of Dennis Duhigg and brother-in-law Marshall Wilmarth. The two comrades-in-arms lie with many Duhiggs and Wilmarth's widow, Honora. Go to the ridge beyond, where a tall flagpole stands beside an 1865 Parrot cannon, in the cemetery's GAR Lot. Beginning in 1886, elaborate Memorial Day commemorations honored Lyndon's war dead. A procession including local GAR post members and later WRC members, St. Johnsbury GAR members, schoolchildren, the Lyndon band, and many townspeople, formed in Lyndonville and marched here. After flowers were placed on soldier graves, everyone gathered at the GAR lot for speeches and music. The

Lyndon Coronet Band, later known as the Lyndon Military Band, always performed. That band, formed in 1867, became the best known in the state. Indeed, it performed at several national GAR encampments, including those in Cincinnati in 1898, Montreal in 1899, Boston in 1904, Denver in 1905, and Salt Lake City in 1909, where it became the first band ever to play in the Mormon Tabernacle. At the close of the Memorial Day ceremonies, a trumpeter from the band blew taps, and another, standing at the highest point in the cemetery, answered with taps.

From the town hall, continue on Center Street, cross the covered bridge, and turn right on Stevens Loop. In 0.5 mile, cross Route 5 onto Route 114 north. In just over 1.5 miles, turn right on Burrington Bridge Road, and follow it 1.3 miles to a hilltop farm on the left.

Jesse and John Simpson were born of Scottish immigrant parents, who kept a hotel in Quebec City. When the parents died, their young orphan sons were apprenticed to a farm in southern Quebec. On turning eighteen, John ran away, crossed the border, and ended up in Lyndon. A year later, he went back north and brought Jesse to Lyndon, where they both became loggers. John Simpson enlisted in August 1862 as a private in the 3rd Vermont. He died May 12, 1864, at Spotsylvania's Bloody Angle. His body never came home, though a stone commemorates his life in the family plot in the Lyndon Center cemetery. His brother Jesse did not serve, and after the war, he bought this hilltop farm. He named his first son John.

Return as you came to Route 114, turn south on Route 5, to Lyndonville.

SOURCES
FISHER, HARRIET FLETCHER. *IMAGES OF AMERICA: LYNDON*. DOVER, NH: ARCADIA PUBLISHING, 1998.
FISHER, HARRIET FLETCHER, ED. *LOOK AROUND LYNDON*. LYNDON, VT: LYNDON BICENTENNIAL BOOK COMMITTEE, 1978.
HARRIS, LUTHER. MANUSCRIPT OF WAR REMINISCENCES. SPECIAL COLLECTIONS, BAILEY/HOWE LIBRARY, UNIVERSITY OF VERMONT, BURLINGTON.
"LYNDON CIVIL WAR HERO DIES IN ACTION 100 YEARS AGO." *CALEDONIAN RECORD* (ST. JOHNSBURY), 1964.
LYNDON TOWN RECORDS.
SHORES, VENILA LOVINA. *LYNDON: GEM IN THE GREEN*. LYNDON, VT: TOWN OF LYNDON, 1986.
WITH THANKS TO WILDER SIMPSON AND THE COBLEIGH LIBRARY (CHESTER) STAFF.

NEWARK

In his 1990 book on Newark, *Walk Through a Hill Town*, Newark resident Bill Jackson wrote: "When the Civil War began . . . Vermont stood up, inspired by the Freedom Spirit who delights to dance in Green Mountains, and who was grieved over slavery and was prepared to sacrifice self for freedom."

The Newark Union Church, almost unchanged since it opened in 1862, stands beside Newark Street, which leads north from Route 5A, north of East Burke. Some forty-two Newark men served, and many attended this church. Indeed, a list of deceased members in the vestibule includes the names of seven Civil War veterans. Among them is Hiram Spencer, listed with his wife Angelina, longtime attendees of the church. Both Hiram and Angelina grew up in Newark. He joined the 7th Vermont as a private in September 1864 and served until the war ended. He wrote regularly to his wife, always expressing concern about how things were going on their farm. Writing from near Mobile, Alabama, in April 1865, Hiram said, "Bee as careful as you can and get along as easy as you can Till I get home and then I will try and help you so that you wont have to work so hard I should like to be at home now but I cant as things ar now I have got to work for Uncle Sam now." And he wrote to his wife mentioning William, someone helping with the farm. He said, "William must try and find someone to take the sugar . . . on the chandler place if he can and if he cant he must get up some logs and . . . wood if he can so as not to have it lay till next spring he must tend to this worre at home." His words "tending to his worre [war] at home" speak well to the concerns of many a distant Vermont soldier. Hiram came safely home.

Just south of the church, Schoolhouse Road crosses Newark Street. At the intersection is an old school, site of Newark town meetings during the Civil War. Voters meeting here October 4, 1862, approved the town's first bounties of $25 for nine-month enlistees and $50 for three-year men. By war's end, Newark was paying bounties of $600 and more. On June 25, 1869, the *Vermont Union,* a local paper, said in a story on Newark, "The war debt will be mostly paid this year."

From the school, go east on Schoolhouse Road to Pleasant View Cemetery. Near the front is a stone marking the graves of Hiram and Angelina Spencer, who lived in Newark all their lives. He died at seventy-eight in 1916, and she died a year later at seventy-six. Their funerals took place in the Union Church.

Behind their grave is a single stone that appears to tell a story of the war's ruination of a family. The names of Francis West and his sons Levi and Francis Jr. are on the same stone. Levi joined the 3rd Vermont in the summer of 1861 and died of sickness the following January at age twenty. He is buried in Washington, D.C. Father Francis died on March 26, 1864, at fifty-two. Francis Jr. is listed as having died at eighteen at City Point, Virginia, near Petersburg, on July 25, 1865, though it is unclear in which unit he served.

Continue on Schoolhouse Road 1.25 miles and turn right on Maple Ridge Road. The first house on the right was the Corliss farmhouse, and it is believed that Dennison Corliss enlisted from here in the 15th Vermont, marched to Gettysburg, and came home.

Just beyond the Corliss house, go right on Brook Road. In 0.4 mile is a house on the right, with a barn across the road. James Smith lived here after the war, who enlisted at twenty-two in the 8th Vermont in February 1862. Captured at Boutte Station, Louisiana, the next fall, he was paroled after two months. Smith became a lieutenant and served until the war ended.

Return to Maple Ridge Road, go right, and the first house on the right was once the home of Henry Hoffman, a private in the 9th Vermont the last two years of the war.

Continue on Maple Ridge 0.4 mile, and go left on Shady Lane. Soon, go right at a Y, entering a rough and very narrow road. In 1 mile, the cape on the right was the home of Ansel Foster, 17th Vermont private. Foster was captured at Petersburg and survived only two months in Andersonville.

Return to Maple Ridge Road; go 0.75 mile and turn left on Ball Farm Road. At the end of this lane is one of the oldest houses in Newark, set into a bank, home of Albro Ball. He enlisted in the 4th Vermont as a private, served two years, and was wounded at Third Winchester.

Back on Maple Ridge Road, pass Schoolhouse Road, and soon go right on East Hill Road. Descend to East Haven village, and go left on Route 114. In just over 2.5 miles, a small white frame house on the right faces a small barn across the road. This was the home of Samuel Drew, who served the war's last year as a private in the 10th Vermont; he saw his 26-year-old younger brother, Thomas Drew, killed in the June 3 assault at Cold Harbor.

SOURCES
JACKSON, BILL, AND MARCIA PLANT. *WALK THROUGH A HILL TOWN: BEING A WALK THROUGH NEWARK, VERMONT, A NORTHEAST KINGDOM TOWN.* WEST BURKE, VT: NORTHERN LIGHTS BOOKS, 1990.
SPENCER, HIRAM. LETTERS. COURTESY OF NEWARK TOWN OFFICE.
NEWARK TOWN RECORDS.
NEWARK UNION CHURCH RECORDS. NEWARK TOWN OFFICE.

PEACHAM

Enter Peacham from the north, from Danville, and on reaching Peacham Corner, note the old store on the right. People gathered here during the war to hear the best reader among them read the newspaper that had just arrived on the stage.

Peacham was hit hard by the Civil War as 32 of the 122 men who enlisted died. And the total cost of the war to his small hill town was $22,668. But that is only a small part of the Peacham story.

Turn right at the store, and the Congregational Church is on the right. When news of John Brown's execution reached Peacham, Leonard Johnson climbed to the church belfry and rang the bell for an hour, not to the pleasure of all the locals. Johnson was a firebrand, much opposed to slavery, and at one time he used "unchurchful language," apparently in the church. Threatened with expulsion from the congregation, Johnson signed an apology but noted beside his signature that "time has shown that I was right on the anti-slavery question." The church has a fine pipe organ, and a plaque says that Oliver Johnson, Leonard's brother, gave it as "an enduring symbol of peace and harmony." His hope was that feuding within the church would end. Apparently, during the Civil War era, such issues as abolition, colonization, and temperance had caused disagreements among parishioners.

Oliver Johnson was an important player in the abolition movement and was, of course, a member of the Peacham Congregational Church. Born in Peacham in 1809, he left his father's farm at sixteen to learn the printer's trade and became a newspaperman in Boston, where he became friends with William Lloyd Garrison, Henry Ward Beecher, and other prominent abolitionists. During the Civil War, while in Washington on antislavery business, Johnson twice met Abraham Lincoln. He traveled extensively, speaking against slavery, and attacked it in the papers he edited, including the *New York Tribune*. Johnson brought Garrison to Peacham to speak, probably in the Congregational Church, and gave him a tour of the local countryside. In 1879, Johnson was a pallbearer at Garrison's funeral.

Peacham town meetings at the time of the war were held in the church basement. There on April 22, 1861, thirty volunteers signed a document indicating their willingness to serve. In 1864, voters approved bounties of up to $900.

Continue up the hill, and two houses past the church, on the right, is the house to which Ziba Johnson moved his family, from a farm high in the hills, apparently so that his sons, Leonard and Oliver, could be close to Peacham Academy. Oliver later lived here, and two of his daughters, Martha and Caroline, went south during and after the Civil War to teach newly freed slaves in freedom schools in occupied Union territory. Martha died in 1871 in Beaufort, South Carolina.

Continue uphill and, at the green, bear left and enter the main entrance to the cemetery. Straight ahead, enclosed by an iron fence, is the gravestone of Sarah Morrill Stevens, mother of Thaddeus Stevens (see Danville). Stevens erected the stone for his beloved mother and paid for its perpetual care.

Just across the road is the Peacham Civil War memorial. Peacham voters meeting at the church in 1867 refused to approve funds for a memorial, likely because of the town's indebtedness due to the war. But in 1869, the money was voted, and the monument was dedicated on July 4, 1870. The main address was by C. A. Bunker, principal of Peacham Academy, which had been attended by more than half of Peacham's soldiers. He said, "Whether on that ever memorable field of Gettysburg, where the contending hosts trod the earth to bloody mire, or in that Golgotha, that wretched sepulcher, where death and the furies and the demons of southern treason held hell's high carnival—Andersonville—anywhere, everywhere, a grateful nation, redeemed, blood-bought, will hold in everlasting remembrance the resting place of the sacred, martyred dead."

Leaving the cemetery, bear left, soon go straight through a crossroads, and in 1.5 miles on the right is a modern home with old foundation stones evident along the road. Here stood a house from which John and Harvey Hand went to war, both in the 15th Vermont. John died of disease in March 1863. Continue just under 0.25 mile, and on the right is the Green Bay School. Peacham people also met here during the war to hear the reading of newspapers.

Return toward Peacham Corner, pass a large hilltop farm on the left, and descending the hill just beyond it, look to the left, to a large farmhouse across the fields. There lived Hazen Hooker, a private in the 3rd Vermont, killed on May 5, 1864, at the Wilderness.

Returning to Peacham Corner, at the crossroads go right and quickly see historic markers that note the site of Peacham Academy, founded in 1797. Among its pupils were Oliver and Leonard Johnson and Thaddeus Stevens.

Return to the crossroads and bear right on Old Cemetery Road. On reaching the crossroads at the hamlet of East Peacham, go straight ahead onto Thaddeus Stevens Road. In 0.5 mile, the large hillside house on the right is the home that Stevens built for his mother. During his long stay in Congress, Stevens sometimes visited her here. Continue past the house, and in 0.25 mile, come to a Y. Just ahead is an old house surrounded by a high hedge. Isaac Watts from here enlisted as a private in the 11th Vermont and served the last two years of the war. Home in September 1865 he wrote that "everything is the same. I should hardly think I had been gone a week instead of over two years." A week later he was sick with an "intermittent fever," perhaps malaria contracted in the service, and he was never a well man until he died in 1881.

Go right at the Y, and at the next Y, leave Thaddeus Stevens Road and quickly turn left on Somers Road. In 0.5 mile, come to a farm little changed since Marcus Wheeler left to enlist as a private in the Vermont Cavalry late in 1861. On June 29, 1864, he was captured near Petersburg and taken to Andersonville. He survived and came by train to Barnet,

reaching home after several people gave him rides. When his mother saw his emaciated self, she said she never would have recognized him.

Return to the Thaddeus Stevens Road and turn right. In 0.8 mile at a T, turn left. In 0.2 mile on the left is a house with barn. Horace Rowe, a private in the 4th Vermont, who lived here, was captured at the Weldon Railroad but survived Rebel prisons. Continue on and take a left on reaching the paved road. In East Peacham, take Hollow Wood Road, and in 0.25 mile, on the left, is the house to which Sally Stevens moved, from Danville, with her young family. Crippled Thaddeus walked nearly 1 mile from here to Peacham Academy every day, taking a road that once passed in front of the house.

Another way to reach Peacham is by the scenic Mack Mountain Road from Route 2, east of Marshfield. Going that way, you follow the route of the sled that brought the body of Edwin Palmer home from Sloan Hospital in Montpelier. Palmer, a 4th Vermont private, had been severely wounded at the Wilderness. While he was away, his wife and daughter lived in many homes. Seamstresses, they moved in with families who needed their services making clothing, women's dresses or suits for men. Palmer is buried in the Peacham Cemetery.

SOURCES
BOGART, ERNEST L. *PEACHAM: THE STORY OF A VERMONT HILL TOWN.* MONTPELIER, VT: VERMONT HISTORICAL SOCIETY, 1948. *THE STORY OF PEACHAM.*
BONFIELD, LYNN, AND MARY C. MORRISON. "THE PEACHAM WAR MEMORIAL." *THE*

Peacham Patriot 2, no.1 (May 1966).
——. *Roxanna's Children: A Biography of a Nineteenth Century Vermont Family.* Amherst: University of Massachusetts Press, 1995.
Johnson family papers. Vermont Historical Society.
With thanks to Lynn Bonfield and Lorna Quimby.

RYEGATE

In their history of Ryegate, published in 1913, Edward Miller and Frederic Wells wrote, "Surely Ryegate paid its full share for the maintenance of the Union. But who can calculate the loss to the town of the young men who never returned, or came home only to die; who can measure the terror and dread of those four years of war to the parents, the wives and children of those who went to the army?" Ryegate sent 121 men to war, and 32 died.

Route 302 long ago cut through the village of South Ryegate. On the south side stands the tall 1847 Reformed Presbyterian Church, of which David Wright was a prominent member. At age fifty, in September 1861, this father of eighteen joined the 6th Vermont and served two years, then reenlisted in the 3rd Vermont. While at the Wilderness, his eyes became inflamed, making him nearly blind. Near Cold Harbor, he became detached from his regiment and wandered in the woods for three days, until found nearly starved by New York soldiers. Wright came home, but his health was broken, and he died in 1869. Son Henry Wright, a 6th Vermont private, was killed at the Wilderness. Son James served in the Vermont Cavalry and was honored for bravery. Son David was a 35th Massachusetts soldier.

From the church, cross Route 302 onto Creamery Road, and soon on the right is the old South Ryegate School. Directly across the road, on a knoll, is a frame house that was the home of Lydia Brown. Her husband, Private Thomas Brown, Company F, 1st U.S. Sharpshooters, was struck dead by a bullet in the center of his forehead while shooting from a tree during the fighting at Spotsylvania's Bloody Angle. Lydia moved here after the war and lived until 1898, never remarrying.

Return to Route 302 and go east; pass under Interstate 91 and reach Route 5 in the village of Wells River. Go north on Route 5, paralleling the Connecticut River, and in 4 miles, turn right on Paper Mill Road. Quickly turn right on School Street, then left on Farm Street. Thomas Nelson owned the farm below the road, on the right. Nelson raised a company in the Ryegate area, which became the 3rd Vermont's Company I. Surviving a wound at Savage's Station, he became regimental major and was for a time the tent mate of regimental commander Samuel Pingree.

Return to Route 5 and go north 1.25 miles to a farmhouse on the left, with a barn across the road. Alexander Beattie lived here. He became a lieutenant in the 3rd Vermont, then a captain and company commander. At Cold Harbor, he crawled into the no-man's land between Union and Rebel trenches to rescue a wounded comrade. Later, he received the Medal of Honor.

Return south of Route 302 1.75 miles

and go right on East Road to the hamlet of Ryegate Corner. Turn right on Witherspoon Road to the 1855 Ryegate town hall. The 1913 town history states that eleven war meetings were held here during the four years of war. On September 2, 1862, voters approved the town's first bounties, $100 each. The town history states: "We hear a great deal in these days about the sacrifices of the men who went to the army; it is by cold figures like these that we comprehend the pressure of the war on those who remained at home. On the 14th of June (1864) a bounty of $300 was voted to all who would enlist . . . At a later meeting on July 27, a further bounty of $400 was voted in addition to that previously promised to all who would enlist for three years, $200 additional for two years, and a bounty of $300 for enlisting for one year. The pressure upon the country for men to serve . . . is shown by the vote of the town of the 7th of September, to pay a bounty of $900 each to three men who enlisted under the last call." Total monetary cost of the war to Ryegate was $16,229.

From Ryegate Corner, take the Bayley-Hazen Road north 3.3 miles and look up to an old farm and barn on the hill to the left. From here, Edwin Gibson went to McIndoe Falls to join the 15th Vermont. Less than three months later, he was hospitalized at Fairfax Seminary, near Washington, with typhoid fever. He died at 3 AM on December 30, 1862, and his mother brought his body home.

Continue north on Bayley-Hazen 1.25 miles to a long frame house on the left, which James Hunter bought after returning from three years of service. He had enlisted in the West and for a time carried mail for the army in Kansas and Missouri. He served for a time under Major General Sterling Price and toward the end of the war fought Indians in the Southwest.

Continue on Bayley-Hazen 0.5 mile into Mosquitoville, pass the cemetery, and come to the Mosquitoville Meeting House, built in 1831, a building that once rang with antislavery words. Though this structure is just into Barnet, it's included here because Reverend James Milligan once preached here. Milligan was a Ryegate resident, coming to town in 1817 as pastor of the Reform Presbyterian church in Ryegate Corner, long ago destroyed by fire. A powerful presence in town, some fifty Ryegate children were named after him. According to the Ryegate 1913 history, "His frame was large, his features dark and strongly outlined, his voice powerful and well modulated. His sermons abounded in metaphor; he exercised a singular fascination over his audience, and held its close attention for hours at a time."

Milligan was an abolitionist, his "denunciations of slavery were uncompromising," and he was president of the Ryegate and Barnet Anti-Slavery Society. A son of Milligan's also became a preacher and strong opponent of slavery. He corresponded with John Brown in his Charles Town, Virginia, jail cell while Brown awaited hanging.

Return to the Mosquitoville Cemetery and turn right on Mosquitoville Road. In just under 2 miles, go right, north, on the Groton/Peacham Road, and in 0.75 mile, the 1808 stone Whitehill home stands on a knoll. From here, brothers Calvin and

Peden Whitehill enlisted as privates in the 7th Vermont's Company E. Both were shipped to Fort Barancas, Florida, where the regiment was stationed, and the following September, two weeks apart, both died of sickness.

SOURCES

MILLER, EDWARD, AND FREDERIC P. WELLS. *HISTORY OF RYEGATE, VERMONT: FROM ITS SETTLEMENT BY THE SCOTCH-AMERICAN COMPANY OF FARMERS TO PRESENT TIME.* ST. JOHNSBURY, VT: CALEDONIAN CO., 1913.

RYEGATE TOWN RECORDS.

WHITE, DWIGHT A., AND EDWARD MILLER. *THE DOWN OF THE THISTLE: 20TH CENTURY RYEGATE.* RYEGATE, VT: TOWN OF RYEGATE, 2006.

WITH THANKS TO PETER SINCLAIR, DWIGHT WHITE, AND CARLIE WHITEHILL.

SHEFFIELD

A 2002 study of Sheffield's Civil War history concluded that 118 men with connections to the town served, and 28 died. Route 122 passes through the village, and at the main intersection, Berry Hill Road goes north. Just up the hill on the left is the 1800 meetinghouse and the 1829 Sheffield Baptist Church. Town meetings were held at the meetinghouse, and on August 25, 1862, voters displayed some Yankee practicality by approving a total of $1,200 for bounties, $25 to be paid when enlisting and $25 after nine months of service. A year later, bounties of $300 were voted. On December 28, 1863, voters authorized the hiring of Josiah Miles, a former private in the 4th Vermont discharged for disabilities, to serve as town recruiter. Records of the church next door note unusually large attendance at services during 1864, the war's bloodiest year.

Continue up Berry Hill Road, pass under Interstate 91, and you soon are among fields once owned at the time of the Civil War by the Berry family. Their descendants are still here. Some 2 miles along is a large white farmhouse on the left, with a barn across the way, where Alexander Berry lived for a time. Alexander saw sons Aylmer, Edwin, Richard, Stephen, and Thomas go to war. Private Edwin Berry, 7th Vermont, died of disease at Fort Barrancas, Florida, in August 1862. Private Richard Berry, 8th Vermont, died of disease in May 1864. The other Berry boys returned home, and former Private Aylmer Berry, 6th Vermont, lived here after the war. A niece of Alexander's, Elizabeth Berry Hodgdon, also lived here for a time. Three of Elizabeth's twelve children served. Her son Private Carlos Hodgdon, Vermont Cavalry, was shot dead in September 1864 as the Shenandoah Valley Campaign began. Brother Samuel, also a cavalry private, died of disease the following May.

Returning toward Route 122, note that all the fields with their long views would have been well known to all the Berry and Hodgdon boys. On reaching Route 122, note the large yellow house across the way at the corner of Chesley Hill Road. The place was a tavern in the 1860s, and its owner, N. Folsom, was among those men exempted from duty. Town records say he suffered from heart and lung disease.

SOURCES

BERRY-WILLIAMS, NORMA L. *THE FAMILY HISTORY OF ALEXANDER BERRY AND HIS*

Wife Joanna Gray. Privately printed, 2006.

Sheffield church records, 1800–1885.

Sheffield town records.

Simons, John M. *Civil War Veterans with Connections to the Town of Sheffield, Caledonia County, Vermont*. Sheffield, VT: Sheffield Historical Society, 2002

··

STANNARD

Stannard is named for the state's most famous Civil War hero George Jerrison Stannard (see Georgia). However, at the time of the war, it was called Goshen Gore. Private Allen Batten, 3rd Vermont, went to war from here and was wounded at the Wilderness. In 1914, at age seventy, Batten compiled a list of 34 men from Goshen Gore who served. From a population of about 200 in the 1860s, it appears that at least 8 died while serving. The *Brattleboro Phoenix* on March 3, 1864, reported:

"Goshen Gore, of Caledonia County, has sent almost its entire arms bearing population to war, but unfortunately they are nearly all placed to the credit of adjoining towns." Since this was an unorganized town at the time of the war, local enlistees were credited to the towns in which they signed up, including Walden, Lyndon, Wheelock, and Hardwick.

Leave Route 14 at Greensboro Bend and ascend Mountain Road 3 miles to Stannard. About 0.5 mile short of the town hall, on the left, is the Stannard Cemetery. Front and center is a small marker placed by the Women's Relief Corps that honors "the unknown soldiers" of the war. Among the many Civil War markers here are those for Privates George Sawtelle and George Flanders, both 3rd Vermont and killed at the Wilderness; Private Martin Bachelder, 4th Vermont, died of disease at the Bandy Station encampment in March 1864; Private Cyrus Perrin, 11th Vermont, died of sickness at Brattleboro in September 1864; and Private George Stevens, 10th Vermont, died of illness in September 1864. The Gore also lost men at Spotsylvania's Bloody Angle, at Cold Harbor, at Cedar Creek, and in the Andersonville and Goldsboro, North Carolina, prisons.

Near the cemetery center is the Batten family marker. Among those buried by it are Susan Hood Batten and husband, Albert James Batten, parents of ten children, including their eldest son, James. Susan lost her husband, a private in the 3rd Vermont, at Lee's Mill in 1862. James, 10th Vermont, was killed at Mine Run in the early winter of 1863.

Continue up Mountain Road, quickly turn left on Flagg Pond Road, then left again on Winchester Road. The house at the end was the Batten home. It is said of Susan Batten that after she learned of the death of James, she never again smiled. Return to Mountain Road and continue uphill to the center of what was the little town of Goshen Gore. After the war, finally heeding the pleas of Gore residents, the legislature, effective August 19, 1867, gave Goshen Gore independent status as a town, naming it after Gettysburg hero General Stannard. But so far as is known, the general never visited here.

SOURCES

Stannard town records.

SWIFT, ESTHER MONROE. *VERMONT PLACE-NAMES: FOOTPRINTS OF HISTORY.* ROCKPORT, ME: PICTON PRESS, 1977. WITH THANKS TO ANNE BATTEN, JAMES BATTEN, RACHAEL HEXTER, AND JAN LEWANDOWSKI.

ST. JOHNSBURY

Any Civil War tour of St. Johnsbury should begin just south of town along Route 5, by the interstate overpass. Here a flagpole and monument mark the site of Camp Baxter, where in the early summer of 1861 the companies that made up the 3rd Vermont gathered at the St. Johnsbury Fairgrounds. The marker stands approximately in the center of the old fairgrounds, set in a natural amphitheater of surrounding hills. The main fair building was enlarged to a length of 340 feet to serve as a barracks with bunks for one thousand men. The drilling regiment became the biggest attraction in the Northeast Kingdom. On July 4, 1861, ten thousand spectators saw the ladies of St. Johnsbury present a handmade regimental flag to the 3rd. St. Johnsbury's own Governor Erastus Fairbanks was on hand, and a witness recalled, "The scene was imposing. The long line of soldiers in new uniforms, their arms glittering in the light of an unclouded sun; the vast concourse of people on all sides filling the seats of the great amphitheatre and occupying the windows, cupola and roof."

Not all was rosy at camp. A sutler named Pike operated a refreshment saloon, and one night some soldiers decided to take what they wanted. A guard fired at the would-be thieves trying to batter down the door, and Sergeant John Terrill, of Canaan, was killed and another soldier wounded.

The time soon came for the regiment to go south. The *Caledonian Record* reported on July 26 that it departed at 6 a.m. on a train of twenty cars, pulled by two engines. Hundreds of citizens assembled, and "there were many touching scenes of parting between parents and sons, husbands and wives, relatives and friends." As the train pulled out, the soldiers returned the spectators' cheers.

Go north on Route 5, following the 3rd's march route to the train. On coming in sight of the depot, note Federal Street on the left, associated with the soldier and diarist Henry Herrick. More on this later. A cannon placed in 1921 by the local GAR post overlooks the depot era, where no Civil Ear–era buildings remain. But it was here that the 3rd Vermont departed. Many touching farewells and welcomes took place here during four years of war, none more poignant than the arrival of the body of Colonel Addison Preston (see Danville). St. Johnsbury people escorted the casket up the hill to Main Street, where Danville people waited to take it to his hometown.

Pass the cannon and quickly go left on Eastern Avenue, going uphill, as did Preston's procession. At the hilltop at Main Street, the Caledonia County Court House is on the left, where the 3rd Vermont band practiced, including musician Henry Herrick. Soon after the war commenced, a war meeting was held in the courtouse yard. In 1863, when some companies of the 15th Vermont stopped at St. Johnsbury, the *Caledonian* reported that a "public entertainment" was held in the yard "in which fire companies of the village and the citizens generally participated."

On August 20, 1868, St. Johnsbury's Civil War memorial was dedicated in the courthouse yard, now known as Monument Square, a Larkin Mead's (see Brattleboro) marble sculpture *America* carved in the artist's studio in Florence, Italy. The names of 80 St. Johnsbury men who died in the war are inscribed on its sides, a high total from the 400 men of the town who served. At the dedication, the names of the dead were read, and a prayer was given by Jonathan Woodward, former Vermont Cavalry chaplain (see Westford). Larkin Mead was introduced to the crowd. When the monument was unveiled, thirty-six young ladies representing the states of the restored Union deposited floral offerings at the base. Years later, two Parrot guns, once aboard U.S. Navy ships during the Civil War, were installed by the monument.

Go south on Main Street, and the South Congregational Church, or South Church, is on the left. Many war-related events took place here, including an October 1863 address by a black man named Freeman, about to depart for Liberia, who advocated colonization as the "best future for the Negro." In May 1864, the *Caledonian* reported on "a contribution taken up at the South Church last Sabbath in aid of the Christian Commission amounted to about $90." Many soldier funerals were held here, including one for Private William Green, 11th Vermont, captured at Weldon Railroad and sent to five Confederate prisons, including Andersonville. Released in December 1864, Green was sent to Annapolis, Maryland, where his father went to meet him. But Wiliams was dead on arrival, and his father brought home the corpse. Those who saw said it was "nothing but a skeleton." Young Green was well known throughout town because he delivered milk. On April 9, 1865, when word came of Richmond's fall, Reverend L. O. Barstow's sermon in this church was based on a passage from Isaiah, "The Lord hath done great things for us, whereof we are glad."

South Church was, of course, familiar to the students of adjacent St. Johnsbury Academy, many of whom ended up in Vermont regiments. Many were in attendance on April 19, 1865 for a memorial service honoring Abraham Lincoln. It began with a long moment of silence "broken by low tones from the organ and the chanting of a psalm," according to Edward Fairbanks, who was there. By the church, turn right, west, on Route 2, and on going down the hill, look up to the right at the old mansion that was once the home of Horace Fairbanks, a son of Governor Erastus Fairbanks. Continue past a motel, turn left, cross a bridge, and quickly turn left again onto Factory Street. Stop here and look ahead along the Sleeper River at the area once occupied by the Fairbanks family's massive manufacturing complex, the E. T. Fairbanks Company, makers of platform scales. During the war, the company also made bridles and stirrups for the Union armies. Many young men who worked here went to war, including Henry Herrick. Asa

Blunt, who commanded the 12th Vermont and for a time the entire 2nd Vermont Brigade, was an official of the company.

Return to the courthouse. Across the street is the St. Johnsbury Athenaeum, a gift to the town of Horace Fairbanks. North of the Athenaeum is the St. Johnsbury House, at the corner of Center Street, a former hotel with double-deck porch. While the 3rd Vermont trained at Camp Baxter, two of its young officers, Wheelock Veazey and Thomas Seaver, both newly married, brought their brides to this hotel. One evening, the regimental band assembled in front of the hotel to serenade the couples. Veazey and Seaver were destined to win the Medal of Honor, Veazey at Gettysburg and Seaver at Spotsylvania. In late July 1865, when Company A, 11th Vermont came home, a dinner for its seventy men was held here.

Note the intersection of Central and Main streets. Lee's surrender at Appomattox prompted a grand St. Johnsbury celebration, with muskets and cannon firing, bells and steam whistles sounding, as people poured into the streets. The highlight was the burying of a casket, representing the Confederacy, borne here in a procession led by mounted cavalry veterans and buried in the intersection. Apparently, it is still there.

Continue past the hotel, and soon on the right is the Fairbanks Museum. You are now in that area of the town where the Fairbanks presence is most obvious, and the museum was a gift to the town of Franklin Fairbanks. Across the street is the big stone First Congregational Church, whose organ is dedicated to Erastus Fairbanks. This building replaced the Civil War–era edifice of which he was a member. Fairbanks, Vermont's first Civil War governor, died November 20, 1864. Henry Herrick, a member of the choir, was attending services that day and wrote, "Mr. Cummings began his sermon this morning by an allusion to the sickness and apparent near approach of death of Gov. Fairbanks and while he was yet speaking, word was brought to him and announced to the congregation that he was dead. Mr. Cummings stopped a while quite overcome by emotions and there were many tears shed in the congregation for the good old governor." So the man who had informed Abraham Lincoln that Vermont would do its "full duty" was gone.

Pass the church, and Frost Avenue is on the right. The story-and-a-half frame house at the intersection was the home of Captain Edwin Frost, 4th Vermont, killed at Cold Harbor. Henry Herrick wrote on June 7, 1864, "The news came today that Capt. Frost is killed and the news seems to have made a profound sensation as he was well known and much liked here. What a fearful price we are paying for the maintenance of the government." Before the war Frost had been studying medicine with his doctor brother C. P. Frost. A chaplain wrote to the brother describing Edwin's long and agonizing death after being shot in the abdomen by a sharpshooter. The letter concluded, "He rests in a good spot, if he must be away from home. We buried him while the cannon were roaring about him his requiem. His life went out as the sun goes down at evening."

Continue along Main Street to the

park, bear left, and where the road turns sharp right, go straight on Mount Pleasant Street to the gateway of Mount Pleasant Cemetery, containing scores of Civil War graves. Many with the most interesting inscriptions are located behind the Victorian cemetery office and crematorium. Governor Fairbanks is buried here as is Colonel George Chamberlin of the 11th Vermont, killed at Charles Town in the Shenandoah Valley. He was writing a letter to his wife in St. Johnsbury when interrupted. "Picket firing in front is quite sharp," he wrote, "increasing for the last half hour, and it seems nearer, as though our pickets were falling back." He died an hour later. A family member wrote soon after his burial, "Forest trees bend over his grave, there birds sing; kindest hands administer to make it beautiful, but when all is done, it is still GEORGE'S GRAVE." The St. Johnsbury GAR Post Number 1 was named for Chamberlin.

A funeral was held in the cemetery for the Reverend Thomas Kidder, who enlisted as a private in the 9th Vermont at age sixty-two in November 1863. Kidder had previously served as chaplain of the Windsor Prison but in recent years had lived in St. Johnsbury and preached in local churches. His age soon took a toll on his soldiering, and he was detailed for hospital and chaplain duties. He contracted diarrhea and died on November 29, 1864, at Point of Rocks, Maryland. St. Johnsbury's *Soldiers' Record* says, "There was so much delay in transporting the body from Virginia to St. Johnsbury, that it became expedient to observe religious services on the occasion of its burial at the Cemetery."

The cemetery contains a GAR lot with a monument, a stone soldier with rifle.

From the cemetery, return as you came to the end of Mount Pleasant Street, turn left down the hill, and on reaching Route 5 take it north 2 miles to St. Johnsbury Center and the Congregational Church. A funeral was held here for Private Roseme Bacon, 15th Vermont, who killed himself in early March 1863 in the regiment's winter camp by cutting his throat. He is buried in the church cemetery.

Return to St. Johnsbury and take Route 2 east 4 miles to East St. Johnsbury and the Third Congregational Church on the left. On July 10, 1864, a funeral was held here for Private Joseph Hutchinson, 11th Vermont, killed at Cold Harbor. The *Caledonian Record* reported, "At the close of the services the sympathies of the congregation were tendered to the widow and her two orphan children, the parents, and other relatives of the deceased by reading the following resolution:" That resolution honored Hutchinson for his part in suppressing a rebellion by a government "so profane as to demand . . . their right to chattelize four millions of its population, and their children for all time to come."

Return as you came to St. Johnsbury; turn south on Route 5, pass the depot, and turn right on Federal Avenue. Proceed to the stop sign where, at the time of the Civil War, Federal Avenue ended. A house stood across the street where the avenue now continues and in it lived Henry Herrick, in a rented upstairs room. Herrick served for a year in the 3rd Vermont band, endured the Peninsula Campaign, then resumed his job at E. T. Fairbanks. He kept a diary during his service, then through the remaining war years. The Herrick diary, preserved at the Fairbanks Museum, is certainly the finest home-front Vermont diary yet discovered. Every night Herrick returned here to his room to record the events of his day and those of this town:

June 10, 1864, he wrote: "After tea I opened the Journal and looking down a long list of killed and wounded almost the first name that arrested my attention was that of C. H. Perry—died of wounds received June 3d. I sat for a moment utterly stupefied and incapable of taking in the truth of which the types declared— unable to realize that among that 'noble army of martyrs' was the friend that I had known and loved so well; then as the bitter truth came plain, I cried out in bitterness of spirit."

July 3, 1864: "There is a call for a meeting at the Town Hall to-morrow evening to consult in the matter of celebrating the coming 4th, but I don't see how they can feel like it—for my part anything of the kind seems to jar on my feelings, while it is such a time of intense anxiety, and the fate of the nation seems trembling in the balance, and while there is such wide-spread sorrow in the land, mourning for loved ones who are not. A time of rejoicing and merrymaking seems like 'sweet bells jangled out of tune and harsh.'" The last quote is from *Macbeth*.

SOURCES
CALEDONIAN RECORD (ST. JOHNSBURY), 1861–1865. ST. JOHNSBURY ATHENAEUM.
CHADWICK, ALBERT G. SOLDIERS' RECORD OF THE TOWN OF ST. JOHNSBURY, VERMONT, IN THE WAR OF THE REBELLION, 1861–5. ST. JOHNSBURY, VT: C. M. STONE & CO., 1883.
FAIRBANKS, EDWARD T. THE TOWN OF ST. JOHNSBURY: A REVIEW OF ONE HUNDRED TWENTY-FIVE YEARS. ST. JOHNSBURY, VT: COWLES PRESS, 1912.
HERRICK, HENRY. DIARIES 1861–1865. FAIRBANKS MUSEUM.
JOHNSON, CLAIRE. I SEE THE PEOPLE: AN INFORMAL HISTORY OF ST. JOHNSBURY. ST. JOHNSBURY, VT: COWLES PRESS, 1987.
SHERMAN, RACHEL CREE. "ST. JOHNSBURY PUTS THE CIVIL WAR TO REST." VERMONT HISTORY: THE PROCEEDINGS OF THE VERMONT HISTORICAL SOCIETY 76, NO. 1 (WINTER/SPRING 2008): 63.
ST. JOHNSBURY ALMANACS AND TOWN MAPS. COLLECTION OF FAIRBANKS MUSEUM.
ST. JOHNSBURY TOWN RECORDS.
WITH THANKS TO PEGGY PEARL, FAIRBANKS MUSEUM, AND LISA VON KAHN, ST. JOHNSBURY ATHENAEUM.

··

SUTTON

The village of Sutton is conveniently reached from Route 5 in West Burke by going west up the steep Sutton Road. The 1833 redbrick Sutton School overlooks the village at its north end. Here, Civil War–era town business was attended to, and in 1860, the town gave Lincoln 96 votes and Douglas 29. In 1864, Lincoln was favored, 109 to 46, over McClellan. On January 23, 1864, $300 bounties were voted to pay men "drafted under the last call of the president." Voters approved raising $5,900 in September 1865 "to pay the indebtedness of the town for soldier bounties."

From the old school, go directly downhill on Underpass Road, and note the fourth house on the left, in 2011 much concealed behind trees and a fence. From here, Luther Harris enlisted in the 4th Vermont when it was formed. He ended up in Andersonville and wrote a book about it (see Lyndon).

Return up the hill and go sharp left on Calendar Brook Road. The second house on the left, with addition and central chimney, was the home of Aylmer Berry, a native of Canada, who served a year early in the war in the 6th Vermont. His brother, Stephen, 4th Vermont, survived a wound at Petersburg in March 1865 that sent him home. Another brother, Thomas, was in the 15th Vermont.

Continue on Calendar Brook Road, and soon on the right is the old Baptist Church. It is believed that a funeral for another member of the 15th Vermont was held here in late March 1863. Danville's *North Star* reported: "We are grieved to learn of the death of another soldier from this section, as we do by the following communication—Lieut. William M. Tibbetts, of Co. I, 15th Regiment Vt. Volunteers, died of fever near Fairfax Station, Va., on Tuesday the 17th instant, aged 28 years. He was an only son of Hon. John C. Tibbetts, of Sutton. His remains were brought home to his father's, on Saturday evening, the 21st. Lieut. Tibbetts leaves a young wife, who, with the wife of Col. Grout, attended him in his last illness." Reverend Lucius Harris, father of Luther Harris, was pastor of the Baptist Church during the war.

Continue on Calendar Road 1 mile, go right on Pudding Hill Road, cross the bridge, and go left on Dexter Road. In the only house on the road lived the Scott family, which lost two sons. Israel joined the 2nd Vermont at Newport in August 1861 and was killed May 18, 1864, at Spotsylvania. His brother, Nelson, a private in the 3rd Vermont, had already died of sickness, at twenty-two. Another brother, Henry, also a 3rd Vermont private, served three years and came safely home.

Return to the village, pass the school, and soon, on the right, is the Sutton Village Cemetery. The many Civil War graves here attest to the number of soldiers Sutton sent to war. Nelson and Israel Scott lie side by side in the family lot.

SOURCES
DANVILLE NORTH STAR, 1862. VERMONT STATE LIBRARY.
HEMENWAY, ED. *THE VERMONT HISTORICAL GAZETTEER.*
SUTTON TOWN RECORDS.
WITH THANKS TO DEBBY OGDEN, TOWN CLERK.

....

WALDEN

The tiny village of Noyesville in the town of Walden lies along Route 15, and there, Noyestar Road turns north. Take that road and note the first building on the left, formerly Rogers' Store, owned by Civil War veteran John Rogers, a lieutenant in the 15th Vermont. Rogers, apparently working as a sutler, was at City Point, Virginia, where Ulysses Grant had his headquarters, when the war ended. He wrote home to Walden on April 5, 1865, "Saw Mrs. Grant and Lincoln the other day. They were rather rough specimens of female beauty." And he noted, "Rebel prisoners are as plenty here as flies."

Continue on Noyestar Road 0.2 mile and turn right on Cahoon Farm Road, quickly stopping at the cemetery on the right. On a knoll in the center is the prominent stone of Private John Cole, 10th Vermont, who "lost both eyes at the battle of Petersburg April 2, 1865." Cole said that he looked over the top of an earthwork and was hit by a Confederate marksman. Cole came home a blind man; he bought a farm, married, and fathered several children. Return to Noyestar Road, turn right, and in 0.5 mile, come to an old house on the left with a bay window, where Cole lived for a time.

Continue on Noyestar 1.3 miles, and on the right, is a shallow old millpond. Along the pond once lived the Capron family, and when a heavy rain came, the four Capron boys rushed to father Freeman Capron's "thundershower mill" to saw wood with the sudden waterpower. Freeman enlisted early in the war at age fifty, with his oldest son Hiram, both apparently joining the 4th Vermont. The father served only briefly. Soon, sons Henry and Nathaniel joined the 3rd Light Artillery Battery. Hiram was mortally wounded near White Oak Swamp on June 27, 1862. Henry died in an army hospital near Washington and is buried at Arlington National Cemetery. Nathaniel died in a military hospital in Brooklyn, N.Y. Son Marshall did not serve.

Continue on Noyestar, and in just over 1 mile, Orton Road turns right. If you wish, turn here and follow Orton .1 mile, then turn right on Cole Pond Road. Follow this narrow, twisting road through high country with long views just over 2 miles and see Cole Pond on the left. The July 9, 1876, *Caledonian Record* reported on the death of John Granville Horn, seventeen. "He went to the pond with two or three other boys," the paper said, "and . . . announced that he was going to wade across it, and dared them to follow. He then deliberately walked into the water where it was over his depth, and was drowned before help could be obtained . . . His father died in the war, and Granville lived with his grandfather, Israel Farrar, and was the main support of his grandparents."

Return to Noyestar, turn right, and quickly on the left is a large, old, redbrick house. From his family's home, George P. Foster went to war as commander of Company G, 4th Vermont. Foster rose to command the regiment and was brevetted brigadier general for gallantry at the Wilderness, where he was badly wounded. He recovered to command the Vermont Brigade at Fisher's Hill and Winchester. A gentle giant loved by his troops, after the war Foster became Vermont's first U.S. marshal, and once waded into a crowd of agitated Fenians, intent on invading Canada, to arrest their leader. He died of diabetes in 1879, and in Burlington, thousands of people, including hundreds of veterans, watched as a pair of white horses pulled the hearse through a snowstorm.

Continue along Noyestar and quickly see, on the right, the house known as The Belfry, the home of Charles James Bell, who enlisted at age seventeen in the 15th Vermont Regiment. Bell made the long march to Gettysburg, then reenlisted in the Vermont Cavalry. Corporal Bell was wounded April 8, 1865, the day before Lee's surrender, as the Vermont horsemen captured eight Confederate cannon near Appomattox Court House. After the war, Bell became a successful farmer, served in the Vermont legislature, and was elected governor in 1904. In the 1890s, he remodeled the family home, adding columned porches and a small turret, in essence "Victorianizing" a Vermont farmhouse. To celebrate his gubernatorial nomination in 1904, and a century of the Bell family living on the farm, a party, which attracted five thousand, was held at The Belfry on July 8. A platform was erected across the road from the house, and after dining, the multitudes assembled on the hillside facing the house. Several Vermont Civil War veterans spoke, among them Redfield Proctor and Urban Woodbury. Oliver Otis Howard, who used the occasion to boost the presidential candidacy of Theodore Roosevelt, reminisced on the war.

Return on Noyestar Road and go 0.3 mile, then turn right on the historic Bayley-Hazen Road. In 1.7 miles on the right is a large farmhouse with central chimney, set back from the road. The Eddy family once lived here. A diary kept by Sally Gould, a Walden girl, in November 1861 noted, "The Committee brought articles of clothing, which they had collected for the soldiers, to Mr. Eddy's."

In 0.7 mile farther on Bayley-Hazen is the 1825 South Meeting House, in whose basement wartime town meetings were sometimes held. Bounties approved by the town reached $1,000.

Continue downhill to Route 15, turn left, and in 2-plus miles, go right on Route 215. In 0.4 mile, the large farmhouse on the right was the home of the Burbank family. Nathaniel Burbank served in the navy, on ships in the Gulf of Mexico enforcing the blockade of the Confederacy. His granddaughter, Ilene Burbank Miles, recalled, "Grandpa was a dear old man . . . Grandma used to listen to his stories but after a while told us kids war wasn't as glorious as he made it sound. It was hard on those who fought and hard on those at home."

SOURCES
HATCH, ELIZABETH P. "WALDEN'S PART IN THE CIVIL WAR." *WALDEN 200 HISTORIC PUBLICATIONS* 20, NO. 1 (SPRING 2000).
WALDEN TOWN RECORDS.
WITH THANKS TO BETTY HATCH, JANET MCKINSTRY, AND EARLE CAPRON.

··

WATERFORD

From England to the New World, not long after the Pilgrims landed, came two Lee brothers. One arrived in the Massachusetts Bay colony, and thus a branch of the family was established in New England. Another brother went south, to the Virginia colony, and thus the Virginia Lees began. That branch eventually produced Robert E. Lee, Army of Northern Virginia commander. Some New England Lees settled in the Northeast Kingdom town of Waterford in 1801. Go east on Route 2 from St. Johnsbury 3 miles and turn south on Route 18. Quickly cross Interstate 93 and just ahead see an imposing old farmhouse and a huge red barn.

From this farm in 1862, Edward Payson Lee enlisted in the 11th Vermont. A year later his brother, Oscar Lee, also joined that regiment. Both served in the defenses of Washington, D.C. when their regiment was an artillery unit. When the regiment joined the Vermont Brigade at Spotsylvania, the 11th became an infantry outfit, fighting in the Overland Campaign against the Army of Northern Virginia. So the Lee boys were fighting an army commanded by distant cousin General Lee. When the Vermont Brigade was ordered to the Shenandoah Valley as part of Philip Sheridan's army, it faced a Confederate army under Jubal Early, ordered to maintain Rebel control of the valley by Lee. Edward entered the 11th with the rank of sergeant but rose to captain. Wounded in an arm at Cedar Creek, he came home here to recuperate, then returned to duty and served until the war's end. Oscar, also a sergeant, was promoted to captain. He also fought at Cedar Creek, where he was killed when a piece of shell carried away his shoulder.

Continue south on Route 18 from the farm, and in 6 miles, turn right into Lower Waterford, with many houses that stood during the Civil War. An old photograph of the village shows a flagpole standing in front of the Congregational Church, just across from the hotel, both of which survive. The *Caledonian Record* reported that on May 17, 1861, "People of all parties assembled at Lower Waterford to participate in the ceremony of giving to the breeze the American flag . . . and to declare their devotion to the constitution and the Union. At about 2 o'clock p.m. the assembled audience formed into line, headed by the St. Johnsbury East Village Band . . . and formed into a hollow square, surrounding the liberty pole. The flag was brought forth and flung to the breeze, while the band discoursed the national air, the *Star Spangled Banner* amid cheers." After speeches, a committee that included F. R. Carpenter was appointed to draft resolutions for the crowd's approval. One said, "By the unfurling of our national banner today we express our loyalty to our country and do hereby publish our solemn vow to do all we may for the untarnished honor of our country's flag."

Just past the hotel, a short street turns right. The last house on it was the home of Carpenter. In 1880, Waterford published its *Soldiers' Record of the Town of Waterford,* the work of a committee led by Carpenter. He wrote, "The rebellion has been suppressed and the soldiers from Waterford who survived the hardships of the camp, the sufferings of the prison house, and the perils of the battlefield, have returned to mingle again with us in the common walks of life, and there is little left now except the page of history to remind us of the fearful struggle through which we have passed. And although the eye may moisten and the heart be sad at the thought of some vacant chair at our fireside, yet we will rejoice in the unity and redemption of the country."

Continue past the hotel and soon note an old schoolhouse above the road on the right. In 0.25 mile is a farmhouse, on the right, with views to the White Mountains and with a small barn across the road. Charles Ross went to war from this house, joining the 11th Vermont in August 1862 as a corporal and then winning a lieutenant's commission. Ross taught at times in the school you just passed and attended the Congregational Church. He kept a journal, and these excerpts are from August 1862:

"Tuesday 5. I have taken a very important step today. Went over to a war meeting at St. Johnsbury with Cousin Harlan & we both enlisted for three years unless sooner discharged in the U.S. Service. Father was very much opposed and feels bad, but Mother is not so bad."

"Wednesday 6. Went down to the river mowing this morning and have cut a good piece. Went down and saw James and Warren to night they both want to go to war but are held by folks at home."

"Saturday 9. Went over to St. J. with Warren & James to have them enlist. Both have put down their names. All hands are rushing in pell mell."

"Monday 11. This morning I put a few shirts into a little trunk and sent them over to St. J. . . . then made calls on Grand Father & Grand Mother . . . Then over on foot with Harlan & James drilled as soon as I arrived."

Ross soon became a corporal. At home, his family followed the war closely. His mother wrote him in early June 1864: "You are pretty near Richmond & pretty near the swamps I should judge by the maps . . . We are at work doing all we can for the wounded soldiers. Have sent two barrels of hospital articles & shall continue to work as long as we are furnished with the means to work with, which I hope will be as long as there are sick & wounded soldiers to need the things we make."

Ross and fifty-six other members of his company were captured at Weldon Railroad two weeks later. Confined in Andersonville from July 11, 1864, until November 15, he was released and hospitalized in Annapolis, Maryland. He came home on a ninety-day furlough, then rejoined the 11th and served until the war ended, receiving a lieutenant's commission. Ross said that only fifteen of the fifty-seven members of his company survived Andersonville.

F. R. Carpenter wrote in this *Soldiers' Record* of prison survivors: "To us who have seen for ourselves the crippled and emaciated frames of some of those who did survive and come back to us from that charnel house of misery and death we need the gift of tongues and the vocabulary of the infernal regions to express our abhorrence of such deliberate and diabolical cruelty."

Continue past the Ross house 2 miles, turn right on Duck Pond Road, and in 0.3 mile come to a Y. Look in the field to the right for a cedar grove on the site of the Civil War–era Waterford town hall. Carpenter wrote that while Waterford had strong support for suppressing the rebellion when the war began, "We had no man or set of men standing high above the great mass to mould and guide public sentiment and action." Town records show that voters early on were indecisive, approving and then rescinding some appropriations to support bounty payments. At the outset, the town did approve support payments for needy families of men at war. Carpenter: "Although at times it might seem that we were far behind, yet when the count was made we were found to be in the forward rank fully up to the requirements of the hour . . . when the last man was called for he was promptly furnished and paid, and our burden was gone." According to Carpenter, Waterford furnished 130 soldiers, of which 7 were killed in action and 7 died of illness. He said the town's "entire cost for war purposes" was $27,807.54. At March meeting in 1865, Westford appropriated $50 to produce a "soldier record" so that "what Waterford has done for the preservation of the Union may be written." It would be fifteen years before the record came off the press.

Bear right, continuing on Duck Pond Road, and soon come to the West Waterford Cemetery, where the stones include those for:

Marcus Hovey, eighteen years, five months, and eleven days old when he "died at Washington February 22, 1864."

John V. Goodell, twenty-one years and ten months when he "died in U.S. Hospital Baltimore, Md."

Austin Goodell, thirty-three, when he was "killed in battle near Charlestown, Virginia, Aug. 21, 1864."

George Harvey, forty-four years and three months when he was "killed at Cold Harbor June 3, 1864."

According to *Soldiers' Record,* he was killed by a Minie ball through the breast. "He was seen to turn around, put his hand to his breast, and fell and died without a groan. He was buried on the field by our own men." The body never came home.

More Carpenters lived in the large farmhouse beyond the cemetery, including Amos Carpenter, who was a bit old to soldier and did not serve. But well into the war, he told a discouraged neighbor, "No, the South shall not win; before that should happen we will all rise in a body and drive them into the Gulf of Mexico."

SOURCES

CARPENTER, F. R. SOLDIERS' RECORD OF THE TOWN OF WATERFORD, VERMONT, IN THE WAR OF THE REBELLION, 1861–5. ST. JOHNSBURY, VT: C. M. STONE & CO., 1880.

HARRIS, C. E. A VERMONT VILLAGE. YARMOUTH PORT, MA: REGISTERED PRESS, 1941

ROSS, CHARLES. "A VERMONTER IN ANDERSONVILLE: DIARY OF CHARLES ROSS, 1864." EDITED BY CHESTER MACARTHUR DESTLER. VERMONT HISTORY: PROCEEDINGS OF THE VERMONT HISTORICAL SOCIETY 25, NO. 3 (JULY 1957), 229–351.

WESTFORD TOWN RECORDS.

WITH THANKS TO JANE JURENTKUFF, TOWN CLERK, AND SHARON PAYEAR.

WHEELOCK

Six miles north of Lyndonville on Route 122, the Wheelock town hall faces a small green in the village of Wheelock, known as Wheelock Hollow during the Civil War. There stands the town Civil War memorial with the names of 86 Wheelock men who served from an 1860 population of 845. Dedicated May 29, 1915, the *Boston Globe* ran a story on the event, noting that Wheelock native Fred Chase, a veteran of the 6th Vermont who owned a hotel in the Adirondack Mountains, had donated the Barre granite monument to his hometown. Among the speakers was U.S. Senator William

Dillingham (see Waterbury). A soldier history of Wheelock was quoted, that day noting that of the 30 men of the town did not return, 3 died at Andersonville and 1 in the Rebel prison on Belle Isle, in Richmond. The number of war deaths among Wheelock men was 11.

Once the Wheelock town house stood beside the Baptist church here. But it burned, and the church was moved onto its foundation and is now the town hall. In her history of Wheelock, Eleanor Hutchinson wrote, "It would seem that the period 1861 to 1865 shows the town and its people in their finest hours. For nearly twenty years they had been listening to the slavery sermons of their native born pastor Elder Jonathan Woodman . . . sermons that took an added eloquence after he became pastor of the Freewill Baptist Church at Wheelock Hollow in 1859. However, it was more of the sense of union, the need to preserve the entirety of the nation that animated the volunteers of the town and sent over ten percent of its population to the battlefield."

Woodman delivered his message in the old church building that is now the town hall. Civil War–era town meetings took place in the building that preceded the church as the occupant of the present building's old foundations. In that building, Wheelock voters approved war expenses that totaled $25,584.51, including a total of $21,150.85 in bounty payments.

Several war meetings took place in the present town hall, with one held on September 31, 1861. A local lad noted in his diary, "Judge Cree made a Patriotic speech, followed by C. H. Davis & Chas. Rogers for the purpose of getting enlistments for the 6th Regiment of this state of which he, Mr. Davis, is recruiting officer. Got 8 in this town."

Also, in the old town hall, women gathered right after the fall of Fort Sumter to make a flag to fly along Wheelock village's Main Street. The Wheelock history said, "The women of the town gathered at the meetinghouse and with ready fingers wrought their country's emblem. Although the ruthless hand of secession had sought to efface eleven stars from the constellation on its field of blue, in faith they placed 'a star for every state' with the fervent prayer that in God's good time there would be 'a state for every star.'"

While the flag making went on, according to Mrs. Hutchinson, "The young men . . . procured two handsome poles from the swamp near Ramsay Corner across the street north from my father's store, in such a way that no one could escape doing honor to the flag by passing under it. The flag was raised, with appropriate ceremonies, on July 4, 1861."

Women's work at the meetinghouse did not cease with the flag. Mrs. Hutchinson: "As long as the war continued their needles were busy and their pens were active in sending what comfort they could to their soldiers." Among their 1864 output were eighty pillowcases, eighty-four pillows, and 76 pounds of bandages

In 1884, Wheelock veterans formed the Colonel Elisha Barney GAR Post, named for a colonel of the 9th Vermont killed at the Wilderness. The post often met at the town hall.

From the green, go north on Route 122,

quickly turn sharp right up Sutton Road, and in 0.5 mile, go right on Matthewson Hill Road. From the first house on the right, a cape, Charles Matthewson saw his twenty-two-year-old son, Ozias, depart to become a private in the 6th Vermont in the fall of 1869. Ozias Matthewson died the following spring of disease, and his body came home to this house, to be buried in the Wheelock Village Cemetery.

Return to Route 122, go right into Wheelock village, and the village store is on the left. During the Civil War, this building was a house, the home of Henry Chase who joined the 11th Vermont at eighteen in November 1863. Taken prisoner near Petersburg the following spring, he died at Andersonville in October 1864.

It was in the area of the present-day store that the giant flag made by Wheelock women spanned the road.

Continue north on Route 122 and quickly go left on Peak Road. Follow it for 3 miles to a crossroads in South Wheelock, where a Baptist Church stands on the left. In the house on the right lived the John Coffran family. Sons John and Roswell Coffran joined Company E of the 6th Vermont in the fall of 1861. John died two months later of sickness, at Camp Griffin, Virginia. His remains came to this house. Brother Roswell was promoted to corporal before he deserted and made his way to Canada a year after his brother perished. He later returned and became a four-term mayor of Topeka, Kansas.

From South Wheelock, go right on South Wheelock Road, and soon go right on Minister Hill Road. The little red schoolhouse in the Y was attended before the war by Daniel, Stephen, and William Jones, all sons of William and Mercy Jones, whose house once stood just up the hill. Daniel served three years in the 4th Vermont, Stephen served three years in the 6th Vermont, while William gave three years to the 8th Vermont. All came home safely.

In February 1863, the *Caledonian Record* reported on Wheelock: "Out of a population of 845, there have been 60 deaths in town, and eight soldiers in the army died and two were killed the past year. Fifty of the above deaths were by diphtheria." Evidence of this may be found in Wheelock's cemeteries.

SOURCES
CALEDONIAN RECORD (ST. JOHNSBURY), 1861–1863. VERMONT STATE LIBRARY.
HUTCHINSON, ELEANOR JONES. *TOWN OF WHEELOCK: VERMONT'S GIFT TO DARTMOUTH COLLEGE*. BOSTON: LITTLE, BROWN & CO., 1961.
NORTH STAR (DANVILLE), 1863. VERMONT STATE LIBRARY.
WHEELOCK TOWN RECORDS.
WITH THANKS TO MICHELLE TROTTIER.

chapter five

Chittenden County

In Burlington's Battery Park, William Wells, in bronze, moves to saddle up for the 1st Vermont Cavalry's doomed charge at Gettysburg. His statue is on ground where John Lonergan drilled his Irish lads who led the assault on Pickett's Charge the same fateful July 3, 1863. A mile north in Lakeview Cemetery, George Stannard, who led the 2nd Vermont Brigade at Gettysburg, also stands frozen in time. Nearby are buried Wells and another important Gettysburg figure, Oliver Otis Howard, in command of the Union forces for a time in that great battle, who later led the Freedmen's Bureau. Along Route 2 in Colchester are the homes of three friends who went to war in the 13th Vermont's Company D. William Munson led the company against Pickett's Charge; John Lyon fought well, while Jules Densmore had his skull shattered by a Rebel shell. He was brought home to die. High on Lincoln Hill in Hinesburg is the house from which the Langley brothers went to war, African Americans who enlisted in the 54th Massachusetts. Before the war, they gave refuge to a fugitive slave. In Westford, John Woodward's statue overlooks the town green, in front of the church he once served as pastor. Reverend Woodward became the "Fighting Chaplain" of the Vermont Cavalry. He came home with the body of his son, fellow cavalryman Captain John Woodward, after the young man was killed in a skirmish soon after Gettysburg. The funeral was held in the church, then a procession made its way to Cambridge, where the son was buried beside his fiancé, whose death had made the lad reckless. When the Confederate capital of Richmond, Virginia, fell, people from surrounding towns flocked to Richmond, Vermont, for a grand celebration. Years after the war, Buffalo Bill, a Civil War veteran, visited Cambridge and, while deer hunting on a well-identified hillside, lost a valuable ring that has never been found.

....

BOLTON

This mountainous town, divided by the Winooski River, sent 52 men to war from a population of 650. From exit 11 on Interstate 89, go east on Route 2 through Richmond and Jonesville to the village of Bolton. Go left on Bolton Valley Road, and from the second house on the right, two McGee boys went to war. Andrew was twenty-six when he enlisted in the 11th Vermont in June 1863. He was wounded at Cold Harbor. Neal, twenty-two, of the 13th Vermont, survived Gettysburg and came home to live in West Bolton, where he worked as a mill hand and clerk.

Return to Route 2 in the direction you came, and turn right on Bolton Notch Road, headed for West Bolton. In just over 4 miles, arrive at a T; go right on Stage Road and quickly come to a four-way intersection in the hamlet of West Bolton. On the cellar hole to the right once stood the home of Robert and George Cunningham, who enlisted in late 1863 as 5th Vermont privates. Robert, thirty-three, died of disease the following October and is buried at Antietam National Cemetery. George, twenty-three, was wounded on May 5, 1864, at the Wilderness and was soon discharged. He came home to live

until 1923. Look to the first house beyond the cellar hole where it is believed Cassius Chase lived, who joined the 5th Vermont at eighteen and was also wounded at the Wilderness.

From the intersection, continue straight onto Cemetery Road and cross a narrow bridge over a rushing mountain stream that once gave West Bolton power for at least seven mills. You now enter a military firing range, thus the fences along the road. Soon on the left are the front steps and cellar hole of the West Bolton Baptist Church, which stood during the Civil War. Beyond is the church cemetery, with several headstones of Civil War veterans. Harrison Smith's stone says he "died for his country's cause in the Rebellion of 1861." Smith enlisted at eighteen in the 5th Vermont as a private with the Cunningham boys and died of disease seven months later in July 1864. He is buried near Petersburg. A total of five Smiths served from Bolton. John Smith, a lieutenant in the 5th, was killed at Petersburg on April 2, 1865. The peace of this cemetery is often disturbed by the boom of big guns or the pop and rattle of small arms from the nearby firing range.

Return to Stage Road and turn right. Soon pass a golf course, and the next house on the right was a Tomlinson family home. Five Tomlinsons went to war from Bolton. Private Philo Tomlinson, 5th Vermont, was killed at thirty-two at Cold Harbor. Private George Tomlinson, a 13th Vermont musician, helped bury the Union dead at Gettysburg. After the war, he moved to Kansas.

SOURCES
BOLTON TOWN RECORDS.

LANE, GARDNER. "A HISTORY OF BOLTON."
UNPUBLISHED MANUSCRIPT, UNDATED.
BOLTON TOWN OFFICE.
STURTEVANT AND MARSH. *PICTORIAL HISTORY
OF THE 13TH REGIMENT VERMONT
VOLUNTEERS.*
WITH THANKS TO THE MULLIN FAMILY.

....

BURLINGTON/ SOUTH BURLINGTON

With a population of 7,700 in 1860, Burlington was Vermont's largest community. A Civil War tour should begin by departing Interstate 89 at exit 13 and taking the I89 connector to Route 7, Shelburne Road. Turn north and immediately look left at the busy shopping complex at the corner of Home Avenue. Here stood the old unused Marine hospital, which in 1862 became the Baxter military hospital after Vermont suffered its first heavy casualties at Lee's Mill. Baxter was the first of the state's three military hospitals to go into operation. The *Burlington Free Press* said in late May 1862 that, based on the patients' condition, "the rebels must have fired low since most wounds were in the legs and thighs . . . One man had a wife, who had a visit yesterday from her, who had heard and supposed until within a day or two, that he had been killed."

A cemetery was located behind the hospital, but all traces have disappeared. After the war, the hospital became a home for destitute children. The *Free Press* said on June 1, 1871: "The committee appointed to visit the graves of the soldiers at the old Baxter Hospital grounds on Decoration Day, were assisted by the children of the "Home" in their floral offerings. There were about 30 of these little ones in attendance, and the most of them are orphans of deceased soldiers . . . It has become a practice of these children to visit these graves on Decoration Day."

Continue north on Shelburne Road and note that in July 1865, the 8th and 11th Vermont regiments marched along it. Indeed, most Vermont regiments marched this route, from their welcome-home festivities at City Hall Park to a campground in the hospital area. Quickly turn west on Flynn Avenue, toward the lake. On reaching the railroad tracks, look left at the spur track paralleling the main line, built so that ailing soldiers could be unloaded as close to the hospital as possible. The *Burlington Weekly Times* reported on May 10, 1862: "76 of the wounded soldiers of the Vermont Brigade arrived in town yesterday morning at 5 o'clock after a long journey from Fortress Monroe. The train arrived at the crossing near the Marine Hospital at 5 o'clock. Here a convenient platform had been constructed . . . and a goodly number of our citizens were waiting with easy-going carriages and commodious springs to convey the wounded to the hospital. The work of removing them which had to be done with great care and caution, occupied some two hours . . . About half of the wounded were obliged to be lifted onto the wagons."

The following Civil War sites may be seen in Burlington:

1. City Hall Park. The wartime city hall stood on the site of the modern structure. The park, circular at that time, was the scene of many war-related events. The 3rd Vermont, according to G. G. Benedict, "Arrived in Burlington in the afternoon of [July 14, 1865]. They were received with a salute of cannon, were escorted to the city hall by a mounted escort of citizens, were welcomed in an address by Rev. George B. Safford, and entertained at a dinner in the city hall, served by the ladies of Burlington." A Burlington welcome for returning regiments at city hall became a tradition, with among others, such an honor accorded the 8th Vermont on July 2, 1865; the 9th on July 6, 1865; and the 10th on June 27, 1865.

The June 26, 1900, *Free Press* ran the following reminiscence: "Thirty five years ago, June 22, 1865, at about six o'clock in the afternoon, there arrived in Burlington the first detachment of the Vermont troops to return home at the close of the war. Six hundred and sixty-one boys in blue and three commissioned officers, from the 'Old Brigade,' dusty, tired and hungry, were given a 'welcome home' by the good people of Burlington, that has never been surpassed . . . A sumptuous banquet was served by the ladies in the city hall. After doing ample justice to the occasion, the 'sojer boys' were marched to the Marine hospital (Baxter hospital), where they camped till paid off, received their discharges and went home."

In 1891, when the body of George Stannard came home from Washington, D.C., the *Free Press* reported: "For nearly an hour before the procession formed hundreds were gathering in City Park and on all sides of the square, awaiting the time when the funeral cortege should take up the line of march. The scene was one of deep interest—the great multitude awaiting in hushed expectation, flags drooping from their staffs at half mast, public and private buildings draped in black, stores and places of business all around closed . . . As the troops forming the military escort began to assemble, the measured tramp of many feet, the tap of muffled drums, the low command, the reverent bearing of the troops, all conspired to enhance the deep solemnity of the occasion."

2. Civil War monument. The Burlington Civil War monument, at the park's northeast corner, was dedicated on Memorial Day, 1907, with Urban Woodbury, the first Vermonter to lose a limb in the war, presiding. The 17-foot Barre granite stone's inscriptions put the number of Burlington men who served at 779, of whom 38 were killed or mortally wounded, 47 died of disease, 101 were discharged for disability, and 68 deserted. Also, 68 were listed as missing in action.

3. *Burlington Free Press* building. The building occupies much of the south side of College Street between Church Street and South Winooski Avenue. The *Free Press* was published here during the war, owned by the Benedict family, including George Grenville Benedict, who won a Medal of Honor at Gettysburg. Benedict edited the *Free Press* for forty years. The older parts of the building are best seen from the rear.

4. Leavenworth Block. This block, on the corner of College Street and Winooski Avenue and opposite the Fletcher Free

Library, was built in 1847. The *Free Press* of May 31, 1861, noted: "Capt. Lonergan's company now have a drill room in Leavenworth Block . . . They drill daily." Lonergan, a native of Ireland and a dry goods dealer in Burlington, tried to raise a company for the 2nd Vermont Regiment early in the war. But his unit, made up mainly of fellow Irishmen, was not accepted into a Vermont command until formation of the 2nd Vermont Brigade a year later. It became Company A of the 13th Vermont and led the attack on Pickett's Charge at Gettysburg.

5. Unitarian Church. At the north end of College Street, the pastor before the Civil War was the abolitionist Joshua Young. Reverend Young offered the final prayer at the funeral of John Brown, at North Elba, New York (see Vergennes), and he wrote years later of the Sunday after his return. "How vividly I recall that Sunday, my text, the sermon, my subject, Christ's example of lowly service, washing his disciples' feet, the symbol of willingness to serve for love's sake. I remarked the appearance of the congregation, many new faces seldom or never seen there before; many familiar ones conspicuous by their absence; and, in the atmosphere, a certain unmistakable indication that things were different. But nothing visible occurred; only a short sea-turn had set in and a chilling mist hung in the air. Next day I learned what had happened. Six of the wealthiest families from my parish had taken an oath and gone over to a neighboring church . . . On all sides the arrows of public rebuke began to fly." Young was soon dismissed from the church.

The *Free Press* on April 4, 1865,

described a funeral service for Lincoln held in the Unitarian Church. A minister named Ware told the congregation, "For ourselves, for the stricken country, we spend our sorrow now, but none for him in the noble, full accomplishment of his work, and his entering into his reward." Ware then quoted from Shakespeare's *Macbeth,* probably Lincoln's favorite play:

After life's fitful fever he sleeps well,
Treason has done its worst; nor steel, nor poison,
Malice domestic, foreign levy, nothing can touch him further.

In 1909, funeral services were held here for Major General Oliver Otis Howard.

6. George Stannard house. General Stannard bought this brick house, on the corner of Pearl and George streets, with front door columns, in about 1870. He lived here while he was collector of customs in Burlington.

7. 111 College Street. The home of Colonel Thomas Canfield who, 1861–1862, served as assistant manager of military transportation in the national War Department. Canfield was credited with hastening troops into Washington, D.C., to defend the capital at the war's start.

8. 275 College Street. Theodore Peck, born here, enlisted at age eighteen in the Vermont Cavalry. Serving also in the 9th Vermont Regiment, he was awarded a Medal of Honor for bravery at Newport Barracks. Later, he was wounded in the attack on forts Harrison and Gilmer near Richmond. Peck was among the first Union officers to enter Richmond, and he returned home a war hero. To the everlasting thanks of those who delve into Vermont's Civil War history, as adjutant general, Peck saw to it that the *Revised Roster of Vermont Volunteers and Lists of Vermonters Who Served in the Army and Navy of the United States During the War of the Rebellion 1861–66* was compiled and published in 1892. Known as Peck's Roster, every one of the 34,238 Vermonters who served is listed.

9. 337 College Street. George Hagar at twenty-five joined the 1st Vermont Infantry at the war's outbreak, thus becoming the first Burlington man to enlist. He fought at Big Bethel and later served in the 12th Vermont. Hagar built this house in 1871.

10. 254 South Union Street. William Greenleaf built this home in 1887. He enlisted in May 1861 in the 2nd Vermont and later served in the Vermont Cavalry, receiving three severe wounds at Hagerstown, Maryland, as the cavalry pursued Lee's retreating army from Gettysburg. Recovered, he rejoined the cavalry and was again badly wounded in Wilson's Raid on June 23, 1864, when he was captured.

11. 158 South Willard Street. This grand home was built by William Wells, the former commander of the Vermont Cavalry, after he became a wealthy Burlington businessman.

12. 31 South Prospect Street. In 1871, George Grenville Benedict moved his family into this house, returning to his boyhood home. The family had, before the war, been involved in moving fugitive slaves to freedom in Canada. Benedict today is best remembered as the author of the two-volume *Vermont in the Civil War.* A member of a prominent Burlington family, Benedict for four decades after the Civil War owned and published the *Burlington Free Press* until his death in 1907.

13. 98 South Willard Street. Here lived Josiah Young, the Unitarian Church pastor who participated in John Brown's funeral. Young said that his wife was involved in sheltering fugitive slaves.

14. 272 Church Street. Lucius Bigelow, a key Underground Railroad activist and outspoken abolitionist, lived here. Bigelow accompanied Joshua Young to the funeral of John Brown. He later served as a sergeant in the 5th Vermont.

15. Old Mill. This great Victorian structure, with tall peaked cupola, has overlooked the University of Vermont (UVM) green from its east side since its completion in 1829. The Marquis de Lafayette participated in laying the cornerstone. The building housed troops during the War of 1812. The Old Mill was familiar to all UVM students who served in the Civil War. In late June 1865, when the 2nd Vermont arrived in Burlington, home from the war for good, Wilbur Fisk (see Sharon) wrote about a visit to what he called "the College belfry," atop Old Mill. He said, "I don't know of anything that could be more delightful to a four-year soldier than to stand upon the tip top of an institution like that in his own native State, which he has not seen in its verdure and beauty since the day he first left for war, and look at what he has so long wished to see from a standpoint like that. Quite a respectable portion of the country that a man may be proud to say he was born in, can be seen from there. The smooth lake on one side, pent in by rugged mountains all around and on the other side the hills and valleys, fields and forests, entertain the eye for miles around, while Winooski and Burlington seemed almost under our feet. If anybody should tell me that a man could live in that beautiful region and be a copperhead, I should want to tell him he lied." In Old Mill's John Dewey Lounge is a plaque with the names of nineteen UVM students who died in the war.

16. Wheeler House. Now the home of the UVM History Department, Wheeler House, on the corner of Main and South Prospects streets, was the home of university president John Wheeler, a key supporter of the colonization movement, which advocated freeing and returning slaves to Africa.

17. 26 Summit Street. Major General Oliver Otis Howard moved to Burlington in 1892 to be close to his eldest son, Colonel Guy Howard, then supervising construction of nearby Fort Ethan Allen. Colonel Howard also oversaw the building of this house, which his parents occupied in 1897. A Maine man, O. O. Howard, at First Bull Run, commanded the brigade in which the 2nd Vermont served. Howard also led the Army of the Potomac's 11th Corps, which was overwhelmed by Stonewall Jackson at Chancellorsville. On the first day at Gettysburg, Howard was briefly in command of all Union forces and selected the high ground of Cemetery Hill as the army's fallback position. He later served with distinction at Chattanooga and Missionary Ridge and in William Sherman's army on the March to the Sea. After the war, he fought in the Indian wars in the West and was superintendent of West Point. He was also selected by Lincoln to head the Freedmen's Bureau. Howard also founded two schools for blacks, Howard University and Lincoln Memorial University. Taken ill in his downtown Burlington office on October 26, 1909, Howard walked home and to his bedroom on the third floor of his home, where he died. He was said to have been the last surviving commander of a Civil War army.

18. 83 Summit Street. Stephen Perry Joselyn bought this house in 1907 and enlarged it for his retirement. Joselyn served in the 6th Vermont, then in 1864 became an officer of the 115th Colored Regiment that battled guerrillas in southwestern Kentucky. Late in the war, Joselyn was posted to the Army of the James and took part in operations around Richmond.

19. 189 Cliff Street. Before the Civil War, railroad and steamboat magnate Le Grand Cannon created on this hilltop a grand estate he called Overlake. The carriage house is a remnant of what once was a 60-acre enclave. Cannon during the war served on the staff of Major General John Wool. Assigned to Fortress Monroe in Virginia, he witnessed the battle between the *Monitor* and *Merrimac* and wrote an account of it for the Navy Department.

20. 241 Church Street. Here lived Dr. Samuel Thayer, dean of the UVM College of Medicine when the Civil War began. Appointed Vermont's surgeon general, he supervised care of Vermont casualties in the three Vermont military hospitals. After the

Battle of the Wilderness, Thayer helped care for Vermont wounded at Fredericksburg. The following is from a death notice in the *Free Press* April 3, 1891: "Death of Mrs. S. W. Thayer. During the war, Mrs. Thayer was a member of, and a prominent laborer in, the work carried on by the Christian Sanitary Commission, her home being the distributing point for goods sent to soldiers from this locality."

21. 4 Loomis Street. Urban A. Woodbury lived here after the war. A comrade said of him, "He has the honor of wearing the first empty sleeve from Vermont in the war for the Union." He ran for governor in 1894 with a fellow amputee, seeking the lieutenant governorship. "One good pair of arms between us," was their slogan. It worked, and Woodbury served two one-year terms as Vermont's chief executive.

22. 239 North Street. The wife of George Stannard bought this house in 1875. During the war, Mrs. Stannard joined her husband in Virginia, after he assumed command of the 2nd Vermont Brigade, and helped care for soldiers in field hospitals.

23. The Old Fairgrounds/Camp Underwood. The area in Burlington's North End bordered by Blodgett Street, Pitkin Street, Manhattan Drive, and North Avenue was once the Burlington fairgrounds. Used as a military camp during the war, and named Camp Underwood for wartime Lieutenant Governor Levi Underwood, regiments that trained here included the 2nd Vermont, 17th Vermont, 1st Vermont Cavalry, and the 3rd Vermont Light Battery.

24. 161–163 North Street. Burling-

ton's last survivor of the war, Peter Lander, lived here from 1880 until his death in 1936. Lander enlisted in the 1st Vermont Cavalry at sixteen and participated in Judson Kilpatrick's raid on Richmond. He served as a personal aide to Major General Winfield Scott Hancock, commander of the Army of the Potomac's 2nd Corps, during the Battle of the Wilderness.

25. 18 Pearl Street. William Wirt Henry, commander of the 10th Vermont, lived here from 1869 to 1890.

26. Battery Park. Overlooking Burlington's waterfront, this was the site of a battery and encampment during the War of 1812. Before it went south as part of the 2nd Vermont Brigade, John Lonergan's Company A of the 13th Vermont sometimes drilled here. A monument to William Wells, a gift of the Wells family, was dedicated here on May 30, 1914. The statue is a replica of one erected the previous year on the Gettysburg battlefield, near Round Top, where a portion of the 1st Vermont Cavalry, led by Wells, began its doomed charge after the defeat of Pickett's Charge.

27. Lakeview Cemetery. Off North Avenue just north of Burlington College, the cemetery contains a remarkable grouping of Civil War graves. Drive to the rear, toward Lake Champlain, as far as possible and see a statue of General Stannard marking his grave; the statue depicts him with an arm missing, as a result of a wound at Fort Harrison in 1864. Vermont's great war hero faces toward the grave of another major figure in the Battle of Gettysburg, Oliver Otis Howard. Howard's modest monument, with two stars denoting his rank as major general, is 100 yards distant in a circular plot of stones. Closer to the Stannard stone, to his left front, are the graves of Colonel William Wirt Henry and Adjutant General Theodore Peck. Nearby, look for a huge boulder with a bronze plaque, marking the grave of William Wells.

From downtown Burlington, drive east, following signs to Burlington Airport. Just after turning from Williston Road to Airport Drive, note an old cemetery on the right, in South Burlington. In the southeast corner is a marker for twenty-four men who died nearby, smallpox victims, "waiting the call to action" in the War of 1812. Just west is the grave of Lieutenant H. J. Barstow, a local man, who joined the 36th Illinois Infantry. As his gravestone says, he fought in many of the big western battles, at Pea Ridge, Perryville, Lookout Mountain, and Chickamauga. He died back in Burlington in 1870.

SOURCES
BENEDICT, GEORGE G. VERMONT IN THE CIVIL WAR. 2 VOLS. BURLINGTON, VT: FREE PRESS ASSOCIATION, 1888.
BLOW, DAVID. HISTORIC GUIDE TO BURLINGTON NEIGHBORHOODS. 3 VOLS. BURLINGTON, VT: CHITTENDEN COUNTY HISTORICAL SOCIETY,1991–2001.
BURLINGTON FREE PRESS, 1881–1865. VERMONT STATE LIBRARY.
STURTEVANT AND MARSH. PICTORIAL HISTORY OF THE 13TH REGIMENT VERMONT VOLUNTEERS.
ZIRBLIS, RAY. FRIENDS OF FREEDOM: THE VERMONT UNDERGROUND RAILROAD SURVEY REPORT. MONTPELIER, VT: VERMONT DIVISION OF HISTORIC PRESERVATION, 1997.
WITH GREAT THANKS TO DAVID BLOW.

CHARLOTTE

Go south On Route 7 from the traffic light in the center of Shelburne village, and in just over 3 miles, note a large old farmhouse on the left. From it, Cassius Newell went to war as a private in the 6th Vermont. He died on August 31, 1862, at Fort Monroe, Virginia, after becoming sick during the Peninsula Campaign. His body was brought home for burial in Charlotte's Barber Cemetery. To reach the cemetery, continue south 2 miles on Route 7 and go right on Ferry Road. In 0.2 mile, turn left on Greenbush Road, and in 0.5 mile, the cemetery is on the left. From the far entrance, Newell's grave is halfway down the hill. Almost beside it, a stone marks the resting place of Alonzo Root, a corporal in the 14th Vermont. He died of sickness at Fairfax Courthouse, Virginia, on February 18, 1863. Charlotte historian William Wallace Higbee wrote, "The burial in the one day of two soldier boys, Cassius Newell and Alonzo Root, in the west [Barber] cemetery reminded us of the horrors of war in which men died."

Return as you came to Route 7, cross it onto Church Hill Road, and in 0.4 mile, the Congregational Church is on the left. During the Civil War, Charles Seaton was pastor, whose son Charles William Seaton served as a lieutenant in Company F, 1st U.S. Sharpshooters. Historian Higbee wrote, "During the enlistment of Berdan's sharpshooters . . . Charles Seaton had charge of target practice here for a time, and the firing stand was from the grounds opposite and back of the Congregational church to an object at the base of the hill, north of the parsonage, where many a minie ball is today buried in the gravel bank."

According to Higbee: "Meetings of the women were held in different parts of the town, but generally in the Congregational vestry to prepare lint and bandages for the front and army hospitals." The vestry is just east of the church.

The building east of the vestry is the Congregational parsonage, where Reverend Seaton lived and where his son recovered from wounds received near Malvern Hill, the last battle of the Peninsula Campaign.

Continue east on Church Hill Road to the intersection of Hinesburg Road. The old store at the corner was once known as Alexander's. Townspeople gathered here to hear war news read from newspapers. "Saturday night was always sure of a full house," Higbee said. Across Church Hill Road from the store is the brick home of the Charlotte Historical Society, once the town house, or town hall. Here Charlotte voters gave selectmen discretion in paying the necessary bounties and, late in the war, some reached $1,000. Charlotte's war spending totaled almost $25,000. War meetings to encouraged enlistments were held here and in the Congregational Church.

From the store bear right on Hinesburg Road and look to the field on the right, where local militia drilled and sometimes fought mock battles. Pease Mountain rises beyond and Higbee said, "Many an imaginary confederate was forced to retreat into the woods and bushes of Pease Mountain before the advancing skirmishers."

Continue on Hinesburg Road 0.5 mile to Mount Philo Road. From the prominent redbrick house on the left, at the intersection, Milo and James Williams went to war with the 14th Vermont. The brothers fought at Gettysburg.

Cross Mount Philo Road and continue on Hinesburg Road for 1.75 miles and turn right on Spear Street. The old Baptist Church is quickly on the right. Higbee: "At one time there was a call for men and a war meeting was held at the Baptist church at East Charlotte. About midnight, the quota was filled by volunteers. It was proposed to join with men from Hinesburg, but the call proved to have been made by mistake and the men were released."

Just up Hinesburg Road, on the left, is the redbrick home, with porch supported by graceful columns, of Dr. William Varney, who treated many Civil War veterans after the war. In 1863, Varney performed an autopsy on the body of Private Henry Dunn, a murder victim. More later.

Continue South on Hinesburg Road, and in 1 mile, turn left on Pringle Road. In 0.25 mile, the yellow brick farmhouse on the right, with barn across the road, was the home of Cyrus Prindle. A Quaker, Pringle objected on religious grounds to serving but was forcibly drafted into the 4th Vermont. Refusing to perform any war-related duty, he was discharged after four months of abuse and came back to this farm.

In just over 0.5 mile, Hinesburg Road turns rather sharp left. Just before it does, note a barn set back from the road on the right, all that remains of Guy Willoughby's farm. Willoughby, a healthy thirty years of age in 1863, farmed 120 acres and raised bees and apples. He procured a substitute and did not serve.

Continue 0.3 mile to where Roscoe Road enters from the right and go straight ahead up the little hill. Look closely just before the hilltop, on the right, for a low stone wall, by which Henry Dunn was shot dead. Private Dunn was home on a brief leave after fighting at Gettysburg and was about to return to Brattleboro for discharge from the 14th. But he and neighbor John Burns, a Copperhead who opposed the war, got drunk one evening and commenced an argument. Burns shot Dunn here, apparently with a shotgun, killing him almost instantly. Burns was arrested, tried, and convicted, though not hanged.

Return downhill and turn left on Roscoe Road. Cross the pre–Civil War covered bridge, and just across it, where the road turns right, the Burns home stood on the left, just before the driveway.

A total of 102 Hinesburg men served, and about half moved west soon after the war.

SOURCES

CHARLOTTE TOWN RECORDS.

HIGBEE, WILLIAM WALLACE. *AROUND THE MOUNTAINS: HISTORICAL ESSAYS ABOUT CHARLOTTE, FERRISBURG, AND MONKTON.* CHARLOTTE, VT: CHARLOTTE HISTORICAL SOCIETY, 1991.

BURLINGTON FREE PRESS, JULY 28, 1864. ACCOUNT OF DUNN MURDER. VERMONT STATE LIBRARY.

WITH THANKS TO DALE COLE.

COLCHESTER

Colchester, and Milton just to the north, supplied eighty-four men for the 13th Vermont's Company D. So this is Gettysburg country in Vermont.

Leave Interstate 89 at the Colchester exit and proceed north on Route 7. In 2 miles on the west side is an old two-story farmhouse with barn behind—the Densmore house. Here lived Jules Densmore, a private in Company D who was the victim of an exploding shell as the company advanced against Pickett's Charge. Another Colchester man, Private John Lyon, saw a lieutenant "raise him sufficiently to see who had fallen and heard him say 'poor Jule' as we passed on." Densmore's skull was shattered, but he lived to come home and die here in the care of his family on August 31, 1863. His funeral here was attended by many members of the company.

One-half mile north along Route 7 is another old white frame house, which was formerly the Munson family home. An 1834 graduate of Norwich University, William Munson organized and commanded Company D of the 13th Vermont. By the time the regiment reached Gettysburg, Munson had risen to second in command of the entire regiment. He was slightly wounded in the battle.

Continue north on Route 7 and soon come to the cemetery where Munson and Densmore are buried. Munson died in 1904, and members of his old regiment gathered here on July 3, 1908, to dedicate a monument in his memory. Music was provided by Munson's Orchestra, a band founded by the colonel. Among the speakers was Henry Clark, a comrade from the 13th Vermont. He said, "In Pickett's Charge he was wounded, and might, and would have been justified in doing so, have withdrawn from the action, but he continued with his command till the engagement was ended."

The monument's plaque reads, in part: "July 3, second in command, he participated with the regiment in the deadly assault on the flank of the confederate charging columns, bravely doing his full duty in that terrible hour, which turned the tide of battle at the point since called "The high water mark of the rebellion."

Just north of the cemetery, Munson Road bears west and the only house along it is the grand brick home where Colonel Munson lived out his years.

Return to Route 2 and continue 0.4 mile to the junction of Route 7. Just beyond it on the right is a small frame house with small barn behind. George Brownell left here to enlist in the Vermont Cavalry in September 1862 at age twenty-one. He died at Gettysburg some nine months later, in the futile cavalry charge launched after Pickett's Charge.

Continue north 2 miles and note an old farmhouse on the east side of Route 7, in 2012 much hidden by a hedge and adjoining an automobile business. This was the house from which John Lyon went to war as a private in Colonel Munson's company. A letter he wrote on July 5, 1863, sent from "the battlefield near Gettysburg Penn," was received here:

"Dear father

We have had a hard battle . . . Jule Densmore is badly wounded in the head. Am afraid he will die, four or five others are wounded not dangerously . . . The fight was fearful, but we have whipped them well, and they are on the retreat and our forces are chasing them also trying to cut them [off]. Our corps remains on the field. Are burying the dead."

Another 0.25 mile north on the east side of Route 7 is a big farmhouse, once the home of Lemuel Platt. In the fall of 1861 Platt met with Secretary of War Simon Cameron in Washington and received permission to organize a cavalry regiment in Vermont. Platt gathered the 1st Vermont Cavalry Regiment at Burlington, the only mounted regiment Vermont sent to the Civil War. He resigned before it went into battle, saying he was too old to fight.

Return south along Route 7 and go east on Route 2A into the old center of Colchester. On the right is the Colchester Congregational and Baptist Church. The 13th Vermont held a reunion here on the day in 1908 that it dedicated the Munson monument. The veterans were welcomed here by Miss Hattie McBride, speaking to "You who, 43 years ago this day, executed the order, 'Battalion, change front forward on first company!' and thereby gained immediate and lasting renown." She said, "The news of the victory at Gettysburg was sent flashing to every city, hamlet and rural home of the North, prominent in which was the action of Stannard's Second Vermont Brigade and particularly the execution of the order by the 13th."

Just beyond the church, go north on East Road, and in 0.25 mile, the Wolcott farm is on the right, with a large frame house with extensive porch and a barn beside it. Edgar Wolcott went from here to enlist in the Vermont Cavalry and was wounded in the charge at Gettysburg. The monument to the Vermont Cavalry at Gettysburg, a statue of Colonel William Wells, has a plaque on its base depicting the charge. Wolcott is shown at the moment he was shot. He recovered and came home.

Lake Champlain's beautiful Malletts Bay lies along the Lake Champlain shore in Colchester. During his Vermont visit in 1869, Philip Sheridan, according to the *Burlington Free Press* of August 3, "enjoyed the scenery, fishing, and quiet of that beautiful bay."

SOURCES
COLCHESTER TOWN RECORDS.
MUNSON FAMILY PAPERS.
STURTEVANT AND MARSH. *PICTORIAL HISTORY OF THE 13TH REGIMENT VERMONT VOLUNTEERS.*
WITH THANKS TO REBECCA MUNSON AND BILL STRONG.

....

ESSEX

The Essex Free Library is beside Route 15 in Essex Center, just east of where Route 128 branches north. During the Civil War this redbrick building served as the Essex town hall. Several war meetings were held here as the conflict began. The town's Civil War history is documented in *The Memorial Record of Essex, Vermont,* compiled by Dr. L. C. Butler at war's end and first read at a town meeting here in 1866, when voters decided to print 600 copies.

According to the *The Memorial Record,* at times during the war town selectmen paid bounties larger than authorized by town voters. "These officers had thus nominally exceeded the limits of their authority, though not considering themselves as having transcended the line of their duty . . . but as having kept in view the best interests of the Town, in respect to any future requisitions for men. At a town meeting held Nov. 11, 1864, the Town was asked to indemnify them for the money thus expended. The motion to raise a tax of forty cents on the dollar for the purpose was lost on a division of the House. At a subsequent meeting, the Selectmen were magnanimously relieved of the responsibility they had assumed, and fully indemnified for all the expenditures they had made in filling the quota of the Town, as well as the surplus enlistments. A tax of fifty-seven cents on the dollar was voted to make up the deficiency. It is hardly necessary to add that these votes met with a strong and determined opposition from men belonging to both political parties,—not from a desire to repudiate any such obligation, but from a feeling that the people were burdened almost beyond endurance, with taxation. Taxes had accumulated rapidly—piling up like mountain upon mountain, and still larger bounties were constantly demanded . . . The amount expended by the Town for bounties and attending expenses was thirty-seven thousand five hundred and sixty-seven dollars; equivalent to nineteen dollars for each man, woman and child in Town, according to the Census of 1860; and more than one hundred dollars to each voter; or nearly eight hundred per cent of the Grand List."

Essex met all its draft quotas. "The whole number of men furnished by the Town during the continuance of the war," said *The Memorial Record,* "was one hundred and forty. Of this number twenty-six died—mostly from diseases incident to camp life; seven were killed in battle; nine were taken prisoners; eight deserted; and thirteen were wounded."

To best understand the toll on Essex during the war, go east from the old town hall to another redbrick building, the Essex Memorial Hall, on Towers Road. Above the entrance, in marble, are the names of the Essex men who perished, put there "In grateful remembrance of the brave soldiers of Essex who lost their lives in the service of their country during the war for the preservation of the Union 1861 & 65." After the war, the local chapter of the GAR met here.

Among the names of the town's war dead are those of Oscar Siebert, James Nichols, and Edward Sands, all 6th Vermont privates killed at the Wilderness May 5, 1864. Also, Private Mortimer Lister, 6th Vermont, captured at Cedar Creek, who died at the Salisbury, North Carolina, prison two month later; Private Joshua Day of the Vermont Cavalry, captured near Cold Harbor on June 1, 1864, he died at Andersonville four months later; and Albert Whitcomb, 17th Vermont, died of wounds received at Spotsylvania. His father, Warrren, also a 17th Vermont private, died of illness the following July 30.

SOURCES

Butler, L. C. *The Memorial Record of Essex, Vermont.* Burlington, VT: R. B. Styles Book and Job Printer, 1866.

With thanks to Penny Pillsbury, Brownell Library (Essex), and the staff.

HINESBURG

Hinesburg's main street is Route 116 and Erastus Boswick's town history, written in 1861, described the village: "Dwelling houses, stores and shops are built on each side of the street, and neatly painted. Sidewalks of planks and gravel inclosed with a railing, pleasantly shaded with the locusts and maples, with dooryards adorned with shrubbery and flowers. Upon the sidewalks you see the man of business with a hurried step, to be in time to compleat the object of his pursuit. You also see the laydes in their enlarged skirts and flowing robes making calls of friendship and sociability. Benevolence dwelled with them."

In just over four years, the *Free Press* reported on an April 11, 1865, celebration when word came of Lee's surrender: "Men talked in low tones. They wept. Someone thought the feeling could best find utterance in the church bells. They rung. Guns were fired, not in any concerted way, but here and there from each man's doorstep. Boys began to shout. Girls brought out the dinner bells and rung them from almost every door up and down the street. Then came the drums, fifes, tin horns . . . The joyous, multitudinous din rolled up in increasing volume till darkness gathered over us. Then some patriotic householder placed lights in the front windows, and other followed him till the whole village was brilliantly lighted up. Then all the lanterns were lighted and brought out, moving and waving up and down the street. Bonfires flashed, and the voice of singing mingled with the other sounds of joy.—This was all kept up till a late hour in the evening—making a night to be remembered by old and young to their latest day. Glory to God in the highest; peace on earth."

Hinesburg's 1830 Baptist Church rises prominently along Route 116, where Rev. William Arthur was pastor 1833 to 1834. The congregation surely heard words about human freedom, for Arthur was a determined abolitionist.

From the large house on a knoll across the road from the church, Guy Boynton went to war, as a corporal in the 14th Vermont's Company G, in which many Hinesburg men served. He was promoted to sergeant on the battlefield at Gettysburg the day of Pickett's Charge.

South of the present town hall, at the corner of Route 116 and Charlotte Road, the house where Reverend Arthur and his family lived still stands. His son was future president Chester A. Arthur (see Fairfield).

Go south on Route 116, and where it turns sharp left, go straight on Silver Street. In 1.5 miles, pass a cemetery on the right. From the big brick house just beyond, Charles Mead enlisted as a corporal in the 14th Vermont. Killed at Gettysburg, the family learned the details when Charles's fellow soldier, Guy Boynton, came home. Charles's brother Elisha wrote, "It was at the time that the rebels were making one of their desperate charges upon our center. Guy said he had seen Charles and talked with him not two

minutes before he was struck he said that Charles had just fired and loaded his gun when they were ordered to reserve their fire until the enemy came nearer. At that time he was struck but not disfigured. They buried him under a large oak tree and set up a board with his name at the head of the grave." Mead is buried in the Gettysburg National Cemetery.

Return on Silver Street to Route 116 and turn right, south. Look across the road from the modern school to a long, old, wooden building beside a gas station, now a store. Built in 1815 as a schoolhouse, it was later the GAR hall. The veterans formed here each Memorial Day to march to the village cemetery.

Continue south, and four buildings past the restaurant on the left is a long old wooden house, the home of John Allen, first lieutenant of the 14th's Company G. Allen fought at Gettysburg, came home to resume his trade as a harness maker, and served Hinesburg in the legislature.

Continue 0.8 miles south on Route 116 and bear right on Gilman Road. In 0.6 mile on the right is the part brick and part frame home of eighteen-year-old Emulous Landon, private in the 11th Vermont, who died of sickness on June 6, 1864.

Return to 116, go straight across it onto Beecher Hill Road, go left on North Road, then quickly turn right on Lincoln Hill Road. A marker at the intersection notes that a community of blacks thrived on this hill for a century, beginning in 1765, among them a Langley family. Brothers Newell, Lewis, and Loudon Langley, and cousin John, all served in the 54th Massachusetts. Loudon also served in the 1st South Carolina Colored Infantry and in the 33rd Colored Infantry, where he rose to the highest rank a black could attain, that of sergeant major. After the war, Loudon stayed in South Carolina and became auditor of Beaufort County. Go up Lincoln Hill Road 3 miles, and just before reaching the Huntington town line, a small frame house with wraparound porch is on the right, believed to have been the home of the Langley brothers. Before the war, the Langleys gave refuge to at least one escaped slave. In 1854, Loudon spoke out in opposition to colonization. And he asked fellow citizens to "lend their influence with intent of giving us liberty and equal rights in the land of our birth."

Return along Lincoln Hill Road and turn right on North Road. Turn left on Richmond Road and in 1 mile is a large white house on the right, with barn behind. George Patrick enlisted from here in the 9th Vermont in the fall of 1862. Private Patrick was killed at Chapin's Farm, near Petersburg, on September 29, 1864.

Go past the Patrick house 0.5 mile and turn left on Mechanicville Road. Look closely in 0.3 mile on the left for an aged farmhouse set behind trees and shrubs. Arthur Post lived here who served in the 14th Vermont's Company G. His descendants say that he had to hitch rides to Virginia to join the regiment, but he fought at Gettysburg.

Quickly come to Route 116 and go north 0.5 mile, turning left on Shelburne Falls Road. In 2 miles on the left is a farm, with a large house. From here, two Russell boys enlisted as privates, Hiram in the 9th

Vermont and Thomas in the 6th. Thomas was wounded at Banks's Ford but recovered to fight at the Wilderness, where he died on May 6. His body never came home.

Return to Route 116 as you came.

SOURCES

CARPENTER, LEONARD E. *HINESBURG, VERMONT FROM 1762*. LONDON: SHELDON PRESS, 1962.

CHILD, HAMILTON. *GAZETTEER AND BUSINESS DIRECTORY OF CHITTENDEN COUNTY, FOR 1882–83*. SYRACUSE, NY: JOURNAL OFFICE, 1882.

DELAIRE, PENELOPE. "THE STORY OF HINESBURG, VERMONT USA. SENIOR SEMINAR, CHAMPLAIN VALLEY UNION HIGH SCHOOL." UNPUBLISHED ESSAY, 1967.

FULLER, JAMES R. JR. *MEN OR COLOR, TO ARMS!: VERMONT AFRICAN-AMERICANS IN THE CIVIL WAR*. LINCOLN, NE: UNIVERSITY PRESS, 2001.

MEAD, CHARLES. CIVIL WAR LETTERS AND FAMILY PAPERS. SPECIAL COLLECTIONS, BAILEY/HOWE LIBRARY, UNIVERSITY OF VERMONT, BURLINGTON.

ZIRBLIS, RAY. *FRIENDS OF FREEDOM: THE VERMONT UNDERGROUND RAILROAD SURVEY REPORT*. MONTPELIER, VT: VERMONT DIVISION OF HISTORIC PRESERVATION, 1997.

WITH THANKS TO CATHERINE MEY, JEAN MINER, AND JOHN MEAD.

HUNTINGTON

The majestic shape of Camel's Hump, which rises above the upland town of Huntington, was a welcome site to returning soldiers, including many from the town who fought at Gettysburg.

Facing Huntington village's small green, along Main Road, is the old village schoolhouse, where Civil War town meetings were held. The building, with stone foundation, is attached to the south side of a store. Here on December 5, 1863, voters approved $350 bounties. The following October, a tax of 230 cents on each grand list dollar was approved to support such payments, whose future amounts voters left to the discretion of the selectmen. In this building, thirteen Huntington men enlisted in the 13th Vermont's Company F, known as the Richmond Company, destined to attack Pickett's Charge.

From the store, go south on Main Street, and on the left is another village store. The house just south of it was built by Dr. Alwyn Chessmore in 1868. Chessmore, in the fall of 1862, joined the 5th Vermont as its surgeon. He later became 1st Vermont Brigade surgeon.

Continue south on Main 1.75 miles, and go right and uphill on Sherman Hollow Road. In 1 mile, the frame house on the right, with peaked roof over the porch, was the home of Andrew Kenyon. He fought at Gettysburg with Company F, came home here, then joined the navy and served on the gunboat Penobscot.

Return to Main Road and go back to Huntington village, pass the old schoolhouse where town meetings took place, and go straight onto East Street. In just under 1.5 miles, bear right at a Y, then again right at a second Y, and keep climbing until crossing a height of land. The road soon ends at a farm with a long view down the Green Mountains. Oscar Tomlinson from here enlisted as a private in Company D of the 13th Vermont. He recalled after the war: "I had the opportunity of going over that portion of the battlefield where Pickett made his charge:

there were dead men swollen to twice their natural size, so near you could step from one to the other." Tomlinson also saw General Winfield Scott Hancock wounded at Gettysburg.

Return to the beginning of East Street and go south, left, on Main Road 1.75 miles. As you cross the Huntington River, the Ellis farm is ahead, from which Sergeant John Ellis enlisted in Company F, 13th Vermont. He fought at Gettysburg and came home to farm here.

Continue south on Main Road, and on entering Huntington Center, go left on Camel's Hump Road. Bear right at a Y in 0.5 mile, and in just under 2 more miles, go left on Fielder Road to its end at an upland farm. From here, Levi and Milo Taft joined the Vermont Cavalry as privates. Levi was twice captured, at Broad Run and Ream's Station, but survived imprisonment to come home and live until 1921. Brother Milo, captured once, was soon released. He served until the war ended and came home to live until 1928. After the war, James Chipman lived here for a time. He was surgical assistant to Dr. Chessmore in the 5th Vermont.

Return to Main Road and continue south. Pass the Huntington town office on the left, and in 3 miles, go left on Carse Road. In the house just across the bridge lived George Burnham, a corporal in Company F of the 13th, who fought at Gettysburg.

Continue south on Main Road, and the first house on the right, past Carse Road, was the home of Hiram Cook. He joined the 5th Vermont when it was formed, and became commander of Company B. Wounded at the Wilderness, he recovered to serve until the war ended.

SOURCES

HANSON, BERTHA BROWN. *HUNTINGTON, VERMONT 1786–1976*. HUNTINGTON, VT: TOWN OF HUNTINGTON, 1976.

HUNTINGTON TOWN RECORDS.

WITH THANKS TO HEIDI RACHT, TOWN CLERK.

....

JERICHO/ UNDERHILL

Jericho and Underhill have a Civil War history so intertwined that they will be dealt with together. Indeed, along Route 15 is a triangular green that is bisected by the Jericho/ Underhill town line, on which is a GAR monument.

From the green, go east on Route 15, and the Methodist Church is quickly on the left. The house just across the street was the home and office of Dr. Henry Burdick, who served eight months as assistant surgeon of the 5th Vermont, treating wounded from the first and second battles at Fredericksburg.

Proceed 0.8 mile on Route 15 east, and turn left on Brown's Trace Road. In 3 miles, turn left into Jericho Center Circle, where the Jericho Congregational Church faces the green. A flag raising took place on the green June 3, 1861, and according to the *Rutland Herald*, "as the people were beginning to disperse, the gun carriage with the cannon upon it was started down the eminence where it had been standing, by a company of boys, when one of their number, Frank Stoddard, aged fourteen, was run over by the wheels, and so much

injured that he died in about two hours."

The Congregational Church basement was a meeting room in which several war meetings were held to encourage enlistments. Wartime town meetings also took place here. In memory of its Civil War soldiers, the town of Jericho published in 1868 a *Soldiers' Record of Jericho, Vermont*. The book noted that at a town meeting in September 1864 voters approved a tax of 200 cents on each dollar of the grand list to pay the cost of bounties. It continued, "Then in December 1864 came another call, for 12 Jericho men. The work of recruiting had become extremely difficult . . . The competition between towns was great, some of which were offering extravagant bounties." By war's end, Jericho was paying $800 bounties. The *Soldiers' Record* stated: "The amount of money expended by the town, for bounties and attending expenses, was thirty thousand eighty-four dollars. The taxes voted and assessed for this purpose were as follows, viz: seventy cents on the dollar of the Grand List of 1862; one hundred and forty cents on the dollar of the Grand list of 1863; three hundred cents on the dollar of the Grand List of 1864; and sixty cents on the Grand List of 1865, voted at the annual March meeting—making in all, five hundred and seventy cents on the dollar of the Grand List of the town, and raising a sum equivalent to a little more than eighteen dollars for each man, woman and child in the town."

The book also noted, "Added to this, the patriotic and liberal efforts of the ladies of the town, in collecting and sending forward, every article, which only the ingenuity and sympathy of women can devise, to add to the comfort and alleviate the sufferings of sick and wounded soldiers." It also said that collections of money and goods were taken for hospitals and that "almost every family, rich or poor, contributed something." Also, several boxes of goods were sent to the Sanitary Commission. The women often met in the Congregational Church basement.

Also facing the Jericho Center green is a village store. The large frame house beside it was the home of Benjamin and Lura Hatch. Sons Truman and Byron, both privates in the 5th Vermont, died of wounds received at the Wilderness on May 5, 1864, Byron expiring at Baxter Hospital in Burlington.

From the green turn left and continue on Brown's Trace, and in just over 1 mile, go left on Nashville Road. In 1.5 mile, the old farmhouse on the right was the home of Albert Parker, a private in the 118th New York, who fought under George Stannard when his division captured Fort Harrison, near Richmond. In 0.75 mile beyond, on reaching a bridge, see Bentley Lane on the right. In the last house lived Hubbell Smith, a private in the 6th Vermont, who took a bullet in the groin at Third Winchester. Though it could never be removed, he later fathered four children.

Return to Jericho Center, pass the green, and soon go left on Lee River Road. In 2 miles on reaching Jericho Center and the traffic island, look to the house on the right, half of which is brick. The stonework around it was part of the foundation of a carriage shop capably operated by Spafford Wright, despite the fact that

he lost an arm at the Wilderness as a private in Company F, 1st U.S. Sharpshooters. Turn left on Route 15 and note the small house on the left, just before the bridge. Michael Martin lived here after the war. Though he returned from service in Louisiana with the 7th Vermont in broken health, he became an expert mechanic, repairing farm implements.

Turn around, go east on Route 15, and in just under 0.4 mile note the frame house on the right with a porch across its front. Bliss Atchison lived here, a private in the Vermont Cavalry with his brother Blinn. The brother was wounded and captured in a skirmish with John Mosby's men.

Continue east on Route 15, and in 2 miles, the house on the right, just beyond the park entrance, was the home of Edward Whitcomb. The Jericho town history calls him "a strong abolitionist" and said that "during the Civil War when sick soldiers were dying and begging to come home, Mr. Whitcomb was the one to go to Washington, see Pres. Lincoln and secure their release; and once to bring home the dead body of Lieut. Lucius Bostwick." Bostwick, commander of Company F, 13th Vermont, was taken ill in camp and died in a Washington hospital.

Continue past the Whitcomb house 0.3 mile to the Episcopal Church on the right. Bostwick's funeral was held here in the early spring of 1862. The local GAR post was named for him.

Continue on Route 15 and quickly turn left on Palmer Lane. Simeon Palmer lived late in life in the first house on the right. In 1862, Simeon, the mainstay of his parents' farm, was intent on going to Richmond and enlisting in the 13th Vermont. But his younger brother Cornelius rose early on the appointed morning, donned his sleeping brother's uniform, and announced to Simeon, "I am going to war and you are going to stay with father and mother." Cornelius survived Gettysburg and came home.

Return to Route 15, go past the triangular green 0.5 mile, and turn right on Poker Hill Road. From the first redbrick house on the left, A. C. Humphrey and his brother William enlisted. A. C., a 2nd Vermont private and later a stalwart of the Bostwick GAR post, was wounded at First Fredericksburg but served until 1864. William, a lieutenant in the 2nd U.S. Sharpshooters, was severely wounded at Petersburg. Continue on Poker Hill Road for 2.2 miles to a large frame house on the right. Byron and Edward Ward, both privates in Company G, 2nd Vermont, lived here and both were wounded at the Wilderness. It is believed that Byron freed George Washington Henderson from slavery and brought him to Underhill.

Return to the triangular green, turn north on Park Street, and soon go left on River Road. In 1.3 miles, English Settlement Road enters on the left. In the first house past the road, on the left, lived brothers Daniel and Eli Ross. Both privates in the Vermont cavalry, they were captured June 29, 1864, at Stony Creek, Virginia, and sent to Andersonville. Daniel, twenty-three, died there on August 16. Eli, paroled in December, came home a broken man and died in this house.

Continue on River Road into Underhill

Center, turn right on Green Street, and take a quick left stopping at the bridge, by the 1853 Green Mountain Academy building. Here, Underhill voters met to approve bounties that, in part, resulted in 157 men serving, of a population of about 1,600. A total of thirty-one died. When the local GAR post was formed, it met on the second floor of this building. One of the academy's distinguished graduates was George Washington Henderson (see Craftsbury), born a slave in Virginia, he apparently came to Vermont late in the war with Lieutenant Byron Ward, of Underhill, and the 5th Vermont

Return to the main road, now Pleasant Valley Road, and turn right. In 0.25 mile, turn right on Stevensville road and in 1.5 miles, where Maple Leaf Road bears left, note the house on the right, once owned by the Leander Tillotson. Leander served only five months, as a private in the 2nd Vermont's Company E, having been discharged for disability. His brother Charles, in his late forties when he enlisted in 1862, worked as a hospital orderly for most of the war. He was lost overboard from a hospital ship in June 1864. At least three other, younger Tillotsons, served in the 2nd Vermont. Two were wounded at the April 2, 1865, breakthrough at Petersburg.

Return to Pleasant Valley Road, turn right, and the first house on the left, at the top of the rise, belonged to David Story. A private in the 5th Vermont, Story was having this home built for himself and his wife when he was wounded and taken prisoner at Savage's Station. He died of wounds in a hospital in Philadelphia. Continue on Pleasant Valley Road and see the wood frame house that sits above the road, on the left. From it, Josephus and Horace Ellsworth enlisted as privates in Company F, 13th Vermont. Both fought at Gettysburg and returned here.

SOURCES

BOSTWICK POST. CIVIL WAR MEMORIAL BOOK. UNDERHILL TOWN CLERK'S OFFICE.
HAYDEN, CHAUNCEY H., ET AL., EDS. THE HISTORY OF JERICHO, VERMONT, 1763–1916. JERICHO HISTORICAL COMMITTEE. BURLINGTON, VT: FREE PRESS PRINTING, 1916.
LANE, E. H. THE SOLDIERS' RECORD OF JERICHO, VERMONT. BURLINGTON, VT: R. S. STYLES PRINTER, 1868. COURTESY OF VERMONT HISTORICAL SOCIETY.
JERICHO TOWN RECORDS.
TILLOTSON FAMILY LETTERS. SPECIAL COLLECTIONS, BAILEY/HOWE LIBRARY, UNIVERSITY OF VERMONT, BURLINGTON. COURTESY OF THE TILLOTSON DESCENDANTS.
WITH THANKS TO SETH SOMERS, GARY IRISH, AND VERNA GRANT.

MILTON

From exit 17 on Interstate 89, take Route 7 north, and in 0.6 mile, a small 1836 farmhouse is on the left, with its back to an industrial park. George Stannard, commander of the 2nd Vermont Brigade, apparently purchased it in 1866. The general had recently been appointed customs collector in Burlington, and he began amassing a considerable amount of property. The barn that once stood behind the house had door latches made especially for a one-armed man. Stannard had lost an arm at the Battle of Fort Harrison, near Richmond, in 1864. He owned the property until 1872, selling it after he got into financial difficulty, probably in part because of the number of real estate holdings he acquired.

Continue north on Route 7 just over 2 miles and turn left on West Milton Road. In 1.5 miles, go right on Bear Trap Road and cross the Lamoille River. On ascending the riverbank, the second left turn is Rowley Road, and the first house is believed to have been the home from which William B. Reynolds went to war. Reynolds was captain of Company I, 6th Vermont, when captured at Savage's Station. Soon paroled, in 1864 he was appointed major of the new 17th Vermont Regiment. In command at the Battle of the Crater near Petersburg, he led the regiment's advance after the explosion of a mine under the Rebel works. Fighting in the crater itself, according to historian G. G. Benedict, he was struck by a musket ball in the left breast. Carried to the rear on a rubber blanket, he expired within minutes.

Proceed uphill on Bear Trap Road, and quickly, on the left, is the West Milton Cemetery, on land that was once part of the Reynolds family farm. A memorial stone for Major Reynolds states: "Killed while leading the 17th Vt. Vols. in an assault before Petersburg, Va., July 30, 1864. Buried where he fell by rebel hands." He was twenty-four.

The building across the road was once a school, built on the site of an older school, which Reynolds attended. The building on the river side of the school stands on the site of the West Milton church, where a memorial service was held for Reynolds.

Return to Route 7 and turn left, north, to Milton village. In 2.5 miles, turn right on Main Street. As you do, note that the Milton Civil War monument once stood in the middle of the intersection of Route 7 and Main. On September 6, 1909, two thousand people gathered here for the monument dedication.

Proceed up Main Street and quickly turn right on School Street. Soon come to the Milton Historical Society on the right, with the Civil War memorial on the front lawn, facing south as it did in its first location. The monument bears the names of 200 Milton men who served and a plaque lists 44 who died.

Albert Clark, a lieutenant in the 13th's Company G, spoke at the monument dedication. Noting that thirty-four Milton men served in the 13th's Company D, he said, "We look back upon our part and it seems all a dream now, but vacant chairs and empty sleeves and this monument remind us that it was no dream to them. We place ourselves in imagination upon those fields of value, well may we say with the martyred Lincoln: 'The world will little note nor long remember what we say here, but it can never forget what they did here.'"

Return to Main Street and turn right. The second house on the left, brick with a long porch, was the home of Dr. Benjamin Fairchild, who began a practice in Milton in 1838. Fairchild was one of the Vermont doctors who hastened to Fredericksburg, Virginia, after the Battle of the Wilderness, to treat Vermont wounded.

Continue on Main Street, and quickly, on the right, is the old Milton Congregational Church. In 1869, the fighting chaplain of the Vermont Cavalry, Jonathan Woodward (see Westford), became pastor of this church, serving until his death in 1895. His funeral was held here, and he is buried in the adjacent cemetery.

Return along Main Street to a huge brick house on the right, just above the monument site. The local GAR post, named for William Reynolds, met on the second floor.

SOURCES

HOLLENBECK, BARBARA F. *MILTON'S STORY, 1763–1976*. MILTON, VT: MILTON BICENTENNIAL COMMITTEE, 1976.
MILTON TOWN RECORDS.

RICHMOND

For one hundred men from surrounding Chittenden County towns in the late summer of 1862, "on to Richmond" meant making their way to Richmond, Vermont, where Company F of the 13th Vermont assembled. On September 10, according to company historian Henry Mudgett, "A hundred boys brought together from the farms, stores and shops of Chittenden County, all full of fun and frolic made Richmond a pretty lively place during our stay. Yet I don't believe there was a low, dirty or mean act committed, just simply boyish frolicks, the overflow of youth." When the company arrived, Mudgett said, "the boys slept together with the rest of the company on straw thrown upon the floor of J. H. Ranson's Hotel."

Enter Richmond today along Route 2, and at the southwest corner of the main intersection, where a convenience store now stands, Ransom's hotel was located. Turn south here and stop by the railroad tracks. The Richmond depot once stood on the near side of the tracks. The long freight building, on a stone foundation, dates to the 1860s, as does the old store. Company F drilled for several days in Richmond, then boarded a train here for Brattleboro. The company would, of course, end up at Gettysburg. Cross the tracks and on the left is the Village Cemetery. On its north side, by a marker whose inscription has long ago weathered away lies Pvt. Henry Russell of Company F. From an old Richmond family, Russell married Julia Robinson in January 1859. He was thirty when he went to war. At Gettysburg, Russell was killed just before the 13th Vermont made its flank attack on Pickett's Charge. Buried on the field, his comrades marked the spot with a wooden headboard. According to the company historian, "After the company had been mustered out and returned to Richmond, Vermont, Private Amos Brown went to Gettysburg and removed the body of Corporal Russell to its final resting place."

Continue south, and just before reaching the Winooski River, Volunteer Field is on the right. It is believed that Company F drilled here. Continue across the Winooski, to Richmond's famous Round Church, begun in 1812. Town meetings once took place here, and on September 22, 1862, Richmond voters, asked to approve $300 bounties, approved only $100 bounties. Meeting the following December, they voted against paying bounties to drafted men but approved $100 payments to volunteers. In Decem-

ber 1863, $300 bounties for volunteers were approved, and Richmond continued providing that sum through the remainder of the war. A Richmond woman, Betsy Flagg, noted in her diary on November 20, 1863, "Jones and his wife Mary have gone to the Round Church to a war meeting. Full house."

From the Round Church, take Huntington Road for 0.5 mile and turn right on Hinesburg Road. In another 0.5 mile, at Fay's Corners, left from the old frame house on the right, Arnold Fay enlisted with Company F, serving as first sergeant, later a lieutenant. After Gettysburg, he came home to work as a recruiter, then reenlisted, joining the 17th Vermont. Fay was brevetted a captain for meritorious service in the April 2, 1865, assault at Petersburg.

Return to Richmond village. On May 11, 1865, the *Burlington Free Press* reported, "Nowhere, outside of Burlington and Winooski, was the surrender of Lee so fitly and enthusiastically rejoiced over as at Richmond . . . The bells were rung all day, and flags were displayed everywhere, and the people from neighboring towns flocked in to participate in the rejoicings over Gen. Grant's grand success." Vermonters flocked to Vermont's Richmond to celebrate the fall of the Confederate capital of Richmond.

On reaching the main intersection, turn east (right) on Route 2. In 2.75 miles, note the large old house set back from the road and surrounded by maples, an early 1800s building once known as Whipples Tavern. At a time well before the Civil War, a militia muster took place in the field across the road from the tavern. That day, Winfield

Scott, hero of the War of 1812 and the Mexican War, happened along. According to the historian Lilian Baker Carlisle: "Scott inspected the troops and inquired if any soldiers belonged to the 11th Regiment which fought with him at Lundy's Lane or Bridgewater. One soldier—Orderly Sergeant William Humphrey, a Richmond resident, stepped forward. Gen. Scott gave a rousing speech praising the men who had fought so valiantly under his command. After the speech, Humphrey remarked, 'One name you forgot.' 'Who?' asked Scott. 'Gen. Winfield Scott!' shouted Humphrey, whereupon thunderous cheers arose from the spectators." Scott, though very elderly, was in charge of all U.S. forces when the Civil War began, but soon he went into retirement.

SOURCES
CARLISLE, LILIAN BAKER, ED. *LOOK AROUND CHITTENDEN COUNTY, VERMONT*. BURLINGTON, VT: CHITTENDEN COUNTY HISTORICAL SOCIETY, 1976.
FLAGG, BETSY. DIARY, 1860S. COURTESY OF HARRIET RIGGS, RICHMOND.
RICHMOND TOWN RECORDS.

SHELBURNE

Approaching Shelburne from the north, on Shelburne Road, which is Route 7, go left on Allen Road, and in 0.7 mile, turn right on Spear Street. In another 0.7 mile, go left on Barstow Street, and soon, on the left, a sign marks the site of the Barstow estate, from which John Barstow went to war, as a captain in the 8th Vermont. Barstow was promoted to major before he led the regiment on an assault at Port Hudson. He came home in June 1864 in poor health, but was soon serving in the Vermont legislature and was well enough that fall to take command of some of the troops assigned to watch the Canadian border after the Confederate raid on St. Albans. He served as Vermont governor, 1882 to 1884.

In 0.9 mile, turn right on Dorset Street, and in 0.2 mile on the right is the brick Sutton homestead. John Sutton joined the 12th Vermont at twenty-eight, one of nineteen Shelburne men in Company C. He died of disease on April 25, in Virginia, and his body came home for burial in Shelburne's Spear Street Cemetery.

In 2.2 miles, turn left on Pond Road. Proceed past the entrance to the Shelburne Pond fishing access, and in another mile look closely at the swampy area to the left for the faint trace of a farm lane leading to a knoll. Once, the Isham family home stood there. Among the eighty Shelburne men who served was Private Gilbert Isham, 1st Vermont Cavalry. Captured soon after the Battle of Gettysburg, he spent six months in Richmond prisons. Isham returned home a broken man, unable to work. One day in 1865, his wife, Sarah, twenty-eight, came down this lane in a buggy and turned left, on the road you are following. Approaching the corner of the main road just ahead (Route 116), the horse ran away, and Sarah was killed when the buggy overturned. Gilbert was left with three young children.

Return to Dorset Street and go left 0.4 mile, and the house on the right, just before the intersection, is the much-altered home of Private Francis Douglas, eighteen when he joined the 10th Vermont. Fourteen months later, on November 27, 1863, he was severely wounded at Orange Grove, during the Mine Run campaign, and died less than three weeks later. Return north on Dorset Street to Barstow Road, take Spear Street south 1.2 miles, and go right on Webster Road. In 0.6 mile, the house on the left was the home of William Harmon, Shelburne's town clerk and treasurer during the war years. His son Argalus enlisted in the Vermont Cavalry at nineteen, in the fall of 1861, and died of disease less than a year later.

Continue west on Webster Road to Shelburne Road, Route 7, turn left, and in the center of Shelburne village, go left at the traffic light and quickly park by the green. Across Route 7, is the brick building that was once the town's largest store, built in 1851 by John Simonds. Simonds was appointed Shelburne's wartime postmaster by President Lincoln. He was one of a dozen Shelburne voters who petitioned the town to hold a special town meeting on April 27, 1861, after the fall of Fort Sumter. At the meeting, the town voted to appropriate $1,000 to pay $30 bounties to each volunteer.

Return to the traffic light, go straight across Route 7, and in just under 1 mile, go left through the south gate of Shelburne Farms, once the Webb-Vanderbilt estate. Shelburne farms was begun by William Seward Webb, the brother of Alexander Stewart Webb, who, as a brigadier general, won a Medal of Honor on Cemetery Ridge at Gettysburg, leading a Pennsylvania brigade. The general was a frequent visitor here.

When William Webb created his estate, he purchased thirty-two farms on the west side of Shelburne, including the Morehouse family farm. Their house remains. From the South Gate of Shelburne Farms, proceed 0.9 mile through the estate's farmlands and turn right toward Quaker Smith Point. Soon come to a cemetery, and just beyond is a long private drive that leads to a large brick house, the central core of which was the Morehouse home.

In 1933, Jennie Morehouse Edwards recalled her Civil War–era childhood in Shelburne saying, "Our home was in one of the most charming spots in New England. Our farm sloped to Lake Champlain about a mile away." Jennie wrote that, just before the war, her father raised a flagpole in the yard for the presidential ticket of Lincoln and Hannibal Hamlin. Jennie said that two of her brothers enlisted. Roderick crossed the lake to join in the 142nd New York and was wounded at Chaffin's Bluff in 1864. Private George Morehouse joined the 13th Vermont and fought at Gettysburg. Jennie also wrote that another brother, in Texas when the war began, was drafted into the Rebel army but eventually escaped to fight with the Union.

According to Jennie, many of the burdens of running the 70-acre Morehouse farm fell on younger brother Hawley, a "happy joyous handsome little fellow but not rugged enough to stand the strain upon him that came too soon," In 1865, he was taken ill in "an epidemic of what was called dysentery." He steadily weakened until a doctor saw no hope. Jennie said, "Not only the family, but church and other friends came into his room. To some he said, 'Come up higher,' and this is on his stone in the little cemetery on what was then a part of our farm . . . Before morning he was gone." The old cemetery here contains the names of many people who once farmed what is now estate acreage. The Webbs are also buried in the old cemetery, in a fenced enclosure. Hawley's stone stands in the graveyard, with a carved hand pointing skyward.

Return to Route 7 as you came and turn right, south, and soon come to the Shelburne Museum, also a creation of the Webb family. Houses have been moved to the museum from several Vermont locations, including two that offer a remarkable sense of what life was like to Vermonters of the Civil War era. From the Settlers House, built in Charlotte in 1832, Henry Wilder enlisted as a private in Company F of the 1st U.S. Sharpshooters and served three years. Before the war, two sisters and a brother died of tuberculosis in the little house, with its log walls, low ceiling, and large fireplace. The Dutton house, built in 1782 in Cavendish, was for many years a tavern. Solomon Dutton lived here and served as a lieutenant in the 1st Vermont and a captain in the 7th Vermont. His sister Emily Jane was married in the large tavern room to Redfield Proctor, who would one day command the 15th Vermont.

SOURCES

LANG, ROBERT. SHELBURNE FARMS: FARM BARN DEVELOPMENT REPORT. BURLINGTON, VT: UVM DEVELOPMENT ECONOMICS GROUP, 1984.
MOREHOUSE FAMILY PAPERS. VERMONT HISTORICAL SOCIETY.
PHISTERER, FREDERICK. NEW YORK IN THE WAR OF THE REBELLION, 1861–1865. ALBANY, NY: L. R. LYON, 1912.
WEBSTER, TRUMAN M. SHELBURNE PIECES OF HISTORY. SHELBURNE, VT: SHELBURNE HISTORIC SITES COMMITTEE, 1994.
WITH THANKS TO DAN COLE AND INA ISHAM.

ST. GEORGE

From exit 12 on Interstate 89, take Route 2A south and a sign soon marks the town line of St. George, Vermont's smallest town. In 3.5 miles from the interstate, on the right, is the old Hinsdale farm, with the original farmhouse and very old barn set far behind it. From here Mitchell Hinsdale, at nineteen, joined the 17th Vermont in September 1864. He served until the war ended and was engaged in heavy action around Petersburg, including the Battle of the Crater. But he came home safely and lived here until his death in 1923.

Just past the farm entrance, on the right and close to the road, is an odd-shaped house built by Hiram Tilley, who saw three sons go to war. Hiram, Silas, and Sydney Tilley all were privates in Company G, 2nd Vermont, enlisting in the fall of 1861 and serving three years. Hiram, twenty, was wounded at Second Fredericksburg.

Go 0.3 mile past the Tilley house and look closely for the narrow entrance to the St. George Cemetery. Several veterans of the Revolutionary War and War of 1812 are buried here, as are St. George Civil War veterans Mitchell Hinsdale and Hiram Westcott, a private in the 12th Vermont, who was discharged for disability before the Gettysburg campaign.

Just beyond the cemetery, also on the left, is an old tavern where George Isham grew up. He joined the 17th Vermont at seventeen in September 1864 and served until the war ended.

Past the tavern 0.1 mile, also on the left, is the St. George School, built in 1829. The only school in town, among the future soldiers who attended were the three Tilleys and George Isham. This one-room school was the center of St. George activity, and Civil War era town meetings were long held here.

Continue south on Route 2A and look left, to the long, 1,00-foot ridge that runs the length of town. Known today as St. George Hill, and long ago as Pritchard Mountain, its named changed during the Civil War. When Anson Weed returned home after serving eight months as a lieutenant in the 2nd Vermont, he named the ridge Lincoln Mountain, in honor of the president. The name stuck for a time. Weed lived along the south end of the ridge, just across the line in Hinesburg.

SOURCES

CARLISLE, LILIAN BAKER, ED. *LOOK AROUND ST. GEORGE AND SHELBURNE, VERMONT.* BURLINGTON, VT: CHITTENDEN COUNTY HISTORICAL SOCIETY, 1975. WITH THANKS TO INA ISHAM.

···

WESTFORD

The Civil War monument that faces the common in Westford, along Route 126, lists 108 Westford men who served. It was dedicated on July 4, 1912, with a speech by former governor Urban Woodbury, the first Vermonter to lose a limb in the Civil War. Atop it is a statue of the town's most famous soldier, the fighting chaplain of the 1st Vermont Cavalry, Jonathan H. Woodward. Reverend Woodward was fifty when he recruited Company M of the regiment, leaving the pulpit of the former Westford Congregational Church, which overlooks the monument. Elected regimental chaplain by the men, he soon won a reputation as a fighter. In the Shenandoah Valley in 1862, Chaplain Woodward pursued an enemy soldier to his home, barged in, and, in front of his terrified mother, led the young man away as a captive.

Jonathan W. Woodward joined his father in the Vermont cavalry in the late fall of 1862, after graduating from the University of Vermont, becoming captain of the company his father had recruited. Young Woodward left behind in Cambridge his fiancé, Hattie Chadwick (see Cambridge). Woodward served at Gettysburg, and about that time, he heard of Miss Chadwick's death, from disease. On July 6, 1863, while pursuing Lee's retreating army near Hagerstown, Maryland, the Vermont horsemen got in a hot fight. Chaplain Woodward wrote, "It was while bravely attempting to rally his company to face this overwhelming attack that Captain Woodward was shot simultaneously through the brain and heart."

The chaplain came home with his son's body and never returned to war. Services were held in a packed Congregational Church, with the Reverend O. G. Wheeler of Grand Isle presiding. The congregation sang a hymn composed by Wheeler for the occasion, the words of one verse being:

Charge, soldiers, charge the trait'rous foe,
God bids you strike the avenging blow!
His work is done, and angels bear
To the loved that wait him there.

According to a woman in attendance: "All the services, music, prayers and sermon were appropriate, impressive and in keeping with the subdued and solemn spirit of the occasion, stirring large and at times strong emotion, and conveying a wholesome lesson to all whose privilege it was to be present."

Chaplain Woodward said of his son, "Thus ended the earthly career of one who so lately went from among you in all the bloom and promise of early manhood. You will not see his face again; that clear, ringing voice, which so often sounded forth the praises of God in this house and who so often cheered his comrades on to daring and victory on the bloody field, you and they will hear no more."

Woodward was buried next to his fiancé, in East Cambridge.

The Congregational Church, now known as the United Church of Westford, held another soldier funeral on June 5, 1864. Local farmer Alney Stone noted in his diary, "Marcia, Billie & I went to meeting. Dr. Foster preached forenoon, in afternoon preached funeral sermon for Lieutenant John G. Macomber." A soldier in the 6th Vermont, Macomber was mortally wounded at the Wilderness on May 5, 1864.

Face the church and note the house to its left with long side porch, once the church parsonage in which Reverend Woodward raised a boy. Look far across the common to the other Westford Church. Built in 1828, early worshippers there certainly heard a good deal about the evils of slavery as preached by Baptist Reverend Alvah Sabin, an abolitionist (see Georgia).

Six Westford men died in battle, 15 of wounds or disease, and 1 in Andersonville prison.

SOURCES
STONE, ALNEY. DIARY. SPECIAL COLLECTIONS, BAILEY/HOWE LIBRARY, UNIVERSITY OF VERMONT, BURLINGTON.
BURLINGTON FREE PRESS, 1863–1864. VERMONT STATE LIBRARY.
WESTFORD TOWN RECORDS.

WILLISTON

From Interstate 89 exit 11, take Route 2 west, and in 1.5 miles, go right on Governor Chittenden Road. In just under 1 mile is the historic farm, on a bluff, once the home of Vermont's first governor, Thomas Chittenden. Lucius Chittenden grew up here to become a prominent lawyer and member of the Democratic Party. Not long before the Civil War, he made the acquaintance of Salmon Chase, and when Chase became treasury secretary, he appointed Chittenden to a position in the U.S. Treasury Department. There, Chittenden signed all the wartime bonds issued by the federal government. In fact, his hand became so sore from signing bonds that he sometimes returned to Vermont to take a break. Present when Abraham Lincoln entered the Confederate capital of Richmond on April 4, 1865, Chittenden wrote:

"Multitudes of the emancipated crowd craned and sought to touch the garments of the benefactor, as with streaming eyes they shout their thanksgivings. Truly, as Lincoln said, 'It is a great thing to be responsible for the freedom of a race.' Note the historic picture as he removes his hat and bows in silence to the old Negro who exclaimed, 'May the good lord bless you, President Lincoln.' Truthfully did he write at the time, 'That bow upset the forms, customs, and ceremonies of centuries.'"

Return to Route 2, continue west, and on entering the village of Williston, Johnson Lane turns left to the farm where Lucia Brown lived most of her life. Lucia, 5 feet 4 inches and petite, was born on October 10, 1833, and died at eighty-seven in December 1920. She began keeping a diary at age twenty-five and continued for fifty-seven years. Lucia was baptized a member of the Williston Methodist Church, and she spent Sundays going from one Williston church to the next, attending services. She was active in a choir, a ladies' aid society, a church donation society, a Sabbath school, and a missionary society. She also attended gospel meetings. Lucia married Frank Pinney in 1859, but he soon left, with Lucia's brother Charles, for the California gold fields. Frank never returned, and Lucia divorced him in 1867. She soon remarried, to a cousin, Will Darling. Her life became miserable as he was often away from home and generally neglected her.

She wrote, "The more I see of men, the more I like dogs."

Go east past Johnson Lane, pass through Williston village's busy main intersection, and quickly come to a group of old brick buildings. On the right is the 1832 Congregational Church. Its members in 1844 adopted several antislavery resolutions, including one stating that the church "will not receive to our communion table and to our pulpits, ministers and members of churches who are living in or justify slavery." Directly across the road is the Williston town hall, which was a Universalist church during the Civil War. Just west of it is the town hall annex, formerly the Methodist Church. Beside it once stood the Civil War–era town hall, long gone, and just past it was Williston Academy, where many young men who served went to school. It burned in the 1950s.

When Company F of the 13th Vermont formed in 1862, twenty-three Williston men volunteered who would fight at Gettysburg. With them as regimental chaplain went Reverend Joseph Sargent, pastor of the Universalist Church. Sargent spent much of his time caring for the regiment's sick, and, on April 20, 1863, he died of typhoid fever at Fairfax, Virginia. Back home, Sargent was replaced as pastor by Reverend Edward Randall, brother of Francis Voltaire Randall, who commanded the 13th Vermont.

The grouping of old brick buildings was the setting for much of the story told by Lucia Brown's wartime diaries:

March 15, 1863: "The funeral sermon of Charlie Chase was preached today from the words If in this world only we have hope in Christ." (Chase, a private in the 7th Vermont, died of disease at Fort Barancas, Florida.)

April 20, 1863: "Mrs. Sargent got a telegraphic dispatch to go immediately to Fairfax [Virginia] . . . as Mr. S. was very sick—starts tonight."

April 23: "Dr. Welch had got a telegram that Mr. Sargent was dead. Come down here found them [the Sargent family] almost broken hearted at the loss of their excellent father."

April 24: "It seems lonely to walk through the street and see the flag at half mast. I suppose it has to be that Mr. Sargent was to die for his country. Oh how many families are left desolate by this awful war."

April 28: "Went down to Mr. Sargent's this afternoon his body come last night. The officers of the Regt. went to the expense of having it embalmed and sent home."

April, 30: "The funeral took place this afternoon . . . There were at least a thousand people there and all mourning."

August 6, 1863: "Today is National Thanksgiving [for the Gettysburg victory]. The people of Williston had a Thanksgiving in the Congregational Church and Town Hall. Good speeches, nice refreshments, a good contribution for the wounded soldiers and one for Mrs. Sargent."

August 10, 1863: "I got a letter from Esther containing the sad news of [brother] Edgar's death. He died at Yorktown, Virginia, but she had learned little of the particulars. He leaves five little children. Oh dear why has he been taken from them, poor brother has given his precious life for his country & we are left to mourn his loss."

August 14, 1863: "Ironed this forenoon and this afternoon went to the Ladies Aid Society. I want to sew and do all I can for the poor soldiers."

Reverend J. W. Hough, pastor of the Congregational Church, wrote of the war years in Williston: "It took away our young men. It colored the tone and quality of the sermons. It turned our thought and life into new channels. It linked every farm and every home with the battlefields of the Rapidan & Rappahannock. Possibly some of you will recall . . . the debate in the old Academy Hall on the question of Emancipation, and the meetings in the Town hall for the enlistment of soldiers— Many, I am sure, remember the sad day, when Charley Chapin's wasted form, brought home from Andersonville, was placed before our pulpit, on its way to the cemetery—I do not know what I preached about on that day, but I know that when I held up one of those testaments, well-thumbed and marked, and nearly worn out by being carried in Charley's pocket, it spoke more effectively than any words of mine."

Charles Chapin, a Vermont Cavalry private, was captured near the Wilderness on May 5, 1864, imprisoned at Andersonville, and exchanged six months later. He died in January 1864 in a hospital near Washington. His brother Cornelius, an assistant surgeon in the 6th Vermont, had died in September 1863.

On April 13, 1865, Williston celebrated Lee's surrender, and the *Burlington*

Free Press said, "The streets of our usually quiet village were enlivened by the strains of martial music and the singing of patriotic songs. The church and Academy bells were rung with enthusiasm, and a salute of 100 guns fired in honor of the great event."

Stephen Thomas, 8th Vermont commander, made three recruiting appearances in Williston. One of those he persuaded to sign up was fifteen-year-old Francis Forbes. From the town hall, return east on Route 2 to the main intersection and go right, south, on Oak Hill Road. Cross Interstate 89, and in 2.2 miles, a large brick house stands above the road on the right. Young Forbes was working here on the Grove Talcott farm in 1861, and he remembered, "One day I saw a hay-rack pass the house. It had the Stars-and-Stripes flying from a pole, and men in it were shouting and singing, 'Come on boys, come on.' That was a short time after the battle of Bull Run, and the North was realizing that the war was a big thing and calling for men.'" Forbes, who heard Colonel Thomas speak, enlisted in the 8th Vermont in December 1863 and fought at Winchester and Cedar Creek, returning safely.

Return to Williston village's main intersection and note the large brick house with prominent cupola at the southwest corner, long known as the Miller/Bradish House. Forbes said of the spring of 1861, "Soon a great flag-pole was erected on the village 'Green' on the three-cornered plot in front of the Bingham house . . . It stood 150 feet high . . . The great pole stood during the war." Dr. A. L. Bingham lived in the house in the 1860s and spiritualist

gatherings were held there. During the war at one Williston séance, the deceased Reverend Sargent was contacted and said that he intended to return to town and preach. At another, Abraham Lincoln supposedly spoke from beyond the grave to criticize his successor, President Andrew Johnson, as a man more dangerous than Jefferson Davis.

Return south on Oak Hill Road, and immediately after crossing the interstate, turn left on South Road. In just over 3 miles, the large farmhouse on the left was the home of Williston Congregational Church deacon William Yale. His son John Yale led the 13th Vermont's Company F, in which twenty-four Williston men served. Soon after reaching Virginia, Captain Yale contracted typhoid fever. Deacon Yale went south and brought his son home to this house in March, where he fully recovered.

Return to Williston village; two houses beyond School Street, on the right, is a large frame house behind maples, once the Winslow home. Three Winslow boys became ministers, among them Gordon, born here in 1803. He was an Episcopal pastor in New York City when the Civil War began and became chaplain of the 5th New York Volunteers, a Zouave regiment. It is said that he drowned in June 1864 helping his wounded son across the Potomac River. Just past the Winslow house, turn right on Old Stage Road, and in 0.5 mile a horse farm is on the left. Here, before the war, the Byington family gave shelter to fugitive slaves. Return to Route 2, go right to busy Taft's Corner, and turn left on St. George Road. Pass under

Interstate 89, and in 1.25 miles is an 1856 brick house, set back on the left. From here, it is believed that George Baldwin went to war, as a private in the 13th Vermont's Company F. During the cannonade that preceded Pickett's Charge on July 3, 1863, a shell fragment struck Baldwin, and he was carried to the rear by comrades. He lived until July 30, dying, at twenty-three, in a field hospital at Gettysburg. He is buried in the national cemetery there.

Williston sent some 127 men to war.

SOURCES

BARBER, AIMEE ANGUS. "A HISTORY OF THE RELIGIOUS LIFE OF WILLISTON, VERMONT." UNPUBLISHED PAPER, 1940. VERMONT HISTORICAL ROOM, DOROTHY ALLING MEMORIAL LIBRARY, WILLISTON.

CARLISLE, LILIAN BAKER, ED. *LOOK AROUND ESSEX AND WILLISTON, VERMONT.* BURLINGTON, VT: CHITTENDEN COUNTY HISTORICAL SOCIETY, 1973.

FORBES, J. ET AL., EDS. *A HISTORY OF THE TOWN OF WILLISTON, 1763–1913.* WILLISTON, VT: HISTORICAL COMMITTEE, 1991.

FORD, FRANCIS. "A SOLDIER OF SHERIDAN: FIRST RECOLLECTIONS OF THE CIVIL WAR." UNPUBLISHED MANUSCRIPT, UNDATED. VERMONT HISTORICAL ROOM, DOROTHY ALLING MEMORIAL LIBRARY, WILLISTON.

GOODRICH, J. E. "CAPTAIN HIRAM HENRY HALL OF THE FIRST VERMONT CAVALRY." SPEECH GIVEN AT THE 21ST ANNIVERSARY MEETING OF THE VERMONT COMMANDERY OF THE MILITARY ORDER OF THE LOYAL LEGION, NOVEMBER 19, 1912. PAMPHLET, 1912. BURLINGTON FREE PRESS PRINTING.

MOODY, F. KENNON, AND FLOYD D. PUTNAM. *THE WILLISTON STORY.* ESSEX JUNCTION, VT: ROSCOE PRINTING, 1961.

NAHRA, NANCY, AND RANDALL WILLARD. *THOMAS CHITTENDEN'S TOWN.* WILLISTON, VT: WILLISTON HISTORICAL SOCIETY, 1991.

YALE, JOHN. PAPERS. VERMONT HISTORICAL ROOM, DOROTHY ALLING MEMORIAL LIBRARY, WILLISTON.

ZIRBLIS, RAY. *FRIENDS OF FREEDOM: THE VERMONT UNDERGROUND RAILROAD SURVEY REPORT.* MONTPELIER, VT: VERMONT DIVISION OF HISTORIC PRESERVATION, 1997.

WITH SPECIAL THANKS TO MARTI FISKE AND DEBORAH RODERER OF THE DOROTHY ALLING MEMORIAL LIBRARY.

WINOOSKI

At Winooski, mill buildings still line the southern bank of the Winooski River, some standing on the foundations of manufacturing complexes that made wool for Union army blankets and uniforms. One structure survives that was part of the great industrial complex that ran full steam during a time of war. From the center of Winooski and its wide roundabout, go west from Main Street on Canal Street. From the corner of River Street to the corner of Main Street, a long two-story brick structure survives that once was a dormitory for women mill workers. During the Civil War, country girls who came to the big town to work in the mills lived here.

Winooski at the time of the Civil War was part of the town of Colchester. In 1862 when the Second Vermont Brigade formed, Company D, commanded by William Munson of Colchester, drilled on Weaver's Field. That field, named for a local manufacturer, is now filled with houses. But the Kennedy house, once owned by the Weaver family, stands at the corner of Main and Mansion streets, up the hill from the roundabout. That big old house with a cupola, on a knoll, overlooked the sizeable drill field to its north.

When Company D went to war, it

departed from the Winooski depot, located west of the roundabout on Malletts Bay Avenue. The depot complex was on both sides of the tracks where they cross the avenue. The return of Company D three weeks after Gettysburg, according to the *Burlington Free Press,* was "long to be remembered by soldiers and citizen." The paper reported, "A telegram having announced that they would arrive on the seven o'clock train, at about that hour the bell began to ring, and soon every avenue leading to the depot was thronged with expectant, joyful relatives of our brave, returning 'boys' . . . As the cars approached they were greeted by tremendous cheers from the assembled multitude." From the depot they were marched through Allen and Main streets "to the stirring notes of the fife and drum." After speeches in front of the Congregational Church, at the northeast corner of Allen and Weaver streets, a building that no longer stands, the ladies of the village served a feast. The boys, most of them, were home.

Continue east a block and make a quick right on Maple Street. The house with columned front porch, at the top of the hill on the right, was the home of Winooski's most prominent Civil War soldier. William Greenleaf took part in the cavalry charge at Gettysburg, after Pickett's Charge, which took the life of another Winooski boy, Private George Duncan. Near Hagerstown, Maryland, ten days later, Greenleaf was shot from his horse, wounded in the arm and hip. Left behind enemy lines, he was found the next day by Union soldiers. He recovered to fight the next spring and was again wounded, on May 5, near the Wilderness. This time he was captured, though soon exchanged. He came home to Winooski a hero and became a successful businessman.

SOURCES

CARLISLE, LILIAN BAKER, ED. *LOOK AROUND WINOOSKI*. BURLINGTON, VT: CHITTENDEN COUNTY HISTORICAL SOCIETY, 1972.
FEENEY, VINCENT. *THE GREAT FALLS OF THE ONION RIVER*. WINOOSKI, VT: WINOOSKI HISTORICAL SOCIETY, 2002.
WITH THANKS TO DAVID BLOW, VINCENT FEENEY, AND REBECCA MUNSON.

A bend in the Connecticut River in Essex County

chapter six

Essex County

In 1862, Maidstone people looked down from a favorite hilltop picnic spot, with a commanding view of the Connecticut Valley and the White Mountains, and saw something new. Five bends of the Connecticut River spelled the word *union*, for which the Civil War was being fought. Men drilled along the main street in Concord, then one day marched away in a procession led by

women, to St. Johnsbury, to become part of the 3rd Vermont. From a farmhouse set above the main road through Granby, Captain George Ford went to war, destined to be shot through both legs during the desperate early morning struggle for the 8th Vermont's flag on a knoll above Cedar Creek. After the war, the North's greatest hero, Ulysses Grant, stepped from a train at the depot in Island Pond. Guest of honor at a grand luncheon, he shook hands with three hundred local men who fought for him. Was he told, during his visit, of the local widow who sent three sons to war? Who built a house mostly with her own hands while they were away? And did he hear that two of the sons died far away, and that other came home a broken man?

AVERILL

From the village of Norton on the Canadian border, go east 4.5 miles on Route 114 and turn right at a small store onto Lake View Road. Soon on the right is an old hotel, built soon after the Civil War as a dormitory for loggers. A sawmill was also located here, giving good testimony to the fact that Norton was a logging town. Census records state that Norton had twelve inhabitants in 1860. At least one was a Civil War soldier.

Chauncey Brunell joined the 3rd Vermont on January 6, 1865, and served until the war ended. Thus he was involved in the Petersburg siege, the April 2 breakthrough, and the pursuit of Lee's army.

Brunell lived along the eastern edge of Norton, near Wallis Pond. Return to Route 114, continue east, and as Wallis Pond comes in sight on the left, you are in the area of his home, though most, if not all, of the pond is in the town of Canaan.

SOURCES
WITH THANKS TO JOHN COWAN AND CLIFF BIRON.

BLOOMFIELD

Approaching the village of Bloomfield from the south, along Route 102, one encounters a railroad underpass over which run the tracks of an old line known as the Grand Trunk. The Grand Trunk played a little-known role in a famous chapter of the Civil War.

On November 8 1861, the United States warship *San Jacinto* intercepted, in international waters, the British mail ship *Trent* and removed from it two Confederate diplomats, John Slidell and James Mason. The two were steaming for England and negotiations with its government, as the Confederates held fond hopes that the British might be persuaded to enter the war on their side. The British government reacted sharply to the incident, considering it something of an act of war, and began strengthening its limited forces in Canada. Abraham Lincoln quickly ordered Secretary of State William Seward to commence negotiations aimed at mollifying the Crown. In the end, Slidell and Mason were released, and tensions eased. The whole matter went down in history as the Trent Affair. According to historian Samuel

Elliott Morrison, "During the Trent crisis, Britain strengthened her Canadian garrison of 6,400 regulars by over 14,000 men. Many of these reinforcements were glad to avail themselves of Seward's tactful offer to be landed at Portland, Maine, instead of Halifax [Nova Scotia], and proceed to Quebec over the recently built Grand Trunk Railway. Thus, the Trent affair cleared the air in Canada, too."

Morrison was wrong, for thousands of British troops did not pass along the Grand Trunk to Canada. They landed on Canadian soil and proceeded overland to Montreal. But the Grand Trunk was a tool in the Trent negotiations. But it is believed, that some of their officers went by train to Montreal from Boston and made use of this rail route.

Go through the underpass and enter the little village of Bloomington, where Vermont Route 105 goes west. From here, look east, and slightly north to a frame house on the bluff. There lived Frank Roby, a private in the 9th Vermont. Go north 200 yards on Route 102 and on the left is an old schoolhouse. Attached to the rear is an older school, now the town office, in which Bloomfield held its 1860s town meetings. The town sent 34 men to war, of whom 7 were credited to other towns. Six men died of disease, and 4 were killed in battle. Among them were three 10th Vermont men. Private Alvin Martin died of wounds received at Mine Run, while Private Daniel Morse was killed at Cold Harbor on June 1, 1864, two days before his brother, Daniel, was shot dead there. It is believed that they all enlisted in the old school here.

SOURCES
BLOOMFIELD TOWN RECORDS.
WITH THANKS TO PAULETTE ROUTHIER.

··

BRIGHTON

In Brighton's Island Pond village where Routes 114 and 105 join, stands the 1904 railroad station and Brighton's Civil War memorial with the names of 110 men who served. The Civil War era station stood a bit east of the present building and at noon, August 12, 1865, four months after Appomattox, Ulysses Grant arrived. On a train trip from Portland to Quebec City, Grant, his wife Julia, his children, and some friends, were riding the Grand Truck. According to the *Newport Express,* as Grant stepped onto the platform "three rousing cheers were given the distinguished guest." Grant then walked to the eighty-room Island Pond House, which stood on the hill behind the old depot. A walkway spanned the tracks, as one does today, though the one Grant climbed stood well east of the present structure.

According to the *Express,* "A large arch was erected in front of the hotel covered with evergreen and festooned with U.S. flags, and showing in large letters 'Welcome the Hero.'" After Grant and his party attended a luncheon in the 300-seat dining room, "He was presented to our returned soldiers in a body each of whom he took by the hand and during his stay there seemed to be a general shaking of hands with every one." Grant was soon on his way north.

From the depot, go south on Cross Street, which is Route 105. In 0.3 mile,

Pleasant Street turns left. Three houses before the turn, on the right, stands a frame house with a double-deck porch, the postwar home of Lieutenant William Currier, Brighton's first man to enlist. Currier was one of twenty-four men from the town who joined Company D, 3rd Vermont.

Quickly turn left on Pleasant Street, then right into the second entrance of the Old Protestant Cemetery at the top of the hill. Here are the graves of John and Samantha Stevens, parents of three Civil War soldiers. Susannah Aldrich married John Stevens in 1840, and on his death in 1852, she was left with five children. When the war began, sons Orlando and Russell joined the 3rd's Company D. Orlando was soon dead of Rebel bullets at Lee's Mill, age twenty. Russell served until killed July 11, 1864, at Fort Stevens, near Washington. A third son, Calvin, who also joined Company D, served three years and came home an invalid. Orlando and Calvin lie by their parents, and a cenotaph honors Russell, who is buried in Washington.

Continue on Pleasant Street 1.3 miles to where a road branches left, leading to the Island Pond state park. The house on the right, at the turn, was built during the war by Samantha Stevens. Historian Abby Hemenway's Brighton chapter says of the enlistments of sons Orlando and Calvin: "Soon a recruiting officer made his appearance . . . Though hard to part with her main supports . . . she set about getting them ready and accompanied them on foot to the village at 12 o'clock at night through the untrodden snow, saw them sign their names; receive the loving kiss, bid them goodbye." Later, when Orlando was killed, Russell wrote his mother, "Brother Orlando was shot in the breast and died instantly, but while he lived he fought like a tiger; and thank God he died in a noble cause."

Night after night, throughout the war, widow Stevens walked into the village to join other Brighton women in making items for the soldiers. As you return to the village on Pleasant Street, you follow her footsteps. Return to the railway station, and across the street and to the east is a large frame building that houses the Brighton town offices. The top floor was long used by the local Erastus Buck Post of the GAR where Samantha Stevens was, for years, a welcome guest. The GAR gatherings were often presided over by Zophar Mansur, a native of the town of Morgan, who came to Brighton after the war and served as collector of customs at Island Pond. He was elected lieutenant governor of Vermont in 1894, after serving in the state senate. During the war, Mansur was a corporal in the 10th Vermont and was wounded at Third Winchester.

SOURCES
BRIGHTON TOWN RECORDS.
HISTORY OF THE TOWN OF BRIGHTON.
  BRIGHTON, VT: BRIGHTON HISTORICAL
  SOCIETY, UNDATED.
WITH THANKS TO CLIFF BIRON.

....

BRUNSWICK

From the junction of Route 102 and 105 at Bloomfield, go south 1.25 miles to the 1838 Brunswick School, which also served as a town hall. Voting here in 1860, Brunswick went for Lincoln over Douglas, 15 to 14. Town records list 21 persons eligible for duty in 1861. Brunswick sent 12 men to war.

In April 1864, $200 bounties were voted for three-year enlistments. In July, bounties of $100 were voted for a one-year enlistment, $200 for a two-year enlistment, and $300 for three years. Obviously having trouble finding men, the town, in February 1865, voted to pay an additional $400, added to the earlier amount, to any a man who would enlist.

Behind the old school, a trail leads to mineral springs along the Connecticut River where a resort once flourished here, with people drawn by the supposedly healing waters. Indeed, the Brunswick list of eligible men includes Edwin Bailey, the innkeeper. He procured a substitute and did not serve.

But brothers Franklin and Frederick Roby were soldiers. Franklin, a private in the Vermont Cavalry the last ten months of the war, was in on the breaking of Lee's Petersburg lines and the Appomattox Campaign. Frederick joined the 9th Vermont as a private and served the last eighteen months of the war, including the Overland Campaign and Petersburg siege. They both came safely home to the house that stands just north of the new town office, just across the street from the old school.

SOURCES
BRUNSWICK TOWN RECORDS.
WITH THANKS TO SHARON GRAHAM.

CANAAN

At this state's northeast corner, where Vermont meets New Hampshire and Canada, the village of Canaan centers on Fletcher Park. On the north side, in 2011, a Civil War monument was dedicated with the names of sixty-five Canaan men who served. On the park's south side is the old schoolhouse where town meetings were held during the Civil War. Town records state:

August 21, 1862: "Voted to raise 50 cents on the dollar on the list of polls and rateable property of inhabitants of Canaan on the present grand list to pay a bounty to the three-years men. Also voted to raise seven cents on the dollar on said grand list to pay each 9-months man the sum of $70, and each three-year man $100 when mustered into the United States service."

December 5, 1863: "Voted to raise not exceeding $1,200 to procure volunteers under the call of the President of the United States, it being the quota for Canaan. Voted that the selectmen of town procure 6 volunteers at a sum not exceeding $200 each volunteer."

Meeting on June 27, 1864, Canaan approved bounties of $500 and appointed two men, William Rich and Joseph Cooper, recruiters. Three months later, faced with a quota of six men under another call from Abraham Lincoln, Canaan approved bounties of $1,000 each for not more than six men.

On the park's west side is an 1840s house that is now the Alice M. Ward Memorial Library. Local legend holds that the house harbored fugitive slaves. More

certain is the fact that a Civil War veteran, Hiram Harvey, lived his last years in a small room added to the building's south side, which is now a library office. Harvey served the last ten months of the war in the Vermont Cavalry.

The Civil War experience of northern New Englanders was often affected by the closeness of Canada. That was true for the family of Osburn Gray, of the central New Hampshire town of Bristol. In 1863, Osborn joined a New Hampshire regiment and served until the war's end, suffering a wound. On his enlistment, his wife Mary Jane (Ackerman) Gray, headed north in a buckboard with her four sons and three daughters, bound for Canada. Her great-grandson George Edward Carr said in 2008, "Her husband had gone. She knew those boys would be drafted. So she came up here." Mary Jane first settled just across the Connecticut River from Canaan, believing that she had reached the safety of Canada. In 1863, the border was a line little heeded, as people moved freely back and forth across it. When Mrs. Gray discovered that she was still in the United States, she headed farther north, to Hereford, Quebec, just north of Canaan. When the war ended and her husband came back, Mary Jane took her kids back to Bristol, NH. But one son, Charles, stayed in Hereford, where he married and fathered eight children. Most of those children remained in and around Canaan, and there are many Grays in the area today. One child, Ellis, bought a house in Canaan about the time of the First World War. Go south from Fletcher Park, pass the athletic field on the left, and the fifth house beyond it, on the left, was Ellis Gray's home.

SOURCES
CANAAN TOWN RECORDS.
WITH THANKS TO JOAN COWAN AND VIRGINIA
AND GEORGE GRAY.

....

CONCORD

The Concord veterans' memorial on Route 2 in the center of Concord village honors all the town's veterans, including the 124 who served in the Civil War. Of them, 18 died, including 9 in Rebel prisons.

As the war began, a Concord resident writing for the *Caledonian Record* reported on April 21, 1861, that "soldiers of Essex County have been drilling in our village for two weeks." That happened along Concord's main street, Route 2. The paper said that the ladies of Concord presented each soldier with "a Havelock cap and a thousand and one of the necessary articles of convenience." Most of the men served in the 3rd Vermont, which organized at Camp Baxter in St. Johnsbury. According to the *Caledonian,* when the time of departure came, "The company marched from the hall, preceded by the ladies, for Camp Baxter."

That farewell event took place in Concord's town house, which stood on the location of the present town hall, north along Route 2 from the memorial. There, Concord twice voted for Lincoln, 214 to 40 over Douglas in 1860 and 188 to 45 over McClellan in 1864. Bounty payments that reached $500 were voted there, including one $400 payment that apparently resulted in the signing of a man recruited in the southern states and credited to the town.

Beside the plaza where the memorial stands is a large 1852 building. Now housing town offices, it was once a store, owned after the war by Oliver Cutting, who served in the 11th Vermont as a private and was wounded at Cedar Creek.

Just east of the memorial go left on Shadow Lake Road, and in 2 miles, Mountain Top Farm Road goes right. In the only house on the road lived Oliver Cutting. His sister Lydia married Curtis Stacy in 1860, and thirteen months later, he left her and a baby daughter at home to join the Vermont Cavalry. She apparently spent much time while he was gone at this house. Stacy became an aide to cavalry commander Alfred Torbert. He came home with his health broken and never fully recovered. Lydia had ten brothers and brothers-in-law in the Civil War. All but two came home.

Return to Concord village, go east 8 miles on Route 2, and turn right on Oregon Road. In 3 miles, on entering East Concord, the Methodist Church is on the left. An account in the *Bennington Banner* of April 25, 1861, reported on an event here, with the building "filled to overflowing," even though "the going was bad." It said, "Amid speeches and cheering could be seen the fire of '76 burning in the eyes of the younger portion . . . today a rifle company is being formed." The *Banner* also said that a liberty pole 121 feet tall was soon to be raised here. Likely the men who drilled here joined the 3rd Vermont.

SOURCES

CONCORD BICENTENNIAL COMMITTEE. *TOWN OF CONCORD, VERMONT, THEN AND NOW, 1781–1971*. ST. JOHNSBURY, VT: TROLL PRESS, 1976.

CONCORD TOWN RECORDS.

BENNINGTON BANNER, 1861. VERMONT STATE LIBRARY.

WITH THANKS TO LORRAINE RANEY.

....

EAST HAVEN

The 1870s East Haven Chapel is 5 miles north of East Burke, on Route 114. Two houses south of it is a frame house that once was the home of D. C. Hudson, East Haven town clerk. Hudson contributed information on his town to Abby Hemenway's *Gazetteer* and listed fifty men who served. He wrote, "There was not any bounty paid to a man from East Haven. We furnished ten men for other towns." Despite the lack of bounty payments, it appears that East Haven met its draft quotas.

Just north of the chapel is the East Haven Cemetery, where several men who served from the town lie. No stone bears any inscription referencing the Civil War, including two cenotaphs to men who died and are buried far from home. Henry Hudson, fifty-two when he enlisted at Lyndon as a private in the 11th Vermont, died of sickness as the Overland Campaign began and is buried in Arlington National Cemetery. Horace Ross, an 11th Vermont private who enlisted in Newark, was thirty-nine when captured at Weldon Railroad. He died three months later, of diarrhea, in Andersonville, where he is buried.

Go south 1.25 miles on Route 114, and go right on Walters Farm Road. At the corner is an old frame house, once the home of William Smith, who hired a substitute and did not serve. Walters Farm Road ascends very steeply 0.8 mile to a hilltop farmhouse and cluster of barns with a sweeping mountain view. From here, George Walter enlisted at twenty-one in Burke as a private in the 10th Vermont. He was a corporal two years later when wounded at Cedar Creek. He came home and lived only until 1891.

Return to Route 114 and cross it onto School Street. Soon, on the right, is a former schoolhouse, much altered, where Civil War–era town meetings took place. In 1864, Abraham Lincoln was favored over McClellan here, 28 to 3.

Continue to the end of School Street and go left on Mountain Road. In just over 0.5 mile, Olson Road goes right to a house and barn by a small pond. Once the Hosford farm, from here Eli Hosford joined the 11th Vermont as a private in November 1863. He died at twenty-three at Cold Harbor, probably felled by a sharpshooter. John Hosford enlisted in the 4th Vermont as a private at twenty in August 1863 and served until wounded at the Wilderness. He lost a limb but came home and lived forty more years. Sister Nancy Hosford was a nurse during the war, though details of her service are not known.

Continue up Mountain Road 0.75 mile and go left on Moultrop Road. This narrow and rough road leads 1 mile to a farmhouse in a large clearing. From here, Charles Moultrop enlisted, joining the

15th Vermont and making the march to Gettysburg.

SOURCES

EAST HAVEN TOWN RECORDS.

LUND, RUTH. NOTES ON EAST HAVEN HISTORY, COMPILED IN 1976. EAST HAVEN TOWN OFFICE.

WITH THANKS TO FRANKLIN HIGGINS, TOWN CLERK, AND MARVIN OLSON.

FERDINAND

About halfway between Island Pond and Bloomfield, along the Nulhegan River, Route 105 crosses the Grand Trunk Railroad at Wenlock Station. Here, in the town of Ferdinand, at the time of the Civil War, several sawmills operated, and trains stopped to pick up lumber. Census records put Ferdinand's 1860 population at thirty-four, certainly mostly loggers. One Civil War soldier came from Ferdinand. Joseph Johnson, a native of Canada, went from here to enlist as a private in the 3rd Vermont at Charleston in September 1862. He served until wounded in Upton's attack at Spotsylvania on May 10, 1864. Where Johnson lived isn't known but certainly he was most familiar with Wenlock Station. He was likely a logger.

SOURCE

WITH THANKS TO CLIFF BIRON.

GRANBY

The mountain town of Granby can be reached from Route 2 at North Concord by going north past Victory on the Victory Road, or west from Guildhall on the Granby Road. An 1859 map of the town shows twenty-one households, and from them fifteen men went to war, the majority enlisting for three years in the 8th Vermont. Among them were brothers Ethan and Pascal Shores, Ethan at twenty and Pascal at eighteen. Both survived service in Louisiana and Mississippi, which included the siege of Port Hudson and the fight at Bayou Des Allemand, where Ethan was wounded four times. Then came the Shenandoah Valley campaign. In the early morning stand of Stephen Thomas's small brigade at Cedar Creek, a fierce fight developed around the 8th Vermont's flag. When the color bearer was shot, Sergeant Ethan Shores seized the flag and protected it, bayoneting one man and shooting another. Pascal was shot through a lung, and Ethan knelt and spoke with him before the 8th was forced to withdraw. Later in the day, after the counterattack led by Philip Sheridan, Ethan found his brother's lifeless body on the field.

Also in that early morning fight was Captain George Ford, commander of the 8th's Company K, in which the Granby men served. According to the regimental history, "Capt. Ford was shot through both legs by bullets coming from opposite directions, and fell flat on his face, but refused to surrender, struggled to his feet, and escaped in the excitement." Ford had also been wounded a month earlier at Winchester.

Granby's post office, town hall, and 1845 church are located along the north side of the Granby Road. Go east from the church, and the first house on the north side of the road was the Ford home. From it, Captain Ford went to war, as did his brother Alonzo, a corporal in the company George commanded. Alonzo survived Confederate captivity after he was seized at Bayou Des Almandes in Louisiana but died in September 1863 of disease. He is buried in New Orleans.

Continue past the Ford house and quickly turn left on a narrow road lined with stone walls. Walk 300 yards down this road to the Shores Cemetery. There lies Ethan Shores, who came home in 1865 and lived until 1901. His brother Pascal is buried in the national cemetery at Winchester, Virginia.

Return along the Granby Road to the little village, and go past it 0.3 mile to Shores Road, on the right. The house that Ethan Shores built on returning from the war stands at the end of the road, 1 mile distant. Return to Granby Road, and in 2.25 miles is a tiny cemetery set on a knoll. From their home near here, which no longer stands, Richard and Joanna Boyce saw two sons go to war. Each has a stone in the cemetery. Private J. Wesley Boyce was another member of the 8th Vermont's Company K, but he died at age eighteen at Brattleboro, before the regiment left for war. Private James Boyce enlisted in the 10th Vermont in August 1862 and died a month later, of disease, at twenty-five.

SOURCES

CARPENTER, GEORGE N. *HISTORY OF THE EIGHTH VERMONT REGIMENT, VERMONT VOLUNTEERS: 1861–1865*. BOSTON: PRESS OF DELAND & BARTA, 1886.
THROUGH THE WOODS, DOWN THE RIVER, OVER THE HILL: GRANBY, VT. GRANBY, VT:
GRANBY VERMONT HISTORICAL GROUP, 1990.

WITH THANKS TO RUTH NOBLE AND JOHN REYNOLDS.

GUILDHALL

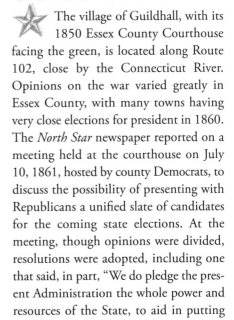

The village of Guildhall, with its 1850 Essex County Courthouse facing the green, is located along Route 102, close by the Connecticut River. Opinions on the war varied greatly in Essex County, with many towns having very close elections for president in 1860. The *North Star* newspaper reported on a meeting held at the courthouse on July 10, 1861, hosted by county Democrats, to discuss the possibility of presenting with Republicans a unified slate of candidates for the coming state elections. At the meeting, though opinions were divided, resolutions were adopted, including one that said, in part, "We do pledge the present Administration the whole power and resources of the State, to aid in putting down rebellion by force of arms, and in bringing its wicked leaders to justice."

A town history published in 1886 says of Guildhall during the war: "One thing is certain, that the inhabitants of Guildhall were unanimous in supporting the Government in its attempts to put down the Rebellion. Party spirit was set aside and everyone was a Union man, and this fact is conclusively shown from the fact that in an election in September 1862 every vote was cast for Gov. Holbrook, the War, or Union candidate for Governor, and there was no difference of opinion relating to the duty of every one to sustain the government at any time during the continuance of the war, although some were not remarkably well pleased when the Emancipation Proclamation was issued, having never had any great love for the abolitionists . . . But at no time was there any opposition to the Government shown, and all the calls for men were promptly filled."

The town of Guildhall's "guild hall," at the southeast corner of the town common, contains a Roll of Honor, with the names of some of the 52 men from the town who served in the Civil War. Among then are 11 who died in the service.

From Guildhall, go south 1.1 miles of Route 102 to a large frame house and barn on the right. John Beaton, twenty-one, left here to join the Vermont Cavalry as a private in the fall of 1861. He died a year later of disease.

Just south of the Beaton home, North Road turns right. In the house at the corner, Charles Barrett lived, a private in the 12th Vermont who marched to Gettysburg.

Continue south on 102, and soon go right on Granby Road. In 0.75 mile, take Maplewood Farm Road to where it ends by an old cape. It is believed that from here Ashbell Meacham joined the Vermont Cavalry in September 1861. He was killed the following May 25 in a skirmish with Turner Ashby's cavalry near Middletown, Virginia.

Return to Route 102, continue south 4 miles, then go right on Fellows Road. In 2 miles, go right at a Y, and in 1.5 miles, pass a clearing on the right. Just beyond it is the stone foundation of the old District Three School. During the Civil War, this

was the District Four School, where many Guildhall town meetings took place.

Town records indicate that when the first call came from Washington for three-year men, some local men advanced their own private money to encourage enlistments. Indeed, at March 1863 town meeting, held here, selectmen and the town moderator were appointed a board to "settle and adjust the claims of the subscribers to the subscription for the three years men." Guildhall voted bounties that peaked at $300 per man. Out of a wartime population of some 550 people, 52 men served.

SOURCES
BENTON, EVERETT C. *HISTORY OF GUILDHALL, VERMONT*. WAVERLY, MA: PRIVATELY PRINTED, 1886.
GUILDHALL TOWN RECORDS.
ROGERS, PATRICIA. *HISTORY OF GUILDHALL, VERMONT*. LANCASTER, NH: NORTH COUNTRY PUBLISHING, 1975.
WITH THANKS TO CAROL WENMARK AND NELLIE NOBLE.

LEMINGTON

The Lemington town office and the old District One School are side by side along Route 102, facing the nearby Connecticut River. From this town with a wartime population of 200, 14 men enlisted in New Hampshire and 14 in Vermont.

Civil War–era town meetings were held in the school, and though town records are incomplete, it is known that $100 bounties were approved in 1862. Also, selectman John Cook was paid one dollar a day for "drafting soldiers."

The first house south of the old school

on Route 102 was the home of Mills Blodgett, town clerk. Well into his forties when the war began, he hired a substitute. The next house south, with a cemetery across the road, was once the O'Neil family home. In the summer of 1863, teenager John O'Neil went from here to enlist in New Hampshire. But he was soon home before being mustered into any regiment, sick with the measles. He died in this house, and his body was hastily buried in the cemetery across the road to keep other family members from becoming sick. It is believed that his funeral was held in the home. John's headstone says "rest in peace" and notes that he died at "17 years 10 months and 15 days."

Go back north on Route 102, pass the town office, and in 1.5 miles, the old cape on the left was the Holbrook home. Manlius Holbrook grew up here and at seventeen, in November 1861, joined Company E, 2nd Vermont Sharpshooters. Holbrook was wounded in the hip and thigh at Antietam's Miller Cornfield. He came home and recovered; the following May, he was back at the front just in time to fight at Chancellorsville. Two months later, he was wounded at Gettysburg. Once again he recovered, and in December 1863, he reenlisted and served until the war ended, becoming a sergeant. A nephew recalled that Manlius, in later years, was fond of showing off "the very bullet that had hit him."

A hired man on the Holbrook farm, John Watson, served four years in the 4th Vermont. He came home and lived in a small house he built on a piece of land the Holbrooks gave him.

Continue north 2 miles on Route 102 and cross the Connecticut, entering Colebrook, New Hampshire, on Bridge Street. The town Civil War monument is soon on the left. Colebrook was the trading place for Lemington people, and Lemington men came here to enlist. After the war, many Lemington veterans joined the local GAR post, and its hall survives on Pleasant Street, now the American Legion.

SOURCES
DALEY, MARION M. *HISTORY OF LEMINGTON, VERMONT*. COLEBROOK, NH: M/S PRINTING & ADVERTISING, 1976.
ELLINGWOOD, MYRA. "A PIECE OF TOWN HISTORY." LEMINGTON TOWN REPORT, 2009.
WITH THANKS TO MYRA ELLINGWOOD.

LEWIS

Along Route 105, just east of Wenlock Station in Ferdinand, is the headquarters of the Silvio Conte Federal Wildlife Refuge. To reach the town of Lewis, to the north, which presently has no year-round inhabitants, stop at refuge headquarters and obtain a map. By carefully following directions on a dirt road nearby, in 14 miles of winding road, remote Lewis Pond in the town of Lewis may be reached. Census records say that Lewis had no population in 1860 and no Civil War soldiers can be associated with the unorganized town. But many veterans were loggers and would have worked the deep Lewis woods.

SOURCE
THANKS TO GINA VIGNEAULT, UNORGANIZED TOWNS OFFICE, LUNENBERG.

LUNENBURG

In the Lunenburg park, a soldier facing due south stands atop Lunenburg's Civil War memorial, erected in 1904 by the Howard Chapter of the GAR. It bears the names of seventy-four men who served. Beside it is a Civil War cannon, installed by the post's Women's Relief Corps (WRC). On the north side of the park is the 1849 Lunenburg town hall. Here, bounties were voted that reached $800 in September 1864, forcing the town to adopt a tax of $2 on each grand list dollar. In November 1864, Lunenburg went for Lincoln over McClellan, 146 to 61.

The Howard Post, made up of men from Lunenburg and East Concord, was founded in 1883, and in 1886, the veterans received permission from the town fathers to install a second floor on the town hall to serve as a GAR hall, where the Howard Chapter of the WRC also met.

Lunenburg lies along Route 2, and a pair of tall stout poles stand on either side of the highway, one in the park. Between them, on special occasions, a giant American flag is suspended, as was an earlier flag from the predecessor posts in Civil War days.

The Balch Memorial Library is just east of the park. Given to the town by Alden Balch, who served as a private in the 15th Vermont, the library has a memorial book compiled by GAR members, which profiles their Civil War service.

Just west of the park on Route 2, the second house on the north side was the home of Albert Brown, three years a private in the 11th Vermont. His brother,

Alonzo Brown, 5th Vermont, badly wounded at Cedar Creek, died here a year later of his wounds.

From the park, go north on Bobbin Mill Road, and in 1 mile, go left on Colby Road. In 0.2 mile, Donning Road goes left and at the end is the Ball Farm. Alden and Daniel Ball were privates in the 15th Vermont's Company E, in which many local men served. Levi Ball, a 4th Vermont private, died of sickness four months after he enlisted in September 1862.

Return to Colby Road, go left, and in 2 miles, take Cole Hill Road. Descend a steep hill for 0.3 mile, and in the farmhouse on the left, Charles Cole lived, a private in the 15th's Company E. At the end of Cole Hill Road, go right on Guildhall Hill Road and soon pass Pierce School, on the left. The barn and silos on the left just beyond it are part of the farm from which Ezra and Artemis Pierce went to war. Ezra, a corporal in the 8th Vermont, was shot at Boutte Station, Louisiana, in a Rebel ambush, but survived. Artemis was a private in the 15th's Company E.

Just past the Pierce place, go straight at the corners and soon return to the Lunenburg park. Go west 0.6 mile on Route 2 and turn left on Baptist Hill Road. In 0.5 mile, Wentworth Road goes right, and at the corner is the home of George Washington Hill, a private in the 4th Vermont, killed May 5, 1864, at the Wilderness.

Continue on Baptist Hill Road 1.25 miles to the Baptist Hill Cemetery. Here in an unmarked grave lies Ida (Snow) Thomas, who lived on a nearby farm. Though Ida hated to be alone, her last two children remaining at home, Saba and Zeruah, both went to Lowell, Massachusetts, when the war began to work in the woolen mills that thrived on war production. Saba came home with tuberculosis in 1865, and soon thereafter her sister returned to take care of her. Saba soon died, but Zeruah lived a long life.

Baptist Hill road leads to the village of Gilman, on the Connecticut River. On reaching Commercial Avenue, go right, and in 1.5 miles, after passing through the village, set back on the right is a large frame house with outbuildings. From here, Frank and Ira Grant enlisted as privates in the 11th Vermont in 1862. Frank was captured at Weldon Railroad and survived Andersonville. Ira, a musician, was also a stretcher bearer.

Return through Gilman, pass Baptist Hill Road, and in 2 miles come to a small turnoff on the left, beside a small wooden building, all that remains of the Hartshorn farm. Elden Hartshorn went from here to attend the U.S. Military Academy. A lieutenant in Company E, 15th Vermont, he also was a captain in the 17th Vermont.

In just under 1 mile, go left on South Lunenberg Road and follow it back to the park.

SOURCES
LUNENBURG CIVIL WAR MEMORIAL BOOK.
BALCH MEMORIAL LIBRARY, LUNENBURG.
LUNENBURG TOWN RECORDS.
WITH THANKS TO CAROL WENMARK.

MAIDSTONE

Mount Byron in Maidstone was a favorite picnic spot long before the Civil War. When the fighting began, local people visiting its summit saw something new. The description of Maidstone in Abby Hemenway's *Gazetteer*, written during the Civil War, said: "From Mount Byron in Maidstone, the bows of the Connecticut river, five of them which are to be seen— spell the word Union, each bow forming a letter sufficiently distinct for recognition. Looking over into New Hampshire and also into Canada for 40 or 50 miles, the landscape is exceedingly beautiful." For the Union, Maidstone sent twenty-two men to war, most serving in the 3rd Vermont's Company I. At least seven died.

From the Guildhall green, go north 1.5 miles on Route 102, and the Maidstone town office is on the right. One-half mile beyond, on the right, is one of Maidstone's oldest houses, set back from the road along a tree-lined driveway. From here, John Rich enlisted in the 3rd's Vermont's Company I as a private in June 1861. He served until killed by a Confederate bullet at Charles Town on August 21, 1863. The thirty-one-year-old is buried in the national cemetery at Winchester, Virginia.

Continue north on 102, and as you drive, look east at the Connecticut River and the New Hampshire mountains. The bends of the river, which seemed during the Civil War to spell *union,* are in this area. The Mount Byron mentioned in Hemenway is believed to be the elevation known now as Bear Hill. It rises west of the road, in this area, now apparently all wooded and affording little or no view.

Go 1.8 miles beyond the Rich house and look for a very old and small frame building on the left, which in 2010 seemed near collapse. This, or a building on its site, is believed to have been the District One School where most Maidstone town meetings took place during the war. At a March meeting in 1863, voters approved $675 for bounties, apparently for nine soldiers at $75 apiece. In September 1864, after twice adjourning meetings without taking action on increased bounties, payments of $500 were okayed.

In 1860, Maidstone voted for Abraham Lincoln over Stephen Douglas, 19 to 11. Four years later, Lincoln carried the town over George McClellan, 22 to 10.

SOURCES
Maidstone town records.
With thanks to Susie Irwin.

NORTON

The Norton town office is just east of Norton village and just south of the Canadian border, by Route 114. Census records show Norton with an 1860 population of thirty, though that year nobody attended school in town. The first town meeting wasn't held in Norton until 1885.

Though no Civil War soldiers can be credited to Norton, at least two veterans made their home here after the war. One was William Bishop, a Syracuse, New York, native, who came to Norton in 1880. At age twenty-six, Bishop joined the 127th Illinois Cavalry. He participated in the siege of Vicksburg and General Sherman's March to the Sea. Bishop died in Norton in July 1889, and his funeral was held in nearby Stanhope, Quebec, where he is buried. A newspaper account said that "members of the GAR bore their comrade to the grave."

From the Norton town office, go north and quickly turn left on Nelson Road. Pass a customs house, go through an underpass, cross a bridge, bear left on Bauman Road, and the first house was Bishop's last home.

Return to the town office and go south 4.5 miles on Route 114, and on the right is a white frame house with shed behind. Also behind the house is the old Grand Trunk Railroad. This area was once part of the Davis farm, and another house once stood on the far side of the tracks. Alonzo Davis lived here for a time after the war. He served from October 1862 until the war ended as a private in the Vermont Cavalry. He, like Bishop, is buried across the line in Quebec.

SOURCES
Andrews, Lydia C. *Three Towns: Norton & Averill, Vermont, Stanhope, Quebec; A History of the Northeast Kingdom.* Littleton, NH: Sherwin Dodge Printers, 1986.
With thanks to Gina Vigneault, town clerk, and Cliff Biron.

VICTORY

Go north at North Concord from Route 2 onto the Victory Road, following the Moose River, and in 2.5 miles cross the town line from Concord to Victory. Just north of the line, the woods open to broad old fields. On the left is an old house that Charles Story built after he returned from the Civil War. A private in the 2nd Vermont, Story served eighteen months until discharged for disability in the spring of 1864. He soon reenlisted in the 3rd Artillery Battery, serving until war's end. Look beyond his house and see an older farmhouse, one that his father built during the war.

Pass another old house on the right, and 0.25 mile north of it, on the right, see foundations, which are all that remain of the Kneeland family home and store. At the time of the Civil War, town meetings were held here by the few inhabitants of this remote town. Reverend J. Evans wrote for Abby Hemenway on the beginnings of the Methodist Church in Victory, noting that "the dwelling house of Willard A. Kneeland" was "the usual place of holding meetings at the river." According to Evans, a church meeting took place here in August 1862, at which he told parishoners, "We cannot speak of great prosperity at this time . . . Some of our brethren have gone to war, and some of our brethren's sons have gone, and some have fallen there in hospital, and a general feeling of sadness is manifest in all our borders."

Continue north, and in 2 miles reach Damon's Crossing, where a small logging community once existed. Albert Shaw went from here to serve but was discharged for illness before being assigned to a regiment. Continue north 3 miles, and just beyond a sizeable bridge, note an old road on the right blocked by a gate. Down this road the Lee family lived and operated a sawmill. Private Ira Lee served the war's last nine months in the 11th Vermont, fighting in the Shenandoah Valley and at Petersburg.

Reverend Evans noted that twenty-two Victory men served and summed up Victory's war experience: "Of this number, six have died from sickness, and have thus been called to lay all, even life itself, upon the altar of our country, and thus become a portion of that costly oblation which she has so willingly offered. They died, not on the field of battle made gory by the blood of thousands of thousands of their fallen comrades—not amid the roar of thundering cannon as their awful death tones hushed, as it were, for a moment, the shrieks and groans of the dying, only to add new horror to the scene—not amid the accumulations of contending armies, as they rush to victory and glory, but they are none the less honored. They have done what they could to perpetuate those liberties and blessings for which our fathers bled and died. They have done what they could to defend our homes, our friends, our sacred altars, and our government— the best upon which the sun ever shone—from tyranny and blood-stained oppression; from a power whose poisonous fangs were seeking to sever the very life-strings of its existence; and their graves are in southern climes—their precise locations doubtless soon to be lost by time's onward march; yet their memories will long be fondly cherished at home."

One Victory soldier, Corporal Augustus Jones, 3rd Vermont, died of wounds received in Upton's Charge at Spotsylvania.

SOURCE
With thanks to George Stanley.

St. Albans's Taylor Park, where Confederate raiders kept the locals under close watch while they robbed the bank.

chapter seven

Franklin County

Many buildings that still stand in St. Albans witnessed the October 19, 1864, Confederate raid. To the north, in Sheldon, from the front yard of a house that survives, the raiders stole a horse, the property of a Vermonter recovering from a wound suffered at the Wilderness. They didn't know the man's uncle presided at a marriage ceremony, in Virginia, for Robert E. Lee and Mary Custis. Not far south of St. Albans, in Georgia, a granite monument marks the birthplace of George Stannard, who led the 2nd Vermont Brigade at Gettysburg. Over in the upland town of Bakersfield, the house yet stands where one of Stannard's able company commanders died. Captain Merritt Williams, who led the 13th Vermont's Company G, was horribly wounded at Gettysburg. He came home to his wife and died in her family home, after two weeks of suffering. In Swanton, Ralph Sturtevant's house faces the village green. There he wrote his remarkable history of the 13th Vermont.

BAKERSFIELD

Routes 108 and 38 meet in the high farmland of Franklin County, in the village of Bakersfield. The town of Bakersfield in 1860 gave Lincoln 140 votes for president, Breckenridge 29, and Vermonter Douglas just 7. The town backed that up by sending 135 men to war.

In the village, Company G, 13th Vermont, known as the Bakersfield Company, assembled. The men boarded in village homes, many of which remain. They marched about the village time and again, under the command of Captain Marvin White, an Enosburg man. When White died of illness in mid-December 1862, command went to Lieutenant Merritt

Williams, of Bakersfield. Promoted, Williams led the company at Gettysburg and, during the battle's second day, suffered a severe wound in the groin, from a shell fragment. His battered body was brought to Bakersfield and the home of his in-laws, the Hookers, where wife, Jesse, family, and friends tried to nurse him back to health. A comrade, Corporal Joseph Hitchcock, also wounded at Gettysburg on the second day, recalled of his friend, "Everything possible was done by devoted friends for his comfort and recovery; and for some time he was very hopeful. A fatal result was doubtless inevitable. After eleven weeks of suffering, patiently and heroically endured, death brought relief. He viewed death calmly and said he was ready to go, in hope of Christian immortality. He gave minute instructions for his funeral, requesting that Company G might be there, and that Rev. E. A. Titus preach the sermon. It was held at the Congregational Church in Bakersfield, attended by a large gathering of citizens and soldiers, with impressive services, and many demonstrations of love and mourning." The casket was taken across the road to Maple Grove Cemetery, where Williams and many other Civil War veterans lie.

The Congregational Church remains, facing the park and cemetery. Beside it is the Bakersfield Historical Society, located in an 1840 building that was once the South Academy.

Take Route 108 south, pass Egypt Road, and the second house beyond it, on the left, above the road, is believed to be Merritt Williams's home. One half mile beyond, on the right, is an old tavern,

once a store part owned by the Hooker family. Their home is the first house past it on the left, above the road. Captain Williams died there.

Return toward Bakersfield village and go right on Egypt Road 0.2 mile to a large frame house above the road, on the right. Corporal Hitchcock, who described Williams's funeral, lived here. On July 2, as the 13th Vermont moved onto Cemetery Ridge, Hitchcock was shot in the thigh. He was treated on the field by regimental surgeon John Crandall (see Berlin).

Continue on Egypt Road to the intersection of Lawyer Road and a brick farmhouse on the right, home of Private George Scott of the Bakersfield Company. On the second day at Gettysburg, when part of the 13th Vermont recaptured a Union battery, Scott was the first man to reach the guns. After the war, he gave many lectures on Gettysburg and became the first Civil War enlisted man invited to address the Vermont Historical Society. He said, "Thank God our brave boys did not suffer or die in vain. Gettysburg avenged Waterloo, America gained what Europe lost. Imperial despotism triumphed at Waterloo; Democratic liberty at Gettysburg . . . Waterloo riveted yet tighter the chains of the European peasantry; Gettysburg broke the chains from 4,000,000 slaves."

Return to Bakersfield village, go north on Route 108, and the village store is across from the park. After the war, it was owned by William Narramore, a private in Company F, 13th Vermont, who survived a brief captivity after Gettysburg, then was a sergeant in the 17th Vermont. During that latter service, a family memoir indicates he may have been a Union spy. A successful local businessman, he owned the first car in Bakersfield.

Continue 1.5 miles on Route 108 and go right on Whitney Road. In 1.75 miles, approaching an unused railway bed, look to the field on the right for a foundation. From the farm that once was here, John McMahon joined the 13th Vermont's Company G. He fought at Gettysburg, helping recapture cannon and defeat Pickett's Charge. He wrote in 1905, "I have in my room the belt for the world's champion collar and elbow wrestler, but I can do no wrestling now; the malaria of the Occoquan has settled in my bones and I am troubled by rheumatism."

SOURCES
BAKERSFIELD TOWN RECORDS.
PELADEAU, MARIUS B., ED. *BURNISHED ROWS OF STEEL: VERMONT'S ROLE IN THE BATTLE OF GETTYSBURG, JULY 1–3, 1863.* NEWPORT, VT: VERMONT CIVIL WAR ENTERPRISES, 2002.
WITH THANKS TO NANCY HUNT.

....

BERKSHIRE

From Enosburg Falls, go north on Route 108 to West Berkshire, as the Pinnacle, a summit in Quebec, rises ever larger to the north. On entering the village, where the road goes sharp left stands the 1835 Phoenix House. A photograph in the Berkshire history shows a full company of Civil War soldiers assembled before the flag-decorated hotel, with many spectators on its porches. Could this be Company G of the 13th Vermont, known as the Bakersfield Company, home from Gettysburg? Several Berkshire men served in Company G.

Just past the hotel, turn right on Cross Street to the old redbrick Methodist/Episcopal Church. Here on June 11, 1863, a funeral for Orloff Whitney (see Franklin) took place with Reverend E. A. Titus preaching from Ecclesiastes: "For a man also knoweth not his time."

A funeral was held here July 19, 1863, for Private Hanson Town, killed in a cavalry fight at Ashby's Gap, Virginia, on June 21. Town, a Fletcher native, was serving in the 8th Illinois Cavalry. On May 25, 1865, Titus presided at rites for Charles Ellsworth, a Vermont cavalryman from Bakersfield who late in the war had joined the infantry, enlisting in the 17th Vermont. Mortally wounded at the April 2, 1865, Petersburg Breakthrough, and a Rebel prisoner for a time, he was back within Union lines when he died a two weeks later. This time Titus's words were from Isaiah, "And the ransomed of the Lord shall return, and come to Zion with songs and everlasting joy upon their heads."

A funeral for Abraham Lincoln took place here on June 1, 1865, a day of fasting proclaimed by Governor John Gregory Smith. Reverend Titus chose his text from Psalms, "Surely the wrath of man shall praise thee: the remainder of wrath shalt thou restrain." Longtime members of the West Berkshire Church were Elias and Sarah Olmstead Babcock and their son Orville.

Return to the Phoenix Hotel and go south on Route 118. Soon pass a schoolhouse on the right, by Mineral Brook Road, and the next house along 118, with maples in front, was the Babcock home. Orville Babcock grew up here and went to

West Point, graduating in 1861. Trained as an engineer, early in the war, he worked on the Washington defenses. Babcock served in the Peninsula Campaign as a member of Major General William Franklin's staff. Later transferred west, he saw action at Vicksburg with the IX Corps. Rising to lieutenant colonel, he became an aide to Ulysses Grant. He then worked as a War Department observer of Major General Philip Sheridan's operations in the Shenandoah Valley, sending reports to Edwin Stanton, secretary of war. Babcock served in the Overland Campaign as a member of Ulysses Grant's staff. When Lee surrendered to Grant at Appomattox Courthouse on May 9, 1865, Babcock was in the surrender room. He soon received a brigadier general's commission. After the war, he became private secretary to Grant.

Continue on Route 118 to a four-way intersection, and go left on Richford Road 2.1 miles to a frame farmhouse on the right. Horace Stutson lived here as a teenager, before joining the Vermont Cavalry and serving three years. Lafayette Stanhope and his wife, Lucinda, bought the farm early in the war. Lafayette and son Horace both joined the Vermont Cavalry, leaving Lucinda to run the farm. Both men came home safely, though Lafayette was captured soon after Gettysburg.

Return to Route 118 and go straight through the intersection to Berkshire Center, pass the town office on the left, and just beyond, on the right, is an old schoolhouse. It stands on the site of an earlier school building, in which Berkshire town meetings were once held. Here in 1860,

Berkshire voted 117 to 21 for Lincoln over Douglas. Four years later, the vote was Lincoln 117, McClellan 21. In February, the town approved its highest bounties, $500. Lewis Cass Aldrich's history of Franklin and Grand Isle counties says of Berkshire: "The town is credited with having furnished a total of 151 men, or nearly nine per cent of its entire population. Of this aggregate 136 actually entered the service, while the records show that but four were drafted. Four men from the town were killed in action, twenty died of wounds and disease, and sixteen others were discharged for wounds or disability."

Pass the school and go left on Reservoir Road to the Berkshire Cemetery, with a gravestone for Hanson Burleson, a private in Company G, 13th Vermont, who fought at Gettysburg. A Berkshire lad who served in the Bakersfield Company, company historian George Scott (see Bakersfield) wrote of him: "Once a year on memorial day his surviving comrades, neighbors, friends and citizens here repair and on his lowly grave scatter the early flowers of spring and raise above his resting place the Stars and Stripes, the flag of his country that he followed on the march and into battle."

Return to Route 118, go east, pass Mineral Book Road on the right, and the first house beyond it was once the King home. Nelson King joined the 5th Vermont in December 1863 and was wounded at the Wilderness and Cold Harbor. Discharged in September 1864, a question arose about him having deserted. But he fought determinedly against any such accusations and for a pension. By a special act of Congress passed in 1933, just before King died, his pension was approved with back pay. King's sister Clara Belle was the wife of Gilbert Lucier (see Jay), the last surviving Vermont Civil War veteran.

Pass the King house 1 mile to where Longe Road goes right. On a farm down this road, which no longer exists, W. R. Hogaboom operated a livestock dealership. His sons, Horatio, twenty-two, and Orrin, twenty-eight, joined the 3rd Vermont in the fall of 1862. Horatio was killed in the June 3, 1864, assault at Cold Harbor. Orrin was shot at the Wilderness and came home to die six weeks later. Continue on Route 118, and you are passing through the fields of the big Hogaboom farm, where the two sons once worked and played.

On entering East Berkshire, where Route 118 meets Route 105, the Catholic Church is on the left. Once an Episcopal church stood here. In 1862, Reverend Ezra Jones became its minister, after having been forced to leave a pulpit in Sumter, South Carolina, due to his Union principles.

The large frame house facing the intersection on the south side of Route 105 was once the Rublee home. Amherst Rublee was a private in the Vermont Cavalry for a year before coming home wounded. He later operated a store with his father in East Berkshire.

Go left on Route 105, quickly go right across the Mississquoi Bridge on Route 118, and soon, on the left, is the 1824 Congregational Church, now the Berkshire Historical Society. Phineas Bailey was once its pastor, and he had a daughter, Cyrena Ann, who, in 1850, married a local man, Amherst Stone, who had recently become a lawyer. The young couple moved to Georgia, settling in Atlanta, where they owned six slaves. Soon, Amherst's brother, Mitchell, also moved to Atlanta and became a respected businessman. Charles also joined a local militia company, which was activated and became part of the Confederate forces when the war began. Amherst and Cyrena made regular visits back home, the last coming in 1861. On the train from East Berkshire to St. Albans, starting back to Georgia, Mitchell made some loud remarks praising the Confederate victory at Bull Run. His words were reported to the authorities, and he ended up in military prisons at New York and Boston Harbor for a time.

Soon, Merritt Stone, a brother of Amherst Stone, enlisted at Berkshire in the Vermont Cavalry. Now the Stone family had one son fighting for the North, and one for the South. In Georgia, Amherst became involved in blockade running, helping the Confederate cause. Charles, in a Rebel uniform, though a captive for a time and wounded at Third Winchester, survived the war. In Atlanta, Cyrena secretly aided captured wounded soldiers. After the war, Charles and Mitchell went west. Cyrena died in 1868, and Amherst soon moved to Colorado, where he eventually became a federal judge.

Return across the bridge, go left on Route 105, and head for Enosburg Falls. Just after leaving East Berkshire, the Episcopal Cemetery is on the right. In the Hogaboom lot is a single stone for W. R.

Hogaboom's two sons, killed in the Overland Campaign.

SOURCES

BERKSHIRE TOWN RECORDS.
LIST OF CIVIL WAR–RELATED ACTIVITIES AT
    THE WEST BERKSHIRE CHURCH.
    UNPUBLISHED MANUSCRIPT, UNDATED.
HISTORY OF BERKSHIRE. BERKSHIRE, VT:
    BERKSHIRE HISTORICAL SOCIETY, 1994.
WELD, JOHN. "CIVIL WAR ON THE
    HOMEFRONT: THE STONE FAMILY."
    UNPUBLISHED MANUSCRIPT, UNDATED.
    COURTESY OF THE AUTHOR.
WITH THANKS TO VIRGINIA MESSIER AND
    JOHN WELD.

....

ENOSBURG

Enosburg sent 184 men to war, of whom 22 died and 25 were wounded. Many served in Company G, 13th Vermont, which attacked Pickett's Charge. The village of Enosburg Falls lies along Route 108, which is its Main Street. From Main go east on Depot Street to the Enosburg Opera House, built in 1892 by the prosperous Kendall Company. On June 7, 1894, the 13th Vermont held a reunion here, with the house filled as local people joined the old soldiers. According to the regimental history, "A fine program of musical selections interspersed. The success of the reunion was largely due to the efforts of Lieut. C. L. Marsh (see Frankin) who was elected president for the next year."

On a January day in 1911, 13th members again gathered here, for Marsh's funeral. According to the regimental history, "The hall was draped in the national colors, and a flag covered the casket. A double quartet sang 'Nearer My God to Thee' and the chants connected with the burial service of the Episcopal Church." Marsh, a stalwart of regimental reunions, invested in the Kendall Company after the war and became wealthy. The company manufactured Spavin Cure, a popular horse liniment.

Return to Main Street, go north, and soon on the right is the large and ornate Victorian home that Marsh built. Two buildings beyond is the Kendall Company building.

Return south on Main and take Route 105 south, quickly crossing the Missisquoi River. From the bridge, look right to an arched bridge on the site of an earlier covered bridge. The Confederates who raided St. Albans on October 19, 1864, crossed that covered bridge on their flight to Canada, splitting into small groups after passing through Enosburg Falls.

Continue on Route 105 south 2.5 miles to West Enosburg, and go right on Tyler Branch Road. In the first house past the United Church lived blacksmith Marvin White, his wife, and two daughters. White was first to enlist in the 13th's Company G and was elected captain. But soon after the regiment reached Virginia, he became sick, was hospitalized, and died on December 13, 1862. His body came home to this house.

Return to Route 105, continue south, and soon turn right on St. Pierre Road. In 1.5 miles, come to a hilltop farm with long views of the northern Green Mountains and Canada. Joel Bliss, only son of Bradley Bliss, left here at twenty to become a private in Company G. But not long after reaching Virginia, he, too, became ill. His father went south and found him in the regimental hospital. According to the regimental history, the father said that he would go to Washington, obtain a discharge for his boy, and take him home to recover. When the father returned, a comrade of Joel's told him, "I think you had better stay with Joel for he will soon obtain his discharge." In a few days, on January 8, 1863, Joel died, and his father brought the body home.

Return to Route 105, turn south, and the first house on the left was the home of Henry Fassett, who joined Company G at thirty-five, fought at Gettysburg, and came safely home. Just beyond the Fassett home is the West Enosburg Cemetery, where Captain White is buried.

Return north on Route 105 to West Enosburg, go right on Tyler Brook Road, and quickly go left on Grange Hall Road. In 1.5 miles on the right, at an intersection, is the home from which Thomas Langley went to join Company G, at age twenty-seven. Private Langley died of typhoid fever two weeks before Gettysburg.

Continue on Grange Hall Road to Enosburg Center, turn right on Boston Post Road, and a church is soon on the left. During the Civil War, a 100-foot pole stood on the church lawn from which flew a giant American flag, visible from much of the town. When the war was going poorly for the Union, the flag was at half-mast, but when the war went well, such as at Gettysburg, it went to the top of the pole.

Go north on Boston Post Road to the first farm on the right past the Grange Hall Road intersection, where once stood the Spooner House, a hotel. Indeed, the existing house may have been part of it.

Company G of the 13th Vermont assembled at Enosburg Center and drilled here briefly, before marching to Bakersfield for final preparations. The company boarded at Spooner House.

Continue north on Boston Post Road to the Missisiquoi River and a modern arched bridge. Once this was a covered bridge, and immediately after the St. Albans Raid, a local man, Gardner Fassett, was stationed here to guard against any further Rebel incursions. One night, hearing noises, he thrice called out, "Who goes there?" Hearing no answer, he shot, killing a large dog.

From the farm opposite the bridge's north end, Guy Woodward enlisted in Company G as a private and fought at Gettysburg.

Go left, west, on Route 105 and return to and pass through Enosburg. Just over 2 miles from the village, soon after crossing the Sheldon line, a handsome brick farmhouse stands on a knoll to the right. Local legend holds that Confederate raiders were seen burying some of their plunder on the hillside behind where the house now stands. Legend further says that the money was dug up by the farmer who lived here, and it paid for the building of this fine brick home.

SOURCES
ENOSBURG TOWN RECORDS.
GERAW, JANICE FLEURY. *ENOSBURG, VERMONT*. ENOSBURG, VT: ENOSBURG HISTORICAL SOCIETY, 1985.
WITH THANKS TO JOYCE GERAW.

FAIRFAX

The 1807 Fairfax town hall, now home to the town historical society, lies on the east side of Route 104 in the village of Fairfax. Meeting here on December 15, 1863, voters approved bounties of $350. By March 1864, recruiting had become so difficult that voters authorized the selectmen to pay bounties "at their discretion." The following August, Fairfax approved a tax of a "300 percent of the grand list" to pay volunteers, on a vote of 110 to 108. Cyrus Leach and J. J. Wilcox were appointed a committee to assist selectmen in recruiting. On April 25, 1865, with the war ending, voters refused to approve an article "authorizing payment of all expenses incurred by individuals of the town in raising the quotas of said town." Fairfax had had enough of war. Some 140 men of the town had served, and 29 died.

Just south of the town hall, where Fletcher Road intersects Route 104, is a square on which the village post office stood during the Civil War. Fairfax people gathered here each day to hear war news read from newspapers.

From the square, continue 0.5 mile on Route 104 and bear right on Route 128. Quickly turn right on McNall Road, and on the left is a large cornfield where, according to local tradition, men drilled when the Civil War began.

Return to the town hall, and just north of it on Route 104, on the left, is the Baptist Building. A photo taken in the front yard in the early 1900s shows a group of aging veterans, in uniform. Apparently, the local GAR post sometimes met here.

Continue 1 mile on Route 104 and Route 104A branches left. Stay on 104 another 0.5 mile, and on the left is a long, obviously very old, frame house. Once the Ufford family home, John Ufford grew up here, and in 1862, he wrote a history of Fairfax for Abby Hemenway's *Gazetteer*. He wrote to Hemenway on July 7, 1862, having heard news of the Peninsula Campaign:

"I do not feel much like work nor play. I had great fear that our armies before Richmond had been cut to pieces, and, do the best I could, a heavy cloud would settle over my spirits. I hope we have heard the worst . . . I have two brothers in the army . . . Both have seen hard service and yet they are willing to endure and suffer for the perpetuity of our glorious Government more free than the world has ever before seen. I feel a pride in my native State, that when nearly every heart is wrung by the fear of the loss of near or dear friends, she still sends forth her sons to the battlefield . . . The harvest of men taken out of the State has weakened the force left at home, and those here must work harder to make up the deficiency, so if our brave soldier-boys should return they would find full garners to welcome—for, though the loving words of friends would be dear, we can imagine how the imagination would wander to the pantry after a long campaign, deprived of the luxuries of home."

That fall, John Ufford tried to enlist in the 11th Vermont, but he failed a doctor's examination. He died of typhoid fever the next summer at twenty-nine. Brother Samuel Ufford, first sergeant of the Vermont Cavalry, was wounded and captured in the cavalry attack at Gettysburg. He returned home in 1864 and lived until 1912. Brother Zadock Ufford, a sergeant in the 2nd Vermont, was killed at the Wilderness. Brother Page Ufford, a corporal in the 11th Vermont, was captured at Weldon Railroad, survived Andersonville, and lived until 1900.

Continue 2.75 miles on Route 104 to where King Road enters on the left. Stop and turn around, returning as you came 0.1 mile and on the left see an old cape farmhouse set back from the road. This was once a Richardson family home, apparently owned by relatives of Israel Richardson. This old house was surely familiar to him. Israel Richardson was born in this northern part of Fairfax, in a house long gone, on December 26, 1815. He spent his youth in Fairfax and won appointment to West Point, graduating in 1841. Serving in the Seminole and Mexican wars, he earned the nickname "Fighting Dick." He finally settled in Michigan, where he recruited an infantry regiment when the Civil War began and served as its colonel. He commanded a brigade at First Bull Run, then a Second Corps division in the Peninsula Campaign. A major general by the fall of 1862, he led a division at South Mountain, then at Antietam. Much admired by his men, Richardson often wore a battered straw hat, having little use for the trappings of rank. Said to be fearless, he told his men, "I won't go ask you to go anywhere that I won't go myself." At Antietam, his division advanced across open ground against the famed Sunken Road and drove the last Confederates from it. But as it did so,

Richardson was hit by a shell fragment. Taken to the Pry House, headquarters of General McClellan, Richardson seemed to be recovering, but infection set in, and he died on November 3, 1862.

SOURCES

Fairfax 1763 to 1976. St. Albans, VT: Regal Art Press, 1980.
Fairfax town records.
Rosentreter, Roger L. "Three Generals and an Unlucky Regiment: Michigan at the Battle of Antietam." *Michigan History Magazine* 92, no. 5 (September–October 2008).

···

FAIRFIELD

Go east from St. Albans 7 miles on Route 36 to reach Fairfield's main intersection, by the town office. Turn south, and the athletic field on the right was once the Fairfield drill field, where it is said men marched when the Civil War began. The 1860s schoolhouse by the field was once the town's meeting hall. Here on December 11, 1863, voters approved $325 bounties. In June 1864, Fairfield voted to raise $20,000 on the grand list "to pay bounties to volunteers to fill the quota of Fairfield under the next call of the President of the Unites States." A month later the town "voted to raise one thousand dollars for each white volunteer to fill the quota of the town." Also approved was the raising of $2,700 on the grand list "to be deposited . . . in the St. Albans bank to the credit of the state treasurer for the purpose of paying $300 each to nine Negro recruits if they should be obtained to fill the quota of the town." It appears that Fairfield was hoping to obtain black soldiers through recruiters operating in the freed parts of the Confederacy. Whether this strategy was successful is not known, but it does appear that Fairfield met all its quotas. Also, there is no mention of whether any of the money deposited in the St. Albans bank was lost during the Confederate raid of October 19, 1864.

A church is across the road from the drill field, and three houses south of it is a home owned after the war by Thomas Kennedy, 6th Vermont. Enlisting in October 1861, in Sheldon, as a private in Company K, Kennedy rose through the ranks to become company commander when Captain Alfred Horton Keith, of Sheldon, was wounded at the Wilderness. Leading his men at Cedar Creek, Kennedy was shot in a thigh. In Julian Scott's Cedar Creek painting at the Vermont State House, Kennedy can be seen in the left foreground being carried back from the front lines. He was taken to a farmhouse owned by a Virginian, Solomon Heater, who punched the wounded Vermonter. Discharged in April 1865 because of his wounds, Kennedy came home to marry a Fairfield lady, Catherine Howrigan, in the Fairfield Catholic Church, January 10, 1870.

From the four corners go east, pass two houses on the left, and come abreast of a large vacant lot. Here once stood the home and blacksmith shop of the Merrill family. Oscar Merrill enlisted in the Vermont Cavalry at twenty-two, was discharged, and then signed on as a sergeant in the 12th Vermont. Romeo, twenty-five, joined the 1st Vermont Regiment and was wounded in the first battle in which Vermonters were engaged, at Big Bethel, on June 16, 1861. After that ninety-day regiment disbanded, he joined his brother's company of the Vermont Cavalry but came home ill just before Christmas 1862. He died at home the next March 3 of chronic diarrhea.

Continue east on Route 36 across a bridge, and the first house beyond it, on the left, was the home of Hamilton Gilbert, a private in the 1st Vermont, wounded at Big Bethel.

Go east 4.3 miles on Route 36, and on entering East Fairfield, note a great boulder on the right with waterfall behind. Just past it, turn right on Bridge Street, cross the covered bridge, and the first house on the right was the home of Wooster Flood, a 10th Vermont private. Captured at Cedar Creek, he was paroled four months later.

Proceed to a T at the end of Bridge Street, turn right, and in 0.3 mile bear right on Lapland Road. After passing through a little gap known as the Pinch of the Rocks, soon come to a small cemetery above the road on the right. The largest stone honors Philander Reed, who served for more than three years as a private in the 2nd Vermont. Inscriptions note that he died on June 18, 1864, "of wounds received in the Battle of the Wilderness May 6" and that he was "23 years, 10 months, and 14 days old." Beneath a carved flag are the words:

**My boy is gone but not lost.
Don't weep mother for I am at rest.**

This is a cenotaph, for Reed's body lies in Arlington National Cemetery.

Return as you came, then go straight past Bridge Street to the green in East Fairfield. Turn right on Route 36, left on New Street, and in 0.8 mile go left onto Dodd Road. In 3 miles, go right on Chester Arthur Road to the Chester A. Arthur State Historic Site. Arthur was born on October 5, 1829, in a log cabin in this area, the fifth child of William and Malvina Arthur. His father was pastor of the North Fairfield Baptist Church. The small house at this site is a replica of the parsonage built here for the Arthur family by parishioners, Chester Arthur's boyhood home for a time. The Arthur family moved to New York State in 1835, where that year William Arthur cofounded the New York Anti-Slavery Society. Chester Arthur became a prominent New York lawyer, well known for his championing of civil rights for blacks. He won a case entitling blacks in the Empire State to have the same accommodations on public transit as whites. During the Civil War, Arthur became a brigadier general serving as quartermaster general of New York. Rising to prominence in New York politics after the war, in 1881 Arthur became the running mate of James A. Garfield, another Civil War veteran. When Garfield was assassinated four months after taking office, Arthur completed the unexpired term, becoming the nation's twenty-first president. In poor health, he declined running for a second term and died less than a year after leaving office.

At the dedication of the granite monument, held here at the Arthur historic site, on a rainy August 20, 1903, Robert Todd Lincoln was the keynote speaker. Lincoln had served as Arthur's secretary of war.

Return as you came to the T; turn right on Duffy Hill Road, and in 0.2 mile, on the left, is the redbrick North Fairfield Baptist Church, built about 1840. Here, Arthur's father preached, certainly speaking against slavery.

Return as you came, and go right on Chester A. Arthur Road. In 3 miles, cross the bed of the abandoned St. Johnsbury & Lamoille County Railroad, at Fairfield Station. In the farm located here, after the war, lived Ephraim Smith, who enlisted at twenty-two in the 1st Vermont, then reenlisted in the 3rd Vermont, where he became a private. Smith served for almost the entire war and lived on this farm until his death in 1917.

Continue past the station to North Road and turn north. In 3 miles, go left on Pond Road, pass the north end of Fairfield Pond, and go left on Sheldon Woods Road. In a mile on the right is a farmhouse set amid maples. From here, Charles Marvin enlisted as a private in Company K, 13th Vermont. Regimental historian Ralph Sturtevant said Marvin was a wheelwright and carpenter who helped build barracks when the regiment assembled in Brattleboro. He then became company cook. According to Sturtevant, Marvin's mother was a spiritualist, and her son, from an early age, believed that dreams foretold the future. Sturtevant wrote, "Company K listened to the dreams of their cook and placed more or less reliance on them." Marvin returned to this farm and worked it until "rheumatism and infirmity incident on army life" made such hard labor impossible.

Continue past the house on Sheldon Woods Road, which ends on Route 105, not far from St. Albans.

SOURCES

BALLWAY, ELEANOR WHEELER, ED. *FAIRFIELD, VERMONT: REMINISCENCES, 1763–1977.* FAIRFIELD, VT: FAIRFIELD BICENTENNIAL COMMITTEE, 1977.

FAIRFIELD TOWN RECORDS.

WITH THANKS TO RICHARD HOWRIGAN.

....

FLETCHER

From the village of Cambridge, go east on Route 15, cross the Lamoille River, and quickly turn left on Fletcher Road. In 4-plus miles enter Fletcher Center, and the Fletcher Union Meeting House is on the left. Here, the Kinsley family of Fletcher worshipped, including War of 1812 veteran Ben Alva Kinsley and his sons, Rufus, William, Alonzo, Jason, and Edgar. Also, cousin Silas Kinsley was a member. William and Rufus both enlisted in the 8th Vermont in November 1961. William, a private, served three years and was severely wounded in both legs during the siege of Port Hudson (see Lowell). Rufus, a corporal, served eighteen months before being put on special duty. More later. Alonzo, a private in the 2nd Vermont, was shot in the chest at First Bull Run. He survived and was transferred to hospital duty. Jason served in the 1st Iowa Cavalry. Edgar Kinsley was a private in the 2nd Vermont, serving two years.

Cousin Silas Kinsley, who also attended services at the meetinghouse, joined the Vermont Cavalry and died in a skirmish in Hagerstown, Maryland, soon after the Battle of Gettysburg, He was fighting dismounted from building to building, when Confederates cut him off and captured him. He died on September 6. A cavalryman from Craftsbury, Alanson Coon, captured with Kinsley, wrote the Kinsley family: "Your son that died in Andersonville. He wished me to write you that he was willing to die and wanted to get through with the suffering."

In 1870, Silas's sister, Miriah Kinsley, went south to teach in a school for blacks in Cuthbert, Georgia. She visited Andersonville and found her brother's grave. "One of the teachers went with me to the national cemetery in this place," she wrote home. "I found it much prettier than I expected. They are buried in plots and sections the ground is very level." She found a white board marked "L. Kinsley Co. D. Vt. Died September 4, 1864." A Bible that was in the pocket of Silas when he died is in the possession of Kinsley's descendants.

Just past the church, on the right, is a frame house and barn set at the top of a large lawn. There lived Charles Blair, three years a private in Company H, 2nd Vermont, in which many local lads served. The lawn was once the Fletcher drill field where soldiers headed for the Civil War marched.

Past that field, at the stop sign, go straight onto Fairfield Road and soon turn right on North Road. In 1.3 miles, on the right, is an old farmhouse with a huge modern stone chimney, from which Chester Leach went to serve as a lieutenant in Company H, 2nd Vermont. During his term of service from June 1861 to June 1864, Leach wrote 237 letters home, most to his wife, Ann, many including a message for their two sons. From the Cold Harbor trenches on June 6, 1864:

"For the last three days we have been where one could not stand on his feet unless he run the risk of getting a bullet through him . . . The rebel works in front of ours are about 30 or 40 rods distant across an open field so you can see it would not be very safe for a man to show himself a great while at a time. A few get hit occasionally by get above the works or by a ball glancing & falling close to the pits. Co. A lost two yesterday . . . Get someone to help you about the work if possible rather than kill yourself out by doing more than you are able to do, & trust and pray that I may be home ere long, to care for things, & do the work myself."

Return to Fairfield Road, go left back to the intersection, and turn right on Fairfax Road. In 0.5 mile, as you enter Binghamville, the first house on the right was the postwar home of Leroy Bingham, who enlisted at sixteen in Company H, 2nd Vermont, and served until wounded in May 1863 at Fredericksburg.

Quickly take Shaw Road on the left, and in 0.6 mile, the single-story frame house on the left was the home of Edgar and Hollis Montague, both privates in Company H. Hollis was a musician.

Return to Fairfax Road and the Binghamville Methodist Church. In the cemetery behind are buried many Civil War soldiers, including Chester Leach and his brother, William, a private in Company H, who died of sickness Brandy Station in the winter of 1864. Ben Alvah Kinsley is also here.

Return to Fletcher Center as you came, rejoining the Cambridge Road as you enter the village. Go past the meetinghouse 1 mile, and on the right is a small cape, the home of Herbert Boomhour, three years a private in the Vermont Cavalry.

Go 0.2 mile and turn left on Rushford Road, and in 1 mile, go left on North Cambridge Road. In another mile, the road passes through the yard of an old farm, where Ben Alvah Kinsley raised his boys, Rufus among them. Before the war, Rufus worked in Boston as a newspaperman and during that time became involved in antislavery activities, living on Beacon Hill close to its black community. After arriving in Louisiana with the 8th Vermont, he was placed in charge of a camp for escaped slaves near New Orleans. His brother, William, soon joined him in the work. In addition to seeing to the needs of thousands of contrabands, Rufus taught at the camp school. He wrote in his diary June 17, 1862:

"Visited during the day several plantations; and saw enough of the horrors of slavery to make me an Abolitionist forever. On each plantation in all this section of the country is a large building called a hospital, with only two rooms. In one may be seen the stocks, gnouts, thumb screw, ball and chain, hand cuffs, whips, and other instruments of torture, for the benefit of those who have been guilty of loving freedom more than life, but have failed in their efforts to obtain the coveted boon."

Later, Rufus was as an officer in a regiment of black troops that served in Louisiana. In 1865, when the war closed, father Ben Kinsley held a party here at the farm for his sons on their return from war.

Return to Cambridge Road and go left to return to Route 15.

SOURCES

FEIDNER, EDWARD J. *THE CIVIL WAR LETTERS OF CHESTER LEACH.* BURLINGTON, VT: CENTER FOR RESEARCH ON VERMONT, UNIVERSITY OF VERMONT, 2002.

FLETCHER TOWN RECORDS.

RANKIN, DAVID C. *DIARY OF A CHRISTIAN SOLDIER: RUFUS KINSLEY AND THE CIVIL WAR.* NEW YORK: CAMBRIDGE UNIVERSITY PRESS, 2004.

WITH THANKS TO H. CARLETON FERGUSON AND CHARLES TINKER.

FRANKLIN

Franklin village is on Route 120, just east of its intersection with Route 236, and not far south of the Canadian border. At the green's east end is the 1875 Franklin Town Hall with five stone plaques erected "In memory of the deceased soldiers of Franklin." The town sent 127 men to war, and most of their names are listed.

In the house beside the town hall lived Dr. Rodman Welch, who served the last eighteen months of the war as a 5th Vermont private. A Berkshire native, Welch set up a medical practice in this house in 1872 and was the village physician for many years.

East of the town hall are the 1866 Methodist Church and the 1828 Congregational Church, both witness to the September 10, 1910 dedication ceremonies for Franklin's Civil War monument. The bronze larger-than-life statue of a Union soldier is atop a granite pedestal that bears the names of all Franklin men who served. The names of the twenty-seven who died are on one side of the monument, but those who came home are given "equal honor to those who dared to die but lived." The monument was given by Franklin native Carmi Marsh, once a lieutenant in the 13th Vermont.

The dedication took place on a Friday, with 1,500 people present, including many veterans of the 13th Vermont, who held a regimental reunion around the occasion. After speeches that included remarks by 13th veteran Henry Clark, who seemed to speak at all regimental occasions, the monument was unveiled. Two young ladies, one a granddaughter of donor Marsh (ill and not present), the other a granddaughter of Orloff Whitney, who died in the war, unveiled the monument by pulling away its red, white, and blue wrappings. George Towle, select board chair, then spoke, to future generations, concluding: "Looking upon the monument and reading the names inscribed thereon of those brave men who went forth to fight the battles of their country it might be an inspiration and lesson to them as to the path of duty in times of danger to the republic."

Across Route 120 just beyond the green, two large almost identical houses stand side-by-side. This is the old Franklin Academy building, cut in half after it ceased being a school, where Civil War–era town meetings took place. Early in the war, the town kept a close eye on its budget, approving bounties of $50 in 1862 and $150 in 1863. But as the task of meeting quotas became more difficult, a

$1,000 bounty was voted in August 1864.

Just beyond the old buildings, bear left on Route 235, and in 0.75 mile take Richard Road, a country lane that once knew the tramp of an army. In the spring of 1870, an armed force of Fenians, Irishmen intent on freeing the Emerald Isle from British rule, assembled at Franklin to invade Canada. On May 24, their commander, John O'Neil, who served in the Civil War as a colonel and was wounded in the Peninsula Campaign, set up headquarters in the town. With eight hundred men in his command, including many Civil War veterans, O'Neil moved along Richard Road toward the international border.

Continue to the end of the road where the redbrick Richard house still stands. O'Neil formed his command into three columns and moved past the house, crossing the border just beyond it. Just to the north, the Fenians were met by Canadian militia, who loosed a volley from their position on Eccles Hill. One Fenian was killed and several wounded. The advance ended. It is said that O'Neil was on the front porch of the Richard house when a bullet passed between his legs and into the front door. That door is preserved by the Franklin Historical Society. Apparently, the Fenians camped along Richard Road after the brief fight.

From Richard Road, go left on Gallup Road 2.75 miles to a crossroads and the Prouty Cemetery. This little graveyard, enclosed by a picket fence and shaded by locust trees, has a view south across Franklin farmland to Lake Carmi. The cemetery contains but eleven stones, and four mark the graves of Franklin soldiers dead in the Civil War. Horace Safford, a private in the 5th Vermont, was thirty when fatally wounded at Cold Harbor. Edgar Anderson, 102nd New York, was twenty-two when he died on April 19, 1864. Joseph Jones, a private in the 6th Vermont, died of sickness at the winter camp at Brandy Station in February 1864, at age twenty-three. Chauncey Elrick was twenty-three years and nine months old when he, a private in the 3rd Vermont, also perished at Brandy Station of sickness. His stone says:

> Far from affliction toil and care
> The happy soul is fled
> The breathless clay shall slumber here
> Among the silent dead

From the cemetery, take Middle Road 0.25 mile to a brick house on the right. Roswell Olmstead went from here to enlist as a private in the 13th Vermont's Company K, as did many Franklin men, and fought at Gettysburg.

Continue on Middle Road 1.5 miles to East Franklin and go right on Route 236. Quickly on the right is a stately brick farmhouse, the home of Orloff Whitney, whose granddaughter helped unveil the Franklin monument. Whitney was captain of the 13th's Company H and also regimental adjutant. The 13th's historian Sturtevant said, "His premature and untimely death fell like a pall over the whole regiment. He was prostrated with typhoid fever in Camp Widow Violet on the Occoquan, Virginia, and removed to Alexandria, Virginia, and placed in a hospital where the next day in an unguarded moment on account of negligence of a nurse, as his comrades believe, and while in a raging fever, without knowing what he did, jumped through an open window into the street below, and died in a few hours on June 4th 1863." Whitney was twenty-three and left a widow in this house.

Just beyond the Whitney house, bear left on Middle Road and in 2.75 miles come to a large frame farmhouse on the left facing barns across the road. From here, Carmi Marsh enlisted and became a lieutenant in the 13th's Company K. Not long after the 2nd Vermont Brigade arrived in Virginia, Marsh contracted typhoid fever. Recovering, he rode through a cold rain in a mule cart to rejoin his regiment at Wolf Run Shoals. Soon, he came down with meningitis. Hearing of his condition, Marsh's parents went south and paid a local woman, Mary Wilcoxson, to take their son into her home. Slowly, Marsh's health returned, but in mid-February he was forced to resign his commission and come home. Marsh later became a wealthy man (see Enosburg), and in 1898, he went in search of Mrs. Wilcoxson and found her an elderly lady living in Manassas. He visited her each of the next four years she lived and sent her a check four times a year. The Marsh home faces perhaps Vermont's largest Civil War memorial, once known as Silver Lake. In 1910 at Franklin's request, the Vermont legislature approved changing its name to Lake Carmi, to honor all Franklin's Civil War soldiers, but named for the man who grew up along its east shore.

A little more than 1 mile past the Marsh house, turn right on Swamp Road. At its end, turn right on Route 120 and soon return to Franklin village.

From the village, go east on Route 120 to East Franklin and its large white church by the Berkshire town line. On May 7, 1865, a funeral took place here for Abraham Lincoln with Reverend E. A. Titus presiding. His sermon came from Samuel, "How the mighty have fallen."

SOURCES

FRANKLIN TOWN RECORDS.
TOWLE, HANNA MARTHA. *A HISTORY OF FRANKLIN: PAST AND PRESENT, FACT OR FANCY, LEGEND OR FOLKSAY 1789–1989.* BURLINGTON, VT: FRANKLIN HISTORICAL SOCIETY, 1989.
WITH THANKS TO SUSAN CLARK AND LISA LARIVEE, TOWN CLERK.

GEORGIA

Georgia's war memorial fronts the town offices on the east side of Route 7, the names of thirty-two men who perished in the Civil War listed. Georgia in the 1860s had a population of about two thousand. Go north from the memorial 2.5 miles and look closely for a large granite monument on a bluff above the road on the right. In Georgia, the most important of all Vermont's Civil War soldiers was born, George Jerrison Stannard, on October 20, 1820. He grew up in the town and is credited with being the first Vermonter to enlist for the Civil War. Stannard served as lieutenant colonel of the 2nd Vermont Regiment and fought at First Bull Run. Named commander of the new 9th Vermont, through no fault of his own, the entire regiment was captured by Stonewall Jackson at Harpers Ferry, just before Antietam. Stannard was then named commander of the 2nd Vermont Brigade after the capture of its Brigadier General Edwin Stoughton. Under Stannard, the brigade won enduring fame at Gettysburg. With just three of his five regiments on the field, Stannard saw Pickett's Charge suddenly veer to the north of his position, the most advanced along the entire Union line on Cemetery Ridge. With the Confederate right flank suddenly vulnerable, Stannard ordered his 13th and 16th regiments to swing out and assault the southern flank of Rebels, massing toward the famous Clump of Trees. Stannard's men inflicted heavy casualties, delivering the telling blow on what may have been the most important assault of the entire war. Stannard was wounded at Gettysburg but recovered to command a division, then a brigade, in the 19th Corps. Wounded again at Cold Harbor, then at Fort Harrison, the last knocked him out of the war for good. Thus he was in Vermont recuperating and available to take over the defense of Vermont's northern border after the St. Albans raid.

The Stannard monument marks the site of his birth, though the Stannard house actually stood just south of the bluff, where a new house now stands, the first structure south of the monument. The monument was apparently placed so that it would be visible from the nearby railway.

The Stannard monument was dedicated in 1908, with the keynote address by Albert Clarke, a Georgia native, once a 12th Vermont sergeant. He concluded, "As the generations shall come and go across this upland scene, may the modest marker here placed serve to remind them of a modest man whose soul expanded to

his country's needs, until their souls shall likewise be exalted, and a glory shall irradiate these hills that may fitly arch with the resplendent scene that nature paints above the watered vale, and God and country shall be their daily thoughts." A poem composed for the occasion by another 2nd Vermont Brigade veteran, W. C. Clark of Lyndon, included:

> Let this memento mark the native place
> Of him whose steps in history we trace;
> Attracting notice from the passerby,
> Throughout the future let it signify
> Vermont does honor to a worthy son,
> And praise bestows for duty bravely done.

To stand on the site is to wonder how many of the veterans of Stannard's brigade who came here noticed the location is on a low ridge looking east across farm fields toward distant mountains. The view from Cemetery Ridge was somewhat similar.

The monument site held a different memory for another Georgia soldier. Corporal Edwin Payson Clark served in the 12th Vermont, in Stannard's Brigade. Clark remembered his homecoming from Gettysburg and getting off the train in St. Albans in mid-July 1863. He started walking home and encountered his wife, walking north, on the rise where the Stannard monument would later stand.

Another of Vermont's better-known soldiers, Captain George Conger of the Vermont Cavalry, resigned his commission in September 1862, to return to St. Albans and care for his ailing wife. Conger was thus at home when Confederate raiders struck the town's banks on October 19, 1864. Conger led the posse that pursued the raiders across the Canadian border. Conger moved to Georgia soon after the war and owned a farm along the main road. Both Conger and Stannard served together before the war in the Ransom Guards, a militia unit based in Brandon. Go back south along Route 7, just under 0.25 mile, to where Conger Road turns east. The old house at the southeast corner was Captain Conger's home.

Continue 0.75 miles south on Route 7, and on the left is a large frame house with large garage attached. Henry Dustin Blatchley lived here, a newly married twenty-year-old farmer when the Civil War began. From the house, Blatchley's mother was watching him hoe potatoes on July 17, 1861, when she suddenly saw him drop his hoe and begin walking toward St. Albans. There he enlisted in the 10th Vermont. Private Blatchley was captured on July 9, 1864, at the Battle of the Monocacy, and died the following January in the Confederate prison at Danville, Virginia, where he is buried.

Continue south of Route 7, pass the war memorial, and quickly turn right, west, on Plains Road. Antislavery sentiment was prevalent in Georgia well before the war, apparently much due to the efforts of Reverend Alvah Sabin. An organizer of the Georgia Anti-Slavery Society that formed in 1836 with 115 members, the reverend served in the Vermont legislature, where he also trumpeted the anti-slavery cause. Follow Plains Road 2.25 miles to the hamlet of Georgia Plains, and the white farmhouse on the left, at the intersection, was Reverend Sabin's home. Sabin

is reported to have been involved in Underground Railroad activities, and a strong local tradition holds that escaped slaves were housed in the large redbrick house beyond the brick church.

Return to Route 7, go south, and in 1.2 miles, note a frame house on the right, much altered, the last before the sharp right turn. An 1858 map identifies this house with the Joy family. It may well have been, for a time, the home of Agnes Elizabeth Joy, who won considerable fame during the Civil War as Princess Salm-Salm. The origins of the princess are vague, and apparently Agnes preferred to keep them that way. But biographers agree that she was born in Vermont, either in Franklin or Swanton, probably on Christmas Day 1844. Her father, William Leclerq Joy, was a Massachusetts native and her mother, Julia Willard, was from Montpelier. There is also agreement that young Agnes lived both in Georgia and Swanton and likely for a time in Phillipsburg, Quebec, where she received some education from Catholic nuns.

A petite lady of rare beauty and a lover of horses, Agnes met and married, in 1862, a German soldier of fortune Felix Constantin Alexander Johann Nepomuk, Prince Salm-Salm, come to America to fight for the Union. Suddenly a princess, Agnes became well known around Washington, galloping about the city on her fine horses and stepping out in the city's society with her handsome husband. Agnes claimed to be friends with the Lincolns, and the first family certainly knew who she was. She also claimed to be related to the president. The prince served on the staff of General Lewis Blenker, and at times, the princess went to war with him. She may have helped nurse wounded soldiers and became much liked by the troops. After the war, the Salm-Salms were in Mexico, he as an aide-de-camp to the Emperor Maximilian. Both the emperor and her husband were arrested and sentenced to death. The princess successfully pleaded for both their lives. From Mexico, the couple went to Europe, where the prince became involved in the Franco-Prussian War. She won a Medal of Honor from Prussia for helping soldiers, but the prince was killed. The princess died in Europe, nearly impoverished, in 1912.

SOURCES

MALLETT, PETER S. *THE HISTORY OF GEORGIA, VERMONT, 1763–2002.* ST. ALBANS, VT: REGAL ART PRESS, 2002.

———, ED. *MEMORIES OF GEORGIA BEFORE 1900.* NEWPORT, VT: TONY O'CONNOR CIVIL WAR ENTERPRISES, 2005.

PICTURESQUE GEORGIA. GEORGIA BICENTENNIAL COMMITTEE. ST. ALBANS, VT: REGAL ART PRESS, 1976.

WITH THANKS TO EDWIN BREHAUT AND FRIENDS.

....

HIGHGATE

The long park in Highgate Falls, a village known in the 1860s simply as Highgate, runs along Route 207 as it comes north from St. Albans. On the west side of the park's north end, an old brick store faces across the road, toward the site of Johnson's hotel. In late August 1862, men from Swanton, Highgate, Franklin, Alburgh, North Hero, and Grand Isle came to the hotel to join Company K of the 13th Vermont, destined to attack Pickett's Charge. On September 11, a large crowd assembled to witness the election of company officers. Ralph Orson Sturtevant, 13th Vermont regimental historian, wrote, "There were present 126 volunteers, selectmen from several towns, fathers, mothers, brothers and sisters, wives and sweethearts relatives and friends of those that had enlisted, numbering many more, all anxious and curious to see and hear, for nothing of this kind had occurred in this quiet village before."

Balloting took place in the hotel, and among the officers elected was Carmi Marsh, of Franklin, chosen a lieutenant. Sturtevant said, "As soon as Carmi, as he was called, was declared elected, he was given a ride around the common on the shoulders of his ardent and enthusiastic admirers . . . while the others cheered and clapped hands."

On September 16, the men reported to the hotel for medical examinations performed by Dr. Hiram Stevens, of St. Albans. Next day, drills began on the common. Sturtevant said that Sergeant George Blake "took us up opposite of the village cemetery where stood a good stretch of fence and placed us up against it, and in this way formed a pretty good line." Drilling continued on and around the park until September 29, when the company marched to Swanton and boarded a train headed south.

The village cemetery is behind the 1829 Episcopal Church, which still overlooks the south end of the park. Beyond the cemetery, the first house was the home of George Sunderland, a private in Company K. George tented with his father Freeman Sunderland. Freeman did the company laundry, and when his son was taken sick during the winter in camp, he nursed him back to health. They both fought at Gettysburg.

Go south from the park on Route 207, and the third house on the left was the home of Sergeant George Halloway, who was wounded in the attack on Pickett's Charge. "A piece of shell hit him on the shin causing blood to flow quite freely," Sturtevant said.

Go back north on Route 207, past the park, cross the Mississquoi River, and turn east on Route 78. Just past the town offices is the Highgate Civil War monument, bearing the names of 196 men who served. The white bronze statue of a Civil War soldier displays on its base the likenesses of Lincoln, Sheridan, Grant, and Sherman. Some 1,500 people assembled under a blue sky for the dedication on July 12, 1911. A contemporary account said, "The principal streets and buildings and many private houses had been elaborately decorated . . . Electric light poles and forty extra poles which had been placed for the occasion were hung with evergreens and red white and blue streamers." Scores of aging veterans listened as the principal address was given by Henry Meigs, a Swanton native, once a private in Company K. After the war, Meigs thrived in the insurance business and eventually gave the monument to his hometown. His speech echoed words set in the monument:

We shall meet and greet in closing ranks
In time's declining sun,

When the bugles of God shall sound recall
And the battle of life be won

Continue east on Route 78 from the monument to the redbrick home of the Highgate Historical Society on the left. In the house just beyond it lived James Judkins, a private in Company K and a shoemaker in civilian life. Ralph Sturtevant, his old comrade in arms, met eighty-five-year-old Judkins on a Swanton street in 1909 and wrote that "his memory of the old days was fresh and life in the army was spoken of with pleasure, and when I remarked to him, 'We all soon shall pass away and be forgotten, 'Yes,' said he, 'but what we did will remain, and for us it does not matter.'"

Take the first right past the Judkins house, and at the Y just ahead, look to the first house to the right, across an open space, where Private James Hogaboom, Company K, lived. According to Sturtevant, at Gettysburg Hogaboom "was in the ranks near Corporal William Church who was torn to pieces by an exploding shell. The concussion doubled up Min, as we called him, and rolled him over like a hoop, but he was soon on his feet again looking to see what had happened . . . and took his place as if nothing unusual had happened."

Return to Route 78 and go back east. From the junction of 207 and 78, continue east on 78 for 0.5 mile, and turn right on the road to Highgate Springs, the Carter Hill Road. In just over 3 miles, before the bridge over Interstate 91, turn right on Lackey Road. The last house on the road was built after the war by Jackson Lackey, a private in the 6th Vermont, wounded at Funkstown. Lackey brought the bullet that struck him home to his wife. Jackson was one of six Lackey brothers, most born in Highgate, who served in Vermont regiments. One, Orange Lackey, 13th Vermont, died of disease in November 1863. Men from Highgate served in every Vermont regiment.

SOURCES
PROGRAM FOR THE DEDICATION OF THE HIGHGATE CIVIL WAR MONUMENT. COURTESY OF HIGHGATE HISTORICAL SOCIETY.
WITH THANKS TO CHARLES NYE AND REBECCA MUNSON.

··

MONTGOMERY

Montgomery's Baptist Church is located where Route 242 leaves Route 118, in Montgomery Center. On May 20, 1886, GAR Post 95 was formed, named Haile Post, for Private Charles Haile, the first Montgomery man to die in the war. He was one of 105 men from this town who served, from an 1860 population of 1,262.

Haile Post lasted until May 1898; by then, its ranks had dwindled, with forty Civil War soldier graves by then in town cemeteries. While it lasted, the post usually met in the Baptist Church. On Memorial Day, observances included a parade that formed on the little green that was once in the intersection by the church. Led by a band and GAR members, the procession proceeded north along Route 118 to the Village Cemetery.

There, a hollow square was formed, prayers said, and flowers placed at graves. Then the procession returned to the church for a meal and speeches.

During its twelve-year existence, meetings of the post were held on the first Saturday of each month on, or after, the full moon. A women's committee on relief helped post members who became ill. In 1890, 12 post members went to Boston for the Grand Encampment of the GAR, which drew 65,000 members.

The post was active in political affairs and in 1887 sent letters to President Grover Cleveland and the Vermont congressional delegation, demanding an overturn of the president's veto of a veterans' pension bill. They also officially voiced objection to the government's treatment of Native Americans.

The house from which the post's namesake Charles Haile went to war still stands. Go south from the church on Route 118, along the route Haile took from home to enlist in Montgomery Center. Proceed 2.75 miles and go left on Reagan Road. In 1 mile, go right on Rushford Road, and the first house, a cape with ell and large stone chimney, was the Haile farmhouse. Charles joined the 5th Vermont in September 1861 but died on December 25, at Camp Griffin, of sickness.

Return to the Baptist Church, take Route 118 to Montgomery village, and by the green, go right on Fuller Bridge Road. Cross Fuller Bridge, and the first house on the right was Albert Kingsley's home. Several Montgomery men joined Company G of the 13th Vermont, which formed at Bakersfield. Sergeant Kingsley was shot in a thigh during the attack on Pickett's Charge but came home to become a member of the Haile Post and lived until 1915.

Return to Montgomery Center, go left on Route 242, and ascend into an upland valley beneath Big Jay Mountain. In 2.25 miles, at the corner of Amidon Road, is the Montgomery District Four School, in 2010 a restaurant. Among its pupils were John Combs, a 13th Vermont corporal wounded in the attack on Pickett's Charge, and Simon Russell, a 9th Vermont private who took sick and died in Louisiana after a year of service.

Continue past the school 1 mile to a house and barn on the left. From here, Joseph Foster, twenty-one, joined the 5th Vermont in 1861. By the spring of 1864, he had become a lieutenant and was wounded at the Wilderness.

The Montgomery town house, where Civil War–era town meetings took place, is gone, once standing where the town office is now located in Montgomery Center. Montgomery voted for Lincoln in 1860, 79 to 10 over Douglas, and in 1864, 153 to 22 over McClellan.

In writing her chapter on Montgomery, Abby Hemenway included a poem honoring two of the town's soldiers, 5th Vermont corporals Talma Morgan and Israel Puffer, killed at the Wilderness. It concluded:

By fairy hands their knell is rung;
By forms unseen their dirge is sung;
There Honor comes, a pilgrim gray;
To bless the turf that wraps their clay;
And Freedom shall awhile repair
To dwell a sleeping hermit there!

SOURCES

Branthover, W. R. "Montgomery, Vermont Soldiers in the Civil War." Pamphlet, 1960.

Branthover, W. R., and Sara Taylor. *Montgomery Vermont: The History of a Town.* Montgomery, VT: Montgomery Historical Society, 1976.

Montgomery town and cemetery records.

With thanks to Scott Perry.

RICHFORD

Richford's brick town hall overlooks Main Street, also Route 105, and across the street is the town war memorial, with the names of 20 Richford men who died in the Civil War. Richford sent 130 men to war from an 1860 population of 1,300.

From Academy Hill, behind the town hall, Fourth of July celebrations began after the war with the firing at midnight of a cannon and the ringing of bells. The war had been an expensive undertaking for this town, with a tax of $3 on every grand list dollar approved in August 1864 to meet bounty payments. In 1864, Richford went for Lincoln over McClellan, 133 to 79. In 1866, sixty-six veterans, who enlisted early in the war and received modest bounties, asked the town to pay them amounts equal to those paid enlistees late in the war. Voters refused.

From the town hall, go north on Main Street, and the last building on the left, before the bridge, is a replica, in stone, of the building in which the famed theater curtain painter Charles Andrus had a studio. Once he painted large canvases of the Civil War here, including the Cedar Creek scene now at the National Guard Museum in Colchester and the multiscene Civil War work now at the Vermont Historical Society.

On the third floor of the brick building just across the bridge, on the left, Richford's Frontier Post of the GAR met. Go right on crossing the bridge to Church Street. The frame house on the left, at the intersection, was Lucian Parker's home. Parker, a stalwart of the Frontier Post, was a private in the 10th Vermont the last eighteen months of the war. His stone in nearby Hillside Cemetery lists the battles he fought.

Return to the old GAR hall and pass it on River Street. In 0.4 mile, turn right on Pinnacle Hill Road, then quickly right on Drew Road. In 0.6 mile, on the left and just before reaching the Canadian border, is a house with barn behind. John Smith, a private and wagoner in the 3rd Vermont lived here, serving from mid-1863 to mid-1864. His brother Richard joined the 10th Vermont in the summer of 1864 and two years later was wounded in the June 3, 1864, assault at Cold Harbor.

Return to the GAR building, go right on Main Street, and turn left on Route 105 East at the Catholic Church. In 0.4 mile, on the left, is a square brick house by the old railroad bed once owned by Charles Lovelette. It may have been from here that he and his twin brother Edward enlisted as privates in Company G, 13th Vermont. They were late reporting, after a disagreement concerning who should go and who should remain at home. Finally, they both joined. Charles soon became ill and remained at the Brattleboro hospital until his discharge in March 1863. Edward fought at Gettysburg.

Go 0.2 mile past the Lovelette house, turn sharp right onto a dirt road, and in 1.25 miles pass a cemetery. Bear left at a Y, and in 0.25 mile, go left and uphill to the first house. William Kinsley lived here after the war (see Fletcher). Kinsley, an abolitionist like his brother Rufus, was a private in the 8th Vermont. While in Louisiana, he helped Rufus run a camp for escaped slaves. Severely wounded during the siege of Port Hudson, after the war he had a difficult time holding a job. But while living in Lowell, he held town offices and was elected to the legislature. He lived the last of his life here, never well, and on a February day in 1891, he hanged himself.

Return to Route 105 and continue east, and in just under 3 miles, go right up Stevens Mill Slide Road. In 0.75 mile is a farmhouse with a barn across the road. It is believed that Eber Wright went from here to enlist as a corporal in the 7th Vermont in February 1862. In Louisiana, six months later, he died of disease.

Continue on Stevens Mill Slide Road, cross a small cement bridge, and on the right is a frame house with a long front porch and small barn nearby. It is believed that Julius Minor lived here before joining the 11th Vermont as a private. He was killed at Cedar Creek.

SOURCES

RANKIN, DAVID C. *DIARY OF A CHRISTIAN SOLDIER: RUFUS KINSLEY AND THE CIVIL WAR*. NEW YORK: CAMBRIDGE UNIVERSITY PRESS, 2004.

RICHFORD TOWN RECORDS.

SALISBURY, JACK C. *RICHFORD VERMONT: FRONTIER TOWN*. CANAAN, NH: PHOENIX PUBLISHING, 1987.

WITH THANKS TO DEAN HOWARTH.

ST. ALBANS

On Main Street of the busy, unsuspecting, railroad town of St. Albans on a fall day in 1864, Confederates suddenly appeared and gunfire sounded in the northernmost land action of the Civil War. The St. Albans Raid of October 19, 1864, was a Confederate victory on a remarkable day that also saw, 500 miles south, a crucial northern victory at Cedar Creek, won very much due to the heroics of Vermonters.

In mid-October 1864, some twenty Confederate soldiers, in civilian clothes, arrived in St. Albans over the course of several days by train, mostly from Canada. Taking rooms in the town's hotels, they attracted little attention since strangers were always passing through the railroad town. Kentuckian Bennett Young, the leader, had once ridden with the Confederate raider John Hunt Morgan. Young and his men had escaped from Union prisons in and around Chicago, crossed into Canada, and made their way to Montreal. In St. Albans, Young posed as a theology student, riding about the countryside studying his Bible.

On October 19, Young gathered his men in a hotel room along Main Street and gave final instructions. In early afternoon, the Rebels, some uniformed, entered St. Albans's three banks with pistols drawn. "Not a word," said a raider to a teller, "we are Confederate soldiers, have come to take your town, have a large force. We shall take your money, if you resist, will blow your brains out. We are going to do what Sheridan has been doing in the Shenandoah Valley."

Startled townspeople were herded into Taylor Park and kept under close guard. Meanwhile, $208,000 was removed from the banks. It was all over in some twenty minutes, but as the raiders prepared to ride away, on stolen horses, some locals opened fire. One raider was severely wounded. Galloping north along Main Street, the Confederates returned fire and threw bottles filled with Greek fire (incendiaries) at and into buildings, intent on starting a conflagration. Partly due to a recent rain, the grenades fizzled. Elnius Morrison, a New Hampshire man in town to build a new hotel, was mortally wounded as he watched the raiders' departure. A posse, commanded by Captain George Conger (see Georgia), was quickly in pursuit, pounding up Main and onto Sheldon Road.

The St. Albans Historical Society stands along the east side of Taylor Park in a building that was the village schoolhouse in 1864. It was built by Elnius Morrison, the only person killed in the raid. Indeed, all the buildings on the park's east side were witness to the raid. When it began, the schoolchildren were meeting in the hall on the school's top floor. When word of the Confederate attack was received, they were hurried to the lower floor for protection, getting a glimpse of the action from stairway windows. That top-floor room has been restored and is once again an auditorium. In the room, Civil War soldiers were recruited and abolitionists spoke. The building's museum contains a diorama, with a narration of Champlain Valley history and of St. Albans at the time of the raid. Some of the currency stolen by the raiders is displayed, as are reward posters and photos of Bennett Young and his men. The museum's military room displays items from many wars, including George Stannard's saddle.

In 1870, Union troops commanded by Gettysburg victor George Meade, camped in Taylor Park, where the townspeople had been kept under guard six years earlier. The troops were called to St. Albans to keep an eye on Irish Fenians, intent on invading Canada. Facing the park is the Congregational Church, where the *Burlington Free Press* reported on June 12, 1863, that Meade "attended a Sabbath School Anniversary" and "made a brief and happy address to the children." With him, and also speaking, was famed Civil War newspaperman Charles Carleton Coffin. The previous evening, Meade had spoken in town, after being serenaded by a band, praising the 2nd Vermont Brigade's performance at Gettysburg. According to the *Free Press*, Meade noted that he was in Vermont doing his duty as a soldier 'however much sympathy I may have for sincere but misguided men.'" Among the Fenians was Gettysburg hero John Lonergan.

Return to the museum, take Church Street north, and go left on Bank Street. Turn left on Main Street, go to the traffic light, and turn right on Lake Street. At the first intersection, the brick and clapboard building on the left, with porches, was one of the hotels in which some of the raiders stayed. Directly on the right at the intersection is the old St. Albans foundry, managed by George Stannard before the war. Ahead and to the right is the railroad station, built on the site of the old station where the raiders arrived. Behind it is a long redbrick building that stood in 1864, part of the station complex.

Return up Lake Street, and on the left, at the corner of Main, is the St. Albans House, another hotel that housed raiders. In one of its rooms, Elnius Morrison died of his wounds. Look to the right to an auto dealership facing Taylor Park, where one of the robbed banks stood. Turn north along Main Street and note the Franklin County Bank, on the site of another pilfered bank. Farther north along Main, at the corner of Kingman Street, a large three-story brick structure stands at the location of the third bank. Two of the three banks went into bankruptcy after the raid.

A bit farther north along Main Street is city hall, built on the site of the hotel in which Young assembled his men just before they entered the banks. Across Main is a white two-story building with a large modern display window. The wounded Morrison was taken here and treated before being removed to the America House.

Return south on Main Street 0.5 mile past Taylor Park to Greenwood Cemetery, where several St. Albans people associated with the raid are buried. Among them is John Gregory Smith, a railroad executive, who in 1864 was serving as Vermont's governor. In Montpelier the day of the raid, because the legislature was in session, Smith had recently warned lawmakers that Vermont's northern areas might well be vulnerable to a raid. His wife, Anna Smith, who lies beside him, guarded the family's St. Albans home and stable with a pistol during the raid. Also in Greenwood

Cemetery is the grave of Captain Conger, who led the posse.

Near the cemetery entrance is a stone that records a family's anger at the death of a son in Andersonville prison. The stone says: "Joseph Partridge Brainerd, son of Joseph and his wife Fanny Partridge, a conscientious faithful brave Union soldier. Was born on the 27th day of June 1840. Graduated from the University of Vermont in August 1862. Enlisted in Company L of the Vermont Cavalry was wounded and taken prisoner by the Rebels in the Wilderness May 5 1864 was sent to Andersonville prison pen in Georgia where he died on the 11th day of September 1864 entirely and wholly neglected by President Lincoln and murdered with impunity by the Rebels, with thousands of our loyal soldiers by starvation privation exposure and abuse." The son's body never came home and lies in the Andersonville National Cemetery.

Partridge's father had once been a strong supporter of Lincoln, playing an important role in the 1860 Republican convention that nominated him.

To follow the route of the raiders, return to the center of the city by Taylor Park and go north along Main Street 1 mile to the intersection of Route 105. Note that along the way, many houses lining the street predate the Civil War and were witness to the raid. Turn right on Route 105, and like the raiders, you are headed north for Sheldon, Enosburg Falls, and Canada. Follow their route using the Sheldon chapter.

SOURCES
HISTORICAL MUSEUM HISTORY WALK. ST. ALBANS HISTORICAL MUSEUM.
ST. ALBANS CITY RECORDS.
WOODWARD JON. "THE ST. ALBANS RAID: REBELS IN VERMONT." *BLUE AND GRAY MAGAZINE*, DECEMBER 1990.
WITH THANKS TO ADMIRAL WARREN HAMM AND DON MINER.

SHELDON

When the Confederates made their escape from St. Albans the afternoon of October 19, 1864, they headed for Canada, with a posse under Captain George Conger some twenty minutes behind. Still, the raiders under Bennett Young planned to rob another bank, in Sheldon. Go north from St. Albans on Route 105 and soon come to the intersection of Route 104. Continue north on 105, and in 2 miles, to follow the Rebels' route, turn right on Pond Road. Somewhere on their way to Sheldon, likely on Pond Road, the raiders met a local man riding south toward St. Albans. They relieved him of his fine horse and let him have a nag they had stolen. The bewildered man continued on his way but soon saw the St. Albans posse approaching. Its members, recognizing the stolen horse and thinking its rider a Rebel, opened fire. The man saved himself by running into an alder swamp. Continue on Pond Road 2.75 miles, and bear left on Woods road, which continues to Sheldon village. Turn right on Main Street, and the prominent house on the knoll to the right, once the home of a Revolutionary War colonel, was a witness to the raiders passing.

Take Main Street to Bridge Street and turn left. Ahead is a cement bridge that spans Black Creek, where a wooden covered bridge stood in 1864. When the Confederates reached the bridge, a farmer with a wagonload of hay was crossing it. The raiders set fire to the hay, hoping to burn the bridge, but the fire was extinguished by Reverend Hawley, pastor of the 1859 Methodist Church. That church stands prominently on the hill across the creek, overlooking the bridge. The covered bridge stood until a night in 1932, when a fire erupted in buildings along Black Creek. St. Albans historian Dorothy Hemenway Ashton wrote of the bridge's last night: "For awhile the old bridge hung on—it seemed to kind of tremble in the heat of it all. I rather like to feel it was human enough to think, 'I've stood freshets, floods and thaws, Rebel Raiders and other town fires, but I've been lonesome lately. I don't somehow fit in this simple age . . . What's this? The old sheds and blacksmith shop going? Then I want to go, too.' It seemed sort of glad to be free."

Cross the bridge and go straight, as did the Confederates, round a sharp left turn and quickly come to a T. Go right there, and a road quickly enters on the right. At the intersection, in the southeast corner, once stood the Mississquoi Bank. Confederates found the bank door locked, and with a posse close behind, they rode on north. But before leaving, they stole a horse from the dooryard across the road. That horse belonged to Alfred Horton Keith, a captain in the 4th Vermont, who had been wounded at the Wilderness and was recuperating here in the family home.

The lovely Keith home still stands, beside the brick Grace Episcopal Church.

The church was built mostly because of the generosity of Captain Keith's father, Alfred Keith, who also built the Keith house. The captain's uncle, Reuel Keith, a minister of the Episcopal Church, years before had moved to Virginia, where he founded the Virginia Theological Seminary in Arlington. On April 30, 1831, Reverend Keith rode through a heavy spring rain to Arlington House, the majestic home of the Lee family standing prominently on Arlington Heights, overlooking Washington, D.C. On arriving, Keith performed a marriage ceremony for Mary Anna Randolph Custis, great-granddaughter of Martha Washington, and Lieutenant Robert E. Lee, who would one day lead the Confederate Army of Northern Virginia.

Reuel Keith returned to Sheldon late in life and lived his last few years in this house.

Meanwhile, in 1864, the Confederate raiders, having stolen the horse of the nephew of the man who married their General Lee, continued on their way north, toward Enosburg Falls and hoped-for safety in Canada.

At the time of the Civil War, Sheldon had a population of 1,655. About 135 Sheldon men served and at least 11 died.

SOURCES
ASHTON, DOROTHY HEMENWAY. SHELDON, VERMONT: THE PEOPLE WHO LIVED AND WORKED THERE. ST. ALBANS, VT: REGAL ART PRESS, 1979.
JOHNSON, CARL E. THE ST. ALBANS RAID, 19 OCTOBER 1864. ST. ALBANS: PRIVATELY PRINTED, 2001. ORIGINALLY WRITTEN IN 1872. VERMONT HISTORICAL SOCIETY.
ST. ALBANS RAID FILES. VERMONT HISTORICAL SOCIETY.
WITH THANKS TO ALBERT SEVERY AND GEORGE STEBBINS.

SWANTON

The Village Green Park, along Route 7 in downtown Swanton, is something of a Civil War shrine. At the north end is a war memorial with a white marble figure of Liberty, holding a flag. A century of north country weather has worn from its pedestal the names of the Swanton men who died in Abraham Lincoln's forces. But modern marble markers around the statue again list those names, including Isiah Ramo, killed at the Wilderness; Erastus Stearns, killed at Baton Rouge; Alanson Watson, killed at Cold Harbor; and Martin Clark, dead at Andersonville. The first name on the list is that of Colonel Elisha Barney, dead on May 10, 1864, succumbing to wounds received at the Wilderness.

Far too many people for a church to hold gathered here in the park for Barney's funeral on Wednesday, May 18, 1864. Colonel Barney, commanding the 6th Vermont, was shot in the head as the Vermont Brigade was raked by a sudden fusillade of musketry as it advanced into the Wilderness on the afternoon of May 5, 1864. Barney, thirty-two, survived a jolting ambulance ride to a hospital in Fredericksburg, where he died five days later. The Reverend J. B. Perry, of Swanton, attended his funeral and wrote:

"His remains . . . reached the railway station of his native town, Swanton, Saturday evening, May 13. Their arrival was awaited by a large concourse of citizens who accompanied them to his father's house, at the hour of twilight, amid the tolling of the bell, the peal of the cannon, and the beat of the muffled drum. The funeral services were held in the open air on Wednesday, the 18th. The body was borne to the park, that all who wished might once more look upon the face of the deceased . . . . Citizens assembled in large numbers from Swanton, and the neighboring towns, to pay the last rites of respect to the departed. Rev. D. U. Dayton preached a discourse commemorative on the virtues of the deceased, founded on the words: 'How are the mighty fallen in the midst of the battle.' A funeral procession was then formed, consisting of the large assembly, followed by the pall bearers, several clergymen, the mourners and the members of the Sabbath-school. The body was borne to the place of burial, and after the singing of the song, 'Wrap the flag around me, boys,' the coffin was lowered, and dust consigned to dust."

Colonel Barney is buried in the Church Street Cemetery, located on Church Street just off Route 7, south of the park. There lie many Civil War soldiers, including Colonel Albert Jewett, who commanded the 10th Vermont early in its service. Near the entrance is an impressive gravestone of one of Vermont's most famous soldiers, Lieutenant Stephen Brown, 13th Vermont. On the long march to Gettysburg, in stifling heat, Brown, disobeying General Stannard's order not to break ranks to obtain water, was arrested and deprived of his weapons. Yet Brown was in the brigade's flank attack on Pickett's Charge and, picking up a hatchet, he forced a Confederate colonel to surrender his sword. The incident became famous, and when the 13th erected its regimental monument at Gettysburg, it chose the incident as its theme. The plan was for Brown to be depicted wielding the hatchet, but the Gettysburg Monument Commission refused to approve a statue that honored insubordination.

Brown reenlisted after Stannard's Brigade came home, joining the 17th Vermont and commanding its Company A. In its first battle, the Wilderness, he suffered a wound that cost him an arm. But Brown survived and was present at Gettysburg on October 19, 1889, for the 13th's monument dedication. Brown is rendered in bronze, with the famous hatchet at his feet. Brown's grave marker is topped by a marble angel, whose upraised hand once pointed a finger toward heaven. But the finger long ago broke away, leaving an upraised fist.

Beside Brown lies Corporal William Church, a Highgate lad who also served in the 13th. His much smaller memorial says, "Loved one rest. He gave his life to his country as a willing sacrifice." Church was hit by an artillery shell at Gettysburg, as the regiment moved against Pickett. "Among all the bodies that I had seen on this gory field, his was the most horribly mangled," said fellow soldier Ralph Orson Sturtevant.

Sturtevant was the 13th Vermont's official historian and compiled the massive *Pictorial History of the 13th Regiment Vermont Volunteers, War of 1861–1865*. A labor of many years, Sturtevant completed the eight-hundred-page manuscript in 1911 but died shortly before its publication. The book remains the finest single source on the 2nd Vermont Brigade's nine months service. Sturtevant, an attorney, completed that imposing task in his home on Church Street, just north of the cemetery, the redbrick house with a double-deck porch facing the south end of the park.

From the park, go north of Route 7, cross the Mississquoi River bridge, and go straight ahead onto Depot Street. At the end, a siding still leaves the main track where trains stopped in the 1860s. Here, men took the train to and from war, including members of Company K of the 13th Vermont, which drilled in Highgate. And it was here that Colonel Barney's body arrived.

SOURCES

LEDOUX, RODNEY. THE HISTORY OF SWANTON, VERMONT. SWANTON, VT: SWANTON HISTORICAL SOCIETY, 1988.

Old stone hall south of Alburgh where 55 local men enlisted.

chapter eight

Grand Isle County

On Grand Isle, the largest island in Grand Isle County, much of the western shore was once owned by Quaker families. Though people of peace, many of their sons chose to go to war against slavery. Among them was Byron Hoag, who enlisted at thirty, and wrote from the 3rd Vermont's winter camp, just before the Overland Campaign: "Oh how I would like to have a permanent peace declared, then go home and find you as happy and contented as you used to be." Days later, Hoag died at Spotsylvania's Bloody Angle. South of Alburgh is the old stone hall, where 55 local men enlisted in an 11th Vermont company. At Weldon Railroad, 17 were captured, and 6 would die in Confederate prisons. At the south end of Isle La Motte, a marker on an old farm notes that Vice President Theodore Roosevelt received word here of the death of William McKinley. He was suddenly president. No mention is made of the three lads who went from here to the Civil War and died. The Methodist Church in North Hero was added atop the county courthouse in 1872. To this day, it is seen as a symbol of the return of peace after the Civil War. Butler Island, off the west coast of the island county, was once owned by the Butler family. That family produced the mother of Wild Bill Hickok, legend of the West and Civil War soldier.

....

ALBURGH

Going north on Route 2, cross the bridge from North Hero and enter Alburgh, Grand Isle County's largest town. Note an old frame house on the left, 1.5 miles from the bridge, with barns behind. From here, Thomas Babcock, forty-four, and his son William, nineteen, enlisted in Company K of the 11th Vermont in the summer of 1862. Thomas, a sergeant, was captured at Weldon Railroad and died five months later of diarrhea in Andersonville. William, a private, was wounded at Cold Harbor and recovered to end the war as a sergeant.

Continue north on Route 2 for 3.75 miles and the big brick building, on the left, was the Alburgh town hall in the 1860s. Not only did Alburgh residents deal with the town's wartime issues here, but in the summer of 1862, a recruiting office was set up in the building. A total of fifty-five men credited to Alburgh, including the Babcocks, here joined the 11th Vermont's Company K. Indeed, the regiment drilled here, under the command of Captain George Sowles, of Alburgh, who would be wounded at Cold Harbor. Going to war as an artillery unit, the 11th became an infantry company and joined the Vermont Brigade at Spotsylvania in May 1864. At Weldon Railroad near Petersburg, seventeen Alburgh men were captured. Six died in Rebel prisons. None of their bodies came home.

Continue north on Route 2 and quickly turn left on Truck Route opposite the intersection of Route 78. In 0.5 mile, the small frame house on the left, with barn to the rear, is believed to have been Jackson Eddy's home. A corporal in Company K, Eddy was captured at Weldon Railroad but escaped on the way to Andersonville. He managed to rejoin his regiment and served until the war ended.

Continue on Truck Route to the lake and go south on West Shore Road. In 0.4 mile, on the left, is a house with double porch that faces the lake. Built by Hardy Ladue after the war, the building was used as a small hotel. Ladue was a private in the 13th Vermont. At Gettysburg on July 3, during the artillery duel that preceded Pickett's Charge, he helped a sick comrade to the rear, with the permission of his company commander. According to the regimental historian, Ladue never returned to his position in line of battle and did not rejoin his regiment until after dark. When asked his reason, the popular soldier replied, "Well, I would rather be a live coward than a dead hero." His comrades forgave him.

Continue on West Shore Road, and in 0.5 mile, by the lake, is an elegant stone house with "1825" and "Joseph Mott" inscribed above the door. Judd Mott grew up here and went west before the Civil War. Enlisting in the 16th Michigan Infantry, Captain Mott was severely wounded while charging a Rebel battery in a skirmish near Middleburg, Virginia, on June 21, 1863. His bravery that day was commended by his brigade commander, Brigadier General Strong Vincent, who died ten days later on Gettysburg's Little Round Top. Mott, twenty-nine, died as June ended in a Washington, D.C., hospital.

Turn around here and go north on Lake Shore Road until it ends on Route 2. Turn left, north, and on the left is a large brick house. George Mott, apparently a cousin of Judd, lived here and enlisted in the 13th Vermont, fighting at Gettysburg.

Continue north on Route 2 through Alburgh village to Bush Cemetery on the right. Several Alburgh soldiers are buried here, including Judd Mott, in the family plot at the cemetery's north end. The large family stone bears his name. He lies by his own small stone that has only the words *Our George*.

Just north of the cemetery is a brick house where Asahel Manning lived. Enlisting in the 13th Vermont at age eighteen, Manning fought at Gettysburg. He joined the 17th Vermont in early 1864 and served until the war ended.

Just north of the Manning house is a stone schoolhouse where Manning, George Sowles, and several other Alburgh lads destined to wear Union blue studied. A total of 136 men were credited to Alburgh. Of them, 17 died.

SOURCES
ALBURGH TOWN RECORDS.
WITH THANKS TO ROBERT KRICK.

....

GRAND ISLE

The main intersection in the town of Grand Isle, which lies north of South Hero and south of North Hero, is along Route 2 where Hyde Road turns west. Just south of the intersection, on the west side, set back from the road is a large and rambling old frame house that once had a dance hall in its upper story and was Melvin Corey's home. Corey at thirty-two became part of the 13th Vermont, and according to Ralph Sturtevant, regimental historian, he was "the only drafted man that served in Company K," but "a good and faithful soldier." Sturtevant added, "He said to the writer that he could have had a substitute, and his wife and her people were anxious to have him procure a substitute, and offered to furnish the money, but he would not consent. He said he was drafted and the Government needed men and a drafted man could do as good a service as any." On the march to Gettysburg, Corey remarked that he "would not now leave if given permission, for I am convinced we shall all be needed before this campaign is over." Corey fought in the attack on Pickett's Charge. When it was over, Corey asked Sturtevant, "What think you of drafted men now?" Corey came home a corporal and lived in Grand Isle until he died in 1901, a highly respected citizen.

From the main intersection, go west on Hyde Road, and quickly, on the right, is the 1854 redbrick church. Brought into being by the Reverend Orville Wheeler, it served both Congregationalists and Methodists. Wheeler was long a Congregational minister in both South Hero and Grand Isle (see South Hero). An opponent of slavery, on the alternate Sundays he preached here, his flock heard condemnations of slavery.

Go west on Hyde Road 0.6 mile to the intersection of Raynolds Road. The house at the southeast corner was the home of Charles Watkins, forty-three when he joined the 9th Vermont at Christmastime 1863 to serve until war's end.

Continue on Hyde Road to Adams School Road, turn left, south, and in 0.2 mile, go right on Quaker Road. The Grand Isle Quaker Cemetery is at the corner. People of the Quaker faith came to Grand Isle in the 1780s, and among the early arrivals were Hoags, Macombers, and Tobiases. The Quaker Cemetery, founded in 1801, is filled with the small and simple stone markers favored by the sect.

Go west on Quaker Road to West Shore Road skirting the west side of the island, an area once virtually all owned by Quakers. Just south of the intersection of West Shore Road, a narrow driveway leads to an old farmhouse by the lake. Here still live Hoags. Two decades before the Civil War, James Byron Hoag was fined for failing to attend militia training. Many Quakers were pacifists. Still, many young Quakers from Grand Isle served in the War Between the States.

From this house, James Byron Hoag's son Byron Hoag, at thirty, signed up with the 3rd Vermont in July 1863. He wrote regularly to his family here, usually beginning his letters "Dearest friends." Early on plagued by illness, he recovered by late winter and was on duty with his regiment in the winter camp at Brandy Station. He wrote on March 11, 1864, "There is a crowd of boys here playing cards and they make so much noise that I shall cut this letter short for I cannot hear myself think. I am in health. Please give me an interest in your prayers."

March 29: "If I live to reach home I want to find the family all there. Oh how much I would like to have a permanent peace declared, then go home and find you all there as happy and contended as you used to be."

May 3 (the eve of the Overland Campaign): "They have commenced packing up and are ready to move . . . We can only trust in Providence. I am hurried so please excuse me. I am well and healthy and hope to remain so."

On May 20, from "Field near Spotsylvania, Va.," an officer wrote to the Hoag family: "When this letter reaches you, you will be mourning over an affliction as great as any that can befall a family . . . He was killed instantly by a musket ball about noon on Thursday the 12th of this month in one of the fiercest battles of this bloody campaign. Our men of the old Vermont Brigade fought that day sometimes hand to hand for a long time with only a breastwork of a few feet in thickness to separate them from the enemy . . . They say he was buried by our men . . . Opposed to war as he was . . . he was a good and brave soldier. From the greater interest he took here in spiritual things he was fully prepared to die." Private Hoag was killed at Spotsylvania's Bloody Angle. His body never came home.

Go north on West Shore Drive 1 mile and, on the left, is a large farmhouse that was the home of Wyman Macomber. Though a Quaker, Macomber joined the 11th Vermont as a private at forty, the last day of 1863. Captured at Weldon Railroad, he survived nearly nine months in Andersonville. He came home a corporal, apparently in broken health, and died eleven years later. Orlando Macomber, a private in the 11th who joined in 1862, was killed at Cold Harbor. Lindley Macomber was drafted into the 4th Vermont in July 1863 but was soon discharged, the records say, "by reason of being a Quaker."

Continue on West Shore Road and go straight, at the curve, onto Adams Landing Road. In 0.3 mile, on the right, is the old redbrick Tobias homestead. This early Quaker family saw three men go to war. Charles and Henry together joined the 11th Vermont in September 1862 as privates. Charles, twenty-one, was captured at Weldon Railroad and sent to Andersonville. Paroled after five months, he served until war's end and came home to live until 1915. Henry, also captured at the Weldon, also went to Andersonville. Transferred to a stockade at Millen, Georgia, he died as the war ended. James Tobias enlisted in the 9th Vermont at eighteen and served the last eighteen months of the war.

Follow Adams Landing Road until it ends at Moccasin Avenue. Turn left on Moccasin, and quickly, on the right, at the corner of Adams School Road, is Adams School, which the Tobias and Macomber boys attended. One-quarter mile beyond, on the left, is the home of Hiram Tobias, who hired a substitute and did not serve.

Proceed on Moccasin Avenue 0.4 mile and go left on Simms Point Road. In 0.8 mile, the road becomes private. But look ahead to the redbrick house by the lake. Homer Hurlburt was a private in the 17th Vermont the last ten months of the war, surviving the Petersburg siege to come home and live here until 1908. He was one of forty-six soldiers from Grand Isle.

SOURCES

GRAND ISLE TOWN RECORDS.

MILLARD, JAMES P. *THE LAKE CHAMPLAIN AND LAKE GEORGE HISTORICAL SITE.* SOUTH HERO, VT: AMERICA'S HISTORIC LAKES, 1977.

STRATTON, ALLEN L. *HISTORY OF THE SOUTH HERO ISLAND BEING THE TOWNS OF SOUTH HERO AND GRAND ISLE VERMONT.* BARRE, VT: PRIVATELY PRINTED, 1980.

WITH THANKS TO DON AND MAY CHAMBERLIN AND JAMES HOAG.

ISLE LA MOTTE

Isle La Motte's Main Street is Route 129, and along it stands the Isle La Motte town hall. Meeting here on February 16, 1863, $350 bounties were approved, but before the meeting adjourned, an additional $150 was added. On August 29, 1864, a $1,000 bounty payment was made to Charles Fleury, who served the last ten months of the war as a private in the 11th Vermont.

The library is by the town hall and the building just north of it, much changed from its original appearance, was the home of Dr. Melvin Hyde, who returned home to practice medicine after graduating from Dartmouth Medical School in 1852. Hyde loved this little island town and, in 1856, when he had to go away, briefly, he wrote:

> Proud Isle! Must I leave thee! And no more thy beauty behold?
> So soon must I leave thee! Thy lovely fields and rocks so bold?
> The forests grand so gaily waving o'er marble shores?
> Fair Queen of the Lake!

For three years, Hyde was a surgeon in the 2nd Vermont, and he wrote often to his wife, Alice, letters, which have been made into a book. From Fredericksburg on May 18, 1864, he described a field hospital on the Wilderness battlefield:

"The soldiers were cut down by the hundreds . . . We put up three large hospital tents, which were crowded with wounded while 1500 men lay on the ground around uttering the most heart-rending cries of agony. We numbered but 5 or 6 surgeons and it took us about 3 days to attend to them and many had to be moved in army wagons and ambulances without their wounds having been dressed at all! All this time the ambulances continued to bring in the wounded of our Division and the cannonading and musketry was almost deafening. O! it was terrible to hear the poor fellows cry for water or in piteous tones cry out to any surgeon that chanced to pass near them for help." After the army moved on, Hyde stayed with the wounded and was captured, though held only four days.

Ten days after the Battle of Cedar Creek, he wrote to Alice, "Our division suffered dreadfully. I was struck on the side of my knee by a piece of shell. I thought I had lost my leg—The cut has healed, but it is some lame yet."

On May 20, 1865, Hyde, always on the lookout for souvenirs, was in Richmond and visited Jefferson Davis's abandoned office. He sent Alice some threads from the president's chair. "I also send a sprig of locust," he wrote, "which I got at Jef Davis's house. His house is plain but richly furnished."

Hyde came safely home to Isle La Motte to long resume his medical practice.

Go north on Main Street 1 mile, and on the right is an old house with a long porch and barn behind. Seneca Pike saw his twenty-year-old son Preston, whom he called Perry, go to war from this house. He served only three months as a private in Company E, 2nd U.S. Sharpshooters, coming home ill in February 1862. He died here the following December.

The next house north, on the left, a log cabin that has been added to and altered to look modern, was the home of another Pike family. From here James, Herman, and Henry Pike enlisted. Henry and James joined the 5th Vermont's Company C in 1861. Henry was killed at the April 2, 1865, Petersburg Breakthrough. James served until war's end, becoming a sergeant. Herman joined the 11th Vermont in 1862, became a corporal, and served through 1864. Their father, Henry Pike, died on December 30, 1865, while bringing the town's mail across the Lake Champlain ice.

Go north on Main Street to the intersection of Shrine Road and note, at the southeast corner, a lot filled with lilac bushes where the Nathaniel Holbrook home stood. Son Augustus was a musician in the 5th Vermont for a year, until discharged with poor health. Son Calvin, a sergeant in 17th Vermont, was wounded at the Petersburg Breakthrough. Son George, a private in the 1st U.S. Sharpshooters, died at nineteen of disease on May 12, 1862, having served but nine months.

Return as you came on Main Street, pass the town hall, and take the first left. The first house on the right was the home of brothers Francis and Lorenzo Holcomb, who both enlisted as privates in

Company C of the 5th Vermont in the fall of 1861. Three months later, Francis, thirty-one, died of sickness. Lorenzo, twenty-one, was soon transferred to serve on a gunboat. He died in June 1862, cause unknown.

Return to Main Street and follow it until it becomes West Shore Drive. Soon, along the lakeshore is a historic marker on the right set before what was once the Fisk family home and quarrying operation. The marker notes that Vice President Theodore Roosevelt was a guest here when news reached him on September 14, 1901, that President William McKinley had died.

Ira Fisk grew up in the stone house here and lived his life in this area. Three of his sons served in the Civil War. John, a corporal in the 11th Vermont, died at twenty-nine of wounds at Third Winchester. Julius, a private in the 5th Vermont, was killed at Savage's Station at twenty-five. Samuel, also a private in the 5th, died of sickness three months after he enlisted in 1861, at twenty-one.

Another Fisk, Edson, probably a cousin, enlisted at eighteen as a private in the 11th Vermont in 1862 and was captured at Weldon Railroad. He died on June 24, 1865, soon after being released from Andersonville.

According to Hemenway, Isle La Motte furnished 73 soldiers of whom 14 died in battle, and 4 in army hospitals.

SOURCES
CHITTICK, GERALDINE FRANCES, ED. *IN THE FIELD DOCTOR MELVIN HYDE SURGEON, 2ND VERMONT VOLUNTEERS*. NEWPORT, VT: VERMONT CIVIL WAR ENTERPRISES, 1999.
ISLE LA MOTTE TOWN RECORDS.
STRATTON, ALLEN L. *HISTORY, TOWN OF ISLE LA MOTTE VERMONT: AN ACCOUNT OF THE DISCOVERY, SETTLEMENT, AND INTERESTING AND REMARKABLE EVENTS*. BARRE, VT: PRIVATELY PRINTED, 1984.
WITH THANKS TO THE MCEWENS.

NORTH HERO

North Hero town meetings took place in the 1824 stone Grand Isle County Courthouse, which stands along Route 2, with a gold-topped cupola. On Monday, December 14, 1863, bounties of $300 were voted, but selectmen were also authorized to borrow "on the credit of the town such sum as shall be needed for the payment of bounties." In February 1865, bounties of $600 were approved to enable the town to meet its latest quota. One study of North Hero during the war has found that only thirty of the men who served from the town can be identified as North Hero residents, perhaps indicating that many men who enlisted here came from north of the nearby Canadian border. North Hero sent sixty-three men to the Civil War.

The Methodist Church is beside the courthouse. The lower portion was built, at the direction of the voters in 1866, as a town meeting hall. In 1872, the church was added above it. To this day the building is regarded by North Hero people as a symbol of the return of peace and good times after the Civil War.

From the courthouse, go north on Route 2 along the island's east shore. Pass the North Hero school and town offices, and the next house, on the right, a long farmhouse with chimney in the front and barns across the street, was owned by Jesse Hazen in 1860. It appears that when the war began, Almon Chapel and Clarence Hazen were working on this farm as hired hands. Chapel, a native of Canada, enlisted at twenty-four in September 1864 as a private in the 7th Vermont and served until the war ended, seeing action in the attack on Spanish Fort at Mobile, Alabama. Hazen, a native Vermonter, enlisted, at twenty-one, in the 6th Vermont in September 1861. But he was soon transferred to serve on a gunboat called the *Flotilla*, probably on the Mississippi River.

Continue north on Route 2 and soon bear right on Lakeshore Drive. In 0.25 mile, on the left, is a large shingled 1850 house in two sections. In the autumn of 1861, Spellman Hazen, a hired man here employed by James McBride, joined the 6th Vermont as a private and served for three years. On May 4, a Rebel bullet tore through his right shoulder in the assault on the heights at Fredericksburg.

Continue on Lakeshore Drive just under 2 miles, and the Best House, an 1860 farmhouse with a wing on each side of the main building, is on the right. Some twenty years after the war, a veteran, whose name has been lost, was entertaining some children with tales of wartime adventure. With musket in hand, he showed them how to fire the old weapon. To his shock, it was loaded and blew a hole in the ceiling of the summer kitchen.

Return south on Lakeshore Drive until reaching Route 2. Before turning south, left, note the big old frame house across

the road, built on land once owned by the Butler family. As you proceed south along Route 2, look left, east, and out in the lake see low and forested Butler Island. At one time, much of the island was owned by Butlers. James Butler came to North Hero in the 1790s to join brother Benjamin who had already settled here. James married Eunice Kinsley, of Fletcher. Among their ten children was Polly, born on August 4, 1804, in North Hero. In 1827, at North Hero, Polly Butler married William Alonzo Hickok. They moved in 1837 to Troy Grove, Illinois, and produced seven children. Among them was James Butler Hickok. The Hickoks' Illinois farm became a stop on the Underground Railroad.

James served with the Union army in Kansas and Missouri as a scout, sometimes operating with William Cody. After the war, he continued to scout for the army, sometimes for George Custer. In 1865, Hickok shot a man in a "quick draw" confrontation, the first ever recorded. His legend began to grow, and soon he had the nickname Wild Bill. By the time he was shot in the back of the head in 1879, while playing poker, he was a national legend.

Return south, passing the courthouse and Methodist Church, and soon on the right is another old church, long since put to other uses. Once it was the Keeler Ladd store, where, in 1826, Polly Butler bought some muslin and linen for a dress she was making, charging it to her father's account.

Continue south 2.25 miles on Route 2, and turn right on South End Road. Pass a cemetery, and the first house on the right beyond it was the home of Asa Mooney. When he was drafted in 1863, Mooney procured a substitute and did not serve.

Proceed along South End Road and turn right on West Shore Road. In 1.3 miles on the left is North Hero's oldest house, brick and set well back from the road, near the lake. Built in 1835, at the time of the Civil War it was owned by Reuben Hyde, whose son, Charles, furnished a substitute to avoid service. That man apparently was Beach Troy Knight, who worked here for the Hydes. Knight served three years as a Vermont Cavalry private, fought in most of its battles, and came home safely.

SOURCES

AYERS, ROBERT. *NORTH HERO MEN IN THE CIVIL WAR 1861–1865*. HERO, VT: S.N., 2009.
NORTH HERO TOWN RECORDS.
STRATTON, ALLEN L. *HISTORY, TOWN OF NORTH HERO VERMONT*. BARRE, VT: PRIVATELY PRINTED, 1976.
WITH THANKS TO WILLIAM AYERS AND WINSTON WAY.

SOUTH HERO

Take Route 2 west from exit 17 of Interstate 89 and soon cross Lake Champlain at Sandbar on the bridge/causeway. The far end is the southern tip of Grand Isle County, in the town of South Hero, where a tollbooth and hotel once stood by the bridge. Benajah Phelps operated both after serving the last eighteen months of the Civil War in the 8th Vermont, surviving the big battles of the Shenandoah Valley. He later represented South Hero in the legislature.

Continue 2 miles on Route 2 to the town's main intersection, marked by an old stone store at the corner. Just north, on the right, is the 1816 meetinghouse where Civil War–era town meetings were held. Vermonters' cherished right to debate and question did not wane here during the war years. On December 19, 1863, at a special town meeting, a motion was made in favor of "raising a bounty" to pay enlistees. It was approved 39 to 29. But, according to the town clerk's minutes, "An appeal was immediately made on the ground there were illegal votes counted and the moderator proceeded to a second division of the house and the result of the count was 47 in favor of raising a bounty and 33 against. So the motion was declared carried."

A motion was then made "by Mr. Wheeler to assess a tax upon the grand list of 1863 sufficient to raise $300.00 for each enlisted soldier to make up the quota of this town under the last call of the President for 300,000 volunteers, one hundred dollars to be paid to each soldier when mustered into the service of the United States and the remaining $200.00 to be divided in equal payments—provided that in case any of said enlisted men be honorably discharged from service it shall be paid upon said discharge in case of death to their legal representatives and the selectmen are hereby authorized to borrow seven hundred dollars to make the first payment."

A Mr. Robinson then offered an amendment to Mr. Wheeler's motion "that there shall be no money paid until the whole quota [of seven men] was raised." The amendment was defeated.

On August 13, 1864, bounties of $300 were approved under a new draft call for ten men, and the selectmen were told to borrow $3,000 to pay them. In January 1865, $400 bounties were voted.

The Mr. Wheeler referred to in the minutes was the local Congregational minister, Orville G. Wheeler, for decades the dominant personage in South Hero. Wheeler had come to town from Underhill in 1840 to replace Reverend Asa Lyon, old and in failing health, in the Congregational pulpit. The locals took quickly to Wheeler, as a town historian explained: "If Mr. Lyon's God was a God of wrath, then Mr. Wheeler's was a God of love." Wheeler preached in South Hero and in Grand Isle for fifty years, served in the legislature, and was a moving force in building the Sandbar Bridge.

His first preaching was in the old town hall, which also housed the Congregational Church. Wheeler, an abolitionist, surely sermonized on the evils of slavery. Also an amateur poet, he started a "select school" in this building for his better pupils, which thrived until the Civil War took most of them away.

Return to the stone store and go right on South Street. Soon on the right is the 1854 Congregational Church, which Wheeler brought into being. Just beyond, also on the right, is Wheeler's home, a large frame house. From here, the reverend saw his eldest child, Henry Orson Wheeler, go to war in early October 1861. Henry interrupted his studies at his father's alma mater, the University of Vermont, to become a sergeant in the Ver-

mont Cavalry. As the cavalry retreated along the Shenandoah Valley in 1862 before Stonewall Jackson's advance, it was struck and scattered by a surprise attack. Wheeler was forced to hide for several days, and word reached South Hero that he was dead. A year later, after Gettysburg, Lieutenant Wheeler was separated from his unit in the fight at Hagerstown. Again, word came home of his death. Soon back in action, Wheeler was shot through the lungs at Craig's Meeting House, during the Battle of the Wilderness. He recovered, returned to action, won a captain's bars, and was captured in the Shenandoah Valley 1864. He survived Libby Prison, came home to eventually become Burlington's superintendent of schools and a UVM trustee.

Return to Route 2 at the stone store and turn right. In 1 mile, turn left on Kibbe Point Road, and the first house close to the road, on the right, was the Conro family home. From here, Henry Conro, a UVM student, enlisted at nineteen in the 2nd Vermont. Private Conro was captured at First Bull Run and held for nearly a year. Back in action, he was wounded at the Wilderness. His brother, A. Bertrand Conro, joined the Vermont Cavalry as a private at twenty in the summer of 1864. Wounded in the Shenandoah Valley in October 1864, he was discharged for disability in March 1865.

Continue on Kibbe Point Road 1 mile to the intersection of Cavendish Cove Road, and look directly ahead to a stone house and barn amid trees, by the lake. Edwin Phelps enlisted from here as a private in the 8th Vermont in early 1864.

Wounded and captured at Cedar Creek, he was locked up, with other prisoners, in a meetinghouse. Managing to hide beneath the pulpit, he went unnoticed when the other prisoners were marched away. Phelps came home a sergeant, one of forty-two South Hero men to serve.

SOURCES

ALLEN, CATHERINE R. "EARLY DAYS OF SOUTH HERO." VOL. 2. UNPUBLISHED MANUSCRIPT, UNDATED. SOUTH HERO LIBRARY.

SOUTH HERO TOWN RECORDS.

STRATTON, ALLEN L. *HISTORY OF THE SOUTH HERO ISLAND BEING THE TOWNS OF SOUTH HERO AND GRAND ISLE.* BARRE, VT: PRIVATELY PRINTED, 1980.

JULIAN SCOTT
1846-1901

Julian Scott, Vermont's most renowned Civil War artist, was born in this Johnson house in 1846. At the start of the Civil War, when only 15, he enlisted as a fifer in the Third Vermont Regiment. Scott was awarded a Medal of Honor -- for rescuing wounded under enemy fire at the Battle of Lee's Mills, Virginia. He later studied art under Emanuel Leutze at the National Academy of Design in New York and in 1870 was elected an associate member of the Academy. "The Battle of Cedar Creek," his monumental 1874 painting, was commissioned as a Civil War memorial for the Vermont State House. Scott's Civil War and Native American paintings are acclaimed for their authenticity, detail, and democratic viewpoint. He died in Plainfield, New Jersey, in 1901.

VERMONT DIVISION FOR HISTORIC PRESERVATION – 1998

Historic marker by the birthplace of Julian Scott,
Civil War artist and Medal of Honor winner

chapter nine

Lamoille County

Civil War–related activity in Lamoille County centered on the square by the country courthouse in Hyde Park, where war rallies took place and men gathered to enlist. Just up Church Street, the Congregational Church waited, where at least three soldier funerals would take place, among them a service for eighteen-year-old Hiram Hall, killed by a sharpshooter at Petersburg. In

Johnson, Julian Scott left the family home on the west side of the village to enlist in the 3rd Vermont. In his future were a Medal of Honor and being chosen to paint the Battle of Cedar Creek for the State House. From Morristown, a widow left her little house and went to Washington to bring her drummer boy son home. She succeeded, with the help of Abraham Lincoln. In Stowe, a wealthy man financed the building of a memorial hall, then had his remains interred within. In the hills above the village, Olive Cheney, with four sons serving, wrote to her daughter from the family farmhouse: "It is strange what makes the boys want to go to war . . . If the boys hated to go as bad as we hated to

have them there would not be much fighting done could there."

....

BELVIDERE

Belvidere's town office along Route 109 in Belvidere Center is the same building that hosted town meetings during the Civil War. For Abby Hemenway, Henry Willey of Belvidere wrote, "From 1861 to 1865, a time when many, of the most sanguine even, believed our nation to have reached its zenith, and that its decline had already commenced, Belvidere was not behind one of her sister towns, in cheerfully giving her sons, as her free contribution, toward effectually preventing a dismemberment of the Union." Willey also stated that forty Belvidere men served and that "several were either killed or died in service."

If a note of skepticism is detectable in the above, it may reflect the fact that in 1861 the town voted 17 to 11 for Stephen Douglas over Abraham Lincoln for president, and four years later, it favored George McClellan over Lincoln, 33 to 15. The town even cast a one-sided vote against the reelection of Congressman Portus Baxter, who by that time had won statewide admiration for his care of wounded Vermont soldiers. Mr. Willey's reference to the town giving men to the Union "as her free contribution" may relate to the fact that Belvidere appears to have paid no soldier bounties. Indeed, records of Belvidere town meetings hold not a single mention of the war. Still, the town appears to have met its draft quotas. It was to this town building that many of the Belvidere men who enlisted came to sign their enlistment papers. Go south on Route 109, following the North Branch of the Lamoille River, and in 2 miles on the left is the 1850 District Two Belvidere School. Town records indicate that at least three of its former pupils served in the Union armies. Augustus Thomas joined the 11th Vermont as a private in the fall of 1863 and died of typhoid fever the following August, at twenty-eight. Charles Potter served two and one-half years in the 9th Vermont, enlisting at twenty-one. Chauncey Shattuck joined the 8th Vermont at thirty and served through most of the war. Student Amasa Hemenway paid commutation and did not serve.

Continue 0.5 mile on Route 109 to Belvidere Junction and note the church on the left. The *Lamoille Newsdealer* reported on June 16, 1861, that a war meeting was held here. "A large portion of the male inhabitants of Belvidere and Waterville met on the green in front of the Belvidere meetinghouse," the paper said, "on the afternoon of the 14th inst. for the purpose of organization and election of officers." (The Waterville town line is just down the road.) The paper continued, "On the report of the canvassing committee it was found that forty-five persons had signed their willingness to enroll themselves in an independent company under the name of the 'Round Mountain Guards.'" Round Mountain, also known as Laraway Mountain, rises behind the church. Chosen first lieutenant of the company was Richard Cull, who with other members would serve in the 7th Vermont. Lieutenant Cull died of sickness in Louisiana in 1862, at forty-two.

Return toward Belvidere Center, and on approaching the village, the Belvidere Center Cemetery is on the right. Several local men who served lie here, among them Augustus Thomas and Henry Carpenter, who became adjutant of the 8th Vermont. A historic marker in the cemetery honors George Washington Henderson, born a slave in western Virginia in 1850 and brought to Vermont by Carpenter.

Continue on 109, pass the old town hall, and in 1.5 miles, an aging house with small shed sits above the road on the left. Henry Carpenter went to war from here and returned with fourteen-year-old George Henderson, who recalled that he began "to learn his letters," apparently here. Henderson had apparently been Carpenter's servant late in the war. The black man went on to become highly educated, studying at Underhill Academy and Barre Academy, graduating first in his class at the University of Vermont, and receiving a degree from Yale's Divinity School. Becoming a well-known educator and clergyman, he was principal of three Vermont schools and once held a pulpit in New Orleans. While there, Henderson authored the first formal protest against the lynching of blacks. His alma mater, the University of Vermont, gave him an honorary degree.

Continue on Route 109 to its junction with Route 118 and go left, north, on 118. In 0.2 mile, on the right, is an old house, close by the road. Look across the road and see a sugarhouse set back against the woods, all that's left of the McGookin farm. Henry McGookin joined the 8th Vermont when the regiment was formed. He was killed a year later at Bayou des Allemands, Louisiana, at twenty-nine, and is buried in Chalmettte National Cemetery. His brother Rodney was thirty-six when he signed up with the 8th, early in the war. Later he served in the 11th Vermont and survived Confederate imprisonment to come home. Both men were natives of Ireland.

Return to the junction of Routes 109 and 118; take 109 for 0.3 mile and see a narrow and rough dirt road that goes left into a swamp. Park here and walk 0.3 mile on this old track to the Burroughs Family Cemetery. The Burroughs farm was in this area, the house close to the cemetery. Alfred Burroughs enlisted in the 9th Ver-

mont as a private at twenty-two and was, at 6 feet 4 inches, said to be the regiment's tallest man. After the 9th Vermont was captured by Stonewall Jackson at Harpers Ferry, Burroughs died of typhoid in Chicago's Camp Douglas Prison awaiting exchange and is buried there. But a cenotaph in this remote cemetery remembers him.

SOURCES
BELVIDERE TOWN RECORDS.
LAMOILLE NEWSDEALER (HYDE PARK), 1861–1865. LANPHER MEMORIAL LIBRARY, HYDE PARK.
WITH THANKS TO SHIRLEY BROWN.

CAMBRIDGE

Enter Cambridge from the east, along Route 15, and the East Cambridge Cemetery is north of the road. A small obelisk marks the graves of Captain John Woodward, of the Vermont Cavalry (see Westford), and his fiancée Hattie Chadwick. Chadwick, eighteen, died of typhoid fever on May 29 at her parents' home. When Woodward learned of her death, he became reckless and was killed in battle near Hagerstown, Maryland, pursuing Lee's army from Gettysburg. The stone says, "These two fondly united in life are not divided in death."

Continue 4 miles on Route 15, and go north on Route 108. In just under 1 mile on the left is a farmhouse and barn. Edgar Paige, twenty-one, went from here to become a private in the 4th Vermont in the summer of 1863. A year later, he was captured at Weldon Railroad and died at Andersonville.

Return to Route 15, continue west, and soon turn left into the village of Jeffersonville. Soon on the right is the redbrick town hall, once a church, where Cambridge town meetings were held. In July 1864, voters approved borrowing $10,000 "to pay bounties to the volunteers of the United States service." According to Reverend Edwin Wheelock, who wrote a town history, "For the war of the Union in 1861–5, the town furnished one hundred and seventy men and paid thirty three thousand dollars in bounties to enlist them. Thirty-seven of these men died in the service."

In March 1863, Colonel Stephen Thomas, 8th Vermont commander, spoke to encourage enlistments in Jeffersonville, probably in the redbrick church. Before Cambridge veterans built a GAR hall, they met here. In January 1871, the GAR held a literary entertainment in this building, and the featured lecturer was Major General Judson Kilpatrick, Union cavalry commander, who ordered the futile cavalry charge at Gettysburg. One of the church's ministers before the war was the abolitionist Alvah Sabin.

Past the town hall and on the left is the Second Congregational Church, built on the site of a hotel once owned by the Chadwick family. Just past the church come to a Y, with a military monument on the right, set against a ledge. In the redbrick house just past it lived the Chadwicks, including Hattie, fiancé of Captain John Woodward.

Loop around the traffic island, return to the church, and there go left on Upper Pleasant Valley Road. In 2.25 miles, on

approaching an old stone house, look to the right across the Pleasant Valley. Along the ridge that is the valley's west wall, sometime in the 1880s, William Cody, better known as Buffalo Bill, once hunted deer. While doing so he lost a valuable ring that has never been found. His hunting companion was Clarence Dyer Gates, who served as adjutant of the 1st Vermont Cavalry. According to Gates's descendants, he met Cody during the Civil War. How that happened is not clear, since Cody served in the West after he enlisted as a cavalryman in 1863. Cody apparently came to Cambridge when his traveling Wild West show was appearing in Burlington.

A mile past the stone house, Westman Road bears left; look along it to the hillside Westman farm. From here, Orson Westman enlisted in the 2nd Vermont as a private in 1861 and rose to the rank of lieutenant by war's end.

Continue on Upper Pleasant Valley Road, and soon turn right on Lower Pleasant Valley Road. In 2 miles on the left is an aging farmhouse with a long barn behind it. Thaddeus Whipple enlisted from here in the 13th Vermont, as a musician, and served at Gettysburg.

Continue 1.5 miles into Cambridge village, crossing a bridge, and the first house on the right was owned by Clarence Gates after the war. Just beyond the house, and set back from the road, is a long low barn. This structure was Gates's home when the war began. Gates recruited local men for the Vermont Cavalry, and he signed them up here. As regimental adjutant, he was in many battles, including a fight at Brandy Station, Virginia, on September 13, 1863. According to G. G. Benedict, "Adjutant Gates charged the enemy's guns with the regiment, and after one gun had been taken, went on with the battalion after the second gun. The cavalry which defended this made a fight of it, and several charges and counter-charges took place in quick succession. After one of the latter, while Adjutant Gates was trying to rally some of the men who had fallen back to a piece of timber, he found himself surrounded by a flanking party of the enemy . . . Gates's horse was wounded, and the Confederates continued to fire on him after he had surrendered, but fortunately without effect." Gates survived Libby and Belle Isle prisons and eventually rejoined the cavalry.

Continue to the intersection of Route 15, and the Cambridge GAR monument is on the right. Dedicated on November 29, 1918, it notes that for a further record of the role played by Cambridge in the war, the GAR record book should be consulted in the town clerk's office.

Across Route 15 from the monument is a large redbrick house that was once the Eli Ellinwood home. According to town historian Wheelock, "He went out in the Second Vermont Regiment, and died in a hospital in the city of New York, at the close of Gen. McClellan's campaign before Richmond, August 5, 1862 . . . He obtained a furlough of twenty days to come home, but died in New York." Ellinwood was forty-six, a man of wealth, who had helped recruit men early in the war.

Cross Route 15 to the Ellinwood house and turn left, moving along broad Main Street. It is said in Cambridge that Civil War soldiers drilled on this street and that Route 15 was named the Grand Army of the Republic Highway for this wide thoroughfare. At the west end of Main, go left, returning in the direction you came. In the house on the left with two storefront windows once lived the Farringtons. George Farrington enlisted at eighteen as a private in the 13th Vermont and fought at Gettysburg. Then he joined the Vermont Cavalry and served until the war ended. He was one of the last Vermonters wounded, hit near Appomattox Courthouse the day Lee surrendered to Grant. Henry Farrington enlisted in July 1863 at twenty-three and served until the end of the war as a private in the 4th Vermont. He was wounded at the Wilderness.

Proceed to the east end of Main Street and note the large frame house on the left with two bay windows, where the road turns left. Reverend Wheelock lived here. On July 21, 1894, a handsome book was given to the town, and Wheelock gave the presentation speech. "I feel proud of the heroic part taken in the contest by the soldiers of Vermont," he said. "And we as citizens of the new born Republic should lose no opportunity to do honor to the memory of the brave men who went forth from our midst to defend the Flag of our Country." The newborn republic was an obvious reference to Lincoln's Gettysburg Address. The book presented that day is preserved at the Cambridge town office, filled with soldier reminiscences of their service.

SOURCES
CAMBRIDGE TOWN RECORDS.

Noble, Winona S. *The History of Cambridge, Vermont*. Cambridge, VT: Town of Cambridge, 1976.

Wheelock, Edwin. *Historical Sketch of the Town of Cambridge*. Montpelier, VT: Freeman Steam Printing House and Bindery, 1876.

Whitcomb, J. A. "Vermonters in the Civil War." *The Vermonter*, July 1941.

With thanks to David Gates, Gena Little, and Richard Westman.

....

EDEN

Hemenway's *Gazetteer* says of Eden, "Ever since the first agitation of the slavery question, this town has been Anti-Slavery. At the last presidential election [1864], but five Democratic votes were cast."

The Eden Congregational Church, at the junction of Route 100 and North Road in the village of Eden Mills, was used by several religious denominations at the time of the Civil War. A Reverend Farrand, a Congregationalist, sometimes presided at services here, and his son, Thaddeus, joined the 17th Vermont at twenty-four as a private in March 1864. Four months later, he was dead of sickness.

On January 15, 1865, a funeral was held here for George Emerson, who left Eden in September 1862 to enlist at Irasburg in the 11th Vermont. Captured at Weldon Railroad in June 1864, the private died less than three months later in Andersonville. His body came home for burial in Eden. On July 17, 1864, a funeral was held here for Abel Hinds Jr., a private in the 11th Vermont. Hinds was shot, surely by a sharpshooter, on June 21, 1864, in the Petersburg trenches while

bringing coffee to fellow soldiers. He was a private, age thirty-two.

Also, a funeral took place here for George Emery, who enlisted at thirty-five in the 11th Vermont in June 1862, leaving wife Mary Belle and six young children on an Eden farm. In the spring of 1864, Emery and the rest of the 11th were serving as artillerymen manning the forts guarding Washington. Convinced that he would spend the rest of the war there, he persuaded his wife to bring the children to Washington. But soon after his arrival, the 11th was made an infantry regiment and ordered to the front. Little more than a month later, Emery was captured at Weldon Railroad and died in Andersonville. Mary, suddenly destitute, enlisted as a laundress for the armies and, with the help of her children, did the work of two laundresses, thus receiving two soldier rations to feed her family. Through the generosity of friends back in Eden, she was able to bring her family home when the war ended. After the war, it took her ten years to win a pension from the government. She lived until 1910, in Eden.

From the church, go north on Route 100 and quickly go right up East Hill Road. In 0.3 mile on the right is a small cluster of buildings, including a house, which may have been the Emery home.

Return to Route 100 and continue north 0.4 mile, and set back on the left, amid trees, is a white one-and-a-half story house with a long porch. Napoleon Bonaparte Hinds built this house in 1866 after returning for two years' service with the 3rd Vermont. He was wounded in Upton's Attack at Spotsylvania on May 10, 1864.

SOURCES

EDEN TOWN RECORDS.
LAMOILLE NEWSDEALER (HYDE PARK), 1861–
1865. LANPHER MEMORIAL LIBRARY, HYDE
PARK.
MACDONALD, PETER I., AND THE STUDENTS
OF GRADES 4, 5, AND 6, EDEN CENTRAL
SCHOOL. *EDEN, VERMONT: THE HISTORY OF
EDEN IN THE NINETEENTH CENTURY*. EDEN,
VT: EDEN CENTRAL SCHOOL, 1984.
MCKAY, ALICE. *A WALK THROUGH THE GARDEN
OF EDEN: A HISTORY OF EDEN*. EDEN, VT:
EDEN HISTORICAL SOCIETY, 1966.
WITH THANKS TO DEANNA FRENCH.

ELMORE

Approach Elmore from the north, on Route 12, and you follow the route a company of men marched along, destined to fight at Gettysburg. Elmore sent sixty-six men to war from an 1860 population of 602 and the most famous was Urban Woodbury, who fought with the 2nd Vermont as a sergeant at First Bull Run, the war's first major battle. As the regiment advanced under fire up Chinn Ridge, a shell fragment mangled Woodbury's arm. The arm was amputated at a field hospital, giving Woodbury the distinction of being the first Vermont Civil War soldier to lose a limb. Woodbury was taken prisoner as the hospital was overrun and confined in Richmond. But he was soon exchanged and back in Vermont to recover. He reenlisted in the 11th Vermont but was assigned to drill troops preparing for war. Thus he was in Morristown to drill Company E of the 13th Vermont as it prepared for war. Company historian Henry Mudgett described an early September day in 1862:

"One day previous to the town fair at Elmore, he (Woodbury) extended an invitation to the whole company to march up in a body the day that the fair was held at Elmore, for he felt an interest in the fair, on account of its being his home town, for his father resided at Elmore Pond village. The company nearly all marched up when the day arrived in good style, for that was the way Company E had of doing things."

Mudgett added that when Elmore was reached, a footrace was held among company members, and the one-armed Woodbury won.

The village of Elmore, referred to by Mudgett as Pond Village, lies close by Lake Elmore. Go just north of the village store and come to Lake Elmore's outflow. A few hundred yards downstream, now in an area of brush and trees, Urban Woodbury operated a starch mill powered by the lake's waters. The Elmore fairgrounds was once located in the area behind the village school and town hall, where on an early fall day in 1862 a company of men destined to attack Pickett's Charge at Gettysburg had a bit of sport.

Elmore voters met during the war in the village school, the 1860s District Three School that still stands opposite the village store. Though only partial records of town meetings are preserved, voters here on September 2, 1862, "voted to raise a tax on the grand list of the town sufficient to pay the sum of $25.00 to each volunteer that shall enlist into the United States Services previous to the 8th day instant of September."

In mid-April 1861, right after the firing on Fort Sumter, a patriotic gathering, which included a flag raising and speeches, took place in the street in front of the Pond House, a hotel that once stood across the street, and slightly south of, the village store.

The Elmore Methodist Church remains on the north edge of the village. There, according to the *Lamoille Newsdealer*, on Sunday, June 11, 1863, Elder Herrick of Wolcott "delivered a discourse" on the death of Sergeant David P. Barnes, of Elmore, a private in the 9th Vermont. Barnes died in a Union prison camp in Chicago on March 16, awaiting, with his regiment, an exchange of prisoners after the 9th's capture at Harpers Ferry.

From the school, go 2 miles south on Route 12 and turn left on Lacasse Road. In just over 0.5 mile, a farmhouse with a huge barn behind it is on the left, the Merriam homestead. John Merriam went to war in February 1862, never to return, enlisting in the 8th Vermont. He went with the 8th to the Deep South and served until his death on September 23, 1863. The regimental history of the 8th states that he perished of disease, while Merriam family history indicates that he was wounded and came home to die.

Proceed past the Merriam farm to the crossroads and go straight onto Hardwood Flats Road. Quickly look to the left for foundation remnants of the District One School, which stood here before and during the war. Among the pupils who once studied here and played in the yard, most probably walking to school along the converging roads, were:

Justin Gale, who enlisted at twenty-four in the 8th Vermont and died two years later, in November 1863. His body never came home.

Franklin Olmstead, a corporal in the 3rd Vermont, who survived a wound at the Wilderness and came home to live a long life.

Bradford Sparrow, who volunteered for the 4th Vermont in July 1863, as a twenty-year-old private, was captured at Weldon Railroad and survived two months in Andersonville.

Charles Stoddard, who joined the 3rd Vermont Light Artillery at twenty-two in August 1864, died the following January in a hospital on Bedloe's Island in New York Harbor. He is buried in a national cemetery in Brooklyn.

Proceed past the school 1 mile and turn left on Tallman Road. In 0.8 mile, look up and to the right to an old farmhouse, from which Franklin Olmstead went to war. Continue on Tallman Road to where it now ends. Ahead is the impassable continuation of the road, which leads to the site of East Elmore, once a thriving community with two mills, a church, a post office, and several houses. Indeed, a soldier from East Elmore wrote to his sister in 1862 that he thought the place would one day be Vermont's capital. "I think East Elmore is high in cultivation," he said. East Elmore has now disappeared, much the victim of Vermont's post–Civil War migration.

SOURCES

ANGELL, ELEANOR. *THREE EARLY VERMONT SETTLERS: AMOS MORSE, GEORGE TROW, EPHRAIM AINSWORTH.* BURLINGTON, VT: VERMONT HISTORICAL SOCIETY, 2000. COURTESY OF VERMONT HISTORICAL SOCIETY.

ELMORE TOWN AND SCHOOL RECORDS.

MEAD, MONICA. "QUEST FOR THE HOMESTEAD OF VERMONT'S 45TH GOVERNOR." *BARRE-MONTPELIER TIMES ARGUS.* JUNE 23, 2009.
RICH, SARAH. "EAST ELMORE: GONE, BUT NOT FORGOTTEN." *TRANSCRIPT* (MORRISVILLE), JUNE 18, 1984.
WITH THANKS TO STANLEY MERRIAM AND ARLO STERNER.

....

HYDE PARK

Courthouse Square in the center of Hyde Park village, just off Route 15, was the center of Civil War activity in Lamoille County. The country courthouse is here, on the site of the Civil War–era courthouse that burned in 1912. Most appropriately, two Civil War cannon stand in front of the present building, placed there in 1913. Across the street, on the Lanpher Memorial Library, a plaque lists the 140 Hyde Park men who served; of them 29 died.

Here in the square men recruited by Captain Edward Sawyer for Company I of the Vermont Cavalry gathered, and then went into the old courthouse to enlist. Moses McFarland (see Waterville) signed up forty men for the 8th Vermont here. And here on August 28, 1862, came Lamoille County enlistees to elect officers for their Company E of the 13th Vermont Regiment, destined to fight at Gettysburg. That took place in the town hall, which once stood on the square.

The *Lamoille Newsdealer* reported that on July 4, 1861, "The people of Hyde Park were entertained by another display of military evolutions by the Green Mountain Union Guards, who paraded and counter-marched through the street

and on the Court House Green. Nearly all day the fife and drum filled the air with martial notes."

The September 12, 1861, *Newsdealer* reported that "a company of men under Captain Benton" were drilling in the village. Reuben Benton served in the 5th Vermont, then became a lieutenant colonel in the 11th Vermont, commanding one of the big regiment's battalions.

Look up Church Street from Courthouse Square to the 1843 Union Meeting House, where several soldier services were held. Among them was a memorial service for Private Henry C. Stewart, known as Chandler, who died in Chicago in early 1862 at thirty-five, while awaiting exchange after the Harpers Ferry capture of his regiment. He is buried in Chicago. On August 7, 1864, a funeral for Hiram Hall, eighteen and a private in the 17th Vermont, killed by a sniper in the Petersburg trenches, was held here. On November 13, 1864, a service honored William Crowell, a private in the 5th Vermont, twenty-four when mortally wounded at the Wilderness. His body came home.

From the square, go west on Main Street and bear left at the Y to the second house beyond the Catholic Church, once Woodbury's home. To this house, after losing an arm at Bull Run and enduring Libby Prison (see Elmore), came Charles's brother, Urban Woodbury, to recover. Charles, in November 1861, enlisted in the Vermont Cavalry and became a lieutenant in Company B. He was killed in a fight with John Mosby's Cavalry along Broad Run in Virginia on January 1, 1863, at twenty-five.

Return to the square and go east on Main Street to the Y where Depot Street turns right. Edward Sawyer, who for a time early in the war commanded the Vermont Cavalry, lived in the white house set back from the road on the right, with tall front windows. In this house, his wife worked to supply goods to the soldiers.

Turn left at the Y to Eden Street, and the second house on the left, with long porch and barn behind, was the Cobleigh home. The *Newsdealer* said in September 1862: "Terrence Roddy, who left this place one year ago the 20th of May, and enlisted in Company D of the 2d Regiment, died in Bellevue Hospital, N. Y. City, on the 23 of August, of typhoid fever and in consequence of debility after amputation of his leg, which was made necessary by an incurable wound in the foot received in the battle of Savage's Station, Va., on the 29th of June last. He leaves a wife and one child, who are now living in this village with A. Cobleigh, Esq."

Continue on Eden Street to Route 100; go right, east, and quickly turn north on Centerville Road. In 0.5 mile, go right on Noyes Farm Road, and in 0.25 mile, Sloboda Road goes left to a large farmhouse and barn. Cornelius Reed built this farm after the Civil War. In March 1863, Cornelius journeyed to Virginia to bring home his brother, Carolus, desperately ill. Carolus and another brother, Henry, were privates in the 3rd Vermont and fought together at Lee's Mill and Fredericksburg. Carolus became sick after the Army of the Potomac's tiring Mud March of early 1863, and when the severity of his condition was learned at home, the boys' father sent Cornelius for him. They came by train to the station in Waterbury and by buckboard home. Arriving on March 23, Carolus told his mother, according to the *Newsdealer,* "It was all I asked to get home to die with father and mother. All is well and I am going to a brighter, and better world, where wars are not known, and the weary are at rest." He died forty-eight hours later. All that remains of the old family home is a pile of stones among maples, by the brook, below the present-day house along Noyes Road.

Return to Centerville Road, take it to North Hyde Park Road, and proceed to the village of North Hyde Park. On reaching Route 100, turn left and quickly, on the right, is 1910 Gihon Valley Grange Hall, now the Hyde Park Historical Society. The local GAR chapter met on the third floor.

Beyond the hall, and across the road, is the 1858 Union Church. In December 1862, a memorial service was held here for James Kimball, an Eden resident, who joined the 8th Vermont in February 1862 at age fifty-four. Serving only six months before being discharged for disability, he died on board the steamer *Fulton* off Cape Hatteras on his way home from Louisiana. Another memorial service was held here in mid-January 1865 for Thomas Newcomb, a private in the 11th Vermont, who died of sickness at twenty-six in December 1864 at a military hospital in Maryland, after evacuation from the Petersburg lines.

Continue south 1.5 miles on Route 100 and go right on Whitaker Road. From the first farm on the road, John Griswold, at eighteen, enlisted in 1863 as a private in the 6th Vermont, as a substitute for a local man, Almon Whitney. Griswold died of illness on June 25, 1864, and is buried in a cemetery near New York City, apparently having been on the way home when he perished. A memorial service was held here on the farm on July 24, probably in the old house that was still barely standing by the road in 2010.

Captain Moses McFarland (see Waterville) of the 8th Vermont, as an old man with failing sight dictated his memoirs to Sarah Chapin in the Hyde Park town clerk's office. The building still stands on Main Street.

SOURCES

HYDE PARK BICENTENNIAL COMMITTEE. *HYDE PARK VERMONT: SHIRE TOWN OF LAMOILLE COUNTY*. HYDE PARK, VT: BICENTENNIAL COMMITTEE, 1976.

HYDE PARK TOWN RECORDS.

LAMOILLE NEWSDEALER (HYDE PARK), 1861–1867. LANPHER MEMORIAL LIBRARY, HYDE PARK.

WITH THANKS TO GARY ANDERSON AND THE LANPHER MEMORIAL LIBRARY STAFF.

....

JOHNSON

Along the north side of Johnson's Main Street (Route 15) is an old red two-story schoolhouse with belfry. Once the Johnson Grammar School, its pupils before the Civil War included the Scott brothers Charles, Julian, and Lucian. One of the teachers here, before the war, was Reuben Benton, who commanded a battalion in the 11th Vermont.

Go west along Main Street and quickly across the street is the 1851 Congregational Church, which the Scott family attended. Once serving as the town hall, the building hosted Civil War–era town meetings. Also, several war meetings were held here. One, in the summer of 1862, saw four Goosey brothers enlist in Company D of the 11th Vermont Regiment. All served as privates, and Alexander, Ambrose, and Joseph came home. But David was wounded at Charles Town on August 21, 1864, dying the next day. On July 1, 1861, Captain Andrew Blanchard, headmaster of Peoples Academy in nearby Morrisville, came to Johnson recruiting men for his Company E of the 3rd Vermont. The event surely happened in the Congregational meetinghouse, and among those who volunteered was fifteen-year-old, 5-foot-4 Julian Scott. Claiming to be sixteen, he was accepted and made a musician, a fifer, though he apparently preferred to play the drum. In the Congregational Church on April 17, 1865, a "funeral service" was held for Abraham Lincoln.

Johnson sent 140 men to the Civil War, and 27 died. In September 1862, voters gathered at the church approved the town's first bounties, $50 each. By December 1863, bounties of $300 were voted.

From the church, continue west on Main Street, following the route Julian Scott would have walked from his home to school, and to enlist. On the way, soon pass a modern church, on the right, and the house beyond it, rambling with many porches, was the postwar home of Darius Holmes. Enlisting at age thirty-three in the 6th Vermont in the summer of 1863, he was wounded at Charles Town thirteen months later and soon came home.

One-quarter mile west, a historic marker on the lawn of a two-story frame house identifies it as the Scott home. Charles Scott enlisted in 1863 at sixteen and was a musician in the 11th Vermont. Lucian Scott, a private in the Vermont Cavalry during the war's last year, survived three months in a Confederate prison.

But it is their brother Julian Scott that history remembers. In this house built by his father, Julian was born on Valentine's Day 1846, one of eight children of Charles and Lucy (Kellum) Scott. The mother died in 1855, but Charles, a jeweler and watchmaker, soon remarried. Julian was the first to enlist from the family, as a musician in the 3rd Vermont. On April 16, 1862, in the Vermont Brigade's first heavy action, at Lee's Mill, the Vermonters waded a millpond to attack Confederate positions. Forced to retreat by superior Confederate forces, many Vermonters were cut down by Rebel fire. Young Scott waded into the water several times to rescue wounded comrades. For that "gallant conduct," in 1865 he became the first Vermonter to win a Medal of Honor. Scott served two years, then studied art with, among others, famed painters John Frederick Kensett and Emanuel Leutze. One of his first major commissions came from the Vermont legislature for the huge State House painting of the Battle of Cedar Creek. Today, four of his Civil War paintings grace the State House's Cedar Creek Room.

But Julian was not the only Scott brother known for wartime bravery. Abby Hemenway's *Gazetteer* contains a brief account by a Massachusetts soldier of an 1864 incident along the Rapidan River involving Charles Scott, also a musician. One evening, a boat was seen in the Rapidan bearing two Union soldiers from the opposite Rebel-held shore. Coming under fire, the men took to the water, and one was wounded. Charles Scott swam to the wounded man and brought him to safety.

Return through the village past the Academy and turn left, north, on Route 100C. In 2 miles, where the road curves left, a house with a small barn is on the right. John Mudgett lived here, who as a private in the 13th Vermont fought at Gettysburg. Continue north, and in 1 mile, go left on Ben Oberhill Road. In 1 mile, go right on Mackey Road and follow it to its end at a big farmhouse with a grand mountain view. Seth Hill lived here, who joined the 8th Vermont in the winter of 1862 as a private. Soon promoted to sergeant, at Cedar Creek, as the 8th Vermont fought desperately at first light, Hill was in the thick of it. The regimental history described how Hill shot a Rebel who had just shot a lieutenant of the 8th and narrowly escaped a Rebel bayonet, knocking flat his assailant. He continued fighting, the history states, "until surrounded and forced into the enemy's ranks, but refused to surrender, when a side shot tore away his belt, cartridge box, and the flesh of his backbone, which crippled him to the ground." Hill then joined a Rebel charge, firing harmless shots until he saw an opportunity. He raced back into Union lines, with both Rebels and Yankees firing at him. There he continued fighting until he sank to the ground from loss of blood. Hill returned to Johnson to live a long life, dying on December 1, 1927, a victim of the great 1927 flood.

SOURCES

JOHNSON GAR MEMORY BOOK. COURTESY OF JOHNSON TOWN OFFICE.

JOHNSON TOWN RECORDS.

SMITH, MARGARET T. *HISTORY OF THE TOWN OF JOHNSON VERMONT.* OREAD LITERARY CLUB. BURLINGTON, VT: FREE PRESS PRINTING, 1907.

TITTERTON, ROBERT. *JULIAN SCOTT ARTIST OF THE CIVIL WAR AND NATIVE AMERICA.* JEFFERSON, NC: McFARLAND, 1997.

WITH THANKS TO FRANK DODGE, LOIS FRYE, JIM HEATH, LINDA JONES, AND JOLLIE PARKER.

MORRISTOWN

⭐ Morrisville village in Morristown is located along Route 12, south of where it meets Route 15. Morristown sent 172 men to war, from a population of about 1,700, with 13 killed in action or dead of wounds. Another 16 died of disease, 15 more were wounded, and 7 were imprisoned. Today, the business center of the town is the village of Morrisville, a political entity that did not exist in the 1860s. Just east of the village's main intersection is the Morristown Civil War monument, one of the grandest in Vermont. Dedicated on Memorial Day, 1911, the Barre granite edifice is 25.5 feet high and cost the town $5,500. A thousand people gathered in Academy Park on a blue-sky afternoon for ceremonies that also marked the fiftieth anniversary of the war's beginning. Mrs. Ila Niles sang "Barbara Fritchie," John Greenleaf Whittier's famed Civil War poem, set to music. Then former governor and Civil War amputee

Urban Woodbury (see Elmore) gave the keynote address. Services then were held in the Congregational Church, with members of the GAR, Women's Relief Corps, and Sons of Union Veterans present. Reverend W. E. Baker said, "The purpose of Memorial Day is not to glorify war. If so it were better abolished . . . I am glad that your memorial committee saw fit to put the flag, rather than the musket, in the hand of the figure on the pedestal, for the time will come, we trust, when all men shall be at peace. But may the time never come when the flag for which these men fought will cease to be revered."

The soldier on the monument looks toward the Congregational Church, located on the north side of Route 12. Before the dedication ceremonies, a parade wound through the village streets led by parade marshall Frank Kenfield. It was a well-deserved honor for the old soldier. Lieutenant Kenfield had been left behind ill when the 2nd Vermont Brigade began its march to Gettysburg. But he rode cross-country to catch up and, with his 13th Vermont, joined in the attack on Pickett's Charge. Wounded, Kenfield came home to recover, then enlisted in the 17th Vermont. On May 6, at the Wilderness, he was again wounded. But he again healed to fight with the 17th at Petersburg in the Battle of the Crater, where he was captured. He survived two Rebel prisons to return at war's end to Morristown, where he enrolled in Peoples Academy.

When the war began, Andrew Blanchard was the academy's headmaster. He enlisted in May 1861 and commanded Company E of the 3rd Vermont for only five months. He took many of his two hundred students with him, some serving in his company. Among the Peoples Academy students who served were two Waterbury men, Henry Janes, the surgeon in charge of all the Gettysburg wounded, and Colonel William Henry, who commanded the 10th Vermont. The original academy building, opened in 1847, still stands on Pleasant Street, near the monument, an aged white frame structure with belfry that now houses an arts center.

From the monument go south on Main Street (Route 12) 0.25 mile to a two-story house with two-story bay windows and attached garage. Here lived Morristown's last surviving Civil War veteran, George Bridge, who died at ninety in 1937. The local paper, on his passing, called him "the last of our boys in blue." Bridge was an 11th Vermont private who served in the forts around Washington, then with the Vermont Brigade in hard fighting. In later years, seated on the porch of his home, he was fond of telling children of his war experiences. "Grampa Bridge" would invite visitors to shake his hand, reminding them that hand once shook the hand of Abraham Lincoln.

Return to the monument and go north on Main Street to the northeast corner of Pleasant Street and the frame house that stands beside the brick church. This was the home of Dr. Horace Powers, who was the examining physician for local recruits. His son George Powers was one of the Peoples Academy students who enlisted as a group in the 3rd Vermont. But soon after reaching Virginia, and Camp Griffin, Private Powers contracted diphtheria.

Doctor Powers, on learning of his boy's sickness, went south, and with the help of Dr. Henry Janes, received permission to bring George home. But his son died in less than a month, in this house. The *Lamoille Newsdealer* reported on February 7, 1862, "His funeral was attended by a vast concourse of people; he laid in his coffin holding in his hand the flag that had cost him his life to defend." In 1864, Dr. Powers joined the group of Vermonter physicians that went to Fredericksburg to treat wounded Vermonters.

From the four-way stop in the middle of the village, go south on Route 100, and in just under 1 mile, turn west on Morristown Corners Road. Drive 0.6 mile to Morristown Corners, proceed straight through the stop sign on Walton Road, turn right on Cote Hill Road, and note the old two-story brick house on the right from which Frank Kenfield went to war.

Turn around and return to Morristown Corners. Go south on Stagecoach Road and soon descend into a dip through which runs an alder-lined brook. Note that on the knoll to the left are the remnants of a foundation. A widow named Gates lived there, who saw one of her two children go to war at age fourteen, enlisting as a fifer in the 5th Vermont. In 1862, her other child, a daughter, suddenly died. Needing her son at home, Mrs. Gates went to Washington in an attempt to secure his release from the army. Unable to see Secretary of War Edwin Stanton, she went to the White House and did see Abraham Lincoln. The president made certain that she met Stanton, and she came home with her son William Preston

Gates. Look toward what is left of that home and know it was a place touched by the Great Emancipator.

SOURCES
LAMOILLE NEWSDEALER (HYDE PARK), 1860–1865. MORRISVILLE CENTENNIAL LIBRARY.
MOWER, ANNA L., AND ROBERT L. HAGERMAN. MORRISVILLE TWO TIMES. MORRISTOWN, VT: MORRISTOWN HISTORICAL SOCIETY, 1982.
WITH THANKS TO DEANNA FRENCH AND FRANCIS FAVREAU.

....

STOWE

Approaching Stowe from the south on Route 100, turn left on Moscow Road and go 0.5 mile to the Moscow store. In another 0.5 mile, take Nebraska Valley Road, and in another 0.5 mile, come to a large old farmhouse on the right, once the Munn family home. Continue past the house, traveling the route along which young Ira Munn once walked to the Mill Valley School, which is the red house just ahead. On a spring day in 1861, with Fort Sumter having been seized and Abraham Lincoln calling for troops, Ira and four friends rose from their desks in this schoolhouse and walked out the door, to enlist in the 1st Vermont Regiment.

Return to Route 100, and on approaching Stowe village, where Turner Road turns right, note the big farmhouse at the intersection. Henry Thomas lived here, who enlisted at seventeen and served three years as a drummer in the 3rd Vermont Regiment. He became a friend of fellow musician Julian Scott, the artist and Medal of Honor winner (see Johnson).

Continue north on Route 100 to the stoplight in Stowe village. On the right is the building that served as the Stowe town hall during the war, now a ski museum. Here Stowe voters approved bounties that rose to $500 late in the war. A Mrs. M. N. Wilkins, for the historian Abby Hemenway, calculated that Stowe spent $28,000 on the war. She further determined that 208 Stowe men served, enlisting for a total time of 165 years service. In August 1864, Stowe, having trouble meeting a new draft quota, authorized selectmen to spend $2,700 on hiring recruiting agents to go south and seek black recruits. There are no indications the effort was successful.

Continue north straight through the intersection, and stop at the Stowe municipal building, a large columned brick edifice with words over the entrance: "Soldiers Memorial Presented by H. C. Ackley."

Some Stowe people claim their memorial building is the largest of all Civil War mausoleums, even bigger than Grant's Tomb. The $48,000 cost was donated by Stowe native Henry Cady Ackely, who moved to Michigan while a boy and served in the 2nd Michigan Cavalry. Ackely made a fortune in the lumber business and returned to Stowe in 1896, at age fifty-two. His offer to build a memorial so fine that "the town won't be ashamed of it in a hundred years" was readily accepted. Local builder Henry Thomas, once a musician in the 3rd Vermont, supervised construction. The building was dedicated on August 19, 1903; a photo taken that day shows old soldiers assembled on the hall steps. Nine years later, Ackely's ashes were interred in a vault in the hall's entryway in an elaborate ceremony, which included the singing of "Onward Christian Soldiers" by Stowe schoolchildren. A plaque beside Ackley's marker denotes where Thomas's ashes were also to have been placed there, but he preferred a cemetery.

The grand building has a memorial room with granite plaques listing 242 men who went to war from Stowe. Stars indicate those who died. The building's entrance is guarded by a pair of Civil War–era Rodman rifled guns, donated by the War Department at the instruction of U.S. Senator Redfield Proctor.

Just north along Main Street is the Stowe Community Church, known during the Civil War as the New Church. A reception was held in the basement's meeting room for local Company C of the 13th Vermont when it returned from Gettysburg late in the night of July 27, 1863. Some fifty members of the company arrived by wagon from the railway station at Waterbury to tables covered with food. According to the *Lamoille Newsdealer*, "Mr. Wilkins spoke, stating that the victory at Gettysburg would give the men 'a warm place in the hearts of all lovers of their country forever.' The paper noted that "Mr. Wilkins's remarks brought tears to the eyes of many, and one poor fellow who had left at home a large family of small children, and came back to find two of them in the grave, wept aloud." The June 27, 1864, *Newsdealer* gave notice of an oyster supper at the new church "with entertainment by trained choir and several singers and Robinson's Band . . . to benefit needy soldiers proceeds to be sent to Hon.

Portus Baxter, at request of his wife."

Across from the memorial hall, take School Street, and in 0.25 mile, turn right on Stowe Hollow Road. Follow it up hill and down to a left turn on North Hollow Road. In 1 mile, a tired old farmhouse is on the right and just past it, on a knoll, is a large white frame house, much added to since the Civil War, when it was the Cheney family home. Here lived Olive Cheney, a farm wife with four sons in the Union armies. Her letters survive, including many she wrote to daughter Jane Watts, living in New Hampshire. Farming was hard for the Cheneys, with their sons gone. Olive wrote to Jane on March 5, 1864, "Last Monday your father took Edwin to the Centre. Ed enlisted for the war . . . to war he must go and said he SHOULD go, if his father did not give his consent for him to go the first chance he got . . . It comes pretty hard for your Father to give him up he has made so much calculation for him to stay at home . . . I could not reason the case with him at all he said it was no worse for us than others that had given up their boys don't suppose it is any worse than it is for a good many others. it is strange what makes the boys want to go to war I suppose it is all right—if the boys hated to go as bad as we hated to have them there would not be much fighting done could there . . . O that their lives may be spared and the boys return to us again but it is not very probably they all will if any of them." The Cheneys' four boys all returned safely.

Return to Stowe village, turn north on Route 100 for 0.75 mile, and go left on

West Hill Road. In 2 miles, reach a T intersection and bear right, continuing on West Hill Road. The first house on the left, an old red farmhouse close by the road, was the house from which Jackson Sergeant went to war. Lieutenant Sergeant, 5th Vermont, wounded at Spotsylvania's Bloody Angle, survived to fight to war's end. On April 2, 1865, when the Vermont Brigade broke the Confederate lines at Petersburg, he was right behind Charles Gould (see Windham) and carried the regimental flag over the earthworks. Years after the war, Sergeant was awarded a Medal of Honor. At veterans' gatherings, including the Ackley building dedication, he always carried the flag.

Return to Stowe; at the stoplight in village center, turn right on Route 108, and in 1 mile a modernistic church is on the right. Built very much due to the efforts of Maria von Trapp, of *Sound of Music* fame, who lived in Stowe, the building honors Ira Dutton, best known as Brother Joseph, who for forty-five years cared for the sick in the leper colony on Hawaii's Molokai Island. Brother Joseph for many years worked as an assistant to the colony's founder, Father Damien. After Damien's death, from leprosy, Brother Joseph ran the colony, never returning to Stowe. Ira Dutton was born in Stowe, in 1843, though his family moved to Wisconsin while he was a boy. In 1861, he became a private in the 13th Wisconsin Regiment and served in the western theater. He remained in the army ten years after the war until 1882, when became a monk, joining a Trappist order. Eventually, he found his way to Hawaii and the leper colony, where he spent the rest of his life. The church stands on land that once was part of the Dutton family farm.

Look to Mount Mansfield and the base of the Nose at the south end of the summit ridge. There a summit house hotel stood during the Civil War, as its life of luxury continued. While vacationing there, the Mead family of Hinesburg learned that their son Charles, 14th Vermont, had been killed during Pickett's Charge at Gettysburg.

SOURCES
CHENEY FAMILY LETTERS. VERMONT HISTORICAL SOCIETY
STOWE TOWN RECORDS.
WILKINS, MRS. M. N. *HISTORY OF STOWE TO 1869.* STOWE, VT: STOWE HISTORICAL SOCIETY, 1987. ORIGINALLY PUBLISHED IN *THE VERMONT HISTORICAL GAZETTEER,* EDITED AND PUBLISHED BY ABBY MARIA HEMENWAY.
WITH THANKS TO ED RIDLON AND BARBARA BARAW.

WATERVILLE

Leave Route 108 just north of Jeffersonville, turn north on Route 109, and in 4 miles, enter Waterville village. The post–Civil War town hall is on the right, and opposite it is an old white house. To its north is an open field where the Waterville Inn long stood. At the time of the Civil War, it was operated by Moses McFarland and his wife, Lovinia. Continue north along Route 109, and after crossing the first bridge, turn sharp left onto Lapland Road. In 1 mile on the left is the house, with a small bay window, where Moses and Lovinia lived.

McFarland joined the 8th Vermont in November 1861, became commander of Company A, and fought in all the regiment's major battles. At Cedar Creek, he commanded the 8th after Colonel John Mead was wounded. In Waterville, the McFarlands operated a hotel, and a starch factory. When Moses went to war, he left his wife in charge of both. To handle the businesses, and raise two sons and a daughter, Lovinia quit her job as a teacher. Her duties at the hotel included cooking, and she also apparently spent a good deal of time sending supplies to her soldier husband, who had a small business of selling items to the soldiers, including highly desired Vermont maple sugar. Throughout the war, she carried on a correspondence with her husband. Tragedy struck the family in early October 1862, when daughter Cora died. Lovinia wrote to Moses on October 11: "O, my dear Moses, it does seem at times that my heart would break. When I think I shall not have her little society on earth. I counted on her company when the boys were in school. But there is no Cora for me today . . . this great trouble appears more than I can bear."

More than three weeks passed before the letter reached Moses, in Louisiana. He wrote on November 4, "Today I received two letters from you and one from Mr. Gavin [a local minister] and oh what news it brought. Good God, I exclaimed on reading it, is our little Cora dead?"

At some point during the war, Moses sent to Vermont a black man, J. A. Millard, apparently to help Lovinia with all her work.

The letters Lovinia wrote to Moses never once complain of the burdens she bore at home. But when he came home in 1865 and began planning a lavish party at the inn for fellow soldiers, she said no.

Return down Lapland Road, and in 0.4 mile, Quinty Road turns right. Look up the road to the house in the field, on the left, once the Wetherell family home. At least four Wetherells served, four as privates in Company H of the 9th Vermont. Ephraim, William W., and William V. were all discharged for disability after the 9th was captured by Stonewall Jackson at Harpers Ferry in September 1862 and confined in a Union prison near Chicago awaiting exchange. Philander Witherell was a private in the 2nd Vermont and was wounded at the Wilderness.

Continue down Lapland Hill to the first entrance to Mountain View Cemetery. Several Waterville soldiers are buried here. Look beyond to the hillside fields above the cemetery, once part of the Beard Farm. The *Lamoille Newsdealer* reported in early October 1862: "Mrs. H. Beard and Mrs. Curtis Beard . . . whose husbands have both gone to war, having harvested the corn raised on their farms, made a husking bee, and invited some eight or ten of the women of the neighborhood, and husked out some thirty or forty bushels of corn." Curtis Beard enlisted at forty-two as a private in the 8th Vermont and served three years. William Harvey Beard joined the 9th Vermont as a private at forty-five and was soon discharged for disability, but went back to serve until the war ended.

Continue downhill on Lapland Road to the lower cemetery entrance. Just to the right of the granite tomb is the grave of the first person buried in this new part of the burying ground, J. A. Millard, the black man Moses McFarland sent to his home.

Return to Route 109, go right, and cross the bridge. On the left, Bean Road comes in, and in the house on a knoll that overlooks the intersection lived James Holmes, a private for less than a year in the 3rd Vermont. His brother Hiram, a sergeant in the 3rd, survived a wound at Cold Harbor.

Return along Route 109 into the village where Church Street turns right, and in the house on the corner lived Hiram Leach, who enlisted at thirty-five as a private in the 7th Vermont and served four years, coming home in 1866.

The 1839 Congregational Church on Church Street was the scene of a memorial service for a father and his son in January 1863. A newspaper account stated that Reverend Micah Townshend, once pastor of the church, at fifty-two tried to enlist as a private in the 7th when it went to war, but was made a chaplain. He took with him his fourteen-year-old son Albert, who wore a private's stripe. The reverend became ill when the regiment was in Louisiana and died in mid-November 1862 of disease in a New Orleans hospital. By then, the son had gone to Florida with the regiment, where he soon died, also of sickness, probably unaware of his father's passing. Both were buried, the paper said, "in the land where they fell."

SOURCES

LAMOILLE NEWSDEALER (HYDE PARK), 1861–1865. LANPHER MEMORIAL LIBRARY, HYDE PARK.

MCFARLAND, MOSES AND LOVINIA. LETTERS. COURTESY OF LORRAINE (MCFARLAND) PEASE.

WATERVILLE TOWN RECORDS.

WESCOTT, MARY WILBUR. *LOG CABIN DAYS OF COIT'S GORE AND WATERVILLE*. ESSEX JUNCTION, VT: ROSCOE PRINTING HOUSE, 1975.

WITH THANKS TO LORRAINE PEASE.

WOLCOTT

Enter Wolcott from the west on Route 15, and on reaching the village, the Nazarene Church is on the right, which was the Wolcott Congregational Church in the 1860s. The *Hardwick Gazette* reported on a funeral held there Sunday, August 9, 1963, for "Harrison W. Jones, only son of Joel and Harriet Jones, who fell by the wayside, June 29th, near Gettysburg, Pa., when on the march to the battlefield in that place, and died very suddenly, as it was supposed, of sunstroke, aged 22." The paper also said that Jones had fought in several battles, including Lee's Mill and the Seven Days. "A very large congregation" attended the funeral.

Continue past the church 0.25 mile into an area of the village occupied by a single business enterprise, its buildings all the same color. On the second floor of the last such building on the right, with a small front porch, the Wolcott chapter of the GAR, named for Lieutenant Colonel George Foster, 4th Vermont, held its meetings.

Just past that building quickly turn right on School Street, and on the right is a large schoolhouse, beside the Wolcott town office, where Wolcott's Civil War–

era town meetings took place. Here in 1860, Wolcott gave Abraham Lincoln 113 votes, Stephen Douglas 31, and John Breckenridge 6. Four years later, the town favored Lincoln over McClellan, 153 to 39. For Hemenway's *Gazetteer*, a Hardwick resident wrote, "Many a hard-fought battle witnessed the bravery of our sons. We have however to mourn the loss of 32 who never returned; many of whom fell on the field while others died in the hospitals, of wounds and diseases; some of whom were prisoners at Andersonville and Salisbury. We can speak of one thing which many towns cannot; we have five to pass to our credit against another rebellion, that is, we have furnished five more than the required number."

Return to Route 15 and go right, pass a cemetery, and go left up East Hill Road. In 1.25 miles, take March Road 0.3 mile to the farmhouse on the left. From a house that stood just across the road, Marcus Scott enlisted in the Vermont Cavalry in August 1864. Less than three months later he was wounded in the Shenandoah Valley battle of Tom's Brook and was soon discharged for disability.

Past the house, on the right, is a large barn, once part of the Currier family farm. Israel Currier Jr. enlisted in the 9th Vermont from here, late in the war, and soon came home ill. He recovered.

One-half mile beyond, on the right, is a state of Vermont wildlife management area. Park here and walk into the woods to a large cellar hole, once the foundation of the William Titus home. Son David Titus joined the 9th Vermont in May 1862, less than a year after marrying a neighbor girl, Elmira Cummings. Within six months, Titus was promoted to sergeant while his regiment was confined in a Union prison camp in Chicago, awaiting exchange after at Harpers Ferry. About that time, Titus became ill and, according to a notice in the *Hardwick Gazette*, on his deathbed, "He requested a fellow soldier to read to him from the Bible, which he did. He also requested him to tell his beloved Elmira to trust in the Savior, and his dear mother, that he died praising God. His body, by request, was sent to his home, and his funeral services attended on the 18th of December last." The funeral was held here in the Titus home. Titus died three months before his twenty-second birthday.

Return to Route 15, go back through the village, and in just under 2 miles, turn right on North Wolcott Road. In 3.5 miles in North Wolcott, note Birch Lane on the left. The first house past it, on the right of Route 15, with a triangular window below the roof peak, was once the North Wolcott Methodist Church. Many parishioners were avid abolitionists.

SOURCES

REED, RUTH ELEANOR. *YESTERYEAR IN WOLCOTT, 1789 TO 1939*. WOLCOTT, VT: GLEE MERRITT KELLEY COMMUNITY LIBRARY, 1939.

WOLCOTT TOWN RECORDS.

WITH THANKS TO BRADLEY AND SHIRLEY ALLEN AND LLOYD PHELPS.

Braintree church where William Lloyd Garrison spoke.

chapter ten

Orange County

The brick church in Thetford Center hosted a funeral for a local man, who, while marching his black regiment through Norfolk, Virginia, was shot dead by a pro-slavery local doctor. Abraham Lincoln got involved in the case. At the church in Brookfield's Pond Village, by the floating bridge, a war meeting took place in 1862 that saw the town enlist enough men in one afternoon to fulfill its draft quota. Those who signed up were rewarded with kisses from the girls. William Lloyd Garrison was so struck by Vermont's beauty that he paused before entering Braintree's hilltop meetinghouse on an October day in 1862. Once inside, he said, "Such a country could be peopled only by those who love liberty, and insist on it for all others." Garrison also spoke in the East Topsham Church, as did William Wells Brown, a fellow abolitionist, who had escaped from slavery. Mourners at the Randolph Center Church heard the minister speak words for the assassinated Abraham Lincoln days after Richmond fell. He said, "We have come to weep and pray. Oh the joy of our hearts is ceased; our dance is turned into mourning." In West Fairlee, a local woman gave work to many needy soldiers' wives through her knitting business; her office still stands. During the Civil War, Justin Smith Morrill, whose elegant Strafford home is now a museum, gave America a mighty gift. Morrill brought to passage by Congress the Land Grant College Act, signed by President Lincoln, which would give countless Americans a chance at a higher education.

BRADFORD

On Sunday afternoon April 28, 1861, a religious service was held in the Bradford Congregational Church for the Bradford Guards, the local militia company about to become part of the 1st Vermont Regiment. Reverend Silas McKeen delivered the sermon, choosing as his theme a quotation from the book of Samuel, the words of an Israeli general named Joab, speaking to his men about to go into battle: "Be of good courage, and let us play the men for our people, and for the cities of our God: and the Lord doeth that which seemeth him good." McKeen said, "The impressive address of Joab to his army is entirely appropriate to the loyal citizens of the United States at this tremendous crisis—especially to the patriotic soldiery, assembling in such great numbers for the support of our government and national honor . . . The people of the loyal states are all moved by the same mighty spirit of patriotism, and, without regard to former political divisions, now stand firmly together." He further added, "Let us then . . . aim to perform our whole duty, courageously and manfully, and submit the resolution entirely to His infinite wisdom and goodness." The company departed four days later.

Bradford's North Main Street, which is also Route 5, is lined with antebellum buildings. The old Congregational Church, now used as a theater, still stands, behind the high-spired Union Christian Church. Just south along North Main is an Italianate house with a cupola, once the home of Roswell and Mary Farnham. Roswell went to war in the 1st Vermont as a lieutenant in the Bradford Guards. Later, as a lieutenant colonel, he was second in command of the 12th Vermont. His wife joined him, for a time, in the regiment's winter camp in northern Virginia. The

morning of January 19, 1862, she wrote, "When I opened my cabin door such a splendid scene I never beheld before. Twenty fires were burning, 600 or more men were hurrying about . . . Beyond glowed the blood red tint of morning . . . There are but a few women here in this country. What are left are all secesh [secessionist] and look as black as night at you." The Farnhams built this house after the war. They lived here when Roswell was elected governor in 1880.

Go north on North Main to where a road enters on the left, and look across the way to a small, white frame house with porch. Calista Robinson Jones once lived here, who, in 1901, was elected national president of the Women's Relief Corps. The corps was instrumental in the preservation of the prison site at Andersonville, Georgia, purchasing and protecting the land. Jones, before being elected national president, served on the corps' Andersonville Committee.

Just north of that house, North Main begins to ascend a hill. Look to the left and see a modest, elongated frame house at the base of a slope. Mrs. Martin, a widow who lived here, sent three sons to war. Moody, Remembrance, and John Martin were privates in the 6th Vermont. John came home safely, but Moody was killed and Remembrance wounded on May 5, 1864, at the Wilderness.

Return south on Main Street and proceed through the Bradford business district to the intersection of Route 25B. Here in a small park is the town Civil War monument, honoring the 236 Bradford men who served. Beside it is a statue of

Admiral Charles E. Clark, a Bradford native. Along with George Dewey, Clark was one of Vermont's two great Spanish American War heroes, particularly for his performance in the battle at Santiago Bay, Cuba. Clark also served in the Civil War, seeing action as a junior officer along the Gulf Coast. Turn onto Route 25B, and in 0.3 mile, on the left, see the redbrick cape that was Clark's home.

SOURCES

Bradford United Opinion, August 16, 1865. Vermont State Library.
Orange County Gazetteer, 1861. Vermont State Library.
Women's Relief Corps. Journals of the nineteenth and twentieth national conventions. Vermont Historical Society.
With thanks to Larry Coffin.

....

BRAINTREE

Go north on Route 12A from Randolph; soon, turn right on Braintree Hill Road, and follow it 3 miles to the open hilltop where the 1846 Braintree Hill Meeting House stands. In the church occupying the building's upper floor, William Lloyd Garrison spoke in mid-October 1862. Already turned away by two other local churches, he was welcomed here at Sunday service by Reverend Ammi Nichols. In Randolph four years earlier, Garrison had said, "The government is the tool of slavery. The national flag waves over execrable commerce in African slaves. Against such a government I am arrayed,—I trample on such a flag." But now a war to end slavery was underway. According to Braintree history, this 1862 day "proved to be one of those charming autumn days, when nature, at her prettiest, wore her most bewitching smile, and could not fail to address the heart as well as the eye." When Garrison arrived, he took a long look at the scenery.

The town history said, "Scarcely ever before had a larger audience gathered in that meeting house . . . Mr. Garrison's appeal for the slave was earnest and effective. He expressed his deep admiration of the beautiful panorama of hills and mountains around him, saying that such a country could be peopled only by those who love liberty, and since they insist on freedom for themselves they should insist on freedom of all others."

In the fields around the meetinghouse, on an early August day in 1881, three thousand people gathered to celebrate the one hundredth anniversary of Braintree's founding. A procession led by a coronet band moved to the Grove, a shaded area a few hundred yards north, for ceremonies. Among the speakers were Colonel Francis V. Randall, former 13th Vermont commander, and Dr. Samuel Thayer, Vermont's Civil War surgeon general.

The basement of the meetinghouse held Civil War–era town meetings. Some 105 Braintree men served, and 25 died, including 5 lost at the Wilderness.

Return to Route 12A, and go north to West Braintree and its old white hall, with cupola, on the left. Opposite it, North Road turns right by the World War I monument, and in the second house on the left along it, Francis Luce lived the last few years of his life. Francis was one of six sons of Stephen and Sophia (Withington) Luce, who were privates in the Civil War. Francis enlisted when the 2nd Vermont was formed, but came home in 1863 sick with malaria. Never a well man again, for years he was a stalwart of Randolph's GAR post. Among his brothers, John served with the 17th U.S. Infantry, until blinded by a bullet at Gettysburg. Brother Lyman, 8th Vermont, was captured in Louisiana and came home with heart and liver trouble. He was never well until his death at sixty-one.

Return south on Route 12A to Randolph, take Route 12 north to Snowsville, and note the small triangular green on the left. The large house facing it with a small porch, known as the fan house for the ornament above the door, was the home of George Flagg. Already a famed collar and elbow wrestler before he joined the 2nd Vermont early in the war at twenty-eight, Flagg defeated all challengers during his four years in the army. He also survived a wound at the Wilderness and came home to continue his wrestling career, traveling even to Chicago for matches. He also raised a prize herd of Cotswold sheep here in Snowsville and commanded the Randolph GAR post.

On Memorial Day 1886, Braintree people gathered in Snowsville for a patriotic observance. The scrapbook of a local woman, Mrs. Orra Peavey Mann, described it: "There were present fully 500 people with 125 teams and 35 veterans accompanying the procession to the West Brookfield Cemetery. At the cemetery the graves of our fallen heroes were decorated, followed by a prayer . . . a selection written by Gen. John A. Logan read by Mrs.

Belle Kinney, and a piece by Miss Lula Allen called 'Cover them Over,' . . . The procession returned to Snowsville headed by the Band and Drum Corps." Among those speaking on return was George Flagg." The West Brookfield Cemetery is north along Route 12.

SOURCES

BASS, H. ROYCE. *THE HISTORY OF BRAINTREE, VERMONT, INCLUDING A MEMORIAL OF FAMILIES THAT HAVE RESIDED IN TOWN.* RUTLAND, VT: TUTTLE AND CO., STATE PRINTERS, 1883.
BRIEF SKETCHES OF THE LIFE AND HISTORY OF GEORGE W. FLAGG. RANDOLPH, VT: BUCK PRINTING CO., 1908.
DUCLOS, KATHARINE F. *THE HISTORY OF BRAINTREE, VERMONT, 1883–1975.* VOL. 2. EDITED BY MURIEL C. THRESHER. BRAINTREE, VT: HISTORY BOOK COMMITTEE OF BRAINTREE, 1976.
WITH THANKS TO PHYLLIS HAWLEY AND CATHERINE MEY.

BROOKFIELD

Take Route 65 uphill from Route 14 to Pond Village, and the Brookfield United Church is on the left. Ira Carpenter, once a corporal in the 15th Vermont, lived to be Brookfield's last surviving veteran. In his ninety-first year, he recalled a war meeting held here in 1862: "People filled the pews on the floor and the gallery. Five of us young men sat in the front pew . . . We had decided to enlist that day. The governor made a stirring speech painting some pictures of the country's need of men as would move a heart of stone . . . It didn't take many minutes for us fellows in that front pew to get onto our feet. We went up together and signed those papers. Then some eight or ten more followed us quickly in volunteering. Every time a man arose the house broke forth in applause and cheering . . . Somewhere about 18 men responded to the call. Then the governor began to make all manner of inducements to get the men to enlist. He even offered to give any man who would enlist his choice of the girls in the church to kiss. There was great excitement. Parents wept. Friends cheered and cheered. We had a great time for about two hours. When the meeting broke up 27 men had volunteered to fill the quota of 24. Half of those men left their wives and families."

From the church, go south on Ridge Road and turn right on Crossover Road; proceed beneath Interstate 89, and go left on West Street. In 0.25 mile, see a cape with a weathered barn behind that was Edwin Hall's home. Hall enlisted from here in the 15th Vermont, then reenlisted in the 10th Vermont. At Cold Harbor on June 1, 1864, he was wounded in a knee. Hall wrote many letters home, in one describing a truce at Cold Harbor:

"No man could show his hand or go 20 yards from the breastworks to the rear without exposing himself to the bullets. On the 7th from 11 to 12 there was a truce and men of both armies sprang over their works to see the bloody work that had been done. Enemies met as friends. There was no boasting, no joking . . . Some had lain dead since they fell 6 days before but now swollen and torn by the iron tempest that had swept over and around them thicker than flakes of a blind-

ing snowstorm . . . Then this sublime hour—holy for its brief lease of life—an hour of peace when the earth was calm and the air so still that the gods of war slept—was at an end—friends were enemies again and all hurried back to renew the contest."

Continue on West Street 0.3 mile to the next house on the same side of the road, once the home of Egbert Allis, who joined the U.S. Navy in 1862. Allis, an assistant surgeon, served on warships along the Mississippi that participated in the bombardment of Forts Phillip and Jackson near New Orleans. Briefly a prisoner, he was exchanged and came home here on sick leave in 1863. Returning to duty, he took with him a neighbor lad, seventeen-year-old Horace Smith, to serve as a surgeon's steward. The two shipped out of New York City on the *Bainbridge* on August 18, 1863, but three days later, the ship went down in a hurricane. The *Bainbridge* sank with Allis and Smith among the hundred men lost.

Return north on West Street past Crossover Road, and soon on the left, above the road, is the state Grange headquarters. From the farm just past it, Urial Clark Jr. went to war with the 10th Vermont and fought at Monocacy, the Wilderness, Winchester, Cedar Creek, and other great battles, then came safely home.

Just beyond the farm, turn right on Northfield Road and pass under the interstate to Stone Road. The big farmhouse to the left at the intersection was Cassius Peck's home, a sergeant in Company F, 1st U.S. Sharpshooters. Two days after Antietam, Peck's company encountered retreating Rebels near Boetler's Ford on the Potomac. According to historian G. G. Benedict, "The enemy's riflemen held the opposite bank but the sharpshooters crossed, fording the stream under fire, and supported by the Fourth Michigan, drove them away. Moving on a short distance, a party of sharpshooters, under Corporal Cassius Peck, discovered a small body of the enemy guarding two guns which had been left by the retreating column. The enemy were driven away with the loss of one prisoner, and the guns were captured and brought off." Peck would eventually be awarded a Medal of Honor for that action. After the war, he returned here, and he and wife, Luna, raised eleven children. He died on September 6, 1906, the same day his friend President William McKinley was assassinated.

Go south on Stone Road to the famous floating bridge built well before the Civil War. Ask local people for directions to remote East Hill Cemetery, high in the hills east of Route 14. Alonzo Whitney is buried there, commander of Company I of the 26th Regiment, U.S. Colored Troops, until he was mortally wounded at Gregory's Farm, South Carolina, on December 5, 1864. A flag is carved on his stone above an epitaph that speaks of freedom.

SOURCES
PRINCE, JOHN CONGER. "A WAR MEETING LONG REMEMBERED." THE VERMONTER 34, NO. 9 (SUMMER 1929): 142–43.
WAKEFIELD, ALICE WEBSTER. WEST BROOKFIELD AND THEREABOUTS. RANDOLPH, VT: HERALD PRINTERY, 1985.
WITH THANKS TO ELINOR GRAY, KAREN ELLIS, ALICE WEBSTER AND PRUDI DEMPSEY.

CHELSEA

Chelsea, the shire town of Orange County, has two village greens, side by side along Route 110. The only house facing the south green was purchased in 1873 by Captain William Henry Harrison Hall. Hall went to California with the Gold Rush, captained a steamboat on the Columbia River, but was back in Vermont to organize Company G of the 6th Vermont Regiment, based in Waitsfield, when the war began.

At the head of the green is the Orange County Courthouse; the lower floor served as Chelsea's town hall in the 1860s. On July 24, 1862, the Democrats of Orange County convened here, summoned by this notice: "All those in favor of preserving the Constitution as it is and the Union as it was, and are of the opinion that abolitionism and secessionism are alike disastrous for the perpetuity of the Union, and are in favor of suppressing both and restoring the Union to its original purity and harmony, are invited to join in nominating and supporting county and district officers, good conservative constitutional Union men."

In November 1862, Eunice Barnes, a young Chelsea woman, noted in a letter to her soldier brother, "I came back from the paring bee it was to the town hall they were paring apples to send to the soldiers."

On town meeting day 1862, Chelsea voters approved purchase of land for a new cemetery. The town's centennial history said, "The purpose of the town to have a new cemetery, for the burial of the dead, has been faithfully carried out, and much of the credit is due to Capt. H. H. Hall . . . The cemetery is situated on a hill and commands a fine view of the village and the beautiful valley in which it is situated."

Pass the courthouse on Highland Avenue and proceed uphill into the cemetery. A marker notes that maples lining the way were planted in 1887 "by ladies and sons of veterans auxiliary aided by the sons of veterans and veterans of the GAR." On the cemetery's arched gateway are the words *Consecrated in 1864*. Highland Cemetery is filled with Civil War graves.

Close by the gateway, Captain Orville Bixby is buried, who led Company E, 2nd Vermont, made up of men from Chelsea and nearby towns. Killed at the Wilderness on May 5, 1864, the popular captain was buried on the battlefield. But thanks to the persistence of his widow, Frances, who contacted many of her husband's fellow soldiers to find the site of his burial, a year later the body came home. Captain Bixby's stone lists the battles in which he fought. Frances outlived her husband by a half century and is buried beside him.

Nearby is the grave of Private John Bliss, 17th Vermont, who died in a Petersburg hospital at fifty-six. Cenotaphs honor two victims of Andersonville: Private John Paul dead at thirty-nine, after his capture at Spotsylvania's Bloody Angle, and Private Francis Skinner dead at thirty, after being seized at Weldon Railroad. Both men lie among the more than thirteen thousand Union soldiers buried at Andersonville. Skinner's widow, Clara Searles Skinner, outlived Francis by fifty years. On his cenotaph here she had carved:

God has marked every sorrowing day
And numbered every secret tear

Return to the village and note the old house with bay window facing the southwest corner of the south green, across Route 110, the Bixby home.

The Congregational Church overlooks the north green. A newspaper account from 1863 noted, "A benefit for the sick and wounded soldiers was held Thursday 15th January in the Congregational Church Chelsea under the auspices of the Soldiers Aid Society. Notwithstanding the storm it was very successful. The house was crowded and the proceeds amounted to upwards of $80."

Go north 0.1 mile on Route 110, and an old gristmill is set back on the left. Charles Tinker lived in the brick house directly across the street, one of four cryptographers who worked at the War Department in Washington. Three were Vermonters, and all were often in the presence of Abraham Lincoln, who frequented the department's telegraph office seeking information from the front. After the war, Tinker operated a chair factory that included the gristmill.

A Chelsea history states that 178 men served, with 5 killed in action, 6 dead of wounds, 6 dead in prisons, 21 dead of disease, and 2 killed by accidents, for a 23 percent casualty rate. And 11 Chelsea men deserted, while 24 were discharged for disability.

SOURCES
CHELSEA CENTENNIAL COMMITTEE. *CHELSEA CENTENNIAL: PROCEEDINGS OF THE CENTENNIAL CELEBRATION OF THE ONE*

HUNDREDTH ANNIVERSARY OF THE SETTLEMENT
OF CHELSEA, VERMONT, TOGETHER WITH THE
ORANGE COUNTY VETERAN SOLDIERS' REUNION,
SEPTEMBER 4, 1884. KEENE, NH: SENTINEL
PRINTING CO., 1884.
CHELSEA HISTORICAL SOCIETY. A HISTORY OF
CHELSEA, VERMONT 1784–1984. BARRE, VT:
NORTHLIGHT STUDIO PRESS, 1984.
CHELSEA TOWN RECORDS.
GILMAN, W. S. CHELSEA ALBUM, 1863–1979:
CHELSEA, VERMONT; A COLLECTION OF
PHOTOGRAPHS, SOME OLD, SOME NEW.
RANDOLPH, VT: HERALD PRINTERY, 1979.
RUTLAND HERALD, 1863–1864. VERMONT
STATE LIBRARY.
WITH THANKS TO EUCLID FARNHAM.

CORINTH

Enter East Corinth along Village Road, coming north from Route 25, and just before crossing the bridge, on the right, is a large frame house with a two-tiered porch. Edward Keenan went to war from here, serving in the 15th Vermont and marching to Gettysburg. Henry Divoll, who enlisted in the navy in Massachusetts, came to this house to live soon after the war with his brother Sabin Divoll. Henry had suffered a head injury during the war, and until his death in 1906, he was severely impaired.

Continue on Village Road, and just up the little incline, Short Street turns right. The first house on the street was Dr. Roswell Jenne's home. He served in the 6th and the 17th Vermont and lost a leg to an artillery shell at the Petersburg Breakthrough on April 2, 1865. After the war, he studied medicine and practiced here, until he died in 1894 of heart disease contracted during the war. The second house on the street, with three roof peaks, was the postwar home of Henry Jackman. He served in a Massachusetts battery and witnessed the battle between ironclads *Monitor* and *Merrimac* from a shore battery.

Continue north on Village Road, and in the tiny red house on the left, after the war, lived George Prescott, once a sergeant in the 9th Vermont. He was with his regiment when it was the first to enter Richmond. He was once named the best soldier in the 24th Corps division, in which the 9th served late in the war, by Major General Charles Devens.

The 1840 East Corinth Congregational Church was once the Union Meeting House. Antislavery Reverend Nathan Robinson Johnston (see Topsham) recalled a night there before the war. "A young man," he said, "a son of a Congregationalist, a native of the town of Corinth, had gone into the South and become an attorney . . . Returning home on a visit he was anxious to convince his old friends and companions that their anti-slavery notions were all erroneous, and that slavery was a good thing, and the Abolitionists fanatics." Three debates were arranged between Johnston and the lawyer, and the building was packed for each. According to Johnston, "At the close of the third evening's discussion, when the whole audience was in the height of agitation...the question was put to the people. The anti-slavery vote was almost unanimous and was followed by long applause."

Just north of the church, on the left, is a former store with display windows that was purchased in 1864 by Joseph Darling. He served in the Bradford Guards of the 1st Vermont, commanded by Roswell

Farnham. Darling read law with Farnham after the war, then opened his own office in East Corinth. The store was bought in 1877 by Joseph Kemp, formerly of the 12th Vermont, who added the two upper stories.

A local GAR post formed in 1866, and on Memorial Day, after a program in the Union Meeting House, its members joined a procession to the East Corinth Cemetery, at the end of Short Street, which holds many Civil War graves. The GAR often met in the church vestry. Corinth sent 157 men to war, and 20 died.

Along Village Road are many prewar houses, and in them the women of East Corinth gathered to make items for the soldiers. In one year, they sent forty-one quilts and puffs, fifty-five shirts, and 116 pairs of socks, among many other items, to the fighting men.

SOURCES
CORINTH TOWN RECORDS.
WITH THANKS TO JUDY DRURY.

....

FAIRLEE

A Doric column on the Fairlee green, beside Route 5, was dedicated August 11, 1926, with a few aging Civil War veterans present. Among those honored by the monument were the forty-four men, credited to Fairlee, who served in the Civil War. Of them, ten died, three in battle.

This area was the center of Fairlee life in the 1860s. Civil War–era town meetings took place in the town house, destroyed by a fire that swept through the village in 1912; it stood on the site of the present town office building.

Recruiting in Fairlee was a challenge, with some men crossing the Connecticut River to New Hampshire, just yards away, to enlist. To meet draft quotas, in December 1864 voters gathered in the town hall and approved bounties for Fairlee men of $900 for three-year enlistments, $600 for two years, and $300 for a single year. Also voted were bounties for men enlisting here from other towns of $600 for three years, $400 for two years, and $200 for a single year.

Here on November 8, 1864, Fairlee voted 75 to 64 for Abraham Lincoln over George McClellan.

At the annual meeting in March 1864, the Fairlee Ladies Sewing Circle presented a hearse to the town. The meeting approved a resolution that began, "The patriotic labors of the Fairlee Soldiers Aid Society in their efforts for the benefit & comfort of our brave soldiers, who are periling their lives for the suppression of a most wicked and gigantic rebellion, shall be a fair and equivalent offset to the labors of the Fairlee Sewing Circle in procuring a hearse."

From the green, go south on Route 5, and on the left is the 1850s railway depot. Fairlee men went to war from here, and some came home here in caskets, among them Benjamin Stratton, Daniel Davis, and Gilman Hammond.

Continue south, and the road to Lake Morey soon turns west. From the second house before the turn, on the right, Royal Morris enlisted as a 12th Vermont private.

Continue south on Route 5 just over 2 miles, and just before the road descends to

Ely village, a stately brick home is on the right. Charles Clogston went from here to join the 17th Vermont in the spring of 1864 and was quickly wounded in his first battle, at the Wilderness.

Return north on Route 5, and just before reentering the village, Bush Meadow Drive is on the right. From the small frame house at the corner, Benjamin Stratton went to join the 12th Vermont as a private at eighteen. He got sick and died in January 1863 at his regiment's winter camp.

Return to the village, and soon Route 25 turns right, to cross the Connecticut River. At the intersection, on the left, is a small mall. Just north of it, on the left, the small frame house was once the Davis family home. Daniel Davis from here crossed the Connecticut to enlist in the 2nd New Hampshire Infantry and fought at First Bull Run. In November 1861, Davis, known to his buddies as Uncle Dudley, joined Company E, 2nd U.S. Sharpshooters, a Vermont outfit. Promoted to corporal, he was shot in an elbow at the Wilderness. When his father learned that Davis was in a Washington hospital, he sent a local man, Ira Freeman, to care for him. But on arrival, Freeman learned that Davis had died when an artery in his wounded arm burst. Freeman brought the body home.

Go north on Route 5 out of the village, passing beneath the towering cliff of Morey's Mountain, and the entrance to the Village Cemetery is soon on the left. Davis is buried here, as are Gilman Hammond and Nathan Hammond. To find the Hammond home, continue on Route 5 for 2 miles to a large and very old stone house on the left. Gilman Hammond went from here to join the 8th Vermont, but died of sickness at twenty-one soon after reaching Louisiana. Nathan Hammond, probably his father, enlisted at forty-four in Company F, 1st U.S. Sharpshooters, but was discharged for disability in January 1862. He died the next year.

SOURCES
DAVIS FAMILY PAPERS. FAIRLEE TOWN OFFICE. FAIRLEE TOWN RECORDS.
ROBINSON, PHILIP G. *THE TOWN UNDER THE CLIFF: A HISTORY OF FAIRLEE, VERMONT.* WEST TOPSHAM, VT: GIBBY PRESS, 1957.
WITH THANKS TO GEORGETTE WOLF-LUDWIG.

....

NEWBURY

The village of Newbury's large common borders Route 5, and on its western side is the Methodist Church, once closely affiliated with the school that stood beside it, the Newbury Seminary. An account published in the *Vermont Journal* of May 4, 1861, said, "The star spangled banner had never waved over our building till Thursday last, when the efforts of the ladies culminated in the presentation to the Institution of a large and beautiful flag, which now stands floating from its heaven-pointing standard." That day a large crowd gathered at the seminary to hear speeches and see the flag raised by J. B. Brooks, a volunteer, while the band played "The Star-Spangled Banner." Brooks, a graduate of the seminary, had just enlisted in the 1st Vermont as a private. Later, he joined the 4th Vermont and served until a wound suffered at the Wilderness brought him home.

From the north side of the common, take Chapel Street west, and soon bear left on Scotch Hollow Road. In 4.5 miles, the 1839 Newbury Center Town House is on the left. Here, town meetings were held, and voters of this town, with an 1860 population of 2,549, approved war spending that totaled $42,622.07. All but $1,400 was spent on bounty payments. Some two hundred Newbury men served.

From the town house, return south on Scotch Hollow Road, soon turn right on Halls Lake Road and skirt the west shore of the lake. In 2.75 miles, come to Tucker Mountain Road; turn left and stop, to look back at the fields along the Lake Road. Once Thomas Tucker owned a farm that included those fields. At age forty-four, when the war began, Tucker joined the 1st Vermont. A story in the *Middlebury Register* of July 3, 1861, said "27 Wells River people turned out recently and hoed T. L. Tucker's corn for him, as he has gone to the war as a drummer."

Go right on Tyler Farm Road, and the 1833 West Newbury Union Meeting House is soon on the right. Thomas Tucker led this church's choir for thirty years and made it the finest in town.

Return as you came, take Snake Road by the West Newbury post office, and in 3 miles, return to Route 5. Go north 2.5 miles, and the common is again on the left. Continue north 1.25 miles to a stately frame house with a large central chimney on the right and a stone historic marker just beyond. From this house, A. K. Heath saw two sons go to war. William, nineteen, joined the 4th Vermont in September 1861 and served as a private until killed at the Wilderness. Everett joined the 3rd Vermont at twenty-one when it formed and served until the war ended.

Continue north on Route 5 for 4 miles, and entering the village of Wells River, a recreation field is on the left. In the third house beyond the field, John Farwell lived after the war and ran the nearby Wells River railway depot. Farwell served in the 13th Vermont and cared for the horse of its commander, Francis Randall, and those of other officers. He fought at Gettysburg.

Continue north, and soon the Wells River Congregational Church is on the right. The house on the church's north side was once its parsonage, and among its residents was Reverend Eugene Ranslow, a navy man who served on the U.S.S. *Brooklyn* and was in the battle for Fort Fisher on the Carolina coast.

Continue into the village, and note the large frame building on the left, beside a store and just north of the Route 5 and Route 302 intersection. On its top floor, the Addison Preston GAR Post held its meetings each month on the Tuesday evening of the full moon week. Organized in 1883, it once had two hundred members. A Women's Relief Corps of the Preston Post was organized in 1885. In 1894, Erastus Baldwin presented the post with a memorial book, in which the war experiences of post members was recorded. He said in a presentation letter, "I would like to do something to show you the respect and honor I feel is due every soldier that took his life in his hand and went to the front to protect our union and the Stars and Stripes." Baldwin, who had paid a commutation fee and did not serve, became Wells River's most prosperous resident.

When word reached Wells River of Lee's surrender, a celebration was held that the *Caledonian Record* said included "the ringing of bells, the firing of cannon, a torchlight procession, and brilliant beacon fire on Carpaean Rock (as Rev. J. D. Butler used to call it) at the west end of the village." Go north on Route 5, and take Route 302 west. In one-half mile, on the left, note a steep-sided rock that rises abruptly to some 50 feet that may have been the rock where the fire was built.

SOURCES
NEWBURY TOWN RECORDS.
WITH THANKS TO PETER SINCLAIR AND
  HORACE "HOD" SYMES.

ORANGE

In the mountains along Route 302, west of Barre, the Orange Civil War memorial stands in front of the 1848 Orange Alliance Church. Listed are the names of 81 Orange men who served, from an 1860 population of 930. Among those whose names are here:

Private Asa Whitcomb, 6th Vermont, killed at the Wilderness

Private William Godfrey, 6th Vermont, killed at Lee's Mill and buried at Yorktown, Virginia

Private Ephraim Webster, 8th Vermont, captured in Mississippi and died at Vicksburg

Private Addison Whitcomb, 6th Vermont, killed at Charles Town, Virginia

Also on the stone is the name of Private John Patterson, 11th Vermont. His regiment had just joined the Vermont Brigade in the trenches at Spotsylvania, when, according to a fellow soldier, he "took an unexploded shell was fooling with it by a campfire. Some one told him it would blow his hand off. None of your damned business if it does [he said]. Shell exploded and killed him and another man . . . and wounded 5 or 6 others."

In the Orange town hall, across the road from the church and monument, town voters approved bounties that reached $500 in 1865.

In the house just east of the town hall lived Orange Fifield, a successful businessman who owned much property in Orange. In the fall of 1860, Fifield was in Boston on business, having driven his prize Morgan mare, Nancy, there. On arriving, Fifield overheard some men planning a trip to Montpelier where, they said, a warehouse was filled with wool for sale at a very cheap rate. With war obviously approaching, they planned to sell it to the government. Fifield immediately hitched up Nancy and headed north, covering 50 miles the first night. He drove his horse all the way to Montpelier, stopping every 50 miles, where he bought all the wool and turned a handsome profit. He was perhaps the first person to profit from the war in Vermont. Fifield, his brother, and their sons did not serve.

Go east on Route 302, and Brook Haven Cemetery is soon on the hillside to the right. By the road, beside where the cemetery entrance is now located, stood a small house, once the home of Hannah Flanders. She was the wife of Royal Flanders, a cobbler also known for his abilities to help the sick and injured. Apparently, he stitched wounds as well as shoes. Royal served in the 2nd Vermont as a hospital steward early in the war, leaving Hannah (Dana) and six sons in a remote mountain farmhouse in Orange. Times were hard for Hannah, and she soon moved her family to a small house in the village. Time and again, Hannah wrote to her husband at war, telling him of the family's hardship, of a lack of food, money, and clothing.

Royal came home for a time in 1863, because of disability, but soon returned to the front, leaving his wife pregnant. In 1864, in desperation, Hannah sent her eldest son to work in the copper mines in nearby Corinth. She wrote her husband, "I want money very bad for the children are perfectly shirtless."

Sometime in 1864, she gave birth, but Royal did not return home until seven months after the war ended, working for a time in the Brattleboro military hospital. He finally came home with chronic diarrhea and died in August 1866. Months later, Hannah had another child. Soon, she was placed in an insane asylum, but she eventually came home to Orange and lived with her children, all of whom became upstanding citizens. She died in 1903.

Royal often wrote to Hannah from the army, and a letter sent in late September 1862 to the little house in the village spoke of the Antietam battlefield. He wrote, "Imagine to yourself the side of the hill above your house all covered with dead and wounded so thick that you would have to pile one upon another to get a chance to pick up the wounded." In

1862, the hillside behind Hannah's house was a farmer's field. Today, the hillside holds the dead of Brook Haven Cemetery.

Across Route 302, the first house east of the cemetery was once the Jackson family home. When Hannah Flanders was institutionalized, her children were sent to live with local families. The Jacksons took two of them.

Turn around and return past the Civil War monument on Route 302, and in 0.5 mile, go left on Tucker Road. Proceed to Route 110 and turn right. The first house on the left was built by Newell Waterman, who cut and sawed timbers for it in 1860. But because of the war's demand for metal, Newell said he couldn't get nails to finish it until 1864.

SOURCES
FLANDERS FAMILY PAPERS. COURTESY OF ELSIE
    BEARD.
FREEMAN, VIVIAN L. ROGERS. *ORANGE,
    VERMONT, TOWN HISTORY: 1781–1981.*
    ORANGE, VT: ORANGE TOWN
    BICENTENNIAL COMMITTEE, 1991.
WITH THANKS TO ELSIE BEARD.

RANDOLPH

Randolph Center, located at the geographic center of Vermont, is just uphill from Interstate 89 at the Randolph exit, on Route 66. Entering the village, go left at the Y, and just past the village store, go right toward Vermont Veterans Memorial Cemetery. Descend the hill to a small stream, Pinney Brook, and look left on the near bank for a cellar hole. Private Oliver Pinney lived here, a 6th Vermont private killed at Savage's Station. A small settlement once thrived along Pinney Brook because a foundry operated here. The only house that remains is the 1802 Langevin House. Another young man who went to war from here was Charles Kelley. As a 10th Vermont private, he lost an eye to a Rebel bullet at Cedar Creek. Kelley's father, Alpha, agitated before the war to make sure that Vermont did not enforce the fugitive slave laws.

The Veterans Cemetery, founded in 1995, contains one Civil War gravestone. It was discovered by Randoph Center historians Wesley and Miriam Herwig in a brook near West Randolph, where the Harlow family lived and made fine baskets. Apparently, a flood had undermined the family cemetery. The stone marked Private Henry Harlow's grave, a soldier in the 17th Vermont, who was taken sick during the Petersburg Siege and died on his way home. The Herwigs had the stone erected in the Veterans Cemetery.

Return to Randolph Center and the Randolph Congregational Church. On June 26, 1838, the Randolph Female Anti-Slavery Society held its annual meeting here. Four years earlier, the abolitionist Orson Murray spoke here and, according to Abby Hemenway, "There was a strong feeling of opposition to this meeting, and boys and men, moved by the seditious spirit, came with eggs and other missiles, and succeeded in driving Mr. Murray from the place of meeting." However, Murray was invited to speak again, and "a temporary police was organized, and the most powerful men, physically, stationed in various parts of the house; and thus the meeting passed off quietly."

On April 19, 1865, a funeral service for Abraham Lincoln was held in the church with an address delivered by Reverend E. E. Randall, who noted that the joy attendant on the war's end had suddenly been turned to sadness. "We have come to this house of prayer," he said, "in the presence of God, to mingle our common sorrow. We have come here to weep and pray. We have come to sorrow over the fearful calamity which has so recently overtaken us in the midst of our rejoicings. Oh, the joy of our heart is ceased; our dance is turned into mourning."

Go straight past the church on East Bethel Road, and 1 mile south, the cape set above the road with a large barn behind was the home from which John Mead went to war. Mead was second in command of the 8th Vermont, until Commander Stephen Thomas was put in charge of a brigade. Leading the 8th at Cedar Creek, Mead was wounded in the regiment's early morning stand.

Continue south 3 miles to a Y, and look uphill to an old farm, on which Jonathan Peckham Miller was born. Miller volunteered for the War of 1812, then fought in the Greek War of Independence against the Turks, where he won the nickname the American daredevil. Returning to Vermont, he represented Berlin in the legislature, where he introduced a resolution calling for an end to slavery in the District of Columbia. Miller attended the 1840 world antislavery conference in London.

Return to Randolph Center and take Route 66 to Randolph. Cross the interstate, and 1.75 miles, on the right, is a redbrick cape, now an office. Albert Chandler was born and grew up here, receiving his early education in the stone schoolhouse across the street. Chandler, during the war, was a cryptographer in the War Department, deciphering war messages from the front and often handing them to Abraham Lincoln. After the war, Chandler made a fortune in the telegraph business. Proceed on Route 66 into downtown Randolph (known as West Randolph at the time of the war), and Chandler Music Hall, Chandler's gift to his hometown, is on the left. On October 19, 1910, the 8th Vermont held a reunion in this building, on the 46th anniversary of Cedar Creek. Sixty veterans were present, and many visited the birthplace of Stephen Thomas before holding an evening "campfire" in the music hall. After Thomas's death in 1903, the 8th's regimental association never filled the office of president, keeping it open in his honor.

Not far past the hall is the Methodist Church, where in 1910 a funeral was held for Ben Robinson. Once a ten-year-old slave in North Carolina, he was plowing a field with a mule when Company C of the 9th Vermont marched past. The lad left his mule and went with the regiment, eventually being brought to Randolph by a local soldier. Robinson worked as a watchman in local mills and lived in Randolph until his death of heart disease.

The Randolph railway station stands by the tracks in the center of town. In 1866, a train carrying Philip Sheridan briefly stopped here. A big crowd was present, and the *Burlington Daily Times* said, "A salute was fired, flags were flung to the breeze from every point, and Gen. Sheridan was obliged to leave the car and take an elevated position on the platform, where he was introduced by Col. H. R. Stoughton, formerly of the sharpshooters."

Continue on Main Street past the depot, go uphill, and turn left on Highland Avenue. This level residential area was once a fairgrounds, and two of Vermont's three sharpshooter companies were organized here, the first being Company F, 1st U.S. Sharpshooters, on September 13, 1861. Company E, 2nd U.S. Sharpshooters, formed here on November 9 of that year. Company F was commanded by Colonel Homer Stoughton, of Randolph, who wrote, "All these men were required to stand the special test of making ten consecutive shots with a rifle, placing each shot within a ten inch ring at a distance of three hundred yards, and must in every way stand the physical examination required of all recruits to the army at the time."

SOURCES
WITH THANKS TO MIRIAM AND WESLEY HERWIG.

....

STRAFFORD

From interstate 89 at Sharon, take Route 132 east to South Strafford, and go north to the village of Strafford and its green. Strafford's magnificent town house, built in 1799, dominates the village, standing on a knoll at the head of the village green. Town meetings and war meetings took place here, the first war meeting held on May 11, 1861, when 75 men joined the local militia company. Hard news was delivered the next year when Strafford learned that it must raise 30 men to serve three years, and another 25 for nine months. On August 25, voters approved the town's first bounty payments, a decision that was to put the town in debt for years. The Civil War hit Strafford hard, with some 30 men perishing. No wonder, then, when word of Lee's surrender arrived on April 10, 1865, the town house bell rang, and this building, and several others nearby, were illuminated.

The Congregational Church, overlooking the green's south end, was attended by Justin Smith Morrill, Strafford's most famous resident, who once complained during the Civil War that the minister, Samuel Delano, did not voice enough support for the conflict. Across the green, the stone and brick building, which now houses the post office and town historical society, was the village store in the 1860s. Morrill was part owner.

In the large white house south of the store, Ellen Janette Harris was born, who married Portus Baxter, of Derby Line, a wartime congressman from Vermont. Ellen and her husband worked in Washington, D.C., hospitals caring for sick and wounded soldiers. Though the Baxters were Derby Line residents, Ellen came home to Strafford to give birth here to son Jedediah Hyde Baxter, who became an army surgeon and was once in charge of the Campbell military hospital in Washington, which cared for fifteen thousand Union soldiers.

Two Strafford men served in the famed College Cavaliers, a cavalry unit mainly composed of Norwich University and Dartmouth students. The cavaliers, unlike some ten thousand other Union soldiers, escaped capture by Stonewall Jackson at Harper's Ferry during the Antietam campaign by galloping out of town. On their return from service soon afterward, Strafford cavaliers Walter Hazleton and Albion Clark were guests of honor at a celebration held in Carpenter's, a hotel that operated during the war. The building remains, just north of the old store.

At the south end of the village is the Justin Smith Morrill Historic Site, with its nineteenth-century Roman Gothic–style architectural masterpiece, the 1853 home designed by Justin Morrill. Morrill, born the son of a Strafford blacksmith, made a fortune as a businessman. At thirty-eight, he retired to Strafford, and began a political career, serving Vermont in the U.S. House and Senate for forty-four years. Surely the most important legislation he sponsored was the Land Grant College Act, signed into law by Lincoln on July 2, 1862. It created financial support for a land grant college in each state, thus bringing into being many prominent colleges and universities. Morrill also chaired the Senate Building Committee, which oversaw construction of several major federal buildings in Washington, D.C., including the Library of Congress, and he was a key figure in congressional funding of the Union war effort. Morrill died in this house in 1898, still a senator.

Return to the green's north end, and in the cemetery behind the town house is the Morrill mausoleum and the graves of Congressman Baxter, his wife, and their surgeon son.

From the green, go north on Justin

Morrill Highway 0.6 mile and turn right on City Falls Road. In 0.5 mile, on the left, is an old farmhouse, now part of a large horse farm. Janet Flanders was fifteen when she married Olcott Bacon just before the war began. Olcott, twenty-two when he joined the 9th Vermont, was captured in fighting near New Berne, North Carolina, on February 2, 1864, and taken to Andersonville, where he died the following August 14. Janet bought this house after the war and lived here until she died in 1933. Never remarrying, she explained that she never found another man "worth her pension." Apparently, marriage would have meant loss of her widow's pension.

From the green, go north on Brook Road just over 1 mile, and turn right on Kibling Hill Road. In 0.4 mile is a large brick house, once the Morey family home. Reuben Morey, who lived to 101, volunteered for the militia in 1814. A son of the old man recalled that early in the Civil War, a young man who had just enlisted came to the house. Taking up Reuben's musket, he began to demonstrate what he had learned. The old man proceeded to put the recruit through a drill long remembered.

SOURCES
STRAFFORD TOWN RECORDS.
WITH THANKS TO GWENDA SMITH AND JOHN
  DUMVILLE.

....

★ THETFORD

Thetford produced two Civil War generals and lost a son to a strange incident in the South that attracted Abraham Lincoln's attention.

Some 175 Thetford men served, with 14 dying of sickness and 2 killed in action.

Leave Interstate 91 at the Thetford exit and go west 0.5 mile on Route 133 to the elegant houses of Thetford Hill, set around a common. The last house on the right before the church, facing the common, was the boyhood home of Gustavus Loomis, born in 1789. In 1863, he was seventy-four and commanding a training post on Governors Island in New York Harbor, when Abraham Lincoln granted him a retirement exemption. He served through the war and retired as a major general in 1865.

Turn south on Academy Road, and on the right is Goddard Hall, an 1845 building once part of Thetford Academy. Among the students who attended the academy before the Civil War was Thomas Morris Chester, a black native of Philadelphia whose family had harbored fugitive slaves in their home. When the war began, Chester delivered antislavery lectures throughout the North, and was involved in the formation of two black regiments, the 54th and 55th Massachusetts. Later, Morris raised two companies of black troops for the defense of Harrisburg, Pennsylvania, as Confederates threatened the city during the Gettysburg campaign. As a reporter for the *Philadelphia Press*, he was present at Richmond's fall, filing one report seated in the speaker's chair of the Confederate congress.

Another student familiar with Goddard Hall was Henry Ellis Beecher, son of Harriet Beecher Stowe. He graduated from Thetford Academy in 1856 and went on to Dartmouth College, where he drowned while swimming in the Connecticut River his freshman year.

Continue on Academy Road, pass modern Thetford Academy, and in 1.5 miles, go left on Burnham Road. In 0.5 mile, in the old cape on the right, Richard Hovey was born in 1827. Hovey moved to Illinois before the war, organized the 33rd Illinois Regiment, and later became a brigade commander. He was wounded in an attack on Rebel positions at Arkansas Post in January 1863. He retired a major general.

Return to Route 133, turn left, and in 1 mile, on entering Thetford Center, note the small white frame house on the right, with a brick house just beyond. Alanson Sanborn lived in the frame house as a young man, the son of abolitionist parents who may have harbored fugitive slaves here. In 1862 in New York City, Sanborn recruited the 1st U.S. Colored Volunteers. In July 1863, Sanborn was marching the regiment through Norfolk, Virginia, when a local man, Dr. D. M. Wright, an ardent secessionist and slaveholder, took offense. Wright shouted an insult at Sanborn, then shot him dead.

Arrested and tried by a military commission, Wright pleaded insanity and self-defense. Both strategies failed, and he was sentenced to death. An appeal was made to President Lincoln, who ordered a review of the case, including examination of Wright by a medical expert. The doctor was found sane and hanged on October 16, 1863.

Past the Sanborn house is the redbrick Methodist Church where Sanborn's funeral was held on December 8, 1863. Reverend Daniel Sidney Frost spoke at length, concluding, "Oh God of heaven and earth . . . consecrate the spot where the ashes of our murdered brother are to rest, who fell in this sacred cause of liberty. Forsake us not in our hour of need, great God of battles. Bless our efforts to maintain the rights of man, and promote that liberty of which thine own spirit is the essence . . . O Lead our armies to victory, and give our country a righteous peace, and in the name of the whole American people, we will ascribe and honor and praise thy name forever more." Sanborn is buried behind the church.

On November 9, 1861, the Thetford Soldier Relief Society was organized in this church. Reverend Frost spoke; a hymn, "The First Gun Is Fired," was sung; and a committee of sixteen women was organized to solicit contributions for the soldiers. A month later, the society staged a concert here, featuring a thirty-voice choir.

From the church, continue on Route 113 for nearly 4 miles, and on entering Post Mills, cross a bridge and look ahead to the foundation of a mill. In 1890, Thomas Henry Chubb opened a factory here that made fine fly rods. Chubb and his father, Commodore Thomas Chubb, both veterans of service on Confederate blockade runners, came to Thetford in 1867, accompanied by black servants. Though the group was initially refused lodging in a local hotel, the younger Chubb eventually established himself in town, providing employment for many local people in his rod factory. In 1882, Thetford sent the former Confederate to Montpelier, as its representative in the legislature.

SOURCES

FROST, REV. D. S. FUNERAL SERMON
PREACHED AT THETFORD, VERMONT.
DECEMBER 8, 1863. THETFORD HISTORICAL
SOCIETY.

SLADE, MARY BROWN CHASE. *THETFORD
ACADEMY'S FIRST CENTURY, 1819–1919.*
THETFORD, VT: THETFORD ACADEMY
HISTORICAL COMMITTEE, 1956.

SPIEGEL, ALLEN D. "ABRAHAM LINCOLN AND
THE INSANITY PLEA." *JOURNAL OF
COMMUNITY HEALTH* 19, NO. 3 (JUNE
1994).

WITH THANKS TO BARBARA CONDICT,
CHARLES LATHAM, AND JOSEPH DEFFNER.

TOPSHAM

South of Groton and north of East Corinth, in the midst of East Topsham, stands the United Presbyterian Church. Reverend Nathan Robinson Johnston became its pastor in 1851, a devout opponent of slavery, who knew many of the major antislavery figures of his time. Indeed, anti-slavery leaders William Lloyd Garrison and Samuel May both spoke in the church on a day in the mid-1850s. They spent the night at Johnston's parsonage. From the church, look to the house directly across the street. The house behind it was the parsonage, the first dwelling on Galusha Hill Road.

In 1859, Topsham closely followed events in Virginia associated with John Brown's raid. As the day of Brown's execution neared, Johnston told his congregation, "A martyr to liberty will John Brown die. His blood will cry for vengeance, and from that blood will rise up thousands of John Browns armed with moral weapons and sworn to conquer and destroy slavery or die."

The Topsham town hall is beside the church. Johnston wrote a memoir he called *Looking Back from the Sunset Land,* and in it he wrote, "The evening after the hanging of John Brown the abolitionists of Topsham held a public meeting in the town hall at which resolutions were introduced and discussed in part." Several more meetings were soon held and at one, Johnston wrote, "Among the speakers who stood in defense of the Charlestown Martyr were young Robert McNiece and Charles Divoll . . . While young McNiece was speaking from his place in the audience, a big stout man walked excitedly and hurriedly to the speaker, and, shaking his weapon at him, ordered to 'stop that talk' . . . But the words were scarcely out of the mouth of the man when two muscular abolitionists rushed up to him, caught him by the arms and, pulling him away, ordered him to sit down and behave himself."

In 1860, William Wells Brown, an escaped slave and abolitionist, spoke in the church. Johnston wrote that he received a note the next morning threatening that if Brown did not immediately leave town, he would be "carried out." But Brown spoke again that night and left town safely. After a subsequent Sabbath service, Johnston saw, on the church wall by the pulpit, that someone had written, "Death to traitors and nigger preachers."

Reverend Johnston traveled throughout the east attending anti-slavery meetings. Early in the war he taught black children in Union-occupied territory along the Carolina coast. Once while in Washington, he met Lincoln, of whom he said, "His countenance was sad."

When the war against slavery commenced, Topsham paid a heavy price. A local historian, William Hodge, has calculated that of an 1860 population of 1,660, 165 served and 41 died.

Soon after the firing on Fort Sumter, Johnston preached a Sunday sermon in his church based on the book of Matthew: "And ye shall hear of war and rumors of wars: see that ye be not troubled: for all these things must come to pass, but the end is not yet."

One of the first Topsham lads to perish was Private Morris Divoll, 6th Vermont, from sickness near Fredericksburg in November 1862. Johnston wrote, "The week preceding our winter communion was one of anxiety and sorrow for many. Death from diphtheria occurred in several families. To others came sad news from the battlefield. One Sunday morning the church bells tolled the death of Morris Divoll." The body came home, and Johnston wrote, "After brief devotion in the house the body was carried to the church and lay in the vestibule while the funeral services were held within. [The covenanters of Topsham objected to the common custom of carrying the dead body into the church and placing it before the pulpit.] A very large assembly filled the house. It was the first case of a soldier's burial and he had many friends." Johnston chose words from the book of Daniel: "Unto the end of the war desolations are determined."

On May 6, 1864, Divoll's brother Charles, also of the 6th Vermont, was severely wounded at the Wilderness. Johnston was in New York City and, in response to a telegram from the soldier's father, hastened to Washington to seek out the wounded lad in a military hospital. He arrived too late, as Divoll had just died, but he did locate his grave. Back in Topsham, Johnston preached a sermon honoring the young soldier who, four years earlier, had spoken at a contentious town meeting in support of John Brown.

In the early winter of 1864, Colonel Stephen Thomas, 8th Vermont commander, spoke at the town hall to encourage enlistments. At town meetings in that hall, soldier bounties were voted beginning with $25 in August 1862. Right after Thomas spoke, the town approved bounties "of a sufficient sum" in addition to the $300 they had just approved.

From East Topsham, take Groton road 0.3 mile and go left on Willey Hill Road. In 0.75 mile, from the old farmhouse on the right with a porch, twins Henry and Nathan Heath went to war, enlisting as privates in the 6th Vermont. Henry joined the 9th Vermont late in the war and died of sickness on October 16, 1865. Not long before, Horace, then an officer of the 3rd U.S. Colored Troops, took sick and died in Jacksonville, Florida.

Just south of East Topsham, in the village cemetery close by the road, is a single gravestone for the Heath twins. The stone notes that Albert and Amada Heath were their parents and that the lads perished at age twenty-three. Henry's body lies in the federal cemetery at Hampton, Virginia. Nearby are stones for the Divoll brothers. Higher up the slope is Reverend Johnston's stone. He lived until 1904.

From East Topsham, go south on East Corinth Road, and on the left at the corner of Swamp Road is the house from which Henry Butterfield enlisted in the 8th Vermont. He was killed May 27, 1863, in the costly, failed assault on Port Hudson.

The village of Waits River, on Route 25, is also part of Topsham. North of the village, where Honey Corners Road intersects Route 25, look across the river to the large level field where Topsham men drilled when the war began.

SOURCES

History of Topsham, Vermont. Topsham, VT: Town of Topsham, 2006.
Johnson, Nathan Robinson. *Looking Back from the Sunset Land; or People Worth Knowing.* Oakland, CA: s.n., 1898. Vermont Historical Society.
With thanks to Bill Hodge.

··

TUNBRIDGE

Tunbridge's best-known Civil War soldiers, Wilbur Fisk and Franklin Aretas Haskell, today would surely recognize the village in the town that was once their home, as prewar structures line the village's main street, which is Route 110. Fisk, a private in the 2nd Vermont, was the best-known Vermont newspaper correspondent of the war. Haskell won everlasting fame for a letter he wrote describing the Battle of Gettysburg.

The town Civil War monument stands in the Tunbridge Cemetery at the south end of the village, and it bears the names of 116 men who served. Just north of the cemetery is the Tunbridge Congregational Church, where Fisk and his family worshipped. The church bell, still in use, rang on several important Civil War occasions, including Lee's surrender to Grant.

The Tunbridge town hall, just north of the church, held Civil War town meetings. In December 1861, a funeral for the first Tunbridge resident to die in the war, Corporal Cyrus Hunt, was held here, a grand patriotic occasion with a band playing and many speeches. Hunt died of disease in the Vermont Brigade winter cantonment, Camp Griffin. Soldier funerals would become quieter occasions as they became more common.

Haskell and Fisk were hill-farm lads. To reach the area of town where they lived, go north along Route 110 from the church and, before crossing the bridge, go right on Strafford Road, and in 1 mile go right on Hoyt Hill Road. In 0.75 mile stop on reaching a Y. The road to the right once led over the ridge to the Fisk home, and hence, Wilbur Fisk walked this road to the nearby school where he taught, which no longer stands. Along the road you just drove, Haskell came walking as a pupil, then as a teacher, to the same one-room schoolhouse. Perhaps the two, the best soldier writers Vermont produced, sometimes met here.

From here, return to Strafford Road and go right. Soon, go right on Moody Hill Road to the intersection by Strafford Road Cemetery. Haskell's parents lie here, as does Private Spencer Noyes, with his family. More on that later.

Continue on Moody Hill Road 0.3 mile and stop where Morrill Road turns right. Walk straight ahead on the narrow road into the woods, and some 100 yards along, in the maples on the left, once stood the Haskell home, now a cellar hole. Franklin Haskell grew up here, then graduated from

Dartmouth College. Moving to Wisconsin, he enlisted in the 6th Wisconsin Regiment and soon became aide-de-camp to John Gibbon, commander of the famed Iron Brigade. Gibbon and his brigade were on Cemetery Ridge as Pickett's Charge approached. Riding about the ridgetop under fire, Haskell brought up reinforcements to bolster the Union line. After the battle, he wrote a lengthy letter, describing the fighting, considered the finest eyewitness account of Gettysburg. He wrote of Pickett's Charge: "Regiment after regiment, brigade after brigade, . . . the red flags wave, their horsemen gallop up and down; the arms of 18,000 men, barrel and bayonet, gleam in the sun, a sloping forest of flashing steel. Right on they move as with one soul, in perfect order, without impediment of ditch, or wall, or stream, over ridge and slope, through orchard and meadow, and cornfield, magnificent, grim, irresistible." Eleven months later, a bullet to the brain killed Haskell in the July 1 attack at Cold Harbor.

Return to Strafford Hill Road and continue uphill 0.5 mile to an aging farmhouse on the left. From here, the Noyes family saw five sons go to war. Privates Charles Noyes and Spencer Noyes joined Company E, 2nd Vermont. Charles died of disease in October 1862. William was killed at the Wilderness. Brother Spencer, a private in the 11th Vermont, is said to have deserted and moved to Canada, saying that he couldn't put his mother through the loss of another son.

Return to Route 110, go north, and in a 0.5 mile, Monarch Hill Road goes left. At the intersection, look to the field along the river where Company E, 2nd Vermont, including the Noyes boys, once drilled, as did Company H, 2nd Vermont.

Go up Monarch Hill 1.3 miles to a farmhouse on the left, with barn across the way. Lieutenant James Farmham from here enlisted in the 12th Vermont. For the nine months he was away, his wife, Sena, skinny and 5 feet tall, ran the farm and cared for three babies and her eighty-year-old father-in-law. She lived to eighty-six.

Here on Monarch Hill, Pete and Kay Jorgensen, in 1993, began publishing *Civil War News,* a periodical that has since kept the worldwide Civil War community informed. The paper has been an essential ingredient in the Civil War battlefield preservation movement of the late twentieth and early twenty-first centuries.

Return to Route 110, go north, and soon go left on Whitney Hill Road. In just over 2 miles, at a crossroads, is a one-room schoolhouse that seven of Phineas Whitney's twelve grandsons attended. All twelve served in the Civil War. The road going left of the schoolhouse once led to the Whitney home, and along it twelve maple trees were planted in honor of the Whitney soldiers. Private Orlando Whitney, 9th Vermont, died of sickness in July 1863, and a cenotaph in the cemetery by the one-room schoolhouse honors him. Another Whitney boy died at Andersonville.

Return to Route 110 and go north into North Tunbridge. Flag-raising rallies to encourage enlistments were held on the little common in front of the white church, on the left.

Tunbridge is, of course, the home of the Tunbridge World's Fair. Founded two years after the war, it moved to its current location in Tunbridge village, along the White River's First Branch, in 1871. Surely, countless Civil War veterans attended the autumn harvest celebrations and, on meeting, paused to recall days spent along the rivers Rappahannock, Potomac, and Mississippi.

SOURCES

BYRNE, FRANK AND ANDREW WEAVER. *HASKELL OF GETTYSBURG*. WISCONSIN HISTORICAL SOCIETY, 1970.
WITH THANKS TO EUCLID FARNHAM

....

VERSHIRE

A history of Vershire published in 1981 said, "113 Vershire men [over 10 percent of its total population] went to fight in the Civil War, leaving farms unattended for four years. Thirteen of those men lost their lives, many were seriously wounded, some totally disabled. Homesteads were vacated. Other farmers, during haying season, went place to place, camping out in derelict buildings, keeping some of the fields open, but brush and forest rapidly reclaimed much of the land."

The history also says, "Between 1860 and 1880 there was another major increase in population. Hundreds of miners were imported from Ireland and Cornwall, England to work in the new copper mines, creating a large village of Copperfield." By the time the Civil War began, the Vershire mines employed several hundred men. Business thrived early in the war with the War Department buying copper. Some local mine workers went to war.

Copper was mined in the southeast corner of town. But in Vershire village, along Route 113, a proud relic of the town's mining past survives. Across the brook from the Vershire town office is the Vershire Historical Society, partly housed in the Methodist Church that once stood in Copperfield. It was built in 1867, surely with the help of former soldiers.

From the town office, go 2.5 miles west on Route 113 to a hilltop intersection and turn left on McIver Road. An old farm reached in 0.8 mile, with a tall white house and barn across the road, was the home of Freeman Norris. He joined the 10th Vermont as a private in 1862 and was killed at Mine Run in November 1863.

Return to Vershire village, take Vershire Center Road to the height of land, and Mountain School Road on the left leads to the Mountain School. On the campus, the stately old white house on the hilltop was Freeman Church's home. He joined the 9th Vermont in the fall of 1862 as a corporal. But he deserted early in 1863 and was never again heard from.

Just past the turn to Mountain Road, on the left, is a narrow track that leads to Vershire Center Cemetery. Close by the entrance is a stone at the graves of William and Henry Tenney, sons of Joshua and Mary Tenney. Henry joined the 10th Vermont as a private, in July 1862, and served until dying of illness in camp at Brandy Station on February 9, 1864, at twenty-six. William enlisted two weeks after his brother, but died at the hospital in Brattleboro before he was assigned to a regiment. From the cemetery, look across the road at Patterson Mountain. The Tenney farm was on its far side.

Return to Vershire village and go east on Route 113. Quickly look left at the house that stands just before the little bridge. In the house, which has since been rebuilt, lived Allen Dearborn, a private in the 9th Vermont, who survived a wound at Chaffin's Farm, Virginia, in September 1864.

Continue on Route 113, passing through Mill Village (where a sawmill once stood), and at the corner of Eagle Hollow Road is a small cape, once the home of Carlo Titus. He was a private in the 9th Vermont the last nine months of the war. According to Abby Hemenway's *Gazetteer*, "After the surrender of Richmond, some of our soldiers were on guard there, and among them was a soldier named Carlo Titus, a member of Co. G, of rather eccentric habits. His orders were to allow none to pass. A file of Johnneys marched in, having surrendered. When they came to our friend Titus, he ordered them to halt. They disobeyed his order, when he presented his rifle and discharged it, sending the ball with which it was loaded entirely through the chests of the first two men, and bringing the remainder to a halt."

Continue 0.8 of a mile on Route 113 to a house and barn on the right, once the Prescott home. Private George Prescott, 15th Vermont, died of sickness two months after going south at twenty. His brother, Luther Prescott, enlisted in the 4th Vermont at eighteen and was mortally wounded at Savage's Station.

Continue on Route 113 into West Fairlee, and turn right on Beanville Road, reentering the town of Vershire. You soon enter the old copper mining area, with stone foundations and reddened soil betraying the place's history, where copper was dug, some of which went to the Union war effort.

SOURCES

ABBOTT, COLLAMER. "GREEN MOUNTAIN COPPER: THE STORY OF VERMONT'S RED METAL AND APPALACHIAN COPPER." PUBLISHED IN SERIAL FORM IN THE *WHITE RIVER VALLEY HERALD*, 1973. VERSHIRE HISTORICAL SOCIETY.

VERSHIRE BICENTENNIAL PUBLICATION, 1981.

VERSHIRE TOWN AND SCHOOL RECORDS. VERSHIRE TOWN OFFICES AND VERSHIRE HISTORICAL SOCIETY.

WITH THANKS TO GARY GOODRICH.

······························

WASHINGTON

Washington's Civil War monument stands along Route 110, in Washington village, in front of the 1848 Baptist Church. Listed on four bronze plaques are the names of 157 men who served, a number that seems too great for a town this size. Erected by the local S. C. Smith Post of the GAR, its members had all their names inscribed on the tablet facing the road. The post was named for Shubael Smith, a 4th Vermont private, who enlisted September 21, 1861, and died just twenty-six days later of sickness. He was Washington's first war casualty. Child's *Gazetteer of Washington County, Vt., 1783–1899* says of this town, "Over 50 men were lost in the Civil War, either to the war itself, to war diseases, or were so badly disabled as to be no use to the community." Young Smith's funeral took place in the Baptist Church.

The monument was dedicated in 1906, and a photograph of the occasion, in the Calef Library, shows a parade coming north along Route 110, led by a fife and drum corps and flag bearers, followed by veterans in blue uniforms and schoolchildren. A speakers' stand decorated with flags was erected in front of the church.

Washington's wartime town meetings took place in the church basement. In August 1862, voters approved appointment of an agent to pay each volunteer a $25 bounty and $5 "for the comfort and support of such volunteer's family." Bounties rose to $200 the following November and to $525 in August 1864. In March 1865, voters met here to approve a tax of $3 on each grand list dollar "to pay in part the indebtedness of the town for town bounties."

In October 1863, according to the *Windsor Journal,* "The citizens of Washington, on the 3d inst., presented a beautiful sword to one of their own esteemed sons, Lieut. P. C. Cheney, of Co. C., 1st Vermont Cavalry Regiment, who was wounded at the Battle of Gettysburg, and is now on furlough to his native State to regain his health." Perley Cheney was wounded soon after Gettysburg, in a skirmish near Hagerstown, Maryland, with Lee's retreating cavalry. The presentation is believed to have happened in the church basement.

From the church, go south on Route 113, and in 0.3 mile is a small frame house, set above the roadway on large granite blocks. Royal Ordway lived here after fighting at Gettysburg with the 13th Vermont.

Just past the Ordway house, turn left on Turnpike Road. In 0.5 mile, come to the Cheney Cemetery, set on a knoll and surrounded by farmland once owned by the Cheney family. Gilman Cheney, who lived nearby, joined the Vermont Cavalry on December 19, 1863, and died two weeks later at Camp Stoneman, near Washington, D.C. His monument, beside his parents, says he was fifteen years and four months old. Martin Newman's stone, also by his parents, is a cenotaph. He died of sickness in August 1864, six months after enlisting in the 9th Vermont. He lies at City Point, near Petersburg. Robert Bohanan, also 9th Vermont, is buried nearby, dead at twenty, also of illness. Six Bohanons served from Washington.

Return to the village, go north on Route 113, and quickly go right on Creamery Road. In the farmhouse on the left, by the bridge, barely standing in 2011, Thomas Sanders lived for several years after the war. A corporal in the 9th Vermont from July 1862 until the war ended, Sanders suffered the effects of his service for the rest of his life. At fifty-five, he was still trying to receive a pension and signed an affidavit stating that he had become a shoemaker, because he was unable to farm. He added that he was able to work, at most, a half day and "a large share of the time unable to do anything." He stated, "I contracted fever and ague . . . In the spring of 1863 while we were defending Suffolk, Va. . . . We were not allowed to take off our equipments for ten days and we laid in rifle pits while on duty here and weathered fire."

SOURCES
CHILD, HAMILTON. *GAZETTEER OF ORANGE COUNTY, VERMONT, 1762–1888.* SYRACUSE: NY: SYRACUSE JOURNAL COMPANY, 1888.

———. *Gazetteer of Washington County, Vt., 1783–1899.* Edited by William Adams. Syracuse: NY: Syracuse Journal Company, 1889.

Donovan, Constance Flint, and Terry W. Dorsett. *A History of Washington Baptist Church, Washington, Vermont 1848–1998.* Washington, VT: s.n., 1998.

Washington town records.

With thanks to the Calef Library staff and Maudeen Neal.

WEST FAIRLEE

Alvah Bean, West Fairlee's town clerk, gave money to support the building of the big barnlike Bean Hall, which stands along Route 113 and dominates West Fairlee village. For Hemenway's *Gazetteer,* Bean wrote a tribute to the town's soldiers, which concluded:

"In the war of 1861, against Rebellion, I think it must he said of her that she acted nobly her part, faithfully and persistently fulfilling her mission. But few towns in the State have furnished more men according to the number of inhabitants, or paid more money according to their wealth. She furnished 92 soldiers, in all, and seven paid commutation. And in order that they not be forgotten—but that their memories shall live when we have passed away, I subjoin a list of their names, worthy to be written in every patriotic book of Vermont and the Union, and indelibly stamped upon the tablet of every American heart, and then transmitted from sire to son, to generations yet unborn! For who indeed should be remembered and have historic commemoration, if not those who were willing to forego the comforts and pleasures of home—leaving behind them near and dear friends, and all for which at the moment of the momentous call, they were toiling with zest and strength of young manhood—to preserve and perpetuate, and transmit to posterity unimpaired, the principles upon which this great and glorious republic and union was founded. And it would not be going too far if every town should erect a monument of marble, upon which should be engraven their names in letters of gold."

West Fairlee's most famous Civil War soldier was Stephen Thomas, a friend and business associate of Bean. Thomas belonged to the Congregational Church just north of Bean Hall, and he contributed money to its construction in 1855. Late in January 1862, probably in the church, Bean presented Thomas with a sword, as he was about to depart with the 8th Vermont, which he commanded. A brass band played, and several speeches were made. Thomas said, "We may never meet again as we are met upon this occasion, but I hope and trust that my life has been and may be such, that there will be no occasion for regret that I have lived among you. This evening's service will be remembered by me through life."

But Thomas, of course, did return, and after the war, he was elected Orange County state's attorney. One of the dramatic moments of his career came on June 30, 1883, when copper miners rioted and marched into West Fairlee, demanding unpaid wages. To the home of company official Smith Ely they came, one with a noose in his hand. Entering the house, the miners saw Thomas at the top of the stairs with a pistol. (Ely was sick in bed.) Thomas stood his ground and vowed to help get them their money, and the men eventually dispersed. It happened in the first house north of the church, on the same side of the road.

Go north from that house, pass the entrance on the right to the West Fairlee Village Cemetery, and 200 yards beyond, set above the road on the left, is a small house with front porch and garage attached. This was the home of Hiram Russell and his son Franklin, who joined the 15th Vermont together at ages forty-five and eighteen. Both came home, then reenlisted, in Thomas's 8th Vermont. The father served until the war ended and saw his son killed at Cedar Creek. Father and son are buried in the Village Cemetery.

Return past Bean Hall to the junction of Beanville Road, which leads to the Vershire copper mines and down which once came some angry miners. Just south of the intersection is a cinder-block garage, and in the lot just beyond it, on which lilac bushes grew in 2011, Colonel Thomas's house once stood.

Across from the Thomas lot, and slightly north, is a one-and-one-half-story house in which Phineas Kimball lived. His father, a Mormon, went west with Joseph Smith, but came back and built this home. His son Phileas paid commutation and did not serve in the Civil War.

Continue 0.75 mile south of Route 113 to the corner of West Fairlee Road, where a small barn is on the left, all that remains of the farm from which Lyman Colburn went to war as a private in the 15th Vermont.

Take West Fairlee Road, and soon go left on Route 244. In 0.5 mile, go left on Middlebrook Road, and in 3.5 miles, come to a large farmhouse and barn on the right. During the Civil War, Nancy (Niles) Kimball operated a knitting business in the building attached to the right and rear of the house. Affiliated with a Boston company, she hired local women to knit, in their homes. From Boston came wool, patterns, and orders for knitted goods. Documents preserved at the Vermont Historical Society indicate that many orders were for mittens. The business gave many local women badly needed income during wartime..

SOURCES
ABBOTT, COLLAMER. "GREEN MOUNTAIN COPPER: THE STORY OF VERMONT'S RED METAL AND APPALACHIAN COPPER." PUBLISHED IN SERIAL FORM IN THE *WHITE RIVER VALLEY HERALD*, 1973. VERSHIRE HISTORICAL SOCIETY.
DANVILLE NORTH STAR, JANUARY 25, 1862.
WEST FAIRLEE HISTORICAL SOCIETY RECORDS.
WEST FAIRLEE TOWN RECORDS.
WITH THANKS TO JAMES MCDADE.

....

WILLIAMSTOWN

In Williamstown along Route 14, the Congregational Church, the Methodist Church (now the Williamstown Historical Society), and the town hall stand side by side, all built before the Civil War. Between the churches is the town Civil War monument, one of the first erected in Vermont, bearing the names of the Williamstown war dead.

Williamstown voters met in the town hall on May 18, 1861, responding to Abraham Lincoln's first call for troops, and voted to pay 75 cents per day and boarding expenses to the Williamstown men then drilling in Barre. On August 11, voters approved paying each new recruit $300. On town meeting day in March 1868, voters approved spending not more than $2,000 "to erect a monument to the memory of the officers and soldiers who counted on Williamstown's quota in the war of the Rebellion and fell in battle or died of wounds or sickness received in aiding to put down the Rebellion." The monument bears the names of ten Williamstown men who died, but not the names of the Martin brothers.

Drive south from the monument, and on leaving the village, see a stately redbrick home on the right of Route 14. Now part of a retirement community, it was the Martin home in the 1860s. Lieutenant William H. Martin, 4th Vermont, was twenty-five when he died of wounds received at the Wilderness. Brother Francis Martin, 2nd Vermont, was wounded the same day. Francis was again shot, at Cedar Creek, and a leg was amputated. After the war, Francis came back to Williamstown and joined his father, Chester Martin, in running the family farm. On October 11, 1865, Francis was killed in an accident on the farm. His father refused to allow his sons' names to appear on the town monument.

Continue south on Route 14, pass the Chelsea Road, and the first house beyond, with huge barn behind, was once the Jillson farm. From here, Private David Jillson enlisted in the 10th Vermont in September 1862. Wounded at the Battles of Cold Harbor and Cedar Creek, he kept on serving until he was horribly injured in the 6th Corps Breakthrough at Petersburg on April 2, 1865. He returned to Vermont, to his sister's home in South Pomfret (see Pomfret), where he died of his wounds. Take the Chelsea Road, turn left on Gilbert Road, and soon come to the East Hill Cemetery. Private Jillson and his family are buried here. Nearby lies Private Henry Burnham, who enlisted with Jillson and served until his death at Cedar Creek. Burnham was among the 10th Vermont soldiers who recaptured a battery in the early morning of October 19, on the orders of Brigadier General William Ricketts. Just after the guns were safely back within the Union lines, a Rebel Minie ball slammed through Burnham's head.

Continue along Gilbert Road to its intersection with Quarryville Road, and turn right. Soon, bear right on Martin Road, and in 0.5 mile, on the right, stands the Burnham home. Private Burnham faithfully wrote his parents, penning the following letter on September 21, 1864, describing the Vermont Brigade's fighting at Winchester:

"We had to advance under the hottest shelling that I have ever been under and we lost the most men by shells that we ever did our major has lost his leg and died soon after. We advanced a piece and then had orders to fall back again then we advanced again and held our position two or three hours and then we advanced again and drove the rebs from the entrenchments on Winchester heights. The cavalry come around on their flank and captured about one thousand prisoners."

To the Burnham home on October 27, 1864, came a note from E. P. Walton, editor of Montpelier's *Vermont Watchman and State Journal*: "Father Burnham: A letter just rec'd at this office from the surgeon of the 10th Regiment gives the painful announcement that brother Henry was killed in that terrible battle on the 19th. I write you thinking perhaps you have heard it from no other source. I think there is no doubt about it as the list we have seems to have been copied from the official records. We shall print the full list today. May the grace of God sustain us in this sad affliction."

Return down Quarryville Road all the way to Route 14, and turn left to the Congregational Church, where Private Burnham's funeral was held. At that time, on the wall of the sanctuary, were these words:

Honor the brave
Cherish their memory
Our fallen heroes

Henry Burnham's name is on the town monument.

At the town hall on July 2, 1892, veterans from Williamstown and several nearby towns met to organize the William Wells post of the GAR. Also organized was the Wells Chapter of the Women's Relief Corps. At Memorial Day observances, it became the practice for these organizations to march to the Village Cemetery (north along Route 14), where many veterans are buried, and there to sing "Tenting Tonight on the Old Campground."

Take Route 66, which goes sharply uphill from the center of town toward Interstate 89 and in just over 2 miles, Palmer Road goes left. At the intersection is an old house with a wooden front that masks a 1791 brick rear. George Savery, a Vermont Cavalry private, bought this farm in 1865, when he came home from war. Two of George's brothers, Elliott and Oliver, fought for the Confederacy. A third brother, Lawrence, enlisted for the Union in another state.

SOURCES
BURNHAM, HENRY P. CIVIL WAR LETTERS. VERMONT HISTORICAL SOCIETY.
WILLIAMSTOWN HISTORICAL SOCIETY. *A HISTORY OF WILLIAMSTOWN, VERMONT, 1781–1991.* WILLIAMSTOWN, VT: WILLIAMSTOWN HISTORICAL SOCIETY, 1991.
THANKS TO ADAM BOYCE, MIRIAM HERWIG, AND PAUL ZELLER.

chapter eleven

Orleans County

Erastus Buck went west, seeking his fortune in the California gold fields, then came home to Charleston, married, and built a house. He went to war a captain and became one of Vermont's most respected soldiers. When he died, a thousand people came to his funeral at the new house, which still stands. In Derby Line, the grand home of Congressman Portus Baxter still faces the park. He and his wife, Elizabeth, both worked in the Washington, D.C., hospitals, caring for the wounded. Then Portus went south to nurse the Vermont wounded at Fredericksburg.

In Jay is the house where Gilbert Lucier lived, the last surviving Vermont Civil War soldier, wounded at Cold Harbor. He once met Abraham Lincoln. At Gettysburg, three-quarters of a century later, Lucier became angry with his nephew for socializing with Confederate veterans.

It was a Rebel lady who saved the life of Hiram Bedell. Wounded in a Shenandoah Valley skirmish, she hid him in her home and nursed him back to health. Then she and her Confederate soldier husband came to Bedell's Westfield home, which still stands. Along Newport's Main Street, volunteers assembled after word came of the Confederate raid on St. Albans. Some overzealous Norwich University cadets nearly opened fire on a steamer docking at the Newport waterfront, fearing it carried more invaders.

....

ALBANY

Albany's war memorials is along Route 14 in Albany village, in front of the old Albany village school, now the town historical society. A total of 117 men enlisted from this town; 13 died of sickness, 4 in prisons, and 6 were killed in battle. Albany paid $12,200 in bounties to 51 men.

Here, where the memorials stand, marchers in Memorial Day parades once gathered. Led by the Albany Coronet Band and Civil War veterans, the processions moved north along Route 14 to the town's largest cemetery, just north of the village. There, a service was held before everyone returned to the Methodist Church, across the road from the school, for lunch.

From Albany, go north on Route 14 to the Irasburg green, and there turn south on Creek Road, passing the Catholic Church. Moving from one side of Albany to the other can be difficult, due to the steep intervening hills. Drive 6 miles to the hamlet of East Albany and a- four corners by another Catholic Church. Turn right on Daniels Road, and the first house, on the right, was the home of David Green, who served the last year of the war as a private in the 11th Vermont. He was wounded at Cedar Creek.

Continue past the Green home into a little valley through which runs Lord Brook, cross it, and look left to the stone remnants of a dam. Here, Ebenezer Lord operated a sawmill and starch factory. Lord's son Marcus went from here to join the 11th Vermont, a private the last two years of the war. His father sold the sawmill to Charles Rowell in 1860. Rowell went with Marcus Lord to enlist as a private in the 11th and also served until the war ended.

Return to the four corners and turn left, north, on Creek Road. In just under 1 mile, where the road curves right, a house and barn stand on the left. From this farm five Stiles men enlisted. Oliver, Wilbur, Frank, and Benjamin all joined Company D of the 6th Vermont in the fall 1861. Oliver, who became a lieutenant, was captured at Savage's Station but was paroled two months later. He was wounded at the Wilderness. Wilbur, a private, was also captured at Savage's Station, but soon released. Privates Benjamin and Frank Stiles joined at ages twenty-three and twenty-eight, respectively. They both died of sickness in the spring of 1862. Private Milo Stiles served the last two years of the war with the 11th Vermont.

Continue past the Stiles farm 0.3 mile to a farm on the right, with a large Civil War–era barn. From here, Lucian Sanborn also joined Company D of the 6th, as a private. At the Wilderness, on May 6, 1864, a bullet passed through the side of his head, and one struck his arm. Captured and taken to Andersonville, he somehow recovered from his wounds to come home, blind in one eye and nearly blind in the other. He received a $24 monthly pension the rest of his life.

Just under 0.5 mile north, a large farm sits below the road on the left, once the Lunge farm. Joseph Lunge, a private in the 11th Vermont, was twenty when mortally wounded at Cold Harbor. Carlos, a private in the 3rd Vermont, was wounded and captured at Lee's Mill. He died at home, age twenty-five, in January 1865, as a result of his captivity. Isaac, a 15th Vermont private, made the long march to Gettysburg and came home safely.

Continue on Creek Road and soon turn right on Kingdom Road. In 0.75 mile, go left on Noyes Road to the first house. Reuben Brooks from here joined the Vermont Cavalry at twenty as a private and served three years as a teamster.

Look beyond the house along a narrow dirt track that leads to a weathered farmhouse, once the Annis home. George and William Annis were privates in the 15th Vermont, with William serving as a musician.

Return to Creek Road and East Albany. Continue south past the Catholic Church for 2 miles, bear left at a Y, and quickly go left on South Albany Road. In 1.3 miles, on entering South Albany, Saw Mill Lane is on the right. The first house, a large frame structure with long porch, was the Randall home. George, a musician in the 4th Vermont, became sick with diphtheria in the winter of 1861 and was sent to Brattleboro, where his wife went to care for him. She eventually brought him to their Glover home, where he died. George's daughter, staying here with her aunt and grandfather, soon died of diphtheria, likely caught from her father. Two weeks later, the aunt also died of diphtheria here.

SOURCES
RANDALL, GEORGE. CIVIL WAR LETTERS.
    UNIVERSITY OF VERMONT, BAILEY/HOWE
    LIBRARY, SPECIAL COLLECTIONS,
    BURLINGTON.
WHARTON, VIRGINIA. HISTORY OF ALBANY,
    VERMONT, 1806–1991. ALBANY, VT:
    ALBANY HISTORICAL SOCIETY, 1991.
WITH THANKS TO PAUL DANIELS.

....

BARTON

From a wartime population of 1,600, Barton sent 147 men to serve. But the issue that brought the country to war was much alive here well before the Civil War. Enter Barton village from the south, along Route 16, and the red-brick former Methodist Church is on the left. This 1887 building is built on the site of the 1833 Methodist Church, whose membership was very much against slavery. In August 1859, the Radical Abolitionists of Orleans County met here to nominate candidates for county offices who "advance the cause of liberty." Five years earlier, Barton voters had unanimously passed a resolution opposing the appeal of the Missouri Compromise and the extension of slavery westward.

When in May 1859 Bishop Matthew Simpson addressed the statewide Methodist conference in the old church, the crowd that gathered was so large windows were removed to enable people outside to hear. Pastor of the Foundry Church in Washington, where Abraham Lincoln sometimes worshipped, Simpson counted the president as a friend. Simpson delivered the eulogy at Lincoln's burial, in Springfield, Illinois. Pastor of the Barton Methodist Church, at the time, was Reverend Haynes Cushing, an opponent of slavery.

Continue on Route 16 north, and on entering the square, note the old high-peaked building, with double-decked porch, at the southeast corner, once the home of the *Monitor* newspaper, named for the Civil War ironclad. The paper was founded in 1872 by Elergy Webster, a veteran of the 11th Vermont. Private Webster was captured at Weldon Railroad and survived six months in Andersonville.

In the square, on learning of the St. Albans raid, Josiah Grout assembled men to defend the state's northern border. A veteran of the 15th Vermont, Grout returned from war to be a lawyer in Barton. Just north of the square, take Main Street north and quickly go left into Congress Court. Josiah Grout lived in the large Victoria house at the end. Return along Congress Court, and in the first house on the right, bordering the Grout property, Joseph Webster lived, who served with Grout, as a private, in the 15th Vermont.

Return to Main Street, go right, pass through the square, and take Route 16 north. Crossing the railroad tracks, the third house on the left was the home of Dr. Richard Skinner, who graduated at the top of his 1858 Harvard Medical School class and became a Barton doctor and a surgeon in the 3rd Vermont.

Return to Main Street and go left. Soon, on the left, is an old frame factory building with railroad tracks behind. The next building is believed to date to the Civil War era and was part of the Barton Depot. From here, men went to and returned from war. Leander Scott, who lived out his life in Barton, enlisted in February 1864 in the 17th Vermont. His diary of March 7, 1864, the day he went to war, noted, "Left Barton about 8 o'clock for St. Johnsbury." He boarded the train here at the depot. He came home safely at war's end, but three of his brothers perished.

From Barton village, go north on Route 5, then east on Route 58, into the village of Orleans, known as Barton Landing at the time of the Civil War. Just off Route 58, on Maple Street, is a small green with a veterans' memorial. Here, for many years, local Civil War veterans gathered on Memorial Day and marched up Maple Street to the nearby cemetery for memorial exercises. Among those who participated was O. H. Austin, who served in the 11th Vermont throughout its existence and rose to command Company A. He came home to become a highly successful businessman in Barton Landing. Return to the small green, pass it, and go right on North Avenue. Austin lived in the last house on the right, a small frame structure with a long front porch.

SOURCES

GRIMSLEY, ELIZABETH TODD. "SIX MONTHS IN THE WHITE HOUSE." *JOURNAL OF THE ILLINOIS HISTORICAL SOCIETY* 19 (OCTOBER TO JANUARY, 1926–27): 46.

GROUT, JOSIAH. *MEMOIR OF WILLIAM WALLACE GROUT.* NEWPORT, VT: BULLOCK PRESS, 1914.

HOYT, DARRELL. *SKETCHES OF ORLEANS, VERMONT.* NEWPORT, VT: MEMPHREMAGOG PRESS, 1985.

SCOTT, ERASTUS. CIVIL WAR DIARY. COURTESY OF ROBERT W. FREY.

YOUNG, DARLENE. *A HISTORY OF BARTON, VERMONT.* RUTLAND, VT: ACADEMY BOOKS, 1998.

WITH THANKS TO DARRELL HOYT.

BROWNINGTON

In the small hilltop village of Brownington stands a big stone schoolhouse built by Alexander Twilight. There are several ways to reach the place, one of them being from the Orleans exit on Interstate 91 to Route 58 east into the village of Orleans, then following the signs to the Old Stone Schoolhouse.

Twilight, born in Corinth in 1795, was

of mixed race, at least part black. He graduated from Middlebury College in 1823, and that school counts him as the first African American to earn a degree from an American college. Twilight and his wife, Mercy, arrived in Brownington in 1829, he to be principal of the Orleans County Grammar School. Twilight was quickly ordained by the Brownington Congregational Church as its acting pastor. In 1836, Twilight completed the magnificent four-story granite school that dominates Brownington today. He also built a comfortable house that still stands across the road.

Brownington sent Twilight to the legislature in 1836. For a time, he was dismissed from the pulpit of the Congregational church, but returned and preached in the present 1841 Congregational Church. Whether Twilight made it public that he was a man of color is doubtful. Brownington records listed him as a free white male. But he did make known his feelings about slavery. In a sermon delivered in the Congregational Church in 1853, he said, "Subjugation by war and superiority of physical and intellectual strength never gave man the right to reduce his fellow man to his service without his own consent . . . This practice built the mighty pyramids of Egypt, and has handed down to us the errors of those times, when a hundred thousand men could be continued to work upon one pyramid for twenty years . . . From these practices of barbarism, ignorance and cruelty, arose our American slavery, so much detested now by enlightened nations."

A total of sixty-two Brownington men served in the Civil War, and six attended the Congregational Church. Among them was Frankin Buxton, a sergeant in the 11th Vermont, who was discharged after being wounded at Cold Harbor. Captain Edwin Joslyn, 6th Vermont, came home after a musket ball smashed through his right eye and exited his skull at Third Winchester. Private Erastus Spencer, 6th Vermont, was wounded and taken prisoner at Savage's Station. Discharged in 1863, he was never again well and died in 1869.

In the Brownington Cemetery beside the church is a monument to Charles Chamberlin, 3rd Vermont, captured at Savage's Station. He was twenty-eight when he starved to death in the Belle Isle prison at Richmond. Another stone honors the memory of the Baxter family, including wartime congressman Portus Baxter (see Derby).

Many pupils of Twilight's in the stone school served in Vermont units during the war. Among them were private Charles Cook, 4th Vermont, Edson Fairbrother, 6th Vermont, and Lorenzo Nye, 9th Vermont, who died of disease. Private Horace Cook, 4th Vermont, was wounded at the Wilderness.

The school educated both men and women, and among the students in 1849 was Emma Scales, whose father at the time was the school principal. She later moved to Kansas and wrote home in a letter dated April 11, 1865, "We had a great time here yesterday over the surrender of Gen. Lee. Firing of cannon & ringing of bells continued from 3 AM to 9 PM."

The Old Stone House is now a

museum with many Civil War artifacts, including the desk believed to have been used at the Glover recruiting station.

SOURCE
WITH THANKS TO THE OLD STONE HOUSE MUSEUM STAFF.

CHARLESTON

The 1856 Congregational Church is on the north side of Route 105 in East Charleston, along the Clyde River Valley. In a speech on the church's one-hundredth anniversary, George Dale, grandson of Vermont's U.S. senator Porter Dale, said, "When the church was built, Vermont was the important 20th state in population . . . Franklin Pierce was the president of 23 million people; 20 million were free, the other three million were slaves. Our secretary of war was Jefferson Davis, future president of the Confederate States. Vermont had not heard of Abraham Lincoln. In East Charleston lived Erastus Buck, a Forty-niner, who had come here with some California gold, not realizing that a few years hence he would again return home for burial as a war hero, the best known in the Clyde River Valley."

Several denominations met in the church, including the Free Will Baptists. Their church records state that, on August 23, 1862, "a few of the brethren and sisters met in monthly meeting; all seemed to have a fixed principle to live religion, yet the wars and tumults and commotion on earth seem to depress our feelings." On January 10, 1863, the records state: "Two of our dearest brethren have fallen asleep in Jesus, We mourn deeply their loss.

Brother Chester Stephens and Harrison Switzer died in the army." Stevens, a sergeant, and Private Switzer, of the 10th Vermont's K Company, in which many local men served, both died of sickness shortly before Christmas 1862.

F. B. Gage, the son of Royal Gage, the local reverend, attended services here. Young Gage spent his boyhood in East Charleston and became a poet. As the abolitionist John Brown awaited execution in his Virginia cell, Gage wrote a poem titled "Hang John Brown," which began:

> Hang the fearless old man, he deserves it
> For doing what Christ might have done:
> There is peril in being a Christian,
> When a nation containeth but one!

Most of Charleston's Civil War–era town meetings were held in the church basement. Voters on August 20, 1864, approved $500 bounties.

Across the street is a store once owned by a son of William Moulton, whose father was a private in Company K of the 10th. The father was captured at Cold Harbor and spent seven months at Andersonville. He came home a human skeleton, but recovered to live until 1916, sometimes working in the store. Once beside the store stood a large building that included a livery stable and a meeting hall. The cupola was built by former private Moulton. When the building was torn down, the cupola was saved, and the Charleston Historical Society in 2011 planned to erect it on the building site as a war memorial.

Just east of the church is the East

Charleston post office, added to the front of a building erected on the site of the Goodwin Hotel. The Goodwin family lost a son, Private Edmund Goodwin, 2nd Vermont, at Spotsylvania's Bloody Angle. Another son, Ivora, of the 10th Vermont's K Company, survived a wound at Mine Run.

Go east on Route 105 onto Buck Flats, turn right on Hudson Road, cross Buck Brook, and the large house on he left was the home of Erastus Buck. Born on this farm in 1830, Buck went to California in search of gold and apparently found some. He came home, built this house, and when the war began was living here with his wife, Martha, and two sons. When the war began, Buck enlisted as a sergeant in Company D of the 3rd Vermont, in which many local men served. By the time the 1864 Overland Campaign commenced, he commanded the 3rd's Company I and was much loved by his men, particularly because he shared all the hard tasks. Wounded at the Wilderness, he was taken to a Fredericksburg hospital. The captain wrote his wife on May 10, "I improve a few moments this morning to let you know how I was wounded in two places. Through the left hand, and right leg my wounds are doing well our Brigade is badly cut up and nearly half killed or wounded." Buck died twelve days later.

His body came home, and a Masonic funeral service was held here beside his home. A thousand people attended. The *Caledonian Record* of May 3, 1864, said: "The services were very solemn and made a lasting impression upon the audience. His last words were, 'Have you heard from the front?'" Buck was buried in the Old Protestant Cemetery in Island Pond, in the lot of his wife's family.

Pass the Buck home, cross Mad Brook, and look to the left for an old building on a high foundation, once the Buck School, that Erastus Buck attended. In the school yard, a funeral, attended by hundreds, was held for Chester Stevens. Sergeant Stevens, 10th Vermont, died of illness in camp in Maryland two months after enlisting.

Just beyond the school site is the Buck Cemetery, where lie the parents of Erastus Buck, Private Stevens, and Stevens's mother, who died the spring after her son's death.

Continue on Hudson Road 1.5 miles to see a long and low farmhouse, by a barn, where Chester Stevens grew up. Continue on Hudson Road for 1.25 miles to Center School Road, on the right. Go past it 0.75 mile to a farm, from which George and Albert Lawrence went to war as privates in the 10th Vermont. Albert died of illness at Brandy Station, Viriginia, in 1864, soon after his brother succumbed to wounds suffered at Mine Run.

Turn here and return as you came, soon turning left on Center School Road. Proceed to Route 105 and turn right. Soon on the right is the Bly Cemetery. The Lawrence boys share one stone, on which is carved:

Parents, sisters, mourning friends,
Fainting hearts with anguish sends,
Know they lived to honor you,
Know they died as heroes do.
Know the cause was great and true.

Mourn, but know the glory too,
Look you up through streaming eyes,
God will bless this sacrifice.

From the cemetery, go west on Route
105 into West Charleston. Just before
reaching the stone church on the left, turn
right on Durgin Road then quickly left on
Corkins Road. The West Village Cemetery, on a knoll to the left, above the roaring Clyde River, holds the graves of many
soldiers. Among them are William and
Francis Barnard, sons of Deacon James
Barnard. William, a private in the 9th Vermont, and Francis, an 8th Vermont private, both died of sickness.

Across the street from the entrance to
Museum Drive is the West Charleston
GAR hall, with porch across the front.
The post was named for Isaac Blake, who
served for a time as a musician in the 8th
Vermont, before becoming chaplain of a
Louisiana regiment of blacks.

SOURCES
BALZER, JOHN E. *BUCK'S BOOK: A VIEW OF THE
THIRD VERMONT INFANTRY REGIMENT.*
BOLINGBROOK, IL: BALZER AND
ASSOCIATES, 1993.
HAMILTON, ESTHER B. *HISTORY OF THE TOWN
OF CHARLESTON, VERMONT.* CHARLESTON,
VT: CHARLESTON BICENTENNIAL
COMMITTEE, 1978.

COVENTRY

The soldier atop Coventry's Civil
War monument, on the small
common in front of the old Congregational Church, faces north. The gift of
Riley E. Wright, who organized and com-

manded Company H of the 15th Vermont, the monument was dedicated on
August 14, 1912. The *Express and Standard* of Newport reported that the sky was
blue with broken clouds and that "teams,
and autos, and pedestrians were seen cen-
tering in from the four or five different
routes leading into the town. They formed
circles around the common . . . filled the
chairs between the veiled monument and
the speakers stand, and lined the banks far
up under the beautiful maples that bordered the village front . . . Even after the
exercises opened the audience continued
to enlarge until it was estimated that
between 1500 and 2000 people were on
the ground."

After the singing of "Tenting Tonight
on the Old Campground," Civil War veterans delivered three cheers for the monument. Wright then spoke: "They died for
their country," he said, "that their country
might live on, undivided and reunited for
all time." Former governor, and veteran,
Josiah Grout said, "I wish here to express
the hope that sometime, somewhere in the
most prominent place for national observation, the gratitude of our people will
take form, in the shape of a monument of
the most lofty and enduring character, in
honor of and to the memory of, the
women of the Civil War, who at home, in
the hospital and on the field did so much,
in so many ways to encourage him who
bore the brunt of the battle and to soften
the severity of his privations and to relieve
the anguish and suffering of his hardships."

The monument includes the likenesses
of Abraham Lincoln, Ulysses Grant,
George Dewey, and George Stannard. A

wreath of flowers, sent for the ceremonies by three of Stannard's daughters, was placed beneath their father's portrait. Also on the monument are the names of Coventry's soldiers and some of the places where they fought: Gettysburg, Cold Harbor, the Wilderness, Cedar Creek.

During the Civil War, the Reverend Pliny White, an outspoken foe of slavery, was pastor of the Coventry Congregational Church. It is believed that the funeral of Amasa Bartlett, who led Company E of the 9th Vermont, was held here. Bartlett died of sickness in 1864. The Reverend White, in his eulogy, called Bartlett "the Christian Patriot." He said, "He looked after the moral and religious interests of his men as diligently as he cared for their health and discipline."

In the church in April 1865, White spoke at a memorial service for Lincoln. He said, "Hardly had the joyous peals with which the bells announced the fall of Richmond and the surrender of Lee died upon our ears, when they were saluted by the melancholy knell that bewailed the nation's bereavement. Such a transition from the delirium of joy to the delirium of woe, has had no parallel since that event in Judea." And he said, "Had the rebellion been crushed in 90 days from its outbreak slavery could not have been crushed. It would only have been exasperated, and would it not have nursed its wrath, and its strength, till another more favorable opportunity? God permitted it to triumph, but overruled its victories to its complete and perpetual overthrow."

In the area of the green, Lieutenant Enoch Bartlett, brother of Amasa, organized and drilled Company B of the 3rd Vermont. Amasa Bartlett was killed at the Wilderness, May 5, 1864.

From the church, go uphill on Covered Bridge Road, and the first house on the left, set well back from the road, was a postwar home of Charles Branch. Enlisting as a corporal in the 9th Vermont from his hometown of Orwell, Branch won a promotion to major based on bravery displayed in combat late in the war near Richmond. Family legend holds that Branch once removed, with his own knife, a bullet that had hit him in the leg. That experience may have influenced him to later become a doctor, and he practiced in Coventry.

Take Main Street north to Route 14, turn left, then quickly right on Coventry Station Road. On the left is the Village Cemetery, where many Coventry veterans lie. Among them are Corporal Almon Priest, killed at Cold Harbor on June 1, 1864, and Reuben Pierson, a Vermont Cavalry corporal, twenty-three when killed at Weldon Railroad.

Continue past the cemetery 2 miles to an intersection and turn right to the Coventry Center Cemetery. To the rear, side by side, are stones for Amasa and Enoch Bartlett. Enoch's says that "his men buried him on the Battlefield."

Three-quarters of a mile past the cemetery, turn left on Webster Road, and in 0.25 mile, come to the Guild farm, from which Martin Guild enlisted in the 11th Vermont. Captured at Weldon Railroad, he died on November 19 in Andersonville, where he is buried. Proceed 1.25 miles on Webster Road, cross the Barton River, and the house on the left by the bridge was the home from which Amasa and Enoch Bartlett went to war.

SOURCES

BITS AND PIECES OF COVENTRY'S HISTORY. BARRE, VT: COVENTRY BICENTENNIAL COMMITTEE, 1977.
COVENTRY TOWN RECORDS.
WITH THANKS TO CYNTHIA DIAZ, ROBERT DIAZ, FRED WEBSTER, AND MONA ROUNSEVELLE.

....

CRAFTSBURY

Craftsbury Common occupies a hilltop above the Black River and is surrounded by white clapboard buildings, many of which predate the Civil War. The Craftsbury war memorial here, dedicated in 1922, lists 149 men who served, of whom 28 perished.

Craftsbury Academy, at the common's north end, was founded in 1829, and many lads who attended served in the Civil War. Among its principals was George Washington Henderson (see Belvidere), who ran the school from 1877 to 1880 and again from 1886 to 1888. He was an escaped slave who came to Vermont with Union soldiers. The 1879 academy building, at the common's northeast corner, replaced the former school building, which was destroyed by fire. Henderson led rebuilding efforts. Henderson also served as pastor of the church at the northwest corner of the common.

On the common's south side is Simpson Hall, now a part of Sterling College, once Augustus Paddock's home. Paddock joined the Vermont Cavalry in September 1862 as a private. On April 1, 1863, during a fight with Mosby's cavalry along Broad Run, Virginia, he was shot through the right shoulder and lung. He was eventually treated at a hospital in New York City, then at the Brattleboro hospital. Discharged for disability, he again saw service after the St. Albans raid, patroling the Canadian border.

From the common, take South Craftsbury Road and pass through Craftsbury village to Whetstone Brook Road on the right. The first house on the left, beyond the turn, was Charles McRoy's home. He was a private in the 2nd Vermont for two and a half years, until discharged for disability in January 1864. At age twenty-four, his brother, John, enlisted as a private in the 3rd Vermont at Guildhall, in June 1861. Wounded at Savage's Station, he survived Libby Prison and Belle Isle. At the Petersburg Breakthrough on April 2, 1865, he was shot through both thighs, but survived.

Take Whetstone Brook Road, and the first house past the cemetery, on the left, above the road with barn attached, was the Tallman home. William Tallman, a sergeant in the 11th Vermont, was captured at Weldon Railroad. He died of dysentery two months later at Andersonville.

Return to Craftsbury village, go left on Cemetery Road, then left on Guy Lot Road. Cross Route 14, continue on Guy Lot 0.5 mile, and see a farm above and on the right. Lewis Cass, who lived here, served the last nine months of the war as a private in the Vermont Cavalry.

Return to Route 14 and go north just over 5 miles to a cape on the left, with barn across the road. Once the home of the musical Bagleys, father John Bagley saw four sons go to war, three as musicians. George, a fifer in the 9th Vermont, played his regiment into Richmond as the Confederate capital fell. Moses and Richard were musicians in the 3rd Vermont. Brother Henry served the last year of the war in the 17th Vermont, as an infantryman. Another son, Edwin, wrote the famous "National Emblem March."

Go south 0.8 mile on Route 14 south and turn left on North Craftsbury Road. Quickly, cross the Black River and reach the top of a knoll, and a small turnoff is on the right. From here, look right to where a tall tree stands above the river. The Boutwell home once was there, and the Boutwell family worked these fertile fields, and swam in the winding river. Then came war, and four sons, Rodney, Robert, William, and Thomas, enlisted. Rodney joined the 11th Vermont as a private in July 1862. At Cold Harbor, he was shot through both hips and died five days later at age twenty-two. Robert, a private in the 4th Vermont, was shot through the knee at Spotsylvania's Bloody Angle. Next day, his leg was cut off at a field hospital, but he died from the effects of chloroform. William went to New Hampshire to enlist in that state's 16th Regiment, but died in June 1863 of sickness, in Louisiana. Thomas joined the 4th Vermont as a private in September 1861, but was home in three months, disabled by disease.

SOURCES

CRAFTSBURY TOWN RECORDS.
METRAUX, DANIEL A. *CRAFTSBURY: A BRIEF SOCIAL HISTORY.* LINCOLN, NE: iUNIVERSE.COM, 2001. ORIGINALLY PUBLISHED BY THE AUTHOR IN 1977, REVISED IN 1980.
SPRAGUE, GEORGE F. *SOLDIERS' RECORD, TOWN OF CRAFTSBURY, VERMONT, 1861–1865.* CRAFTSBURY, VT: S.N., 1914.
WITH THANKS TO DAVID LINCKS AND ANNE WILSON.

DERBY

The Civil War took an especially heavy toll on Derby, and the town was Vermont's first to erect a Civil War monument. Dedicated October 31, 1866, it stands on Route 5 in Derby Center. The *Stanstead Journal*, published in nearby Stanstead, Quebec, reported, "The services on this occasion were attended by a very large concourse of people from Derby and neighboring towns including Stanstead. The Stanstead band was in attendance and discorsed sweet sounds. An introductory prayer was made by [former Vermont Cavalry chaplain] Rev. Mr. Woodward of Irasburg, Vt. Gen. P. T. Washburn, late adjutant general of Vermont delivered the oration." The principal address was given by B. H. Steele, of Derby. "Fifty-three of the soldiers of our town lost their lives in the great work," Steele said, "and such lives, young, ardent, promising lives around which clustered our fond hopes and tender aspirations . . . Today there are American citizens standing upon a common ground of a common reverence for the memory of the soldiers of the Republic. The monument we this day consecrate is a monument to Liberty erected in memory of men who performed an honorable share of the work of removing the element of despotism from our glorious constitution." In 1884, fifty maples were planted adjacent to the monument. In July 1917, a rededication took place, with five hundred people present. The town of Salem, which existed during the Civil War, had recently been made part of Derby, and the names of Salem soldiers were that day added. The main address was given by Josiah Grout.

Go north on Route 5 to where Beebee Road enters from the left. The small frame house in the Y was purchased soon after the war by Lucius Kingsbury, one of three Kingsbury brothers who served in the Confederate armies. The family had gone south from Derby some forty years before the Civil War, where the father, Charles, had become a successful Georgia businessman.

Go south on Route 5 from the monument, and quickly on the left is the entrance to Derby Junior High School. The old 1840 frame building, set back from the road, is old North Hall, once part of Derby Academy. According to a history of the school, "the Civil War years came on and had their effect on the school. In the fall of 1863 there were registered only 76 students, two teachers plus music teacher who may have been only part time. Before the year was over Mr. Eri Woodbury left to join the army." Attendance was up to 154 students in 1866.

Principal Woodbury became a lieutenant in the Vermont Cavalry and won a Medal of Honor at Cedar Creek. In the grand cavalry charge that turned the battle into a rout, Woodbury rode down four Rebels and ordered them to surrender.

Noticing that one was concealing something, he ordered that it be handed over. What he received was the 12th North Carolina's regimental battle flag. Woodbury accompanied George Custer to Washington and presented the trophy to Edwin Stanton, secretary of war.

Just south of the academy, across the green, is the Dailey Memorial Library. Its entryway is all that remains of the Derby Town House, the hall used for town meetings during the war. Derby voters here in July 1864 approved bounties of $225 "to all such veterans who have enlisted to the credit of Derby and in cases of those killed or died, paid to their legal heirs." One of Vermont's famous Civil War personalities, Willie Johnson, likely enlisted here. Signing on as a drummer boy at eleven, he endured the Peninsula Campaign, said to have come through the fighting with drum in hand. Secretary Stanton gave the lad, who grew up in Salem, a gold medal.

Go south from the library 2.75 miles on Route 105, go left on Hayward Road, and on the left is the Salem Cemetery, located in the old town of Salem, close by Salem Lake. Harrison Lyon is buried here, a 15th Vermont private, who died of sickness at Fairfax Courthouse, Virginia, in early March 1863. He lived on a Salem hillside farm just across the lake. Pliny White, writing for Hemenway's *Gazetteer*, said of Salem, "The town always kept in advance of its quota, and was in advance when the order came to discontinue recruiting in April 1865." Salem was credited with sending thirty-nine men to war.

Return to Derby Center. Three miles north, on Route 5, is the village of Derby

Line, on the Canadian border. The large park is Baxter Park, given to Derby in 1923 through the will of Elizabeth Baxter, in memory of her husband, Portus Baxter. At the soldier memorial in the park's center is a 12-pound Napoleon, given to Derby in 1971 by a Baxter descendant. A Vermont congressman during the Civil War, Baxter went to Fredericksburg during the Overland Campaign to care for Vermont's wounded. According to Hemenway's *Gazetteer*, "When the crisis was past, and he returned to Washington, those who saw him could scarcely recognize the man, so emaciated—so utterly had he entered into and shared the life and sufferings of our soldiers." The Baxters lived in the large Victorian house, fronted by a low granite wall, facing the northeast corner of the park. Throughout the war, Elizabeth gathered materials for the aid and comfort of Vermont soldiers. She and her husband also worked as nurses in Washington hospitals. The congressman was appointed a member of the official committee that accompanied Abraham Lincoln's body from the capitol to its burial in Springfield, Illinois.

In mid-November 1861, the *Stanstead Journal* reported: "Saturday was quite a stirring day in Derby Line, just over the border. The Lieut Col. [Edward Sawyer] of the Vermont Cavalry was present to purchase horses to mount his men, and bought some 35 in the course of the day at an average price of $92 per head."

SOURCES
DERBY TOWN RECORDS.
GROUT, JOSIAH. *MEMOIR OF GEN'L WILLIAM WALLACE GROUT AND AUTOBIOGRAPHY OF*

JOSIAH GROUT. NEWPORT, VT: THE BULLOCK PRESS, 1919.
HAY, CECILE B., AND MILDRED B. HAY. *HISTORY OF DERBY.* LITTLETON, NH: COURIER PRINTING CO., 1967.
HUBBARD, BETHIA L. *DERBY ACADEMY: THE STORY OF A COMMUNITY INSTITUTION.* PRIVATELY PRINTED, 1954.

GLOVER

Route 16 is Glover's main street, and side by side along it, in the center of the village, stand the Union House and the Congregational Church. On the ground floor of the Union House (now a nursing home), a recruiting office operated early in the war. After the war, a GAR post named for Glover's Captain Daniel Mason met on the building's upper floor, as did the local Women's Relief Corps (WRC) chapter, named for Captain Erastus Buck (see Charleston). A photo taken about 1895 shows the WRC members assembled on the upper porch with the GAR men on the front steps.

A local historian wrote soon after the war for Hemenway's *Gazetteer*: "As soon as there was open opposition to our government on the part of the South, public meetings were held and the grounds of complaint were fully discussed by the clergymen of Glover, and addresses patriotic and stirring were made." Such patriotic words were heard in the old Congregational Church. It is believed that in that building, funeral services were held for Captain Mason on February 4, 1866. Mason, a local farm boy, died of disease in Brownsville, Texas, on November 20,

1865, while serving as a company commander in the 19th Regiment of black troops. Mason also soldiered for three years in the 6th Vermont, and during 1863, he kept a diary. Among his entries:

April 8: "Cold and cloudy, chill wind. Corps reviewed by Pres. Lincoln near Falmouth. Great display of military. Generals Hooker, Sedgewick, How[e], Brooks and several other generals were present with staff."

May 3, writing of the recent attack on the Fredericksburg heights: "About 11 o'clock we charged on the heights and took them under heavy fire. Took 15 pieces of cannon and 400 prisoners."

Mason's final entry, written on December 23, 1863, at the end of a leave spent in Glover, said: "Expect to start for Brattleboro tomorrow morning. I have now filled this and will now present it to Hat."

Hat was his nickname for Harriet Clark, his sweetheart, who he married during another leave, on March 20, 1865. He never saw her again, but she was surely present at the Congregational Church to hear the funeral sermon delivered by Reverend Sidney K. B. Perkins. In it, Perkins read a resolution adopted by Mason's fellow officers in Texas: "We lose one whose sterling qualities as a soldier and gentleman made him dear to us his associates, enlivening our most gloomy hours by his most brilliant genius and sparkling wit, by his wise counsel, congenial disposition and even temper endearing himself to all who knew him." Perkins then spoke to the widow, "To you . . . let me present the promise of our heartfelt sympathy and of our prayers, that you may be sustained under your affliction and enabled to submit to the holy will of God."

From Route 16, just north of the church, take Bean Road uphill into the hamlet of West Glover. The old Congregational Church, where Perkins was pastor, is on the right. Mason was fond of attending group sings at the church, surely with Harriet. The Coburn family were longtime church members, including Amanda. When her brother Henry joined the 3rd Vermont, she followed him to war as a volunteer nurse. She served throughout the war, assisting in operations, caring for the wounded, and driving an ambulance. When requested, she kept her patients' valuables in her tent for safekeeping. One night when a soldier tried to steal them, she shot him. Both Amanda and her brother came home safely. Continue across the bridge, and on the right is the old creamery, now an ambulance station. The house just beyond it was the Clark home, where Harriet grew up and where she likely received the terrible news of her husband's death, at age twenty-six.

Return to Route 16, turn right, and proceed south to the Westlook Cemetery, on the left. Mason's tall monument stands to the front and center. Though Harriet remarried another local man and had a family by him, she chose to be buried here beside Daniel, her husband of only eight months. Alexander Davis, a Glover man, served with Mason in the 6th Vermont. Then he also reenlisted to command black troops. Mason was a captain of the 19th Regiment, Davis of the 39th Regiment. Their commands were stationed together for a time and were involved in the Battle of the Crater at Petersburg. Davis had come home to Vermont before Mason died, and in a reminiscence of his former comrade in arms, he said, "The first I knew of Dan's death was in passing the cemetery at home I saw a burial party and learned by inquiry that it was the friends of Dan."

Directly behind Mason's monument, on the crest, are the graves of George Randall and his wife, Emma. The little stone beside them marks the resting place of their daughter Hattie. George enlisted as a musician in the 4th Vermont and served until he was brought ill to the Brattleboro hospital. Emma and her two children had been sharing a house in the hills above Glover with her sister, Persis Stone, whose husband was also at war, and her four children. When Emma went to Brattleboro to bring George home, she left daughter Hattie with George's sister. George, thirty-six, died soon after reaching Glover, and a few days later, Hattie died of illness. Soon a ten-year-old son of Persis's perished. In Westlook Cemetery lie 52 men who served in the Civil War. By one count, Glover, a town of 1,200 people in 1860, sent 90 men to war, of whom 17 perished.

SOURCES

ALEXANDER, JOAN. *GLOVER'S CIVIL WAR PLACES*. GLOVER, VT: GLOVER HISTORICAL SOCIETY, 2006.

DAVIS, ALEXANDER. *REMINISCENCE OF DANIEL MASON*. FEBRUARY 4, 1866. COURTESY OF JEAN BORLAND.

FISKE, MARGUERITE BEAN. *THE UNION HOUSE OF GLOVER, VERMONT*. GLOVER, VT: GLOVER HISTORICAL SOCIETY, 1999.

GLOVER BICENTENNIAL COMMITTEE. *HISTORY OF THE TOWN OF GLOVER, 1783–1983*.

GLOVER, VT: GLOVER HISTORICAL SOCIETY, 1983.

MASON, DANIEL. CIVIL WAR DIARY, 1863. COURTESY OF JEAN BORLAND.

PERKINS, SIDNEY K. B. SERMON AT THE FUNERAL OF DANIEL MASON. 1866. COURTESY OF THE GLOVER HISTORICAL SOCIETY.

WITH THANKS TO JOAN ALEXANDER, JEAN BORLAND, AND REBECCA MUNSON.

GREENSBORO

As the war began, local men formed the Greensboro Sharpshooters, and on June 12, 1861, according to the *Caledonian Record,* a "grand march" took place. The sharpshooters stopped before the home of a Mrs. Wheeler, elderly and in poor health, and seventy-five former members of her Sunday school class stepped forward from the ranks. She cried, as did many of her former pupils. Then they marched off, many destined to go to war in real companies, and Mrs. Wallace died eleven days later.

Greensboro village is close by Caspian Lake, and in the village center is the general store, with a small green across the street. From the store, take East Street, and the fourth house on the left, with two peaked roofs, was Mrs. Wheeler's.

Return to the store, turn left onto Breezy Avenue, and quickly on the left is the Greensboro Historical Society. Go to the building's rear and look down upon an old square barn by the brook. Amos Dow came home from war to run his father's sash and blind factory, in this building. Dow served less than a year as a private in the 11th Vermont, but fought in the Overland Campaign.

The large house beside the historical society, with apartments added, was the boyhood home of Sherman Pinney. He enlisted at twenty-two as a private in the 3rd Vermont in the spring of 1861. Plagued with poor health, early in the Peninsula Campaign of 1862 he was too sick to march. He soon returned to Vermont and died in November 1864.

Down the street, a bell is displayed on the site of the old Presbyterian Church. Three houses beyond is the home in which Elliot Kenniston grew up. He joined a Massachusetts regiment in August 1862, but died the following spring of diphtheria.

Return past the village store and the Congregational Church is on the left. The abolitionist reverend Kiah Bailey, pastor, gave the dedicatory address when this church opened in 1829.

Beside the church is the Grange Hall. During the Civil War, this building was the Greensboro town hall, where Greensboro voted for Lincoln twice, 102 to 26 over Douglas and 122 to 54 over McClellan. Here, soldier bounties reaching $300 were approved. As filling quotas became difficult, bounty amounts were left to the selectmen's discretion. In 1864, the town made a deposit with the state to help pay for seeking recruits in the South that could be credited to Greensboro. A total of 114 Greensboro men served: 6 were killed in action, 7 died of wounds, and 19 of disease.

Proceed north on Craftsbury Road, and in 1.75 miles go right on Gebbie Road. In just over 0.5 mile, turn onto Atherton Way and look to the farm on the

hill ahead. John Paddleford left his wife Caroline in charge of this farm to serve nine months in the 15th Vermont. She wrote him on January 4, 1863, "It has been frozen most of the time, though it is thoughing some today. I am quite alone today excepting Grand Mother and the baby and Jennie. O how I wish you was by my side." She discussed managing the farm, the high price of oats, the excellent work of the hired man, and the need to buy a horse from a neighbor she called "Mr. Lincoln."

Return to Craftsbury Road and continue north, pass Shadow Lake Road, and just beyond is an old cape set amid large maples. William Macomber lived here and saw two sons go to war. William Jr. served in the 15th Vermont and came home safely. Soon after he returned, Carlos joined the 6th Vermont, reaching it at its Brandy Station winter camp. But he was soon sick with typhus and died in a field hospital on March 4, 1864. His body came home to this house.

Turn around here and quickly go left on Shadow Lake Road. Soon, go right on Hanks Hill Road to its end, at a farm once owned by John Calderwood. At the end of August 1864, his sons Luther, eighteen, and Andrew, twenty, joined the Vermont Cavalry. Luther was wounded in a brush with Confederate riders near Berryville in the Shenandoah Valley the following November 12. He spent the rest of his enlistment in hospitals, including Burlington. Andrew served in several engagements. Local historian E. E. Rollins wrote, "Once, while away from camp for water, he was taken prisoner, but made his escape by running from his two captors, preferring the risk of being killed by a bullet to the horrors of a rebel prison. He was killed near Petersburg, by a Minnie ball entering his side and passing through his heart."

SOURCES

GREENSBORO TOWN RECORDS.
ROLLINS, E. E. *THE MEMORIAL RECORD OF THE SOLDIERS OF GREENSBORO*. MONTPELIER, VT: FREEMAN PRINTING HOUSE, 1868.
WITH THANKS TO SUSAN COFFIN AND DIANN ROSS.

....

HOLLAND

From Route 11 at Morgan Center, along Lake Seymour, go north on Valley Road to the Holland United Methodist Church, on the left. Built on the site of an 1844 meetinghouse, it stood beside a school that once hosted town meetings. There, Holland voters in 1860 voted for Lincoln over Douglas, 55 to 30. In 1863, bounties of $300 were voted. In early 1865, having difficulty meeting a quota, voters appropriated $900 "for the purpose of securing soldiers in the States in Rebellion."

From the church, go back south on Valley Road (Holland's main street) and quickly bear right on Holland Pond Road. Turn right on Page Hill Road, and the first right is Smith Road. In 0.1 mile, the first house on the left was the home of James Smith, who joined the 8th Vermont when it formed and was wounded at Port Hudson on June 14, 1864. He came home.

Continue on Page Hill Road 0.3 mile to a farm lane on the left that ends at the Rumery farm. Albert Rumery left here in August 1864 to enlist in the 2nd Vermont

Artillery at twenty-three. He served until the war ended and fought in the Petersburg Siege. Later he became a faithful member of the G. F. Spaulding GAR Post in Derby Line. When he died in 1917, his widow, Elizabeth, applied for and received a $25 pension, which in 1920 was increased to $30.

Continue on Page Hill Road 2.5 miles and bear right on Truscott Road. In 1.25 miles, on the left, is an old house with outbuildings. John Woodward enlisted from here as a private in the 2nd Vermont at the end of 1864. He was wounded in the Petersburg Breakthrough.

Continue past the Woodward house until again reaching Valley Road. In a 0.5 mile, Mead Hill Road leads to Mead Hill Cemetery. Buried here are 35 Civil War soldiers. Holland, with a population of 748 in 1860, sent 53 men to war, and 12 died.

Return to Valley Road, and go left 3.25 miles to the Whittier Road intersection, with a farm on the right. Here, George Tice grew up who served three years in the 10th Vermont and was wounded at Cedar Creek.

Continue on Valley Road 0.75 mile, go right on Goodall Road for 0.8 mile, and a farm lane on the left leads to the Goodall farm. Richard Goodall, a private in the 3rd Vermont for three years, surviving wounds at Second Fredericksburg and the Wilderness. After the war, he went west.

Return to Valley Road and proceed as you came, in 2 miles passing Tice Road, where in the field on the left George Tice long ran a sawmill, though plagued by his Cedar Creek wounds and with poor health.

SOURCES

FARROW, ELLA. *HOLLAND HIGHLIGHTS (HISTORY OF HOLLAND)*. BURLINGTON, VT: QUEEN CITY PRINTERS, 1979.

HOLLAND TOWN RECORDS.

RUMERY FAMILY RECORDS. COURTESY OF PENNY TICE.

WITH THANKS TO PENNY TICE.

....

IRASBURG

Exit Interstate 91 at Orleans and take Route 58 west to Irasburg, the shire town of Orleans County at the time of the Civil War. In just under 0.5 mile, on the right, is a large "Victorianized" farmhouse with barns behind. According to Irasburg's town history, a man who fought for the Confederacy lived here. Sydney Beauclerk, a British aristocrat, came to America as a boy and was schooled at Virginia Military Institute. Serving in the rebel army, he was wounded with both saber cuts and bullets. After the war, Beauclerk met an Irasburg lady and moved here. According to the local history, "His wit, charm and generosity became more important to his neighbors than his early career as a 'Reb,' and when he died in 1938 his casket was decorated with the Stars and Stripes, with a Union Jack displayed at its head."

Continue on Route 58 three miles to the Irasburg common. On its north side is a Masonic hall, a building that was the town hall during the Civil War. Here, Irasburg voters approved bounties that peaked at $800. The town sent some one hundred men to war.

At the time of the Civil War, Irasburg was the legal, political, and military center of Orleans County. Indeed, in the rear of the brick store, facing the common, a portion of the county jail survives. A recruiting office operated in the county courthouse, about where the library now stands. Two companies were organized here, and both drilled on the common, one being Company I of the Vermont Cavalry in which thirteen Irasburg men served.

Amasa Bartlett (see Coventry), a lawyer who lived and practiced law in Irasburg, in just nine days in June 1862 recruited Company E of the 9th Vermont, which included six Irasburg men. In 1891, Lucy Jameson Scott, an Irasburg native, published *The Gilead Guards,* subtitled *A Story of War-Times in a New England Town,* based on events she witnessed in Irasburg. She described a ceremony held in the Congregational Church as Bartlett's company departed: "The people looked at him through tears as he stood there so handsome and fearless; and, just as he began to speak, the sunlight burst through the mists, falling like a morning blessing upon his bare head and untarnished uniform. An involuntary murmur of applause again rose around him, and he smiled in response and begged the sorrowful hearts before him to accept it as an omen of good." By the common, the company boarded wagons to head for war. "The last kisses were exchanged," Scott wrote, "and last blessings bestowed. The officers gave their orders, the company drew up in position, and the next moment all was ready for departure. The band began to play, caps were lifted, handkerchiefs waved, eyes met and spoke one more mute farewell, and with cheers and music and flying flags the boys in blue rode away."

The 1829 church facing the southeast corner of the common was the Congregational Church during the Civil War. On June 12, 1863, the *Vermont Journal* reported: "Capt. Henry C. Flint of the Vermont Cavalry, who was killed in the late fight at Drainsville, Va., was buried at Irasburgh on the 12th inst. Appropriate services were held in the Congregational church which was filled to overflowing . . . An eloquent and patriotic discourse was delivered on the occasion by Rev. Thomas Bayne. Capt. Flint greatly distinguished himself by his courage in the affair at Drainsville. He had a hand-to-hand conflict with Mosby, the rebel guerilla captain." Flint died at twenty-three.

In 1864, the Reverend Jonathan Woodward, former chaplain of the Vermont Cavalry (see Westford), became pastor of the Irasburg Congregational Church. Later, the Irasburg GAR post was named for him.

Just east of the church, the house beside the post office was the home of Thomas Fisher, 17th Vermont, who was wounded at the Wilderness. Look south down the street to the Methodist Church. According to the Scott novel, announcements made from both its pulpit and that of the Congregational Church led to the founding of a ladies' aid society organized to make and gather materials to be sent to the soldiers.

From the common, go 1.3 miles south on Route 14 to an old frame house set above the road on the left. Captain Henry Flint went to war from here, and his body came back here.

Return to the common, and go north on Route 14, to the cemetery on the left. Many Irasburg soldiers are buried here, and a prominent obelisk marks Captain Flint's grave. Nearby is the grave of Lewis Ingalls, an 8th Vermont private, who won a Medal of Honor in fighting at Boutte Station, Louisiana, in 1862.

Pass the cemetery and stop at the intersection of Route 58, where three roads approaching Irasburg meet. After the Rebel raid on St. Albans on October 19, 1864, many local men were mobilized to guard north county roads. In the Scott novel, the author describes one lonely boy stationed in the night at this intersection: "A dead limb fell with a thud a few rods away; then, snap, snap! Twigs were breaking in a thicket like the click of many rifles. Then the wind swept over the hill, and Benjie was sure he heard the echo of horses' hoofs." He gave the command halt and asked for a countersign. Then something crashed through the bushes, and he fired. The shot produced a "moo," as a terrified cow ran away, unharmed.

Go west on Route 58 for 0.75 mile to a large farm with a round barn. Eben Grant, who served most of the war with the Vermont Cavalry, lived here.

SOURCES
IRASBURG TOWN RECORDS.
ORCUTT, MARJORIE A., AND EDWARD S. ALEXANDER. *A HISTORY OF IRASBURG, VERMONT.* RUTLAND, VT: ACADEMY BOOKS, 1989.
SCOTT, MRS. O. W. (LUCY JAMESON). *THE GILEAD GUARDS: A STORY OF WAR-TIMES IN A NEW ENGLAND TOWN.* NEW YORK: HUNT & EATON, 1891.
WITH THANKS TO ROY INGALLS.

JAY

From Route 100, go 1 mile west on Route 242 to the village of Jay, where Cross Road crosses Route 242. On the right, in a former school, is the Jay town office. Jay held its town meetings during the Civil War in the District One School, which stood on this site. Apparently a town of very limited resources, Jay spent little money funding enlistments. Hemenway's history of the town states that "Jay furnished for the Army of the Union 39 volunteers on its own quota, and many others to apply on the quotas of other towns, in which money was more abundant than patriotism." Town records show that at March meeting in 1864, Jay voters passed over a resolution asking whether a sum of money might be appropriated to pay volunteers. In August 1864, a total of $1,000 was voted "for the purpose of providing recruits on the call of 500,000 for the army of the United States."

Among the local men who signed up in Jay was Gilbert Lucier, who was born in St. Hyacinthe, Quebec. His family came to Jay when Gilbert was a child, and at seventeen, he enlisted on October 27, 1862 in Company F of the 11th Vermont. Lucier served until the war ended, and on June 1, 1864, he was wounded in a thigh at Cold Harbor. He nearly died, and the leg hurt him at times throughout the rest of his long life. Lucier came home to Jay and married Lucy Ann King, of Berkshire, in 1868. He was Jay's road commissioner and twice represented the town in the legislature. In 1938, his nephew, Graham Lucier, drove him to Gettysburg for the seventy-fifth reunion. Lucier's grandniece, Peg Barry, recalled that the nephew got bored one evening and went for a walk. On returning, his uncle wanted to know where he'd been. Visiting with some of the Rebel veterans, was the reply. Lucier told his nephew to start packing. For him, after three quarters of a century, the war still had not ended. Lucier lived another six years in Jay, and his great-grandnephew, Duane Lucier, said in 2009 that the old man was short and stocky and spoke fluent French Canadian. He also was "kind of fiery, kept to himself, and he did his work and wanted everyone who worked for him to do theirs." In his last months, Lucier became bedridden but was still fond of recalling that he had once met Abraham Lincoln, while the 11th was at work building forts around Washington. When he died on September 22, 1944, at ninety-seven, in Newport's Orleans Memorial Hospital, Lucier was Vermont's last surviving veteran.

Lucier's last home stands behind the Jay town offices, a neat little house with barn attached to the rear that faces, and fronts on, Cross Road. Here, in this house with a small front porch and a glassed-in side porch, his funeral was held.

The next house on Cross Road, just beyond the bridge and on the same side of the road as Lucier's, was Henry Chamberlain's home, which looks more like a hotel than a house. He served five months in the 3rd Vermont, before being discharged for disability.

Return to Jay village and turn right, west, on Route 232. In 1.25 miles, go left on Lucier Road, and in 0.25 mile, come to a T. The old house above the road to the right was the home of Charles Lucier, Gilbert's father. Charles first enlisted in the 5th Vermont as a private and was wounded as Savage's Station. He recovered and joined Company F of the 1st Sharpshooters in the summer of 1864 and served until the war's end. His wound plagued him until he died, not long after the war.

Continue on Cross Road almost 1 mile, turn right on Cemetery Road, and quickly enter the Jay Village Cemetery. Here lie many of Jay's veterans, including Gilbert Lucier, buried beside his wife, Lucy, who died at ninety-one, four years before her husband.

SOURCES

JAY TOWN RECORDS.
NEWPORT EXPRESS, 1860–1865. GOODRICH MEMORIAL LIBRARY, NEWPORT.
VERMONT HISTORY: PROCEEDINGS OF THE VERMONT HISTORICAL SOCIETY 33 (JANUARY 1955).
WITH THANKS TO FRANK BARAW, DUANE LUCIER, AND PEG BARRY.

LOWELL

Lowell, from an 1860 population of 830, sent 80 men to war, of whom 8 perished. The town voted for Lincoln over Douglas in 1860, 78 to 24, with 1 vote going to Buchanan. Those votes were cast in the Lowell Corners School, where all wartime town meetings took place, a building that no longer stands.

To find its location, go to the junction of Routes 100 and 58 and turn east on 58, the Hazen's Notch Road. The old school stood beside the Catholic Church, where a modern building is now located.

Continue on 58 through Lowell village, cross a bridge, and soon atop a rise is an aging farmhouse on the left, with a modern house across the road and old barns beyond. This was the postwar home of abolitionist soldier Rufus Kinsley (see Fletcher), who came home from the war a sick man and suffered the rest of his life from chronic diarrhea. Dr. T. T. Dutton often came here from the village to give Kinsley a strong dose of morphine. In 1886, Kinsley was confined to his bed all summer. A neighbor said that his teeth were falling out, he had an irregular heartbeat, and his body was emaciated. Sometimes, his brother William, who suffered the effects of a wound he received at Port Hudson, helped him on the farm here. Rufus lived until 1911, never well, but a respected citizen who held several town offices.

Return to Route 100, and on passing through Lowell village, note Lower Village Road, on the right. The first building on the road's left was once the Parker and Harding Store. At the time of the Civil War, H. B. Parker and F. D. Harding lived as neighbors along Lower Village Road and at some point jointly operated the store. Neither went to war, as both paid $300 to avoid serving.

But that was not the general rule for the men from Lowell. As proof, proceed on Route 58 across Route 100 and quickly turn left into Mountain View Cemetery. Rufus Kinsley is buried here. So is William Allen, who joined the 2nd Vermont Artillery at twenty-six as a private in 1863. He came home in poor health and died three months after the war's end. "Though lost to sight, in memory dear," says his epitaph. David Davenport is buried nearby. Enlisting as a private in the 6th Vermont at thirty-nine, he was wounded at Lee's Mill and soon came home to die. His son Henry, at eighteen served in the 17th Vermont and was wounded at the Wilderness.

Few houses remain in Lowell that were occupied by Civil War soldiers. Yet continue east on Route 58, rising into old farm country well up in the hills, and in 3 miles, see a modern log cabin on the left. From here look right, uphill, to an old house almost hidden by trees. Seth Alger lived there and joined the 7th Vermont as a private in early 1862 at age forty-two. He died of disease the following September, soon after the regiment reached Louisiana. He is buried in Chalmette National Cemetery.

Continue on Route 58 just under 2 miles to where narrow Rabtoy Road comes from the north. Once the Stiles farm stood along this road, and down it Elmore and James Stiles came to enlist as privates in the 11th Vermont, and Myron and William Stiles to join the 3rd Vermont. Elmore and Myron were wounded at Cedar Creek. William was shot at Spotsylvania's Bloody Angle, then at Charles Town. They all made it home.

SOURCES
LOWELL TOWN RECORDS.
RANKIN, DAVID C. DIARY OF A CHRISTIAN SOLDIER: RUFUS KINSLEY AND THE CIVIL WAR. NEW YORK: CAMBRIDGE UNIVERSITY PRESS, 2002.
WITH THANKS TO CAROLYN MURPHY AREL.

MORGAN

Overlooking Seymour Lake, the Morgan Historical Society occupies the 1870 Morgan Center Union Church, at the south end of Morgan Center along Route 111. Coming north from Island Pond, take Toad Hill Road at the old church, and on the left, at the corner of Williams Road, is the Norton District School, where town meetings once took place. Here in 1864, the town went for Lincoln over McClellan, 71 to 13, and approved bounties that reached $500. According to Morgan's sesquicentennial history, published in 1941, the town furnished 47 men, with 13 killed in action or dead of wounds.

Take Williams Road 1 mile to a dilapidated farmhouse on the right, at a Y. Here Joel Williams lived, who joined the 11th Vermont at twenty-eight and was wounded in an elbow at Cold Harbor. The wound troubled him the rest of a long life, which ended in 1916. Go straight at the Y to the farmhouse at road's end, the home of Eugene Burroughs, a private in the 2nd U.S. Sharpshooters. He was wounded at the Wilderness.

Return to Route 111 and turn right on Valley Road. In 1.5 miles, a small frame house sits above the road, on the right, across the road from modern barns. From this farm, David Elliott enlisted in the 3rd Vermont at twenty-three and the following spring was captured at Lee's Mill. He survived.

Return to Route 111 and continue north, turning left at the village store on Charleston Road. At Clark Cemetery, go left, and in 0.4 mile, the Brooks house, a frame structure, is set back on the right. Charles, Daniel, and Lyman Brooks all served in the 11th Vermont. Captured at Weldon Railroad, Charles survived Andersonville, but died in captivity at Charleston, South Carolina, just after the war ended.

Return to Clark Cemetery, where a single stone marks the grave of John Piper and his son Lucian, both members of the 10th Vermont's Company K. The father died at forty-two, while home on furlough. The son perished at Cold Harbor, at eighteen.

Return to Route 111 and go back south, pass the historical society, and in 2.5 miles, Jordan Road turns right. Amos Batchelder joined the 15th Vermont at age twenty-six and died on December 12 at the regiment's winter camp. He is buried here, close by the family farm, now modernized and overlooking the cemetery, at the corner of Jordan Road.

Continue 2 miles south on Route 111, and on the left is Whitehill Loop, with the Whitehill farm at its end. From here, Brothers Matthew and Moses Whitehill joined the 15th Vermont and came home safely. Moses then enlisted in the 17th Vermont. The morning of the April 2, 1865, attack at Petersburg he was judged too ill to fight, but insisted on joining the ranks. He was shot dead in the breakthrough assault.

SOURCES

HISTORY OF MORGAN. NEWPORT, VT: ORLEANS COUNTY PRINTERS, 1976.
MORGAN TOWN RECORDS.
MORGAN, VERMONT: SESQUICENTENNIAL OF VERMONT STATEHOOD, 1791–1941. MORGAN, VT: TOWN OF MORGAN, 1941.

WHITEHILL FAMILY RECORDS. COURTESY OF CARLIE WHITEHILL.
WITH THANKS TO KEN AND CARLIE WHITEHILL AND BEVERLY MAY.

NEWPORT CITY/ NEWPORT TOWN

Perhaps no community, other than St. Albans itself, reacted as strongly to the October 19, 1864, Confederate raid as did lakeside Newport, at the southern end of international Memphremagog Lake. Longtime Newport resident Charles Robinson recalled that the news flashed into the Main Street telegraph office not long after the Rebels had galloped for the Canadian border. On Newport's Main Street men assembled to form a militia for the town's protection. Some fell into line as infantry; some were mounted. Then they paraded to stand in formation in front of the Memphremagog House. After all, the border was only 5 miles distant.

Next day, Norwich University cadets arrived by train. As a steamboat was seen approaching from the direction of Canada, the cadets formed on the docks with arms at the ready. Coming in from Canada was the steamer *Mountain Maid*, George Fogg captain. The cadets seemed about to open fire on the boat, until cooler heads prevailed. That night, under cover of darkness, a pair of recently discharged veterans launched a pair of rockets from Pine Hill. Panic spread until the two were sought out and, for a time, jailed.

Robinson summed things up: "An

entire outfit of arms for a cavalry company and for an infantry battalion arrived in Newport the next day and the men were regularly armed and equipped but not uniformed, and their organization was kept up a number of months, or to about the close of the war when the arms were mostly returned to the State arsenal."

Newport's Main Street today is both Routes 5 and 105. Along it few of the buildings that witnessed the raid scare remain. But the long, brick state office building stands on the site of, and looks a bit like, the Memphremagog House. Behind the building is a lakefront walkway located where a big dock accommodated steamboats and where the cadets once took aim.

Go to the east end of Main Street and look up to Pine Hill, topped by a large Victorian mansion, once the home of Captain Fogg.

Go west on Main and the Goodrich Memorial Library is on the right, where the Ladies Reading Circle of Newport sometimes met. Henry Bedell (see Westfield) lived most of his postwar life in Newport and was often visited here by Bettie Van Metre, the woman who had hidden him in her Shenandoah Valley home and likely saved his life. After Bedell died, the club sent Van Metre a letter, which said, "A few of our ladies are proud to say that they have met and talked with you during your visits here and all wish to tell you of their admiration of your bravery and daring."

Bedell was a faithful member of the local Portus Baxter GAR Post. Its building is gone, but the post flag is displayed at the library. Also preserved there is the post's *Memorial Book,* in which many veterans wrote of their war experiences. The book was given to the GAR by local attorney George Prouty in 1894. In his presentation speech, Prouty recalled, as a lad, walking along Main Street on April 15, 1865: "As I went along, I felt something was wrong. The people whom I met looked strange. I noticed the flag was at half-staff. Just as I turned from the lake to the skating ground, one of my companions . . . said to me that President Lincoln had been shot the night before, and that word had just come that he was dead . . . The air was charged with sadness."

Go north on Main to the corner of Third Street, where a service station stands. Look behind it to the top of an old frame house, set back from both Main and Third streets. When Henry Bedell moved to Newport soon after the war, he first lived here, where Van Metre visited several times. Bedell worked in the local customs house. Also, as a local paper noted on his death, "He served the public as an auctioneer, getting about on one limb, the other resting on a stub crutch."

Continue north on Main and the fourth house on the left, east of Third Street, was the home of Joseph Rutherford. Dr. Rutherford was one of the men who assembled after the St. Albans Raid. When the war began, Rutherford had recruited local men, before becoming assistant surgeon of the 10th Vermont. He later was chief surgeon of the 17th Vermont.

Take Third Street, which is Route 105, and soon on the right is the former Orleans County Hospital. In it, the last surviving Vermont Civil War soldier, Gilbert Lucier (see Jay), died in 1944, with his uniform at his bedside.

Continue 5 miles on Route 105 into Newport Center. Go right on Cross Road, cross the railroad tracks, go quickly left, then right, and the first house on the right was the home of Nathaniel Rogers. He joined the 15th Vermont at age fifty-seven and was one of several soldiers captured with Brigadier General Edwin Stoughton the night of March 9, 1863. On his return home, Roger's son, Nathaniel Jr., joined the 11th Vermont and lost his right leg on May 18, 1864, in the regiment's first battle at Spotsylvania. He came home and farmed for many years here. Henry Smith, who served most of the war in the 8th Vermont, lived in the house across the street.

Return on Cross Road into the village to the Methodist Church on the left. Across the street, where the town office now stands, was the Newport Center School, where many Civil War town meetings were held. There, Newport went for Lincoln over McClellan, 272 to 70, in 1864. That same year, Newport voters, having trouble meeting draft quotas, decided to seek black recruits. To do so, they approved bounties of $300. They also voted to pay white men $500.

Continue past the church on Vance Hill Road for 3 miles, and go left on Lake Shore Road. In 2.5 miles on the left is an aging farmhouse, with barn beside, less than 0.5 mile from the Canadian border. This was the home of Israel and Adiva Scott, parents of eight children. Son Nelson joined the 3rd Vermont at twenty-three in 1861 and died eighteen months later of sickness in a Philadelphia hospital. Son Israel was seventeen when he enlisted in the 2nd Vermont in October 1861. He was killed May 18, 1864, at Spotsylvania.

Return as you came, and soon, on the right, is the Newport Center Cemetery, where the Rogers boys lie side by side.

SOURCES

MALLOY, BARBARA KAISER. *NEWPORT AND THE NORTHEAST KINGDOM.* CHARLESTON, SC: ARCADIA PUBLISHING, 1999.

NELSON, EMILY M. *FRONTIER CROSSROADS: THE PEOPLE OF NEWPORT, VERMONT.* CANAAN, NH: PHOENIX PUBLISHING, 1978.

NEWPORT EXPRESS, 1860–1865. BIXBY MEMORIAL LIBRARY, VERGENNES.

WITH THANKS TO SANDY MCKENNEY AND ERNESTINE PEPPIN AND THE BIXBY MEMORIAL LIBRARY STAFF.

NORTH TROY/ TROY

Just south of the Canadian border, in the village of North Troy, at the intersection of Route 105 and Main Street, is a triangular common with a modest Civil War monument. On it are the names of the veterans who made up the Bailey Post No. 67 of the GAR. Among them are Gilbert Lucier (see Jay), the last Vermont Civil War soldier to die, and George Bailey, for whom the GAR post was named. Bailey, a sergeant in the 6th Vermont, died at Fort Monroe, Virginia, two weeks after being severely wounded at Lee's Mill.

From the common, take Main Street east and quickly come to the local historical society, on the right, in the former St. Augustine Episcopal Church. Here, on

February 27, 1887, a memorial service was held for Colonel Orion Elkins, a North Troy businessman who gave much of the money that built the church. That day, the Reverend Joseph Hooper delivered a long eulogy that traced Elkins's life. He noted that Elkins, in 1856, had gone to Kansas and "was on the side of absolute liberty, and aided in the escape of many slaves from Missouri." Back in Troy when the war began, Elkins did not serve, but "carefully looked after the wives and children of friends and neighbors who had bravely marched from their homes to meet death and exposure in the Virginia swamps." In 1863, Elkins became a member of Governor John Gregory Smith's staff. The eulogy stated, "In company with the governor . . . he made several visits to Washington and the seat of war in Virginia, carefully inspecting the Vermont troops and providing for their necessities. To the wounded who returned on sick leave he was a true friend. For the families of those who died he spared no exertion." In response to the St. Albans Raid, Elkins organized a home guard and helped patrol the Canadian border. For that, Governor Smith made him a colonel.

Four houses beyond the church, on the right, is a two-story frame house that was, for a time, the home of Chester Wheeler, a private in the 6th Vermont the last two years of the war. Wheeler, a member of the Bailey Post, faithfully kept a record of all its members, noting their term of service, whether they were wounded, and how they died during and after the war. The book is preserved at North Troy's Rand Memorial Library.

At the Wheeler house, turn left on School Street, then take Railroad Street north. Passing Elm Street, on the left is a large frame house set back from the street, that is now an inn. From this property, perhaps this house, Charles Bailey went to war and his death on the Virginia Peninsula.

Return to the triangular common and go south on Route 105. Soon, on the right, is a row of large houses, set above and back from the road. The big house with a barn-type roof, at the end of a long drive, was the home of John Currier. Born in a house that stood on this site, Currier grew up in Massachusetts and enlisted in the 10th Massachusetts Regiment. Late in the war he was in charge of supplying uniforms and equipment for officers of the Army of the Potomac and, during the Petersburg Siege, he worked at the City Point headquarters of Ulysses Grant. He returned to North Troy and built this house after the war.

Continue south 6 miles to the village of Troy. At its center is another triangular common, with a lone house on its east side. Here lived Samuel Sumner, who wrote a history of Troy for Hemenway's *Gazetteer*. "Most of the soldiers furnished by Troy," he wrote, "proved their devotion to their country by faithful service in the army, and many families in the town deplore the loss of a loved and worthy son and brother who has fallen on the field of battle. It has been the sad lot of the writer of this article to know how deep is this affliction, in the loss of a noble son who fell while bravely leading his Company in one of 'the seven days' battles on the

Peninsula in 1862." Samuel Sumner Jr. went to war from this house, to become a lieutenant in the 5th Vermont's Company D in September 1861. He was killed the following spring at Savage's Station.

SOURCES
BAILEY POST 27, GAR, MEMBERS. RECORD. RAND MEMORIAL LIBRARY, NORTH TROY.
BUTTERFIELD, ANNE HUCKINS. *MEMORIES OF THE EARLY DAYS IN THE TOWN OF TROY, VERMONT.* TROY, VT: S.N., 1977.
HOOPER, REV. JOSEPH. "TRUE MANHOOD." SERMON PREACHED ON THE DEATH OF COLONEL O. N. ELKINS AT NORTH TROY, VERMONT. FEBRUARY 27, 1887.
WITH THANKS TO GLORIA WILLIS.

....

WESTFIELD

Westfield lies along Route 100, south of Jay and north of Lowell, and the village is centered on a small green. Town meetings were held in a town hall that no longer exists but that stood beside the Congregational Church, fronting on the green. In 1864, Westfield went 130 to 37 for Lincoln. According to Hemenway's *Gazetteer*, "During the early part of the war volunteering was quite brisk, the young men of Westfield particularly coming forward without much thought, or expectation of any bounty; but as time passed it was found that heavy bounties must be offered or a draft submitted to. The selectmen paid as high as $1,000 for several recruits, and for several more a less sum, so that the close of the war found the town in debt several thousand dollars." From a wartime population of 600, 63 local men went to war.

From the green, take North Hill Road 0.6 mile to a frame house just past the turn to Kingdom Mountain Road. Henry Hitchcock lived here and, according to Hemenway's *Gazetteer*, "He joined the 3rd Vermont Co. B June 1 1861. He served till August 1, 1862, when he was discharged on account of ill health. In December 1863 he enlisted in the 39th N.Y. At the battle of the Wilderness, May 6, 1864, his leg was shattered by a shot. The next day his limb was amputated and he was started in an ambulance for Fredericksburg, but the guerillas turned the train of wounded and dying men back to Chancellorsville. The next day, May 8th, he died. His age was 29 years." The body came here and is buried in the cemetery just past the house.

The first house beyond the cemetery, on the left, was the wartime home of Westfield's best-known soldier. Henry Bedell enlisted in the 11th Vermont in the summer of 1862, leaving here on the family farm his wife Emeline, three children, and an adopted nephew. Having served through the Overland Campaign and in the Petersburg trenches, the 6-foot, 2-inch soldier was in a skirmish in the lower Shenandoah Valley on September 13, 1864, when a Confederate artillery shell shattered his left leg and severely injured his right hand. The leg was amputated two days later. Too weak to travel, Bedell was left at a farmhouse near Berryville, Virginia. A local woman, Bettie Van Metre, learned of his plight, and as Aldace Walker, 11th Vermont, wrote in *The Vermont Brigade in the Shenandoah Valley,* "The Lieutenant had been . . . entirely neglected for a day or two or longer; he had resigned himself to death, when this good woman entered his chamber and with kindly words called back his spirit from the mouth of the grave." Bettie was the wife of a Confederate soldier, James Van Metre, who at the time was confined in a Yankee prison, having been captured at Spotsylvania. Bettie nursed the Yankee soldier back to health, keeping his presence a secret. Time and again, she journeyed to the Union garrison at Harper's Ferry to obtain medicines and other supplies. In November, when Bedell had regained some strength, Bettie concealed him in a wagon and drove him to safety within Yankee lines.

Bedell and the Virginia woman then went to Washington and were presented to Secretary of War Edwin Stanton, who, in gratitude, gave them a pass granting freedom to James Van Metre. They found him in the Union prison at Fort Delaware. Bedell brought Bettie and James here, to his home, where they remained until the war ended. Then the Van Metres returned to their Shenandoah Valley home, where Bettie was never forgiven by her neighbors for harboring a Union soldier. Not long after the war, the Bedells visited the Van Metres in Virginia. The Bedells soon moved to Newport, where Bettie, who long outlived her husband, visited for many years. In 1915, Bettie Van Metre was honored by the Vermont legislature, which passed a resolution in her honor.

Return to the Westfield green and go south 0.6 mile on Route 100, then go left on Cemetery Road. At its end, go right, and soon Fuller Road turns right to a small cape at its end. Willard Farnham from here enlisted at twenty-three in the 6th Vermont and served a year that included the Overland Campaign.

Continue past Fuller Road, cross the Mississquoi River, and on reaching the top of the hill, on the left, is the former home of Ara Miller. He was a private in the 3rd Vermont for three years, until discharged for disability.

SOURCES

WALKER, ALDACE. *THE VERMONT BRIGADE IN THE SHENANDOAH VALLEY*. BURLINGTON, VT: FREE PRESS PRINT, 1869.
WESTFIELD TOWN RECORDS.
WITH THANKS TO CONNIE LaPLUME.

WESTMORE

In Westmore, at the southern end of Lake Willoughby, there is a public beach at the intersection of Routes 5A and 16. Augustus Lyon's home once stood here and from the beach Lakeview Cemetery can be seen, to the east. Lyon's stone is the most prominent on the hillside and it bears this inscription: "In memory of First Lt. A. M. Lyon of Co. I Third Vermont Vol. who served his country four years and three months during the great struggle for the Union receiving five wounds, two severe, three slight. Died Nov. 21 1915 in his eighty-third year. 'I now surrender to my friends and enemies, if any, to my country and the world.'"

Lyon joined the 3rd Vermont as a private when the war began and eventually became a first lieutenant. He was wounded at the Wilderness and Cold Harbor and, apparently, three other times.

In her book on Westmore, Harriet Fisher states that 34 men from the town served. Hemenway's brief chapter on Westmore says that 5 of them died. Also noted are 5 men who, having been drafted, "run to Canada." According to a militia record in the town clerk's office, the town's draft pool included 92 farmers, 4 mechanics, 2 merchants, 2 masons, 2 innkeepers, a clerk, and a machinist.

From the public beach, go west on Route 16, proceed up a hill, and on the left is a farmhouse, once part of the Hunt farm. It is believed that from here, John and Bradbury Hunt enlisted. Bradbury was twenty-one when he became a private in the 10th Vermont, as 1864 began. Wounded at Cedar Creek the following October, he died two days later. A cenotaph honors him in Lakeview Cemetery. John Hunt was thirty-four when he joined the 3rd Vermont just before Christmas 1863. Wounded the following May at the Wilderness, he recovered to serve until war's end.

Return past the public beach and go south 1 mile on Route 5A, and the 1857 Westmore District Two School is on the left, now the Westmore town office. Among the pupils here were future soldiers John and Bradley Hunt, Augustus Lyon, and James and Hiram Cummings, who both served as privates in the 15th Vermont.

Continue south on 5A, and leaving the lake behind, go abruptly uphill 0.25 mile to a pull-off on the right. Note foundations in the trees, some of which were likely part of the Willoughby Lake House. The deep lake, set between steep mountains, was a tourist attraction well before the Civil War. The first large hotel built here, the Lake House often hosted Westmore town meetings.

In November 1860, Westmore voted for Lincoln, 37 to 20, over Douglas. On December 14, 1863, townspeople approved bounties of $100 each. In May 1864, $300 bounties were voted. In July 1864, meeting here, Westmore approved a tax of $2 on each general fund dollar "to pay the soldiers" and decreed that it be collected "by the first of January next." But two months later, an additional $350 in bounties was approved for each enlisting soldier, necessitating an additional $3 per $100 grand list dollar tax increase.

The first Tuesday in November 1864, Westmore voted 35 to 12 for Lincoln over McClellan. Two months later, at a special town meeting, with quotas becoming more difficult to meet, the selectmen were authorized "to pay such bounties as they think best."

SOURCES

FISHER, HARRIET F. WILLOUGHBY LAKE LEGENDS AND LEGACIES. BROWNINGTON, VT: ORLEANS COUNTY HISTORICAL SOCIETY, 1988.

THE WESTMORE STORY: A BICENTENNIAL PROJECT. WESTMORE, VT: WESTMORE ASSOCIATION, 1976.

WESTMORE TOWN RECORDS.

WITH THANKS TO ART FRENCH.

chapter twelve

Rutland County

Before the war, Southerners came, some with slaves, to the still elegant, old hotel in Clarendon Springs, seeking relief from their homeland's summer heat. The Congregational Church's great spire towers over Rutland, as it did during the Civil War. In the church, women met to make things for the soldiers, after long days of work made so much more difficult by the absence of so many able-bodied men. Not far away in the upland town of Tinmouth, a study has shown that most of the soldiers who came home from war were somehow disabled, and many of those who returned soon left, to go west. In Chittenden, the town Civil War memorial seems to be the work of a master carver, a stone soldier deep in thought as he looks, eternally, due south, toward the old battlegrounds. In Brandon, where abolitionists spoke for human freedom, a grand Civil War monument erected in 1886 stands in the village center. At its dedication, seven thousand people listened to the words of Louis Addison Grant, former Vermont Brigade commander. Grant had seen many killing fields, including the Wilderness and Cold Harbor, and he had seen enough. "Let us labor," he said, "to hasten on the glorious day when peace shall prevail and nations shall learn war no more. That day is coming. It shall be a day of rejoicing, the like of which has not been known since when the morning stars sang together and the sons of God shouted for joy."

BENSON

A single story filled the April 27, 1871, *Rutland Herald*'s front page. It began: "A large concourse of citizens assembled at Benson on Wednesday to pay the last tribute of respect to Capt. John Quincy Dickinson, who was murdered at

---

Clarendon Springs House, where Southerners vacationed before the war.

Marianus, Jackson County, Florida, on the 3d of April. At an early hour, from every direction, people might be seen coming into the quiet town to attend the services, until near a thousand had gathered to witness the sad ceremonial."

Dickinson served in the 7th Vermont, its quartermaster for a time, including the regiment's assignment to Fort Barrancas in Florida. After the war, Dickinson joined the Freedmen's Bureau and was assigned to the Jacksonville area, where championing the rights of freed blacks was dangerous. He had recently been appointed a judge when, in the darkness of an April night in 1871, he was shot to death.

Enter Benson from Route 22A, and on arriving in the village, turn right, north, on Stage Road. Quickly, the old Methodist Church is above the road on the right, now a community center, in which "The Misses of the Methodist Church" gathered during the war to make hospital supplies. Dickinson's grave is in the cemetery behind the building. A funeral had been held in Florida, then the body came back to his hometown of Benson. According to the *Herald,* at Dickinson's wish, a service took place at early morning. Friends gathered for prayers at his home, then moved to the cemetery, where a poem was read:

Oh! bury me in the morning, mother,
And let me have the light
Of one bright day on my grave, mother!
Ere I am alone at night.

A thousand people, including many veterans, came to bid farewell to the captain, and after the burial, a lengthy memorial service was held at the Congregational Church. There, the Reverend W. W. Child said, "His name had become a charm to the freedmen, who loved and trusted him like a father." Reverend William Smart, an old friend, said, "He was one of those souls that was willing to give up all to do the world good, and they never die." Another friend, Vermont governor John Stewart, said, "He died for his country, and was as much a martyr to liberty as those who have died on the field of battle."

From the cemetery, return to Stage Road and continue north. The Congregational Church, where the Dickinson's services were held, is on the left. On April 20, 1862, Reverend Smart, then pastor of the church, had delivered a sermon to his congregation called "Lessons of the War." He said, "As war changes its nature, have we become blind to its true character, because it is our war? Are the widow's tears and the orphan's cries for those who fall in battle to be esteemed less because they come from our neighbors and friends? . . . There are better uses we can make of our noble sons than send them to be slaughtered upon battle-fields, or pine in hospitals." In late summer, Reverend Smart joined the 14th Vermont as its chaplain.

Three buildings beyond the church on Stage Road, a huge sycamore stands in the front yard of an old house, planted in memory of Captain Dickinson when his body came home.

Return along Stage Road to the village center, go right on Lake Road, and in 1 mile on reaching a four corners, turn right on North Lake Road. One-half mile along, the first house on the left was Dr.

John Mahana's home, once a private in the 4th Michigan Cavalry. Mahana was involved in the pursuit of Jefferson Davis after the Confederate government abandoned Richmond. Davis was seized near Macon, Georgia, and a controversy has raged since concerning whether Davis tried to disguise himself as a woman. Late in life, Mahana told a newspaper, "The only thing Davis had on of women's attire was a veil tied over his own small felt hat. He had his own dressing robe and officer's poncho, folded like a shawl, and he really did look like a woman as he hurried away from the tent."

Return along North Lake Road to the crossroads, and continue straight onto Park Hill Road. In 1 mile just beyond where Money Hole Road turns right, the first house on the right was the Aiken family home. James Aiken, a corporal in Company D, 14th Vermont, fought at Gettysburg. While the regiment was at war, Aiken's sister received here, by mail, a present from Company D's commander, Captain Charles Abell, of Orwell—a dried leaf and flower. Abell wrote on the leaf, "Magnolia leaf from Mt. Vernon May 25/63 Presented by Capt. Abell. To Miss Hattie." They were married when he returned from the war.

SOURCES
BENSON TOWN RECORDS.
"DEATH OF COLONEL DICKINSON." *RUTLAND HERALD,* APRIL 27, 1871. HOWARD COFFIN COLLECTION.
RUTLAND HERALD, 1871. VERMONT STATE LIBRARY.
WITH THANKS TO GERALDINE TUTOR.

BRANDON

Brandon's Civil War monument, topped by a granite soldier, is at the intersection of Routes 7 and 73, or Main and Park streets, in Monument Square. On it are listed 53 Brandon men who died, including 13 killed in action and 6 who died of wounds. The Wilderness killed 5 and Savage's Station 4. On Memorial Day 1886, 7,000 people gathered here for the monument dedication. The granite soldier faces where the speaker's platform stood, about where the flagpole on the Triangle now stands. Lewis Addison Grant, once commander of the 1st Vermont Brigade, was the featured speaker. Stephen Thomas was among scores of veterans present.

Grant, according to the *Rutland Herald,* "Was saluted by tremendous cheers which burst forth afresh at different times throughout the eloquent address." Near the conclusion, he said, "The war tore the manacles of bondage from millions of people and bade them go free. It raised them in the eyes of the law from the condition of chattels to that of free men. It lifted them from degradation and slavery to citizenship and sovereignty."

He then addressed the parents of those who died. "My dear friends, father and loving mother, the sacrifice of your loving son . . . has produced glorious results. The blood mingled with the blood of thousands and tens of thousands of sons and brothers and has made the atoning sacrifice, and this great crime against Christianity and the age has been washed away, and you live to see your nation rising in newness and life, not yet perfect, not yet what it shall be, but better and purer while undergoing the great work of regeneration."

Then he spoke of his "Old Brigade," saying, "My feeling toward the soldiers of that brigade is akin to brotherly love . . . We have helped to guide our nation into the paths of peace. Let us labor to hasten on the glorious day when peace shall prevail and nations shall learn war no more. That day is coming. It shall be a day of rejoicing, the like of which has not been known since when the morning stars sang together and the sons of God shouted for joy."

In 1860, on the Triangle, a band played, while native son and presidential candidate Stephen Douglas was welcomed at a reception in the Brandon House, located where the Brandon Inn now stands.

Across the street from the monument is the home of Ebenezer Ormsbee, commander of the 12th Vermont's Company C. Ormsbee was a prime mover in the monument's erection and was serving as Vermont's lieutenant governor at the time of the dedication. He was elected governor of Vermont in 1886.

From the monument, go west on Route 73 for 2.25 miles to Forest Dale. Look for a monument on the lawn of an old house on the right, designating it the home of Thomas Davenport, inventor of the electric motor. His son, Captain George Davenport, 5th Vermont, died at the Wilderness. Young Davenport's widow, Frances, later married Ebenezer Ormsbee.

Return to the Brandon monument, take Route 7 north, and quickly see a long brick block of stores known as the Conant Block. On its upper floors, the local GAR post

met. Just north, along Route 7, is the 1861 Brandon Town Hall. James Flint, eighteen when the war began, quit work building the hall to enlist in the 1st Vermont. The November 10, 1864, *Rutland Herald* reported on a war meeting in Brandon: "the Town Hall was packed almost to capacity by an audience that listened with breathless interest to the thrilling voice of Senator Foot [see Rutland], as he administered his telling blows upon rebels and traitors in thin disguise—the copperheads, and eloquently depicted the heroic deeds of our armies and the success of the administration in subduing the rebellion." The 15th Vermont held its sixteenth reunion here, and the speaker was its commander, Redfield Proctor. "The Green Mountains, termed the backbone of the state," Proctor said, "suggested the thought that the Vermonter, narrow, and bigoted and prejudiced as he might sometimes seem, never lacked that saving quality of back-bone; he always had spine and some to spare, even if he sometimes lacked the most perfect breadth of soul."

Just north of the town hall, go left on Pearl Street and quickly see an imposing brick house with tall columns that dominates the right side of the street. Home of the wealthy lawyer and abolitionist Rodney Marsh, fugitive slaves were harbored here. On Marsh's death, John Greenleaf Whittier said in a letter to his widow, "Thy husband's name was well known among anti-slavery folks beyond the limits of his state."

Returning to Route 7, note the Baptist Church on the left where abolitionist meetings were held. Orson Murray was a prominent member, an outspoken and controversial opponent of slavery. A funeral was held here for Captain Charles Ormsbee, brother of the future governor, killed while commanding the 5th Vermont's skirmish line at the Wilderness. Pass the Stephen Douglas home on the left, and turn north on Route 7. In 1 mile, drive into Pine Hill Cemetery and park by the tomb. On the knoll behind it is a single gravestone for three brothers killed in battle. Private John Ford, twenty-three, 10th Vermont, died at Mine Run; Private Hadley Ford, nineteen, 2nd Vermont, died of wounds received May 18 at Spotsylvania; Private Charles Ford, 5th Vermont, was twenty-two when killed in the Petersburg Breakthrough. The monument tells us his last words were, "Come on boys the works are ours." The Ford boys were the sons of Orville and Susan Hall Ford. The *Rutland Herald,* reporting on the Brandon monument dedication of 1886, said of Mr. Ford: "it is a sad reminder of the war to see this lonely father on the streets, still mourning the loss of the sons he so much relied upon."

Return to Brandon and the Douglas house. A monument with a bas-relief portrait of Stephen Douglas, nicknamed the "Little Giant," stands on the tiny green by the house. Here on April 23, 1813, Stephen was born, son of Dr. Stephen Arnold Douglass and Sarah Fisk Douglass. (Stephen Douglas later dropped the second *s* in his last name.) One summer evening two months later, Dr. Douglass was sitting by the fire holding the infant Stephen and talking with a friend, when he was suddenly stricken with a fatal heart attack. Stephen was dropped into the fire, but the friend rescued him.

The Douglass family soon moved to a farm north of town. Later, Stephen moved to Middlebury, where he learned cabinetmaking. At age sixteen, Stephen moved to western New York and soon acquired an interest in politics, fascinated by the Democrat Andrew Jackson. Then he was off to Illinois, where he rose swiftly, having served as Illinois secretary of state and one of its congressmen by age thirty-two. In 1846, he joined the U.S. Senate, becoming its dominant member during the 1850s. In 1858, Abraham Lincoln, a member of the new Republican Party, challenged his reelection bid. A series of debates were held in seven Illinois communities, eloquent exchanges that both defined the great issue of the day and brought about Lincoln's rise to national prominence.

Douglas won the election, but in 1860 they faced each other again, in a contest for the presidency. Lincoln triumphed over Douglas and the divided Democratic Party. Eighty percent of Vermont voters favored Lincoln.

The night Fort Sumter was attacked, Douglas visited the White House to pledge to Lincoln his support for the Union cause. Then the Little Giant went west, speaking in support of the war effort. Within weeks he died of typhoid fever, in a Chicago hotel room.

Douglas had returned to Brandon, in 1860, while campaigning for the presidency, and was honored with a parade and reception. In 1851, as the Middlebury College commencement speaker, he said, "Vermont is a good state to be born in, a good state to be brought up in provided you emigrate early."

Brandon celebrated the fall of Richmond April 5, 1865. According to the *Rutland Herald,* "Bells were rung, flags unfurled, guns fired, business suspended, and the wildest enthusiasm prevailed, in which old and young men, women and children heartily joined. A large procession was formed under the efficient marshallship of Capt. Cook and, escorted by a large cavalcade of men on horseback, and joined by the students, girls and boys, from our seminary and other schools, marched through our streets . . . Our citizens are out en masse—joy on every face—guns firing, cheer after cheer at every corner—all feeling the end of this terrible war is at hand."

A muster of Vermont militia companies was held in Brandon the summer of 1858. Some ten companies participated, many of which would make up the 1st Vermont Regiment. They used Park, Center, and Pearl streets for drilling.

SOURCES

BRANDON UNION, JUNE 4, 1886. VERMONT HISTORICAL SOCIETY.
GAY, LEON S., ED. *BRANDON VERMONT: A HISTORY OF THE TOWN DEDICATED TO ITS CITIZENS, 1761–1961.* BRANDON, VT: TOWN OF BRANDON, 1961.
RUTLAND HERALD, 1884 AND 1886. VERMONT STATE LIBRARY.
WITH THANKS TO KEVIN THORNTON.

CASTLETON

Leave Route 4 at the Castleton exit and turn right (west) on Castleton's Main Street, where troops bound for the Civil War drilled. The first residence on the left, a large brick structure, was the home of Erastus Higley. His granddaughter recalled that her parents had spoken of fugitives slaves sleeping on the floor, while food was prepared for them for continuing their journey.

Two military companies formed at Castleton. Captain James Hope, soldier and artist, brought together his Company B, 2nd Vermont here. Two years later, Company F, 14th Vermont, assembled and drilled here.

Continue on Main Street, and on the right is the Federated Church, once known as "the brick church." In early October 1862, a funeral was held here for Captain Selah Perkins, commander of the Vermont Cavalry's Company H. The *Rutland Herald*: "The sudden death of Captain Perkins has cast a gloom over our community . . . His funeral was largely attended by the people of this and adjoining towns." Perkins, son of the Castleton Medical College dean, was killed September 22, 1862, leading a charge with Addison Preston in the Shenandoah Valley. On July 9, 1863, the bells of this church joined all bells in the village in celebration of the Union victories at Vicksburg and Gettysburg.

Continue on Main Street to an old brick building on the right, now the Castleton town hall. During the Civil War, a bank and hat-maker's shop operated there. Just beyond is the Castleton library, with a modern school building behind it. The Civil War–era town hall stood on the site of the school. Though long gone, it's worth noting some of the wartime events that took place there:

December 12, 1861: A concert by the Middlebury College Quintet Club to benefit the Soldiers' Aid Society.

December 11, 1863: A lecture by the noted Civil War journalist Charles Carleton Coffin on the battles from First Bull Run to Gettysburg.

March, 1864: A tableau to benefit the Soldiers' Aid Society that included "the washer woman scene, representing two buxom Irish girls over the wash tub, their brogue talk, and their rubbing and wringing clothes."

June 25, 1864: A strawberry festival to raise money "for the soldiers" during which a twelve-year-old girl donated "her pet doll," which was sold for the benefit of the soldiers.

November 1864: According to the Herald, "Capt. Hope's painting of the Army of the Potomac will be on display at the Castleton Town Hall the rest of the week."

Just past the library, go left on Seminary Street to the campus of Castleton State College. On the left is Old Chapel, once the Castleton Medical College. Among its graduates were Dr. Samuel Allen, 4th Vermont surgeon, who became medical inspector of the 6th Corps; Dr. Willard Child, surgeon in both the 4th Vermont and 11th Vermont; Dr. Charles Kidder, 11th Vermont surgeon; Dr. John Crandall, a 13th Vermont surgeon; Dr. Lucretius Ross, the 14th Vermont surgeon; and Dr. Selah Perkins, commander of the Vermont Cavalry's Company H.

Castleton College was once Castleton Seminary, where, in November 1864, the students held a mock election. The results were 150 votes for Lincoln, 20 for McClellan, and 5 for a Miss Haskell, principal of the school. In front of the seminary's main building was a park, located in front of the present Woodruff Hall. The *Herald* reported on June 14, 1861: "S. D. Myers, a colored man from Liberia, gave a lecture . . . in Seminary Park, on the subject of emigration of the colored people of his country to Africa. He was for 11 years a slave in this country . . . At the conclusion of the address Mr. Gilbert, also a colored man, sang 'The Star Spangled Banner' and 'The Bereaved Slave Mother.'" According to the *Herald*, on April 22, 1865, six to eight hundred people gathered in Seminary Park and marched to the brick church for services memorializing Abraham Lincoln.

Return to Main and continue west, go left on South Street, and on the right, on a knoll, is the distinctive Victorian home and studio of James Hope, 2nd Vermont captain. His paintings of Antietam, based on sketches he made during the battle, are displayed in the visitors center at Antietam National Battlefield. After the war, Hope became an accomplished landscape painter, much admired by, among others, Frederick Church.

Go past the Hope house for 0.75 mile, and the white frame house on the right, much added to, was the home of Lieutenant George French, 11th Vermont. Wounded at Cedar Creek, he recovered to serve until April 2, 1865, when he was killed in the Breakthrough at Petersburg.

Beyond the French house, go through the underpass, and at the top of the rise on the right is the 1840 Meadow Brook

School, attended by French and eighteen other Castleton boys who served.

SOURCES

CASTLETON TOWN RECORDS.

FRENCH, GEORGE OSCAR. CIVIL WAR LETTERS. VERMONT HISTORICAL SOCIETY.

RUTLAND HERALD, 1861–1865. VERMONT STATE LIBRARY.

WITH THANKS TO JOE DORAN.

··

CHITTENDEN

In the mountain town of Chittenden, the roads join in the village by the Civil War memorial. A stone soldier with a rifle-musket looks south, and he seems to be deep in remembrance, focused somewhere a long way off toward the battlefields. Nobody knows who sculpted him, but there is no finer Civil War monument in Vermont. It honors the men of the local GAR post, the Azra P. Noyes Post, named for a Chittenden private in the Vermont Cavalry killed at Meadow Bridge, near Richmond, Virginia, on May 12, 1864. Listed on the monument are the names, and units, of the 86 men from Chittenden who served. At its dedication, October 22, 1912, John A. Mead, governor and Civil War veteran, spoke. Eva Stickney wrote a poem for the event, which concluded:

This sculpted form will proudly tell
To generations yet to be,
Of men who did their duty well
For the grand cause of liberty.

From the monument, take Holden Road west, and soon on the right is the Chittenden town hall. In the second-floor hall met the Noyes Post, founded in 1897, and the Noyes Post Women's Relief Corps (WRC), begun in 1907. The day of the monument dedication, the WRC provided a free dinner for the town, as it did each subsequent Memorial Day for many years. The town history indicates that the WRC was working, even after its founding, helping families who had lost men in the war and those with war victims still living. The town hall has a theater curtain painted by Charles Andrus that depicts an unidentified Civil War battle.

Continue on Holden Road, through intersections and zigs and zags, finally going right on Middle Road. In 1.5 miles, Bump Cemetery is on the right, and the first house beyond it, on the right, was the home of Velarous Bump. At twenty-five, he joined the 1st Vermont, came home, then reenlisted in the 7th Vermont in February 1862. Six months later, he died in Louisiana, of sickness. Buried in the Chalmette National Cemetery, a cenotaph in the Bump Cemetery honors him.

The first old house on the left, above the cemetery, was built by Columbus Churchill after the war. A private in the 10th Vermont, he survived wounds at Cold Harbor and Cedar Creek. Columbus was one of five Churchill brothers who served. A first cousin, Azem Churchill, a private in the 12th Vermont, died in winter encampment at Wolf Run Shoals, Virginia, at twenty.

Return to the Civil War monument and go left on Mountain Top Road. In the second house on the right, a large frame house with a long porch, Edwin Horton lived. A corporal in the 4th Vermont, he survived a wound at the Wilderness. Back in action, during the Siege of Petersburg he wrote home on January 5, 1865: "well, this part of the country is nothing but a burying ground there is thousands buried here without as much as a stick to mark the place."

Return to the monument, go straight across the bridge, and turn right. In 1.3 miles, a very large frame house, with a long, columned porch, is on the right. Once the Eddy family, world-famous spiritualists, lived here and held séances, often at a grotto near their home known as Honto's Cave. Francis Eddy joined the 5th Vermont as a sergeant in the fall of 1861 but was discharged three months later due to illness. In 2011, some Chittenden residents recalled the Eddy family and how they could make a walking stick dance across a floor.

SOURCES
CHITTENDEN TOWN RECORDS.
CHITTENDEN, VERMONT: A TOWN HISTORY. CHITTENDEN, VT: CHITTENDEN HISTORICAL SOCIETY, 2008.
WITH THANKS TO KAREN WEBSTER.

CLARENDON

From West Rutland, take Route 133 south 2 miles to Clarendon Springs Road. In just under 1 mile, enter Clarendon Springs and confront a scene that might have been from the antebellum South. The Clarendon Springs House, with great verandahs overlooking a lawn and a small pond shaded by immense trees, could well be a southern plantation house. Built in 1834, as the Clarendon history notes, "Soon after the turn of the century, the invention of the cotton gin gave a magic shot in the arm to the raising of cotton in the Southern states. The plantations tripled production and the slave trade boomed . . . Plantation owners with their new-found wealth began to look for ways to spend it pleasantly . . . These people were, for the most part, not ill, just in search of pleasure. The waters at Saratoga, high in sulphur and with its unpleasant odor, drove people to seek other cool pleasant places to spend those hot humid summers."

To Clarendon Springs they came, as many as five hundred at a time. The Clarendon history continued, "Of the Southern clientele a few dowager ladies, an occasional woman with a few children, a smattering of dashing young men, who rode well, played cards and danced well . . . But by far the largest percentage were charming, affected young women with a trunk full of beautiful clothes and, as far as the natives could see, a head full of butterflies, giggles, incomprehensible chatter and nonsense. They might have a maiden aunt in tow and always a mammy or maid to supervise everything." Those maids and mammys were, of course, slaves. The gaiety and ambiance of it all didn't fool all the locals. The man who operated the store in the stone building that fronts on the inn lawn, Orville Barlow, was an anti-slavery activist. Indeed, the Clarendon history states that "As a station on the 'Underground Railway' the Springs occasionally saw one of the runaway slaves, frightened, scrawny, scarred by whippings or dogs, uncommunicative and pathetic examples of what slavery was supposed to be."

Again the Clarendon history: "The Clarendon Springs House was, in 1861, busily preparing for the usual June opening when suddenly on April 12, Fort Sumter was fired upon and a nation was at war. The hundreds of guests never bothered to cancel their reservations. No one came."

But the place does not seem to have totally shut down. The *Rutland Herald* reported on "religious services" held at the hotel the afternoon of August 6, 1863, a Thursday, in response to a proclamation issued by Abraham Lincoln, giving thanks for the victories at Gettysburg and Vicksburg. "The weather was beautiful," the *Herald* said, "and the services were held beneath the ample shade of the trees in front of the veranda, which was occupied by ladies."

A flag raising had been held at the hotel soon after the war began, in mid-June 1861, with the *Herald* reporting that "hundreds of people came from all directions."

Across Route 133 from the hotel is narrow Peters Lane and, set back well along it on the right, behind trees, is a story-and-a-half brick house. Once the Congdon home, the family in 1862 took in young nephew Bradford Congdon, whose parents had died. Bradford shared a room with an older cousin, Martin Congdon, who had been present at John Brown's execution. Young Bradford kept a diary, and he wrote of a rather happy boy's life in the little village, seldom mentioning the war. One exception concerned a day at the Clarendon Springs School, which still stands. From Peters Lane, go south on Walker Mountain Road, and the brick house soon on the right, set back from the road, was the schoolhouse. Bradford wrote on March 1, 1863, "We had quite a number of visitors among whom was David Quinsy. He was a member of the 7th Re'gt Ver't Vol that were sent to New Orleans and had their colors taken away from them on account of Cowardice at the battle of Baton Rouge." David Quincy, a private in the 7th Vermont from Clarendon, had been discharged the previous October for disability, after having fought at Baton Rouge. General Philip Sheridan later restored the 7th's flag and honor.

From the old school, continue south 2 miles and, on entering Chippenhook, turn left on Firehouse Lane to the Chippenhook Cemetery. A prominent obelisk marks the grave of Theophilus Harrington, a farmer who came to Chippenhook from Rhode Island in 1786 and became Vermont House Speaker and supreme court justice. But Harrington is best known for a decision rendered as judge of the Rutland County Court. Years before the Civil War, a man came before the court requesting a warrant that would allow him to extradite an escaped slave to the South. Inquiring of Judge Harrington as to what evidence would be adequate to establish title, the reply was, "A bill of sale, sir, from God Almighty."

Continue past the cemetery to the Chippenhook School at the corner of Quarterline Road. Judge Harrington's funeral was held in a church that stood on the school's site, and the procession that bore his body to the grave passed along this road.

Go left on Quarterline Road 1.5 miles to a frame house on the left with a small distinct window above the front door, once the Sherman home. Three Sherman sons served in C Company, 11th Vermont: Miron, a corporal, Edwin, a sergeant, and Merritt, a sergeant and lieutenant. Edwin at nineteen was wounded at Winchester. Miron served eighteen months and came home sick at Christmastime 1864. He died four months later. Merritt was killed at Weldon Railroad.

Return on Quarterline Road to its end at Walker Mountain Road and go left, east. In 2.25 miles, turn right on Middle Road, and Clarendon's Brick Church is soon on the left. On a Sunday afternoon in September 1864, a funeral was held here for Lieutenant Gilbert Steward, Vermont Cavalry, killed June 28, 1864, at Stony Creek, Virginia.

Pass the church and soon on the right is a large greenlike area with an old house, once a tavern, facing its southern side. On May 31, 1861, the *Rutland Herald* reported on a flag raising here: "The people met at 2 o'clock, after which the procession formed in front of the old brick Tavern. Speeches were heard, a glee club sang, a band played, with it all concluding with "three cheers for the Union and President Lincoln."

Continue on Middle Road, soon cross Route 4, and bear right on narrow Gorge Road. In 1.4 miles, on entering East Clarendon, turn right on East Road and cross the 1836 covered bridge. In 1 mile, see a large farmhouse on the right, with a long curving porch; Thomas Steward saw his son, Gilbert, go to war from this, the family home.

SOURCES

CLARENDON TOWN RECORDS.

CLARENDON, VERMONT 1761–1971. RUTLAND, VT: ACADEMY BOOKS, 1971.

RUTLAND HERALD, 1861–1863. VERMONT STATE LIBRARY.

WITH THANKS TO CAROLINE BRADLEY, JOYCE PEDRONE, AND FRANCES WILSON.

DANBY

South of South Wallingford and north of East Dorset, along Route 7, turn west on Mount Tabor Road and enter the village of Danby. The Civil War monument on the left was given by the family of Private John McIntyre, 1st Vermont Cavalry, captured in the futile charge ordered by Brigadier General Judson Kilpatrick after Pickett's Charge at Gettysburg. McIntyre died at Andersonville a year later, leaving a widow and two children.

The village was crowded with people on October 18, 1863, as the *Rutland Herald* reported: "The usually quiet peace of Danby was yesterday in a state of some excitement, owing to the arrival and burial of three of our brave defenders who fell at the battle of Gettysburg. The martyrs to the cause of liberty were Orderly Henry H. Vaughn Co. B. 14th Vt.; Elisha Swett, Orderly of Co. K, 14th Vt., and Private George S. Baker of Co. B [14th Vermont]. Orderly Vaughan said to Captain [John] Thompson [of Danby] as they were marching to battle, 'This is the last time we shall be permitted to march together.' He was instantly killed by a shell, part of the same shell exploding a caisson within ten feet of Co. B. Orderly Swett was wounded in the head, living three days after. Private Baker was killed by a sharpshooter. There were upwards of five hundred people to witness the solemnities, besides fifty of the deceased soldiers' comrades, who marched in military order, headed by Captain Thompson . . . The Rev. H. H. Smith preached a most eloquent sermon, taking his text from the 33d chapter of Exodus."

Just beyond the Civil War Monument, turn left on Main Street, and the 1838 Union Meeting House is just ahead, on a knoll. Reverend Smith was a pastor of that church in 1863, which was then shared with Baptists and Quakers, thus it is believed that the services held for the three soldiers took place here. The three had been buried on the battlefield at Gettysburg, but in October, a group of Danby people are said to have gone to Gettysburg, disinterred the remains, and brought them home.

From the church, the bodies were taken to Danby cemeteries for burial, probably in a procession. Two of the bodies went to the Scottsville Cemetery, north of the village. The route of the procession would have been from the church north along Main Street 1.5 miles to what is now Route 7. The cemetery is 0.75 mile ahead on the left. The graves of Privates Vaughan and Baker are near the south end, well up the hill. The Danby town history notes that Vaughan was "kind hearted, patriotic and brave" and that his

remains were laid beside those of his father. It says of Baker that "he was a good soldier; highly esteemed by his comrades, and was the pride and hope of his patriotic parents." The artillery shell that killed Vaughan and Swett blew up an ammunition wagon, causing 2nd Vermont Brigade commander George Stannard to seek, and receive, permission to move his command to a low area forward of the main Union line on Cemetery Ridge. The brigade was thus in a perfect position to launch its attack on the southern flank of Pickett's Charge.

The 14th Vermont was commanded by Colonel William Nichols, a Danby native, who grew up on the Nichols homestead, which occupied land south and east of the Scottsville Cemetery. All the Nichols houses appear to be gone. Many Nicholses, relatives of the colonel, are buried in the cemetery. Nichols, before the war, was a Rutland lawyer who had served as Rutland County state's attorney and then was elected to the legislature. After the war, in the autumn of 1865, he and a brother boarded the steamship *Republic* at New York City and set sail for New Orleans, in search of their fortunes. But the ship *Republic* sank in a gale off the Georgia coast. Both men survived.

At Gettysburg, when Pickett's Charge came on in the afternoon of July 3, the 14th remained in its advanced position. As Nichols ordered it to fire, the southern portion of the Confederate mass turned abruptly northward, bringing it across the Vermonters' front. All three regiments of the 2nd Brigade fired into their exposed foes. When the 13th and 16th Vermont swung to the front to hit Pickett's right flank, the 14th stayed in place. Soon after the main attack was defeated, the 14th faced a supporting attack, which was smashed by a flank attack by the 16th Vermont.

The Danby history states, "Out of the one hundred and three men, which Danby furnished for the war, nearly thirty laid down their lives to preserve to us our nationality—our government—our country—and the flag of our country."

SOURCES
DANBY TOWN RECORDS.
RUTLAND HERALD, 1863. VERMONT STATE
    LIBRARY.

FAIR HAVEN

Depart Route 4 at exit 3, not far east of the New York border, and go south on Route 4A, which becomes Fair Haven's North Main Street. Look along the right side for 130 North Main, once the home of John Williams, a Welsh lad who served with many Fair Haven men in the 14th Vermont. Williams was a member of a family drawn from Wales by the slate industry, which began to flourish in this area about two decades before the Civil War. He kept a diary throughout his nine months of service, written in Welsh. He wrote home regularly, several letters going to his pastor, a Reverend Herbert, who lived next door at 132 North Main.

Williams served in Company F of the 14th, commanded by his friend and neighbor, Lieutenant Julius Bosworth, who was severely wounded at Gettysburg.

More Fairhaven men served in the 14th than in any other Civil War regiment. Williams, after returning home, helped care for Bosworth. Williams wrote the night of July 3, 1863, after his regiment had helped repel Pickett's Charge and a follow-up attack, "We killed many, took colors and captured hundreds of prisoners. Lieut Bosworth was badly wounded. Merling [Private George Merling, of Poultney] was killed. Lieut Hamilton [William Hamilton, a New York man who enlisted in Fair Haven] mortally wounded and many others killed and wounded. It was a fierce battle. In the evening we were released from the front and came to the rear to sleep. It was a great victory."

Proceed along Main Street to the large tree-shaded park, pass through the business district, and down the hill, soon turning left on River Street. Turn right on Depot Street, and go to the old Fair Haven railroad station, which stood during the Civil War. Well after the war, a large crowd gathered here to greet President Ulysses Grant, but his plans changed, and the people got only a fleeting glimpse of the Civil War hero as the train never stopped. More importantly, on July 4, 1887, some four hundred veterans of the 14th Vermont arrived here by train. The occasion was a grand reunion of the 14th Vermont, and waiting at the station to greet the Gettysburg veterans was the Fair Haven GAR post, the Bosworth Post.

From the station, led by the Fairhaven Cornet Band, the old soldiers marched along Depot Street to Main Street and the park. The 14th Vermont's history states:

"The village had been made to put on a holiday appearance; nearly all the places of business, public buildings and principal residences were decorated with flags, evergreens, and bunting; and large flags were hung across the main streets. The large public park, of five acres or more, in the center of the village, had been selected as the place in which to hold the reunion. A grandstand had been erected in the east end of the park, near the band stand . . . decorated with flags and evergreens, and in the center of it, on a stand was a floral decoration prepared by Mrs. James Pottle, with the inscription '14TH VT. 1863–1884,' upon it. A large flag just to the south of the stand was an object of interest to many; it being the first flag that was raised over Fort McPherson, after the surrender of Natchez, Miss. . . . The west side of the park had been fitted up with tables capable of seating about 600 people . . . The day was a perfect one; there was a slight breeze throughout the day, so that the heat at no time was oppressive."

The park today looks much as it did in 1884. Its walkways converge like the hub of a wheel at the center, and the bandstand mentioned stood just east of the hub. The long tables were on the far, or west, side. The day produced a long list of speakers.

Captain W. C. Dunton, commander of the 14th's Company F said: "We meet . . . for the first time as a regiment, since we left the United States service in 1863 . . . As the rebel lines approached, the men upon the run, yelling like demons, and came within range of their muskets, these Vermonters quickly sprang to their feet and by several well-directed volleys, made the hitherto victorious rebel columns stagger and waver."

Major General Abner Doubleday, commander of the corps in which the 14th served at Gettysburg, in a letter read at the reunion, first praised the caliber of the Confederate soldiers who made up Pickett's Charge. Then he said: "It was against these veterans that the untried troops of Vermont were to measure their strength in the greatest battle of modern times; a battle upon which the fate of a nation depended. Thank God they did not falter in the great emergency . . . Civilization and progress owe a debt that can never be repaid to Stannard and his men at Gettysburg."

Regimental Chaplain William Smart said: "O, fallen comrades, heroes of the mighty epoch, may your memory be green while the mountains of your loved State remain, may your graves be strewn with the freshest flowers of spring, while spring shall return, or flowers bloom."

An incident at the reunion that caught the attention of many was the meeting, for the first time, of Captain William Munn, commander of the 14th's Company K, and a Mrs. Swett, a widow from Danby. Her son, Private Elisha Swett, was mortally wounded at Gettysburg and died in Munn's arms. Both mother and captain wept as they talked.

That night, by lantern light and a bonfire, a regimental campfire was held with more toasts and speeches. A glee club sang "Keep the Campfires Burning Bright."

At the park's south end stands a huge Civil War artillery piece, an 1864 Parrott rifle capable of firing a 100-pound shell, "ERECTED IN MEMORY OF OUR FALLEN COMRADES 1861–1865," according to an inscription. In the darkness of the night before July 4, 1907, some local lads loaded the big gun with dynamite and set it off. The result was the breaking of most windows around the green. Fair Haven spent that Fourth cleaning up the mess. The barrel was promptly and permanently plugged.

Fair Haven voters in 1860 voted funds to expand the brick village school to include a hall where town meetings could be held. It opened in 1861 with a program that included a reading of Abraham Lincoln's inaugural address. The May 10, 1861, *Rutland Herald* stated: "The flags are flying from many of the principle buildings in the village . . . A large meeting convened at the beat of the drum on the common in front of the meeting house on Saturday evening for the purpose of enrolling a company of volunteers when about 45 good fellows and true put their names to the paper . . . The multitude again assembled, pursuant to adjournment at the Town Hall, on Monday evening at 7 o'clock . . . After the roll call, a committee was appointed to procure arms for the company . . . The company immediately commenced drilling." The same paper reported on February 10, 1864: "The ladies of Fair Haven are doing a noble work for our brave volunteers, who are laboring and suffering on behalf of their country. Last Tuesday, under their auspices a festival was held at the Town Hall, Fair Haven . . . The contributions consisted in Tableau Vivants, of rare excellence, and amusing pantomime, and excellent vocal and instrumental music . . . The proceeds, amounting to one hundred dollars, are to be devoted to the purchase of materials to be made into hospital comforts."

The redbrick Fair Haven town office building, the Civil War–era town hall, stands at the park's north end. Meeting at the town hall, Fair Haven voters approved bounty payments that reached $800. The town's total war expenditures were calculated at $26,368.33. A tax of 200 cents on each grand list dollar was approved in 1865 to help defer that cost.

From the park, go south on Main Street, which here is Route 22A, pass by River Street, go up the hill and across the railroad tracks, and in 0.75 mile, go right on Cemetery Street. Cedar Grove Cemetery is soon on the left, with many Civil War stones, and near its center is a flagpole, standing in the GAR lot. Several soldiers are buried here beside a granite GAR monument.

Return back toward the park on 22A and note on the corner of Academy Street, on the left, a large brick house. Once the home of Zenas Ellis, the area behind was a drill field on which a barracks was located. The forty-five men raised in the war meeting at the town hall camped and drilled here and, according to the Fair Haven town history, went to war as part of a New York cavalry regiment, the Harris Light Cavalry, commanded early in the war by Judson Kilpatrick. In 1862, a company led by Captain James Hyde, of Castleton, camped here for a time. It became Company C of the 11th Vermont.

Return to the park on 22A and go north through the village, pass under Route 4, and in 0.25 mile see a house above the road on the right with a stone garage. Joel Hamilton, a 14th Vermont private who fought at Gettysburg, went to war from here. Continue north, and in just over 0.5 mile, on the left, is a large old frame building, once a hotel. Leman Wood fought with the 14th at Gettysburg, was wounded, and returned here to a long career as an innkeeper.

SOURCES

ADAMS, ANDREW N. *A HISTORY OF THE TOWN OF FAIR HAVEN, VERMONT.* FAIR HAVEN, VT: LEONARD & PHELPS, 1870.
BFAIR HAVEN TOWN RECORDS. COURTESY OF TOWN CLERK'S OFFICE.
PELADEAU, MARIUS B., COMPILER. *BURNISHED ROWS OF STEEL.* NEWPORT, VT: VERMONT CIVIL WAR ENTERPRISES, 2002.
RUTLAND HERALD, 1861. VERMONT STATE LIBRARY
WILLIAMS, JOHN. CIVIL WAR LETTERS. VERMONT HISTORICAL SOCIETY.
WITH THANKS TO PETER LARAMIE.

HUBBARDTON

Depart Route 4 at the Castleton exit and proceed north, along the East Hubbardton Road, following signs to Hubbardton Battlefield. Hubbardton is best known for the July 7, 1777, Revolutionary War battle, the only true battle ever fought on Vermont soil. Approaching the field, pass the Battle Abbey Church, turn left on St. John Road, right on Frog Hollow Road, then right into Hubbardton Cemetery. Some of the Hubbardton battle dead may lie here. Certainly, some of the civilians who lived in this tiny uplands community at the time of the battle are buried here. Also in this burying ground lie several of the forty-five Hubbardton men who served in the Civil War. A stone in the far corner marks the grave of Charles Root, a private in the 17th Vermont, who died of sickness in an Alexandria, Virginia, hospital on August 28, 1864, one of nine Hubbardton men who perished. The stone notes that he was an only son. Nearby is the stone of Stephen Allen, a 12th Vermont private, who lived until 1912.

Return to Battle Abbey and go left, soon pass the Hubbardton Battlefield visitors center, in the area where the last fighting in the 1777 battle took place. Continue 3 miles, as the road becomes Monument Hill Road, and note a one-room school set in the trees on the left. Some Civil War–era Hubbardton town meetings were held here. According to Hemenway's *Gazetteer:* "In Hubbardton, at a meeting held . . . in Aug. 1862, $2,800 were subscribed mostly in sums of $100 each, to be expended in filling up the quota of the town: 18 young men came promptly forward and enlisted in the service of their country, generally for nine months, each receiving a $100 bounty." Hubbardton records state that in December 1863 the town voted $500 bounties for seven volunteers. In August 1864, selectmen were authorized to pay bounties ranging from $600 to $900. The town's total war expenditure was $10,600.

Continue on Monument Hill Road 2.5 miles to Route 30, and look left to the Hubbardton Congregational Church. In the frame house across the road, Marcus Gibbs is believed to have lived for a time, a private for three years in the 2nd Vermont Artillery. He saw action at Port Hudson.

Go north on Route 30 and left on Hortonia Road. In 2 miles, a farmhouse on the right, with barn across the road, was the home of Ezekiel St. John, who served less than a year as a private in the Vermont Cavalry. Continue 0.4 mile to an old farmhouse on the right. It is believed that Sumner Jennings lived here, who paid commutation and did not serve. In 1.25 miles, entering Hortonia, the frame house with small front porch on the left was once the Crone family home. At least eight Hubbardton men fought at Gettysburg with the 14th Vermont, including Corporal Joseph Crone. James Crone, a private in the 5th Vermont, served the last four months of the war, at Petersburg.

Go past the Crone house to the intersection of Route 144, cross it, and, bearing slightly left, go uphill. The second house on the left, at the top of the hill, was the home of Edward Bird, a 5th Vermont private during the war's last ten months. Return to 144 and go right. The first house on the right, a large frame house, was once the Gibbs family home. James Gibbs joined the 5th Vermont at eighteen and served three years as a private. Samuel Gibbs, also eighteen, a private in the 2nd Vermont Artillery, served just six months before being discharged for disability. Edward Gibbs, a 9th Vermont private, deserted in January 1863, but he returned to duty until the war's end and won a sergeant's stripes.

Route 144 goes west to Route 22A, or east to Route 30.

SOURCES
HUBBARDTON TOWN RECORDS.
SONDERGELD, DONALD R. *HISTORY OF HUBBARDTON, VERMONT.* COLLIERVILLE, TN: INSTANT PUBLISHER, 2005.
WITH THANKS TO ROBERT GIBBS, CARL FULLER, AND HOLLY HITCHCOCK.

IRA

A group of pre–Civil War buildings stands along Route 131 in Ira. Close beside the road is the distinctive redbrick Ira town hall, built around 1800. Just to the south is the 1852 Ira Baptist Church, behind which is the old District Two School. The town war memorial, unveiled in 1922, in front of the church, is dedicated to those who "sought not glory but their country's good" and lists forty-one Ira men who served in the Civil War.

According to S. L. Peck, Ira's town clerk for more than forty years, a giant Stars and Stripes once waved from a tall flagpole in front of the town hall, which proclaimed the town's allegiance to the party of Abraham Lincoln. Peck wrote, "In 1864 or thereabouts, the Republican County Committee of Rutland County offered a large flag as a premium to the town that should cast the lightest Democratic vote at the coming September election. After the contest as the polls closed, and the votes were counted, it was found that not a single Democrat vote had been cast in Ira, and accordingly the flag belonged to Ira. The flag was brought to town on a day designated by the committee, and duly presented to the citizens in a ringing patriotic address by Col. C. H. Joyce of Rutland. The response and acceptance on the part of the town was accepted by S. L. Peck." Joyce had served briefly as second in command of the 2nd Vermont early in the war.

Apparently another flag waved over Ira for some time before the event mentioned by Peck. The *Rutland Herald* said of an event here on May 18, 1861: "On Saturday afternoon . . . the ladies of Ira erected a flag at the Meeting House. The flag was gotten up by the ladies, and is some sixteen feet in length, nicely suspended from a pole sixty-five feet high to the church. It was flung to the breeze amid the stains of martial music and enthusiastic cheers." After a church service, everyone again gathered round the flag and "gave three cheers for the *Stars and Stripes,* each thus expressing his patriotic devotion to the Union, and love of liberty."

Ira voters gathered in the town hall in December 1862 and voted to raise money through an unspecified tax on the grand list to pay the amount of money the selectmen "have paid and have agreed to pay to the soldiers that have been mustered into the Unites States service and credited to the said Town of Ira and to pay the expenses for raising said men." That faith in the judgment and honesty of the town officials continued through the war, as in December 1864 voters authorize selectmen "to borrow money or whatever course they will take to pay the bounties."

Meeting in early 1865, voters approved two $100 payments, one to the widow of Henry Peters, a private in the 7th Vermont who died on July 31, 1865, of disease. The other went to Levi Plumley, also a private in the 7th, who enlisted in December 1862 and again in September 1864. The payment rewarded his reenlistment. Plumley soon deserted, but returned voluntarily and served until the regiment disbanded in 1866.

From the town hall, go north on Route 131, and in a 1.5 miles, see Pyka Road on the left. From their family home still standing at the road's end, in September 1861, came brothers Harrison and Charles Peck, bound for the Rutland fairgrounds and a sharpshooter tryout. Years later, Harrison recalled: "In the morning of the day set for the test, two boys, brothers, go down from the hills with a horse and buggy, and, after hitching their horse under the Meeting House shed in the village with their rifles saunter down to the fair grounds, where they find a large crowd of people who have assembled to witness the shooting which was under the control of Wm. Y. W. Ripley, who afterwards became lieutenant colonel of the regiment . . . When the targets were in place and the distance measured, the elder of the boys stepped to the line and, carefully loading his rifle, commenced firing. The first shot was a little wild, but inside the ring; so were all the ten consecutive shots, many of them being almost in the center of the target. The younger of the boys then walked to the line and, although somewhat nervous at first, he succeeded in placing ten bullets within the ring. As each shot was fired and the target master placed a black patch over the bullet hole, a cheer went up from the crowd, which encouraged the boys in their efforts." Both Pecks qualified and became corporals in Company F, 1st U.S. Sharpshooters. Charles served little more than a year, wounded early in the Peninsula Campaign. Harrison came home in the late summer of 1862 after being shot at Second Bull Run.

SOURCES

Charles, Sheila. *The History and Archaeology of the Ira Town Hall Site.* Montpelier, VT: State of Vermont Division for Historic Preservation, 1990.

Ira town records.

Peck, S. L. *History of Ira, Vermont.* Rutland, VT: Charles E. Tuttle, 1970.

Rutland Herald, 1861. Vermont State Library.

With thanks to Alta Johnston.

....

KILLINGTON

Known as Sherburne at the time of the war, the little village of Killington in this mountainous town is located beside Route 4, as it begins its ascent to Sherburne Pass from the east. Turn right on River Road at the church, which stood during the war, and note the large frame building on the left with two entrances, once the Union Store. Lacking a town hall in the 1860s, town meetings were held in several locations, including here. Meeting here on November 28, 1863, Sherburne voted to "pay each volunteer two hundred dollars" and to raise 125 cents on each grand list dollar. By January 1865, a tax of 200 cents on the dollar was voted to fund bounty payments

with the provision that those paying the tax by June 1 "be entitled to three percent discount." One history of Sherburne says the town spent $13,500 in bounties and that 70 men went to war from a population of about 525. All the town's quotas were met.

Continue on River Road to Riverside Cemetery, where several Sherburne soldiers lie, and 0.3 mile beyond, on the right, is the very large old house built by Daniel Taylor. He served Sherburne in the legislature, held every important town office, and during the war advanced $780 to Sherburne so it could avoid a draft. At least one bee was held here to make quilts for the soldiers.

Continuing on River Road 2 miles, and Wolf Hill Road goes right. This narrow and very steep road ends 0.75 mile at a farmhouse that was once the home of Ezekiel West, a private in the 8th Vermont the last six months of the war. A Sherburne history states that West "sold his war services to someone who had been drafted and didn't want to go. When he returned he used the $500 to buy the upper farm of 180 acres, later 300 more. It was very steep and rocky, but suitable for raising sheep."

Continue on River Road, and quickly come to an old schoolhouse on the left, where in 1864, eighteen-year-old Susan Adelia Colton was a student. Just beyond the school, Steinway Road turns right, and Colton lived in the only house on it. In 1864, she kept a diary, and a few entries mention the war:

January 16: "School is half out. Heard of Albert's death, very unexpected. He died yesterday. [Albert Hastings, a private in the 11th Vermont, died of sickness.]"

January 22: "Went to Albert's funeral. Mr. Wild preached a good sermon the text was in Mark 13: 31–37. [Heaven and Earth shall pass away, but my words shall not pass away.]"

February 27: "Have been to school . . . I pieced up a bed quilt block for the soldiers this evening."

March 23: "Went to Mr. Taylor's to a quilting (soldier's quilting). There were 13 ladies and gentlemen."

Continue on River Road to Route 100 and turn right, north. In 0.25 mile, note Doubleday Hill on the right. William O. Doubleday and his wife, Asceneth, lived on a mountainside farm up this road. In the fall of 1862, William came down to join the 14th Vermont's Company H, at Rutland. Just beyond Doubleday Hill, turn left on Coffee House Road. The long building just ahead, now a hostelry, has long been known as the Coffee House, and since before the Civil War was a tavern and stagecoach stop. William Doubleday boarded a coach here that took him to Rutland. No doubt Asceneth and their four sons were here to see him off. Soon, Asceneth left the farm and took her sons to Sharon to live with some of William's relatives until his enlistment expired.

William wrote home frequently during his nine months of service. In November 1862, from northern Virginia: "You said you was not agoing to have any Thanksgiving, but would have it when I come home. So we will, asceneth, let it be what time of the year it will . . . I don't want you to think I am homesick but I can't help think-ing of you & the rest of the folks & of you pretty often." William had a dark premonition, he mentioned in a letter written June 24, 1863, speaking of a dream in which Asceneth had taken another husband. He added, "Kiss the boys for me, from Willie down to little Fred."

On July 3, as Pickett's Charge advanced, the newly promoted Corporal Doubleday was wounded in a leg. Left in a field hospital at Gettysburg when the rest of the 2nd Brigade returned home, he seemed to be improving. Then he took a turn for the worse, and an uncle named Avery hastened to Gettysburg. Finally, doctors amputated the lower third of William's mangled limb and administered "stimulants and injections" in a desperate attempt to save his life. Doubleday died on August 12. His last letter told Asceneth to "kiss the boys for me." He is buried in the Gettysburg National Cemetery.

Return to Route 100, go right, 2.5 miles to Route 4, and turn east. In 0.3 mile, go left on Thundering Brook Road, cross Kent Pond dam, to the first house on the left, set back from the road. Daniel Hadley lived here, a 3rd Vermont private, who served from 1861 to war's end and survived a brief imprisonment. His brother, John, served with William Doubleday in the 14th Vermont.

Return to Route 4, continue east, and go right on West Hill Road, which leads into Killington Basin. Now the site of a massive ski development, at the time of the war, it held a small community with a school and several sawmills. In 0.5 mile, reach the Killington access road. Though it might seem impossible to find a remnant of long ago, go left on this busy road, and in 1.2 miles, on the left, is a large restaurant with an office building just beyond that was clearly once a schoolhouse. The Russell family lived in a house located about where the restaurant stands, and Haskell Russell attended the school. In November 1863, he went to West Lebanon, New Hamphsire, and enlisted in the 1st New Hampshire Cavalry. The unit was soon sent to Louisiana, but Russell came home on furlough in July 1864. Back in the South, he became ill with typhoid fever and chronic diarrhea, dying on December 2, 1864, at age twenty. His gravestone in Riverside Cemetery says he died in New Orleans. With the help of Daniel Taylor, the poor Russell family was able to secure a pension.

SOURCES

COTTON, SUSAN ADELIA. DIARY, 1864. SHERBURNE MEMORIAL LIBRARY.
DOUBLEDAY, WILLIAM O. CIVIL WAR LETTERS AND MEDICAL RECORDS. COURTESY OF "DOC" DOUBLEDAY, HARTLAND.
FLEMING, MADELINE C. AN INFORMAL HISTORY OF THE TOWN OF SHERBURNE. RUTLAND, VT: S.N., 1941. SHERBURNE MEMORIAL LIBRARY.
LIST OF HISTORIC BUILDINGS IN SHERBURNE. SHERBURNE MEMORIAL LIBRARY.
SHERBURNE TOWN RECORDS.
WITH THANKS TO MAUDEAN NEILL FOR INFORMATION ON THE HASKELL FAMILY, INCLUDING MILITARY AND PENSION RECORDS.

MENDON

East of Rutland along Route 4, in the village of Mendon, the 1860 Mendon meetinghouse is on the south side of Route 4. The *Rutland Herald* of May 15, 1861, reported on a war meeting here: "The people of Mendon village had a flag-raising on Saturday afternoon. The flag, which we learn was some fifteen feet in length, was given to the breeze amid cheering and other appropriate and patriotic demonstrations by the large gathering of people present. After which some stirring speeches were delivered by citizens of the place eliciting the hearty and loud applause of the assemblage. In the evening, among other things, a procession was formed and marched through the streets, with music, cheering at different dwelling-houses, and receiving cheers there from, in return, all conspiring to make a lively and good time. The gathering broke up at about 10 o'clock."

Across the road from the meetinghouse, Meadowlake Lane leaves Route 4. Take it, quickly cross Mendon Brook, and go uphill to a small schoolhouse, now a residence, below the road on the left. Mendon held several wartime town meetings in this District Seven School. Voters in mid-1864 approved bounties up to $800 and by early 1865 had authorized the selectmen to borrow money to pay whatever amounts were necessary to secure recruits. By war's end, Mendon spent $13,000 on bounties, sending 94 men to war and meeting all quotas. Of those serving, 63 were farmers, 21 lumbermen, 3 mechanics, 2 sawyers, 1 livery worker, and 1 store and post office proprietor. Their ages ranged from nineteen to forty-four.

Among them was Marquis Tenney, a farmer's son, who had attended this District Seven School. He joined the 2nd Vermont as a private in September 1861 and was wounded at Second Fredericksburg May 3, 1863. Promoted to sergeant in late 1864, he won a lieutenant's commission as the war ended.

Past the school 0.1 mile is the house from which Tenney went to war, a large farmhouse on the right facing a small field across the road. Just beyond is Tenney Cemetery, in which Marquis and his wife, Hannah (Wedson) Tenney, are buried. He died in 1926, and she in 1930. Markers by their stones indicate that she belonged to the Women's Relief Corps, and he to the GAR.

Return to Route 4 and go right, into the large parking lot on the right. At the rear of the lot, on a large boulder, is inscribed:

The Grave of
Gen. Edw. H. Ripley's
OLD JOHN
Of the great
Civil War
1861 to 1865

Brigadier General Edward Hastings Ripley rode Old John when he led the 24th Corps brigade he commanded into Richmond, Virginia, on April 3, 1864—the first Union troops to enter the Confederate capital. Within the brigade was the 9th Vermont, a regiment Ripley had long led. Ripley wrote, "Densely packed on either side of the street were thousands upon thousands of blacks, till that moment slaves, down upon their knees, throwing their hands wildly in the air, while floods of tears filed down their wild faces, and shouting 'Glory to God! Glory

to God! the day of Jubilee has come.'" Reaching the Virginia state house, the Confederate capitol, Ripley dismounted from Old John and ascended its steps. There Major General Godfrey Weitzel put Ripley in command. Ripley promptly ordered his troops to extinguish the fires raging in the city and stop looting. He also dispatched soldiers to Libby Prison, where seven thousand Union soldiers were liberated.

After coming home to Rutland, Ripley returned to the family marble business. But he soon was involved in banking, opened a hotel in New York City, and founded a railroad and a steamship line. Ripley married in 1878 and that year he founded an estate here in Mendon. On Memorial Days, late in life, General Ripley drove a buggy down to Rutland for the Memorial Day parade, with his long gray hair streaming out from under his old Civil War hat as he clopped down the mountain. He lived until 1915, leading a parade on horseback at his alma mater, Union College in Albany, New York, three weeks before he died.

The main Ripley house stood where the parking lot now is. The red wooden building to the lot's rear dates to the heyday of the Ripleys in Mendon, once part of their carriage shed. Across Route 4 are two frame houses about the same size. The westernmost was the home of General Ripley's daughter, Alice Ripley Jones, built for her by her father.

From the Ripley site, go 2 miles west on Route 4, left on Town Line Road, and in 2.3 miles go right on South Mendon Road. In 0.25 mile on the right is an athletic field, long a public space. Here, according to the *Rutland Herald,* soon after Fort Sumter surrendered, "The citizens of South Mendon and vicinity, met in large numbers yesterday afternoon, for the purpose of raising the Stars and Stripes. The ladies had the honor of running up the flag, and as it floated out on the breeze, it was greeted by round after round of enthusiastic cheers, and a cannon which had been procured for the occasion opened its iron throat in deafening notes. Speeches were made by a number of gentlemen, which were well received; and an excellent glee club favored the audience with several patriotic songs."

SOURCES
The History of Mendon, Vermont.
    Mendon, VT: Town of Mendon, 1976.
    Courtesy Mendon town offices.
Mendon town records.
Ripley, Edward Hastings. *Vermont
    General.* New York: Devin-Adair, 1960.
Rutland Herald, 1861. Vermont State
    Library
With thanks to George Bradley, Ann
    Singiser, S. Kendall Wild, and
    Gretchen Sharp.

....

MIDDLETOWN SPRINGS

Go east from Wallingford on Route 140 to where Route 133 goes south, by the Middletown Springs green. In the green's center is the town Civil War monument, a zinc statue of a soldier mounted on a Barre granite pedestal with a plaque bearing the names of sixty-eight Middletown Springs men. The soldier, and two cannons beside him,

face south toward the old war zone. Dedicated on Memorial Day 1904, the monument was a gift of Edwin Hoadley, a former private in the 10th Vermont's C Company, who was wounded at Cedar Creek. Ceremonies included a recitation of the Gettysburg Address.

A local woman recalled of the war's beginnings: "While there were as yet only rumors and fears the Middletown Springs boys had formed themselves into a company of soldiers. They called themselves 'The Wide Awakes'; sent away for uniforms, (consisting of long shiny black capes and caps) also wooden guns. They secured a retired army officer for Drill Master and began to learn Militarism. When war was declared and regiments formed, 'The Wide Awakes' boys became valuable members. Mrs. [Helen] Buxton's younger son, Edwin Rublin, the only one left at home—was busily shingling a barn which 'must be finished before haying.' A recruiting officer from Rutland called to see him and before the barn was finished, before the officer left, Edwin Rublin Buxton was an enlisted private in Company C, 10th Vermont Regiment." The Wide Awakes drilled on the green, and twenty-four members joined the 10th's C Company.

The Middletown Community Church, facing the green, was, in the 1860s, a Congregational church. According to the December 3, 1863, *Rutland Herald,* "An enthusiastic war meeting was held in the Congregational Church in Middletown on Monday evening last. An address was delivered by Henry Clark, Esq., of Poultney." (A frequent speaker at war meetings,

Clark was secretary of the Vermont senate and editor of the *Rutland Herald*.) In early October 1862, a funeral was held here for Charles Dayton, once of the Wide Awakes and a private in the 10th Vermont, who died of sickness on September 26. It was Middletown Springs' first soldier funeral, and a local woman recalled, "His mother planned the funeral. The church was filled to overflowing with mourning relatives and friends. Six young ladies were selected by his mother for special bearers . . . All were his schoolmates. They wore . . . black silk dresses, with crepe shawls and flowers in their hair . . . Later on soldiers' funerals became too frequent and too tragic to be spectacular."

The town garage, facing the green's west side, was once a Baptist church. Aaron Haynes was minister during the war, and his son, Delet Haynes, was a private in the 12th Vermont.

Facing the southeast corner of the green, beside the modern store, is an old building that was once the Middletown Springs post office. Here, the truth about Benjamin Hall was discovered. Hall, a local lad, joined Company C of the 10th Vermont. But he deserted and promptly enlisted in the navy, under the name William Gray. He served a year, failed to report to his ship, and joined the 88th New York Infantry, using the name John Riley. In 1917, back in Middletown, he visited the post office to collect a pension check for John Riley, later returning for William Gray's check. The postmaster reported this to Washington, and inspectors were sent. Hall was soon deprived of his pensions. But the many-named soldier

appealed on the grounds that he had, indeed, served three years, and in 1921, a special act of Congress once again gave him a pension.

From the green, take North Street to the frame house, just north of the old Baptist Church, where Warren McClure lived, of Company C, who played coronet in the 10th Vermont band. Four houses beyond is the postwar home of Warren's brother, Charles, also a private in C Company. In the house just north lived William Grover, one of four Middletown Springs men who served in the 2nd New York Cavalry. Grover died of sickness.

Continue on North Street, and soon go left on Spruce Knob Road. From the first house on the right, Royal Coleman enlisted in the 9th Vermont in July of 1862. He died of sickness in October 1863.

Continue on Spruce Knob Road until it ends at a farm in the shadow of Spruce Knob. Reuben Spaulding lived in the old house here, which looks as it did in the 1860s. He was one of seven men from this town who served in the 14th Vermont, fighting at Gettysburg.

Return to the green, go south on Route 133, and the second building on the left, erected in 1781, is the current Middletown Springs post office. From the house close beside it, William Hoadley went to war with C Company. (He was the brother of Edwin Hoadley who donated the Civil War monument.) Before enlisting, Hoadley was employed in the local A. W. Gray's factory, which made horse-powered treadmills. Hoadley, on October 10, 1862, wrote to his former boss, A. W. Gray, "We are very sad since we witnessed

Charley's [Dayton's] death . . . I was detached to go to Georgetown with his corpse and got it embalmed and sent it home and it cost $65 to send him home and the Company paid it."

The house across the street, with a porch across its front, was the Congregational church parsonage and home of Reverend Calvin Granger. Henry Clark wrote in the *Rutland Herald,* November 24, 1864, that Reverend Granger addressed the ladies of the local Soldiers' Aid Society, "cheered hearts with soul-stirring music," and volunteered to head its bounty donation effort. Two of Granger's sons served as privates, Charles in the 12th Vermont and James in the 11th. Both returned safely.

Continue south on Route 133, cross the bridge, and a historic marker denotes the A. W. Gray factory site. To his home across the street, with the wide front porch, in the summer of 1864 came Private Horace Green, of the 2nd New York Cavalry, with a severe wound suffered in fighting along the Danville Railroad near Petersburg. He died here on June 29.

Continue south on 133, and in 0.3 mile, take Buxton Avenue. Soon on the left is a long frame house with a very large barn just beyond. The house was once a barn, which, it is believed, Edwin Buxton was shingling when the Rutland recruiter showed up. Buxton, a sergeant, survived wounds at Cold Harbor and Cedar Creek.

SOURCES

FRISBIE, BARNES. *THE HISTORY OF MIDDLETOWN, VERMONT.* BICENTENNIAL EDITION. MIDDLETOWN, VT: MIDDLETOWN SPRINGS HISTORICAL SOCIETY, 1975.
KIMBALL, CHARLOTTE EDMUNDS. *A MEMORIAL TO HELEN BUXTON HENDERSON.* 1931. COURTESY THE MIDDLETOWN SPRINGS HISTORICAL SOCIETY.
MIDDLETOWN TOWN RECORDS.
RUTLAND HERALD, 1863 AND 1864. VERMONT STATE LIBRARY.
WITH THANKS TO GRANT REYNOLDS, DAVID WRIGHT, AND JOHN MATHEWSON.

MOUNT HOLLY

At a special town meeting on September 23, 1862, Mount Holly voters "[R]esolved that while making ample provision for those who have gone or may go from among us to fight the Battles of our Country, and while we are ready cheerfully to endure every sacrifice that may now, or in the future be necessary, for the perpetual welfare of our Glorious Republic we at the same time deem it our Right and our duty to express our decided and earnest conviction, that every obligation of right, and every consideration of expediency, unites to demand, that the whole legitimate authority of the Government should be employed for the Complete Extinction of American Slavery, the great Cause of the trouble, and Sanguinary Struggle in which our Country is involved."

From Route 103, south of Cuttingsville, go south on Belmont Road 1.75 miles, and on the left, at the corner of Teer Road, as Star Lake comes in view, is a large frame house. From here, Henry Barrett enlisted as a 14th Vermont private and fought at Gettysburg. A year later, he joined the 4th Vermont and served until the war ended.

Proceed into Belmont village, known

as Mechanicville at the time of the war, and in 0.3 mile, a cemetery is on the right. Across the road is an open area with a low stone foundation, all that remains of the village school. In the early 1900s, the Decoration Day parade formed here, led by children bearing flowers and Myron Pettingill, once a drummer in a Massachusetts regiment.

Continue along Belmont Road with the procession, and on the right, in the fourth house beyond the cemetery, lived Charles Tarbell, a 7th Vermont private, who enlisted in February 1862 and died eight months later of sickness. He is buried in the Chalmette Cemetery near New Orleans.

Across the road at the near corner of Lake Street is the home of Phillips Chase, who joined the 2nd Vermont early in the war. He survived a wound at the Wilderness and came home to join his brother in operating a toy factory in Mechanicsville.

Just across Lake Street is the house where Benjamin Parmenter lived. A 2nd Vermont corporal, he deserted, returned, then was discharged for disability after eighteen months service. After the war, he was Mechanicville's only Democrat, and when Democrat Grover Cleveland was elected president, Parmenter was appointed village postmaster. The small post office he added to the rear of his house survives. When Republican Rutherford B. Hayes became president, Parmenter lost his job, but he got it back when Cleveland returned to office.

Continue past the village store and village green onto Maple Hill Road to Mechanicsville Cemetery, destination of the Decoration Day parades, where flowers were placed by graves and patriotic speeches made. Then everyone marched down the lane across the road to the home of Charles Priest. The Civil War veteran gave each child an orange and a banana.

Former drummer Myron Pettingill lived in the house just past the cemetery, on the left. Pass it, and at the top of the hill, on the left, fronted by maple trees, is the house where three Priest boys grew up. Charles Priest's father at first paid commutation to keep his youngest son at home. But in the summer of 1864, Charles joined his brother, Darius, as a private in the 2nd Vermont. Charles was wounded at Cedar Creek. Darius had been shot the previous May at Spotsylvania's Bloody Angle. Brother, Ethan Allen Priest, enlisted in the 2nd, when the war began. He was wounded three times, at Bull Run, at Golding's Farm on the Peninsula, and at Spotsylvania.

Return to the village center, go right on Healdville Road, and in 2 miles, on the left, is an old cape, much added to, and a small garage. Henry Fletcher, who lived here, joined the 7th Vermont as a private in July 1862. Captured at Newport Barracks in February 1864, he survived ten months in Andersonville to return home.

Continue on Healdville Road 1 mile, and turn right on Station Road, soon bearing right into the Healdville Station parking lot, by the railroad tracks.

The August 30, 1869, *Herald* reported on Ulysses Grant's passing through Mount Holly on a train taking him from Bellows Falls to Rutland. The paper noted that the president, from Ludlow to East Wallingford, sat with the engineer to best see "the rock cuts and the mountain scenery." Onlookers here would have seen the former general passing slowly by in the train's engine as it chugged up the long climb to Summit Station just ahead.

Mount Holly, with a wartime population of 1,522, saw 122 men go to war. Of them, 28 died, while 13 men paid commutation.

SOURCES

TARBELL, CARROLL R. *TARBELL'S MOUNT HOLLY: HISTORY OF A VERMONT TOWN.* MOUNT HOLLY, VT: PRIVATELY PRINTED, 1987.
"MAP AND GUIDE: HISTORIC DISTRICT, BELMONT, VERMONT." MOUNT HOLLY HISTORICAL SOCIETY, 2008.
RUTLAND HERALD, 1861 AND 1869. VERMONT STATE LIBRARY
WITH THANKS TO DENNIS DEVEREAUX.

MOUNT TABOR

From Route 7, with the village of Danby on the east, turn west on Mount Tabor Road into the hamlet of Mount Tabor. The town clerk's office is soon on the right, in a schoolhouse where Civil War town meetings took place. The *Rutland Herald* reported that townspeople voting here in 1860 "gave Mr. Lincoln 28 votes and none for any other man. In 1864 they gave 36 for Mr. Lincoln and none for the other man." The mountain town of Mount Tabor, with a wartime population of about 360, sent 30 men to Mr. Lincoln's armies. Like all towns, Mount Tabor wrestled with how to meet its quotas. On December 5, 1863, voters assembled at the schoolhouse to approve

bounties of $300, plus a per month payment of $7 to each enlistee. But on August 16, 1864, voters decided that "the selectmen are hereby empowered to hire volunteer soldiers to serve in the U.S.A. on such terms as said selectmen may judge to be for the best interest of the town and also to borrow money on the credit of the town to pay such volunteers who are enlisted."

From the town office, continue east on Mount Tabor Road and soon climb steeply into the Green Mountain National Forest, leaving houses, even camps, far behind. In just under 3 miles, pass the Long Trail parking lot, and in another 3.4 miles, cross a small bridge. Continue exactly 2.5 more miles, and see a rough road go left into the woods. Park here and walk some fifteen minutes along this stone wall–lined track, until coming to a small cemetery along a little woodland ridge. On seeing for the first time Harvard's memorial hall honoring her Civil War soldiers, the writer Henry James expressed amazement that the war reached "even here." What would he have said here, in the midst of this mountain forest, 2,000 feet up, looking upon two Civil War gravestones. One states that Leroy Britton was twenty-six when he died at Rockville, Maryland, on December 17, 1862. He was a private in the 10th Vermont and surely perished of disease. The other stone is for Joseph Buffum, a Vermont Cavalry private, thirty-two when he "fell in action at the Battle of Gettysburg July 3 1863." Buffum was shot in the cavalry charge ordered by Judson Kilpatrick. His body was brought home to this quiet mountain place.

Return through the village of Mount Tabor to Route 7, go south 2 miles, and turn left on a road that quickly crosses railroad tracks. Just beyond them is the little hillside Tabor Cemetery, with two soldier graves. Benjamin Stafford, a private in the 4th Vermont, died of disease at Camp Griffin on February 2, 1862. Calvin Billings joined the 11th Vermont in September 1862 and was discharged a month later, when it was discovered that he was a man of color. His stone, set beneath a giant maple, has been broken.

SOURCES
Mount Tabor town records.
Rutland Herald, 1860–1862. Vermont State Library.

PAWLET

In the Pawlet library, at the center of Pawlet village, where Routes 30 and 133 meet, a plaque lists 176 Pawlet men who served, with an additional 30 names of those enlisting in other towns and states. Since Pawlet's western border is the New York line, some local men joined New York units. In the basement of the Pawlet Congregational Church, just north of the intersection on Route 133, Civil War town meetings took place. On November 11, 1863, bounties of $300 were approved. A month later, the bounties were raised to $500. As filling quotas became more difficult, on August 3, 1864, a three-man committee was appointed to seek volunteers, and the amount of bounties paid was left to the selectmen's discretion. At March meeting

in 1865, a $100 payment was voted for the support of Clarisa Mosier, widow of Thomas Mosier, a private in the 7th Vermont. Mosier died of sickness in November 1862 in Louisiana. At the same meeting, Pawlet approved $100 payments "to any soldier widow who shall have one or more children" and directed that payments of $25 be made on February 1 for four consecutive years.

The Congregational Church apparently witnessed some disagreements over slavery. According to a town history written in 1867, church members Ozzias Clark and Paul Hulett were "steadfast old wheel-horses" of the antislavery cause. "On one occasion when we were present the trustees of the old Congregational church refused to open their doors for an anti-slavery lecture, and when Deacon Clark sent for the key it was refused. 'I can get that key' said he, and strode off down the road—and he got it.'"

The Pawlet Soldiers' Aid Society often met in the church. The October 6, 1864, Rutland Herald said that the society sent to the Troy, New York, branch of the Christian Commission "44 lbs. of dried apples; 17 lbs. dried currants; 36 lbs. dried blackberries; 11 bottles blackberry wine; 10 bottles highly spiced blackberry syrup; 33 towels, 6 pair slippers, 3 dressing gowns, 6 shirts, 18 pillows, 19 rolls bandages, and a quantity of other things including lint, newspapers, etc."

Take Route 30 north, cross a bridge, and immediately go right on Cemetery Road. The second building on the left is believed to have been the home of Henry and Betsy Bostwick, who in October

1861 saw their eighteen-year-old son, Noble, depart to join the 5th Vermont. He wrote his parents on January 22, 1863, describing the recent march of the Army of the Potomac ordered by Major General Ambrose Burnjside:

"I am well and if I want tough as a bare I couldn't stand what we have to endure we started from camp day before yesterday to cross the Rappahannock and we're about twelve miles from it. We would have been across yesterday but it commenced to rain night before last and has rained ever since. So that it is so muddy we cant move our pontoon bridges . . . we had to work all afternoon yesterday in the mud up to our knees at getting the pontoon bridges through . . . the wheels go in to the hubs and we didn't get through until abought 8 in the morning." That failed advance up the Rappahannock River came to be called the Mad March.

Bostwick was promoted to sergeant in December 1863. The next spring, at Spotsylvania's Bloody Angle, he was severely wounded and died three days later. His body came home to this house and is buried in the village cemetery, just up the road.

Return to Route 30, and go north 3.3 miles to North Pawlet and a small redbrick schoolhouse on the right. In front of this 1846 building is a stone with a historic marker noting that, in September 1777, 2,500 American troops under Benjamin Lincoln camped in Pawlet. Later that fall, an American ranger company under Ebenezer Allen was in this vicinity, and on November 28, Allen wrote a dispatch that has become a key part of Ver-

mont's freedom story. Allen and his men had returned from a scouting mission with two black slaves, Dinah Mattis and her two-year-old daughter, Nancy, who had been in British hands. Allen gave Mattis a letter stating that she and her daughter were to be henceforth free for "it is not right in the sight of God to keep Slaves." Allen stated that the two were to be free "to pass and repass any where through the United States of America" and "to Trade and Traffic for her self and child as though she was born free, without being molested by any Person or Persons."

Continue north 0.8 mile on Route 30 and go left on Route 153. In 1.5 miles, on the right, is another redbrick schoolhouse, the Braintree School. In 1830, Marcellus Jones was born in this area of Pawlet and may have attended, for a time, a school on this site. The son of a wagon maker, Jones at age seventeen went west, and when the Civil War began, joined the 8th Illinois Cavalry. Jones's E Company of the 8th, part of John Buford's command, was posted west of Gettysburg on the morning of July 1, 1863. Seeing the approach of Confederates, Jones took a rifle from one of his men, placed the weapon in the fork of a tree, and fired a long distance shot. It was the first shot of more than a million fired in the Battle of Gettysburg.

SOURCES

HOLLISTER, HIEL. *PAWLET FOR ONE HUNDRED YEARS*. ALBANY, NY: J. MUNSELL, 1867.
OFFENSEND, DOROTHY BACKUS. *PAGES FROM MY PAWLET SCRAPBOOK: BOOK TWO*. RUTLAND, VT: ACADEMY BOOKS, 2002.
RUTLAND HERALD, 1864. VERMONT STATE LIBRARY
WITH THANKS TO STEPHEN WILLIAMS.

PITTSFIELD

Pittsfield village surrounds a long village green, along Route 100. According to the *Rutland Herald,* when word of Lincoln's assassination reached here, "the citizens of Pittsfield formed in procession near the hotel, under the marshalship of Lieut. G. L. Parmenter, and after marching through the principal streets, entered the Methodist Church, which had previously been draped in mourning fitting the solemn occasions . . . The choir sang a hymn suitable for the occasion. Prayer was then offered by Rev. Ira Beard; then music by the choir." Several resolutions were then approved, including these:

"Resolved: That we have unswerving fidelity and confidence in President Johnson, and pledge him our undivided support in the carrying out of the great work of restoring the Union and emancipating the slaves, so nobly begun by Abraham Lincoln.

"Resolved: That we deeply deplore that there are some in our community who rejoice in the death of Abraham Lincoln. To such we would say, beware; the time may come, (if not already,) when the atmosphere may become so tainted by your foul breath as to be no longer sufferable."

The Methodist Church where that happened is on the east side of the green, now the Pittsfield town hall. Indeed, voters in 1864 gave approval to the purchase of the old church for a town meeting place. Previously, town meetings had been held in the District Five schoolhouse, which stood across the road at the near corner of the cemetery, and in Gibbs Hotel, a building that is still a hotel on the west side of the green. There, the Lincoln funeral procession to the Methodist Church began, and in that building, a war meeting took place on July 1, 1862 in response to Lincoln's call for 300,000 men. The *Rutland Herald* said that it began with "stirring remarks by townspeople that gave the assembly the feel that men were needed and men must be had." However, "There were but two ready to offer them selves on the altar of southern rebellion and those were of dreadful physical ability. The ship seemed about ready to ride her anchor and dash on the shore of disappointment." The meeting was adjourned until the next Wednesday. On reconvening, "The fire of patriotism began to burn . . . eight of our best young men came forward."

The Pittsfield cemetery contains many graves of Civil War soldiers, including that of William Breed, twenty when he left the family farm to enlist in the 5th Vermont, over the mountains in Pittsford. Private Breed was captured in early May 1863 at Banks' Ford. In the Overland Campaign, he was wounded at Spotsylvania's Bloody Angle and shot in an arm at Cold Harbor. He eventually lost the use of the arm. Breed returned to the family farm in Pittsfield and lived until age seventy-four, dying in 1915. His funeral was held in the church along the green, beside the old hotel. Laverne (Breed) Dutton, Breed's granddaughter, recalled his funeral and that it happened during several days of rain. The casket was borne from the church to the cemetery by fellow soldiers. When the committal service began, the sun suddenly broke through. It shone until the old soldier was lowered to his final rest, then the rain came again in torrents.

From the green's northwest corner, take Upper Michigan Road just over 2 miles to an old farmhouse that sits above the road on the right, William Breed's lifelong home.

Return to Route 100; go north 0.75 mile and take Liberty Hill Road. As you turn, look in the field to your left at an old schoolhouse now used as a barn, the old District One School. According to local legend, Liberty Hill was so named in honor of the many young men who lived along it and served in the Civil War. Among those who attended this school were John Brown, a private in the 16th Vermont who fought at Gettysburg; James Crossman, a private in the 4th Vermont who served from January 1864 to war's end; Lorenzo Parmenter, 6th Vermont, who served the last two years of the war; and Rufus Parmenter, 7th Vermont, who died of disease at Fort Barrancas, Florida, in April 1864. At least six Parmenter boys from Pittsfield served.

A list of Pittsfield's "male citizens liable to enrollment," compiled in January 1864, is displayed in the Pittsfield town office. It lists 96 men and their occupations. All were farmers save for 2 peddlers, 3 laborers, 2 blacksmiths, 1 painter, 1 joiner, 2 shoemakers, 1 carpenter, 1 student, 2 ministers, 1 physician, 2 mechanics, and 1 manufacturer.

SOURCES

PITTSFIELD TOWN AND SCHOOL RECORDS.
PITTSFIELD TOWN OFFICES.
RUTLAND HERALD, 1862 AND 1865. VERMONT STATE LIBRARY.
WITH THANKS TO JOHN BARROWS, INCLUDING THE REMINISCENCE OF HIS GRANDMOTHER, LAVERNE DUTTON.

....

PITTSFORD

Approach Pittsford village from the south on Route 7 from Rutland, and Parker Road goes right. The frame house just past the corner was the boyhood home of Edwin Hudson, who enlisted in the 10th Vermont in August 1862. Assigned as a hospital steward, he contracted typhoid fever, likely from one of his patients. He died at the Fairfax Seminary Hospital, near Alexandria, Virginia, on August 23, 1863, twenty-one years old.

Continue just over 1 mile north on Route 7, and the last house on the right, before the bridge, was Thomas Hennessey's home. He enlisted in the town of Jamaica as a private in the 10th Vermont. Hit by a musket ball at Cedar Creek, an arm was amputated in a field hospital fourteen hours later. Hennessey recovered at Baxter Hospital in Burlington and returned to this house in the spring of 1865. He soon opened a livery stable, which late in his life became a garage, operated by a one-armed mechanic.

Continue north on Route 7 for 2.25 miles, and on the right is a rambling frame house, much added to, facing a barn across the road. Edward Phalen, a native of Ireland, lived here and enlisted in the 7th Vermont in 1861. Taken prisoner in Florida in November 1864, he survived Andersonville to return home. His daughter Edna for many years was a teacher in Pittsford, and when she taught the Civil War, she vividly told stories of her father's imprisonment. In 2001, Margaret Armitage, of the Pittsford Historical Society, said that her mother, a student of Edna's, recalled having nightmares from the stories Edna told, as her "black eyes snapped."

Just north of the Phelan house, the first house past the funeral home was Isaac Peabody's. The 10th Vermont sergeant was wounded at Monocacy on July 9, 1864, and taken to a hospital in nearby Frederick, Maryland, where he died, at twenty-one.

Continue north on Route 7, and go right on Furnace Road. The first house past the cemetery, on the left, a small cape with a stone chimney, was Joseph Kelley's house. In 1856, his daughter Samantha Kelley went to Alabama to teach school. She kept a diary and wrote on June 4, "Oh how miserable warm this day and this room is . . . Finished reading Uncle Tom for the second time this morning. I read it with intense INCREASED interest. Many of the expressions that were new and strange when I read it before are now strangely familiar. Oh Slavery. And I a native born New Englander am living in the midst of it."

June 23: "Had strange conversation with Aunt Hattie the other day . . . She says I was sold away from my mother when I was a little girl, but I remember the spot now and after they went away I used to go to the spot and feel like I should die I'd strike right out crying and never would stop."

Samantha's brother George joined the 7th Vermont, leaving his wife Kate in Pittsford. Soon after the regiment departed in the winter of 1862, the family heard that George had deserted in New York City, and they assumed he was absent without leave. But a cousin recently moved from Pittsford to Wisconsin saw a notice in a newspaper about George's death, of illness on a ship carrying the regiment to duty in Louisiana. She wrote to Kate in Pittsford:

"I had been very sick all winter . . . and thinking a walk would do me good, I went to see one of our neighbors. The walk tired me very much and I laid down on the lounge to rest. A paper was lying by my side. I picked it up and began at the bottom of one of the columns, glancing at different notices; suddenly my eyes fell on those dreadful lines. They seemed to burn deep into my heart. How I ever got home I do not know, but when I did, it seemed as if my brain was on fire, as if everything was turning round on me . . . I knew nothing about George's enlisting till Aunt Lydia wrote me that he had joined the army and the company had left."

Because military records showed her husband deserted, after the war Kate Kelley was forced to wage a long legal battle to secure a widow's pension.

Continue on Furnace Road to the large ornate three-story Wedding Cake House. Elisha Pike Hitchcock, an elderly former soldier, lived here and, at the war's outbreak, drilled Pittsford men eager to enlist.

Continue on Furnace Road to a big brick house with tall columns, on the left, home of the Granger family who ran a blast furnace and foundry here. Edward Granger, born in Pittsford, joined a New York cavalry regiment when the war began and was mortally wounded at Third Winchester. His cousin, Lyman Granger, appointed an assistant surgeon in the navy in 1862, served in Admiral David Farragut's fleet and was wounded in the attack on Fort Jackson, on the Mississippi. He died here while home on furlough, apparently of the wound.

From Furnace Road, a long drive leads to the Vermont Police Academy, once the Vermont tuberculosis sanitarium. The sanitarium was created by a $250,000 gift from Redfield Proctor. Early in the war, young Lieutenant Proctor, 3rd Vermont, while serving in Virginia, contracted tuberculosis and ended up in an army hospital in Philadelphia. He recovered and later commanded the 15th Vermont.

Return to Route 7 and go north to Pittsford Common, overlooked by the 1837 Congregational Church. On the common, Elisha Pike Hitchcock drilled young men as the war began. Pittsford sent 155 to war, of whom 21 died. The town paid $19,079 in bounties, which placed it in debt for years after the war.

SOURCES

CAVERLY, A. M. HISTORY OF THE TOWN OF
    PITTSFORD, VERMONT. RUTLAND, VT:
    TUTTLE AND CO., 1872.
KELLEY, SAMANTHA. DIARY, 1856. PITTSFORD
    HISTORICAL SOCIETY.
PITTSFORD NOW AND THEN. PITTSFORD, VT:
    PITTSFORD HISTORICAL SOCIETY, 1980.
SOLDIERS' DEATH RECORD. PITTSFORD
    HISTORICAL SOCIETY.
WITH THANKS TO MARGARET ARMITAGE.

POULTNEY

Enter Poultney from the north on Route 30, turn right on Main Street, and the Methodist Church is on the right. According to the *Rutland Herald,* a musical entertainment took place there on February 27 to benefit sick and wounded soldiers at the military hospital in Brattleboro. The *Herald* of January 26, 1864, said that a concert here "under the direction of Mr. Wm. Coxe, of New York City, and Prof. R. H. Green, assisted by a quartet of ladies and gentlemen from the town" raised funds for the Sanitary Commission. The paper on June 17, 1864, said, "Funeral services over the remains of Capt. Samuel Darrah, late of the 10th regiment Vermont volunteers, took place . . . on Thursday at 4 o'clock PM At an early hour the citizens of Poultney began to assemble at the M. E. church, and long before the hour appointed for the commencement of the services had arrived, the house was densely crowded." Darrah died at Cold Harbor on June 6. On April 19, 1865, the *Herald* reported on a memorial service here for Abraham Lincoln. "The desk, galleries, and flags were draped in deep mourning . . . At one o'clock the house being filled to overflowing" the service began. It included readings, prayers, a eulogy, the singing of the national anthem and "America."

Proceed to the end of Main Street to Green Mountain College's oldest building, which once housed the Ripley Female College. In early November 1864, the *Herald* reported that as a result of an entertainment staged by Ripley students,

$78 was sent to the "New England Association for the sick and wounded soldiers."

Return along Main Street through the Route 30 intersection and note the elegant brick house on the right built by Henry J. Ruggles. Ruggles and his brother, Francis, were born on a Poultney farm. Francis Ruggles moved to New York State, became a judge, and, during the war, served in the State Department. In 1862, an Indian conflict known as the Dakota War erupted in Minnesota. When it was supressed by government troops, 303 Indians were sentenced to be hanged. President Lincoln asked Judge Ruggles to investigate, and as a result of his report, Lincoln commuted 265 of the sentences. Still, the hanging of 38 Sioux warriors at Mankato, Minnesota, on December 26, 1862, is the largest mass execution in American history. A nephew of Henry and Francis Ruggles, Captain Charles C. Ruggles, 7th Vermont, died of typhoid on Ship Island off the Louisiana coast July 24, 1863.

Continue on Main Street, now Route 140, to the green at East Poultney, and go right on Bird Street. The house at the corner was the home of Dr. Lucretius Ross, assistant 14th Vermont surgeon, who treated Gettysburg wounded. Later, Ross was a physician at the Brattleboro military hospital.

Turn left from Bird Street, and cross behind the Baptist Church. The old house ahead, with a small historic marker on the lawn, was the *Northern Spectator* office when Horace Greeley (see West Haven) apprenticed there 1825 to 1829. Greeley went on to found the *New York Tribune,*

the most influential of all America's newspapers during the Civil War. The opinionated and brilliant publisher was a strong opponent of slavery who, at times, took Abraham Lincoln to task for not aggressively pursuing its destruction. Greeley's constant urgings of "forward to Richmond" were a key factor in bringing on the battle of First Bull Run.

Go left and note the store on the right. In a store that predated the current structure, Horace Greeley's friend George Jones worked as a lad. Jones, born in East Poultney in 1811, was in 1841 invited by Greeley to help him launch the *New York Tribune.* In 1851, Jones cofounded the *New York Times,* another influential paper during the war and a strong opponent of slavery.

In the Eagle Tavern, on the corner Greeley roomed during his apprenticeship. He wrote in his autobiography of an incident when an escaped slave arrived in the village pursued by his owner: "I never saw so large a muster of men and boys so suddenly on our village green as his advent incited; and the result was a speedy disappearance of the chattel, and the return of his master, disconsolate and niggerless, to the place whence he came. Everything on our side was impromptu and instinctive; and nobody suggested that envy or hate of 'the South,' or of New York, or of the master, had impelled the rescue. Our people hated injustice and oppression and acted as if they couldn't help it."

On October 7, 1864, a funeral took place in the Baptist Church on the green for Corporal William Broughton, a Poultney lad who served in the 11th New York

Battery and was killed at Petersburg.

Turn right on Route 140 at the Eagle Tavern and soon come to the East Poultney Cemetery. The Poultney Civil War memorial was moved here long ago from its original location at the head of Main Street. It was given to the town in memory of Lieutenant Judson Lewis, 11th Vermont, who late in the war was an aide to Lieutenant General Ulysses Grant. As president, Grant appointed Lewis U.S. consul to Sierra Leone. The stone soldier honors the men who served from Poultney, 171 by one count. One of them was Private Julius Lewis.

Return to Eagle Tavern and turn right, north. Soon, bear left on Lewis Road, and in 2 miles cross a small bridge. The second farm beyond was Lewis's boyhood home. He was twenty-nine when shot dead in the skirmish at Charles Town, Virginia, on June 21, 1864, as the Shenandoah Valley Campaign began. He had enlisted in the 5th Vermont at the beginning of the war, becoming a sergeant.

SOURCES

JOSLIN, JOSEPH. *A HISTORY OF THE TOWN OF POULTNEY, VERMONT: FROM ITS SETTLEMENT TO THE YEAR 1875*. POULTNEY, VT: JOURNAL & PRINTING OFFICE, 1875.

RUTLAND HERALD, 1864–1865. VERMONT STATE LIBRARY.

TUTTLE, CHARLES E., JR. "VERMONT AND THE ANTISLAVERY MOVEMENT." HONORS THESIS, HARVARD UNIVERSITY, MARCH 1, 1937. UNIVERSITY OF VERMONT, BAILEY/HOWE LIBRARY, SPECIAL COLLECTIONS, BURLINGTON.

WINTER, KARI J., ED. *THE BLIND AFRICAN SLAVE*. MADISON: UNIVERSITY OF WISCONSIN PRESS, 2004.

WITH THANKS TO RICHARD HINSON AND THE LEWIS FAMILY.

PROCTOR

Go north from Center Rutland on Route 3, and entering the village of Proctor, much built of marble, note the Proctor mausoleum in the cemetery on the right. Within it lie the remains of Redfield Proctor, marble magnate, governor, U.S. senator, secretary of war, and Civil War veteran. It is because of Proctor that the town of Proctor exists, created from parts of Rutland and Pittsford in 1886. Previously, the village now known as Proctor was called Sutherland Falls, after the falls of the Otter Creek here.

Redfield Proctor (see Cavendish), educated at Dartmouth and Albany Law School, enlisted in the 3rd Vermont early in the war and served as its quartermaster. Forced to return home with tuberculosis, he recovered and was appointed commander of the 15th Vermont. His men remembered that he allowed tired soldiers to ride his horse on the long march to Gettysburg. After the war, Proctor formed a law partnership in Rutland with his friend Wheelock Veazey, 16th Vermont commander. In 1869, Proctor entered the marble business, moved to Sutherland Falls, and eventually became president of the Vermont Marble Company.

Past the cemetery, go left across the marble Otter Creek Bridge, and bear right on Main Street. Soon on the left, past the YMCA building, is an old stone structure, once a schoolhouse, that now houses Proctor's town offices. When the Civil War began, Sutherland Falls residents held war meetings here.

In 1904, celebrating his seventy-third

birthday, Redfield Proctor hosted a reunion of 15th Vermont veterans. The fact that Proctor was up for reelection to the U.S. Senate, and that workers of the Vermont Marble Company were on strike at the time may have been factors. According to the *Lyndonville Journal,* on June 4, 1904: "Arrangements had been made for a special train which left Newport at five o'clock on Wednesday morning, going from there to Wells River, stopping at many of the stations along the way and adding new members to the number each time. From Wells River the train went to Montpelier and from thence to Burlington and on this road as on the other one the numbers kept increasing. At Montpelier word was sent to Mr. Proctor that there would be at least two hundred and fifty people on the train when it reached Proctor and that was about the number which did arrive shortly before noon."

On arrival, those veterans were joined by comrades from southern Vermont, swelling the total attendance to three hundred. Lunch was served in the YMCA hall, then everyone assembled outside for a group portrait. A highlight of the day was a walk to a monument marking the grave of Proctor's warhorse Old Charley. The *Journal* noted, "Around the slab gathered many of the old boys with their colonel and many were the incidents which were related by them."

To find Old Charley's grave, return up Main Street and recross the marble bridge. At the intersection, go straight ahead up the hill on Ormsbee Street. At the hilltop, a long stone wall borders the estate of Proctor's son, Redfield Jr. Look to the

front of the house for the horse's grave-stone—a low rectangular marble block with sundial.

The evening of June 4, 1904, the 15th Vermont veterans assembled in Rutland for a dinner. Next morning, a train took the group to West Rutland to visit the company quarries there. After lunch, back in Rutland, the train departed on its roundabout journey, taking the veterans home.

Proctor sent each of his comrades a copy of the photo taken at the Proctor YMCA. Letters of thanks poured in. Among letters sent by invitees unable to attend the reunion, was one written on June 1, Proctor's birthday. It said, "I did so want to send you some flowers today, but am quite sure you will understand why I carried them to the cemetery instead. It is just 18 years today since Papa left us." It came from the daughter of 2nd Vermont Brigade commander George Stannard.

Many of the 15th's veterans returned to Proctor three years later for their former commander's funeral. Proctor died while serving in the U.S. Senate.

From the Proctor mansion, return down Ormsbee Street, and at the foot of the hill, turn right on East Street. In just under a 0.25 mile, the Masonic lodge is on the right, once a church. Two men who served from Sutherland Falls were Myron Warner, a Vermont Cavalry private, and Charles Stiles, a private in the 12th Vermont. A history of Proctor states that here, before the war, the two "often met on the level ground near the base of Patch Hill for an hour or more of target practice. The target was placed near a little knoll. If it were standing today it would be in the way of the Greek Church. It had a nine-inch bulls eye and the men stood eighty rods away."

SOURCES

GALE, DAVID C. PROCTOR, THE STORY OF A MARBLE TOWN. BRATTLEBORO, VT: VERMONT PRINTING CO., 1922.
REUNION OF 15TH VERMONT REGIMENT, 1904. REDFIELD PROCTOR PAPERS. PROCTOR FREE LIBRARY.
WITH THANKS TO JOHN REYNOLDS.

RUTLAND CITY/ RUTLAND TOWN

The soaring spire of the Rutland Congregational Church is visible on approaching the city from any direction, and the church is a good place to begin a Civil War tour of Rutland. With some seven thousand residents in the 1860s, Rutland was Vermont's second largest town. It's largest church was the Congregational Church, with a chapel to the rear, on Court Street, near the intersection of Routes 4A and 7. The *Rutland Herald* carried this notice on December 1, 1863:

"The annual meeting of the Soldiers' Aid Society will be held in the chapel of the Congregational Church, on Tuesday, Dec. 1st, at one o'clock PM A full attendance is earnestly requested. The society acknowledges the reception of $64.54 which will be equally divided between the Christian Commission and the Sanitary Commission."

A memorial service was held here in April 1865 for Abraham Lincoln. The *Herald:* "The interior of the church was . . . tastefully and elegantly draped in mourning . . . after all the available space was occupied more people were outside unable to gain an entrance than were in the large church." Resolutions were adopted at the service, including: "That we charge upon the slaveholders' rebellion the entire responsibility and guilt of this atrocious murder; and impartial history with its iron pen will consign its instigators, its aiders and abettors, to an infamy so deep and damning that, in the comparison, utter oblivion would be an unspeakable boon."

Also on Court Street is the Rutland Free Library, a building designed by State House architect Ami Young. At the time of the war, Rutland's post office was on the ground floor. Upstairs was the federal courthouse, and the room that housed it is well preserved, with a marble fireplace at each end. The *Herald* noted in 1864 that a man named N. P. Simonds opened a recruiting office in the courthouse and was paying a $402 bounty to veteran volunteers and $302 to raw recruits. When news reached Rutland of Lee's surrender, a procession formed under the command of Colonel Wheelock Veazey. The paper said, "The marchers came to a halt in front of the U.S. Court House . . . The Rutland Mendelssohn Chorus sang patriotic songs . . . In the evening there was a grand illumination, a torchlight procession, bonfires and impromptu fireworks. Bells rang and guns sounded."

In March 1866, a more solemn occasion took place here, as the body of Solomon Foot, president pro tempore of the U.S. Senate, come home. Foot died in Washington, and a funeral was held at the capitol. Among those who eulogized him was fellow senator Charles Summer, the abolitionist. "In the long warfare with slavery," Sumner said, "Mr. Foot was from the beginning fairly and constantly on the side of freedom." According to the *Herald*, Foot's casket was taken from a train at the Rutland depot and a procession accompanied it via "Washington Street to Main Street, thence to and down West Street to Court Street, and then to the courtroom in the United States Court House." The *Herald* continued, "There the casket was placed on a catafalque with evergreen pillars and a canopy with beautiful festoons and drapery." A service had been planned at the depot, but because of bad weather was moved inside to the crowded courtroom. Among those who eulogized Foot was Colonel William Nichols, former commander of the 14th Vermont Regiment (see Danby).

Downtown sites in Rutland are best seen by walking. Down the hill along Route 4 west (West Street) is Trinity Episcopal Church, of which Wheelock Veazey was a member of the vestry board. For many years after the war, Cyrus Williams, a former private in the 54th Massachusetts Regiment, was janitor at the church. Rheumatism and lung disease contracted while a soldier left him unable to do hard manual labor. The 1860 census counted ninety-two blacks in Rutland. Since blacks could not belong to white regiments, the Rutland blacks enlisted, or were drafted into, the 54th Massachusetts, commanded until his death at Fort Wagner by Robert

Gould Shaw. Rutland sent twenty men to the regiment.

In the Rutland Park, where Routes 7 and 4A meet, on a day in 1863 newly conscripted soldiers gathered after marching through the town's principal streets. After a prayer and speeches, cheers were given for the Union.

South along Route 7 (Main Street) from the park, on the west side, along a narrow park, is the graceful 1832 brick house, with arches, once Solomon Foot's law office.

Across Main Street, at the corner of Washington Street, is an old brick house with an identical structure beside it on Washington. The houses are built of bricks from the Baptist Church that once stood here. In 1835, during an antislavery meeting in the church, people stamped their feet so loudly that abolitionist Samuel May was unable to speak.

Pleasant Street lies west of Main, and the house at number 55 was the postwar home of Wheelock Veazey. After the war, the former 16th Vermont commander practiced law in Rutland with his close friend, Redfield Proctor (see Cavendish). Veazey rose to national prominence, serving as a member of the Interstate Commerce Commission and in 1890 was elected commander in chief of the national GAR.

In downtown Rutland, the brick Bardwell Hotel along Merchant's Row faces the Rutland shopping center constructed on the site of the Rutland railroad depot. On December 5, 1859, a train bearing the body of John Brown, accompanied by widow Mary Ann Brown, arrived here.

Mrs. Brown spent the night at the Bardwell. As she did so, souvenir hunters at the depot carved chunks from the box holding her husband's casket.

The Bardwell was a busy place during the war. The *Herald* reported that in late August 1863, "Mrs. Abraham Lincoln, accompanied by her son Robert and another younger son, arrived at the Bardwell House in this village yesterday forenoon from Saratoga. They left on the 4 o'clock PM train for Manchester." In May 1864, the paper reported: "A large number of ladies and gentlemen, friends of Capt. Harry Brownson, assembled at the Bardwell House on Wednesday evening for the purpose of presenting him with an elegant sword." Brownson was quartermaster of the 12th Vermont.

Varina Davis, former first lady of the Confederacy, stopped briefly at the Rutland depot in April 1866, on her way to Montreal. The *Herald* said, "She was plainly dressed in black, with a short loose cloak, or sacque—and is a large handsome looking woman."

On July 25, the *Herald* reported that "Gen. W. F. Smith stopped at the Bardwell on his way to St. Albans." Smith had shortly before been relieved of command by U.S. Grant. In April 1865, the *Herald* said, "Gen. Geo. J. Stannard was yesterday at the Bardwell House, where he was visited by some of his numerous friends. He was looking very well and every inch the gallant soldier that he is." Stannard was recovering from a wound suffered the previous fall at Fort Harrison.

From the Bardwell, go south on Merchant's Row, which becomes Strongs Avenue, and continue to the intersection with Route 7 (Main Street). The Rutland fairgrounds are just south along Route 7. The First Vermont Regiment assembled here on May 2, 1861. The first night in camp, the men got a rude awakening to army life as a frigid wind blew down tents. As the time came for departure, Governor Erastus Fairbanks presented the regiment with American and Vermont flags, as a large crowd cheered. The regiment had been mustered into federal service at Rutland by Lieutenant Colonel Gabriel Rains, a man the Vermonters did not trust. Their feelings proved well founded, as Rains soon resigned for the Union army and went south to eventually be in charge of the torpedo branch of the Confederate military. Colonel William Y. W. Ripley held tryouts for his Company F of the 1st U.S. Sharpshooters at the fairgrounds in September 1861. The requirement was that a man be able to shoot ten consecutive bullets from a rifle, offhand, without a rest, into a 10-inch ring at a distance of 40 yards (see Ira).

Return north to Merchants Row, and before reaching the Bardwell Hotel, turn west on River Street and cross the Otter Creek Bridge. Quickly turn right on Dorr Drive, and on the left is a large white house on a knoll, now a church. Once the home of Julia Dorr, half-sister of Edwin Hastings Ripley and William Y. W. Ripley, Dorr was a well-known poet who entertained many literary luminaries at her home, including Ralph Waldo Emerson. She composed a poem that was read at the dedication of the Vermont Monument at Gettysburg, which concluded:

Oh beautiful one, my Country
Though fairest daughter of Time,
To-day are thine eyes unclouded
In the light of faith sublime!
No thunder of battle appals thee;
From thy woe thou has found release;
From the graves of thy sons steals only
This one soft whisper,—"Peace!"

Continue on Dorr Drive, and soon cross Otter Creek again. On reaching Route 4 (West Street), bear right with Evergreen Cemetery on the right. The first house past the cemetery on the right was the Ripley home. William Young Ripley made a fortune in the marble business, and his children grew up in comfort, spending summers at Saratoga Springs. Son Edward Hastings Ripley, who commanded the 9th Vermont Regiment, was later given command of a brigade, which he led into Richmond when the city fell in 1865. Son William Y. W. Ripley served in the 1st Vermont Regiment. His brother, Edward, said, "William enjoyed his reputation as a marksman and liked to demonstrate his ability by throwing two potatoes in the air and sending a bullet through both." William organized Company F of the 1st U.S. Sharpshooter Regiment. He commanded the regiment until badly wounded at Malvern Hill. Father Ripley wrote to son William from this house on July 28, 1861, "This is a war of the people, and the men at Washington—will find that they are only agents in the matter—if they go ahead and lead, with vigor, the people will follow & support them—if they falter, another Cromwell or Napoleon will make his appearance on the

stage, and tell them to make room for more competent men."

Enter the main gate of Evergreen Cemetery, and proceed to the high ground toward the cemetery's northwest corner. The Ripleys are buried around the tall marble family monument. Above the Ripley monument, on the highest point within Evergreen, is the large monument marking the grave of Senator Foot.

Foot's stone faces the Baxter family plot, on much lower ground. The graves are set in a circle around a column topped by a female figure, where H. Henry Baxter is buried. Baxter was Vermont adjutant general early in the war. Also in the plot is the grave of Colonel George Roberts, who commanded the 7th Vermont until mortally wounded at Baton Rouge on August 2, 1862. The *Herald* of August 8, 1864 ran this item: "A VISIT TO COL. ROBERTS' GRAVE.—On Sunday the members of the Seventh regiment who are in town, formed themselves into a company and visited the grave of the lamented Col. Roberts, their former commander."

Along the east wall of the cemetery is a Civil War memorial stone with a quotation from the Gettysburg Address: "That from these honored dead we take increased devotion to that cause for which they gave the last full measure of devotion." More than twenty veterans are buried by it.

SOURCES
EISENSCHIML, OTTO. *VERMONT GENERAL: THE UNUSUAL WAR EXPERIENCES OF EDWARD HASTINGS RIPLEY.* NEW YORK: DEVIN-

ADAIR, 1960.
RUTLAND HERALD, 1863–1866. VERMONT
   STATE LIBRARY.
WITH THANKS TO JIM DAVIDSON AND S.
   KENDALL WILD.

SHREWSBURY

Along Route 103 in Cuttings-ville, a village in the town of Shrewsbury, is a unique mausoleum. Outside a tomb in Laurel Glen Cemetery, which holds the remains of the Bowman family, is a statue of Charles Bowman, peering sadly into the tomb. Across the highway is the Bowman family mansion. Charles Bowman operated a tannery in New York State during the war, selling boots, saddles, and other leather goods to the federal government for the armies. He made a fortune, and the tomb and houses apparently are products of his war profits.

Just past the cemetery is the Shrewsbury Methodist Church, whose pastor, Reverend Eastman, was active in the Sanitary Commission during the war. In March of 1864, Eastman spoke at a benefit in Cuttingsville for the local Soldiers' Aid Society, reporting on a recent Sanitary Commission fair he attended in Washington, D.C.

Beyond the church, cross the Mill River Bridge on Route 103, and 0.5 mile beyond, on the right, is a house and large barn. From here, Duane Barney enlisted in the 7th Vermont in February 1862 and soon was serving as a private in Louisiana. Taken sick the following summer, he was sent home. Brother Jeffrey Barney recalled a July morning at the Barney Farm when "I took the milk pails to the barn, I said, 'I will pray for Duane's return.' I set down the pails and kneeled down on the hay and asked God to bring him home. That evening after the chores were done, Mother and I stood in the doorway looking down the road . . . We saw a horse and buggy coming. I said, 'that's Allen's horse' as they came nearer and I said, 'It is Allen and Duane.' Yes, it was a happy homecoming. Duane Barney was home among the Green Mountains where he could rest and get well. And for supper that night, Grandmother Barney had a strawberry shortcake made with wild strawberries from the Shrewsbury pasture."

Return along Route 103 to Cuttingsville, cross the bridge, and immediately go left on Town Hill Road. Cross the railroad tracks and note the siding along the tracks by the Shrewsbury fire station. Here stood the Cuttingsville depot, where many Shrewsbury soldiers departed and arrived. Among them was Edwin Pierce, one of twenty-three Shrewsbury men in the 14th Vermont. Private Pierce fought at Gettysburg and, after Pickett's Charge, found his close friend, Billy Cairns, of Middletown Springs, dead beside him of a bullet to the forehead. On July 22, 1863, a tired Pierce reached the depot at Cuttingsville. Shouldering his pack and rifle, he started the 4-mile uphill trek to his family home near North Shrewsbury, surely hoping that someone would give him a ride. Nobody did. Fifty years later, Pierce boarded another train at the Cuttingsville depot that took him and fellow Shrewsbury veteran John Quinlan, once a private in the 1st U.S. Sharpshooters, back to Gettysburg and the fiftieth reunion.

From the depot, proceed up Town Hill Road following the footsteps of Edwin Pierce on July 22, 1863. In 1.5 miles, the 1852 Shrewsbury Community Meeting House is on the left. The upper floor of the building is a church, while the lower floor is still the site of town meetings. On June 15, 1861, the *Rutland Herald* reported that Shrewsbury people gathered here "to raise a flag at the center of town." The *Herald* said, "Thirty-four young ladies dressed in white, and bearing the Stars and Stripes for their banner, represented the undivided Union." At the appointed hour, the new flag, measuring 20 by 30 feet, was run up a flag pole "amidst the tumultuous cheers of the people." A war meeting was held in the town hall in early December 1863, and 16 local men volunteered. Some 94 Shrewsbury men served in the war.

Continue with Private Pierce past the town hall, and soon turn left on Kieffer Road. Go the length of Kieffer Road, cross Cold River Road, and take Wilmouth Hill Road to the Upper Cold River Road. Turn right, and in 2 miles, note an old road trace on the left. A few yards along this road, on the left, is the cellar hole of the Pierce family home. As Edwin Pierce's long walk ended in the night, he stepped through the door and collapsed from exhaustion.

Continue on Upper Cold River Road to Cold River Road and go left into North Shrewsbury. In the 1840 church on the left, Edwin Pierce's funeral was held in 1919. Just beyond the church, turn left on the CCC Road. The old farmhouse on the left, in just under 0.5 mile, was the home

of Pierce in later years. In the living room, his granddaughter Marjorie Pierce, when a young girl, often heard him singing the old songs of war, including "Tenting Tonight on the Old Campgound" and "Just Before the Battle Mother," while seated in his favorite rocking chair before the fire.

Return to Northam, and note Pierce's Store on the left. Many old soldiers gathered round the woodstove here in the early 1900s to swap stories. Just past the store, bear right on Town Hill Road, and just before again reaching the Shrewsbury town hall, turn left on Russellville Road. In 1.8 miles, bear left at the Y, cross an old millpond, and the house on the left just beyond was the home of Lyman Russell. Russell avoided service in the Civil War by paying $300 in commutation, but the town apparently didn't hold it against him, for it elected him to legislature three times after the war.

SOURCES

HANCE, DAWN D. *SHREWSBURY, VERMONT: OUR TOWN AS IT WAS.* RUTLAND, VT: ACADEMY BOOKS, 1980.

PERRY, TED. *THE STORY OF RUSSELLVILLE VERMONT.* PRIVATELY PRINTED, 1980.

RUTLAND HERALD, 1861. VERMONT STATE LIBRARY.

WITH THANKS TO MARJORIE PIERCE AND GLENDON PIERCE.

SUDBURY

Sudbury's town meetings took place in the Sudbury Meeting House, which still stands beside Route 30, an ornate white clapboard structure built in 1807. Meetings were in the basement hall, while the upstairs was a Congregational church. Perhaps because the town was close to the home of Stephen Douglas, Sudbury voters in this building went for Douglas over Lincoln in the 1860 election, 62 to 50, with 4 votes going to Breckenridge. Four years later, George McClellan bested Lincoln here, 61 to 53.

At a town meeting on February 14, 1863, Sudbury voted 47 to 46 for a tax to repay townspeople who had contributed their own money to pay bounties several months earlier. In December 1863, by a 52-to-25 margin, bounties of $500 were approved. Six months later, a tax of 150 cents on each dollar of the grand list was approved by voice vote to support more bounty payments.

The *Rutland Herald* reported that, on January 22, 1864, "an exhibition . . . to consist of Dramatic and Miscellaneous rehearsals, songs, etc." was held at the Congregational church. One of the beneficiaries was the Soldiers' Aid Society.

Directly across Route 30 from the town hall, a frame house sits slightly below the road. It is believed that from it James Lillie went to war, enlisting as a private in the 5th Vermont. Wounded and captured at Savage's Station, he came home to live until 1911.

From the church, go 2 miles north on Route 30 and turn left on Vail Road. In 0.75 mile, on the left, is a handsome brick house. From here, Martin Ketchum joined the 12th Vermont, as a private. He died of illness on February 18, 1863, in the regimental camp at Wolf Run Shoals, at twenty-five.

Return to the meetinghouse and go south, quickly coming to a stone school-

house at the intersection of Routes 30 and 73. Among those who attended this 1824 structure were James Lillie and Harrison Williams, a 5th Vermont private, who survived a wound at Petersburg.

SOURCES

RUTLAND HERALD, 1864. VERMONT STATE LIBRARY.
SONDERGELD, DONALD R. *HISTORY OF SUDBURY, VERMONT*. COLLIER, TN: INSTANT PUBLISHER, 2011.
WITH THANKS TO STEVE SGORBATI.

TINMOUTH

On a summer day in 1905, on the ball field just downhill from the village, Tinmouth held an old home day. The speaker, one Learned Noble, said, "The boys of Tinmouth answered the call and left their businesses and their homes and their loved ones and started south, to battle and die." He proceeded to name those who perished, then he named other local soldiers "who came back to us but with wounds and broken health."

Grant Reynolds, who has studied the town's Civil War history, believes that most of the men who went to war and survived became in some way impaired. Also, he has concluded that 53 Tinmouth men served and that 18 from other towns enlisted here, as the town bounty rose to $550. Of the local boys, 2 were killed in action, 9 died of disease, and 14 were discharged for disability. Most who went, Reynolds has found, were farmhands, as only two owned farms. Tinmouth's Civil War was thus a poor man's war. Also, Reynolds has discovered that of the

Tinmouth soldiers, only 14 came back to town and lived for any length of time. Indeed, of the 53 Tinmouth men who enlisted in town, only 8 are buried here. Soon after the war, most went west. Only eldest sons were entitled to inherit the family farm. For the others, there was little to keep them in town. Obviously, the war's effect on this small upland town, population 615 in 1860, was profound.

Turn west from Route 7 in Wallingford onto Route 140 and proceed uphill into Tinmouth. Go 3.75 miles then turn sharp right on North East Road. The first house on the road was part of the farm where hired man Joseph Carpenter worked, who enlisted in the Vermont Cavalry, coming home a year later, after being discharged for disability. The second house was the home of Lieutenant Jeffrey Ballard, 5th Vermont, also discharged for disability after serving less than a year, and dead in 1874. George Phillips was a hired man at the latter house, and he returned safely to live a long life in Tinmouth after serving in the 7th Vermont. But a brother, Ephraim, a corporal in the 9th, died soon after returning home.

Return to Route 140, and soon come to the Tinmouth Cemetery, where thirteen Civil War soldiers lie. One of them, Dwight Holland, moved from Tinmouth to Massachusetts after his father died in 1856 and served in two regiments from that state. While away, his mother died while employed on a local farm. Dwight came home to Tinmouth from the war a sick man and died in the home of a local person who took him in.

Proceed back to Route 140 and uphill

to the Tinmouth green and follow Route 140 out of the little village. The first big farmhouse, on the right, was the home of Private Charles Miner, 5th Vermont, twice wounded at Cold Harbor. Private Henry Houghton worked at the farm just beyond, returning safely from Gettysburg with the 14th Vermont.

Return to the green and go straight onto Mountain View Road. Private Joel Grover, who twice enlisted in the Vermont Cavalry and was twice sent home for disability, owned the store on the left that is now the town clerk's office. Continue on Mountain View, and in just under 1 mile, approaching two silos on the right, look to the right to a large old farmhouse on the hill. Stephen Corey worked there as a hired man, before enlisting as a private in the Vermont Cavalry. Corey was part of a detachment, under Addison Preston, that got in a hand-to-hand fight with some of John Mosby's men near Catlett's Station, Virginia, on May 30, 1863. They captured a cannon from Mosby, but Corey was wounded and taken prisoner. His brother, Sergeant Job Corey, was killed. Stephen was released six months later.

SOURCE
WITH THANKS TO GRANT REYNOLDS.

....

WALLINGFORD

At Wallingford's main intersection, where Routes 7 and 141 meet, a fountain statue, on the front lawn of the old Wallingford Inn, depicts a boy holding a boot from which water drips. During the Civil War, the hotel was operated by Arnold Adams and his wife, Matilda. Their son Gilbert, a 10th Vermont lieutenant, was known as the best rider and tenor singer in the regiment. At the Battle of Winchester, October 19, 1864, a shell fragment hit him just below a knee. The leg was amputated, but a week later, when Hill heard an enemy attack might be imminent, he stood up from his hospital bed and began shouting commands. He hemorrhaged and died. His body came home for a funeral at the hotel. Around 1900, the fountain was erected by the Hill family in his memory.

Diagonally across the square from the inn is the Gilbert Hart Library, given to the town by a Civil War veteran. Hart, at the time he enlisted, was angry at his hometown, apparently because a local store had refused him credit. He went to Dorset to sign up. Serving less than a year as captain of Company H, 2nd U.S. Sharpshooters, he came home and became a rich man. Inside the library, Wallingford's Roll of Honor lists those who served in the Civil War. Wallingford's population in 1860 was some 1,750. The late local Civil War enthusiast Gary Wade calculated that 142 men were credited to the town of whom 5 were killed in battle, 5 died of wounds, 2 died in prisons, and 16 died of disease. Also, 34 were discharged for disability.

Go east on Route 140, and quickly, the Baptist Church is on the left. Lemuel Haines served as pastor here for a year, before he was dismissed in 1859. Haines enlisted from Wallingford as chaplain of the 10th Vermont and in 1870 published a history of the regiment. Just past the church, the brick town hall is on the left,

and just beyond it, turn left on narrow Taft Terrace. The second building on the right was the town hall at the time of the war. Meeting on May 21, 1861, as the war began, Wallingford voters, resolved:

"That we as a Town fully approve of the action of the State at the recent special session of the Legislature and . . . we will by subscription raise a sum of not less than two thousand dollars for the purpose of aiding recruits from our Town to serve in our present struggle for the preservation of our government and perpetuation of our glorious Union."

"That as a Town and community we pledge a good comfortable support [to] the families of such patriotic persons as enlist in the service of their country."

Those pledges proved expensive, as some bounty payments soared to $900 and the total cost of the war reached $11,350.

In the Wallingford's town clerk's office is a notebook kept by Samuel Rogers, a selectman in the 1860s. Rogers attended a meeting of Rutland County towns held at the Rutland town hall in 1862 to draft men for the 2nd Vermont Brigade. He wrote that the names of all eligible men were placed in a box, which was rotated several times, then "the slips were drawn from box by Mr. Reynolds of Pittsford, a distinguished and respectable person who has been totally blind for years." Rogers was careful to note "there was not a man that was drafted that went into the Army as a drafted man . . . from the Town of Wallingford." They, of course, enlisted.

Return to 140, continue east into the mountains 4 miles, and turn left on

Hawkins Road. From the hillside farmhouse, at the road's end, brothers Jewett and Joseph Hawkins enlisted as privates in Company B, 14th Vermont, fought at Gettysburg, and came home safely. Continue east into East Wallingford and come to the village church. The *Rutland Herald* reported that Reverend Aldace Walker preached a funeral service there on July 31, 1864, for Private Henry Mattocks, of nearby Tinmouth, a sharpshooter killed at Spotsylvania's Bloody Angle.

Return west on Route 140 to the main intersection in Wallingford, then go south on Route 7 into the Green Hill Cemetery. At the highest point, a group of Civil War gravestones faces an 1864 rifled cannon, overlooking the Valley of Vermont. Notice that the cannon appears to be placed at an awkward angle, set so that it faces due south. The cannon was the gift of the local Kearney Post of the Women's Reserve Corps.

Return to Route 7, and go south 3.5 miles into South Wallingford. The old store on the left was once owned by Oscar and Mercy Eddy. Mercy Eddy kept a diary for twenty-three years, including the war years, a time of sadness for the busy homemaker. The war years were bracketed by the death of two children: Albert, at age eight, in 1860, and Eugenia, at age three, in 1865. The following are excerpts from her 1864 diary, written as the Overland Campaign began 500 miles south:

May 4: *"lowry morning I have a very bad cough about these days."*
May 5: *"Eclipse of the Sun I am sick today."*
May 6: *"pleasant warm day Army of the*
Potomac moved across the Rappidan lee falling back."
May 8: *"Grant's Army is going to Richmond fought 8 days + are still fighting Gen Sedgewich killed."*

The May 5 entry is the most intriguing, given that it was the costliest, and probably the most glorious, day for Vermont in the Civil War. There was no solar eclipse anywhere in the world on that day when one thousand Vermonters fell at the Wilderness.

On September 2, 1865, Mercy's daughter died of a respiratory illness. After writing a vivid description of her death, she wrote the next day, September 3: "This morn is bright and beautiful, as the sweet flower we are about to consign to the grave. Funeral at one o'clock Mr. Balch preaches. Genie is dressed for the grave in muslin + wreaths of flowers. There comes up from amidst all this gloom, I am the Resurrection + the life, parents + friends this is the way of all the Earth, I have only gone on before you. Prepare to meet me in yonder Heaven where parting is known no more."

SOURCES
KLOCK, JOYCE, ED. *A HISTORY OF WALLINGFORD VERMONT*. RUTLAND, VT: ACADEMY BOOKS, 1976. COURTESY GILBERT HART LIBRARY.
RUTLAND HERALD, 1864. VERMONT STATE LIBRARY.
THORPE, WALTER. *HISTORY OF WALLINGFORD VERMONT*. RUTLAND, VT: TUTTLE, 1911.
WADE, GARY. "CIVIL WAR SOLDIERS FROM WALLINGFORD, VERMONT." UNPUBLISHED MANUSCRIPT, UNDATED. WALLINGFORD TOWN OFFICES.
WITH THANKS TO JOYCE BARBIERI.

WELLS

The Methodist Church, where Civil War–era town meetings took place, faces the small Wells village green along Route 30 in the village center. In her history of the town, local historian Grace Pember Woods wrote: "The Town adopted the policy of paying . . . bounty taxes promptly, so at the close of the war the town had but a small debt. The Town paid for the preservation of the Union $15,057 as certified by the Selectmen. Bounties ranged from $100 for 9 months service to $1,000 or $1,050 for 3 years, only one man received the $1,050 bounty. The surviving soldiers when the victory had been won, and our Union preserved from destruction, returned to their homes. However, 'Many a patriot who escaped death during the War returned with health so impaired, that they were soon laid to rest.'"

Just west of the Methodist Church is the village store, which at the time was owned by the Lewis family. Alfred Lewis and his brother-in-law, David Youngs, enlisted as privates in Company K, 14th Vermont. Youngs won promotion to corporal, and they both fought at Gettysburg. Youngs died at Brattleboro on his way home, likely of exhaustion.

At the store, take South Street 0.25 mile to a small pond on the left. Once known as Norton Pond, William Norton lived in a house on the far side of the pond. He enlisted in nearby New York State, serving in the 123rd New York Regiment with four other Wells men. At Gettysburg, Norton lost his left arm. But he recovered and became a wheelwright in Wells. The Wells Historical Society preserves a tool that Norton had made for his one arm, an iron drawshave, for shaving wood.

Return to the Methodist Church and note the house just east of it, on East Wells Road. During a patriotic celebration years after the war, a cannon exploded in its front yard, blowing a hole in a wall.

Proceed 2.75 miles on East Wells Road, and at the corner of Wells Brook Road, on the right, is a farm once owned by the Clemons family. Martin Clemons, a private in the Vermont Cavalry, was killed in a skirmish in the Shenandoah Valley on September 21, 1864. Before the war, brother Hugh Clemons had moved to Georgia, where he was forced to enlist in a Confederate regiment. At Gettysburg, he crossed into Union lines.

Continue east just under 0.5 mile, and an old farmhouse stands on the left, at the corner of Lamb Road. From here, Elisha Wales joined Company K, 14th Vermont, one of fourteen Wells boys in the regiment. Private Wales fought at Gettysburg, but the forty-three-year-old died of exhaustion while on the march in Maryland, pursuing Lee's army, just before the regiment came home.

Return to Wells village, and at the green, go north on Route 30, 1.75 miles. Note a farm on the right where the road turns sharp left. Here, at the Howe Farm, on October 3, 1927, the Ku Klux Klan held a meeting that included the burning of a cross. A poster advertising the event stated that "America is in danger!" and said that "all Protestants are welcome."

The rally apparently was held to oppose the presidential candidacy of Catholic Al Smith.

Continue north on Route 30, moving along the east shore of Lake St. Catherine, and in 1.3 miles, look closely for a waterfall that plunges down a cliff. In the house directly across the road, hard by the lake, lived Tracy Castle, and in September 1861, his only son Charles enlisted in the 2nd Vermont. The father walked with his son to Rutland and watched the train depart. Private Castle died on January 4, 1863, of sickness in a military hospital at Windmill Point, Virginia.

SOURCES

HILAND, PAUL. *HISTORY OF WELLS, VERMONT, FOR THE FIRST CENTURY AFTER ITS SETTLEMENT.* RUTLAND, VT: CHARLES E. TUTTLE, 1869.

WELLS TOWN RECORDS.

WOOD, GRACE ESTHER PEMBER. *A HISTORY OF THE TOWN OF WELLS, VERMONT, FROM ITS SETTLEMENT: WITH FAMILY AND BIOGRAPHICAL SKETCHES AND INCIDENTS.* WELLS, VT: PRIVATELY PRINTED, 1955.

WITH THANKS TO JIM CAPRON.

WEST HAVEN

Though Horace Greeley began a monumental journalism career in Poultney, which profoundly effected the Civil War era, his roots may be said to have been in West Haven.

Go north from Route 4 on Route 22A at Fair Haven, and in 2.5 miles, go west, left, on the road to West Haven, known as Main Road. Quickly come to Doran Road on the left, and look down it to a mansion with tall columns, once the Minot home, a

building very familiar to young Greeley. Though born in New Hampshire in 1811, in the winter of 1821, Horace and his family moved to West Haven. "When we first set out stakes there," he wrote, "father was thirty-eight and mother was thirty-three. I was not quite ten, my brother and two sisters, eight, six and four, respectively. A third sister was born two years later . . . we now made the acquaintance of genuine poverty . . . Father went to chopping, at fifty cents per day . . . Before the spring of 1821 opened, father had taken a job clearing fifty acres of wild land, north of our cottage; and here he and his sons were employed, save in winter, for the next two years."

The exact location of the "cottage" isn't known, but Greeley said it was "within a few rods" of the mansion of Christopher Minot, for whom his father worked. Minot had made a fortune in Boston as a banker, before settling in West Haven. A Greeley biographer has said that, as a lad, Greeley was never without a book and that his mother encouraged his reading. The writer further stated that Christopher Minot "took some interest in Horace, and though he would not lend him books, allowed him to come to the house and read there as often and as long as he chose."

The Greeleys had three homes in West Haven, apparently all little more than cabins. For a time, his father worked in a sawmill along the Hubbardton River. Continue on Main Road 1 mile and, just before crossing the Hubbardton River, turn sharp left on River Road. The mill where his father was employed was on this pond. And it was here on a summer day that Horace and his brother were paddling about the millpond on a log, when both fell off and nearly drowned.

Continue on Main Road 0.25 mile, and as you go uphill, look into the pasture on the left, on a low knoll, for a cellar hole filled with trees and brush. It is believed this was the foundation of one of the Greeley homes. It was perhaps from this place that, in 1826, Horace began his 12-mile walk to East Poultney, successfully in search of a newspaper apprenticeship with the *Northern Spectator*. He founded the *New York Tribune* fifteen years later. Reflecting on West Haven many years later, Greeley wrote that the town was "too honest to need a lawyer, and too wise to support a grog shop."

Continue on Main Road 1.75 miles and come to an area known as the Center. Go left on Book Road, and quickly come to the 1831 Baptist Church. Here, an event took place in early June 1861 involving a local militia company, the Benson Guards. The *Rutland Herald* said "the company was present, by invitation, at a flag raising which came off at West Haven last Saturday, and the precision and admirable manner in which they went through their drill, and different evolutions, was remarked on by all . . . Their reception and treatment by the citizens of West Haven was highly gratifying to both officers and men." On departing, the guards gave "three cheers for West Haven." A *Herald* correspondent also reported, about that time, on a West Haven town meeting:

"We are an agricultural people and somewhat removed from the great thoroughfares of our State, and therefore may not as readily catch the enthusiasm of the passing moment as many more highly-favored towns; but when real danger is apprehended, we think no people can boast of a more self-sacrificing devotion to the common weal, than can the citizens of this town . . . After some deliberation and discussion as to the amount of the bounty that should be offered, it was voted that the Selectmen be authorized to pay each volunteer that should be mustered into the service of the United States, the gratuity of fifty dollars." The *Herald* said on December 7, 1863, "At a town meeting held in West Haven on the 1st December, five hundred dollars bounty was voted for every volunteer accepted on the quota of the town." West Haven sent 56 men to war, of whom 8 served in the Navy, perhaps reflecting the town's location on Lake Champlain. Serving in the 14th Vermont were 11 West Haven men.

Among those in the 14th were Samuel and Herbert Rice, both privates, the sons of Volney and Adeline Rice. The Rice family lived on the Lake Champlain shore, at a place known as Cold Springs. The boys wrote home throughout their nine months of service, which began when a local company was formed at Castleton that became the 14th's Company F. Both boys survived illness in the Virginia winter encampments. In mid-summer, word reached West Haven of an impending battle. Not knowing that her sons had already fought at Gettysburg but fearing that some battle had taken place, the mother wrote her sons from Cold Springs on July 5:

"I have a great many fears in regard to your safety we learned that you were on the march ere this and may have been obliged to face the cannon's mouth to stand your chance with many others in the dredful carnage that must follow . . . I hope you will have the good luck to come home soon we understand there has been a battle in the direction you were going."

In fact, Samuel was wounded at Gettysburg, and he wrote home from McDougal Hospital in Fort Schuyler, New York, on July 13, "I got a clip on the head just above the right ear with a piece of shell. It is doing first rate nothing but a flesh wound." Both Rice boys soon came home. Samuel later opened a resort hotel, the Cold Springs House, which became a favorite destination of Lake Champlain travelers.

To see Cold Springs, it is necessary to drive to Whitehall, New York, along Route 4. On reaching that New York town, go north on Route 22, paralleling Champlain, 10.5 miles and turn right on Dresden Road. In 0.4 mile, go right on Pit Road, and the first building is an old store with a double-decker porch, beside the lake. The location of Cold Springs Resort is directly across the narrow lake. The Rices came by boat to Dresden Station to get their mail, and the old store was familiar to them.

SOURCES

GREELEY, HORACE. *RECOLLECTIONS OF A BUSY LIFE.* NEW YORK: J. B. FORD AND COMPANY, 1886.
RICE FAMILY. CIVIL WAR LETTERS. UNIVERSITY OF VERMONT, BAILEY/HOWE LIBRARY, SPECIAL COLLECTIONS, BURLINGTON.
RUTLAND HERALD, 1861 AND 1863. VERMONT STATE LIBRARY.
TUTTLE, CHARLES E., JR. "VERMONT AND THE ANTISLAVERY MOVEMENT." HONORS THESIS, HARVARD UNIVERSITY, MARCH 1, 1937. UNIVERSITY OF VERMONT, BAILEY/HOWE LIBRARY, SPECIAL COLLECTIONS, BURLINGTON.
WEST HAVEN TOWN RECORDS.
WHEELER, JOSEPH. "HORACE GREELEY IN WEST HAVEN." UNPUBLISHED MANUSCRIPT, UNDATED. WEST HAVEN TOWN OFFICE.
WITH THANKS TO CAROL RICHARDS AND JOSEPH DORAN.

WEST RUTLAND

On a hilltop above the village of West Rutland, west of Rutland along Route 4A, the marble Saint Bridget's Church stands, a monument to the Civil War era. Work began in 1860, using marble cut from the hill on which the church stands. A history of the town noted, "The men of the parish labored strenuously to cut the marble from the hill with the hand tools then in use. After a long day's work, the men went back to work about 7:00 in the evening until about 11:00 PM, either at the church yard, or at the marble yards, they cut the face and the pieces of the marble into the beautiful edifice. After dark, they worked by lanterns or torchlight. All this work was donated to the parish." That work was done after the standard twelve-hour workday in the quarries. The church was completed in the fall of 1861 and the building was "dedicated to God's service" on November 11, 1861, by the first Catholic bishop of Burlington, Louis DeGoesbriand.

At the time of the Civil War, West Rutland was a village in the town of Rutland, not becoming an independent town until 1894. To the quarries in West Rutland in

1862 came John Longergan to recruit men for his Company A of the 13th Vermont Regiment, an Irish unit. He gained some forty recruits here, most coming from the West Rutland quarries. Most were Irishmen. Two West Rutland men were elected officers of the company. John Sinnott, a schoolteacher, served as first lieutenant, and David McDeavitt, second lieutenant. Lonergan and Sinnott became close friends. On July 3, 1863, just before the 13th led the attack on Pickett's Charge, the regiment lay behind a hastily constructed breastwork made of fence rails. Some of the men occasionally stood up, under fire, and Sinnott raised up to caution the men, "Boys, lie down or you'll surely be hit." Suddenly hit himself, in the head by a shell fragment, Sinnott died two days later. Lonergan saw his friend lying wounded and came to him after the charge was repulsed, bandaged his head, and wept for his friend.

Sinnott is buried in West Rutland's St. Bridgett's Cemetery on Main Street, his grave just left of the tomb at the end of the central drive. The stone notes, as do many in the cemetery, his place of Irish birth. County Westford was Sinnott's. Apparently coincidentally, beside his stone is a monument to a Lonergan family, including another John Lonergan. Many members of Company A lie in the cemetery, including Private Patrick Corey, a native of County Tyrone, killed in the attack on Pickett's Charge. Among other members here are Lieutenant David McDevitt, of County Tyrone, who died in 1897, and Private John Patten, a big quarry worker who was involved in haul-ing the guns of Gulian Weir's battery, recaptured July 2 at Gettysburg, back to Union lines. Most of these men's funerals were held in Saint Bridget's, and it is believed that a service there honored Lieutenant Sinnott.

Also buried in this Irish cemetery is Hugh Corey, who because of a crippled leg did not serve. But he was a leader of the draft resistance that occurred in the West Rutland marble quarries in 1864, and he was arrested. The Civil War period was a troubled time in this community. As the war began, quarry wages stood at $1 a day. The workers went on strike, and many were evicted from their company tenement housing. At the same time, the disgruntled workers refused to be drafted. Unannounced, troops arrived one afternoon from Brattleboro, surrounded the quarries, and forcibly pressed some of the workers into the army. The old quarries where the strikes, and the resistance, occurred are located behind Saint Bridget's, at the base of the hill.

In front of the West Rutland town offices, on Main Street, a town war memorial lists the names of seventy-three men who served in the Civil War.

At the east end of the village of West Rutland, Route 133 goes south from Route 4A. Take 133, and just before reaching the Route 4 underpass, note a large, old, brick house with wide front porch on the right. From here, Charles Mead went to war at twenty-two, serving in Company F, 1st U.S. Sharpshooters. An aspiring writer, Mead kept a diary throughout his service. In the midst of the Overland Campaign, he wrote, "I am sad,

I am sick, at the slaughter in our company and army. I have seen enough to sicken any soul to the very soul. We are winning victories, but at a fearful cost. I feel the danger at every skirmish I go in . . . Never fear for me, but pray for the country." Just after the campaign ended, a Rebel sharp-shooter ended sharpshooter Mead's life in the trenches at Petersburg.

On September 8, 1864, the *Rutland Herald* said: "We are pained to hear of the death of Eugene A. Kelley, who enlisted between three and four months ago. He was taken sick with the typhoid fever on the 10th of August . . . and died on the 17th. It will be remembered that he was the young man who, on learning of the death of Charles B. Mead of West Rutland, so promptly determined to take his place in the country's service . . . He was a good scholar, a fine young man, and as his acts proved, a patriot. His death occasions much sorrow among all who knew him."

SOURCES

HANNON, REV. PATRICK T. *HISTORICAL SKETCHES ON WEST RUTLAND, VERMONT.* RUTLAND, VT: ACADEMY BOOKS, 1986.

RUTLAND HERALD, 1864. VERMONT STATE LIBRARY.

WEST RUTLAND TOWN RECORDS.

chapter thirteen

Washington County

Vermont's Civil War participation officially began at the State House in Montpelier when senators and representatives from throughout the state assembled for an "extra session" of the legislature on April 23, 1861. They first heard a stirring call to arms from Governor Erastus Fairbanks, then appropriated $1 million to launch the state's war effort. The State House today looks much as it did that fateful day and can be said to be a Civil War monument. The magnificent Battle of Cedar Creek painting, in the Cedar Creek Room, is by Medal of Honor–winner Julian Scott. A work by another Vermont artist, Larkin Meade, a bust of Abraham Lincoln that was a study for statuary at his tomb in Springfield, Illinois, graces the lower corridor. Plaques and other paintings honor Vermont's Civil War heroes. In Waterbury, the town library was once the office of Dr. Henry Janes. As an army surgeon, he was in charge of all the Gettysburg wounded. Janes was honored with a place on the speakers' platform when Lincoln gave his Gettysburg Address. Janes came home to be Waterbury's village physician, once more. At Berlin's Congregational Church, a funeral was held for Major Richard Crandall, killed by a sharpshooter at Cold Harbor. Nearby, his gravestone faces Berlin Pond, across which is the cellar hold where the Crandalls lived. Richard's brother John was a surgeon at Gettysburg with the 13th Vermont. A fellow member of the 13th returned to Gettysburg after the battle and brought home the body of his friend, James Wilson, for burial in the East Warren Cemetery. Private Wilson was killed the day of Pickett's Charge. His fiancée, Delia Porter, died soon after learning of his death. Wilson's farmhouse home survives with its grand view of the Green Mountains, towering across the Mad River Valley

···

BARRE CITY/ BARRE TOWN

The Civil War history of Barre (Barre Town and Barre City were one political entity during the Civil War) is perhaps best told in the gravestones of this Granite City. Barre sent some 200 men to war, of whom 31 died.

Barre's Main Street lies along Route 302 and at the west end is a park, with a granite statue of a kneeling, naked warrior, a World War I memorial known locally as "the naked man." On approaching it from the west, look to the last block of stores on the left. The only wooden building among them was, in the 1860s, the Barre town hall. Voters meeting there approved bounties that reached $500 for the nine months soldiers who served in the 2nd Vermont Brigade. Barre's costs for the entire war totaled $71,336.09.

Continue on 302 past the naked man to the old Spaulding High School building, with its statue of the poet Robert Burns on the front lawn, honoring the city's Scottish heritage. It's said in Barre that when Civil War veterans looked upon that statue, they expressed frustration that no monument honored them. They needn't have worried, for the building no longer houses a high school but the Vermont Historical Society. Within the 1892 brick walls is the finest of all Vermont

Civil War collections, preserving thousands of Vermont Civil War manuscripts and relics. Thus, the building is today something of a Civil War monument, and the ghosts of the veterans should be well pleased.

Continue along Route 302, up the hill, and soon turn left into the main gate of Elmwood Cemetery. Proceed north to the rear of the cemetery and see, near the tallest pines, that Barre's veterans eventually took matters into their own hands. A handsome stone bears the inscription:

**In Memory of Those Who Fought
1861–1865
That the Country Might Live**

The monument was erected in 1914 by the Barre GAR post, the Crandall post, named for Major Richard Crandall, of nearby Berlin, killed at Cold Harbor. Beside the large marker is the grave of a Civil War soldier, G. W. Foster, of the 3rd Missouri Cavalry. Foster died well after the war while visiting Barre, and since a grave was needed, the local veterans welcomed his burial here.

Some ninety-four Civil War veterans are buried in this cemetery. Among them, in the northeast corner, is Colonel Homer Stoughton, a Randolph native, who organized and commanded Company E of the 2nd U.S. Sharpshooters, surviving a wound at Spotsylvania and four months in a Confederate prison.

Along the west fence, in front of the old brick schoolhouse, is the grave of Weston Averill, killed at the bloody battle of Franklin, Tennessee, where Confederates, under John Bell Hood, lost more men in a frontal assault than fell in Pickett's Charge.

Go to the east side of the cemetery, and along the road, find a tall monument, with urn atop, marking the grave of Lieutenant Ozias Thompson, 3rd Vermont. Thompson was a sergeant in the fall of 1862 when he ordered Private William Scott, of Groton, to stand guard two consecutive nights in place of a sick comrade. Scott, the famous "sleeping sentinel" (see Groton), was found asleep at his post, and the rest is history.

Go out the main entrance onto 302, turning left, and make a quick left on Hill Street. In 0.6 mile, turn right on Cobble Hill Road, and in just over 1 mile, at the end of a long right turn, an old farmhouse is close to the road at the top of the hill. Here, three Averill brothers spent much of their early childhood. David moved to Michigan in 1860 and enlisted in the 23rd Michigan. He was also killed at the Battle of Franklin, with a thirty-day furlough in his pocket. His brothers, John and James, joined the 8th Vermont in 1864. John contracted chronic diarrhea and eventually was sent to the Sloan Hospital in Montpelier, where he recovered. James remained at the front and lost a foot when hit by a shell at Winchester. He also was treated at Sloan Hospital.

Return down Cobble Hill Road and Hill Street, cross Route 302, and continue on Hill Street to Route 14. Soon, go left on Quarry Hill Road and follow it uphill, then turn left into Wilson Cemetery. Proceed to the flagpole, and go 30 yards east to the Dodge family plot. Six Dodge cousins from Barre served in the Civil War, and only one returned alive. Two of the cousins lie here, Private Leroy Dodge, 10th Vermont, who died of wounds received at Fisher's Hill in the Shenandoah Valley, and Private Wesley Dodge, Vermont Cavalry, mortally wounded and captured at Nottoway Court House, Virginia, on June 23, 1864. He died the next day.

Beyond the Dodge stones and between two small obelisks is the grave of Major Lemuel Abbott, who went to war from East Barre. Abbott attended Norwich University before joining the 10th Vermont. Wounded at Monocacy in 1864, he was hit twice at Winchester two months later.. He wrote of his Winchester experience, "My first wound was from the butt end of an exploding shell in the breast which knocked me down and simultaneously as I fell a minie ball fired but a rod away in my front just grazed my forehead, tore through my upper lip crushing both jaws and carrying away 11 teeth; the most painless dentistry I have ever done; but Oh! the shock it gave my system and the misery I suffered that night!"

Leave Wilson Cemetery and return down Quarry Hill Road to Route 14, turning right. Follow Route 14 back to the stoplight by the naked man, and proceed straight ahead, continuing on 14 through city streets, and in 1 mile, turn left through the grand gates of the famous Hope Cemetery. Within its carefully maintained acreage rest twenty-nine Civil War veterans.

Return to Route 14 and bear right on the Route 14 Truck Route. In 0.3 mile, go right on Brook Street, and approaching North Seminary Street, the last three houses on the right have a Civil War story. The house on the corner was built in 1867 by Albert Dodge, 10th Vermont, the only one of the Dodge cousins to come home. There he lived with his wife, the former Laura Bacon. Dodge built the house beside it on Brook Street. The house beside that, also on Brook Street, was a cooper shop operated by John Bacon and his son James, brother of Laura. James was a private in the 2nd Vermont whose head was grazed by a bullet on May 5, 1864, at the Wilderness. James Bacon died in 1876 of skin cancer, which, the family said, began at the site of his head wound.

While in Barre, it must be noted that the city has a Civil War history that ranges, in a way, throughout the nation. Barre granite has been used for Civil War memorials that stand on countless village greens and on the hallowed ground of many battlefields, including Chickamauga and Gettysburg. The Vermont monument at the Wilderness, a likeness of Vermont's most famous mountain, Camel's Hump, was carved here in Barre from a granite block quarried on Barre's Quarry Hill.

SOURCES

ABBOTT, LEMUEL ABIJAH. *PERSONAL RECOLLECTIONS AND CIVIL WAR DIARY, 1864.* BURLINGTON, VT: FREE PRESS PRINTING COMPANY, 1908.

BLAKE, MARION E. LISTING OF CIVIL WAR GRAVES IN BARRE CEMETERIES, 1939. ALDRICH PUBLIC LIBRARY, BARRE.

BRALEY, ARTHUR W. *HISTORY OF THE GRANITE INDUSTRY IN NEW ENGLAND.* BOSTON: NEW ENGLAND ASSOCIATION OF GRANITE INDUSTRIES, 1913.

HISTORICAL SOUVENIR OF BARRE. BARRE, VT: NICKERSON & COX, 1894.

WITH THANKS TO WHITNEY MAXFIELD.

BERLIN

Leave Interstate 89 at exit 7 and go to the stoplight, then turn right, and in 0.3 mile, come to the Berlin Congregational Church. Richard Crandall went from a Berlin farm to attend Dartmouth College for a year before joining the 6th Vermont in 1861. Fighting in the major battles of the Vermont Brigade, and rising to major, a friend said that he came to believe Crandall was not destined to die at the hands of the enemy. But on June 7, 1864, a Rebel sharpshooter felled him with a mortal wound in the trenches at Cold Harbor. His body came north by train, arriving at Montpelier on June 15. A funeral was held at the Congregational Church on Friday, June 17, 1864.

Another member of this church was Edward Stone, who served as chaplain of the 6th Vermont for the first year of its existence. He had just become a minister before he left for the army and likely preached in this church. He began his letters to his family with "Dear home."

Richard Crandall had a gift for writing, and his diary, which survives at the Vermont Historical Society, contains eloquent passages. From the trenches at Spotsylvania he wrote: "Skirmishing all day on our front . . . the evening is rainy, the first since we crossed the river. A band is playing 'Departed Days.' Oh, the memories it awakens."

After his death, a poem he wrote in the winter encampment at Brandy Station was discovered in his pack, composed exactly two months before his death: "The White Crossed Banner" was a tribute to the 6th Corps and its Greek cross emblem. It concluded:

Sound the clarions of war, be the battle begun
And the night of our land shall be changed in the morning.
But oh! if I fall in a cause so sublime,
I shall join the brave souls that already have bled;
Tell parents and friends to let the bells chime
In slow plaintive airs for her sons that are dead.

A friend of Crandall's wrote a tribute that was published in the *Vermont Watchman*. "He was a friend," wrote A. W. H. "He had always been so. Born near each other, our earliest days were passed together—side by side we sat in school, side by side roamed in the field, in all the ecstasy of wandering boyhood . . . As a scholar, he was diligent and enthusiastic; as a friend, he was faithful and true; as an officer, he was fearless and patriotic; as a man, he was generous and high minded . . . The Army of the Potomac is not the same army to his friends now, for one whom they loved is not there."

Just east of the Congregational Church is a large cemetery. Proceed to the fifth entrance, and Crandall's grave is on the right, a small obelisk facing across Berlin Pond toward his home. Some 50 yards above him is the Evans family lot. Side by side lie Private Edward Evans and his brother, Ira Hobart Evans, who both grew up in Berlin and enlisted as privates in the 10th Vermont. Edward was wounded at Cold Harbor and forced to leave the service. Ira, in December 1863, was made an officer and spent the rest of the war commanding black troops. Promoted to major for bravery, he was awarded a Medal of Honor for gallantry in leading the 116th U.S. Colored Troops at Hatcher's Run in the final assault at Petersburg on April 2, 1865. Evans moved to Texas after the war, where at age twenty-three he was elected Speaker of the Texas House of Representatives, still the youngest person to hold that position.

To find the homes of Crandall and Evans, return toward Berlin Corners and turn left on the Crosstown Road. Quickly, go on left Paine Turnpike and turn right on Brookfield Road. In just under 1 mile, pull into the small parking area on the right. The Crandall cellar hole is in the woods, 200 yards ahead. Crandall's brother, John, studying medicine with a Barre doctor when the war began, enlisted in the 6th Vermont as a hospital steward. He returned home to study medicine at the University of Vermont and on graduating was named assistant surgeon of the 13th Vermont. He treated wounded at Gettysburg. Later, Dr. Crandall was a physician at the Burlington and Montpelier Civil War hospitals. After the war, he served for a time as a surgeon in George Armstrong Custer's 7th Cavalry, but left well before Little Bighorn.

From the parking lot, a hiking trail follows the old road to West Berlin, and in 0.3 mile are foundations of a house and barn. From this 1790 Stewart homestead, Rollin Stewart, twenty-one, enlisted in the 13th Vermont, serving as a corporal and fighting at Gettysburg.

Return to the parking lot and continue south on Brookfield Road, pass the southern end of Berlin Pond, and go left on Paine Turnpike. The first house on the right, above the road, is believed to have been the home of Cornelius Nye, who enlisted in the 2nd Vermont in September 1862 at thirty-three. He was killed at the Wilderness on May 5, 1864. According to a 1992 history of this town, two Berlin men were killed at the Wilderness and six were wounded, of whom two died.

Continue on Paine Turnpike the length of Berlin Pond, and turn left on Crosstown Road. In 0.25 mile, come to a T intersection. In the woods ahead is a stone marker on the site of the first church built in Berlin, in 1803. It was likely here that the sixty-three members of the Berlin Anti-Slavery Society, formed in 1837, held their first meetings. At the T intersection, turn left and follow Crosstown Road 0.8 mile to where Rowell Hill Road goes right. Ira and Edward Evans went to war from the large frame house just beyond the turn.

Some 140 Berlin men served, and 29 died. Berlin in the 1860s was much larger than today, in terms of acreage, for the town included most of what is now Montpelier south of the Winooski River.

SOURCES

GILLIES, PAUL, ED. *A PLACE TO PASS THROUGH: BERLIN, VERMONT, 1820–1991*. BERLIN, VT: BERLIN HISTORICAL SOCIETY, 1993.

TURNER, RICHARD, AND VERNON TURNER. *LETTERS OF THE SAMUEL COOK TURNER FAMILY, 1859 TO 1889*. PRIVATELY PRINTED, 1995.

VERMONT WATCHMAN, JUNE AND JULY 1864. VERMONT STATE LIBRARY.

WITH THANKS TO DAVID PERRIN, HENRY PERRIN, RICHARD TURNER, VERNON TURNER, AND NORBERT RHINERSON.

CABOT

Many Civil War–era buildings still face Cabot's common, which witnessed an event on July 13, 1861, that introduced the village to war. St. Johnsbury's *Caledonian* reported that the "Calais Company passed through Cabot on its way to Camp Baxter, in St. Johnsbury, to become part of the 3rd Vermont. The paper said, "The people took them into their houses and treated them with good dinners and the coronet band turned out to cheer them on their way." The Civil War monument on the common bears the names of 36 Cabot men who died in the Civil War, among them Erastus Scott, Charles Perry, and brothers Abel and Edwin Morrill.

Go south from the common 1 mile and the first farm north of the Cabot/Marshfield town line was the Morrill farm. Major Abel Morrill Jr., adjutant of the Third Vermont, was killed May 6, 1864, on the second day of fighting at the Wilderness. On March 12 of that year, he had married Miss Nancy Morse, of Danville.

Abel's brother, Captain Edwin J. Morrill, commander of the 11th Vermont's Company A, was captured at Weldon Railroad June 23, 1864. According to a letter written by Captain James Eldredge, a Warren man who also served in the 11th, published in the *Caledonian* in July 1864, he and Morrill tried to escape from a prison train (likely bound for Andersonville). Eldredge wrote, "When we got two miles out of Appomattox Station . . . Captain Morrill . . . and myself tried to make our escape by jumping out of the car window when they were running about twelve miles an hour. The guards which were on top at each end of the car saw us and fired, and I think gave Captain Morrill a mortal wound. I got him back to the station and stayed with him until daylight, and then left him in the care of the stationmaster and some negroes. I think he could live but a short time." Morrill died at Appomattox Station. Eldredge returned to Union lines after traveling cross-country 170 miles, obtaining food and shelter from slaves.

Captain Morrill's body was returned to Cabot in 1866. On learning in 1864 of her fiancé Edwin's death, Josephine Lance became a recluse, spending most of her days until her death in 1894 in the family home in Cabot. Her will bequeathed $850 to the Cabot Methodist Church for the purchase of an organ. The instrument was moved to the United Church, on the northern side of the common (formerly a Congregational church), when the Methodist Church closed. The organ, dedicated to her father, is still played. The church displays a portrait of Lance, showing a lovely dark-haired young lady with a rather faraway look in her eyes. Cross the bridge by the firehouse at the southern end of the village and the first house on the right was the Lance home.

Also on the Cabot monument is the name of Private Erastus Scott, 3rd Vermont, killed at twenty-five at Spotsylvania's Bloody Angle. In 1861, Scott married Margarette C. Hartshorn, in Reading, Massachusetts. On learning of her husband's death, Mrs. Scott wrote her sister: "He is dead I never shall see him again Oh I cannot have it so all my hopes in life are oer." The Cabot Civil War monument was dedicated July 4, 1876. A large crowd heard the principal speaker, J. P. Lamson, proclaim, "Their country called, and in the cause of humanity they died. And though their bones lie bleaching on a Southern soil, far away from friends and home, yet ever fresh will be their memories in the hearts of the living and the loved. And their records will remain from everlasting to everlasting, after this monument dedicated to them shall have crumbled."

On the south side of the village, about where the fire department building now stands, was the home of the Herrick family, the boyhood home of the diarist Henry Herrick (see St. Johnsbury). Herrick is buried in the cemetery just past the Lance house. He lies near his close friend, Private Charles Perry, killed by a sharpshooter in the trenches at Cold Harbor on June 5, 1864.

SOURCES
CABOT TOWN RECORDS.
PITKIN, CALEB. *A COLLECTION OF MEMORIES FROM THE CENTURY PAST.* CABOT, VT: CABOT ORAL HISTORY COMMITTEE, 1999.
WITH THANKS TO DAVID BOOK.

CALAIS

Funerals for two very different Civil War soldiers were held in the church in East Calais, which stands at the south end of the village along Route 14, north of East Montpelier and south of Woodbury.

Charles Bancroft joined the 4th Vermont in September 1861 and died the next spring. His father, Smiley Bancroft, wrote in his journal, at his home in the Kents Corner section of Calais on May 5, 1862, "I took my horse and went to O. A. Wilbur's got his horse and wagon he going with me to Montpelier after the remains of our Charles he having died in the Army of the Potomac on board the steamer Richard Willing April 30th 1862." On April 6, he wrote, "The body of Charles came into Montpelier this morning about 9 o'clock AM and we took it and came to East Calais and put it in the tomb and then went home." He wrote April 8, "Sunday, had the funeral of Charles at East Calais."

On January 11, 1888, a funeral for Melvin Dwinell was held at the East Calais Church. Dwinell, raised in East Calais, moved to the state of Georgia in 1863 and became a newspaper publisher. In 1861, he joined a Confederate regiment and served more than two years as a lieutenant, fighting at First Manassas. He wrote his parents, "If I should meet any of my relatives on the battle field in Lincoln's army they will be considered as my enemies and treated as such." Dwinell left the army in late 1863 because of illness and after the war was elected to the Georgia legislature. He made his first postwar visit to Vermont in 1867 and occasionally returned until his death in 1887. His brother, Ira, brought his body home.

Just north of the church, a road turns east behind the church, then goes abruptly uphill to the East Calais Cemetery. Dwinell's stone is large and prominent in the first (downhill) row of stones. A descendant, Harold Dwinell, wrote in 1962, "In the days when the school children marched to the cemetery on Memorial Day to place flags on the graves of soldiers, I remember that a flag was always placed on his grave but there was strictly no comment."

From the cemetery, return to Route 14 and go north. Quickly note a prominent house on a knoll to the right, with stone steps leading to the lawn. The Dwinell family home, it faces a millpond and old mill, which was part of a complex owned by the family. Turn left off Route 14 by the mill, cross the brook, and quickly bear left at a Y. Go two miles to a T intersection, turn right, and in 0.5 mile, go left on Number 10 Pond Road. Quickly pass GAR Road on the right, and look right at the spit of land that extends into the pond. The Calais GAR hall can be seen, owned and operated by a still-functioning Women's Relief Corps post. Beside the grand building, which was erected in 1885, is the 1921 Calais war memorial listing the names of veterans from the Revolution to World War I. About 150 men served in the Civil War from Calais, and 29 died.

Return as you came, but on reaching the turn that would take you back to East Calais, go straight, and in just over 1 mile come to Gospel Hollow, with a meetinghouse to the right and the town clerk's office just ahead. Go straight onto Pekin Brook Road, and in 1.8 miles, look up Pekin Hill Road. On the left, the first building is the old Pekin School. Winters from 1859 through 1861, the Calais

Central Debating Society met at the school to formally discuss various matters, mainly concerning the growing national crisis. The topic in February 1860 was "The South has an equal lawful right with the North to emigrate to the territories belonging to the United States and carry with them their peculiar institution." The topic a year later concerned the proposition that the secession of the southern states might be beneficial to the North. At another session, the question was whether the federal government should send the navy to occupy southern ports.

Return to Gospel Hollow and turn left on Kent Hill Road. At the hall on the left, built in 1866, Calais voters met to face a war debt that arose out of bounty payments of as much as $300. Continue on Kent Hill Road for 1 mile, to Kents Corner, and turn right on Robinson Cemetery Road. Cross a brook by an old mill, and the first house past it, on the right, is believed to have been the home of Smiley Bancroft, who buried his soldier son. Continue past the house and soon come to a cemetery on the left. By the main entrance is a prominent monument to Josiah Livingstone, a captain in the 9th Vermont, who was awarded a Medal of Honor for gallantry at Newport Barracks on February 2, 1864. Many soldiers are buried in this cemetery, including members of the Robinson family, victims of a Civil War tragedy.

Continue on Robinson Cemetery Road and bear right at a broad Y where it joins with the County Road. The first house ahead on the left was the home of Charles Watson, a private in the 13th Vermont and a lieutenant in the 17th Vermont. Watson was wounded during Pickett's Charge at Gettysburg and at the Crater two years later. Family tradition says that his life was once saved when a bullet struck a Bible he carried in a breast pocket.

From the Y, go left on County Road 0.75 mile and turn right on the Worcester Road. In 0.5 mile, go left on Robinson Road to the brick house at the end. Here lived the Robinson family, whose son Joel served as a private in the 13th Vermont. Sick with typhus when he arrived here after Gettysburg, he died on July 28, 1863. Within weeks, four more members of the Robinson family perished of typhus. Return to Worcester Road and Maple Corners, and turn right on County Road, which leads to Montpelier.

SOURCES
CALAIS TOWN RECORDS.
DWINELL, HAROLD A. "VERMONTER IN GRAY: THE STORY OF MELVIN DWINELL." VERMONT HISTORY 30 (JULY 1962): 220–37.
WITH THANKS TO WESTON CATE, LORRIE JUSTUS, AND ELLIOTT MORSE.

DUXBURY

Turn north off Route 100 onto Route 100B and soon come to the hamlet of South Duxbury and its 1855 church, now home to the Duxbury Historical Society. A funeral was held here in 1862 for cavalryman George Magoon. Proceed north less than 0.5 mile, and bear right on Turner Hill Road. Where Tobin Hill Road soon turns left, look to the hillside farm above you. The barn survives from the Civil War era when the farm was owned by the Turner family. The original house burned in the 1920s, but was rebuilt on its foundations. Samuel Turner bought the farm in 1855, the year his wife died. His first-born child was Henry, followed by sons Harrison, Edwin, Charles, and Leslie. Before the war, Henry Turner moved to Wisconsin, where he joined a local regiment. He survived, but died of tuberculosis contracted while in the service not long after coming home. Harrison Turner moved north to Coventry before the war, enlisted there, and served for nine months in the 15th Vermont. On June 15, 1863, just before his regiment began the long march to Pennsylvania, Harrison wrote home concerning the unpopular commander of the 2nd Vermont Brigade, Edwin Stoughton. "I saw Major General Reynolds and Meade today," he wrote, "They looked dusty and rusty. I could not but compare them with our snotty little Stoughton who in reality was nothing but a colonel but was in his own mind the greatest man in the service." Harrison returned home in July 1863 with measles. Soon he had epilepsy, which plagued him all his long life.

Edwin Turner, serving in the 2nd Vermont, was wounded at First Fredericksburg, a ball passing through a leg and exiting through the hip. He was a long time recuperating, spending months at the hospital in Burlington. Never well again, he died in 1867. Charles Turner went south with the 8th Vermont but died of illness in June 1862, in New Orleans. Leslie Turner did not enlist.

A sister, Addie Turner, a schoolteacher, married George Crandall, brother of Major Richard Crandall and Dr. John Crandall (see Berlin). At first, they lived on the Turner farm, but then bought a house 0.5 mile up Turner Hill Road from that farm. It stills stands close by the road, on the right. Addie wrote to a friend in 1863 concerning brothers Richard and John: "Poor soldiers. My brothers are all but one younger than myself, and when mother died and left them mere children I felt that they were my peculiar care. And whether I have done what I could for them or not, I have loved them fondly tenderly."

In a letter written June 28, 1864, she mentions attending a soldier funeral in the South Danbury Church. "There was a funeral here at our church this afternoon. Magoon, a cavalryman died in hospital, and his wife had a funeral. It was rather a dull affair, but I suppose her feelings required it." Private George Magoon joined the Vermont Cavalry just after Christmas 1862 and died less than five months later of disease. On July 24, 1864, Addie wrote to Harrison Turner about the death of her brother-in-law Richard Crandall at Cold Harbor. "He was killed on the 7th of June by a sharp shooter. Was shot in the morning and died at night. O it is a sad blow to our family."

On June 25, 1865, with the war ended, Samuel Turner, who had lost three of five sons, with another sickened, summed up his feelings in a letter to son Harrison: "Well the Rebellion is put down—peace restored and our good President assassinated & all done in a few short weeks. I sometimes think is this a reality or do I dream? It has been the strongest desire of my heart for many years that slavery should be destroyed, but I never expected to see it . . . But God has so ordered and overruled this war that the enslaved are free. This compensates in part at least for the sacrifice of life and property wasted or destroyed in this unholy Rebellion." But Samuel also wrote, "I have done what I could to render those dependant on me as comfortable as possible and help my children in starting in life, tho some of them have never manifested the least obligation to me for what I have helped them." The war had left him bitter, perhaps because his boys had gone off to serve, rather than help farm his hillside acres.

In 2004, Duxbury dedicated a marker in the Crossett Hill Cemetery, on Crossett Hill Road. Long known as a Civil War cemetery, the burial ground is believed to hold the graves of five Civil War soldiers. Among them are said to be Private Hiram Foster, a Duxbury lad who enlisted at age eighteen in the 13th Vermont. Foster never made it to Gettysburg, dying of illness in the regiment's winter encampment on March 26, 1863.

Duxbury is credited with having sent 152 men to war. To do so, the town paid $36,500 in bounties, a total that put Duxbury in debt for years.

SOURCES
DUXBURY TOWN RECORDS.
TURNER FAMILY LETTERS, VERMONT
   HISTORICAL SOCIETY.
WITH THANKS TO THE CRANDALL FAMILY.

EAST MONTPELIER

From Montpelier's main intersection, where State and Main streets meet, go north on Main for 1.75 miles and pass Culver Cemetery on the right, where Medal of Honor–recipient William Noyes (see Montpelier) is buried. Just past the cemetery, turn right on Center Road, and in just under 1.5 miles, on entering East Montpelier Center, note a large old house on the left with Palladian window. Here lived Perley Pitkin who enlisted in the 2nd Vermont early in the war and soon was placed in charge of the regiment's supplies. He proved to be so good a quartermaster that Ulysses Grant appointed him a colonel and put him in charge of supplying the entire Army of the Potomac, through the Overland Campaign to the war's end. His responsibilities included the four-thousand-wagon supply train that followed the army from the Wilderness to Petersburg. When massive casualties were suffered at the Wilderness and Spotsylvania, Pitkin organized the system that evacuated the wounded from the battlefield to hospitals around Washington.

Just beyond the Pitkin house, on the right, is the Old Meeting House, where East Montpelier town meetings were held during the war. War expenses, mainly bounty payments, amounted to nearly $12,000 and caused voters meeting here in 1864 to approve a 200 cent tax on every grand list dollar. Soon after the war began, a 120-foot-high Liberty Tree was raised here to fly a giant flag measuring 30 by 12 feet. A total of 119 East Montpelier men served from a population of 1,300, and 27 died. Company C of the 13th Vermont Regiment was organized at East Montpelier, probably here at the meetinghouse.

From the meetinghouse, continue on Center Road, through several intersections, for 2.5 miles and come to a redbrick house on the right with large barn behind. Addison Peck, a lifelong Democrat who became a Lincoln supporter when the war began, lived here and on one occasion, well before the war, discovered a fugitive slave hiding in his hayloft. That wasn't surprising since considerable activity on behalf of escaped slaves took place in East Montpelier.

Continue past the Peck house for 0.5 mile on Center Road and come to an old cape set above the road on the left. Five East Montpelier men were killed at the Wilderness, among them Private Elhanan Ormsbee, 4th Vermont, son of Caleb and Sarah Ormsbee, who lived here. Their son, Orvis, also a 4th Vermont private, died of disease. A memorial service was held at the Old Meeting House for Elhanan, who is buried at Fredericksburg. A newspaper account said: "In the Battle of the Wilderness he received a Minnie ball near the eye and instantly expired . . . He was buried by his comrades that same evening, near the place where he fell. He was respected and beloved by all the soldiers who shared his acquaintance . . . He leaves a young wife, father, brother and sisters. This is the third funeral we have attended in the family within a year."

Continue downhill past the Ormsbee home to Adamant village and look right to Sodom Pond. William Lawson, a local boy, was a private in the 13th Vermont, and one spring afternoon near Union Mills, Virginia, while in his regiment's winter camp, he stole a goose by baiting a hook and casting it into a farmer's fenced-in yard. In doing so, he "bethought himself of the days when he caught bullfrogs in Sodom Pond."

Turn around in Adamant, return on Center Road 1 mile, and turn left on Sibley Road. In 0.3 mile, the farmhouse and barn on the left was the home of Nathan Dodge, who is said to have given refuge here to fugitive slaves. Indeed, the house contains a hidden room.

Return to Center Road, and in 2 miles, turn left at a cemetery on Dodge Road, and in 1.3 miles, bear left at a Y onto Snow Hill Road. In just over 1 mile, the hilltop farmhouse on the left was the home of Willard Snow, a private in Company C of the 13th Vermont. Wounded fighting Pickett's Charge, he died two weeks later. Seven other East Montpelier men were wounded at Gettysburg.

Turn around here, return on Snow Hill Road 1 mile, and go left on Vincent Flats Road. In 0.8 mile, bear right on Cherry Hill Road, and note the cemetery on the hill to the right. This was Montpelier's Quaker Cemetery, part of a Quaker community that thrived before the Civil War. The Quaker meetinghouse once stood in front of the cemetery. Against the wishes of his fellow Quakers, including his parents, young William Byrd Stevens enlisted in the 4th Vermont. The grandson of the abolitionist Robinsons of Ferrisburg's

Rokeby (see Ferrisburg), Stevens was captured in the fall of 1863 and survived imprisonment. He came home ill, but recovered, and soon was back at the front. On June 8, 1864, he was wounded in the trenches at Cold Harbor. Stevens died of gangrene in an army hospital at Alexandria, Virginia, and was buried nearby. Here in the Quaker cemetery is a small memorial stone to Private Stevens.

Continue past the cemetery for 0.75 mile, and the long gambrel roof house on the left is built on the site of the Stevens Farmhouse. As at the Robinson home of Rokeby in Ferrisburg, fugitive slaves are believed to have worked in the surrounding fields, for wages.

Quickly come to Town Hill Road and turn right. In 3 miles, turn right on Main Street, completing a complex circle tour. Go up the hill to Cutler Cemetery and bear left on County Road. Follow it 3.75 miles and turn left on Horn of the Moon Road. In 1 mile, cross Jacobs Road, and from the first house on the right, with a large barn, Private William Dillon enlisted at seventeen in the 6th Vermont in 1862, against the wishes of his parents, Michael and Ann. When Williams was wounded at Charles Town in August 1864, his mother went south, visited the White House, and received a pass from Abraham Lincoln to go through Union lines. She found her son in an army hospital, brought him home, and nursed him back to health.

SOURCES

BLACKWELL, MARILYN. *ACROSS THE ONION: A HISTORY OF EAST MONTPELIER, VERMONT, 1781 TO 1981.* EAST MONTPELIER, VT: EAST MONTPELIER HISTORICAL SOCIETY, 1983.

EAST MONTPELIER TOWN RECORDS.

ZIRBLIS, RAY. *FRIENDS OF FREEDOM: THE VERMONT UNDERGROUND RAILROAD SURVEY REPORT.* MONTPELIER, VT: VERMONT DIVISION OF HISTORIC PRESERVATION, 1997.

WITH THANKS TO MARILYN BLACKWELL.

FAYSTON

Between Moretown and Waitsfield, 1 mile north of where Route 100B leaves Route 100, take North Fayston Road into the mountain town of Fayston. In 2.75 miles, the North Fayston Cemetery is on the left, with the 1830s District Four School across the road. At the entrance to the cemetery is Fayston's Civil War memorial, dedicated in 1900, with the names of 64 men who served from the town. Counting those who enlisted in other towns, the total is believed to be about 75. The maples that front the cemetery were planted at the time of the dedication.

George Marble went to school in the District Four School. Marble joined the 6th Vermont when it formed in 1861, served there years, and reenlisted. Captured at Cedar Creek, he was held in Richmond's Libby Prison, where he died on January 20, 1865 at thirty-four. His wife, Hannah, outlived him by fifty-three years, dying in 1918. When word of his death reached Fayston, Marble's friends and neighbors crowded the school for a memorial service. The bell in the school belfry was rung, as it still is for funerals. Also attending the school was George's brother, Calvin, who served with him as a private in the 6th Vermont and at nineteen was wounded at the

Wilderness. Royal Haskins, who fought at Gettysburg with the 13th Vermont, was also a student here.

In the first house past the school, on the left, lived Catherine (Barry) Posnett, widow of Daniel Posnett, a veteran of the 13th Vermont. Daniel, a private, on February 5, 1863, fell into a chill Virginia stream and was forced to march 2 miles and stand picket before getting dry. Though able to fight at Gettysburg, for the rest of his life he was crippled and forced to walk with a cane. He still managed to operate a sawmill in Fayston until he died in 1881. For a time his widow, known as Kate, operated a post office in this house.

Continue on North Fayston Road 1 mile to a Y and the old District Two School on the right. Among those future soldiers who were pupils here were George Boyce, a private in the 6th Vermont, killed at the Wilderness at twenty-two. His body never came home.

Just past the school, turn right on Sharpshooter Road and go 1.3 miles to a gravel pit on the right. In the woods, on the far side of the pit, a tree once stood in which was embedded the blade of a scythe. Several stories concerning scythe blades and the Civil War are told along the Mad River Valley. This one, typically about a soldier who drove the blade into a tree when he decided to enlist, has a ring of truth. The blade and branch in which it is embedded are preserved by the Fayston Historical Society. Disagreement exists concerning the soldier involved.

SOURCES

BRAGG, ANNA BIXBY. *THE EARLY YEARS FAYSTON, VERMONT, 1798–1898*. FAYSTON, VT: FAYSTON HISTORICAL SOCIETY, 1898.
FAYSTON TOWN RECORDS.
POSNETT FAMILY RECORDS. COURTESY OF MAUDEAN NEILL.
WITH THANKS TO ZELDA LEVANWAY, MAUDEAN NEILL, AND MIRIAM HERWIG.

MARSHFIELD

In Marshfield village, along Route 2, the Cabot Road turns north. A brick house built in 1802 stands within the Y of the two roads, once the home of Stephen Pitkin Jr. and his wife, Hanna, both stalwarts of the Plainfield Methodist Church (which no longer stands) and opponents of slavery. Stephen died at sixty-two in 1834, but Hannah lived on beyond the Civil War and wrote the history of Marshfield for Abby Hemenway's *Gazetteer*. She said of the town's soldiers, "In the vigor of young manhood they went, one and another, who were household treasures . . . Perhaps the last news of them was 'seen on the battle-field,' or 'taken prisoner,' and then the long months elapsed ere one word could be heard to stay the anguish of suspense. At last came the fearful, 'Died at Andersonville.'" According to her, 98 Marshfield men served, and 28 perished. She also noted that of the 34 men drafted from the town in 1863, 22 "paid their commutation money" and avoided serving.

Behind the Pitkin house is the Marshfield Village Cemetery, which Hannah Pitkin administered. In the third row from the rear is the gravestone of Thaddeus Bullock, a private in the 4th Vermont, twenty when he died of illness in December 1862. His stone states that he was "a soldier of the Potomac who died near Fredericksburg" and says, "Sleep dear Thaddeus sweetly sleep, your sufferings are o'er." Before he enlisted, Bullock was a member of the Green Mountain Rifle Company, Marshfield's militia company that formed in 1856. Though most of its members went to war, enough remained in town to form an escort when Bullock was buried here with military honors.

Across the Cabot Road from the Pitkin house, beside the old Jaquith Library, is a house built after the war by Eli Pitkin, a sergeant in the 13th Vermont who fought at Gettysburg. Where the Y begins on Route 2, Gilman Street turns south, and the first house on the right was, in wartime, the home of the Johnson family, who operated a sawmill powered by the Winooski's North Branch. Norman Johnson was a member of Company F, 2nd Vermont, joining the regiment in January 1864. Johnson served in the Overland Campaign, keeping a tightly worded diary. On May 5, he wrote of the terrible fighting at the Wilderness, "Skirmishing commenced with cavalry about 11. Infantry went in. Our loss was very great." Johnson fought at Spotsylvania's Bloody Angle and wrote, "Started for another battlefield about nine in the morning. Was hit in the right side and wrist. Got to the hospital about four in the afternoon." He eventually was sent home to recuperate, cared for in the Brattleboro and Montpelier hospitals. He recovered and came home here.

West of Gilman Road along Route 2, note, on the right, a stone wall made of large granite blocks. On the knoll, which it supports, where a house now stands, once the Old Brown Schoolhouse was located, where Jacob Trussell came to teach in 1859. Much admired by his pupils, Trussell enlisted in the Vermont Cavalry in 1861 and served three years; he was wounded once and became a sergeant. Partly due to his example, at least ten students of the school enlisted, several of them in the cavalry. Former students George Nownes and Eri McCrillis, both cavalry privates, died at Andersonville.

Continue west 1 mile on Route 2, and Sass Avenue turns left. The house just across the bridge was the home of Private Asa Winch, 1st Vermont Light Artillery, who died from sickness in December 1862 in Louisiana.

Just past Sass Avenue, Pike Road turns right. From the house at the intersection, Ira Ormsbee enlisted. A private in the 4th Vermont, he was wounded while on picket duty as the fighting began at Charles Town, Virginia, on August 21, 1864.

Continue west on Route 2, and in just under 1 mile, turn right on Beaver Meadow Road. In 0.4 mile, Tibbetts Road turns right. Look up it to the only house on the road, the home of Robert Tibbetts, who enlisted in the 11th Vermont in the summer of 1862. He was mortally wounded at Cedar Creek.

SOURCES
MARSHFIELD TOWN RECORDS.
PITKIN FAMILY PAPERS.
WITH THANKS TO THE PITKINS.

MIDDLESEX

Depart Interstate 89 at the Middlesex exit, go left on Center Road, turn east on Route 2, and quickly turn left on Gallagher Street by the old railroad depot. The Middlesex village cemetery is behind the station, and near its center is a small marble obelisk, erected by Calvin and Elmira Farrar in memory of their son Waldo. Waldo Farrar moved to Minnesota shortly before the Civil War and joined the 1st First Minnesota Regiment. He enjoyed a leave at home in Middlesex shortly before his regiment moved to Gettysburg, where on the afternoon of July 2, 1863, it made a suicidal charge at the request of Major General Winfield Scott Hancock to buy time for the hard-pressed Union forces on Cemetery Ridge. Among those killed was Farrar, who is buried at Gettysburg. Lieutenant Farrar's Middlesex cenotaph says:

He died like a soldier.
He died at his post.

The Civil War–era depot stood just beyond the cemetery. In this area along the tracks, the Farrars likely said a final farewell to their son. The house beside the cemetery, on the west side, is believed to have been the home of Corporal Zerah Hills, a member of the 2nd Vermont Light Artillery, who died of disease in June 1863, in Louisiana.

Return to Route 2 and go right, or west, pass Center Road on the right, and in 0.6 mile is an old house on the left, with large field behind. Across the road, look hard for the trace of a road that leads into the woods. This long-abandoned track was once the Notch Road that led to a part of Middlesex long ago cut off by the interstate. About a 0.5 mile up the road the widow Esther Shontell lived, who signed her name with an X and had seven sons in the Union armies. Among them were Benjamin, 6 feet 8 inches tall, Frederick, 6 feet 4, and Leander, 6 feet 3, all privates in the 8th Vermont's Company E. Frederick died in May 1862 of disease. Private Augustus Shontell fought at Gettysburg with in the 13th Vermont. Joseph and William served in the 3rd Vermont Light Artillery, and Joseph died in March 1864 of sickness. Lewis, a private in the 6th Vermont, survived a wound at Charles Town in 1864. Apparently, only Frederick returned to live in Middlesex. The seven big Shontell boys would have come down Notch Road, once a main Duxbury thoroughfare, to enlist. The Farrars also lived along that road.

Return on Route 2, and take Center Road, passing under the interstate. In 1 mile, see two very similar houses on the left. The second was the home of Elisha Scott, a private who served from autumn 1861 to autumn 1864 in the Vermont Cavalry. Just beyond the Scott house, at an intersection, in the house on the left with a barn across the road, Lieutenant Clesson McElroy lived, who fought at Gettysburg with the 13th Vermont.

Continue on Center Road 2 miles and look to a large field on the right. A farmhouse that was the home of Henry Nichols, who served the last year of the war as a private in the 4th Vermont, stood on the prominent rise in the middle of the field. In a letter written home just after Cedar Creek, he nicely summed up that battle saying, "the rebs drove us a piece in the morning but just before night we drove them a good ways farther than they were in the morning we camped that night on the same ground we had been camped on for a number of days."

Continue on Center Road 1 mile, reach a T, and turn left to continue on Center Road. At another T, take a quick right and note an old school house on the left. The aged farmhouse just behind it was once the Chapin house, and attached to the rear was a large hall, where Middlesex held its wartime town meetings. Voters here on September 2, 1862, authorized "the civil authorities to offer such bounties as they may think best for the volunteers that may be called on in the future." Middlesex, a town of about 1,250, sent 152 men to war, of whom 27 died.

Continue on Center Road past the Chapin house 0.5 mile, and turn left on Molly Supple Road that soon becomes Shady Rill Road. In 1.8 miles turn left on East Bear Swamp Road, and in just over 1.5 miles turn right at a T, staying on East Bear Swamp. In 0.4 mile, the road crosses a small stream. In a small house that stood here on the near side of the brook, on the right, lived Josiah Hasbrook, a black man who served in the Civil War. Hasbrook, his wife, Jane, and children, came to Middlesex several years after the war and moved away by 1900. Josiah, before the Civil War, was a member of the Timbucktoo community of blacks at North Elba, New York, where he knew John Brown well.

Return to the beginning of East Bear Swamp Road, go straight on Shady Rill Road, and in 1 mile come to the Shady Rill Church, on the left, where anti-slavery preacher Ichabod Cummings was a minister before the war. Continue 0.5 mile, pass Cummings farm on the right, and in 0.75 mile reach Route 12.

SOURCES
MIDDLESEX TOWN RECORDS.
WITH THANKS TO PAT WILLEY.

MONTPELIER

Of the 2,400 people who lived in Montpelier in the 1860s, 236 served and 51 died. The Overland Campaign took the especially heavy toll of 10 lives. The State House, built in 1859, is a Civil War treasure. The Pavilion Building next door contains the Vermont Historical Society museum with a fine Vermont Civil War exhibit, which includes, among other treasures, George Stannard's uniform and pistols and the famous sword taken from a Confederate officer at Gettysburg by Stephen Brown, armed only with a hatchet. But much more Civil War history is to be found in Montpelier.

Go west 1 mile from the State House along State Street to Evergreen Cemetery overlooking the Winooski River. A monument near the chapel honors five Civil War winners of the Medal of Honor who lie here. Among them is Stephen Thomas, 8th Vermont commander, buried in the far, upper right-hand corner of the cemetery. His modest stone is marked with crossed swords.

Proceed back toward the State House,

and on the left, note the large white house at 159 State Street, once the home of Reverend Chester Wright, who harbored fugitive slaves here. Turn left at the stoplight onto Bailey Avenue, then left on Terrace Street, and at the top of the hill is the Gothic redbrick and sandstone mansion known as Redstone. Professor John W. Burgess, a well-known political scientist, built it in 1891 as a summer retreat. In the summer of 1899, Burgess hosted here, for several weeks, the former first lady of the Confederacy, Varnia Howell Davis, widow of Jefferson Davis. She and Burgess took buggy rides in the surrounding countryside.

Return to State Street and proceed to the State House, noting the reconstructed Pavilion Hotel to its east. Many legislators roomed at the Pavilion while the general assembly was in session during the war. On June 17, 1864, the local *Vermont Watchman* said: "You are soon to have amongst you the brave boys who have been disabled by wounds or disease while nobly fighting the battles of their country. We shall be in want of sheets, pillow cases, blankets, pillows, comforters, dressing gowns, towels, rags, lint and cloth for dressings—Books and magazines will help the patients to beguile many a weary hour. Jellies, preserves etc. . . . Window curtains, tables, chairs. Send to hospital or to the Surgeon William B. Casey at the Pavilion." Montpelier was about to be the site of a Civil War hospital, and supplies for it were being gathered at the Pavilion.

In mid-April 1864, four hundred members of the 8th Vermont, recently reenlisted and home on furlough, were welcomed here. Danville's *North Star* reported, "The multitude greeted them with hearty cheers, by ringing of bells, by bonfires etc. A public reception took place in the State House grounds, and the regiment (under the command of Colonel Stephen Thomas) was drawn up in line, and Charles Reed Esq., from the balcony of the Pavilion, in behalf of the people, welcomed the officers and soldiers to the capitol in an appropriate speech; to which Col. Thomas, in behalf of the veterans, also appropriately replied." In May 1865, a gallows was erected just west of the Pavilion when news was received of the capture of Jefferson Davis. Whether his widow knew of this in her later visit isn't known.

Across the street, between the large granite office building and the ornate Gothic state agriculture building, is a small Victorian building with cupola, all that remains of the Montpelier railway station complex. Arriving at the station on a winter morning in 1870 were women from throughout the country to attend a meeting of the American Woman Suffrage Association. Among them were Julia Ward Howe and Mary Livermore. Howe, author of "The *Battle Hymn of the Republic*," was a well-known abolitionist. Livermore, promiment in the Sanitary Commission, was once praised by General William Tecumseh Sherman for her work on behalf of soldiers. He said, "she ranks me." That cold morning, Howe happily spotted a familiar figure at the station and exclaimed, "Oh you great big Livermore."

Governor Davis Avenue runs along the east side of the Pavilion to a white-brick building at the head of the street. Once a school, among its pupils was George Dewey, the admiral of Spanish American War fame. Many years before, as a young officer serving along the Mississippi River near Vicksburg, Dewey qualified for a Medal of Honor by saving lives when his ship was sunk by Rebel guns.

Continue along State Street to the Washington County Courthouse. On July 30, 1860, presidential candidate Stephen Douglas spoke on the courthouse steps, defending his doctrine of "popular sovereignty," saying it was simply "minding one's own business and leaving one's neighbor alone." He also stopped by the State House that day. In 1866, Vermont officers of the Civil War began a reunion with a meeting in the county courtroom, with George Stannard presiding, awaiting the arrival of Philip Sheridan. Several officer reunions commenced here, before proceeding to the State House. Continue on Main to the city's main intersection. Look straight ahead at the old brick building, which now houses a restaurant, once the office of the *Vermont Freeman.* The antislavery paper employed as its chief war correspondent Wilbur Fisk, a private in the 2nd Vermont (see Sharon). Fisk's Civil War letters, now gathered in a book called *Hard Marching,* constitute the finest Vermont first-person account of the war. Go past this building on East State Street 0.5 mile uphill to the Vermont College campus, once the site of one of Vermont's three Civil War hospitals. Sloan Hospital, named after W. J. Sloan, U.S. medical inspector of the Department of the East, had a capacity of five hundred beds and

was arranged around a circular covered walkway. The twelve ward buildings were more than 100 feet long, extending from a central point like the spokes of a wheel. It stood in the area of the present college green. Under the direction of Gettysburg surgeon Henry Janes (see Waterbury) for much of its existence, Sloan Hospital treated 1,670 soldiers. The hospital was filled to capacity by the 1864 Overland Campaign, in which Vermont suffered nearly 3,000 casualties.

Vermonters rallied to support the hospital. An unsigned letter in the *Vermont Watchman* on July 1, 1864, stated: "In behalf of the sick and wounded soldiers in this hospital . . . sincere thanks to the residents of this, and neighboring villages for their liberal and timely contributions of numerous articles which were needed at the hospital . . . Acknowledgements are especially due to the ladies . . . It is only necessary to say at present that every town and village for miles around have contributed its share." The letter also thanked residents of "places as distant as" Orford, New Hampshire, and Middletown, Connecticut, for their contributions.

The Montpelier facility's long wards, when it closed, were cut into sections and sold as houses. Many survive on streets near the college green. Turn left on College Street and look at the houses that stand at numbers 64, 80, and 84 College Street. Their front sections are parts of the old hospital, one-and-a-half-story buildings. Search the residential areas around the campus and soon you will begin to see similar structures. Back by the college green, the long building on the north side, a story-and-a-half house connected to a barn was the hospital guardhouse. The hospital included a chapel, and in late May 1865, a memorial service was held there for Abraham Lincoln. Reverend A. Webster based his sermon on the biblical quotation from Samuel, "Know ye not that there is a Prince and a great man fallen this day in Israel?"

The hospital was built on the Montpelier fairgrounds, and in the late summer of 1861, the 6th Vermont Regiment assembled here. Private Seth Eastman (see Groton) remembered, "The camp at Montpelier was the most pleasant camp ground that we ever saw while in the U.S. service. We had good tents to sleep in and straw to sleep on . . . We drilled eight hours a day and, all being young boys, we learned easy and soon became as well drilled as U.S. regulars."

Return down East State Street, go left on Hubbard Street, left on First Avenue, to the small frame house at number 9, home after the war of William Noyes. He went to war as a teenager, substituting for a man who bought his way out of service. On November 12, 1864, Noyes was fighting with the 2nd Vermont at Spotsylvania's Bloody Angle, where the Union and Confederate armies were separated only by an earthwork. Seeing a friend killed, the young private leaped atop the earthwork and fired down at the Confederates until his comrades pulled him back to safety. He won a Medal of Honor. On April 2, 1865, at the Petersburg Breakthrough, Noyes was wounded, but recovered and returned to Montpelier. In his sixties he was working as a carpenter on Montpelier's brand-new Blanchard Block, at the intersection of Main and State streets, when he fell to his death.

Return to State and Main and go north on Main Street, turning right on School Street. When General Sheridan visited Montpelier in 1867, he was the star of a parade that wound its way through town from the State House along State Street to Main, to School Street, then left on Loomis Street, and eventually back to the State House.

Return to the Main and State intersection, take Main south, cross the Winooski River Bridge, and proceed straight ahead on Northfield Street. The ornate house above the road on the right was the home of the artist Thomas Waterman Wood. Though not a Civil War veteran, Wood produced many popular paintings of the war.

By far the most intriguing and important Civil War site in Montpelier is the 1859 State House. To this building on April 23, 1861, in the wake of the firing on Fort Sumter, came the Vermont General Assembly, its senators and representatives called into "extra session" by Governor Erastus Fairbanks. The lawmakers were welcomed to Montpelier by the firing of two brass cannons captured from the British at the Battle of Bennington in 1777. One remains, on the State House portico.

The State House was two years old in the spring of 1861, as its predecessor had burned in January of 1857. The main building looks today about as it did then, though the dome in 1861 was painted red. On April 23, Fairbanks stood at the rostrum in a packed house of representatives and declared, "Gentlemen of the Senate and House of Representatives we are convened today in view of events of an extraordinary and very alarming character. The element of disunion which, in a portion of the United States, for many years, vented itself in threats and menaces, has culminated in open rebellion."

Fairbanks asked legislators to appropriate a half million dollars to begin Vermont's war effort. But Representative Stephen Thomas, of West Fairlee, destined to play a major role in the war, rose to declare, "I trust that the whole strength and power of Vermont, both of men and money, will be put into the field to sustain the government." The legislature voted a full million dollars. Thomas returned here in late October 1863, after having led the 8th Vermont in the Deep South. "I am soon to return to my duty," he said. "If it shall be my lot never to enter this hall again, let it be remembered that it is my highest hope (save that of a hold upon eternity), that this infamous rebellion is destined to a certain and everlasting overthrow; and that with it, by the blessing of God, the institution of human slavery, GOES DOWN FOREVER."

The governor's office contains a bust of Governor Fairbanks. Surely, he was seated in the old governor's chair made of wood from the U.S.S. *Constitution* (Old Ironsides) before he walked into the State House to, in effect, call his state to war. On the office walls are portraits of Vermont's two other Civil War governors, Frederick Holbrook and John Gregory Smith. The portrait of Governor Urban A. Woodbury shows a man with an empty sleeve. Woodbury, at First Bull Run, became the first Vermonter to lose a limb to hostile fire.

The house chamber today looks about as it did in 1861, though with nearly one hundred fewer seats, due to the one-man-one-vote reapportionment of the 1960s. The desks and chairs are the same. The rostrum is the one from which Fairbanks spoke. Stephen Thomas sat in the back row of the chamber, to the left as you enter the main door, under the far corner of the balcony. The chandelier is the same that gave light on that historic day, and it contains four reproductions of Hiram Powers's famed sculpture, *The Greek Slave* (see Woodstock).

Reunions of Vermont Civil War officers were often held in the State House, bringing many of the war's prominent figures to the house chamber. Philip Sheridan once spoke here, as did Benjamin Butler. At the reunion of Vermont officers held in 1880, the speaker was Martin McMahon, former 6th Corps adjutant general. McMahon talked of corps commander John Sedgwick and said that it was during the last day of the long march to Gettysburg that "Sedgwick directed me to 'put the Vermonters ahead and keep everything well closed up.' It was not the only time that he complimented the soldiers from Vermont. His compliments many times cost them very dear, for they were the high compliments of placing them on many battlefields in the foremost position of danger."

In November 1864, the legislature passed an act allowing the firing of the two cannons, on the State House portico, captured in the Battle of Bennington in 1777, to salute Abraham Lincoln's reelection.

On May 9, 1865, the legislature met in special session to consider a new amendment to the U.S. Constitution, the Thirteenth, that outlawed slavery. Vermont lawmakers voted here for its ratification, 217 to 0.

In the lobby, also known as the Hall of Flags, Vermont's Civil War battle flags were once displayed. When Sheridan saw the old flags here in 1867, he said, "I do not know but I can say that I never commanded troops in whom I had as much confidence as those of this gallant state." Most of the old flags are now stored for preservation, and some may be seen by arrangement with the State House curator. However, three battle flags still hang in the Old Supreme Court Chamber, now a legislative lounge, to the rear of the building.

The senate looks almost exactly as it did in 1861, with all furnishings and the chandelier original. Nearly one hundred Civil War veterans served in the senate, and Stephen Thomas presided as lieutenant governor.

Look for bronze tablets throughout the State House honoring Vermont's Civil War heroes, including Thomas, Lewis Grant, William Wells, and George Stannard.

The Cedar Creek Room vies with the senate and house for being the most beautiful room in Vermont. Dominated by the Julian Scott (see Johnson) painting of the Battle of Cedar Creek, the 10-by-20-foot canvas depicts Vermont troops engaged in the October 19, 1864, battle that won final control of the Shenandoah Valley for the Union. A Confederate surprise attack before dawn had driven Phil Sheridan's Union army more than 3 miles. But Sheridan, absent from the field at the outset, returned to rally his forces and launched a midafternoon counterattack that turned defeat into victory. The painting depicts the Vermont troops at the beginning of that attack. Scott visited the battlefield and accurately depicted the terrain, dominated by high Massanutten Mountain in the left background, from which the Confederates spotted a weakness in the Union defenses. Scott, a Medal of Honor winner for bravery at Lee's Mill in 1862, incorporated many portraits of Vermont soldiers into the painting. The shattered boulder in the center foreground symbolizes the divided Union.

Cedar Creek was chosen as Scott's subject, after considerable discussion, because more Vermont units were involved than in any other battle. The painting, funded by the legislature, went on display at the State House in 1874. Among those who gave it their approval was General Sheridan, who saw it as a work in progress, and said it showed the Vermonters as they looked "going in." On the wall near the painting is a Thomas Waterman Wood painting of Stephen Thomas, another hero of Cedar Creek.

Other paintings in the Cedar Creek Room include Scott's *The Vermont Brigade at White Oak Swamp*, showing the brigade meeting Stonewall Jackson's assault during the Peninsula Campaign of 1862. Scott's little *Mounted Sentry* depicts a lone cavalryman scanning a war zone horizon, probably at dawn somewhere on Virginia's Peninsula. The large portrait of William Farrar Smith, a St. Albans native, honors his finest moment in the Civil War when he established a vital supply line to Ulysses Grant's army at Chattanooga in 1862. In the background is Chattanooga's Lookout Mountain and the tents of Grant's army.

On the State House's lower floor is Larkin Mead's (see Brattleboro) bust of Abraham Lincoln. Mead was hired to create the statuary for Lincoln's tomb at Springfield, Illinois, for which the bust was a study. It was given to the State of Vermont in 1910 by Mead's widow and faces a bronze plaque by the main doorway that bears the words of Lincoln's Gettysburg Address.

SOURCES
BURLINGTON FREE PRESS, RUTLAND HERALD, AND VERMONT FREEMAN, 1861–1865. VERMONT STATE LIBRARY.
ROBBINS, DANIEL. THE VERMONT STATE HOUSE: A HISTORY AND GUIDE. MONTPELIER, VT: VERMONT STATE HOUSE PRESERVATION COMMITTEE/VERMONT COUNCIL ON THE ARTS, 1980.
TITTERTON, ROBERT. JULIAN SCOTT: ARTIST OF THE AMERICAN CIVIL WAR AND NATIVE AMERICA. JEFFERSON, NC: MCFARLAND, 1997.
WITH THANKS TO DAVID SCHUTZ.

MORETOWN

The Moretown veterans' memorial, at the Methodist Church along Route 100B, honors 125 men who served from an 1860 population of 1,410. Go north on 100B to the 1835 Moretown town hall, with cupola and columned porch. Here Moretown's Civil War–era town meetings were held, with the first bounties approved on September 4, 1862, $25 apiece for men enlisting in the 2nd Vermont Brigade. In November 1863, bounties of $300 were voted "to fill the quota of Moretown on the last requisition of the United States Government for 300,000." At the March meeting in 1865, with the war nearly ended, bounty payments had driven Moretown well into debt, necessitating the approval of a tax of 425 cents on every grand list dollar.

To the town hall in the late summer of 1862 came recruits to enlist in Company B of the 13th Vermont, made up of Mad River Valley men. Some twenty-three from Moretown served in the company, which gathered in Waitsfield on August 15, but soon moved to Moretown for drill. Surely, they marched along the main street as they learned soldiering, drilled by an experienced Norwich University instructor. It is believed that the company held meetings in the town hall. Then they were off to Brattleboro to join the 2nd Vermont Brigade and fight at Gettysburg.

One who enlisted at the Moretown town hall was Russell Dutton Silsby, Dutton to his friends. Silsby, his wife, Marinda, and three young daughters lived with his parents on a Moretown farm. Soon after the 13th reached Virginia, Marinda wrote Dutton: "I hear that the Valley Guards and others intend on giving you a warm reception when you come home. I guess others besides the Valley Guards will give you a warm reception also, and I don't believe the latter would care to have you go back to Dixie." Sergeant Silsby was captured in March 1863, apparently while on a foraging expedition. Exchanged two days later, the agreement under which he was released prevented him from fighting at Gettysburg. He wrote to his wife right after the battle: "You may think it strange, but I could not help shedding tears that I was not allowed to take my place with the Co. . . . I picked up a gun . . . but the Col sent for men and told me not to as the rebs would hang me from the first limb." Silsby came home safely and soon took his family west.

From the town hall, go north on 110B along the Mad River 0.5 mile to a farm with cape on the left, the home of Henry Murray. He joined Company B of the 13th and fought at Gettysburg. Soon after returning, he joined the Vermont Cavalry, where he became a sergeant. In the pursuit of Lee's retreating army toward Appomattox, Murray was wounded four days before Lee's surrender. He came home and recovered.

Continue on 100B, cross the Mad River, and go sharp right up Moretown Common Road to the Moretown Common Cemetery. William Hathaway is buried here beside his parents, his grave marked by a small stone that says Willie. Just beyond the cemetery, go left on Northfield Road, then quickly take the left-most road, Howes Road. In 1 mile, on the left, is a large old farmhouse that was the Hathaway home. William Hathaway was a fifer in Company B of the 13th Vermont. Regimental historian Edward Fisk wrote, "He was a small, slender light-haired boy, pleasant and patient under hardships which he was not able to cope with successfully. He was universally liked by his comrades, who tried to favor him as much as possible. He was taken sick and

went to general hospital in March. I think he was one of those who had measles. He lived to come home but died a few months after our discharge." Willie Hathaway died in this house.

One-third mile past the house, go left on Northfield Road, and in 0.75 mile reach the height of land. Descending, a clump of lilacs soon stands close by the road on the left, just before an old farm on the right. The lilacs are all that remain to mark the farm from which John Wesley Clark went to war. One of twenty-two Moretown men who served in the 6th Vermont, on July 28, while in pursuit of Lee's army after Gettysburg, Clark was in charge of a wagon train that was attacked near Warrenton, Virginia. Though severely wounded, he brought the train into Union lines. He was later awarded the Medal of Honor.

SOURCES
DUTTON LETTERS. NEBRASKA STATE
  HISTORICAL SOCIETY.
MORETOWN TOWN RECORDS.
WITH THANKS TO DENISE GABAREE AND
  CEDRIC REAGAN.

NORTHFIELD

Inscribed on Northfield's Civil War monument, on the village common beside Route 12, are 332 names of men who, it says, "heroically risked their lives in defense of their country in the war of 1861." By war's end, 41 Northfield men died in service. The common was the center of Northfield life at the time of the war, and the railroad depot survives at the west end, the central portion dating to the Civil War. The Universalist Church still faces the common on the north, though now minus its steeple and converted to a commercial building, with two display windows. Years before the war, Pastor John Gregory spoke there against slavery, once declaring it to be "in everlasting hostility to the true spirit of Jesus Christ." On the hill above, to the south, the Congregational Church towers over the green, as it did in time of war.

A resident of Northfield, Reverend W. C. Johnson, described patriotic rallies on the common early in the war, saying that speeches "for sustaining the Union" were made from platform cars parked by the depot and that torchlight parades followed. Northfield resident Walter Davenport wrote of one war meeting that "the bands played and speeches were made, and then the call was given for volunteers, and I can today see those men, rude and untutored farmers, slowly walking up the crude steps of the platform, sitting down at the improvised table and inscribing their names." And he wrote, "Later on, I was taken to the church on the village green to listen to the words of eulogy spoken by the Congregational pastor, as he officiated at the funerals of those who had fallen upon the field of honor."

The first Northfield men to go to war, members of the local New England Guards Militia Company, served in Company F of the 1st Vermont, organized by a local butcher, Captain William Boynton. On Sunday April 28, 1861, Boynton was presented with $500 in gold coins to help meet expenses, then the men attended services at the Methodist, Congregational, and Episcopal churches.

On April 16, 1863, four hundred members of the 8th Vermont, on leave after having agreed to reenlist, passed through Northfield by train. The *Vermont Watchman* reported, "The arrival of the train at Northfield bearing these brave defenders, was duly signaled by the ringing of bells and ere the train arrived a multitude of people swarmed the depot and railroad grounds, who loudly cheered as the train rested."

When word of Lee's surrender reached Northfield, according to an eyewitness by the arrival of the mail train, "feet were busy carrying the joyful news from house to house; men threw up their caps, jumped, ran, wrestled, embraced each other, and hurrahed for everybody and everything." At 3 PM "the people began to assemble from the hills and valleys and one hundred guns were fired."

In October 1867, the train bearing Philip Sheridan to his heroic welcome at Montpelier stopped at the depot. The *Rutland Herald* reported: "At Northfield the train was welcomed by a ringing salute fired by the cadets of Norwich University . . . A tremendous crowd filled the depot, and the general was obliged to leave the train and take the platform in front of the depot, so the people might see him."

On Memorial Day 1885, a large crowd assembled to dedicate the Civil War monument. Before ceremonies, a procession wound its way through town, led by a coronet band and including a wagon bearing thirty-eight young ladies dressed in white, each representing a state of the

Union. The route was south along Central Street, then east on South Street, north on Main to Vine Street, then north on North Street to Elmwood Cemetery, where graves were decorated.

Take that route today, and one passes all three churches where the New England Guards attended church and where the Congregational minister presided at soldier funerals.

From the common, go north on Route 12, turn left on Vine Street, and right on North Street to the village cemetery. On June 23, 1893, veterans of the 13th Vermont gathered in Northfield for their sixth annual reunion and to dedicate a monument at the grave of their commander, Lieutenant Colonel Francis Voltaire Randall, who had led them at Gettysburg. Rain poured down that day, thus the dedication was held indoors. Randall lived in Northfield at the time of his death, operating a hotel, formerly having served as vice president of Norwich University. His former comrade-in-arms Albert Clarke spoke: "He was not only an adroit leader, but he was also a merciful man. He saw before his men did that Pickett's men were throwing down their arms and he gave the order to cease firing. The order was not heard and he broke through his line and faced it, waving his hat and sword and shouting until he was understood." The Randall monument stands at the east end of the cemetery, overlooking the village. Also buried here is Alonzo Jackman (see Norwich), longtime stalwart of Norwich University who drilled Vermont volunteers for Civil War service. By his grave is an iron arch, topped by a cross, apparently a small likeness of the gateway to the military school when it was located in Norwich.

On the fifty-second anniversary of the Battle of Cedar Creek, veterans of the 1st Vermont Cavalry gathered at Norwich University to dedicate a flagpole, with granite base. The monument still stands on the university's Upper Parade, and its tablet lists the battles in which the regiment fought. The university's Centennial Stairway, dedicated in 1919, leads to the Upper Parade, and its steps bear the names of the famous who were associated with Norwich. Among them are Alonzo Jackman, Navy Secretary Gideon Welles, Admiral George Dewey, and Oliver Otis Howard. Howard was a longtime trustee of the university, and its athletic fields are named for him.

The university's Sullivan Museum has exhibits depicting Norwich's Civil War history.

SOURCES

GREGORY, JOHN. *CENTENNIAL PROCEEDINGS AND HISTORICAL INCIDENTS OF THE EARLY SETTLERS OF NORTHFIELD, VT*. MONTPELIER, VT: ARGUS AND PATRIOT BOOK AND JOB PRINTING CO., 1878.

NORTHFIELD TOWN HISTORY COMMITTEE. *GREEN MOUNTAIN HERITAGE: THE CHRONICLE OF NORTHFIELD, VERMONT*. NORTHFIELD, VT: NORTHFIELD TOWN HISTORY COMMITTEE, 1974.

RUTLAND HERALD, 1866. VERMONT STATE LIBRARY.

WITH THANKS TO GARY LORD AND JIM WILSON.

PLAINFIELD

The Plainfield town hall, a Unitarian church at the time of the Civil War, is in the middle of Plainfield village along Route 2. Turn south just east of it, immediately cross the Winooski River, and enter a group of buildings that would easily be recognized by a Civil War–era person. Bear right to the Methodist Church where Reverend Nathan Robinson, the Topsham abolitionist, recalled speaking in 1856 and having "a slight encounter with the minister who took exception to what I said." If that indicated some local opposition to Robinson's antislavery sentiments, Plainfield within a decade would write a record in the freedom war that saw 68 men serve from an 1860 population of about 700. Of them, 3 died of wounds and 11 of disease.

On August 22, 1862, Plainfield selectmen Orin Cree, William Foss, and John Bancroft completed a census of able-bodied males in the town between the ages of eighteen and forty-five. Of the 107 men listed, the town fathers noted 62 farmers, 15 farm laborers, 3 laborers, 3 blacksmiths, 2 dentists, 2 harness makers, 2 shoemakers, 2 physicians, 2 lawyers, 1 tinsmith, 1 wagon maker, 1 mason, 1 clerk, 1 cooper, 1 grocer, 1 teamster, 1 machinist, 1 clergyman, 1 innkeeper, and 1 deputy sheriff. The men that selectmen excluded from that list had the following physical difficulties: right leg short, no teeth, hernia, large veins, deformity of feet, false teeth, disease of lungs, and blind in right eye.

Proceed past the front of the church, quickly turn left on narrow Hudson Avenue and the last house on the left, a large frame structure with a two-deck porch, was the home of Rufus and Sally Lease. Rufus and sons Joseph and Julian all enlisted as privates in Company D, 4th Vermont, on December 21, 1863. Rufus served until June 15, 1864, when he died at sixty of dysentery in an Alexandria, Virginia, hospital. Joseph, like his father a maker of saddles, died three weeks later at age twenty-eight in a Washington, D.C., hospital of wounds at Weldon Railroad. Brother Julian was shot on May 5, 1864, at the Wilderness but survived.

Turn left at the end of Hudson onto Creamery Street, and note the two flat-roofed houses on the left, side by side. Both were built by Ira Batchelder years after he served in the Vermont Cavalry and was discharged for disability. He lived his last years in the larger of the two houses. On February 3, 1910, at eighty-seven, he died from a fall on the ice suffered near here, walking home from a visit to old friend and neighbor Ervin Nye, a fellow veteran who served eighteen months in the 4th Vermont.

Proceed to the end of the street and drive straight into the parking lot behind the Plainfield fire station, located in a building that was the Civil War–era Congregational church. Enter the main gate of the cemetery and go right four rows. Halfway along is Henry Martin's stone, which bears no reference to his service as a private in the 13th Vermont. Wounded in a leg at Gettysburg, Martin came home to outlive two wives, who lie beside him. Proceed up the hill at the cemetery's rear and on the crest is the small stone of Ezekiel Skinner, a corporal in the 4th Vermont, who served from September 1861 until discharged for disability in December 1863. Beside the grave is a plaque that reproduces the words of a certificate given by the State of Vermont to all its Civil War veterans in 1873 for "having borne an honorable part as a volunteer from the State of Vermont in suppressing the rebellion and thereby preserving the integrity of the Union, the supremacy of law, and the liberties of all men under law."

From the cemetery, return to Route 2 and turn east. On the right is a row of houses, with backs to the river. Ezekiel Skinner lived in the last one, just before the Plainfield-Marshfield town line. Turn around and return along Route 2, pass the town hall on the right, and in 1.2 miles, turn right on Coburn Road. In just under 0.5 mile is a large farmhouse, just before the Coburn covered bridge. Henry Martin bought this farm after the Civil War, living there with memories of the day he was wounded attacking the flank of Pickett's Charge as a private in the 13th Vermont.

SOURCES

CHILD, HAMILTON. *GAZETTEER OF WASHINGTON COUNTY, 1783–1899.* EDITED BY WILLIAM ADAMS. SYRACUSE, NY: SYRACUSE JOURNAL COMPANY, 1889.

PLAINFIELD HISTORICAL SOCIETY. *THE TOWN OF PLAINFIELD, VERMONT: A PICTORIAL HISTORY, 1870–1940.* PLAINFIELD, VT: PLAINFIELD HISTORICAL SOCIETY, 1993.

PLAINFIELD TOWN RECORDS.

WITH THANKS TO STANLEY MARTIN, DALE BARTLETT, AND BRIAN PFEIFFER.

······································

ROXBURY

Along Route 12A, in the village of Roxbury, the 1848 Roxbury railroad station is now the town office. On October 2, 1861, one hundred Washington County men making up Company H, 6th Vermont, boarded a train here. The company had elected David Davenport, of Roxbury, its captain and with him to war went his ten-year-old son Henry, a drummer. Company H joined the rest of the 6th at Montpelier and saw its first action at Lee's Mill on April 16, 1862. Captain Davenport was wounded and his son helped to drag him to safety. The captain recovered but died of disease in an army hospital in Alexandria, Virginia, the following September. Young Henry came home for a time, but in 1864 he reenlisted as a drummer at age thirteen. Shot in the leg at the Wilderness, he returned home for good in February 1865.

Of a wartime population of about 1,000, Roxbury sent 103 men to war, exceeding its enlistment quotas by 23 men.

North of the railroad station along 12A is the Roxbury town hall in which voters on September 5, 1863, approved $300 bounties. At the March meeting in 1864, selectmen were empowered to pay whatever amount necessary to meet quotas. But by March 1866, after voting two special taxes during the war years to pay the cost of recruiting, Roxbury voters said no to a proposal for paying additional bounties to men who had served.

Across the road, and slightly north, from the town hall is the old Methodist Church, attended at times by Roxbury's Ellis family, including son Henry. Henry Ellis taught school for a time in Williamstown, then moved to Iowa, then Arkansas. Enlisting soon after the war began in the Confederate 13th Arkansas, he wrote to his family in Roxbury, "I will try to forget that there is a blockade between us for I cannot realize that within five miles of me are the lines of an enemy in whose numbers perhaps are found brothers and friends of long ago . . . Nor will I believe that I am forgotten by the friends at home because I wear the rebel uniform and fight for the land of my adoption." Ellis fought at Shiloh and ended up in a Yankee prison, though he survived the war.

Go north 0.3 mile on 12A, and note the old frame house on the right, in the midst of a summer camp complex. Langdon Nichols, a corporal in the Vermont Cavalry, lived here. He was captured at Middletown in the Shenandoah Valley in the spring of 1862 and died a prisoner in Lynchburg, Virginia.

Continue north 0.75 mile to the cemetery on the right, with many Civil War graves. Near the highway are the stones of George and Samuel Richardson, both privates under Captain Davenport in Company H, who lie beside their parents, Chandler and Sarah Richardson. George had served less than two months when he died of illness at Frederick, Maryland, on December 9, 1862. His brother Samuel, twenty-three, died a year later, soon after having come home sick from the front. Close by is the grave of Byron Batchelder, a private in the 17th Vermont, who died at age twenty-two, three weeks after suffering a wound at the Wilderness on May 6, 1864. He lies beside his parents, Otis and Adeline. Toward the rear of the cemetery is a stone for Samuel Shepard, a black man who was a member of the 56th Massachusetts Regiment. The stone notes that he "enlisted at his country's call" and "laid down his life at Petersburg, Va." on June 21, 1864.

Return south into the village and turn right, west, on Warren Hill Road. In 0.8 mile, the old frame house on the right, along a flat, is believed to have been the home from which Byron Batchelder went to war.

Return to Route 12A and go north past the cemetery toward Northfield. In 3.3 miles, just beyond the second railroad underpass, see Bull Run Road on the right. The road leads high into the hills to parallel Bull Run Brook. It is believed that the name came from the Civil War. Whether there is a connection to the fact that the first soldier credited to Roxbury killed in action, Private Victor Goodrich of the 2nd Vermont, fell at First Bull Run, isn't known.

A long, high ridge divides Roxbury. Continue north on 12A to Route 12 in Northfield, and turn right, south. In 3.3 miles, after reentering Roxbury, note a huge old metal cow barn on the right. The farmhouse just beyond it was the home of Edmund and Roxana Pope, whose son, Edmund, was a sergeant in the Vermont Cavalry. Taken prisoner on June 29, 1864, Pope was soon confined at Andersonville. On September 3, he wrote in his diary, "Cloudly all day but no rain. The nites begin to grow cold and rations grow small. It is a pretty hard site for living. The report is now that there is to be no exchange during the war but I guess that don't amount to much." By late October, Pope had been transferred to the prison at Salisbury, North Carolina. His last diary entry was November 2, 1864: "Rained all day and pretty cold rain. Drew a little beef and musty meal. Pretty tough living and intense suffering in camp."

Continue south 0.5 mile to the East Roxbury Cemetery on the right. In the house facing the cemetery Ozra Boyce lived, who served the war's last eighteen months as a private in the 4th Vermont. He apparently was assigned for a time to the headquarters of 6th Corps commander Major Gen. Horatio Wright. In a letter written to Edmund Pope Sr., father of the doomed Edmund, on December 2, 1864, Ozra said, "I have been taking care of two cows for the general, I have plenty of milk to put in my coffee." The elder Pope was handling Boyce's business affairs. Boyce wrote, "I should like to have you see to my business another year if you would. I will pay you whatever it is worth. Will leave it to you to chose as you are administrator about leasing the farm."

In the cemetery is Edmund Pope's grave, close by his parents. The stone says he "endured with patience the privations of Andersonville and other prisons until Dec. 12 when went on board of transport at Charleston where he died Dec. 14 before reaching Anapolis, Md." Edmund Pope Jr. was twenty-four. Also buried here is Ozra Boyce, who returned home to a long life on this farm.

SOURCES
BOYCE, OZRA. CIVIL WAR LETTER, EDMUND POPE PAPERS. VERMONT HISTORICAL SOCIETY.
BRIGHAM, LORIMAN S. "AN ADAPTABLE YANKEE." ESSAY IN "HENRY M. ELLIS LETTERS, 1858–1868" BY HENRY M. ELLIS. UNPUBLISHED MANUSCRIPT, UNDATED. VERMONT HISTORICAL SOCIETY.
POPE, EDMUND. CIVIL WAR DIARY. VERMONT HISTORICAL SOCIETY.
ROXBURY TOWN RECORDS.
TEDFORD, TED. "THE LITTLEST SOLDIER." LIVIN' MAGAZINE. JULY/AUGUST 2006.
WITH THANKS TO TAMMY LEGACY.

WAITSFIELD

In 1867, the town of Waitsfield published *The Memorial Record of Waitsfield, Vermont,* on the town's Civil War history. In the introduction, the author, Reverend A. B. Dascomb, pastor of the Waitsfield Congregational Church during the war, wrote:

"One by one the lovers of their country joined the Union army till their number was two million, and their strength, employed as it was in the interest of justice, righteousness and liberty, irresistible. Our town, containing a population of about one thousand, contributed its proportion of voluntary offerings on the national altar. Though far removed from the scenes of conflict, and employed in the most quiet of vocations—the industrious cultivation of a fertile soil—yet she felt the large pulsations of the large patriotic heart of the country."

Go south on Route 100 from Duxbury to the Route 100B junction and continue south 1.5 miles to a farmhouse and barn on the right, in 2012 a bed & breakfast. Edwin Palmer grew up here and served as a lieutenant in the 13th Vermont, participating in the flank attack on Pickett's Charge. In 1864, he published a book on his wartime experiences called *Camp Life*. In it, he described a winter funeral in northern Virginia: "He is now laid in the ground four feet deep; twelve of his comrades fire their farewell shots; the chaplain speaks consoling words, offers a prayer to God and pronounces the benediction; and we turn away, not as when we came, with a slow and measured tread,—the drummers beating the dead march,—but with quicker steps, a livelier air, Yankee Doodle."

Just beyond this farm, take Meadow Road, cross the Mad River, and soon go left on North Road. In 1 mile, on the right, is a house and large barn, once the farm home of Albert Blanchard. He joined the local militia company, the Driftwood Company, which became Company B of the 13th Vermont. Blanchard survived Gettysburg but came home exhausted. A comrade recalled, "those last marches and the battle proved to be more than he could endure, and he reached home sick and died on August 12, 1863." He died in this house, at twenty-one.

Return to Route 100 and continue south 0.6 mile to a farmhouse and barn on the right. Orcas Wilder, captain of Company B, went to war from here and returned safely, to live a long life.

Continue south on Route 100, and near the center of Waitsfield village, on the west side, stands the Waitsfield Civil War memorial, erected in 1907 "in memory of the boys in blue who marched from this town on to the battlefields of the Civil War." The Granite monument, with the names of eighty-six men, stands between the Odd Fellows Hall and the Methodist Church, both of which contributed land for the memorial. Proceed south on Route 100 and turn left on Bridge Road. The large building at the southeast corner was once known as Lakes Hall, and in its basement meeting room, some town meetings

of the Civil War era took place. Voters here approved bounties that reached $800, and Reverend Dascomb said the total town contribution to the war effort was $10,433. 40.

Pass through the covered bridge, and the second house on the left, red brick, was a tavern where, according to a town historian, "A society was organized, auxiliary to the Christian Commission, and many army supplies, prepared by bands of devoted women that met regularly in the hall of the brick tavern in the village, were shipped directly to the front."

Return to Route 100 and continue south; go through the village of Irasville, pass the intersection of Route 117, and Fiddler's Green Road quickly turns left. Just past it is a frame house set back from the road with shed behind. William Tell Stoddard lived here and saw four sons go to war. Private Horace Stoddard, 2nd Vermont, was killed at the Wilderness. Private Lathrop Stoddard, 13th Vermont, survived Gettysburg and reenlisted in the 17th Vermont, only to die of wounds received in the Battle of the Crater. Private Harlan Stoddard, 2nd Vermont, survived a wound at Savage's Station and imprisonment to return to Waitsfield. Private William Stoddard, 6th Vermont, came home unharmed.

Cross the Mad River, go right on Lareau Road, and directly ahead is the Stoddard homestead, once home of Dr. Simeon Stoddard. The father of William Tell Stoddard, ten of the doctor's grandsons served, including the four previously mentioned. Another grandson, George Walker, of Randolph, a private in the 8th Vermont, died of disease in Louisiana.

Return north on Route 100 through Irasville and Waitsfield, and soon a picnic area is on the right by the Mad River. Just north of it, the road ascends, and on the right, a barn stands close by the road. Directly opposite it is an old farmhouse where lived Private George Jones, 2nd U.S. Sharpshooters. He was killed at the Wilderness while trying to help a wounded comrade.

SOURCES

DASCOMB, REV. A. B. *THE MEMORIAL RECORD OF WAITSFIELD VERMONT.* PUBLISHED BY VOTE OF THE TOWN. MONTPELIER, VT: FREEMAN STEAM PRINTING ESTABLISHMENT, 1867. WAISFIELD TOWN RECORDS. WITH THANKS TO FRED MESSER AND RICHARD BISBEE.

....

WARREN

Some 90 men served from Warren, and 10 died. People met to conduct town business in the River Meeting House, now the Warren United Church, which survives in the middle of Warren village just off Route 100. Here on November 12, 1863, faced with meeting a quota of 14 men, voters appropriated $4,410, or $315 per man. On March 1, 1864, a payment of $1 per day was approved for selectmen "for time spent in enlisting men in the U.S. service." On February 21, 1865, bounties of $600 were voted.

The graveyard behind the church contains many soldier graves. Headstones mark the resting places of, among others, Sergeant Aretus Thayer, twenty-three, of the 13th Vermont, who died soon after returning from Gettysburg; Sergeant Merrill

Bucklin, twenty-one, 6th Vermont, who died of disease in 1862 at age twenty-one; Sergeant Joseph Eldredge, twenty-one, 11th Vermont, who died of disease at the close of the Overland Campaign; and Sergeant Benjamin Edgerton, 11th Vermont, who died of wounds at Third Winchester. A memorial stone remembers Private Oscar Kelsey, mortally wounded at Savage's Station, and whose body never came home.

Side by side lie Private Willard Thayer and his wife, Esther Thayer. She died at eighty-three in 1913. Thayer enlisted in the 10th Vermont in August 1862 and was wounded three months later at Mine Run. The Thayer family letters are preserved at the Vermont Historical Society, mostly letters written by Willard to the wife he called Et, on their upland farm just off Lincoln Gap Road. On November 9, 1862, he wrote, "Well, Et, tell the little children to be good and that father will come home as soon as he can . . . Oh hon, I wish I could see you all. I hope I shall have that privlege sometime."

January 2, 1863, "Well, Esther, what do people think of this war? I tell you the boys are getting out of patience and there is but a few but what say if they was at home they would not enlist again on any consideration."

She replied on January 23, reporting on local people and the Thayer children: "Sarys man ses if he lives to see another new year he shall see pees dclard Oh I pray he will with out eny more lives lost . . . Jed thinks that the war will end soon . . . Sister feeds her self to the table Willie and Libby are runing and holring . . . Burty at his school Willy ses tell Father to send a leter and a kiss to him he kis this for Father." January 12, 1864, Willard wrote, "If I could have a farm out here in Virginia in some places where we have passed along I would come here to live if the Lord should spare my life when this infernal war is ended." His last letter was written in the trenches at Spotsylvania in May 1864. "I have been on the skirmish line three days of the time where if we showed a head it was popped at . . . the shot and shells fly like hail. Oh, I shall be glad when this is through & we can have some rest."

Willard, promoted to corporal, was soon severely wounded. He started for home but died en route, at the home of his wife's sister, Ella, in Brooklyn, New York. She apparently had removed him from a military hospital. Ella wrote to Esther not long after his death, "Esther, how do you get along with your little family this winter. God knows my heart bleeds for you."

Esther's brother, Sergeant James Miller, 10th Vermont, died of disease at Annapolis, Maryland, in February, 1865 after his capture at the Weldon Railroad and subsequent confinement in Confederate prisons.

Take the Lincoln Gap Road west from Warren, and a bit over 1 mile along, on the left, is an old schoolhouse. Willard and Esther lived in this area, probably in a house on what is now called Hanks Road, just beyond on the right. Willard likely attended this school, or a previous building on its site. The steep and rocky landscape here may have inspired Willard's desire for a Virginia farm. Many former soldiers left Vermont soon after the war.

Return to Warren village and take Roxbury Mountain Road to an upland crossroads, once in the center of East Warren, a thriving community during the Civil War. Little remains save for a school, a handful of houses, and the East Warren Cemetery. Toward the rear of the burying ground is the grave of James Wilson, 13th Vermont, whose stone says, "Killed at Gettysburg."

Return to the crossroads and go east, uphill, on Roxbury Mountain Road, and in 0.6 mile, turn right on Senor Road. In just under 1 mile, the farmhouse on the right, with barns beyond, was James Wilson's home. Private Wilson went to war, leaving behind a fiancé, Delia Porter, in East Warren. He was a faithful writer of letters to his family and friends, and when the 13th assembled at Brattleboro, he wrote, "We are sworn in today and tomorrow. We are to bid adieu to the Green Hills of Vermont for nine months. Then we shall be home again. All I hope." Ever mindful of home, he wrote on April 9, 1863, "Who is going to teach our school this summer? . . . Tell Bub that I want to know how the little calves get along and the yearlings too how have they stood the cold?"

Wilson's mother, Rosalin, wrote him on June 28, "Keep up good courage and put your trust in God of battles and I hope that he will care you safe through all your trials." A friend recalled for the 13th Vermont's history an incident on July 3, 1863, just before Pickett's Charge: "Dexter Parker received a very painful wound from a piece of shell which cut through one of his hands and he was in such agony that Corporal

O. G. Miles and James H. Wilson started to help him to the rear, one on each side. They had only gone a short distance when a shell struck in a pile of stones and burst. All three fell to the ground and it was found that a small piece of shell had pierced Wilson's heart, killing him instantly." The reminiscence continued, "Wilson's body was buried on the field with a carefully marked board placed at the head of the grave. Late in the fall of 1863, S. J. Dana of our company was sent to Gettysburg to bring his body home which task he successfully accomplished and he lies buried in the little cemetery in East Warren. Some of his comrades tell the story that while on the march towards Gettysburg they said to Wilson, 'Our time will soon be out and we shall go home.' To which he replied, 'I shall never go home alive. We shall have a fight and I shall be killed' . . . The missile that pierced his heart, like cases without number in the war, slew another in the home town, who was to become his wife on his return. She lived only a few months after the terrible news reached her."

SOURCES

HARTSHORN, KATHERINE. *COMMEMORATION OF WARREN'S BICENTENNIAL, 1789–1989.* WATERBURY, VT: BUY MONTHLY PUBLISHING, 1989.
THAYER, WILLARD, AND ESTHER THAYER. LETTERS. VERMONT HISTORICAL SOCIETY.
WARREN TOWN RECORDS.
WILSON, JAMES. CIVIL WAR LETTERS. VERMONT HISTORICAL SOCIETY.
WITH THANKS TO RITA GOSS.

WATERBURY

Exit Interstate 89 at Waterbury, go left on Main Street, and soon on the right is the Waterbury library, given to the town by longtime village physician Henry Janes. In his younger days, Dr. Janes was the surgeon given charge of the more than twenty thousand wounded, Union and Rebel, left at Gettysburg after the Civil War's biggest battle. So well did Dr. James perform the monumental task that he was on the speakers' platform at the dedication of the Gettysburg National Cemetery on November 19, 1863. Thus, Janes heard Abraham Lincoln deliver his Gettysburg Address. The large house that housed Janes's office in Waterbury is now the town library, west of the village center on Route 2. On the second floor is a display that includes the doctor's medical saddlebag, his uniform, the doctor's wartime photo, and an 1865 *New York Herald* announcing Lincoln's death. Framed on the wall is Janes's copy of the Gettysburg Address. The house across the parking lot was Janes's home. Janes was also in charge of the Sloan Hospital at Montpelier and of the South Street General Hospital in Philadelphia. By one calculation, he supervised the care of forty thousand soldiers. In Waterbury, the good doctor saw to the needs of local men suffering the effects of their Civil War service for many years after the war.

East along Main Street, across the street, once stood the home of Colonel William Wirt Henry, who led the 10th Vermont Regiment in the latter part of the war. Henry went west before the war, joining the California gold rush. He enlisted as the war began, serving at First Bull Run with the 2nd Vermont. He commanded the 10th in most of its major battles, including the Wilderness, Spotsylvania, Monocacy, and Cold Harbor, where he had a finger shot away. In the surprise Rebel attack at Cedar Creek, the 10th Vermont was personally ordered by General James Ricketts to retake a battery. Henry and his color bearer were the first to reach the guns, which were drawn back to Union lines under heavy fire. The colonel was four times wounded that day. Awarded a Medal of Honor, the citation stated, "Though suffering from severe wounds, rejoined his regiment and led it in a brilliant charge, recapturing the guns of an abandoned battery." Henry was often a guest at the Janes home. He is buried in Burlington's Lakeview Cemetery.

Just down Main Street is the Waterbury Congregational Church, of Gothic design. Reverend Charles Carroll Parker was its pastor, preaching against slavery and in support of the Union, until he left the pulpit for a time in 1864 to serve the United States Christian Commission, the Civil War's equivalent of the Red Cross. Parker joined the winter encampment of the 10th Vermont under neighbor Colonel Henry at Brandy Station, ministering to the spiritual needs of the soldiers. On his way home, the reverend attended a White House reception. "Mr. Lincoln looked like nature's nobleman," he wrote, "& when a smile came over his ordinarily intensely solemn face & he was about to make a funny speech, his face was singularly pleasant—every rough feature radiant with the kindness & humor & geniality of his soul."

Just east along Main Street by the village's main intersection, a plaque by the door identifies a brick house as the Dillingham home. Prominent local attorney Paul Dillingham and his wife, Julia (Carpenter) Dillingham, here raised two sons who served. Edwin Dillingham joined the 10th Vermont and survived Libby Prison to rise to the rank of major. At Winchester on September 19, 1964, one of his legs was shot away. As he died, his last words were, "I am willing to give my life for my country and I am not afraid to die." A comrade described him as "young, handsome, and brilliant."

Another Dillingham son, Lieutenant Colonel Charles Dillingham, rose to second in command of the 8th Vermont and led it in some of the heaviest fighting during the Siege of Port Hudson, the last Confederate bastion to fall on the Mississippi. Father Paul Dillingham was elected governor of Vermont in 1865.

Behind the Dillingham and Janes houses is Hope Cemetery, where many Civil War–era figures are buried, including Henry Janes and the Dillinghams. On September 4, 1893, veterans of the 10th Vermont, in Waterbury for a reunion, gathered at Edwin Dillingham's grave to pay respects.

East of the main intersection on Main, past the fire station, is a large brick office building, a replica of a house on this site in which William Wells was born. Wells enlisted in the 1st Vermont Cavalry as a private and eventually commanded the regiment. The Wells house burned as the twentieth century closed. Wells went to war from here and survived two wounds and a time in Libby Prison. He won a Medal of Honor for his service at Gettysburg, leading Vermonters in the cavalry charge ordered by Judson Kilpatrick. Some sixty Vermonters became casualties in the brave but fruitless assault.

Wells led the Vermont Cavalry at Cedar Creek, joining in the decisive charge under George Custer. He wrote to his parents, here, two days after the battle: "The 1st Vermont was in the charge also the 8th N.Y. we pressed them back to the creek charging several times . . . we charged the enemy through Strasburg distance of about four miles, capturing prisoners, artillery wagons, etc etc . . . it is the *biggest thing of the War.*"

Go north on Stowe Street (Route 100) from Waterbury's main intersection, and soon come to the Waterbury Civil War monument, dedicated on Memorial Day 1914. Scores of veterans were present, and Colonel Henry was master of ceremonies.

Continue north on Route 100 out of the village, and 1 mile along, turn right on Kneeland Flats Road to Waterbury Center. Maple Street runs along the far side of the common and on it is a large ornate house, now a bed & breakfast. Built by Ebenezer Foster, a musician in the 10th Vermont, Foster, after the war, became a friend of Mary Baker Eddy, founder of the Christian Science Church, who apparently provided the funds for this grand home.

Return to Route 100 and go north to a redbrick church, on the right. Here in early January 1914, a funeral was held for Jacob Wrisley, a private in the 2nd Vermont for most of the war. He survived

thirty-four battles and was wounded at the Wilderness. Many members of the local Ezra Stetson GAR Post attended, having passed a resolution in Wrisley's honor, stating that he had "gone to swell the ranks across the river."

Return to Waterbury and go west on Route 2 to Little River Road. At the end of the road, by the flood control dam, is Little River State Park. Maps of its hiking trails can be obtained at the park entrance. Well back in the hills is the foundation of a house that was known in Waterbury as the "syphilis house." Apparently, Waterbury men who came home from the war with venereal disease were made to live there.

SOURCES

LEWIS, THEODORE GRAHAM. *HISTORY OF WATERBURY VERMONT, 1763–1915.* WATERBURY, VT: THE RECORD PRINT, 1913.

YAEGER, W. PATRICK. *THE BEAUTIFUL VALE ABOVE THE FALLS: THE LITTLE REGION OF WATERBURY, VERMONT COMES ALIVE ONCE AGAIN.* WATERBURY, VT: PRIVATELY PRINTED, 1995.

WELLS, WILLIAM. PAPERS. UNIVERSITY OF VERMONT, BAILEY/HOWE LIBRARY, SPECIAL COLLECTIONS.

WOODBURY

Going north along Route 14 from South Woodbury to Woodbury Center, one retraces the route taken sometime in the late 1850s by a young Viola Heath. She remembered, "There had been many indications that fear of war lurked in the minds of the people both North and South, and there was a general feeling in some quarters that if such an event were impending, a 'War Comet' would appear. One evening while driving to the Center from South Woodbury with Orwell [her brother], we saw what looked like a comet with a tail which was short or lost below the horizon. The next night it was higher and the tail was longer, and eventually it stretched clear across the heavens. It occasioned much excitement and settled the question of war in the minds of thousands of people. Also I remember that the Northern Lights were especially bright."

Following the route of that long-ago journey, arrive in Woodbury Center, and on the left is the town hall. Across the street, at the southeast corner of Cabot Road, is a large house built in 1844 that was once the Towne Hotel. Viola Heath lived there. She recalled, "When the news of the dreaded 'War Draft' became known there was much excitement and resentment. George Wells headed a mob that cut down the 'Liberty Pole' which carried a big flag in front of the Towne Hotel." She said, "One of my beaux, named Charles Buxton, starved to death in Andersonville." Private Buxton, who joined the Fourth Vermont in Plainfield, was captured at Weldon Railroad, and died at Andersonville. And Viola wrote, "So many left Woodbury for the War, either as the result of the draft, voluntary enlistment, or the selling of services as 'substitutes,' that there was not enough remaining to attend to the business of the town. The first time some townsmen came home on furlough, there was a great reception at the Towne Hotel followed by a dance in the ballroom."

Despite the small draft riot, according to Child's *Gazetteer of Washington County,* "In the late war Woodbury claims, and is justly entitled to, an excellent and honorable war record. One hundred forty-four of her patriotic sons enlisted . . . a number that more than filled her quota, who came forward without being stimulated by public meetings, or the offer of excessive bounties. No other town in the state, with a population as small, sent more men to war than Woodbury."

Across Route 14 from the old hotel is the Woodbury town hall, where voters on January 23, 1865, voted to "authorize the selectmen to pay bounty to soldiers and be discretionary with them how much to pay." At the annual town meeting six weeks later, in an action likely related to the war, Woodbury voted to spend $200 on a new town hearse. At the 1869 annual meeting, Woodbury voters were still dealing with a debt of $1,650.

From the old hotel, go north on Route 14 to the north end of the village, and the house on the right, above the road, just before Town Farm Road goes right, was the home of Carroll McKnight. He joined the 13th Vermont, deserted, was captured, and was sentenced to nine months in a Union prison. But he reenlisted in the 11th Vermont and was wounded at Cold Harbor. Though permanently disabled, McKnight came home to pursue a career as a carpenter and builder and served four terms in the legislature, representing Woodbury.

Return south on Route 14 to South Woodbury, and opposite the town offices, on the left, turn right on Foster Hill Road. In 0.75 mile, take King Pond Road, and in 1 mile, take Chartier Hill Road. From the first house on the left, Norman Lawson joined the 2nd Vermont in 1861. Wounded and taken prisoner at Savage's Station, he was imprisoned at Belle Isle, but was exchanged two months later. The following May 3, he was shot in the foot at Second Fredericksburg. He survived and came home.

Return to Route 14, go south to Woodbury Pond, and on the left is a large house with long porch, once the Lake View House hotel. Abraham Holt was a sergeant in the 10th Vermont. Wounded at Cold Harbor, then again at Cedar Creek, he recuperated at the Sloan Hospital in Montpelier. In the mid 1870s, he bought the Lake View House and ran it for several years.

SOURCES
Waite, Marcus W. "History of the Town of Woodbury, Vermont from the beginning to the Civil War period with Family Records." Unpublished manuscript, undated. Courtesy of Woodbury town hall.
Woodbury town records, 1860–1870.
With thanks to Eleanor Angell.

WORCESTER

The least populous town in Washington County in the 1860s, Worcester still sent eighty-one men to war. Twelve died. Go north from Montpelier on Route 12, and 0.75 mile north of the hamlet of Putnamville, note the sign marking the Worcester town line. The first house on the left, north of the line was the home of Captain Lemuel Hutchinson, who took command of Company E, 8th Vermont, after fellow Worcester resident Captain Edward Hall was killed at Cedar Creek. In March of 1863, Hutchinson and his wife, Kate, lost their three-year-old son Willie to disease, but the soldier father could not return to Worcester at the time.

Continue on Route 12 into Worcester village, and the Methodist Church is on the left. Harriet Hinkson, a member for eighty-four years, was a Worcester native and a nurse at the Sloan military hospital at Montpelier. Harriet is said to have married a soldier she met at the hospital, Private Clark J. Holmes, of Worcester, 11th Vermont, who lost a thumb in the war. Harriet lived until 1945, dying at 102. By then, two of her great wishes had been fulfilled—to live ten decades and to see the end of World War II.

A little north of the church the postwar Worcester town hall stands on the right. Turn right by it on Calais Road, and in 2 miles, bear left on Eagle Ledge Road. In just under 1 mile on the left, at the outflow of Worcester Pond, once stood the large Wheeler sawmill. Lyman Hinkson, father of Harriet, worked in the mill. He served in the 13th Regiment, fought at Gettysburg, and came home disabled. A brother, Private Edward Hinkson, was in the 11th Vermont until he died of disease in March 1863. Continue past the mill site just under 0.25 mile to an old house above the road on the right, where the Hinkson home was located. The present structure may be that house. Lyman's son, Calvin Hinkson, enlisted in the 2nd U.S. Sharpshooters at eighteen and wrote several letters home, including one on April

25, 1864, just before the Overland Campaign. "We have marched today and now are encamped in a large field and about one mile from Pony Mountain . . . We can see the Rebel camp from whare we are encamped and they probly can see ours. You must excuse my short letter as it is getting late and I am very tired. Now mother please write as soon as you get this bit of a letter and if you got the money I sent you send me a half dollars worth of postage stamps." The family soon received a letter written May 12 at Fredericksburg, from a Union hospital, by a member of the Sanitary Commission: "I am requested by your son Calvin C. Hinkson to write you a line to inform you that he is here in Hospital slightly wounded in the back of the head. His wound is quite painful at present though not probably dangerous. He wants you to pray for him and says he has tried to be a good boy since he was in the army and prays for himself. We will make him as comfortable as we can." Calvin died nine days later.

Somewhere in the area of the Hinkson house, in that part of Worcester known as Eagle Ledge, young Mary Loomis was sexually assaulted and murdered in early August 1863. Two local men were arrested, Austin Loomis and Orrin Carr. Charges were dismissed against Loomis, on the condition that he enlist. He promptly joined the 10th Vermont and served until the war's end. Carr served time in Windsor Prison and was released. But he committed another murder, and at 2 PM, on April 19, 1881, he was hanged at Windsor.

Return to Worcester village, and on reaching Route 12, the house to the right, on the corner, in the 1860s was a hotel owned by Ebenezer and Roxanna Kellogg. Their son Truman, a lieutenant in the 8th Vermont, died of typhoid fever in Louisiana.

Go north on Route 12, soon reaching the Worcester Cemetery. Calvin Hinkson is buried next to his parents in the front row. Nearby are the graves of Captains Hutchinson and Hall, two of the twenty-five Civil War veterans interred here. To the rear is a memorial for nurse Harriet Hinkson Holmes, erected in 2007, to "Vermont's Last Known Civil War Nurse." The monument says that she was a Native American, an Algonquin.

Go north from the cemetery 0.5 mile, and the old farmhouse on the left was Cresmon Hancock's home. Joining the 13th Vermont at age fifty, the regimental history notes that "he was a patriot of the old school and ever had been hostile to the institution of slavery." After Gettysburg, Hancock returned home briefly, then reenlisted in the 11th Vermont and served until the end of the war. He lived until 1891.

SOURCES
Early History of Worcester, Vermont.
    Worcester, VT: Worcester Historical
    Society, 2003.
With thanks to David Book.

*In this field Vermont soldiers camped
and drilled before going to war.*

chapter fourteen

Windham County

A monument on the Brattleboro Union High School grounds marks the site of Vermont's most important Civil War encampment. The 2nd Vermont Brigade's five regiments, destined to attack Pickett's Charge at Gettysburg, were among the units that assembled there. A Civil War hospital, where thousands of sick and wounded soldiers were treated, was also located here. A young Vernon girl wrote in her diary in the early summer of 1864 of watching, from her front porch, trains filled with wounded soldiers chug past. They were bound for the Brattleboro hospital, bearing the human wreckage of the Overland Campaign's great battles. In the summer of 1856, Henry David Thoreau was a guest at the home of friends in Brattleboro, in a house that survives. On departing Vermont, Thoreau wrote that he sensed the coming of a great war. Indeed, the son of his Vermont hosts would die in that conflict. Clarina Howard Nichols's home still fronts on the Townshend common. Nichols championed abolition as she edited newspapers in Vermont and in bloody Kansas. During the war, she cared for orphaned black children in Washington, D.C., earning the thanks of Mary Lincoln. The last house in which Daisy Turner lived survives in Grafton. Very late in her long life, she became a star of Ken Burns's Civil War public television series. Her father had escaped from a southern plantation, then returned to kill his former master. Outside the village of Saxton's River is the farmhouse in which Joseph Drury died. Captured at Weldon Railroad, he barely survived Libby Prison and Andersonville, returned home a human skeleton, and soon perished.

ATHENS

In her history of Athens, Laura Wyman wrote, "By September 1862 . . . Athens had sent fifteen volunteers to the front. More followed until 1865 when a total of forty-three native sons of Athens had joined the service. Twenty-five of these enlisted from Athens plus four substitutes for men unable to serve. Fourteen others were born and raised in town but away from home at the time of enlistment. Forty-three represented a large proportion of Athens' male citizens, the population being 362 in 1860." To reach this town whose population has little changed 150 years after the Civil War, take Route 131 west from Bellows Falls through Saxtons River to Cambridgeport, and turn south on Route 35. In a just over 2 miles, go right on Meetinghouse Road to the 1817 Athens Brick Meeting House. Civil War–era town meetings were held here.

On August 26, 1862, Athens voted bounties of $500 for three men signing on for three years and $100 for nine months enlistees. On December 8, 1863, the town agreed to pay five men $600 apiece. By January 1864, the selectmen were authorized to procure men "at the best terms they can." In December 1866, a tax of $2 on every grand list dollar was approved, to meet war expenses.

From the meetinghouse, continue south 2.3 miles on Route 35 to a white cape on the right with small barn attached. Phineas Bemis from here joined the 4th Vermont in September 1861. Wounded at Fredericksburg in December 1862, he soon returned to the ranks, but was captured on June 23 at Weldon Railroad. Bemis was confined in Andersonville until transferred to North Carolina early in 1865. He died on February 26, the day after receiving a parole.

Return north on Route 35 and 1 mile past the meetinghouse, go sharp right on Brookline Road. Soon pass the town office and in 2 miles, a large frame house stands on the right, with a barn directly across the road. Silas Powers lived here before going to California in search of gold. The 6-foot, 3-inch Powers enlisted in a California artillery battery, fought for the union in twenty-five battles, and returned to Athens. As an old man, he returned to this house in 1927 to be cared for in his last days.

Continue south 0.5 mile to a small brick school on the right, the South School. Among the future soldiers who studied here were Powers and Franklin Oakes. The first house beyond it on the right was once the Robbins family home. Eugene Robbins joined the 4th Vermont as a private in late December 1863 and served until the war ended. For several years after the war he was unable to talk above a whisper.

Continue on Brookline Road, and in 0.5 mile, go left on Valley Cemetery Road. In 0.75 mile, on the right, is a frame house and barn, once the Oakes farm. Franklin Oakes joined the 4th Vermont as a private in the fall of 1861, serving until captured at Weldon Railroad. At Andersonville, according to the town history, "he suffered severe injury to his health from which he never wholly recovered. When at last the order for discharge came, the prisoners were herded onto a train for the North. Pvt. Oakes was so weak from near starvation that he almost missed the train. Just as it was pulling out, a southern guard pushed him through the door." He died in Athens in 1884.

A half mile past the Oakes house is Valley Cemetery, where several Athens soldiers are buried, including Powers and Oakes. According to the Wyman book: "The first memorial decoration of soldiers' graves in Athens was in the summer of 1874 and was directed by Miss Mina Carter, the teacher at the South Brick School . . . She, in sympathy with the growing spirit of the times, to honor the memory of our Soldiers, prepared her school with appropriate exercises, and they marched to the cemetery, where Uncle Elisha Edwards offered prayer and raised the flag, while the little group of teacher and scholars sang America, and placed around the flag their tokens of honor and respect for fallen heroes."

According to Wyman, "Of the forty-odd men who went to war, few returned to take up the broken threads of life in their home town. Many were caught in the new tide of western migration . . . They bade good-bye to the small fields and cold climate of their Vermont homes, often reluctantly nevertheless irresistibly drawn to new frontiers. Eleven men did return to Athens to live and finally to be laid to rest in Athens cemeteries."

SOURCES
ATHENS TOWN RECORDS.
WYMAN, LORA M. *HISTORY OF ATHENS, VERMONT, WITH GENEALOGIES, 1779–1960.* ANN ARBOR, MI: EDWARDS BROTHERS, 1973. WITH THANKS TO LOIS SIPPEL.

BRATTLEBORO

Brattleboro saw more of the Civil War's effects than any other Vermont community, and certainly no acreage is more important to Vermont's Civil War history than the Brattleboro campground and hospital site. To reach it, leave Interstate 91 at exit 1, turn north on Route 5, and quickly go right on Fairgrounds Road. On entering the grounds of Brattleboro Union High School, note the granite monument by the school's main entrance. Its two bas-reliefs depict a soldier about to depart for war, and that same soldier returned from war. The former stands at attention, wearing a neat uniform, looking very serious. The latter has a bandaged head, appears considerably older and very tired, and is waving his cap and smiling. A plaque reads, "Upon this ground during the War for the Union A.D. 1861–65 10,200 volunteers in the Eighth, Ninth, Tenth, Eleventh, Twelfth, Thirteenth, Fourteenth, Fifteenth, and Sixteenth Regiments and the First Light Battery encamped and were mustered. 4,666 survivors were mustered out." The monument was dedicated in 1906, and former Vermont governor Frederick Holbrook sent a message that was read at the ceremony, though he died that year at age ninety-six. Holbrook took exception to the 10,200 total, saying it should have been 13,856.

The campground and hospital occupied

the entire high school grounds and more, with the hospital located behind where the high school now stands. Ralph Sturtevant, 13th Vermont historian, wrote of arriving at the Brattleboro encampment with his regiment in 1862: "The barracks were 74 by 22 feet, each designed for one company of 100 men, doors at each end, a narrow hall through from end to end and on either side bunks built about 4 by 6 feet, two stories high, each calculated for two persons, and made out of boards, simply a box six inches deep nailed up to posts, just space enough between for one at a time to pass and climb over in and when in, just lie down, no room to sit up or would hit their heads on the bottom of the bunk above, or the roof overhead. Some had straw for their bunks and others not." Sturtevant wrote of the next day, "During the afternoon the clouds broke and cleared away, and everything appeared more pleasant in and about camp, and as we looked to the south and west the wooded hills and mountains beyond and the beautiful and thriving village with its white painted houses on the high banks of the broad Connecticut River on its way to the sea made an attractive picture." Around the perimeter of this area some tall pines still stand, surely the children or grandchildren of those mentioned in soldier letters. Edwin Stoughton, first commander of the 2nd Vermont Brigade, marched his five regiments from the camp along the streets of Brattleboro as their time to go to war drew near.

Sickness was common in the barracks. The *Brattleboro Phoenix* noted in March 1864, "We learn that 22 recruits died at the barracks in this place during the win-

ter . . . They were of the average age of 18, five of them below 17."

In mid-February 1863, the *Vermont Standard* said, "Almost a mutiny occurred at Brattleboro on Saturday last, when the colored soldiers were ordered to leave their regiment, in consequence of their not having received any government bounty. They expected throughout to be treated in this respect the same as white soldiers . . . That they were not so treated is a burning shame, which Congress ought to right without a moment's unnecessary delay."

A military hospital operated here much due to the efforts of Governor Holbrook, a Brattleboro man. The governor was convinced that ill and wounded Vermont soldiers would fare better back in their home state than in federal hospitals to the south. It took some convincing, but Holbrook finally persuaded Secretary of War Edwin Stanton to allow Vermont to operate, on a trial basis, three hospitals, one on the drill field at Brattleboro, one in Montpelier, and one at Burlington. All were an instant success, with high cure rates. (Many of the more desperate cases could not endure transport to Vermont.) Indeed, of the 8,574 patients admitted to the three state hospitals from May 1862 to December 1865, only 175 died. According to Holbrook, of the 4,500 soldiers treated at Brattleboro, just 95 perished. Mary Cabot's Brattleboro history published in 1922 states, "Before the end of the . . . summer (1863) the hospital was full, some men having been sent from neighboring states to occupy room not needed by Vermonters. During the summer and autumn, hospital tents were erected to enlarge accommodations, and they were occupied by men from several other states, so that from 1,500 to 2,000 patients were treated at a time, those who had recovered being sent to the front again and new cases taking their places. The hospital was soon credited by the United States medical inspector with perfecting a larger percentage of cures than any United States military hospital elsewhere could show . . . The ladies of Vermont, with most commendable zeal, patriotism, and philanthropy, furnished mainly the equipment for beds and other necessities, as well as many luxuries." Indeed, the *Brattleboro Phoenix* of March 11, 1864, noted, "The Young Ladies Soldiers Aid Society of this village, having learned that the hospital of the 4th Regiment was destitute of supplies, filled and forwarded a barrel containing the following articles: four bed ticks, seven pillows, three pairs of socks, 15 sheets, 12 pillow cases."

Continue on Fairgrounds Road past the baseball grandstand and turn left on South Main Street. The house on the left, at the corner of Grove Street, is believed to have been a part of the hospital, moved here after the war. Continue on South Main and soon come to Prospect Street and a cemetery. Governor Holbrook, farmer, musician, and the inventor of a plow, is buried here, not far from a group of twenty-one Civil War gravestones set around a flagstaff. Men from Vermont, Maine, New York, Pennsylvania, New Hampshire, and Ohio and an unknown soldier, who died at the hospital are buried here.

Continue on South Main past the cemetery and turn left on Canal Street. In 0.3 mile, note a very old two-story house with a slate roof on the left, number 192. Abby Fuller grew up here, and after the war she married Levi Fuller, who became governor of Vermont. Abby's collected essays describe wartime Brattleboro: "Brattleboro, at the beginning of the war, had business interests in the south . . . Our water cures were patronized by people of Southern wealth. They brought some of their slaves with them; gay turbaned black nurses were a common sight on our streets in my childhood." She wrote of 1862, "I think that but few weeks passed when in my early home we did not have as guests there those who came to say 'goodbye' to some son or brother or husband who was going off with this regiment." She remembered her father welcoming a minister's family and sharing a bed with their daughter. "I shall never forget the sorrow of that poor girl and her tears, for she had a lover as well as a brother who was going to war the next day. We wept and prayed together."

She wrote of the hospital's opening and that "some good women from our village were nurses. How much good they did and how many lives they saved we can never tell, or realize . . . It was a great relief to the people of Brattleboro whose homes were on South Main and Canal Street, for before the hospital was built, nearly every house had a sick soldier in it to care for, and many of them died." And she recalled, "After every battle, a call was made for old linen, cotton, bandages, and money for supplies. The young women were the ones to solicit in different parts of the village, and we all had our beats. One friend, a school mate, and I, had our part of our side of the brook, and I remember we collected $100 in an hour after the battle of Gettysburg."

Fuller wrote, "The games of children on the streets during those war days partook of the war spirit. Amputating arms and legs; carrying each other about on improvised stretchers, and in case of a difference of opinion, battles were fought between 'the Yankees and the Secesh.' . . . During the war, the woolen factory in Thomasville was started . . . where woolen blankets were made, good ones, too, for the army, from which they had a contract." (The mill building still stands 0.25 mile up Whetstone Brook, which runs below Canal Street.)

Abby summed up the war experience: "The memory of those four awful years seems to those who lived through them like a dreadful dream. How often some of our own dead were brought back here for burial. The military funeral, the flag-draped coffin, the muffled drums, will long be remembered by us who were born in the '40s."

Turn around and return along Canal Street, and just before reaching the Connecticut River, stop on the right by the railroad. Soldiers arriving at Brattleboro, departing for war, and returning either safe or wounded, took or left the train at the Brattleboro station that stood just south of here. The large white brick building here was part of the wartime station complex. Fuller said, "Three days after Gettysburg, men wounded in that battle were brought in here. It seems as though I can hear now the rumble of John Ray's hacks as they went by after the late train at night, taking the poor fellows to the hospital."

The *Brattleboro Phoenix* on September 29, 1861, reported that the 4th Vermont marched through the streets to the depot. *The Phoenix* printed a poem by a local writer, inspired by the scene:

Slowly through the misty street
Comes the measured tramp of feet,
And a thousand forms sweep by
Going forth to win or die.
Waving colors o're their head,
Blue, and white, with bars of red,
Proudly greet the evening sky.
O'er the hearts that beat so high.
Stepping to the roll of drum
Down the darkening street they come,
Ready each to bear his part,
To resign, it may be, life,
Eager but to join the strife.
Cheers, oh cheers, rise to the sky,
Barely comes their last good-bye:—
Though the aching heart be weak
Trembling lips are forced to speak.
Leaving they for coming years
Childhood's sobs, and woman's tears.
Sadly here to watch, and wait
For the footfall at the gate,
For the step upon the floor,
That may come, perchance, no more.
Will they tread the homeward track?
God in mercy bring them back!

The *Rutland Herald* of February 2, 1864, said, "Every man of the 54 colored troops that left the encampment at Brattleboro, recently, for the seat of war, could write his name. Why did they not receive their bounty, is the question." The *Phoenix* of May 2, 1864: "170 horses were sent from the depot . . . Monday last, destined for the Army of the Potomac." The paper noted in June of that year, as the Overland Campaign produced record casualties, that trains bearing wounded sometimes stretched to Walnut Street.

Return uphill and turn right on Main Street. George Harper Houghton (see Dummerston) worked in a photographic studio on the third floor of the Granite Block, the stone building on the right at the top of the hill.

Turn left on Elliott Street, and the Brattleboro fire station is at the intersection of Carter Street. Some of the town's popular mineral springs, which Southerners visited before the war were in this area. Among the visitors, in the summer of 1860, was an instructor at the Virginia Military Institute named Thomas Jonathan Jackson. The man soon to be known as Stonewall was seeking relief from eye problems and stomachaches. Some antebellum houses survive in this area, particularly on Carter Street.

Return to Main and go north. At the Y intersection in front of the Brattleboro Memorial Library is a granite fountain designed by the McKim, Mead & White architectural firm. Here in 1857, a young Brattleboro man, Larkin Mead, created an ice sculpture, *The Snow Angel*, which brought visitors from near and far. In 1802, Mead went to war at the invitation of Vermont Brigade commander William Farrar "Baldy" Smith, apparently to make drawings of enemy fortifications. Soon, he was selling war sketches to *Harper's Weekly.* But he came home during the Peninsula

Campaign after a near miss from a rebel bullet. After the war, Mead became a famous sculptor, with a studio in Florence, Italy. He was, nonetheless, commissioned to create the statuary for Abraham Lincoln's tomb. Walnut Street turns right by the fountain. The local paper noted that hospital trains sometimes stretched here from the station.

Brattleboro's Main Street was a busy place during the war years. At the town hall, which stood where the post office is now located, war meetings were frequently held. Speakers here included Frederick Douglass, Oliver Wendell Holmes, Henry Ward Beecher, and Wendell Phillips. The funeral of Charles Cummings, once editor of the *Phoenix,* was held at the town hall, and the funeral procession stretched far along Main Street. Cummings served as an officer in the 11th Vermont, as second in command of the 16th Vermont, then led the 17th Vermont until his death near Petersburg on September 30, 1864.

On September 2, 1864, the *Phoenix* reported on the return of the 7th Vermont: "The day was bright and beautiful and Main Street was gay with national flags, which looked as gay and cheerful as if the Republic was destined to stand forever."

The Brattleboro common, at the north end of town, borders the west side of Main Street. In the early summer of 1861 a war meeting was held here which one local historian said produced 75 recruits for the Second Vermont Regiment. Brattleboro's Civil War monument here proclaims that 385 Brattleboro men served of whom 31 died. A bas-relief includes the words of Lincoln's Second Inaugural: "With malice towards none, with charity for all." The monument was erected, in its words, "by a grateful town."

Pass the monument on Park Place and the elegant Greek Revival house straight ahead at the intersection was the home of Governor Holbrook. He generally managed the affairs of state from a hotel in downtown Brattleboro, which no longer stands, with the exception of the few weeks each year the legislature met in Montpelier. Enter Chapin Street, which runs along the left side of the Holbrook house, and the last house on the left, at the intersection of Forest Street, was the home of Larkin Mead.

Turn right on Forest, and at the corner of Chase Street, on the right, is the home of Luke Ferriter, a native of Ireland who enlisted in the 3rd Vermont at age seventeen. Ferriter was a member of the firing squad formed to execute William Scott, the Sleeping Sentinel, (see Groton). After the war, Ferriter three times served as commander of Brattleboro's Sedgwick GAR post. Turn right on Chase Street and note the house on the right beside the Ferriter home. Addison Brown lived here, a man known locally as "the learned shoemaker," and his wife, Ann. In September 1856, Henry David Thoreau based himself in the Brown home for five days of exploring the nearby countryside. Soon after returning home to Concord, Massachusetts, he wrote in his journal of sensing a strong possibility of war: "I seem to hear its distant mutterings, though it may be long before the bolt will fall in our midst. There has not been anything which you

could call union between the North and South in this country for many years, and there cannot be so long as slavery is in the way." A son of the Browns, Addison Jr., served in the 4th and 5th Vermont regiments, rising to lieutenant colonel. He was discharged for ill health in December 1864 and died soon after, at twenty-six.

Return to the common, go north on Putney Road, and soon on the right is brick St. Michael's Church, which was located in downtown Brattleboro during the war. Brattleboro's Lieutenant Colonel John Tyler, second in command of the 2nd Vermont, was shot in a leg at the Wilderness on May 5, 1864, and taken to a Washington hospital. Judge Royal Tyler hastened to Washington to bring his nephew home, but on the way the young man died in a New York City hotel. On hearing the news of his death, cousin Gertrude Tyler Brown wrote:

He fell for his country's good,
Write neath his glorious name
And paint in letters of blood
The scroll of his wondrous fame.

Colonel Tyler's funeral took place in St. Michael's and the local paper said that, as the twenty-one-year-old soldier was borne from the church to his final resting place, "The shadows of the evening hours fell from the darkening sky."

In West Brattleboro, west of Brattleboro along Route 9, the redbrick Baptist Church was once a Universalist church. On Sunday July 10, 1864, a funeral was held there for Sergeant Luke Kendall, 4th Vermont, killed at the Wilderness.

SOURCES
Brattleboro Phoenix, 1861–1865. Brooks
Memorial Library, Brattleboro.
Cabot, Mary R., ed. *Annals of
Brattleboro, 1681–1895.* 2 vols.
Brattleboro, VT: Press of E. L.
Hildreth, 1921.
Derleth, August. *Concord Rebel: The Life
of Henry David Thoreau.* New York:
Clinton Book Co., 1963.
Fuller, Mrs. Levi (Abby Estes). Addresses
before the Brattleboro Chapter of the
Daughters of the American
Revolution. Vermont Historical
Society.
Rutland Herald, 1864. Vermont State
Library.
With thanks to John and Mary Carnahan
and the Brattleboro Historical
Society.

···

BROOKLINE

Brookline's round brick school-house faces Grassy Brook Road, the town's main thoroughfare, which runs north from Route 30 in Townshend. Legend holds that a Dr. John Wilson got the school built in 1822 and became its first teacher. Later, it was discovered he once was a Scottish highwayman, and suspicions are that the round building allowed him to keep watch in all directions for the law, which never came. Among the pupils here were three future Civil War soldiers: Edwin Stebbins and Denny and Herbert Mason. Denny Mason, a private in the 9th Vermont, was wounded in the attack on Fort Harrison in 1864. Herbert Mason fought at Gettysburg, as a sergeant in the 16th Vermont.

Go north from the school 0.3 mile, and the first house on the right was the home of Edwin Stebbins, who joined the 11th Vermont as a corporal in the fall of 1862 and rose to lieutenant, serving until the war ended.

The next house north, built in 1795, was William Adams's home. A cousin, George William Adams, born in Indiana, sometimes visited here. A newspaper correspondent throughout the Civil War, he later became part owner of a Washington, D.C., newspaper. He was in the lobby of Ford's Theater when Lincoln was assassinated.

Return south on Grassy Brook Road, pass the round school, and in 0.4 mile is a large barn on the left, all that remains of the Holden farm. From here, Hebbard Holden joined the 4th Vermont at nineteen in the fall of 1861. He was severely wounded at Fredericksburg in December 1862.

Just south is the Brookline Baptist Church where the Adams, Stebbins, Cutler, Mason, Wellman, and Merrifield families worshipped, who all had sons in the Civil War. Marshall Wellman, a private in the 8th Vermont, died at Bayou Des Allemands, Louisiana, in June 1862. He was nineteen.

South of the church, take the first right, onto Hill Road, and in 0.6 mile, go right on Kirsch Road. A cape stands on the right, once the home of Charles Cutler, who joined the 8th Vermont in 1862 as a private and served in the Deep South until becoming ill eighteen months later. He came home and recovered. Henry Cutler was a private in the 11th Vermont for three years, returning home safely.

Return to Hill Road, go right 1.25 miles to a farmhouse with a large barn. Joshua

Shattuck joined the 5th Vermont at nineteen in December 1863. On June 3, 1864, he was shot in the big Union assault at Cold Harbor. Private Shattuck recovered and was promoted to lieutenant.

Continue on Hill Road 0.5 mile to Grassy Brook Road and turn left. In 0.4 mile, on the right, is the Merrifield house. Albert Merrifield enlisted at nineteen in the 8th Vermont in early 1862, fought in all its major battles, and came home only briefly before going west, to Illinois.

Some twenty-six men served from this little town.

SOURCES
ATHENS TOWN RECORDS.
WITH THANKS TO LESTER ALBEE.

DOVER

The tall spire of Dover's 1858 West Dover Congregational Church overlooks Dover's main road, now Route 100. Of the families who owned pews in the church, nineteen sent at least one son to war. Altogether, sixty-four Dover men served, and of them, thirteen perished.

Beside the church is the 1857 Dover town office, housed in a building that, in the 1860s, was the West Dover School, where most wartime town meetings took place. Bounties of up to $700 were approved here, as was the hiring of W. H. Jones in 1864 as town agent charged with procuring soldiers. Dover's proximity to Massachusetts seems to have made recruiting difficult, as local men could so easily seek more generous bounties there. Jones's

expense account exists in the Dover records, and it shows him making trips to Windsor, Somerset, and Brattleboro in search of men. Jones apparently had discretion to pay whatever bounties necessary, and his highest payment was to John Stanley, for $700. Stanley joined the 7th Vermont in August 1864 and served until the war ended.

From the school, go north on Route 100, and quickly go right on Valley View Road. Jones's home was the second house on the right. Just up the hill on the right is a large inn complex that, in the 1860s, was a farm owned by the Estabrook family. George Estabrook joined the 4th Vermont when it formed and served until captured at Weldon Railroad. Sent to Andersonville, he was on his way home when he died at Wilmington, South Carolina in March 1865.

Continue north on Route 100 through a part of Dover much changed by ski development. In 1.5 miles, go left on narrow Fox Meadow Lane, which quickly dead-ends by a modern building. Walk beyond the building, bearing left into a narrow strip of woods, to a small graveyard, where George Smead lies, one of agent Jones's recruits. Smead was working the family farm here for his mother when persuaded to enlist. According to the Dover history, "To ease his mother's objections, she was paid $90.00, and George was given $10.00, with the promise of a further large bounty. Nine months later he was killed at Santiago Island, Texas, on July 3, 1865, at the age of seventeen. He is buried back home in the farm meadow on Smead Hill." Smead was a private in the

7th Vermont, which was ordered to the Mexican border when the war ended. He died of sickness, surely one of the last Vermonters to perish. Sadly, his resting place is no longer a farm meadow but the backyard of vacation homes.

Return past the Dover town office on Route 100, cross a bridge, and turn sharp right on short Bogle Road, with just two houses. In 1863 and 1864, diphtheria visited Dover, taking a heavy toll. Jemina Pike lived in the first house and lost all three children to the epidemic. Her brother, Moses Bogle, in the next house, lost a nine-year-old son. Jemina's brother, Edward, one of twenty-two Dover men to fight at Gettysburg with F Company of the 16th Vermont, learned that he had lost a son to diphtheria on returning home.

Cross the bridge and go sharp right up Dorr Fitch Road. In 5 miles, come to the East Dover Baptist Church. The church historian wrote in 1865, "A large proportion of the families connected with our congregation have been visited by death. Death selected his victims from all ages." In the church vestry, directly across the road, some wartime Dover town meetings took place. The first soldier payments were approved here in September 1862, $7 each to the men who joined the 16th Vermont. Later, bounties of $300 were added to that.

SOURCES
KULL, NELL M. *HISTORY OF DOVER, VERMONT: 200 YEARS IN A HILL TOWN*. BRATTLEBORO, VT: THE BOOK CELLAR, 1971.
HEMENWAY, ED. *THE VERMONT HISTORICAL GAZETTEER*.
DOVER TOWN RECORDS.

DUMMERSTON

Leave Interstate 91 at exit 3, on the north side of Brattleboro, and go north 1.5 miles on Route 5 to Houghton Road. George Harper Houghton lived for a time in the large frame house that still stands at the intersection. Born in Putney in 1824, Houghton was an experienced photographer by the time the Civil War began. From his Brattleboro studio in early 1862, he took his cumbersome photo equipment and went south to the Army of the Potomac's winter camp, linking up with friends in the 1st Vermont Brigade. He recorded images of the Vermonters at Camp Griffin, including a famous photo of the 5th Vermont, aligned in front of its tents. Houghton accompanied the Brigade on the Peninsula Campaign, for a time. Later, he was in the winter camps of the 2nd Vermont Brigade. When the 7th and 4th Vermont regiments returned home, he photographed them in downtown Brattleboro. After the war, like many Vermonters, Houghton went west to Wisconsin, where he died in 1870. Before departing, he presented a set of his wartime photographs to the Vermont Historical Society.

Go 0.5 mile past Houghton Road on Route 5, and turn left on School House Road. Go uphill 2 miles to Dummerston Center, where the Congregational Church also served as Dummerston's wartime town hall. Here, in 1860, town voters went for Lincoln over Douglas 119 to 24, and over McClellan 132 to 14 in 1864. On December 15, 1863, a town meeting was held to deal with a new call for men. Already, seven Dummerston soldiers had died of disease: Private John Morse, 11th Vermont; Private Asahel Ellis, 16th Vermont; Private Frederick Rice, 4th Vermont; Private Loyal Smith, 4th Vermont; Privates Zelotes Burlingame and Henry Everleth, both sharpshooters; and Lieutenant Pascal Laughton, 16th Vermont. Dummerston, already war weary, met this new quota, and all its quotas, throughout the war. Town bounties reached $500, leaving the town nearly $20,000 in debt at war's end. A year later, all but $295 was paid off. Some 120 men served from Dummerston, and at least 14 died.

From the church, look across Middle Road to a two-section house with a long porch. Once the Mansfield family home, from it three sons of Jesse Mansfield went to war. Charles Mansfield joined the 9th Vermont at sixteen and served three years, dying of illness at Newbern, North Carolina, in 1864. Joseph and William enlisted in the 11th Vermont in August 1862. Joseph died of sickness at Fort Slocum, in Washington, a year later. William was discharged for ill health after serving a year. He died in 1867. Another brother, David, too young to serve, wrote a history of Dummerston.

SOURCES

DUMMERSTON TOWN RECORDS.
MANSFIELD, DAVID LUFKIN. *THE HISTORY OF THE TOWN OF DUMMERSTON: THE FIRST TOWN SETTLED BY ANGLO SAXON DESCENDANTS IN THE STATE.* LUDLOW, VT: A. M. HEMENWAY, 1884.
WICKMAN, DONALD H. *"A VERY FINE APPEARANCE": THE VERMONT CIVIL WAR PHOTOGRAPHS OF GEORGE HOUGHTON.* MONTPELIER, VT: VERMONT HISTORICAL SOCIETY. 2011.
WITH THANKS TO DWIGHT MILLER.

....

GRAFTON

Grafton's Main Street, Route 121, is lined with pre–Civil War buildings, including the Grafton Inn. Ulysses Grant stayed there the night of December 19, 1867, during his presidential campaign. Other guests included Henry David Thoreau, an outspoken critic of slavery, and Oliver Wendell Holmes, three times wounded during the Civil War.

Close by the tavern, on Main Street, an 1843 building houses the Grafton Historical Society. Among its treasures are the Grafton Inn registration book signed by Grant, a portrait of local soldier Alonzo Rice, and items relating to Daisy Turner, who very late in life became a national Civil War personality.

Daisy Turner lived most of her 104 years, which spanned most of the twentieth century, in Grafton. The daughter of an escaped slave, Daisy was discovered in her eleventh decade by filmmaker Ken Burns, who, as he said, "made her my Greek chorus" for his acclaimed 1992 production on the Civil War. Among her words heard throughout the nation were: "The green fields of the Southland is fertile with the blood of those Negro slaves, and the true white men who went from Vermont to save us. Every one of those turning battles, where victory was won, it was the Vermont boys who was there."

Daisy's father, Alec Turner, born in

1845, escaped from a Virginia plantation and joined the Union army. He later returned to the plantation and killed his former master. In 1872, Turner came to Grafton with his wife, Sally, and settled on Bear Hill, where the family eventually came to own several hundred acres. Daisy was one of their sixteen children and the last to survive, dying in 1988. Late in life, she lived at the home of a sister. To see the house, go west along Main Street, and at the Y, take Hinkley Brook Road. The small wooden house on the right, squeezed between road and brook, was Daisy Turner's last home.

To reach the site of the Turner farm, where Daisy lived most of her life, go south from the village on Townshend Road and turn left on Turner Hill. This rough and steep road, closed in winter, ends at the Turner farm site.

Back in the village, Chester Road goes north from Main Street. Follow it 0.3 mile, and at the top of the hill, is a wide-fronted three-story house with steep roofs, once the home of Alonzo and Minerva Rice. Alonzo Rice, a schoolmaster, came to Grafton in 1857. Though only 5 feet 7 and slender, he quickly proved his toughness in town when he whipped all the local Eastman School's bullies on his first day of work. Rice married local girl Minerva Hazen in 1859. He enlisted in the 9th Vermont in June 1862 and was discharged the following November for disability. But he recovered and returned to duty, only to be sent home sick again, this time to the Brattleboro hospital. Minerva left their three small children with a neighbor and hastened to Brattleboro to care for her husband, only to find on arrival that he had died. On reaching Grafton with his body, Minerva was told that their youngest child had succumbed to diphtheria. A year later, the same dread disease claimed a second child.

Grafton sent 106 men to war from a population of about 1,200, and 13 died, with 5 seriously wounded

SOURCES
GRAFTON TOWN RECORDS.
RICE FAMILY FILE. GRAFTON HISTORICAL SOCIETY.
WITH THANKS TO JANE BECK, KEN BURNS,
    AND THE GRAFTON HISTORICAL SOCIETY.

....

GUILFORD

The village of East Guilford, also known as Algiers, is south of Brattleboro, along Route 5. From the village, go west on East Guilford Road to Guilford Center, where the meetinghouse is beside the library. The Guilford Historical Society, across the road, displays a broadside announcing that a war meeting, with singing and speeches, and with women invited, will take place in Guilford Center on May 11, 1961, at 1 PM. That meeting happened in the meetinghouse, and the men who enlisted became part of the 1st Vermont Regiment, commanded by Colonel John Wolcott Phelps. Guilford voters that day adopted a set of resolutions denouncing Jefferson Davis and "upholding the government." Four years later, the meetinghouse bell was rung to celebrate Lee's surrender.

Return to East Guilford, and on reaching Route 5, look north to the first house on the east side of the road, where John Phelps was born on November 13, 1813. Phelps grew up in Guilford and at eighteen applied for entrance to the United States Military Academy. Graduating from West Point in 1836, Phelps served in the Seminole and Mexican wars, then resigned from the army in 1859. But he was back in uniform in 1861, accepting command of the 1st Vermont Regiment. An admirer of John Brown, Phelps, in December 1861, published his own emancipation proclamation, which stated: "We believe that every state that has been admitted as a slave state into the Union since the adoption of the constitution has been so admitted in direct violation of the constitution."

When the 1st Vermont came home, after ninety days, Phelps joined Benjamin F. Butler's New England Division, going south to New Orleans. Phelps promptly gave refuge in his camp to escaped slaves, refusing an order from Butler to throw out the fugitives. Phelps soon asked Butler's consent to begin putting black men in uniform. To this, Butler also said no, so Phelps resigned from the army and came home to Guilford. Soon after his return, Phelps accepted an invitation to address the Vermont legislature, On October 13, 1862, he said at the State House: "The sun never looked down upon a greater evil than American slavery. In ruling this great nation of slaves we have to a degree become enslaved ourselves." Phelps ran for president in 1880 on the anti-Masonic ticket.

Christ Church overlooks East Guilford. Drive to the churchyard and look south beyond it. The small white house just past the schoolhouse was Phelps's last home. Sometimes, in his later years, he taught in this schoolhouse. He died in his home here on February 2, 1885, after shoveling snow. His funeral was held here in the church. A stone that makes no mention of his military service stands in the church cemetery.

Phelps was one of 122 men credited to Guilford.

SOURCES

BENEDICT, GEORGE G. *VERMONT IN THE CIVIL WAR*. 2 VOLS. BURLINGTON, VT: FREE PRESS ASSOCIATION, 1888.
GUILFORD TOWN RECORDS.

HALIFAX

Leave Route 112 and turn west, following signs to West Halifax, and soon come to the Halifax town clerk's office and a school, on the left. Just beyond are Civil War–era buildings, including the first house on the right, which was the Miner home. At age forty-five, Thomas Miner enlisted in the 16th Vermont and fought at Gettysburg. With him went a son, Francis, who, after the 16th disbanded, joined the 4th Vermont. He lived to become the oldest member of the local GAR post, dying at seventy-four, accidentally shot while hunting rabbits. Another son, Private Frank Miner, was also a member of the 4th.

The first building past the Miner house, also on the right, was once a Baptist church. The *Brattleboro Phoenix* reported in January 1864 that women of the church delivered $80 to Brattleboro for the military hospital. Among the Civil

War funerals held here were services for the Niles brothers, both 4th Vermont privates. Alonzo Niles died of disease in February 1862, two months before Private Stephen Niles fell to a bullet through the head at Lee's Mill. Stephen left a wife, Clarissa, and a young daughter. A memorial service was held here for Abraham Lincoln, and a newspaper account said: "The church was tastefully draped for the occasion; there was also an engraving of Mr. Lincoln hung over the pulpit trimmed with a wreath of evergreen interspersed with white flowers. The Universalists also had a discourse upon the death of Abraham Lincoln, in their chapel on the afternoon of the same day."

The latter service was held across the road in the 1843 church, which is now the Halifax Historical Society. That building also served as a school attended by many Halifax boys who became soldiers, including Charles Clark, a sergeant in the 16th Vermont, who died from disease before Gettysburg. The Halifax GAR post was named for him.

Return past the town clerk's office and quickly bear left on the Jacksonville Stage Road. Go uphill, and just past the crest, note an old farmhouse set back from and above the road. In the 1860s, Mary Morrison Tucker, a widow in her seventies, lived here with her sons, Albert and George, the latter a Halifax selectman. Mary kept a diary during the war years. Some entries:

March 4, 1861: "Some cooler President
    Lincoln takes his seete today."
September 16, 1861: "Boys went to
    Brattleboro last night . . . there is great
    excitement here, news came the Vermont
regiment was going to start for the war 9
    oclock last night half of Halifax has gone
    to Brattleboro last night today 18 Ladies
    went in one wagon from the hollow."
February 27, 1862: "snows, all gone to the
    funeral of Alonzo Niles."
May 25, 1862: "Sabbath all hands ben to
    the Hollow [West Halifax] to the funeral
    of B. [Stephen Brainard] Niles."
May 16, 1863: "The select men here all day
    making out the tax bills."
January 1, 1864: "George out recruiting
    soldiers."
February 8, 1865: "we are having the
    soldier aid society here today there is
    quite a rush."

Clearly, the Tucker home was a center of activity during the war. Selectmen met there as did the local soldiers aid society to make goods for the soldiers. George Tucker was the town recruiter.

Continue past the Tucker house through Halifax Center to the cemetery on the left. The large stones that make up the style by the gateway are believed to have been the 1784 town hall's front steps. The hall, long gone, was the scene of 1860s town meetings, during which bounties that reached $500 were approved. The town incurred a war debt of nearly $30,000, and it was years paying it off. Private James Crosier, 4th Vermont, mortally wounded at Third Winchester, is buried in the cemetery. His body came home because of an advertisement placed in at least one Vermont newspaper after the September 19, 1864, battle of Third Winchester by the Winchester, Virginia, embalming firm of Wood & Taylor. The ad listed the names of dead Union soldiers "who fell on the battlefield" and stated that Wood and Taylor would send the bodies home for a fee. The Crosiers mailed the money to bring back their son's embalmed remains.

Return to the town clerk's office on Route 112, turn south, and soon take Pennel Hill Road 1.5 miles to Halifax's oldest standing house, the Civil War–era home of the Niles family. James Niles lost sons Stephen and Alonzo to the war. Another son, Orsamas, moved to Ohio, where he became a vocal critic of the war. He wrote to his father in October 1864, "I have been opposed to this war from the beginning. I consider it infamous and those who inaugurated it and keep it up are infamous."

Halifax sent some 124 men to the war, of whom 3 died in battle and 16 of disease. The war's effects were long felt in town, as three veterans many years later committed suicide.

SOURCES

BRATTLEBORO PHOENIX, 1861–1865. BROOKS MEMORIAL LIBRARY, BRATTLEBORO.
HALIFAX TOWN RECORDS.
NILES, ORSAMUS ELLIOT. "COPPERHEAD AND UNIONIST: AN EX-VERMONTER TELLS HIS FATHER WHY HE OPPOSES THE CIVIL WAR." VERMONT HISTORY 41, NO. 1 (1973): 1–6. COURTESY OF THE VERMONT HISTORICAL SOCIETY.
WITH THANKS TO CONNIE LANCASTER.

JAMAICA

Jamaica has long been known as "the birthplace of Vermont abolition," for the first Vermont antislavery society was formed here in 1833. Dr. Joel Holton had a great deal to do with founding that society, and he lived in the building that is now the village store, at the main intersection in Jamaica village. Holton came to town in 1831 and began practicing medicine, with his office in his home. A hater of slavery and secret societies, he was the local antislavery society's first secretary. His son, William Henry Harrison Holton, at twenty-one, joined the 8th Vermont. Lieutenant Holton was wounded at Port Hudson and came home to recover. Brother Warren Holton also served, as a lieutenant in the 16th Vermont, until taken seriously ill. Sent to the Brattleboro hospital, he was soon released to his father's care. He died here at the Holton home on August 1, 1863, at eighteen.

Directly across the street from the Holton house is a building that once was Muzzy's Store. Judge F. M. Butler, after the war, remembered a day from his Jamaica childhood: "The Jamaica company of enlisted men were training backwards and forwards, up and down the Main Street . . . led by the stirring music of a snaredrum and two fifes. A United States flag was strung from the Muzzy Store to the Holton house and it swung over the center of Main Street." Butler said that a spectator "had been talking quite loud and was the center of a small knot of men. He declared that the soldiers were going south to commit murder for a few damned niggers, and Jamaica would pay for it."

It was the wrong town for such remarks. Butler said the marching men seized the man, led him under the flag, and forced him to cheer, between each cheer commanding him to cheer louder. "In less time that it takes to tell it," Butler said, "the bugle called, the soldiers rushed for the line, the command was given, three cheers went up for the flag . . . and the vigorous marching and countermarching went on."

South of the village store is the 1808 Congregational Church, where on July 6, 1844, its members resolved: "That we will not practice slavery ourselves. That this church will not invite slaveholders or those who defend the system of slavery to commune with them at the Lord's table." A ladies' aid society apparently connected to the church was active during the war and in November 1864 held a fair in the village that raised $156 for the Sanitary Commission.

Town meetings were held in the Congregational Church basement, and there voters approved $44,000 in bounties. Jamaica sent 156 men to war from a population of 1,600.

South of the church, on Route 30, the Masonic lodge is, built on the foundation of the old Baptist Church, of which Doctor Holton was a member. The church was staunchly antislavery, and many members surely were involved in the antislavery society. Doctor Holton is buried in the cemetery behind the building, beside the soldier son who died in their home.

Go south 0.75 mile on Route 30 to the large Victorian house on the left, built after the war by Wales Cheney. As a member of the 18th Massachusetts Infantry, Cheney was wounded at First Bull Run.

Return to the village, and two buildings past the store (the old Holton house), on the right, is the Jamaica GAR hall, a building that, in 2011, housed a furniture shop. The Scott Post met here, apparently named for Lieutenant Henry Scott, a Townshend man, who served in the 11th Vermont and survived wounds at Cold Harbor and Third Winchester.

From the village's main intersection, take Mechanic Street, go left on South Hill Road, and in 3.3 miles go right at a T. Soon, a short lane on the right leads to a frame house on a knoll. David Eddy, another opponent of slavery, lived here. It has been said that "many a needy colored men has found shelter under his roof." Eddy's daughter married a son of Doctor Holton, and they turned the Holton house into a store, as it is today.

SOURCES

BRATTLEBORO PHOENIX, 1864. BROOKS MEMORIAL LIBRARY, BRATTLEBORO.
CIVIL WAR FILES. JAMAICA HISTORICAL SOCIETY.
JAMAICA TOWN RECORDS.
WITH THANKS TO KAREN AMIDON.

LONDONDERRY

Enter South Londonderry from the south, on Route 100, cross the West River Bridge, and go straight uphill on Middletown Road. Quickly, on the left, is the steepled town hall, where Civil War–era town meetings took place. In 1860, the vote here was 193 for Lincoln, 18 for Breckenridge, and 15 for Douglas. Four years later, Londonderry went for Lincoln over McClellan, 207 to 53. In this hall Londonderry voters approved total war expenditures of $28,359.98. Though most funded bounties, some supported the Sanitary Commission.

Continue past the church 1 mile to a cemetery on the left. The first house beyond it, on the right, was the home of Nathan and Elizabeth Buxton, who lost two sons in the war. Horace Buxton was a nineteen-year-old private in the 11th Vermont when he died of sickness in April 1863, while his regiment manned the Washington forts. Brother Albert, commander of Company H, 2nd U.S. Sharpshooters, survived a wound at Gettysburg. The gray-eyed, dark-haired captain recovered, only to be killed on May 5, the following spring, at the Wilderness. Albert's widow, Jennie, was treasurer of the South Londonderry Soldiers' Aid Society. According to the *Bellows Falls Times,* in June 1864, the group forwarded to the Sanitary Commission a box of supplies that included eight pairs of pillows, thirty-three towels, forty-four handkerchiefs, sixty-five bandage rolls, forty pounds of dried apples, and much more. The society sometimes met in the Buxton house.

Return to South Londonderry, and on reaching Route 11, take Thompsonburg Road. In just over 2 miles, a modern house, with small barn attached, is on the left. Look closely in the field behind for remnants of a barn foundation from the Churchill farm, where William Churchill grew up here. Family members were stalwarts of the Baptist Church in South Londonderry, which was destroyed by fire in 2010. Church picnics were often held here at the Churchill farm. William, with Albert Buxton, joined the sharpshooters. When Albert was killed, William became

commander of H Company, by unanimous vote of the men. Churchill survived a wound at the Wilderness, only to be killed in October 1864 at the Boydton Plank Road, near Petersburg. One of his men said he was "leading, not ordering the men forward, when he fell." The body never came home, and the family, for some time, held out hope that he might have survived. In February 1864, Churchill's sister received a letter from William Reynolds, a former surgeon with the sharpshooters, answering her inquiry concerning whether he knew her brother's fate. The reply said, "I first saw him in ambulance bleeding profusely from his wound through the leg. He was shivering and palid from the loss of blood and hardly able to answer questions. He was very faint and could not lift his head, simply because his blood had so freely flowed . . . Nothing could be done." A service was held in June 1865 in Churchill's memory at the Baptist Church. When the church burned nearly a century and a half later, a picture of Churchill, in uniform, went up in flames. The church will be rebuilt.

Continue on Thompsonburg Road to Route 100, turn left, then left again on Rest Haven Lane. Churchill and Horace Buxton are buried in the Rest Haven Cemetery, as are several other Londonderry soldiers. Return to Route 100 and go left into Londonderry village. The Congregational Church is on the right. In this 1842 building on May 29, 1864, a funeral was held for Private George Lyon, of nearby Winhall, killed May 5 at the Wilderness. The presiding minister was

Reverend J. S. Goodall of the South Londonderry Baptist Church. Goodall first asked whether Private Lyon's life had been wasted. The answer was an emphatic NO, for Goodall said that Lyon had died for a noble and historic cause. "American citizen," he said, "stand fast therefore in the liberty where with you have been made free. Millions who have been in bondage have been proclaimed free . . . We have prayed to God to remove the accursed system from our land. The bondmen are fixing their lips to shout the song of liberty . . . We will embalm his memory in our minds as a noble, patriotic youth who gave his life to defend his country—to preserve the privileges we this day are permitted to enjoy; and we pray they will be kept unsullied, and handed down to the last generation for them to enjoy."

SOURCES

Bellows Falls Times, 1864–1865. Bellows Falls Library.

Churchill, William. Letters. Courtesy of Melvin Twitchell.

Cudworth, Addison E. *The History with Genealogical Sketches of Londonderry, Vermont*. Montpelier, VT: Vermont Historical Society, 1935.

Londonderry town records.

With thanks to William Twitchell.

....

MARLBORO

From West Brattleboro, go west 6 miles on Route 9, turn left on South Road, and soon enter the village of Marlboro, dominated by the tall spire of the Marlboro Meeting House. This building, in 1931, was built to replace the 1820 Congregational Church, destroyed by fire.

During the Civil War, the pastor was Ephraim H. Newton, who wrote a history of Marlboro. As the Civil War began, he wrote to his daughter on April 27, 1861, "I am too old to go into the field. but I am willing that my children should buckle on the armour to secure a triumphant victory over secession and rebellion." Two weeks later he wrote, "Gen McClellan, the hero of Western Virginia, is a hero indeed. His wife is young, but a host . . . She is the granddaughter of the late Gen. Jonas Mann, formerly of Brattleboro, by his second marriage to Mary Negus, of Newfane, who was an early associate of my boyhood."

Just south of the church is an old hotel, which in the mid-1800s was run by the Prouty family. It is believed that brothers Elias and Harvey Prouty went to war from here, privates in the 8th Vermont from early 1862 until the war ended.

North of the church is the 1822 Marlboro town hall, site of Civil War–era town meetings. Marlboro voted its first bounties, $100 each, in the fall of 1862. Payments reached $300 in December 1863. War costs by 1865 necessitated a tax of $2 for each dollar on the grand list. Twice during the war, voters approved a measure that allowed Marlboro men, with a payment of $100, to be "cleansed from the military service for a term of one year." A total of ten Marlboro men signed up here for Company I of the 16th Vermont, which fought at Gettysburg.

From the little cape across from the town hall, Private Lewis Brayman joined the 8th Vermont when it was formed. When his three-year term ended, he reenlisted, and served out the war, coming home to be the town undertaker.

Take Town Hill Road by the town hall to Route 9 and turn left, west. In 2.5 miles, go left on Butterfield Road, and in 2.3 miles, turn right on Jenks Road to the large farmhouse at the end. Charles Jenks, son of Andrew and Philara Jenks, left here in January 1864, at eighteen to join the 8th Vermont as a private. At Third Winchester nine months later, he was shot in the throat, and a comrade heard him exclaim that he had been killed. His father went south for his body, and Private Jenks was buried on January 1, 1865, in the little family cemetery in the apple orchard, on the hill behind the barn. He rests near his grandfather Boomer Jenks, a Revolutionary War soldier.

Return along Butterfield Road, and in 1.5 miles on the left, the large frame house was the home of Simeon Adams. At eighteen, he joined Company E, 2nd U.S. Sharpshooters, in the fall of 1862, as a private. Wounded at Spotsylvania's Bloody Angle on May 12, 1864, he nonetheless served until the war ended.

Marlboro sent some seventy-five men to war.

SOURCES
MARLBORO TOWN RECORDS.
NEWTON, EPHRAIM H. *THE HISTORY OF THE TOWN OF MARLBOROUGH, WINDHAM COUNTY, VERMONT.* MONTPELIER, VT: VERMONT HISTORICAL SOCIETY, 1930.
WITH THANKS TO NORA WILSON AND FORREST HOLZAPFEL.

NEWFANE

The Windham County Courthouse faces the Newfane Common along Route 30 in Newfane village. The town Civil War memorial, a soldier with a rifle-musket, bears the names of 134 Newfane men who served.

In the courthouse courtroom is a portrait of Newfane native Roswell Martin Field. Born in this village 1807, Field served as Windham County state's attorney 1832 to 1835, trying many cases here. Field moved to St. Louis in 1839, where he quickly became a prominent attorney. He gained a national reputation in 1853 when he represented Dred Scott, a slave seeking his freedom. Field won the case, but the U.S. Supreme Court, in an opinion written by Chief Justice Roger Taney, reversed the decision. The case, which in effect stated that African Americans had no rights as citizens, moved the nation closer to war.

The *Brattleboro Phoenix* of September 29, 1864 carried a brief item: "E. H. Stoughton and Charles B. Stoughton of Bellows Falls . . . were admitted last week as Attorneys at Windham County Court." That ceremony took place in the county courtroom. Having lost command of the 2nd Vermont Brigade, after his capture by John Mosby, and trying without success to resurrect his military career, Edwin Stoughton turned to the law. So did his brother, Charles, who had succeeded Edwin as commander of the 4th Vermont, when Edwin was given command of the 2nd Brigade. Charles was severely wounded at Funkstown, a week after Gettysburg, and was forced to come home. Many lawyers with the Civil War in their future, or past, practiced law in this courtroom, including Lewis Addison Grant, commander of the 1st Vermont Brigade.

In Newfane's 1839 Congregational Church, behind the courthouse, on May 12, 1861, a sermon was delivered that asked for divine help in bringing about military success for the North. It may have been spoken by Otis Warren, who at times was the church's pastor and kept a diary in the 1860s. Warren wrote that, several years before the war, he attended an anti-slavery meeting in Newfane. But with the war underway, on July 16, 1863, he wrote, "Henry has enrolled in Newfane & Putney but escaped both places—very remarkable case—Albert escaped the draft fortunately—we are glad." Henry and Albert were Warren's sons.

Warren and another Newfane diarist, Chestina Merrifield, both noted that troops drilled in the village in late May 1862. Warren wrote that "soldiers came from Brattleboro to board and drill here awhile." The men were likely members of C Company of the 2nd Vermont. Merrifield wrote that on May 19, 1862, the body of Private Frederick Stoddard, a Townshend man and a member of Company C, was "carried through town he having died in the Army at Washington."

On July 6, 1863, Merrifield wrote, "When I got home at 6 o'clock they were firing guns in honor of a Victory by Gen Mead over Gen Lee." Warren said two days later, "All the bells were rang and guns fired in the evening, at the News of the surrender of Vicksburg & defeat of Lees Army in Penn great rejoicing." Then on April 3, 1865, he wrote, "Richmond reported taken—ringing of bells & firing of guns in every village PM and evening—Blowing of horns—beat of drums—Rattling of dinner bells—Great excitement everywhere."

Beside the church is a hotel with tall columns, once the home, in later life, of Marshall Twitchell. Born in Townshend, Twitchell served three years in the 4th Vermont, rising from private to lieutenant and surviving a wound in the face at the Wilderness. Late in the war, he commanded a colored regiment in Louisiana. He became a planter and mill owner in Louisiana after the war, became involved in Reconstruction politics, and was elected to the state senate. Through the locals called him a carpetbagger, Twitchell firmly believed he was making a contribution to Louisiana, providing jobs to both blacks and whites in his enterprises. But ill feeling persisted, and in 1874, his brother and two brothers-in-law were killed in an ambush in the Louisiana countryside. In 1876, Twitchell was shot in an assassination attempt that resulted in the amputation of both his arms. Later, he became a U.S. consul in Canada and lived until 1905.

Across the street from the common is a corner store, and behind it a large house with corner tower, both once owned by Austin Birchard. His son, Sergeant Sardis Birchard, joined the 11th Vermont in the summer of 1863. Having survived the Overland Campaign, his health weakened in the lines at Petersburg, and on June 23, 1864, he was among those captured at

Weldon Railroad. A comrade of Sergeant Birchard wrote Austin Birchard that Sardis should not have been on duty that day. He said that Sardis "stood the journey from Richmond to Andersonville first rate although it was enough to kill anyone he stood it well for one whose health was as poor as his was. We arrived at Andersonville July 13." Sardis died of chronic diarrhea on August 20.

The Windham County Historical Society fronts on Route 30, south of the Common. Among the exhibits is a large chair made of fence rails taken from the position of the 1st Vermont Brigade at Gettysburg.

From the museum, go south 2 miles on Route 30, turn right on Grimes Hill Road, and enter Williamsville. The 1829 store in the center of the village was owned, after the war, by Amherst Morse. Lieutenant Morse was also captured at Weldon Railroad, but he survived several Confederate prisons to return home. He died in 1877 in a buggy accident. Here in Williamsville, Company I of the 8th Vermont, recruited by William Lynde of Marlboro, drilled before going to war, bound for the far South and later the Shenandoah Valley.

Pass the store, go through the covered bridge, and soon on the right is the South Newfane Church. In the 1840s, its members resolved that no owner of slaves, or supporter of slavery, could be a member. Return past the store and go right across the arched cement bridge. In 0.75 mile, the frame house close to the road (in 2011 the office of a landscaping company) was the home of Harrison Aldrich. A captain in the 21st Massachusetts Infantry,

Aldrich served the first two years of the war. He was wounded in the shoulder at the Battle of Newbern, North Carolina, but survived to return here.

SOURCES
Centennial Proceedings and other Historical Facts and Incidents Relating to Newfane, the County Seat of Windham County, Vermont, 1774–1874. Brattleboro, VT: D. Leonard, Steam Job Printer, 1877.
Marr, Joan. "The 11th Vermont Regiment and in Their Own Words: The Civil War." *News and Views*, 2011. Windham County Historical Society.
Warren, Otis. Diaries. Windham County Historical Society.
With thanks to Joan Marr.

PUTNEY

The Putney town common was a center of war-related activity from 1861 to 1865. On July 4, 1863, an Independence Day celebration began on the common included a reading of the Declaration of Independence and an appeal by E. B. Turner "to lay all bickerings and party feelings aside and stand up boldly for the preservation of our country." In the 1864 presidential election Putney went for Lincoln over McClellan, 240 to 57.

The *Brattleboro Phoenix* of April 16, 1865, reported on a victory celebration held in the village, stating that Putney people "each vied with the other in their joy that 'Babylon had fallen.' Exhausting their own supply of powder they sent off for more."

Putney's 1872 town hall, beside the common, is where members of the W. H. Greenwood Post of the GAR and the

Greenwood Relief Corps often met. (Greenwood was colonel of an Illinois regiment who spent his last years in Dummerston.) A late 1890s photo shows 21 aging and uniformed veterans posed on the building's steps, some of the 115 men credited to Putney who served in the Civil War.

A Putney resident writing to the *Brattleboro Phoenix* just before Christmas 1864 said of his town that "we are loyal from center to circumfrance and while we sustain our government with heart and soul in tis efforts to crush forever the unholy rebellion, we take a deep and generous interest in the welfare of our suffering soldiers in the hospitals throughout the land and in the prison pens of the barbarous Confederacy; and also in the sufferings of the thousands of homeless and shelterless refugees who . . . fly with utter destitution within our lines for protection, safety and sustenance. We have just sent to the American Union Common a donation of money, goods and useful articles of clothing $150 in value."

The Putney Congregational Church is just west of the common, and the July 7, 1864, *Brattleboro Phoenix* reported that "Mrs Kingsbury, for some time a teacher at the South, gave a lecture in the Congregational Church last Monday eve. Subject—slavery." According to the *Phoenix* of July 8, 1864, the "Soldier Aid Society of Putney met at Mrs. Isaac Grout's on Tuesday evening, July 5." Mrs. Grout's house is across the street from the church, a two-story house with a small front porch.

Two days after word reached Putney of Abraham Lincoln's assassination, a funeral service for the president took place in the Congregational Church. Five hundred people marched in procession to the service.

Pass the church going west, and soon go left on Signal Pine Road. Soon, on the left, is Phineas White Lane, and the frame house at the corner is believed to have been the home of Corporal James Black. He was nineteen and a member of the 8th Vermont when he was killed in the victorious charge at Third Winchester.

Continue west from Putney and take Sugar Pine Road, then go right at a Y. The first house on the left, after the war, was the home of Patrick Mooney. He joined the 4th Vermont at thirty-eight as a private in January 1864 and six months later was captured at Weldon Railroad. He survived eight months in Andersonville, came home to Putney, and lived until 1895.

Return to the common, go south on Main Street, and soon Old Route 5 branches right. In the first house on the right lived James Willard who served four years in the 4th Vermont and survived a wound at Spotsylvania's Bloody Angle.

Return to the common, go north on Route 5, and in a mile pass through fields where cotton once grew. The *Phoenix* said in August 1864 that Dorr Clough, and other Putney farmers, were "raising that traditionally southern crop."

Continue on Route 5 to take East Putney Falls Road, and on entering the old mill village of East Putney, Cemetery Road goes right. Pass the intersection, and the first house on the right was the home of Alphonzo Cobb, who, at twenty, fought at

Gettysburg with the 16th Vermont. Beyond the Cobb home, on the left above the road, is Pierce's Hall, built in 1830. In mid-August the hall's front yard was the scene of a war rally. The *Phoenix* said, "The people of East Putney had an enthusiastic time on Friday last, it being the occasion of the raising of a flag presented by the good ladies of that place." After several speeches, "Cheers were given for the good old flag of the Union, and also for the ladies who presented the flag, and a very strong feeling prevailed. Two men enlisted on the spot."

SOURCES

PUTNEY HISTORICAL SOCIETY. *PUTNEY: WORLD'S BEST KNOWN SMALL TOWN.* CHARLESTON, SC: ARCADIA PUBLISHING, 2001.
WITH THANKS TO RUTH BARTON.

ROCKINGHAM

From exit 6 on Interstate 91, take Route 103 north 1 mile and turn left on Meeting House Road. Quickly come to the 1787 Rockingham Meeting House, where Rockingham once held town meetings. Bellows Falls is the largest population center in the town, and on April 24, 1861, voters here resolved "[T]hat we, citizens of Bellows Falls, here meeting assembled, do pledge to every patriot of Bellows Falls who will volunteer to defend our country from assaults of rebels, that we will see that his wants and the wants of his family while he is engaged in the service of his country are supplied."

On June 19, 1861, on the motion of Henry Stoughton, who saw two sons go to war, voters "[R]esolved that the selectmen . . . are hereby directed to provide suitable persons to go into every field of battle where there may be any soldier from Rockingham dead or wounded and bring him or his remains home at the expense of said town and said selectmen are also directed to provide suitable means for the proper care of such soldiers in any hospital." Whether any such search was made is not known.

In December 1863, $19,000 was voted to pay bounties for thirty-four men. Also, voters agreed that "selectmen authorize and make special provision as they may deem necessary for the support of the family of Warren M. Henry who was killed at the Battle of Fredericksburg while in the United States service." Warren Henry, twenty-seven, a private in the 6th Vermont, was killed at Banks' Ford on May 4, 1863.

On June 8, 1864, selectmen were authorized to borrow $15,000 for bounty payments. Ten weeks later, voters refused to approve borrowing $46,000 for more bounties, but ended up authorizing the selectmen to procure whatever funds necessary to meet town draft quotas.

Adjacent to the meetinghouse is one of New England's finest old cemeteries, filled with examples of primitive stone-carver art. Several stones mark the graves of Civil War soldiers, including George Roundy, Vermont Cavalry private, who was twenty-one when he died at Belle Isle Prison after his capture near Hagerstown, Maryland, just after Gettysburg.

From the meetinghouse, return along Route 103; take Route 5 south 2.75 miles, and at a Y, take Rockingham Street into the Bellows Falls village square. This area was the center of Rockingham activity during the Civil War. However, fires have taken their toll, and most important buildings of that era are gone. Long preceding the Civil War, a crowd of three thousand turned out in the square to hear an impromptu speech by Daniel Webster, who long worked as a U.S. senator for compromise and to avoid war. Webster spoke here July 8, 1840, from the balcony of the Mansion House, which stood at the southwest corner of the square. Years later, a local man wrote, "Persons present at the time often spoke in later years of the breathless silence of the great audience, except when they gave forth their mighty cheers."

In early November 1858, a reception was held in the square for the local militia company, the Green Mountain Guards, just returned from the state muster at Brandon. According to the *History of Rockingham,* "Lewis A. Grant, then a young lawyer here, later assistant secretary of war, made a speech of welcome." Grant, who came to Bellows Falls in 1857 to practice law with his mentor Henry Stoughton, became commander of the 1st Vermont Brigade.

The May 9, 1862, *Bellows Falls Times* reported: "SAXTON'S RIVER LIGHT INFANTRY—This company, commanded by Capt. Aldrich, paraded our streets on Wednesday and made a fine appearance . . . They were dined by our citizens in Jabez Hill's new building . . . on the corner." The Saxton's River Company would become Company I of the 12th Vermont.

In April 1865, people flocked to the square to celebrate the fall of Richmond. The *Times* reported, "In their rejoicings at Bellows Falls . . . musketry, salutes were fired; and pains enough not being taken to take all the balls out of the cartridges, 18 or 20 went through Jabez Hill's house, one shot narrowly missing a boy." The hill house stood on the west side of the square. Some of the celebrants surged uphill to the Emmanuel Church to ring the bell.

As September 1869 began, President Ulysses Grant stopped in Bellows Falls on a train trip that would take him to Rutland and Saratoga. A reception was hastily arranged, part of which included a drive by Grant in a carriage through the square. The *Times* reported that he "frequently bowed to the people and especially to the ladies."

From the southeast corner of the square, take Bridge Street east across the canal, and you are in a small section of Bellows Falls known as the Island. On its highest point stood the social center of Rockingham, a hotel known as the Island House, where Grant was entertained. A few weeks previous, in late July 1869, one of Grant's best friends visited the hotel. The *Times* of July 30 said, "Gen. W. T. Sherman, the man who 'marched to the sea,' arrived in town of Friday afternoon last, and on his presence becoming known to our people, the flags were immediately hung out, and a salute fired in his honor, and in the evening several hundred of our citizens with martial music marched to the Island House." Sherman spoke briefly, saying in part: "I am glad to see you in your beautiful home—for it is truly beautiful with its mountains, its swift river and peaceful hills . . . I like the prairies of the west better."

North of where the Island House once stood, the Bellows Falls railroad depot is built on the site of the wartime station, where Grant and Sherman arrived. On a chill winter night in late December 1869, the body of Edwin Stoughton arrived here. Stoughton, after his capture by John Mosby, was imprisoned for a time in Richmond. Apparently his health never recovered, and he died, at age thirty, in Dorchester, Massachusetts.

From the Island, return to the square and go south, quickly turning sharp right on Church Street to stone Immanuel Episcopal Church. In its graveyard, around the family monument, Henry Stoughton lies with his boys, Edwin and Charles. Once the youngest brigadier in all the Union armies, all seemed possible for Edwin. When Rockingham created a GAR post, it was named for Edwin Stoughton.

In the now quiet church where the Stoughtons once worshipped, a memorial service was held for Abraham Lincoln. Days earlier, when the wild victory demonstration in the square surged to the church, the *Times* reported: "On the news of Lee's surrender, there was a contest at the church between the people and the sexton, who acting under orders was guarding the bell to prevent it being rung. After one man had received some injuries the sexton as a last resort cut the rope. The crowd then rushed in and threw out the sexton and up stairs went where they got hold of the short end of the rope when

they made the bell ring, amid the cheers of the crowd in the street. They also rushed up to the belfry, where they cheered for the Union and were responded to by the crowd below."

Return along Church Street and quickly turn right on School Street. Most of the houses on this street were draped in black the day of Lincoln's memorial service. At the end of Church Street, turn right on Atkinson Street, which is Route 5. Go 0.25 mile, and the tall frame house on the right, with glassed-in porch, number 113, is believed to have been the house built by Lewis Grant just before he went to war, on land purchased from his boss, Henry Stoughton.

Return on Atkinson Street and take Route 121 west to the village of Saxton's River. Along its main street once paraded the Saxton's River Guards, destined to march to Gettysburg. When news of Lee's surrender reached here, a torchlight parade marched up and down the main street and a "cannon roared over the hills around."

The Baptist Church is on the south side of Route 121. Its membership on April 12, 1843, adopted a strong anti-slavery statement that concluded: "as a church and as individuals we most earnestly and affectionately instruct all our Christian brothers who still hold their fellow man in bondage to put away this fruitful cause of grief and that in the fear of God they unite with us in this our deliberate and solemn purpose to give countenance to the system in no way whatsoever."

The Drury family once worshipped

here. From the church, continue west on Route 121 out of the village and soon turn right on Pleasant Valley Road. In 3 miles the white frame house on the left, with a large barn directly across the road, both stood in the 1860s. Here, James and Mary Drury on July 13, 1863, saw their son Joseph leave to join Company F of the 4th Vermont. Surviving the Overland Campaign, the twenty-four-year-old 185-pound farm boy was captured on June 23, 1864, at Weldon Railroad. Marched with many other captured Vermonters to Richmond's Libby Prison, Drury was soon loaded on a crowded cattle car and taken to Andersonville. On December 13, Drury, a sick and broken young man, was paroled and released. Drury died here on February 12, 1865, weighing barely 100 pounds. Private Drury is buried with his parents in the Saxton's River Village Cemetery, near the Baptist Church.

SOURCES

ANDERSON, RICHARD. "JOSEPH FREEMAN DRURY." UNPUBLISHED MANUSCRIPT, 2010. COURTESY OF THE AUTHOR.

BELLOWS FALLS TIMES, 1861–1869. BELLOWS FALLS LIBRARY.

ROCKINGHAM TOWN RECORDS.

SAXTONS RIVER BAPTIST CHURCH RECORDS.

WITH THANKS TO RICHARD ANDERSON.

SOMERSET

From the center of Wilmington, go west 5 miles on Route 9 and turn north on Somerset Road. In 4 miles, cross the Sandgate/Somerset town line and enter Somerset, now an unorganized town. In a total of 6 miles from Route 9, bear right at a Y, proceeding toward Somerset Reservoir.

Soon on the right is the Somerset Cemetery, where two of the ten Civil War soldiers credited to Somerset are buried. One of them, Asa Burnap, left his father's farm in this area in 1863 to enlist in Dover, joining the 7th Vermont as a private. Burnap served until the war ended, returned home, and later was Somerset's representative in the legislature. Also buried here is Joseph Kellogg, who enlisted as a private in the 2nd Vermont at Shaftsbury and served three years.

Somerset's best-known native-son soldier was Enos Lyman Kimball Knapp, born on a local farm in 1837. His family moved north to Stratton in 1846, and from there, he joined the 16th Vermont. Captain Knapp was wounded leading the regiment's Company I at Gettysburg. Later a major in the 17th Vermont, he was shot in the head at Spotsylvania's Bloody Angle. But he recovered to win a brevet promotion at the April 2, 1865, Petersburg Breakthrough. After the war, he became a newspaper editor, judge of probate, and, in 1889, was appointed governor of Alaska by President Benjamin Harrison.

Continue past the cemetery and soon come to Sandgate's District One School, where some Civil War–era town meetings were held. It is believed that Enos Knapp, Joseph Kellogg, and Asa Burnapp attended school here, at least for a time. Continue past the school and reach the earthen dam that in 1911 was completed on the Deerfield River. The Somerset Reservoir covers much of what was once the logging and farming town of Somerset.

SOURCES

SOMERSET TOWN RECORDS. COURTESY OF THE
  WINDHAM COUNTY COURTHOUSE,
  NEWFANE.
YOUNG, D. K. *ECHOES IN THE FOREST: THE
  FAMILY HISTORY SUPPLEMENT TO THE
  HISTORY OF STRATTON, VERMONT.*
  STRATTON, VT: TOWN OF STRATTON, 2000.

....

STRATTON

Stratton's town center is located along the Stratton/Arlington Turnpike, at the intersection of Jamaica Road. The modern town office stands near the site of Freeman Wyman's big house, where Civil War–era town meetings took place. There, in 1860, Stratton went 57 to 11 for Lincoln.

A memorial service was held at the Union Church here for writer Robert Penn Warren in October 1990. Warren and his wife, the photographer Eleanor Clark, spent their last years in Stratton, a place Warren came to love. Writing in *New England Monthly* of Warren's service, Peter Davidson said, "The Town Center of Stratton, Vermont, consists of four frame structures set in a high saddle among mountains, not one building dedicated to commerce: a town hall, a town office, a school, and an old, unsteepled, seldom-used church, all white, with no houses close by. Mourners were conducting last rites there for a great American writer last Columbus Day weekend, while the highways lower down were jammed with motorists gawking at the flaming forests by way of celebrating the discovery of America. The man his friends and family were burying was known as Red to everyone present . . . He had been born eighty-four years earlier, on April 24, 1905, just north of the Tennessee border in Guthrie, Kentucky, a town of about one thousand people, given over to tobacco farming, chickens, kinfolk, and story-telling . . . Both grandfathers had fought in the Civil War."

Warren, a prolific writer best known for his novel *All the King's Men,* had much to say about the Civil War. In his small 1961 book *The Legacy of the Civil War,* Warren wrote of the racial unrest in his native South, as school integration was hard won. "Does the man who, in the relative safety of mob anonymity," he wrote, "stands howling vituperation at the little Negro girl being conducted into a school building, feel himself at one with the gaunt, barefoot, whiskery scarecrows who fought it out, breasts to breast, to the death, at the Bloody Angle at Spotsylvania, in May, 1864? Can the man howling in the mob imagine General Robert E. Lee, CSA, shaking hands with Orval Faubus, Governor of Arkansas?"

From the town center, proceed west 3 miles on Stratton/Arlington Turnpike and turn right into a clearing in the upland woods where a marker reads: "This rock marks the spot where Daniel Webster spoke to about 15,000 people at Whig Convention July 7 & 8, 1840."

Webster came here to address the 1840 convention of the Whig Party in Vermont's first congressional district. The largest crowd yet assembled in the state heard the fabled orator speak for two hours. Webster was one of the key players in the great congressional dramas that preceded the Civil War, as national lawmakers wrestled with the matter of slavery, left unresolved by the founding fathers. As slavery expanded westward with the growing nation, tensions grew toward Civil War. Webster ever strove to maintain the peace, compromising to postpone the ultimate resolution of the issue, which would come in the 1860s.

Return to the town center and take West Jamaica Road. In 0.75 mile, Mountain Road goes left and, across the way, is a narrow and short driveway leading to a very modern-appearing house, the home of Robert Penn Warren. The house stands on a bluff above Ball Mountain Brook, along which are remnants of the Grout family mill. Three sons of Joel and Lucy Grout worked here before enlisting. James and Joel, 9th Vermont privates, were captured with the regiment at Harpers Ferry and were confined in Chicago's Camp Douglas to await exchange. James died there, of disease, at thirty-three, in March 1863. Joel was wounded in the foot at Fair Oaks, near Richmond, in the fall of 1864 and was soon discharged. Brother John, a 4th Vermont corporal, was wounded in the Petersburg trenches.

Family legend says that when James Grout's wife, Caroline (Pike) Grout, learned that he had enlisted, she became upset and accidentally broke a kerosene lamp. The resulting fire severely burned her, and she died thirteen painful days later, at twenty-eight.

Return to the town center and go left on the Stratton/Arlington Turnpike toward West Wardsboro. In 2-plus miles, go right on Pike Hollow Road and in 0.4 mile look left across a ravine to the old farmhouse where Rufus Lyman lived. Late in the war he was Stratton's recruiter. Soon Pike Cemetery is on the right and just beyond it is the District Six School (now a house). The Pike house is at the road's end.

Lyman Pike joined the 10th Vermont in October 1862 and was killed at Monocacy in July 1863. Regimental commander Colonel William Wirt Henry said, "After the rebels had taken possession of the Thomas House, which was about thirty-five rods (about 580 ft.) on our right front, their sharpshooters were firing upon us quite lively from the second-story windows. Sergeant Pike was one of our best sharpshooters, and was having all the fun he wanted firing at those rebs in the window, while I was watching them with my glass and giving him points. Soon I saw a head and gun coming in sight around one of the window casings, and directed Pike where to look, and almost at the same moment both fired. I felt a bullet go under my chin, and the reb pitched out of the window. The brave Color Sergeant, Billy Mahoney, was watching us, and in a moment he caught me by the coat-tail and pulled me on the ground, saying, 'That will do, Colonel, the blooming rebs mean you.' And in a moment the brave Sergeant Pike dropped upon us, shot dead."

Pike's body came home for burial in the Pike Cemetery beside the schoolhouse he had attended. Stratton sent some thirty-six men to war.

SOURCES
STRATTON TOWN RECORDS.
YOUNG, DAVID KENT. *THE HISTORY OF*

Stratton, Vermont. Stratton, VT: Town of Stratton, 2001. With thanks to D. K. Young.

TOWNSHEND

Where Route 35 meets Route 30, the 1790 Townshend Church overlooks the Townshend Common. Civil War–era town meetings took place on the first floor, and war expenditures of $31,013.71 had been approved by Townshend voters by late 1865, including $400.85 paid to the state for one recruit from the South, identity unknown. Church services were held on the second floor, and the *Brattleboro Phoenix* reported September 9, 1864, that "Rev. John Wood, for many years pastor of the First Congregational Church of Townshend, now in the employ of the American Tract Society, spoke at the church on efforts of the Tract Society and the Christian Commission to meet the spiritual wants of the soldiers in our armies." The event raised $70.

Also facing the Townshend Common, along its north side, is another 1790 building, a large frame house once the home of Clarina Howard Nichols. Volumes could be written about her life, which the Townshend history published in 2003 well summed up:

"Born in West Townshend in 1810, Clarina Howard became an early advocate of women's rights. After a divorce in 1843 she married George Nichols. As editor of the *Windham County Democrat,* she strongly advocated women's property rights, child custody, temperance, and suffrage. In 1852 she became the first woman

to address the Vermont Legislature, and lectured throughout New England and the Midwest. Nichols was a staunch abolitionist who seized the opportunity to move with her family to Kansas where her views on slavery and women's rights were widely accepted. During the Civil War, she was director of a home for orphaned black children in Washington, D.C. She died at her son's home in Pomo, California, in 1885."

Nichols lived in this house while writing for the *Windham County Democrat.* She married George Nichols, publisher of the *Democrat,* here in 1843. Due to his poor health, she became, in effect, the paper's editor. Her strong opinions on many subjects, very prominently her opposition to slavery, became widely read. While in Kansas, she became, in 1857, editor of an abolitionist newspaper. Her friends included Susan B. Anthony and Mary Lincoln, who presented Clarina with an ivory box for her service to orphaned children in Washington.

From the common, go south 1.75 miles on Route 30, cross the West River, and turn right on Forest Road. From the first residence on the left, Charles Holland, after graduating from Townshend's Leland & Gray Seminary, went to Massachusetts to teach. At twenty-one, in August 1862, he joined the 5th Massachusetts Infantry as a private and served nine months. After coming home to this farm, he joined the 8th Vermont in 1864, and thereafter regularly wrote to his sister Mary. Four days after Cedar Creek, he described General Sheridan's arrival on the battlefield, then said, "Checked the enemy. Charge after charge was made, driving them every time until they were in full retreat." He added a note to his mother, "I have been through the hardest fought battle and came out safe and sound . . . I would like to take supper with you would I not eat a lot."

Return to the common and go north 1.5 miles on Route 35 to where Deer Ridge Road turns left. The house at the corner was the home of Pardon Holbrook, one of twenty-three Townshend men in Company D of the 16th Vermont. The company was in the attack on Pickett's Charge, and fellow soldier Samuel Follett wrote home, "We the 16th moved out in order to cut them off when they threw down arms and came into our lines . . . Flint, Baily & P. Holbrook were wounded but were doing well last we heard. Three killed and 11 wounded in our Co." Private Holbrook survived and came home.

Another member of the company, Private John Dyer, was not so fortunate. Continue north on Route 35 for 0.6 mile, and his home was the frame house on the left, just before the East Hill Road goes right. Shot dead in the move against Pickett's Charge, Dyer is buried in the Gettysburg National Cemetery.

Take East Hill Road to Top Notch Farm Road, and the first farm on the road was James Follett's home. He wrote to his family here the night before Pickett's Charge, while on picket near the Emmitsburg Road: "It was the saddest night on picket that I ever passed. The line ran across the field that had been fought over the day before, and the dead and wounded of both armies, lying side by side, thickly strewed the ground. The mingled imprecations and prayers of the wounded, and supplications for help, were heart rending." Follett came home to farm here and become a renowned local builder of stone bridges.

Return to the common, go north 2 miles on Route 30, turn right, and cross the top of the Townshend flood control dam. Soon go right on West Hill Road to an estate with a large house on the right. From here, brothers Henry and Emerson Bellamy went to join the 4th Vermont in August 1862. They both survived the Vermont Brigade's battles, until Funkstown, just after Gettysburg. Emerson wrote home, "Henry was wounded Friday afternoon while on the skirmish line. The ball struck him in the left side and passed through his bowels and lodged just under the skin in his right side, and was taken out by the doctor. He fell to the rear and laid down under a large tree . . . He suffered greatly until 2 o'clock yesterday morning when his spirit took its flight to the one who gavest."

Some 120 men were credited to Townshend.

SOURCES
BELLAMY, EMERSON. CIVIL WAR LETTERS. TOWNSHEND HISTORICAL SOCIETY.
FOLLETT, JAMES O. CIVIL WAR LETTERS. TOWNSHEND HISTORICAL SOCIETY.
FREEMAN, CASTLE. *A STITCH IN TIME: TOWNSHEND, VERMONT, 1753–2003.* TOWNSHEND, VT: TOWNSHEND HISTORICAL SOCIETY, 2003.
TOWNSHEND TOWN RECORDS.
WITH THANKS TO CHARLES MARCHANT AND PETER GALBRAITH.

VERNON

South from downtown Brattleboro on Route 142, along the Connecticut River, Vernon's modern war memorial by the town offices lists 77 men who served in the Civil War. Stars mark the names of the 16 who perished. Look west from the memorial, across Route 142 and the railroad tracks, to a large field. There, on August 25, 1859, three U.S. Army officers sent from Washington by Senator Jefferson Davis, of Mississippi, and the Senate War Committee, watched the testing of a new weapon, an experimental revolving cannon. Something like a big machine gun that fired 24-pound 6-inch shells, the weapon was invented by Cyrus Dodge of Dummerston. Locals called it "the big gun," and it weighed more than 28,000 pounds. The weapon was set up to fire from the near side of the field into the hillside terrace beyond. The test firings lasted two days, and apparently were initially successful. Then a crack developed in the barrel, rendering the weapon unserviceable. The weapon was never put into production, and the Civil War armies never used anything like a machine gun. A model of the big gun is displayed in the Vernon Historical Society museum.

Go south 0.2 mile on Route 142, and on the left is a small house with front porch, on a knoll facing the railroad. Mary Fairman was the daughter of Edward Fairman, a private in the 11th Vermont, who died of disease in early 1864. Mary kept a diary, and during the spring and early summer of 1864, she noted the passing of trains crowded with wounded soldiers headed for the military hospital at nearby Brattleboro, the human wreckage of the Overland Campaign.

A mile south of the Fairman home, turn right on Pond Road, go through the underpass to the first house on the right. Philander Streeter lived here, a 2nd Vermont private who was captured at First Bull Run and is said to have been the first prisoner confined in Richmond's infamous Libby Prison. Released after five and a half months, he went back to his unit and served until the summer of 1864.

Continue south on Pond Road 1 mile and take Huckle Hill Road. In 1 mile, the road starts to climb, then levels where two side roads come in. Park on the right just before the intersection and step up onto the knoll to see a stone foundation among maples. John Sugland, a black man and private in the 54th Massachusetts, lived in a small house here. After the war, Sugland was a popular man in town, said to be a fine dancer and a ladies' man. A man of immense strength, he once saved a local man's life by lifting a fallen tree off him. But Sugland was accused of murder years after the war, and he hanged himself in a Brattleboro jail cell.

Return to Pond Road and go 1 mile south to the Tyler Cemetery, which holds many Civil War graves. In the north part is the grave of Clarke Sweetland, a Mexican War veteran. The stone notes that three of his sons, Samuel, Artemus, and Daniel, "nobly sacrificed their lives in the War of the Rebellion." Private Artemus Sweetland, 2nd Vermont, died of wounds received at the Wilderness on May 5,

1865. The fate of the other two boys is unclear.

Continue south on Pond Road 0.3 mile and turn right on Houghton Hill Road. Just at the top of the hill, look right to a small cape with small barn behind. A sewing circle made up of local women, called the Women's Home Missionary Society, began meeting in this house in 1858, an organization that still exists. When the Civil War commenced the society sewed things for the troops, including uniforms.

Return to Pond Road, go south, and a large farm that comes in view ahead. The Vernon Historians, the local historical society, has identified many homes in town where Civil War soldiers lived. Lieutenant William Dickinson, 11th Vermont, who rose from corporal to officer, went to war from this farm and served until the war's end.

Where Pond Road meets 142, the 1848 schoolhouse across the road houses the Vernon museum. Among the exhibits is the model of the big gun that was test fired in 1859.

SOURCES
BRATTLEBORO REFORMER, 1861–1865. BROOKS MEMORIAL LIBRARY.
WASHBURN, ARTEMUS HENRY. *THE HISTORY OF THE TOWN OF VERNON.* VOL. 5. LUDLOW, VT: A. M. HEMENWAY, 1885.
WITH THANKS TO BARBARA SPRAGUE AND MEMBERS OF THE VERNON HISTORIANS.

....

WESTMINSTER

 Westminster's town hall, on the west side of Route 5, was dedicated January 8, 1890, with a lengthy speech by the Reverend Charles W. Dickinson, of Boston. He told the story of an escaped slave named Frisbie who lived in a log cabin in Westminster village: "His master soon discovered his whereabouts, and attempted to take him back to bondage. At once a company of 30 men armed themselves with muskets, pursued and overtook the southerners at the old Gilson Tavern. They rescued the captive and brought him back in triumph . . . This was long before the Civil War but when that war sent its thunderous call for men throughout our land there was no quicker or heartier response than that which Westminster gave our fathers and brothers." By one count, the town sent 139 men to war.

The former slave Frisbie's log cabin stood 0.3 mile south of the town hall, where an old frame house is now located, and just north of the handsome brick house that dominates the southern end of the village. The Gilson Tavern where the rescue took place is 2.25 miles south along Route 5, sitting slightly below the road on the east side. The 1700s building has three large chimneys.

Return north 1 mile on Route 5 and go left on Piggery Road. A half mile on the left is the farmhouse where Henry Augustus Willard was born, the founder of Willard's Hotel, the social center of Washington, D.C., during the war. His son, Joseph Willard, was a major in the Union armies, and in 1863 he befriended a beautiful young lady named Antonia Ford, who had been imprisoned as a Confederate spy in Washington's Old Capitol

Prison. Ford was believed to have been involved in John Singleton Mosby's capture of 2nd Vermont Brigade commander Edwin Stoughton at Fairfax Courthouse, Virginia, on March 9, 1863. Ford, who lived in Fairfax and was a friend of Confederate cavalryman J. E. B. Stuart, was sometimes seen in Stoughton's company. Joseph Willard won Ford's freedom after she spent two months behind bars, and he later married her. But Antonia lived only four more years, her health said to have been broken by her imprisonment.

Continue on Piggery Road to its end at Patch Road and turn left. In 3.3 miles, in the old farmhouse above the road on the right, with chimney on the front, Asenath Cook lived for a time. Her gravestone notes that she "died March 1, 1857, age 97; a slave by birth, a useful free woman in adult life."

Continue on Patch Road to Westminster West Road and turn right, soon entering the village of Westminster West. Go sharp left and uphill to the Congregational Church, built on the site of the Civil War–era church that was destroyed by fire. During the war, the pastor was Reverend Alfred Stevens, a well-known preacher. On August 6, 1863, funeral services were held here for Private Walter Ranney, 16th Vermont, nineteen when struck in the head by a shell fragment during the attack on Pickett's Charge. Ranney died three weeks later in a military hospital in Baltimore. Reverend Stevens gave a eulogy at the funeral that included these words: "We must not fail today to notice in our thanksgiving that signal victory God gave to our army at Gettysburg. We

mourn for the loved ones that fell there, but we cannot too highly prize the results of that awful battle to our country. It was a victory above all price, dearly bought as it was . . . We thank God . . . that he gave our country such sons; courageous self-sacrificing, and ready to endure the suffering and give their lives that the world might be delivered from the reign of oppression, that defied all liberty in rebel threats to blot our nation from existence, and extinguish all the rights that God has kindled here for enlightening the world."

At the graveside, Private Ranney's aunt, Elsie Miller, sang a song she composed for the occasion:

> **Soldier rest! The cry of battle**
> **Will disturb thy sleep no more**
> **Booming guns and muskets' rattle**
> **With their terrors all are o'er.**
> **Soldier rest, thy couch awaits thee**
> **Strewn with many fragrant flowers:**
> **Sweetly sleep till God translates thee**
> **To his ever blooming bower.**
> **Yes, tis done! We've gently laid thee**
> **Close beside thy mother dear,**
> **No rude foe will e'er upbraid thee,**
> **Oft will fall the silent tear.**

On April 9, 1865, the first Sunday after the capture of Richmond, Pastor Stevens delivered a sermon in the Congregational Church.

"The last week has been one of great excitement and unbounded joy in the loyal states," he said, "and we doubt not in many places in the land of rebellion. Richmond, the rebel capital is fallen, and the army of Lee, which has been the strength of the rebellion from its beginning, is retreating in confusion, before our victorious troops, as the news flies over the land with lightning speed . . . The nation is frantic with joy. The merchant forgets his sales; the mechanic and farmer their work. The white and black unite in demonstrations of joy. None could speak too loud or enthusiastically the joy for the tidings. The shouts of 'glory, hallelujah!' have rolled up from the mouths of hundreds of Negroes, for whose enslavement the war was begun. It has been as when 'Prophetic Babylon' fell, and the nations are in commotion, 'because in her would be bought no more the bodies and souls of men.' City answered to city, swelling the wave of joy until the land was full . . . This is well. It is as it should be."

As those words were spoken, pastor and congregation were unaware that 500 miles to the south that morning, General Lee was about to ride into the village of Appomattox Courthouse to confer with General Grant on terms for the surrender of the Army of Northern Virginia.

In the cemetery by the church lie Reverend Stevens, Private Ranney, and the former slave Asenath Cook. Reverend Stevens lived in the first house beyond the cemetery.

Return to Westminster West Road, and in 2.5 miles, come to McKinnon Road, on the left. Private Ranney went to war from the first house on the road.

SOURCES

MINARD, M. ELIZABETH. *HISTORY OF WESTMINSTER*. WESTMINSTER, VT: TOWN OF WESTMINSTER, 1941.

STEVENS, REV. A. *A SERMON, PREACHED ON THE DAY OF NATIONAL THANKSGIVING, AUG. 6TH, 1861, AT THE FUNERAL OF SERGT. WALTER W. RANNEY, WHO DIED OF WOUNDS RECEIVED IN THE BATTLE OF GETTYSBURG*. BELLOWS FALLS, VT: PHENIX JOB OFFICE, 1863.

ZIRBLIS, RAY. *FRIENDS OF FREEDOM: THE VERMONT UNDERGROUND RAILROAD SURVEY REPORT*. MONTPELIER, VT: VERMONT DIVISION OF HISTORIC PRESERVATION, 1997.

WITH THANKS TO ROBERT HAAS.

WHITINGHAM

Go south on Route 100 from Route 9 in Wilmington, and in 5-plus miles enter Jacksonville in the town of Whitingham. Along its main thoroughfare here, people from Halifax, Readsboro, and Wilmington marched in procession from a meeting hall to "a beautiful grove" on July 4, 1864. There, under a blue sky, they heard a patriotic oration by Captain Henry Dix, who the previous summer led the 16th Vermont's Company F at Gettysburg. That company was made up of men from Whitingham and nearby towns.

Jacksonville was a stronghold of the Democratic Party. In 1864, when word came that George Brinton McClellan had been chosen the party's presidential nominee, according to the *Brattleboro Phoenix,* local Democrats celebrated "by firing cannon, a public dinner, and an amount of drinking limited only by their capacity."

Continue south on Route 100, and in 1.75 miles bear left on Goodnow Road, which soon leads to a recreation area and the Whitingham veterans' memorial on Town Hill. The village of Whitingham Center once occupied this hilltop, and a history of Wilmington published in 1975 said, "For almost the first hundred years of Whitingham's history, the center of the town and most of its business was found atop Town Hill. Now there are but two houses left on the hilltop. Markers on the Old Common show where some buildings were located. The larger marker, just north of the road, is at the site of the old church built by the town in 1799. Farther back from the road was the Center School, built in 1789, and often used for church services and town meetings before the building of a meetinghouse. East of the church, three small houses were located along the east-west road."

The Mormon pioneer Brigham Young was born in Whitingham, and a large stone monument across the road honors him. That area was once a fairgrounds, and on October 4, 1859, the Whitingham Agricultural Society held its annual fair here with cattle, horse, and poultry shows. Just twelve days later, John Brown raided Harpers Ferry, and the Civil War became inevitable. When the war was well underway, a war meeting was held here on August 29, 1862, with the *Phoenix* reporting that almost the entire town was present. After patriotic speeches, it was voted to pay those volunteering for nine months $100 bounties. A total of 26 men promptly signed up, exceeding the town's quota of 22. Most of those men fought at Gettysburg. Only one citizen, John Gates, voted against the bounties, and a resolution was promptly approved stating that he had forfeited his right to citizenship in the town and should be "transported to Haystack Mountain."

Many town meetings were held throughout the war in a meeting hall here, as filling draft quotas became more difficult. Many Whitingham men enlisted in regiments in nearby Massachusetts. Late in the war, two selectmen were employed, at $6 per day, to seek recruits in other towns. When the war ended, Whitingham was credited with 107 men who served. Among them was Hosea Dix who joined Company H, 2nd U.S. Sharpshooters, on the last day of December 1861 as a private. Less than ten months later he was dead of disease. He went to war from a house on this hilltop.

A Baptist church also was located here, and in January 1864, its pastor Thomas Wrinkle left the pulpit and volunteered for the 8th Vermont's Company B, as a private. He fought in the Shenandoah Valley Campaign.

From the hilltop, go left on Poverty Row 0.3 mile, and on the right is the white frame house where Robert Burrington lived after the war. At forty-five, he joined the 4th Vermont as a private when the war began, came home to recruit in the winter of 1862, then returned to the front. Captured at Savage's Station, he was imprisoned at Libby Prison and Belle Isle three months and came home in broken health.

Return to Goodnow Road, go left to Route 100, and turn south. Soon on the left is a Baptist Church and behind it is Green Mountain Hall, built in 1862 as a Methodist church. The *Phoenix* reported on August 26, 1864, that members of Whitingham and Wilmington churches picked wild blueberries for the soldiers being treated at the Brattleboro hospital. Members of this church participated.

Continue south on 100 through the present-day Whitingham Center, and in 1 mile narrow Pike Road goes sharp right. From the farm at the road's end, on a hilltop with a long view north, nineteen-year-old Eli Pike left to join the 25th Massachusetts Infantry. He was killed a year later in battle at Newbern, North Carolina.

SOURCES

BRATTLEBORO PHOENIX, 1860–1865. BROOKS MEMORIAL LIBRARY, BRATTLEBORO.
BROWN, LEONARD. HISTORY OF WHITINGHAM. NORTH ADAMS, MA: LAMB PRINTING CO., 1986.
GRAVES, MARJORIE W. STORIES OF WHITINGHAM. WHITINGHAM, VT: PRIVATELY PRINTED, 1975.
WHITINGHAM TOWN RECORDS.
WITH THANKS TO STELLA STEVENS AND ALMIRA AEKUS, TOWN CLERK.

··

WILMINGTON

At the center of Wilmington is a stoplight where Routes 9 and 100 meet. Some fifteen years after the Civil War, a Brattleboro businessman, Fred W. Childs, decided to capitalize on Wilmington's clear mountain air and cool summer nights by building a resort hotel here. The fact that a railroad line coming up from North Adams, Massachusetts, ended in Wilmington was key to the enterprise. Childs got his big hotel under construction, then saw the need for a concert hall to entertain guests. To design it, he hired the renowned architectural firm of McKim, Mead & White, designers of many masterpieces, including Boston's Symphony Hall. The hotel was in business when the hall was dedicated on December 29, 1902, and Childs decided that it should serve as a memorial to the founders of Wilmington and to the soldiers who had served from the town in the Revolution and the Civil War. Childs spoke at the dedication. "So long as the Deerfield shall flow onward toward the majestic sea," he said, "so long as the sons of Wilmington shall exalt the memory of their fathers, so long may the men, women and children of this historic old town meet to rededicate their hearts and lives to sacred emulation of the deeds of kindred statesmen and recall the unselfish patriotism of those who speak and those who are silent tonight." The hotel and hall still stand, two shingled buildings side by side along the south side of Wilmington's Main Street, which is Route 9. On the walls of the hall are the names of the Wilmington men who fought with John Stark at Bennington and of the 115 Wilmington men who fought for Lincoln.

At the main intersection, where Route 100 goes north, turn south and take the first right onto Shafter Street. Entering the old depot area, take the second left passing through a commercial area and stop to look into a field with an industrial building and house, with woods behind. Once this area was a park known as the Grove. Here on a Sunday in the fall of 1862, Wilmington people gathered to bid farewell to the local company about to depart for Brattleboro and the 2nd Vermont Brigade. Captain Henry F. Dix, about to lead Company F of the 16th

Vermont, was the center of attention that day. After a feast, the reading of several poems composed for the occasion, and a prayer, schoolteacher Sarah Morgan presented a sword to the captain, saying:

"The ponderous doors of war that have so long been closed in our country are again thrown open. Our boasted land trembles beneath the tread of armed men. The war cry has sounded through sunny valleys, over wide prairies, and even on these green hills where quiet had reigned since the brave Green Mountain Boys helped make our land a nation among nations."

Dix accepted the sword saying: "We believe our cause is just; we go to battle for the right, and we have the strongest assurance that you feel a deep interest in our welfare. We know your best wishes will accompany us, and we believe that in a few months when grim-visaged war shall have smoothed his wrinkled brow, when the angel of peace shall revisit our shores, when the clash of war and the din of battle shall be exchanged for the pleasing pursuits of domestic life and we return to our peaceful homes among the green hills of Vermont, the plaudits of a rescued people will welcome us."

The band played, everyone went home, and next day, the men went off to war. Some 32 local men served in the 16th; Lieutenant Cyren Lauton and Private Dana Chandler died of their Gettysburg wounds.

Return to the center of the village and the library is on the right with the town Civil War monument on the lawn.

Turn left at the main intersection, and the third building on the right, the large Victorian house that is now a shop, was once the home of Chandler Russell, a corporal in the 16th. Years after the battle, this seller of insurance took to the road lecturing on the Battle of Gettysburg throughout the northeast. The Wilmington Historical Society owns the hand-painted map he used to illustrate his talks.

SOURCES
Brattleboro Reformer, 1862–1864. Brooks Memorial Library, Brattleboro.
Wilmington town records.
With thanks to Alan McDougal Peter and Morris.

WINDHAM

From Chester, go west on Route 11 to Route 121, then take Windham Hill Road into Charles Gould's hometown. Some 600 miles south of the mountain town of Windham, a Civil War museum stands on the site of one of the war's important events. Just west of downtown Petersburg, Virginia, Pamplin Park interprets the early April 2, 1865, attack by the 6th Corps that finally broke Robert E. Lee's lines after nine months of siege. Prominent in Pamplin Park's interpretation of that mighty day is the story of Captain Charles Gould, of Company H, 2nd Vermont.

Gould grew up in Windham and when two years old fell into a pot of boiling applesauce on his grandparents' stove. Terribly burned, he could not walk until he was six years old. But he soon became a fearless young man, and when war began, he enlisted against his parents' wishes in the 11th Vermont and rose from private to captain. Reenlisting in the 5th Vermont in the fall of 1864, he commanded Company H. In the predawn hours of April 2, 1865, his regiment was at the front of the 12,000-man 6th Corps, massed in a wedge-shaped formation, with the Vermont Brigade at the front. After a thunderous artillery barrage, the attack rolled forward. Gould and a small group of men accidentally veered from the route of attack and suddenly found themselves between the Confederate earthworks and onrushing Union soldiers. Up the ramparts they went. He recalled:

"My appearance on the parapet was met with a leveled musket, which fortunately missed fire. I immediately jumped into the work, and my part in the engagement was soon over. I was scarcely inside before a bayonet was thrust through my face and a sword-thrust returned for it that fully repaid the wound given me, as I was subsequently informed that it killed my assailant. At almost the same breath an officer—or someone armed with a sword—gave me a severe cut in the head. The remainder of my stay in the works was a confused scramble . . . During the struggle I was once seized and my overcoat partially pulled off, and probably at this time another bayonet wound was given me in the back."

Captain Gould was the first Union soldier to breach the Confederates' Petersburg works, and later he received a Medal of Honor. A picture survives of him in uniform, his boyish, handsome face displaying the scar of a bayonet wound.

Proceed south on Windham Hill Road, and soon the 1802 meetinghouse and Congregational Church is on the right. Windham voters here, in 1860, cast 113 of 126 votes for Lincoln. Four years later, Lincoln again carried the town, 137 to 16.

Turn right at the meetinghouse onto Harrington Road, and the first house on the right, looking down on the church, was the home of James Gould, first cousin of Charles, who served four months as a musician in the 11th Vermont, before being discharged for disability. Continue on Harrington Road 0.5 mile to a driveway that turns right. Just past it, on the left, is a large cellar hole. Lemuel and Mary Abbott lived here and saw sons John and Marcus go to war. John, a drummer in the 16th Vermont, died a month after Gettysburg in the hospital at Brattleboro. Marcus enlisted as a private in the 11th Vermont in September 1862 and died the following March of sickness at Fort Slocum, outside Washington.

Return to Windham Hill Road and turn right. Look left for a stone foundation by a house, the remains of the Harris general store, owned by the parents of Charles Gould's first wife, Ella Harris. Continue south 0.3 mile, and the frame house on the right, with long addition on back, was the home of William Cronin, who served with Gould in Company G of the 11th.

Continue south and the Windham Center Cemetery is on the left.

Gould's 5-foot-tall granite stone notes that he was born on May 5, 1845, and that he died on December 6, 1916. Wives Ella and Frances (Davis) Gould, daughter of Vermont quartermaster general George

Davis, are buried with him, as are two daughters of Ella and Charles. In front of the grave is a Medal of Honor marker. Nearby are the graves of the Abbott boys, beside their parents' stones.

Continue south on Windham Hill Road into South Windham. The last house on the south side of the village, on the right, a huge frame house with shop beside, was George Harrington's home. A private in the 8th Vermont, he was wounded during the Siege of Port Hudson. He was a coffin maker and surely made some for his fellow soldiers here in Windham, a town that sent some sixty-five men to war.

SOURCES
WINDHAM TOWN RECORDS.
WITH THANKS TO JONATHAN STEVENS.

*The scarred face of Captain Charles Gould, the first
Union soldier to break the lines at Petersburg.*

chapter fifteen

Windsor County

John Brown came to Cavendish before the Civil War, seeking money and weapons for his antislavery activity. Local people demanded of him a speech, which he gave in a building that still stands. And they well remembered him after he gave his life trying to start a slave uprising in Virginia, an event that made the Civil War inevitable. When the war began, Peter Washburn administered Vermont's war effort from an office that still overlooks the village square in Woodstock. Abraham Lincoln once spoke to him in praise of Vermont troops. In Windsor's Constitution House, Vermont adopted the first constitution in America that outlawed slavery. When the war began, the redbrick factory down the street had a hand in the manufacture of half the rifle-muskets and pistols that won the war. Plymouth people believed their losses were the highest per capita in the Civil War. Their war monument overlooking Echo Lake makes a strong case. But they didn't lose as many men as poor Rochester, which hastened when peace finally came to erect a monument on the green for all those boys who never came home. In the hills above East Barnard, a strange man hid in a cave, then a rock hut he built, to avoid the draft. The cemeteries of West Windsor are filled with the graves of people who died of diphtheria, brought from the war zone by local soldiers.

ANDOVER

From Chester, go 4 miles west on Route 11, right on Andover Road, and in 2.5 miles come to Peaseville and its 1867 church. In the 1860s, the Andover town hall stood just west of here, but long ago was moved to Town Hall Road just opposite the church. At a town meeting on June 1, 1861, Andover voters approved the following: "Resolved: That we honor the Patriotism of those volunteers who have enlisted from this town (as well as others) who have left home and friends for the purpose of putting down the Rebellion, that is now threatening a total annihilation of our free institutions, who are toiling on the hot soil of Virginia to secure for us the continuance of those institutions and to defy the plans of the traitors collected there who seek to destroy our government." Meeting here on December 11, 1863 bounty payments of $500 per soldier were voted.

From the church, go 0.2 mile east, turn left on Pettengill Road, and go to the farmhouse at its end. From here, Olin Pettengill enlisted as a drummer in Company A of the 3rd Vermont. The *Bellows Falls Times* of February 20, 1863 said: "'Olin Pettengill of Andover, and drummer boy in the Third Vermont Regiment, died recently in the hospital at Windmill Point, Va. If we remember correctly, this brave youth went out with the Springfield Company. At the battle of Fredericksburg, he threw away his drum and took a gun declaring his determination to share the danger of the rest. He was deeply affected with the result of that unfortunate battle and was deranged most of the time afterwards, his thoughts perpetually running upon the battle. He was 19 years of age, a remarkably promising young man, and one of the best drummers in the State. His remains were brought to his home in Andover, and very impressive funeral services were held on Tuesday." Sickness killed young Pettengill. He is buried in the small family cemetery near his home.

Return to Peaseville Church, pass it, and in 0.5 mile come to the brick 1820 Peaseville School. Pettengill was a pupil here, as was Abram Rowell, a private in the 16th Vermont who was wounded in the attack on Pickett's Charge. A half mile past the school, turn right on Jarvis Road, and at the end is the farmhouse where Rowell lived postwar.

Back on Andover Road, go right 1 mile, passing through the sharp turns of the Ox Bow, and go right on North Hill. Soon, turn left on Arrau Road and come to a long farmhouse at its end. George Washington Stickney, a foe of slavery and an advocate of temperance, lived here and saw his twenty-one-year-old son Cassius join the Vermont Cavalry as a private. Two weeks previous, Cassius and Rosalie Peabody were married in the house's parlor. In the spring of 1864, fighting near Ashland Station, north of Richmond, Cassius was shot in the arm and was among seven wounded men captured, all of whom would die by summer's end. When word reached here of Cassius's death, in a Richmond prison, on July 20, his mother, Roxcea, went to Ludlow to talk with one of her son's comrades, Michael Sullivan, just home. In a letter written to her husband, then in the legislature at Montpelier, she wrote, "He was Cassius's nurse in the hospital and was with him when he died. He said Cassius was a great sufferer. But was well treated by his surgeon—not withstanding he was a rebel." She went on to describe how Cassius pleaded with the surgeons to amputate, but they refused, saying it would kill him. Finally, they relented, and Cassius died three days later. He was buried near the prison. Her letter concluded, "It was a great relief to know he was well taken care of. But when I think of what his meditations must have been sick and suffering so far from his friends and home and did not know that he should ever learn his fate it causes a sadness that I cannot describe." Cassius's wife lived twenty more years and never remarried, family legend saying that she died of heartbreak. Many years later, one of the world's finest pianists, Claudio Arrau, bought this house and made beautiful music here.

Return to Andover Road, turn right, and in 0.5 mile, go left on Middletown Road to its end. Turn left on Route 11, go quickly right on Simondsville Road, and come to the 1848 church, where, during the Civil War, spiritualists met and war meetings took place. Years after the war, Eldora Wright Stevens recalled a July 4, 1861, event: "The short spire of the white church glistened against a background of maples and birches, their leaves fairly dripping sunshine. White clouds drifted lazily in the blue sky, but perhaps few people noticed, so intense was their excitement." She described a dinner, patriotic speeches made from a platform erected by the church, and singing the national anthem. She wrote: "And now the parade. Excitement mounted among young and old, who followed along, with many flags waving. The course of the parade was toward Chester . . . or perhaps to the red Simondsville schoolhouse opposite the home of Phoebe Edson Chase, mother of Isaac and Ira . . . Ira and Isaac were not present to watch the parade approach their home, for they had been the town's first men to enlist. Isaac was never to return, for he died in Philadelphia on July 4, 1862."

From the church, take Route 11 east toward Chester, following the parade. In 0.5 mile, Howard Hill Road goes right, and in the frame house just past the turn Phoebe Chase lived. She raised two sons after her husband, a doctor, died in the 1840s from a horse kick in the head. Ira, eighteen, and Issac, twenty, both joined the 1st Vermont and served all its ninety days. Isaac reenlisted as a musician in the 6th Vermont and died of illness on the Fourth of July, 1862. Ira joined the 3rd Vermont and served until wounded at the Wilderness. It is said that Phoebe Chase set a place at the table for Isaac as long as she lived.

Just beyond the Chase house is the Simonsville School, where the Chase boys and their sisters, Elmira and Elizabeth, studied, as did Harland Peabody, who served at Gettysburg with the 16th Vermont.

Return to Simondsville Church, and in 0.75 mile, go right on Gates Road. In 0.4 mile, the large house on the left was the home of Colonel Sylvanius Marsh, a War of 1812 veteran whose sons, Henry, John, and Vernon, served in the Civil War. Henry fought at Gettysburg with the 16th Vermont, then served in the 11th Vermont until war's end. John, a 3rd Vermont private, was killed at the Wilderness. Vernon, wounded as a 2nd Vermont private at First Bull Run, was discharged for disability and came home.

SOURCES
GUTTERSON, HILAND H. *THE LOCAL HISTORY*

OF *ANDOVER VERMONT*. EDITED BY ABBY
MARIA HEMENWAY. PERTH AMBOY, NJ:
HEARTMAN'S HISTORICAL SERIES, 1922.
ORIGINALLY PUBLISHED CHICAGO, 1886.

STICKNEY, PETER. "CASSIUS STICKNEY, CIVIL
WAR SOLDIER." UNPUBLISHED ESSAY,
UNDATED. COURTESY OF THE STICKNEY
FAMILY OF SAXTON'S RIVER.

A GATHERING OF VERMONT RECOLLECTIONS.
BURLINGTON, VT: VERMONT RETIRED
TEACHERS ASSOCIATION, 1980.

WITH THANKS TO JONATHAN STEVENS.

BALTIMORE

North of Springfield on Route 106, Route 10 branches west, and soon Baltimore Road turns right, north. In 0.6 mile cross the line from Springfield into Baltimore, which at 3,300 acres is Windsor County's smallest town. In 1 mile, Bemis Road goes left, and from the farmhouse at the end of this short, narrow old track, five Bemis brothers enlisted in the Civil War. Lowell Bemis, a 16th Vermont private, fought at Gettysburg. Brother Henry, 15th Vermont, marched to Gettysburg.

Sidney, Martin, and George Bemis were privates in Company F, 11th Vermont. Sidney ran away from home to enlist at sixteen and, because he was large for his age, was accepted. When he told the family, his father raised $300 and took Sidney to Brattleboro, intending to buy his release. But the lad protested so much that the father relented. Sidney was wounded at Third Winchester in September 1864 and came home to recover. At Weldon Railroad, on June 23, 1864, Martin lost an arm. George was taken prisoner that day and was soon confined at Ander-

sonville. In February 1865, the Bemis family was unsure of George's fate. Martin wrote to Ellery Webster, in Irasville, who had been imprisoned with Martin. Webster replied on February 8: "We left Andersonville, Georgia and went to Charlestown, South Carolina. George was not able to go with us and he was sent to the hospital. Since then we have not heard nothing from him. I suppose I might as well tell you what I think about him. Martin, I think your poor brother George is dead long ago. It was an awful place there and we did not get half enough to eat and poor unwholesome stuff at that. Out of the 50 that was taken I don't think there is a dozen alive ones now."

The Bemises eventually learned that George died of chronic diarrhea on a ship coming north, off the coast of South Carolina on December 7, 1864. He was eighteen.

Continue along Baltimore Road 1 mile to the wooden schoolhouse on the right, now the Baltimore town office. Baltimore town meetings once took place in a stone school on this site. On September 29, 1862, voters here approved a tax of 2 cents on each dollar of the grand list "to pay the soldiers from this town." In August 1864, bounties of $400 were voted for two men to meet the town's quota under "the President's call for 500,000 men."

On September 22, 1864, here, Joseph Leland was elected town moderator. At that same meeting, payments of $100 each were approved for Leland and Edwin Sherman "as a part of the commutation which they paid to clear them from the draft of 1863."

In January 1865, Baltimore voters instructed selectmen to borrow whatever was necessary to fill the town quota. Baltimore met all its small quotas. The stone school was replaced by the present building in 1894.

SOURCES

BALTIMORE TOWN RECORDS.

POLLARD, ANNIE M. *THE HISTORY OF THE TOWN OF BALTIMORE, VERMONT.* MONTPELIER, VT: VERMONT HISTORICAL SOCIETY, 1954.

WITH THANKS TO DEBBIE BEAN, TOWN CLERK, AND JUDY THOMAS.

BARNARD

Barnard village is along Route 12, north of Woodstock, on Silver Lake, where the local general store is set on a sharp curve. Just beyond the curve on Route 12 is the 1844 Barnard Universalist Church, where, in the early summer of 1864, the largest funeral in the town's history was held, for Captain Daniel Lillie. A schoolteacher known since childhood by the nickname Tiger, Lillie raised a company early in the war that became Company I, 4th Vermont. He led it through the war until May 6, 1864, at the Wilderness, when the Vermont Brigade began its early morning advance. The captain had just uttered the command "Forward," when he was shot. Mortally wounded, he lingered until June 6, dying in a Washington hospital.

Three houses beyond the church, on the left, is the fan house, named for its obvious decoration, which during most of the Civil War was the home and office of town clerk Samuel Thayer. Barnard's town

fathers met there, at times, to consider the financial demands of a war effort that, by March 1865, had cost the town nearly $25,000 in bounty payments.

Continue north of Route 12 for 2 miles and turn left up Mount Hunger Road. A half mile along, note a large farmhouse, with gingerbread decorations, set high above the road on the right. Luke Wheat, the only son of a prosperous farm family, lived here and was one of seven Barnard men to avoid military service by providing a substitute. Soon thereafter, Wheat moved west.

Continue up Mount Hunger Road 1 mile to a fork, bear left, and in 0.25 mile on the right, above the road, is an old farmhouse. The Lillies and their eleven children lived here, including Tiger, engaged to local girl Mariah Cox. Return to Route 12 and continue north, and in 1 mile, the one-room Creek School is on the left, where Lillie taught.

Continue 0.2 mile on Route 12 to the redbrick house on the left, where William Newton, Barnard historian, grew up. According to his 1928 town history this house was "often a rendezvous for returned soldiers." Newton said that the "Kendall boys" also lived here and that he often heard Albert Kendall, once a Vermont Cavalry private, relate his wartime experiences. According to Newton, Kendall talked of his captivity at Belle Isle and Andersonville. There he "wrapped the ragged half blanket, the only covering he had, about him and like a woodchuck crawled into the hole dug in the side of the hill to cry himself to sleep as a homesick and heartsick boy." And Newton wrote of hearing his mother tell of Albert Kendall and "how the family were awakened in the dead of night by the Yankee yell, such as he and others were accustomed to give as they rode to the charge, and to hear him bound out of bed, yelling as he had in many a battle, only to be awakened by coming in contact with the furniture or the side of the house and then, soldier like, turn in again almost as though nothing had happened and go off to sleep."

Return to Barnard village, go straight past the store, and in 1 mile, go left on Royalton Turnpike. In 1.75 miles, look left across a large field to an old barn and house on a hillside. Two Leavitt brothers, Amos and Levi, enlisted from here as privates in the 16th Vermont. Amos wrote in his diary the night of July 3, 1863, "the rebels commenced about 11 AM we had a hard fight all day about 4 PM I was wounded in the head there was about 12 killed and 70 wounded." That was one dazed soldier's account of the 2nd Vermont Brigade's attack on Pickett's Charge. Brother Levi returned home unscathed.

Continue on the Royalton Turnpike, and take the East Barnard Road to the village of East Barnard. Turn left on Broad Brook Road, and in slightly more than 1 mile, look closely on the right, where Broad Brook curves toward the road, for a small cellar hole between road and brook. Oliver Plaisted, a sometime schoolteacher, lived in a small house here, and when the war began, he took to the hills to avoid the draft. Plaisted spent the first year of the war in a small cave high in the hills that rise from the north side of the road.

He scratched on its walls "this is hell." Then, he built a substantial stone hut where he lived the remaining three war years. At war's end he returned home and lived fifteen more years.

Inquire locally for directions to Oliver's Cave. The cave and hut are some 2 miles into the woods above East Barnard, along a trail. The hut is well preserved, and the cave can be found in the woods behind it.

SOURCES
BARNARD TOWN RECORDS.
VERMONT STANDARD, 1864. WOODSTOCK HISTORICAL SOCIETY.
WITH THANKS TO THE LEAVITT FAMILY.

BETHEL

Approach Bethel from the west, along Route 107, and Route 12 comes in from the north. Just past the intersection, go left on Old Turnpike Road to a red barn in the Greek Revival style. This was the Bethel town hall during the Civil War, now 1 mile from its original location. The following resolution concerning Bethel's soldiers was adopted at a town meeting in September 1863 in this building:

"Resolved, that their names should be held in perpetual remembrance and especially the names of those who died gloriously on the battlefield . . . and him who died of wounds received while bravely fighting for our homes and our country . . . and those who died of disease while contracted in such honorable service . . . And therefore resolved that the clerk be directed to record the resolution with the proceedings of this meeting that all who may live in this town until it shall cease to be may know who of its freemen gave up their lives for their country in its time of utmost peril."

Continue to Bethel village, go through the railroad underpass, turn right to continue on Route 107 east, and in 0.25 mile go up Christian Hill Road. According to records of the Bethel Historical Society, 17 men went to war from homes along this road. Eight returned, 6 in one piece, 2 missing arms, and 2 died shortly after returning. In 2.75 miles, a redbrick house is on the left, with barn across the road. Faber Benedict enlisted from here, served a year in the 8th Vermont, survived Winchester and Cedar Creek, and came safely home.

Return to Bethel village, and just before the underpass, go right on Route 12 north. Quickly on the left, below the road, is a small park with a monument marking the site of 1780 Fort Fortitude. In this park, larger during the Civil War, Colonel Homer Stoughton held sharpshooter tryouts in August 1862. Those who passed were enlisted and taken to Woodstock for drills, before going south to join the 2nd U.S. Sharpshooters. Among the qualifiers was Charles Fairbanks, who recalled long after: "It was a sultry August day . . . There was a large crowd of townspeople present, who seemed to be about evenly divided in favor of my going to war, but after making the first shot at the ten inch ring, there was a cheer from the spectators, for I had put a bullet nearly in the center of the bull's eye, which was about two inches in diameter. The remaining nine shots were put inside the ring." Since Fairbanks was only sixteen, Stoughton told him he would need a signed permit from his father to enlist. The lad waded the White River, hurrying home.

Just beyond the park is the Bethel railroad station. Company A, 16th Vermont, commanded by Captain Henry Eaton, of Rochester, drilled at Bethel. It left from this station in early October 1862. Wounded commanding the company at Gettysburg, Eaton was back in 1864 to organize a Bethel company for the 17th Vermont. He was killed near Petersburg (see Rochester), serving as regimental sergeant major.

On October 30, 1867, the train bearing Philip Sheridan to Montpelier stopped here. A newspaper said, "A large American flag was hung across the street and everybody cheered loudly. The General appeared on the platform and bowed his acknowledgment of the compliment."

Continue north through the business district, and on the right is the brick Bethel town hall. An 1892 photo shows local GAR members assembled in front of the building, where the Bethel post sometimes met. Turn left and cross the bridge to the redbrick church. Town records state that on August 4, 1862, meeting in the "old brick meeting house," Bethel approved the town's first bounties of $50, plus $7 a month payments for men enlisting. Most town meetings were held across the street, where the old town hall, now serving as a barn 1 mile away, once stood. Continue north on Route 107 to the sharp right turn, and go straight for 0.5 mile. At the Y, bear left, and the first house on the left, with a wide porch, was the Fairbanks home. When Charles Fairbanks reached here after passing his sharpshooter test, his father was in the fields. Realizing the futility of trying to stop his son's enlistment, in Charles's words, "He immediately sat down on the hollow stump and with trembling hand signed the 'death warrant,' as he styled it." Charles and his older brother, Alfred, joined the sharpshooters. Two older Fairbanks boys also served. Alfred was taken prisoner at Gettysburg, confined at Belle Isle, and barely survived.

Return to Route 12, go north 4 miles, and turn left on Gilead Brook Road. In 0.6 mile, on the right, is a brick house owned, in 1863, by sixty-two-year-old David Owen. Known locally as a "peace Democrat," Owen opposed the war. Once a watering trough stood in his front yard, giving Owen an opportunity to exchange views with travelers. He got away with his criticisms of the war until the local lads came home from Gettysburg. One day they arrived here, tarred and feathered Owen, and carried him on a fence rail to Bethel, where he was paraded and made to give three cheers for Lincoln and the armies.

Continue on the Gilead Brook Road 2 miles, and turn right on Macintosh Hill Road. In 1.3 miles, at the height of land, a granite monument marks the birthplace of Stephen Thomas, commander of the 8th Vermont. Thomas spent his boyhood years here. The monument, dedicated October 19, 1914, the fiftieth anniversary of Cedar Creek, bears praise from his comrades in arms:

"Patriot, brave soldier, wise counselor, and beloved of all his men."

SOURCES

BETHEL TOWN RECORDS.

FAIRBANKS, CHARLES. *NOTES OF ARMY AND PRISON LIFE, 1862–1865.* COMPILED AND EDITED BY JANET HAYWARD BURNHAM. BETHEL, VT: MY LITTLE JESSE PRESS, 2004.

WOOD, LEYLAND E. *TWO VERMONT HOLLOWS: A HISTORY OF GILEAD AND LITTLE HOLLOWS.* RANDOLPH, VT: PRIVATELY PRINTED, 1976.

WITH THANKS TO JANET HAYWARD BURNHAM.

BRIDGEWATER

Go west on Route 4 from Woodstock 6 miles, and on entering Bridgewater, the Bridgewater woolen mill complex is on the left. Before the Civil War, Bridgewater thrived, with the mill that stood on this building's foundations in full operation. And gold had lately been discovered in the hills to the west. The mill's production increased during the war, its looms, powered by the Ottauquechee River, producing blankets for the Union armies. It shut down in 1867, with war production halted, but soon reopened.

Past the mill is the 1789 Southgate House that houses the Bridgewater town office. Just past it, Bridgewater Hill Road turns right, and the second building on the right is an 1803 brick structure, with cupola, which has served both as a school and town hall. Beautifully restored, it now houses the Bridgewater Historical Society. A history of Bridgewater, published in 1976, contains a newspaper notice from August 1854, notifying "Whigs and others of Bridgewater" opposed to "The

Nebraska swindle" and the Fugitive Slave Law to meet at the Bridgewater School House and choose a town representative and justices of the peace.

In August 1856, a newspaper notice said: "Freemen of Bridgewater, without regard to past political differences, who are opposed to repeal of the Missouri Compromise, to the policy of the present administration, to the extension of slavery into the territories and in favor of admission of Kansas as a free state, are requested to meet at the School House near Wood's Mills on Saturday to nominate a suitable person to be supported for Town Representative."

At least one 1865 town meeting was held here. Most wartime town meetings took place at Carpenter's Hotel, some 300 yards west along Route 4, a building long ago lost to fire. Meeting in November 1862, Bridgewater voters approved the first town bounties of $50. In August 1864, obviously having trouble filling quotas, Bridgewater authorized its selectmen to pay "from $500 to $1,500 each if necessary." Some 120 Bridgewater men served, and 24 died, 3 in Andersonville.

In 1865, a July Fourth celebration was held here in Bridgewater village, an end-of-war celebration. The day began with an artillery salute at sunrise and "the meeting house gave us a base, the school house a shrill treble, and the factory an alto-tenor accompaniment in way of bell music at the same time." A day of feasting, speeches, and music ended, as "our young men made our little cannon fairly jump in the closing 36 gun salute." In July 1867, a peace convention was held in Bridgewater, probably in the old brick building.

Continue west on Route 4, and at the west end of the village note that Gold Coast Road turns uphill and right. Continue on Route 4 through Bridgewater Corners, along the deep valley of the winding Ottauquechee, 4.5 miles. Turn right and go steeply up Bridgewater Hill Road. In 1.5 miles, pass an old cemetery with views of Killington Peak, and soon turn right at a Y. In 1.25 miles, turn right on Little Sherburne Road, and on the left is an old schoolhouse. Before the war, Francis Clark and his brother Charles F. Clark studied here. Both Clarks served in the 16th Vermont, Francis a lieutenant, Charles, a corporal. Both fought at Gettysburg and came safely home. The night of July 2, 1863, Francis was at a picket post far front of the main Union line, where hard fighting had occurred hours before. He wrote:

"Here and there the moon revealed, amid the trampled grain, prostrate forms, whom no long roll, or reveille, could rouse again. The air was tremulous with a sound, low and almost indescribable, resembling a far-off and just audible moaning of a forest of pines. It was the groaning of the wounded swelling up from field and wood and blending for miles in one low inarticulate moan . . . After fruitless searches for water I wrapped myself in my blanket and, with the wounded on either side, lay down to sleep. With upturned face to the mild majesty of the Queen of the Night as she looked down so calmly upon us, and with flitting thoughts of home, and friends, and other times, breathing a prayer, I fell asleep."

Clark's thoughts would have been of this upland place, for he lived near the school, in a house long gone.

Pass the school and take Dailey Hollow Road down a valley, along which much of Bridgewater's gold mining took place. The road is narrow, and the drop-offs steep. In 3.3 miles, turn right and pass through the hamlet of Bridgewater Center. Continue to Route 4 and turn left, east. On entering Bridgewater village, go sharp left, uphill along Gold Coast Road, and on the left is Mount Pleasant Cemetery, where many Bridgewater's Civil War soldiers lie.

Continue uphill past the cemetery 1.5 miles, and where the road turns sharp right, note a narrow private road entering from the left. From a house that stood 1 mile along this road, nineteen-year-old Henry White went to join the 16th Vermont in 1862. Private White was killed in the attack on Pickett's Charge. His body came to the White home here, then to Woodstock's Methodist Church for a Sunday funeral. The *Vermont Standard* said that the village's other two churches closed for the occasion and that "more attended the services than the house could hold." The paper also said, "We understand that Mr. White, at the time he enlisted, was fitting for the ministry."

Continue on Gold Coast Road to a T and turn left. Go straight for 2 miles, and at a Y turn right on North Bridgewater Road. Quickly, see Atwood Road on the right. Just beyond in the small cemetery is the cenotaph of Isaiah Maxham, a 6th Vermont private. Maxham was captured in June 1864 as the Vermont Brigade departed, in the night, the entrenchments

at Cold Harbor. Taken to Andersonville, he died less than two months later at age twenty-two. He lived in a house that no longer stands, 0.5 mile along Atwood Road. But the high fields that surround this graveyard were part of his family's farm.

Continue down North Bridgewater Road to Route 12 and turn right, to Woodstock.

SOURCES

ADAMS, GLADY S. *BRIDGEWATER, VERMONT, 1779–1976*. BRIDGEWATER, VT: PRIVATELY PRINTED, 1976.

BRIDGEWATER TOWN RECORDS.

CHILD, HAMILTON. *GAZETTEER AND BUSINESS DIRECTORY OF WINDSOR COUNTY, VT., FOR 1883–84*. SYRACUSE, NY: SYRACUSE JOURNAL COMPANY, 1884.

HISTORY HIGHLIGHTS OF THE TOWN OF BRIDGEWATER, 1779–1959. BRIDGEWATER, VT: CHAMPLAIN FESTIVAL COMMITTEE, 1959.

VERMONT STANDARD, 1861–1865. WOODSTOCK HISTORICAL SOCIETY.

WITH THANKS TO THE BRIDGEWATER HISTORICAL SOCIETY.

CAVENDISH

The villages of Proctorsville and Cavendish are side by side on Route 131 in the town of Cavendish. From Route 103 south of Ludlow, take 131 east into Proctorsville and note a large country store on the right. Just before reaching the store, across the street is an ornate house with wraparound porch. Once, Miss Jarusha French lived there, who, after the war, married a former soldier from Plymouth Kingdom, who had an encounter with Calvin Coolidge (see Plymouth). During the war, Rusha, as her friends called her, corresponded with a Cavendish soldier, Private Zacheus Blood, 4th Vermont. He wrote on June 12, from Cold Harbor, "Came here the 2nd of June and our regiment has been in front most of the time since . . . Two men in the 11th Vt. were killed this morning. I went to the burial of one of them. One of the line officers made a prayer by the grave, which is more than is done for most of them. It seems sad to see them buried so far from home and friends but such is the fate of war."

Blood was killed the following September 19, at Winchester. The *Rutland Herald*: "The body of Zacheus Blood was recently brought from the front to his relatives at Proctorsville and buried in the cemetery of that village. The death of this brave soldier has produced a deep and bitter sorrow throughout the community."

Continue past the store to a green, on the right, and across 131 is a tall brick building, once a hotel, that faces Depot Street. (The Proctorsville depot was once by the tracks on Depot Street, just past the surviving brick bank building.) According to two sources—a letter written by attorney Henry Atherton, of Cavendish, in 1882, and an unsigned account published in the *Rutland Herald* in 1867—John Brown was in Cavendish around New Year's Day 1857. Brown had come from his Adirondack home to visit Governor Ryland Fletcher of Cavendish, a fellow abolitionist. The legislature the previous fall had appropriated $20,000 to support free state settlers in Kansas, and Brown apparently hoped to obtain some of that money for his antislavery activities. He also had heard that some old guns were being disposed of by the state. On arriving in Cavendish, surely by train, Brown checked into the brick hotel. With him was a son, apparently Owen, who would survive the Harper's Ferry raid in 1859. Atherton wrote, "As soon as it was known that 'John Brown' was stopping in our village, all manifested a desire to see and hear the man . . . Notice was given that he would meet the people at the school house, and at the appointed hour an audience assembled. We introduced the modest and unassuming old man . . . He went on and told the tale of his struggles with the despotism of slavery. We thought little then how soon John Brown would be mouldering in the ground, but his soul was even at that hour 'marching on.'"

Continue past the green and, on the left, is the modern Proctorsville school. Across the street is a brick house with wooden top story, believed to have been the school building where Brown spoke.

Two buildings beyond is the Cavendish Methodist Church. The December 29, 1864, *Rutland Herald* said, "The funeral of the late John Willey will be attended at the Methodist Church in Proctorsville this (Wednesday) afternoon at one o'clock; Rev. H. Closson conducting the services. Mr. Willey was an exchanged prisoner and died from starvation, adding another victim to southern cruelty and barbarism."

Continue east on Route 121 to Cavendish, and the town's eagle-topped Civil War memorial is on the right, by the old Baptist Church. On Memorial Day 1883, the monument was dedicated with members of many GAR posts participating. A parade led by the Weston Coronet Band marched from the Cavendish depot to Main Street, down Main to the George Davis house, then back to the square by the town hall. There, a dedication took place that centered on Cavendish native, former governor, and 15th Vermont commander Redfield Proctor. Also participating were former governors Fletcher and Frederick Holbrook. A crowd of 5,000 people listened to lengthy speeches and a reading of the Gettysburg Address.

On January 6, 1863, according to the *Rutland Herald,* "A large and enthusiastic gathering in support of the Government was convened at the Baptist Church . . . Able and stirring speeches were made . . . John Parker, a freedman from Virginia, also addressed the meeting. There was but one voice uttered, which was uncompromising hostility to traitors both North and South, and a determination to put down the rebellion."

Continue east on 131 and, where the road curves left, look straight ahead to a tall and imposing redbrick house, once the wartime home of Brigadier General George Davis, quartermaster general of Vermont. Davis was responsible for equipping the Vermont regiments and also for the building of military hospitals at Brattleboro and Montpelier. He maintained an office in Brattleboro but often went to the front to check on the care of Vermont's sick and wounded soldiers. Well after the war, this became the home of Captain Charles Gould, the first Union soldier to breach the Confederate defenses at Petersburg (see Windham). Gould married into the Davis family and occupied this house late in life.

Pass the Davis house and note the stone church on the left. The frame house beside it was the home of Dr. D. W. Haselton, a Vermont surgeon who traveled with Governor John Gregory Smith to Fredericksburg after the Wilderness to treat Vermont wounded.

Continue on 131 out of the village and soon go left on Brook Road. In 1 mile, turn right on East Road, and at the intersection is a small frame house, once the home of Corporal Henry Fillebrown, 4th Vermont. He served four years and survived every major battle until the April 2, 1865, Breakthrough at Petersburg. Though having earned that day off for his soldierly appearance, he fought and was mortally wounded, at twenty-two. Proceed up East Road to the large frame house at the hilltop. Harvey Wiley from here enlisted in the 17th Vermont in March 1864 and was killed in the Petersburg trenches.

SOURCES

ATHERTON, HENRY. LETTER CONCERNING JOHN BROWN'S VISIT TO CAVENDISH. CAVENDISH HISTORICAL SOCIETY.
STEARNS, SANDRA FIELD. *CAVENDISH HILLSIDE FARM: 1939 TO 1957.* CAVENDISH, VT: CAVENDISH HISTORICAL SOCIETY, 1957.
WHEELER, LOIS. *HISTORY OF CAVENDISH, VERMONT.* PROCTORSVILLE, VT: PRIVATELY PRINTED, 1952.
RUTLAND HERALD, 1863, 1864, AND 1867. VERMONT STATE LIBRARY.
WITH THANKS TO GEORGE DAVIS DESCENDANTS AND JIM AND ELIJAH ZIMMERMAN.

CHESTER

Route 11 is Chester's Main Street, and along it, in the village center, is the town's Civil War memorial, a life-size bronze soldier looking south from a marble pedestal. The names of 213 Chester men are on tablets, one of which bears forty-seven names of "those who sleep where they fell." The soldier faces the park, and in this area on July 3, 1878, the 16th Vermont held its first reunion, gathering on the fifteenth anniversary of Gettysburg. The *Rutland Herald* of July 4, 1878, estimated 5,000 spectators were present.

The day began with a parade, and after the veterans were fed, former commander Wheelock Veazey spoke for an hour, wearing the coat he wore at Gettysburg, Veazey said: "Forty millions of people have read of your achievements, and told the story to children since born how the untrained Green Mountain Boys, by their skill and bravery, plucked the first laurels in the greatest and most important battle of the war. Now, after fifteen years of separation, we the survivors of this regiment again meet in happy reunion, to exchange the soldier's greeting, to refresh memories of those heroic days and scenes, to renew the old song and story of camp and march, and to bid each other God speed through the few remaining years vouchsafed to us."

The parade went from this area, then known as South Chester, to North Chester, known today as the Stone Village. To follow the march of the four hundred veterans, go east on Main Street and bear left on Route 103. Soon come to Chester Depot and its 1849 station. Sixteen years before, the reunion, in 1862, Company K of the 16th Vermont, which assembled at Chester, had departed for war from here.

Continue on 103 into the Stone Village and the stone church on the left. Just beyond and across the road is a frame house with a porch supported by four columns, once attorney Luther Adams's home. His law office is the small building by the road. The *Rutland Herald* said, "The procession marched by the depot through North Chester. The houses on the route were decorated with flags, and near Hon. Luther Adams' house in North Chester was an arch of evergreens with 'Gettysburg' inscribed thereon. Here the ladies presented Colonel Veazey with a bouquet, and strewed flowers in the veterans' path . . . On the way back, Capt. Clark struck up John Brown which was sung with the old fervor."

Two of Adams's sons, John and Elmer, went to war from this house, enlisting as privates in Company G, 7th Vermont. John served three years and came safely home. But Elmer served only three months, dying of sickness at eighteen. Elmer's name is on the family stone in Brookside Cemetery, which notes that he was "buried at Ship Island Florida March 24, 1862." Ship Island was, off the Louisiana coast. The cemetery just up the road is where many Chester veterans are interred.

Return through Stone Village and come again to the stone church, where many wartime town meetings were held, including one on November 8, 1863, that approved $500 bounties. By late 1864, Chester was more than $27,000 in debt from the war, and it was years before the town's books balanced. Gideon Lee lived in the stone house just past the church, a private in the 16th who fought at Gettysburg. In the stone house beside his lived Dr. O'Meara Edson, an assistant surgeon with the Vermont Cavalry, then surgeon of the 17th Vermont. He treated the wounded at the Battle of the Crater.

Return to Chester Depot and the railroad station. Company K of the 4th Vermont Regiment boarded a train here in the fall of 1861. On an August day in 1869, a train bearing President Ulysses Grant made a brief stop here, and a large crowd cheered. The *Rutland Herald* said that Grant "bowed and lifted his hat."

Return to the Civil War monument on Main Street, and the cemetery behind with many Civil War graves. Three houses east, in a building that, in 2009, held offices, lived Hugh Henry, quartermaster sergeant of the 16th Vermont. He funded the Chester Civil War monument, and the local GAR post was named in his honor.

Just west of the monument, the old Chester High School is now the Chester Historical Society. The building is partly built of materials from Chester Academy, a three-story 30-by-60-foot structure that stood in what is now the front yard of the old high school. Among its students were Edwin and Charles Stoughton and Peter Washburn, Vermont's Civil War–era adjutant general.

Across Main Street from the academy site is a rambling old hotel, on the site of the Civil War–era Ingraham Hotel, once the center of Chester social life. A ball was held there the night of July 3, 1863, celebrating Independence Day. Since Chester had the only twenty-four-hour telegraph office between Bellows Falls and Rutland, surely reports were reaching the revelers of the great battle that day at Gettysburg. Everyone must have thought it likely that the local K Company, 16th Vermont, was engaged.

In the park fronting the hotel, on April 26, 1861, according to the *Vermont Journal,* a "demonstration . . . by the citizens of this town" took place, with patriotic speeches and "Jeff Davis was burned in effigy."

Proceed west on Main Street, and the second house beyond the old high school, with long front porch, was the Stoughton home. Edwin Stoughton, destined to command the 4th Vermont and then the 2nd Vermont Brigade, until his capture by John Mosby, spent his childhood here. So did brother Charles, who succeeded Edwin as commander of the 4th Vermont. He served until a bullet took away an eye at Funkstown.

Continue on Main and note across the street the large frame building with a Gothic window, next to a church. The Hugh Henry GAR Post sometimes met on its second story.

Continue to the Congregational Church where, on February 27, 1863, a rally was held, with the railroad bringing people to Chester for half fare. The purpose was to raise money for hospitals and to support soldier families. The *Vermont Journal* said, "Our soldiers in the army doing battle for freedom should be told that while they pursue the rebels in front we will take care of those in the rear." The Soldiers' Aid Society of Chester was organized at the church. On September 29, 1863, it reported on a year of operations that produced for the soldiers: "17 sheets, 171 towels, 68 pounds of dried apples and currants, 83 pairs drawers, 49 cotton shirts, 18 quilts, 90 pairs socks, 20 pairs of slippers, 19 pillow cases, 6 dressing gowns, 3 pillows, a pair of mittens, a testament and a hymn book . . . rags, bandages and lint."

On May 5, 1865, the *Rutland Herald* reported on Chester's response to Lincoln's death. "The church was elaborately draped with the emblyms of mourning, and though one of the largest in the state, was densely packed, the aisles and doorways being crowded." The meeting opened with remarks by Hugh Henry, followed by a eulogy, and the singing of hymns. The *Herald* story concluded, "We separated with hearts knowing a sadness they never knew before."

Across Main Street from the church is a small gambrel roof house, once the home of Martin and Lydia Mariah (Paddleford) Church. Lydia died giving birth to their seventh child in 1861. Local legend holds that a heartbroken Martin, saying that he wanted to find a place to die, promptly enlisted in the 4th Vermont. His six children were placed with other families. Private Church served until the war ended.

Back across the street, the stone house just beyond the church, built in 1825, was the home of Major William Rounds, third in command of the 16th Vermont, who fought at Gettysburg. It was through his efforts that the regimental reunion was held in Chester.

Return along Main Street past the monument and turn right, south, on

Grafton Road, which soon becomes Route 35. In 1.5 miles, turn right on Popple Dungeon Road and, in 1.6 miles, on the right, is a farmhouse with several outbuildings. The Jefts family lived here, and three sons served. Josiah, living in Minnesota, joined a Minnesota unit and survived the war. Albert and Byron became privates in the 6th Vermont. Byron, twenty, was discharged for sickness in January 1863 and died in this house two weeks after he came home. Albert, twenty-six, was killed at Banks Ford five months later.

SOURCES

CASS, LEWIS ALDRICH, AND FRANK HOLMES. *HISTORY OF WINDSOR COUNTY, VERMONT.* SYRACUSE, NY: D. MASON AND CO. PUBLISHERS, 1891.

CHESTER TOWN RECORDS.

HILL, JILLIAN. *HISTORIC BUILDINGS OF CHESTER, VERMONT.* CHESTER, VT: 2003. WHITING LIBRARY, CHESTER.

HISTORY OF THE STONE HOUSES IN CHESTER. WHITING LIBRARY, CHESTER.

PELADEAU, MARIUS B. *BURNISHED ROWS OF STEEL.* VERMONT CIVIL WAR ENTERPRISES, NEWPORT, VT: 2002.

RUTLAND HERALD, 1865, 1869, AND 1878. VERMONT STATE LIBRARY.

RICHARDSON, DONALD. *HISTORY OF CHESTER.* 1932. WHITING LIBRARY, CHESTER.

WITH THANKS TO ANDY OJANEN AND CHESTER TOWN CLERK'S OFFICE STAFF.

HARTFORD

White River Junction, the largest village in Hartford, is at the junction of Interstates 89 and 91. Corporal Edward Clark, a 12th Vermont private from the town of Georgia, wrote on September 25, 1862, about his train journey to Brattleboro. He spoke of "local companies getting on at the different stations until the whole regiment was aboard. We reached White River Junction about noon. We staid there about 20 minutes to get some dinner. There was a grand rush for the table you may believe . . . at last got pie and some cheese and . . . sat down on the floor of the depot and made away with it." White River Junction, one of the famous railroad places in New England, where rivers and rail lines meet, was passed through at one time or another by most Vermonters who served in the Civil War.

From the interstates' junction, take Route 5 north into White River Junction. Hartford is a town of several villages, including the Junction, West Hartford, Hartford village, and Quechee. Follow signs to the train station and see the old depot, with tall cupola. Though not as old as the Civil War, it's built on the site of the war-era station.

From the depot, cross the White River and take Route 14 north. Soon on the right is the Hartford Cemetery, where Hartford Civil War veterans met on Memorial Day in 1880. The town had sent 267 men to war, of whom 37 died. After brief services, Colonel Samuel Pingree spoke and proposed that a temporary veterans organization be formed. A year later, the veterans returned here and adopted a constitution and bylaws, and the Hartford Memorial Association was formed. Pingree was chosen president. Later, the veterans founded a GAR post named after Abraham Lincoln.

Proceed to the second level of the cemetery, and at the top of the hill is Stephen Pingree's grave. Nearby is Hartford's Civil War memorial, dedicated Memorial Day 1893. The monument was erected by the Loyal Club. In 1891, members of the Lincoln GAR Post asked the ladies of the town to form a Women's Relief Corps post. The women declined, instead founding an independent society they called the Loyal Club. But they raised money for the monument, made of Barre granite, at a cost of $650.

Return to Route 14, go north 0.5 mile, into Hartford village, the busy business center of the town during the Civil War. Note a very large brick house on the right. Just past it, and set back from the road, is a small brick building, once the law office of Stephen Pingree and his brother Samuel Pingree. Stephen, a 3rd Vermont lieutenant, was wounded at Lee's Mill, eventually receiving a Medal of Honor for his service there. In the slaughter of the Wilderness on May 5, 1864, he suddenly found himself in command of the 3rd Vermont, and he led it until mustered out in July 1864. After the war, Samuel was Hartford town clerk for nearly four decades, became prominent in Republican politics, and was elected governor, serving from 1884 to 1886.

His brother Stephen entered the 4th Vermont as a lieutenant and rose to lieutenant colonel. In the midst of the Overland Campaign, Samuel wrote to their parents in Hartford, "Stephen is now on the skirmish line with his Regt. & part of the 11th Vt. Reg't. He relieved me on the same line on his arrival last night. He is well." The two brothers carried on a successful law practice after the war.

Continue north on Route 14, and quickly on the right are old store blocks. The two wooden ones were once owned by Moses French, and his son, Arthur, worked here as a clerk. Arthur was a private in the 11th Vermont and was captured at Weldon Railroad. Confined at Andersonville, he died on New Year's Day 1865, at Annapolis, Maryland, after his release.

Pass the stores, and four buildings beyond, on the right, is the home of George Brockway, who, like many Hartford men, served in G Company, 16th Vermont. He fought at Gettysburg and came home safely.

Continue past the Brockway house, pass a church, and the next house on the right was the home of Benjamin Dutton, who also fought at Gettysburg.

Continue along Route 14 for 5 miles, enter West Hartford, and the West Hartford Congregational Church is on the right. The abolitionist Rev. Nathan Robinson (see Topsham) presided at an antislavery meeting here and "met Miss Francis Ellen Watkins, whom I was to join in holding a series of meetings." Watkins, a native of Baltimore, Maryland, was involved in the Underground Railroad and wrote and lectured extensively on slavery.

On May 8, 1861, the *Vermont Journal* reported on a war rally at West Hartford. "On Wednesday . . . those who had given their names for the Hartford company met at West Hartford, to be enlisted into three years service. The volunteers assisted in the raising of a large flag . . . A fine salute was fired from a Hartford cannon.

A few years ago the machinists at the Junction wishing a cannon with which to celebrate the Fourth of July, went to work and made one themselves . . . The ladies provided excellent and abundant rations for the volunteers. In the evening there was a torch light procession, when Jeff Davis was burned in effigy." Most of those volunteers, seventy-seven in number, became part of the 3rd Vermont's Company F.

From West Hartford, cross the White River and go straight onto the Quechee road. In 5 miles, enter Quechee village on Quechee's Main Street, and on the left is the Quechee Library and a church. In the house between them lived George Fogg, 3rd Vermont private, who served the war's last sixteen months. Something happened to Fogg during his service, and he returned home sick. His pension records show that he began to have horrible dreams and to scream in his sleep. He eventually became delusional. Admitted to a New Hampshire insane asylum, he died there twenty years after the war.

Continue on Main Street and go right across the covered bridge. Take a quick right on River Street, and the first house on the left was Elmer Flagg's home. He crossed the Connecticut River, enlisted in the 9th New Hampshire, and was killed in action.

Return across the covered bridge, turn right on Main Street, and follow the Ottauquechee 1 mile to the old redbrick Jedediah Strong house on the right. Here, follow Main Street, left and uphill, to Route 4 and turn left, east. Soon, turn right on Center of Town Road, and in 0.5

mile on the left, at the intersection of King's Highway, is a small park. To its rear is a monument marking the site of the old Hartford town hall, where town meetings were held during the Civil War. Meeting here at the geographic center of the town, Hartford voters approved bounties that in 1864 reached $600. The total cost to the town of meeting its quotas was $55,129.91.

Continue on Center of Town Road to Route 4, which returns to White River Junction and the interstates.

SOURCES

BYLAWS SKETCH AND MEMBERSHIP OF THE LOYAL CLUB. VERMONT HISTORICAL SOCIETY.

PINGREE, SAMUEL. CIVIL WAR LETTERS. UNIVERSITY OF VERMONT, BAILEY/HOWE LIBRARY, SPECIAL COLLECTIONS, BURLINGTON.

PINGREE, STEPHEN. CIVIL WAR LETTERS. UNIVERSITY OF VERMONT, BAILEY/HOWE LIBRARY, SPECIAL COLLECTIONS, BURLINGTON.

TUCKER, WILLIAM HOWARD. *HISTORY OF HARTFORD, VERMONT, JULY 4, 1761–APRIL 4, 1889.* BURLINGTON, VT: FREE PRESS ASSOCIATION, 1889.

HARTFORD TOWN RECORDS.

WITH THANKS TO JENEPHER BOREY-BOYCE.

HARTLAND

From Interstate 91's exit 9, go north on Route 5 to Hartland Three Corners, where a stone Civil War soldier faces south atop the Hartland war memorial. Some 190 Hartland men served, and the town went far into debt to meet its quotas, perhaps because of its proximity to New Hampshire towns competing for enlistees. Indeed, Hartland's debt reached nearly $47,000 in 1867, and according to the town clerk in 2011, the debt wasn't paid until 1961. A wealthy resident offered a contribution that year, which was accepted by Hartland voters in Damon Hall, which stands by the monument at Three Corners.

From Damon Hall, go north on Route 12, and soon on the right is the old Methodist Church, whose pastor from 1860 to 1862 was "Lame" John Smith. The house beside the church was the parsonage. Smith is said to have given refuge to fugitive slaves at the many churches where he presided.

Continue north on Route 12 into Hartland Four Corners, and go left on Brownsville Road. In 1.6 miles, a small cape is set below the road on the left, with a small garage beside. Cyrus Bagley, who served in the 12th Vermont, then in the Vermont Cavalry, lived here. He was wounded at Appomattox Station the day before Lee surrendered.

Continue 0.3 mile and go right on Best Road. In 1 mile, a driveway goes right to a handsome hillside farm. From here, Henry Alexander enlisted at twenty on the last day of 1863 and went to Brattleboro, where he died two months later of sickness, before being assigned to a regiment.

Return to Hartland Four Corners and go directly across Route 12 onto Mace Hill Road. In 2 miles, go right on Center of Town Road, and the Center Cemetery is on the right. In the left front portion, where no stones stand, Hartland's Civil War–era town hall stood. Here, voters went for Lincoln in 1864, 208 to 34.

Quickly turn left on Brothers Road,

and in 1.25 miles, an old farmhouse is set back on the right. From here, Private Charles Cleveland joined the 6th Vermont. He was killed in the futile May 18 attack at Spotsylvania Courthouse.

Proceed 0.75 mile to an upland crossroads. The frame house directly ahead, and above, was the home of Private Peter Green, 3rd Vermont, who survived a wound at the Wilderness. Go left on Advent Hill Road, and the first house on the right, with schoolhouse beyond, was Private Lewis Vaughan's home. He died of disease three months after joining the 4th Vermont in the fall of 1861. He was twenty, and his body came home to this house for burial in the Center Cemetery.

Return to the crossroads and go straight onto Draper Road. In 0.3 mile is a long frame house set back on the right, once the home of Thomas Benjamin. He was one of twelve Hartland men who served in the 16th Vermont. Benjamin was wounded at Gettysburg, but came home and recovered.

Follow Draper Road and go left on Quechee Road, and in 0.5 mile, take Clay Hill Road and follow it to North Hartland. Go south on Route 5 here, and in 5 miles, entering Hartland Three Corners, turn left on Depot Road. On reaching the railroad tracks, go right on Ferry Road. From the only house on the road, Henry Holt enlisted in the Vermont Cavalry in 1861. He died a year later, at the front, of typhus. His body came home here.

SOURCES
HARTLAND TOWN RECORDS.
WITH THANKS TO CLYDE JENNE, TOWN CLERK.

LUDLOW

Enter Ludlow from the north on Route 103, which is Main Street, pass the 1865 woolen mill (now apartments), and just before crossing the Black River, take Elm Street. In front of the large brick house on the left on April 24, 1865, five hundred people gathered to honor the assassinated Abraham Lincoln. Led by the Ludlow Cornet Band, Masons, and the local militia, they marched through the village, while all the bells tolled. Thanks to the April 27, 1865, *Rutland Herald*, it's possible to follow their route. Take Elm Street to Pleasant Street and turn right, follow Pleasant to Andover Street and turn right again, then turn right on Main Street to the triangular green in front of the Baptist Church. Here prayers were said, then a local preacher, according to the paper, "assured that though the righteous ruler had fallen and left us in sadness and gloom, yet the throne of God abideth forever and His justice will ultimately prevail in sustaining our nation and inflicting dreadful vengeance upon the dreadful plotters and perpetrators of the atrocious deed which has made a nation of mourners."

Two weeks earlier, the triangular green was the center of a joyous celebration when word arrived of Richmond's fall. The *Herald* said, "The locomotive whistle sounded the key note, long and loud, as it proceeded on its winding way along the adjacent hillsides. Every bell in the place was brought into requisition; guns big and little were fired; Mr. Pelton ordered a barrel of roofing tar to be rolled out and burned . . . The old swivel, which from time immemorial has proved to be a friend in need, uttered forth its soul-stirring, ear splitting, glass breaking tones, and the surrounding hills reverberated as Vermont hills alone know how to do."

Well might the people of Ludlow have celebrated, for the Civil War hit hard here, particularly in 1864, when 10 local soldiers perished. Ludlow, according to a local history, sent 151 men to war.

Up the hill from the green, on High Street, is the 1872 Black River Academy. Its predecessor of the Civil War years stood here, and when Richmond's capture was celebrated, the principal ran up "a splendid flag" on the building's roof. A historic marker honors graduate Abby Maria Hemenway, who was raised on a farm just outside the village. Hemenway compiled a multivolume state history, the monumental *Vermont Historical Gazetteer.* A dedicated opponent of slavery, Hemenway not only labored on her historic research during the war years but joined a women's group that made and gathered items for the soldiers. In 1862, she published a pamphlet, "Songs of the War," a collection of her patriotic verse. These lines were on the cover:

> The Union of lakes, the Union of lands,
> The Union of states none can sever;
> The Union of hearts, the Union of hands,
> And the flag of our Union forever.

Proceed past the academy on High Street and soon reach the village cemetery, with many Civil War graves. Hemenway's stone is not far behind the old vault, in the family plot.

From Main Street, take Depot Street south through the underpass, and quickly, on the left, is the old Ludlow railway station. Here, on August 29, 1888, two hundred 16th Vermont veterans assembled in a hollow square to greet former commander Wheelock Veazey. This was the regiment's second reunion; its first in ten years. Harland Peabody, of Andover, former regimental adjutant, recalled, "the men quickly tossed him [Veazey] on to a horse provided for the occasion, and then gave nine cheers and a tiger for their old commander. Then followed the cordial greetings between commander and comrades, not unmingled with tears as they clasped hands, in many instances for the first time since they charged the flank of Pickett and Wilcox in the final struggle on the third day of the great pivotal battle of Gettysburg." The veterans then marched into downtown Ludlow, where five thousand people had gathered.

A local historian said of Ludlow, years after the war: "Of those spared to return home, nearly all came back wounded, and many maimed for life. Now and then a man is found who served his country faithfully for three years, and passed through the terrible baptism of fire unscathed, but such cases were rare."

SOURCES

CLIFFORD, DEBORAH PICKMAN. *THE PASSION OF ABBY HEMENWAY: MEMORY, SPIRIT, AND THE MAKING OF HISTORY.* MONTPELIER, VT: VERMONT HISTORICAL SOCIETY, 2001.

HARRIS, JOSEPH N. *HISTORY OF LUDLOW, VERMONT.* CHARLESTOWN, NH: MRS. INA HARRIS HARDING AND MR. ARCHIE FRANK HARDING, 1949. REPRINT BLACK RIVER HISTORICAL SOCIETY, 1988.

Rutland Herald, 1865. Vermont State Library. Thanks to the staff of Black River Academy.

....

NORWICH

Enter the village of Norwich on Route 5 from Interstate 91's exit 13, and quickly come to the spacious village green, once the Norwich University parade ground. The Norwich Congregational Church, just north of the green, faces its original location across the street. At the green's west end, a public school occupies the site of the 1830 old north barracks. Beside it, is a newer school where the old south barracks once stood.

The Congregational Church looks much as it did when it overlooked the parade ground of a military academy. Once the cadets assembled in the church for lectures, concerts, and commencements. Some 750 Norwich cadets fought in the Civil War, about 700 for the Union and some 50 for the Confederacy. Among the Norwich men to whom the old church was a familiar space were Horatio Wright, commander of the 6th Corps; Gideon Welles, Lincoln's secretary of the navy; Joseph Mower, corps commander under Sherman; Alfred Terry, a corps commander in the Army of the James, and Thomas Seaver, who led the 3rd Vermont.

Norwich was founded in 1819 as The American Literary, Scientific, and Military Academy, by native Vermonter Alden Partridge, former West Point superintendent. A pioneering educator, Partridge believed in a broad-based curriculum that, in addition to military science, included languages, mathematics, science, literature, elocution, history, and more. The backbone of the Republic, Partridge believed, was the citizen soldier whom he sought to give a well-rounded education. The school was moved to Middletown, Connecticut, in 1825, but returned to its original location in 1834 with the name of Norwich University. More than eighty men of Norwich fought in the Mexican War, among them the university's second president, Truman Ransom, who left the school to serve in a Massachusetts regiment and died leading his men at Chapultepec.

At the Rebellion's outbreak, Norwich cadets and graduates enlisted wholesale. Among those offering his services was faculty stalwart Alonzo Jackman, who commanded all Vermont militia units as the war neared. But Jackman's wish to go to war was rejected by Governor Erastus Fairbanks, who asked that he stay at Norwich and train cadets and Vermont soldiers. Many of Jackman's protégés participated in the drilling of Vermont units as they readied for war.

One of the intriguing stories from Norwich's history is that of the University Cavaliers, a cavalry unit made up of Norwich and Dartmouth students that enlisted for ninety days in the summer of 1862. The 85-man unit, including 23 Norwich lads, was part of the 11,000-man force surrounded at Harper's Ferry by Stonewall Jackson just before the battle of Antietam. Rather than become part of the largest surrender in American military history, the cadets were among some 1,300 cavalrymen who galloped across the Potomac River and escaped. Before returning to campus with tales of glory, they captured some Confederate supply wagons.

On the Norwich green today, a historic marker near the southeast corner is made of bricks salvaged from old south barracks. But the outstanding relic is the Norwich Congregational Church, built in 1817. The building contains its original pews and balcony and grand Palladian front window. It hosted a commencement talk by abolitionist Wendell Phillips in 1864.

Norwich's Main Street is lined with buildings that would have been familiar to cadets, including the 1807 house, facing the green, that is now the Norwich Historical Society. Once it was the home of Brigadier General William Lewis, Norwich class of 1833, who drilled Vermont troops preparing for war.

The brick house next door was Jonathan Gordon's home, a Norwich professor who took in cadet boarders. Beyond the Gordon house is another brick home, the Williston house, where Ebenezer Bancroft lived who taught classics at Norwich. His son Captain Edward Williston Bancroft, a Norwich graduate, went to war as an artilleryman and won a Medal of Honor in the cavalry battle at Trevilian Station in 1864.

Return along Main Street, pass the historical society, cross Elm Street, and the house on the corner was once the Burton home. The Norwich Female Abolition Society, which organized on April 12, 1843, sometimes met here. Much of the society's efforts went to supporting fugitive slaves who had fled to Canada. The Abolition Society gathered here on May 11, 1843, and, after prayers and a reading of scripture, voted that funds be appropriated for the "Canadian mission."

Continue on Main past the Norwich Inn, and in 0.2 mile beyond, on the left, is a two-story brick house with ornate front door and columns supporting a second-story porch. Alden Partridge, Norwich's founder, lived here and sometimes addressed and reviewed cadets from his balcony.

Return to the Norwich Inn and turn right on Beaver Meadow Road. Follow it to the Norwich Cemetery, and near the center find the granite obelisk, within an iron fence, marking Partridge's grave. Return along Beaver Meadow Road, cross the street, and walk behind the Norwich Inn and through its parking lot, angling right. Behind the rear section of the village store see an old frame two-story house, once the Congregational church vestry. On April 12, 1843, Norwich women met in this building to form the Abolition Society, adopting a constitution that began, "Believing slavery, as it exists in this nation, to be a direct violation of the law of God."

Return to Main and go south, turning right on Elm. The white frame house, past the first brick house on the left, was once the Sproat family home. Private Edward Sproat, 4th Vermont, was killed at Fredericksburg on December 13, 1862. In his last letter sent here, he said: "I am going to get my discharge in 1864. I will be old, I'm afraid, by that time. Did you know that I was eighteen?"

The next house, of brick, was the Congregational church parsonage. The Abolition Society often met here.

A war memorial beside the Norwich town offices, facing the green, lists 168 Norwich men who served, thus the town's Civil War history includes much more than the story of Norwich University. On leaving Norwich, the last house on the left before reaching the interstate, once a farmhouse, was the Messenger home. Private Benjamin Messenger served in the 16th Vermont, fighting at Gettysburg. His brothers, Privates Albert and Charles and Corporal George, all of the 6th Vermont like Benjamin, came home safely.

SOURCES

CONE, KATE MORRIS. *A SKETCH OF THE LIFE OF SYLVESTER MORRIS.* BOSTON: ALFRED MUDGE & SON, 1887.

NORWICH FEMALE ABOLITION SOCIETY RECORDS. NORWICH HISTORICAL SOCIETY.

POIRIER, ROBERT G. *BY THE BLOOD OF OUR ALUMNI: NORWICH UNIVERSITY CITIZEN-SOLDIERS.* MASON CITY, IA: SAVAS PUBLISHING CO., 1999.

SPROAT, EDWARD. CIVIL WAR LETTERS. NORWICH HISTORICAL SOCIETY.

WITH THANKS TO BETH BARRETT, JAN FINNEY, GARY LORD, AND MARTHA HOWARD.

PLYMOUTH

Plymouth Notch is just off Route 100B, and at its center is the general store. Late in life, recalling his Plymouth childhood, Calvin Coolidge wrote, "When the work was done for the day, it was customary to drop into the store to get the evening mail and exchange views on topics of interests . . . A number of those who came had followed Sheridan, been with Meade at Gettysburg, and served under Grant, but they seldom volunteered any information about it. They were not talkative and took their military service in a matter of fact way, not as anything to brag but merely as something they did because it ought to be done."

Coolidge, born seven years after Appomattox, apparently early on developed an interest in the Civil War. Indeed, his personal library contains more books on the Civil War than any other subject. As vice president, he spoke at the dedication of the Lincoln Memorial and the dedication of the national military park at Fredericksburg. And he signed legislation, as president, that made a national park of Georgia's Fort Pulaski. President Coolidge once spoke at Gettysburg, saying, "The government of the people, by the people, for the people, which Lincoln described in his immortal address, is a government of peace, not war."

Just west of the store is the Coolidge homestead, where Calvin Coolidge was sworn in as the nation's thirtieth president by his father, a notary public. In the Union Church across the street, where generations of Coolidges worshipped, a funeral for Lieutenant Luther Moore took place October 11, 1863. The church was packed. Moore died soon after fighting at Gettysburg.

Just past the cheese factory, uphill from the church, is the stone Plymouth Notch school. In the wooden school that preceded it on this site, Calvin Coolidge was a pupil. And Achsa Sprague taught here when she was twelve years old. This once sickly farm girl became a nationally known spiritualist before the Civil War, an era when spiritualism was highly popular. Sprague appeared throughout the eastern United States, before large audiences, communing with the dead and speaking words from the spirit world. Sprague's childhood home was across the road from the school. A slight mound in the field is all that remains. Sprague was also a feminist, an advocate of prison reform, and an abolitionist. On a speaking trip to Providence, Rhode Island, years before the Civil War, she attended a women's anti-slavery meeting and heard a report on Underground Railroad activities. She concluded, "Horrible indeed is the necessity that compels the poor negro to fly like a hunted deer to the land of Kings, for that freedom which he cannot find amid the land of the free and the home of the brave." Sprague died in 1862, at thirty-six.

Lieutenant Moore is buried in the Notch Cemetery, south of the village on Lynds Hill Road. He lies close behind the stones of Calvin Coolidge and his family, with a Union banner carved above his name. Still farther uphill, near the crest, with the 6th Corps badge atop each of their stones, are the Lynds brothers, Privates Levi Lynds, 3rd Vermont, and John Lynds, 2nd Vermont. Levi survived a wound at the Wilderness. Go past the Lynds stones to the crest and along the ridge to a marble stone with a heavenly crown. Beneath the name Achsa Sprague are the inscriptions "WENT HOME" and "I STILL LIVE."

Continue past the cemetery on Lynds Hill Road, which soon rises steeply. Where it begins to level off, a very large house on the left, much added to, was the Lynds home. John Lynds, in 1924, recalled that during his life he had either talked with, or seen, seven presidents. He encountered Lincoln, Grant, and McKinley during the Civil War.

Return toward the Notch and go south on Route 100B to Route 100. The large house just across the road at the intersection was once the site of spiritualist meetings, some involving Sprague. Turn north, pass the town office entrance on the left, and the first house beyond it, on the right, was Eleazar Hall's home. As a private in the 2nd Vermont, Hall was shot in the face at Second Fredericksburg, losing eleven teeth. He barely recovered, but came home to Plymouth and lived to ninety-five, dancing a jig on his ninety-fourth birthday. Return south on Route 100, and in 5 miles reach Tyson. At the four corners, turn right on Dublin Road and you are at the site of the Tyson iron furnace. The little Tyson Library here was the furnace office. The Tyson furnace had closed before the 1860s, but reopened in 1864, to meet war needs. Some Tyson iron was sent to Albany, New York, to make ironclads for the U.S. Navy.

Cross Route 100 onto Kingdom Road, and in just over 0.5 mile, turn left on Scout Camp Road to the Tyson Cemetery. Atop the knoll in this steep hillside burying ground is the Plymouth Civil War monument. Plymouth people believe today their town was hit as hard as any in the state by the war, and the thirty-one names of Civil War dead from this small upland town support them. Eleven were killed in battle. Close by the monument is the cenotaph of Private Moses Baldwin, 16th Vermont, twenty-three when killed July 2 at Gettysburg. He is buried in the Gettysburg National Cemetery.

Return to Kingdom Road, and go left, uphill until the road levels and a large open area is reached that once held the village of Plymouth Kingdom. Bear right at the fork and come to an old schoolhouse. In this building's predecessor, on this site, a local farm boy, Hezron Day (see Ludlow), attended school. Day fought at Gettysburg with the 16th Vermont, later opened a drugstore in Bradford, and lived a long life that ended in a sanitarium in Hot Springs, South Dakota. In the summer of 1924, President Coolidge, summering in the Black Hills, paid a visit to the place. According to the *New York Times,* the president, on learning that a Plymouth veteran was present, changed his schedule to include a fifteen-minute chat. The *Times* said, "Mr. Coolidge took off his hat and extending his hand asked the veteran where he was born. 'Right near your birthplace,' Mr. Day said with a show of pride. 'It was at Kingdom Church.'"

SOURCES

BRYANT, BLANCHE BROWN, AND GERTRUDE ELAINE BAKER. *EARLY SETTLERS OF PLYMOUTH VERMONT.* SPRINGFIELD, VT: WILLIAM L. BRYANT FOUNDATION, 1975.

CHIOLINO, BARBARA, BARBARA MAHON, AND ELIZA WARD, EDS. *RECOLLECTIONS AND STORIES OF PLYMOUTH, VERMONT.* PLYMOUTH, VT: PLYMOUTH PUBLICATIONS, 1992.

COOLIDGE, CALVIN. *THE AUTOBIOGRAPHY OF CALVIN COOLIDGE.* NEW YORK: COSMOPOLITAN BOOK CORPORATION, 1929

WITH THANKS TO CYNDY BITTINGER, WILLIAM JENNE, AND ELIZA WARD.

POMFRET

Go north from Woodstock village on Route 12, and quickly turn right on River Road at the Billings Farm and Museum. Soon, pass Woodstock's oldest graveyard, and 1.5 miles beyond, at a Y, bear left and look left. You have entered a piece of Pomfret that juts down to the Ottauquechee River. On a knoll set back from the road is a handsome old farmhouse with a long porch, the home of Captain Ora Paul, who commanded the 12th Vermont's Company B. On the night of December 28, 1862, Paul led two companies that took position, in the darkness, along the Little River Turnpike in northern Virginia. Moving toward the 2nd Vermont Brigade were 1,500 cavalrymen under J. E. B. Stuart. On hearing the clank and jingle of approaching horsemen, Paul ordered his men to fire. One hundred guns banged, and Stuart's approach was ended.

The next house beyond the old Paul place was the Seaver family home. Thomas Seaver grew up here, attended Norwich University, then Albany law school, before practicing law in Woodstock. Named commander of the 3rd Vermont Regiment, he led it bravely, particularly in the storming of the Fredericksburg heights in the spring of 1862. But his finest moment came at Spotsylvania Courthouse, where, on May 10, 1864, Seaver led the Vermonters who participated in the late afternoon assault, known as Upton's Attack, against the Mule Shoe Salient. Seaver's men swept over the first line of Confederate breastworks and also captured a portion of the final line. Colonel Emory Upton, who conceived the attack, and Ulysses Grant, soon saw the futility of the effort and ordered the Vermonters to retreat. But Seaver's men held on, calling for reinforcements. Eventually, reluctantly, they withdrew. The attack's success prompted Grant, two days later, to launch his massive assault that resulted in the fight at Bloody Angle on May 12. In 1892, Seaver was awarded the Medal of Honor for his performance at Spotsylvania.

Return along River Road, turn north on Route 12, and bear right at the Y onto Pomfret Road. In just over 1 mile, at an intersection, is a large farmhouse on the right with barn across the road. Rush Christopher Hawkins was born here on September 14, 1831. At fifteen, Hawkins ran away to enlist in the Mexican War. Later, he became a New York City lawyer, made a fortune in real estate and debt collection, and became a well-known collector of antiquarian books. When the war began, Hawkins raised, and commanded, a New York regiment known as Hawkins's Zouaves. Later, he led a brigade in the 9th Corps and saw action at Fredericksburg and Antietam.

Continue north into South Pomfret and turn left at the store. Passing Suicide Six ski area, the first house on the right, set back from the road, was once the Jillson home. To that house at the end of the Civil War came Private David Jillson (see Williamstown), severely wounded in the April 2, 1865, 6th Corps attack at Petersburg. Jillson died here five days after Christmas, 1865.

Return to South Pomfret and note the Grange Hall on the right. On a winter morning in 1923, the body of Elba Jillson, former 9th Vermont private, was brought here to lie in state. Jillson had died the previous night during a heavy fall of snow in his son's farmhouse. Next morning, townspeople cleared 3 miles of road to bring his body to this hall. Go north on Pomfret Road, and in 1 mile, turn left on Bartlett Brook Road. Go just under 2 miles to the head of the valley, where an old farmhouse stands just above the road on the right. Elba Jillson died here in a back bedroom.

Return to Pomfret Road and continue north 2 miles to the height of land and the colonnaded Pomfret town hall. Civil War–era town meetings took place here. In November 1860, Pomfret voted for Lincoln over Douglas, 125 to 36. Four years later, voters again went for Lincoln, 148 to 48 over McClellan. Pomfret bounty payments peaked at $400 in March 1864 when the town supplied two men for the 17th Vermont. From Pomfret, 120 men went to war and 24 perished.

Go north on Pomfret Road from the town hall, and quickly Galaxy Hill Road goes uphill to the right. Look up the road to the farmhouse some 300 yards up the road where, it is believed, the Chandler family lived. Edward Chandler attended Norwich University then joined the 3rd Vermont in May 1861 as a lieutenant. Wounded a year later at Lee's Mill, he came home to recover and to recruit. Back on duty in March 1864, Chandler took command of the 3rd's Company. On the way home in April 1865, he stood guard at the home of Secretary of State William

Seward after he was attacked, and nearly killed, the night of Lincoln's assassination. After the war, Chandler worked with the Freedmen's Bureau in Virginia.

Chandler's brother Alexander went to sea, then came home to enlist in the Vermont Cavalry in 1861. Commanding Company E in fighting at Weldon Railroad, June 23, 1864, he had three horses shot from beneath him. Six days later, he was captured, but escaped and made his way through a swamp to Union lines. He came home to the family farm in broken health and lived only until 1870.

From the town hall go 1.5 miles north on Pomfret Road, and turn left on Howe Hill Road. In 1 mile, look right to a large white frame house and barn at the end of a long driveway. Once home to the Vail family, Pomfret and Sharon women met here to make items for the soldiers and the Vermont military hospitals.

SOURCES
JILLSON FAMILY PAPERS. HOWARD COFFIN
    COLLECTION.
POMFRET TOWN RECORDS.
VAIL, HENRY HOBART. POMFRET, VERMONT.
    VOL 2. BOSTON: COCKAYNE, 1930.
WITH THANKS TO ARLENE JILLSON
    COFFIN.

READING

North of Springfield and south of Woodstock, the village of Felchville, in the town of Reading, lies along Route 106. At the south end of Felchville is the Reading Community Church, at the time of the Civil War a Baptist church. On September 18, 1862, the men who were to become Company H, 16th Vermont, assembled in the basement meeting room. With Norwich University's Alonzo Jackman presiding, the men elected Joseph Sawyer, of Hartford, captain, and Reading's Elmer Keyes, first lieutenant. As part of the 2nd Vermont Brigade, the one-hundred-man company, including many Reading lads, would fight at Gettysburg.

In late November 1863, four months after Gettysburg, a war meeting here was addressed by the commander of another 2nd Brigade regiment, the 13th Vermont's Colonel Francis Voltaire Randall. Speaking to what the *Rutland Herald* called "a large and enthusiastic audience," the colonel was "very racy in his speech and vivid in his descriptions of the great events now transpiring." And the *Herald* said, "Lieutenant Clark, of the 16th Regiment, who is an excellent vocalist, was present and, with others, stirred the patriotism of those present with soul-stirring music." A month later, William Rounds, former regimental major of the 16th Vermont, spoke in the church to encourage enlistments.

Across the road is the Reading Public Library where plaques on each side of the front door bear the names of 117 Reading men who served. The plaques were dedicated May 30, 1902, Memorial Day, with lengthy ceremonies that began in the Baptist Church. A highlight was the reading of a poem composed for the occasion by Reverend Homer White, a Reading native, titled "Lines in Memory of the Soldiers of Reading." It concluded:

They were but boys, and some I knew;
With them had played in school-boy
   days;
And now to them, so brave and true,
I bring the tribute of my praise.

After several presentations, the ceremonies moved to the library. There a Reverend Roberts, of the South Reading Methodist Church, praised the GAR members present, saying, "There is a class of men in our midst today, that we ought to venerate, and teach our children to hold in highest esteem; remembering them for what they have done—the survivors of the great Union Army, who saved this nation."

Just north of the library at the corner of Tyson Road is the tall shingled Reading town hall. In 1863, Merrill's Hotel opened on this site, and the *Vermont Journal* reported on an event held there on February 25, 1864, sponsored by the Ladies Benevolent Soldiers' Aid Society. Music, speaking, toasts, and a tableau were provided at 75 cents per person. And an extra 25 cents bought an oyster supper. Proceeds benefited "the Vermont soldiers."

Go north on Route 106 and, just before leaving Felchville, note the frame house on the left set well above the road and behind bushes and trees. From it, Levi Cross enlisted as a private in the 17th Vermont, when it was formed in 1864. In the regiment's first battle, the Wilderness, he was reported missing in action and was never seen again, surely killed or mortally wounded.

Continue north and in 0.75 mile approach the intersection of Route 44.

The last house on the right before the intersection, set back from Route 106, was once the Amsden family home. William Amsden enlisted at eighteen as a private in the 6th Vermont and served until he, too, disappeared at the Wilderness.

The 1815 redbrick tavern at the intersection was once owned by the Hawkins family. Floyd Hawkins was a sergeant in the 16th Vermont, and George Hawkins was a lieutenant in that regiment. Both fought at Gettysburg and returned safely.

Continue north on 106 just under 2 miles and turn left on Baileys Mill Road. In 0.3 mile is a neat frame house on the left, on a stone foundation. Lieutenant Elmer Keyes lived here, the adopted son of Washington and Eliza Keyes. He wrote to his wife, Lettie, here, after commanding his company at Gettysburg: "I am sitting on the battle field now . . . We have suffered for want of food on the long march and the fight . . . We have lived on excitement for two days certain for I didn't eat more than two or three hard tacks all the time. We won a great victory and are now following the enemy. I counted 115 dead rebels today on a piece of ground four rods square . . . We are burying the Rebs now and shall leave as soon as we get done. Our Reg't won the admirations of all for its gallantry."

Just over 0.5 mile past the Keyes house, turn right at a Y and soon come to Baileys Mills, which made cloth for the Union armies, including gray uniforms for the 1st Vermont Regiment.

Return to Route 106 and Felchville, and at the town hall, turn right, west, on Tyson Road. In just over 3 miles in South

Reading is the stone church where Reverend Roberts, speaker at the tablet dedication, was pastor. The *Bellows Falls Times* reported on July 16, 1865, that spiritualists gathered at the church to commemorate the anniversary of the spiritualist and abolitionist Achsa Sprague's first public lecture. The headline on the brief story was "I Still Live," Sprague's epitaph on her stone in Plymouth.

SOURCES

Davis, Gilbert A. *Centennial Celebration Together with an Historical Sketch of Reading, Windsor County, Vermont and Its Inhabitants from the First Settlement of the Town to 1874.* Bellows Falls, VT: Steam Press of A. N. Swain, 1874.

———. *History of Reading, Windsor County, Vermont.* 2 vols. Windsor, VT: s.n., 1903.

King, Hazel Hobbs. *Vernon Farms and Buck Family History, 1635–1985.* Reading, VT: s.n., 1985.

Reading town records.

Rutland Herald, 1863. Vermont State Library.

With thanks to Laura Briggs and Hazel Hobbs King.

··

ROCHESTER

Rochester's 23-foot Civil War memorial, topped by an eagle, stands in the Rochester park, along the Main Street, Route 100. Rochester was the second Vermont town to erect a Civil War memorial. The town history states that 196 men were credited to the town, 153 of them Rochester residents. Of them, 40 died and their names are on the monument, made of Barre granite and dedicated in 1868. The history further states that a "full twenty-five percent of all that gallant band who went forth in the full vigor of manhood, in the flush of health, and buoyant in spirit, have passed from the earth. Their names are chiseled in enduring granite on the beautiful monument erected, in grateful remembrance of their names and heroic deeds, by the town of Rochester."

Across Route 100 from the northeast corner of the park, the modern Federated Church stands on a knoll. During the Civil War, the Rochester town hall occupied this site, where voters met and approved bounties totaling $29,500. In front of that hall in the evenings, people gathered to learn the latest war news, the scene sometimes lit by torches. The local history said, "A daily paper was subscribed for to be read publicly at the town hall, whither the people repaired in crowds, coming from distant parts of the town nightly, and, while the intelligence was being read, the almost breathless attention of all present testified to the intensity of interest."

At the park's southeast corner is a rambling frame house with a wraparound porch, once home of Mrs. Chester Pierce, a stalwart of the Rochester Soldiers' Aid Society. She noted in a report printed in the July 1864 *Rutland Herald* that "early in the war the ladies manufactured and furnished to each soldier who went from here a nice, elaborate, and convenient soldier's pocket companion, well furnished with materials for mending, writing, etc." She also said the society had sent "$186 to the Sanitary commission, $23 to the

Christian Commission, and $20 to the Sanitary Fair at Washington."

Three houses east of the Pierce home, Charles Martin lived after the war. One of fifty Rochester men in the 4th Vermont's Company E, he was wounded at the Wilderness. The large house at the northeast corner of the park was Dr. Daniel Huntington's home. The Rochester history said: "Drs. Huntington and [Ira] Belknap of this town attended nearly all the sick and wounded who were allowed to come home on furlough, and furnished medical assistance free of charge until they were able to return to duty in the field; and their generous aid was not confined to volunteers from this town but extended to the suffering soldiers in adjoining towns."

From the Huntington house, go east on Bethel Mountain Road, quickly bear left on Brook Street, and in 0.25 mile, the frame house on the right, with upstairs porch, was the home of Corporal William Henry, 4th Vermont, who served three years, though wounded at Charles Town.

Proceed 2 miles and bear left at the Y onto Middle Hollow Road. In the first house on the right Edgar and Edwin McWain lived. Corporal Edgar McWain served three years in the 4th Vermont. Lieutenant Edwin McWain, 11th Vermont, was captured at Weldon Railroad but survived Confederate imprisonment.

At the next Y, go right on North View Road; in 0.4 mile, go left on North Hollow Road, and the first house on the right was the Chaffee home. Sergeant Henry Chaffee served four years in the 4th Vermont, until discharged after being wounded at Cedar Creek. In 1.5 miles, go right on Town Line Road. From the second house, with a long porch, on the left below the road, Henry Augustus Eaton and his brother Eugene enlisted. Henry attended Middlebury College, then moved to Kansas and became involved in antislavery activity there. Back in Vermont, he raised Company A, 16th Vermont, at Bethel, and led it (see Bethel). Among its members was his brother Eugene, a sergeant. Both were wounded at Gettyburg.

After recovering, Henry was back in Bethel to recruit a company for the 17th Vermont. At Poplar Grove Church, near Petersburg on September 30, 1864, the 17th was on the firing line when suddenly attacked from the right. The initial fusillade mortally wounded both the regimental commander and Major Eaton. The Rochester GAR post was named for Eaton.

Go down North Hollow Road, passing granite quarries, to Route 100 and turn left, south. In 0.5 mile, note the large farmhouse on the right, then look across the road to a small old house among trees. Alfred and Lafayette Richardson went to war from here. Alfred, a private in the 11th Vermont, served two years and came home sick, living less than a year. Lafayette, a sergeant in the 4th Vermont, survived a wound at the Wilderness.

Continue south on Route 100 through Rochester, and go right on Route 73. In the first farm on the right lived Joseph Huntington, a private in the 4th Vermont wounded at the Wilderness. Continue 1.5 miles on Route 73, and where it turns sharp left, go straight onto Bingo Road. Ransom Towle, 4th Vermont sergeant who later won a lieutenant's commission, lived in the house on the left at the corner. Wounded at Savage's Station in 1862, he came home and recovered. Towle reenlisted and was wounded and captured at Weldon Railroad. He escaped, rejoined the 4th, and was killed at Winchester.

Return to Route 73, turn right, west, and soon go right on West Hill Road. In 0.5 mile on the right is a big farmhouse, built in the 1880s, on the site of an older house destroyed by fire. Albert Kinsman left wife Sarah and ten children here to become a sergeant in the 4th Vermont. He survived a wound at the Wilderness.

Just past the Kinsman house is the West Hill Cemetery. Its retaining wall was completed by Kinsman just before he went to war. In the West Hill Cemetery lie several veterans, including Amos Crossman, a private in the 2nd Vermont, killed at Cedar Creek.

Return to Route 73, and on reaching Route 100 go south 1 mile and turn right on Liberty Hill Road. In just under 1 mile, turn right on Campbell Hill Road and soon, near the road's end, is a large house above the road. When the war began John Wood Campbell raised a liberty pole, with large flag, here. It could be seen for miles along the White River Valley. Campbell made several trips to the war zone with food and supplies, made by local women, for the Vermont troops.

SOURCES

CLARKE, ALBERT. ADDRESS DELIVERED ON THE COMMON, AUGUST 15, 1901. VERMONT HISTORICAL SOCIETY.

DAVIS, EARL N., AND MARY O. DAVIS, EDS. ROCHESTER REMEMBERS: 1881–1981. RANDOLPH, VT: HERALD PRINTERY, 1981. COURTESY OF THE ROCHESTER HISTORICAL SOCIETY.

ROCHESTER TOWN RECORDS.

RUTLAND HERALD, 1864. VERMONT STATE LIBRARY.

WILLIAMS, WENDALL WELLS. ROCHESTER, VERMONT ITS HISTORY 1780–1775. ROCHESTER, VT: TOWN OF ROCHESTER, 1975.

WITH THANKS TO MARCUS BLAIR.

ROYALTON

From the intersection of Routes 14 and 110, cross the White River to South Royalton, Royalton's largest village. The 1849 South Royalton House, facing the green's south side, offered a free meal, and room if necessary, to soldiers coming from and going to war. Soldiers took the train at the South Royalton station, once located where the 1886 station now stands. War traffic was never more heavy than during Grant's 1864 Overland Campaign. Many years after the war, a local man, Leslie Sherlock, recalled:

"My father, about 12 years old, with his dad sometimes used to drive down on an afternoon to see the 2:30 northbound train pull in. From four to 10 wounded soldiers might get off, all bandaged, sometimes minus arms or legs. Elisha Beedle was escorted off the train and to the hotel with two railroad men, with the top part of his head shot off . . . Father asked if he could see the wound. 'Oh my gosh, Lish,' [he said], for he could see the pulse beating in his brain. Mr. Beedle was so angry about the war he said he was going to get fixed up and go back. He did, as a Union sniper, and came home alive."

In 1866, Philip Sheridan, on the way to Montpelier, stopped briefly here, and the *Burlington Daily Times* said, "The people, though the rain poured in torrents, were out in force—Gen. Sheridan showed himself upon the platform of the rear car, and shook hands with all."

The Royalton Civil War monument on the green honors the 185 soldiers who served from the town. A close inspection of the granite soldier will show that, like Private Beedle, a part of his head has been knocked away. Dedicated September 19, 1919, and the work of the local Women's Relief Corps, Nettie Waldo recited a poem composed for the occasion that concluded:

> They must not be forgotten—let this monument so fair
> Stand as a fit memorial for those who lived to dare
> To shield their country's honor to protect our flag and home,
> They must not be forgotten through all the years to come.

A GAR post, named after Chelsea's Orville Bixby (see Chelsea), who operated a furniture business in South Royalton at the time of the war, met on the second floor of the building at the west end of the long block facing the green. On the green is a Civil War–era Parrott rifle, procured by the GAR, a type used on naval vessels, though this one never saw action.

Royalton village and its small common are 1 mile north along Route 14. The big yellow federal house across the road housed, for a brief time, Salmon P. Chase, who in 1860 competed unsuccessfully for the Republican presidential nomination against Lincoln. Chase, an abolitionist, served Lincoln as treasury secretary. He wrote in his autobiography:

"Towards Spring it was determined that I should go to Royalton in Vermont [from his home in Cornish, New Hampshire], where my former instructor Mr. Sprague was preceptor of the academy. It must have been early 1824, perhaps in February or March, that I went to Royalton, and was received in the family of Mr. Denison . . . The doctor occupied a very respectable and comfortable mansion . . . with a garden on the north side beyond which stood the Congregational Church. In front of the house was the road—the main village street, across which, situate in an open space in a sort of public square, stood the Academy."

The academy building where Chase studied for a year was destroyed by fire. But its successor, built in 1840 and now the Royalton Town House, survives. The academy operated on the second floor of the town house, while the lower floor was Royalton's town hall. Royalton voters here on August 27, 1862, approved the payment of $50 bounties to enlisting soldiers. A year later, bounties of $300 were voted.

On April 1, 1863, the women of Royalton staged, at the town house, a "tableau and dialogues," raising money for the soldiers. The program opened with a band concert, then a group of local actors staged scenes portraying the 1780 Indian raid on Royalton.

The record book of the Soldiers' Aid Society of Royalton, preserved at the town house, contains its constitution, adopted on February 9, 1863, at a meeting on the second floor. It begins: "Whereas, We, Citizens and Ladies of Royalton, having been at various times engaged in efforts to relieve the sick and wounded soldiers of the Government and wishing still more effectively to forward this work and assist, as far as may be in our power, in CRUSHING THE REBELLION, and deeming a permanent organization a necessary means we do hereby form ourselves into a Society, which shall be called The Soldiers Aid Society of Royalton, Vermont. God Save the Republic."

The society met often in the town house, and in local homes, making items for the soldiers, particularly those recovering at the Brattleboro Hospital. They also provided small pocket-sized Bibles for local men going to war.

In 1861, the academy hired as principal George Sylvester Morris, a Dartmouth grad. The summer of 1862, Morris enlisted in the 16th Vermont, with two of his former students. One was a regimental orderly who had permission to keep his tent light on late into the night. The academy men formed a Shakespeare club that met in the tent at night to read plays, favoring *Hamlet*.

SOURCES
Dunklee, Ivah. *Burning of Royalton, Vermont*. Boston: G. H. Ellis, 1906.
Lovejoy, Evelyn M. Wood. *History of Royalton, Vermont: With Family Genealogies, 1769–1911*. 2 vols. Royalton, VT: Town of Royalton and Royalton Women's Club, 1911.

WITH THANKS TO JOHN DUMVILLE AND MIRIAM HERWIG.

SHARON

The Sharon Congregational Church is just off exit 2 of Interstate 89. The writing is fading on the old church records, but it's possible to determine that in 1845 its members "deem it our duty" to adopt an "expression of opinion" declaring slavery to be a sin. After the Civil War, one of the church's pastors was Pliny Fisk, brother of Private Wilbur Fisk, Vermont's most important Civil War soldier letter writer, born in Sharon.

The brick building beside the church, now the Sharon Historical Society, was once the town hall. Meeting there, Sharon voters approved bounty payments that totaled $16,070 by war's end. Just below the town hall fronting Route 14 is a large frame house with a long porch, home of the Gibson family, owners of a mill on the White River. Gardner Gibson joined the 17th Vermont not long after he and his wife, Clara, lost their only child, Willie, to sickness at age three. Lieutenant Gibson died on June 15 of a wound received a week earlier at Cold Harbor, probably from a sharpshooter's bullet.

Go north on Route 14, and the red-brick house on the right, at the brow of the hill, was the home of Daniel Parkhurst, a shoemaker and Sharon town clerk for forty years. He fought at Gettysburg with the 16th Vermont. Just down the hill, turn right on Fay Brook Road, and in 1.5 miles, a pond and large farmhouse are above the road, on the left. From here, Luther Fay, a private in the 16th Vermont, fought at Gettysburg, came home and promptly reenlisted in the 9th Vermont, serving until the war's end. He returned ill in 1865 and was sickly until his death seven years later.

Return to Sharon village and take River Road across the White River. In 0.5 mile, take Howe Hill Road, and in 0.75 mile, bear right on Moore Road. In 1.3 mile, come to a Y with a farmhouse on the right and a barn with cupola just ahead. Set behind the barn is the old School District Nine one-room schoolhouse, which Wilbur Fisk attended.

Born June 7, 1839, on a farm 0.5 mile beyond the school, Fisk walked to it along the road to the left of the little building. The Fisk family left Sharon in 1852 to work in the Lowell, Massachusetts, mills, then bought a farm in Tunbridge, from which Fisk enlisted as a private in the 2nd Vermont. Serving four years, he was war correspondent for the antislavery Montpelier newspaper the *Vermont Freeman*. A gifted writer, Fisk described crossing the Gettysburg battlefield soon after the battle:

"The rebel dead and ours lay thickly together, their thirst for blood forever quenched. Their bodies were swollen, black, and hideously unnatural. Their eyes glared from their sockets, their tongues protruded from their mouths, and in almost every case, clots of blood and mangled flesh showed how they had died, and rendered a ghastly sight beyond description. My God, could it be possible that such were lively and active like other people so shortly previous, with friends, parents, brothers and sisters to lament their loss?"

When finally arriving back home in 1865, Fisk wrote: "We have seen home so often like a fairy vision in our imaginings and dreams, and so often have wondered whether, in the good Providence of God, we should be permitted to return and find it as we left it, that now the ideal is realized it almost seems as if we were dreaming still . . . If I was asked 'how it seemed' to be a free citizen once more, I should say it seemed as if I had been through a long dark tunnel, and had just got into daylight once more."

Visiting the tiny school where he received most of his formal education one wonders, who was the teacher?

Return to Howe Hill Road and turn right, uphill to Fales Farm Road, and look up it to the farm on the hill. Emma Fales during 1864, in her twenty-second year, kept a diary of a busy life in which she seldom mentioned the war. Emma was teaching school in Hewittville (The school survives.), 3 miles distant at the far end of Howe Hill Road, boarding with local people. She was extremely fond of her sister Josephine, who often accompanied Emma, sometimes with Hiram, Emma's fiancée, on walks to the nearby Howe Hill Cemetery. Typical entries:

Monday, May 9: "I board to Mr. Vail's this week. How beautiful the world looks this spring now it is being dressed in its dress of green it seems as though I never saw it so lovely." (The Vail house is 2 miles beyond on the Howe Hill road, just across the Pomfret line, on the left at the end of a long drive.)

Monday June 13: "How pleasant our little school room looked today. At noon we made a wreath of leaves and laid round the table which was covered with a white cloth and five bouquets were placed upon it. This with the pleasant faces around was a pleasing sight."

Emma sometimes mentioned war:

Sunday July 3: "To day heard Hiram is drafted. I hope it is not so." (Hiram did not serve.)

Wednesday Nov. 9: "News came today that Lincoln was reelected president. May it prove to be a blessing to the nation."

Wednesday November 30: "Party up to Mr. Spaulding made on account of soldiers Spaulding, Barken and Oscar being at home."

On December 18 Emma made mention of visiting a neighbor suffering with diphtheria. At that time, Emma was taking care of her ill sister.

On December 21: "It commenced snowing about noon . . . we are going to have a great quantity of it this winter I guess."

On December 22: "It very hard for the doctor to get through left his team to Mr. Stewart."

That is the diary's last entry as Emma became sick and died on December 30, age twenty-one. Her sister Josephine later married Emma's intended, Hiram.

Turn back toward Sharon on Howe Hill Road 0.2 mile to a slight turnoff on the left. Up over the steep bank is Howe Hill Cemetery, still the quiet country graveyard Emma loved to visit. Hiram's stone is beside his wife Josephine's. Emma's stone is beside her sister's.

Return to Sharon, and go north 5 miles on Route 14. Turn right on Dairy Hill Road, and in 0.75 mile, the Dairy Hill School, now a home, is on the left. Gordon Tuttle, who grew up in Sharon, recalled in 2008 that on Memorial Day 1932 a Civil War veteran, Joseph Metcalf, spoke at the school. Tuttle said that Metcalf "told stories of battlefields and rivers running red with blood." He also recited the poem "Flanders Field." The veteran, Tuttle said, then led the students "up the hill to put flowers on the soldiers' graves."

Opposite the schoolhouse, turn right on the entry road to the Joseph Smith birthplace. The cemetery where the students put flowers on graves is just up the road on the right.

Continue uphill to the Joseph Smith memorial, located on the farm where the founder of the Church of Latter Day Saints was born. In 1833, Smith and his followers were expelled from Jackson County, Missouri, very much due to their opposition to slavery. Smith said at the time, "It is not right that any man should be in bondage to another." Smith believed that the federal government should purchase slaves and set them free.

SOURCES

ERICKSON, A. KEITH. "MEMORY OF JOSEPH SMITH IN VERMONT." MASTER'S THESIS, BRIGHAM YOUNG UNIVERSITY, 2002.

HILL, DONNA. *JOSEPH SMITH: THE FIRST MORMON*. GARDEN CITY, NJ: DOUBLEDAY AND CO., 1977.

MOORE, VIVIAN. *THOUGHTS OF E. B. CHAMBERLAIN*. SHARON, VT: SHARON HISTORICAL SOCIETY, 1997.

WITH THANKS TO VIVIAN MOORE AND GORDON TUTTLE.

SPRINGFIELD

Approaching Springfield from the north on Route 106, Monument Park is on the left. The town Civil War memorial here, a granite block topped by a golden eagle, once stood in the town square. Inscribed "to our Union soldiers" and erected by the local chapter of the Women's Relief Corps in 1901, it honors some 250 Springfield men who served. To the rear of the park, a small marker by an aging maple notes that it was planted by the "daughters of Union veterans of the Civil War" in memory of "our fathers."

Continue along Route 106 into downtown Springfield, an old mill town at the falls of the Black River. On entering the square, the 1834 brick house, on the left, once housed the home and saddle shop of George Washburn, a Stephen Douglas supporter in the 1860 presidential election. Springfield Civil War hero Wheelock Veazey noted that, when word came of Fort Sumter's fall, "all businesses in the town were flying flags, not Washburn."

Continue through the square on Route 106, now Main Street, and the Springfield town office building on the left was the Civil War–era town hall. On April 22, 1861, it was packed for a war meeting in response to Lincoln's first call for troops. Here the Springfield Company of militia was formed, soon to become A Company, 3rd Vermont. Veazey, company commander, spoke at the meeting and later noted in his diary, "This is probably the most important day of my life." It wasn't. At Gettysburg, Veazey commanded the 16th Vermont in the flank attack on Pickett's Charge. Then he ordered his regiment to about-face and launch another successful flank attack on another Confederate attack.

Another speaker at the April 22 meeting was George Washburn who denied he was a traitor, said the prospect of war saddened him, then pledged financial support for the local company. Springfield voters convened here many times during the war, eventually approving bounties of $500. In 1862, they voted to give each man enlisting in the 16th Vermont $100.

Return to the square, turn steeply up Summer Hill, and at the top, on the left, is Springfield Common. Veazey drilled his local company here before it went to Brattleboro to join the 3rd. And the local company that became Company E of the 16th surely drilled here. Across the road is Summer Hill Cemetery, with many Civil War graves.

Return to the square and cross it to Park Street, pass over the Black River Bridge, and the 1836 building ahead and to the right, made of both wood and brick, was the John C. Holmes Cotton Mill, which made socks for the Union armies.

Return to the square and turn left, noting the three-story wooden office building on the left. Springfield's veterans formed a GAR post in 1867, one of the state's earliest, and it met on the third floor. The post was named for 9th Vermont Major Charles Jarvis, of nearby Weathersfield, killed December 1, 1863, in North Carolina. A Springfield Women's Relief Corps chapter, also named for Jarvis, met here.

SOURCES
HUBBARD, HORACE C., AND JUSTUS DARTT.

HISTORY OF SPRINGFIELD, VERMONT.
BOSTON: GEORGE WALKER & COMPANY,
1895.
WITH THANKS TO JOHN SWANSON.

STOCKBRIDGE

Along Route 107, just east of Stockbridge Central School, Ranney Road goes uphill to Mount Pleasant Cemetery. Don Reddick, local writer, said of the cemetery in 2009, "The steep slope is strewn as thick with Union dead as was the ground before Fredericksburg. Here interred, under lichen-encrusted, leaning, and occasionally broken headstones, are more than fifty veterans of the Grand Army of the Republic. Tiny Stockbridge, today with a population of just more than 600, had sent over 120 men to the Civil War."

North of Pittsfield along Route 100, Route 107 branches east. At the intersection is the Stockbridge town office. Across Route 100 are three buildings. Soon after the Civil War the middle one became the home of Edwina Paine. In August 1862, husband Oscar Paine joined the 16th Vermont as a private, leaving her at home with a young son. Paine survived Gettysburg, but soon joined the 5th Vermont and was killed at Weldon Railroad in June 1864. His wife bought the little house soon after the war, living there until she died in 1902, never remarrying. She left her home to the town, and it became a school.

From the Routes 100 and 107 intersection, go 0.75 mile north on 100 to where it crosses the White River. From the first house on the right past the bridge, Amasa Adams enlisted as a 4th Vermont private in August 1862. He served until the war ended, though wounded at the Wilderness.

Just past the Adams house, go straight through a four corners, and the first building on the right, an old tavern, was once owned by Job Strong. Job's son, David Strong, married a local lady, Margaret Fay. On October 16, 1832, their son, George Crockett Strong, was born here in Stockbridge. David Strong died when George was a boy. The son spent the first few years of his life in Stockbridge, and this tavern was a place familiar to him. Soon after his father's death, George went to live with an uncle in Massachusetts. But he was back in Vermont in 1853 entering Norwich University, though soon leaving for West Point. When the Civil War began, he served on General Irwin McDowell's staff. By the summer of 1863, Strong was a brigadier general, commanding a brigade that included Colonel Robert Gould Shaw's 54th Massachusetts Regiment. On Morris Island in Charleston Harbor in mid-July, Strong permitted Shaw's black regiment to lead the assault on formidable Fort Wagner. Strong joined the attack and was wounded, as the 54th took heavy casualties and Colonel Shaw was killed. The battle was the first in which black troops were heavily engaged, and the regiment's bravery erased any doubt that black troops would fight as well as white soldiers.

The wounded Shaw was taken to New York City, where he died on July 31, at thirty-one. The August 1, 1863, *Rutland Herald* said: "Brig. General Strong, who was severely wounded in the recent assault upon Fort Wagner, died in New York

Thursday morning. He was born in Stockbridge, this State, and it is only a few months since we saw him there on a visit to his mother."

Pass the tavern on Stockbridge Common Road and quickly come to Stockbridge Common. The meetinghouse here held Civil War–era town meetings. Stockbridge approved its first bounties in 1862, $100 each. Late in the war, some payments reached $900. In Maplewood Cemetery beside the common lie several Stockbridge soldiers. A cenotaph honors Private Oscar Paine.

From the common, return as you came to the crossroads, and go left, east, on Blackmer Boulevard. In 2.5 miles, go left on Route 107, and in 1.5 miles, crest a steep hill and note the small house on the left. From here, Lyman Smith enlisted as a 4th Vermont private in August 1861 and died of illness a year later.

Proceed into Gaysville village, a place devastated by the White River in the 1927 flood. Go left on Depot Road, and stop at the post office. The Strong family at one time owned a store just across the road, and it may have been in that building that George Strong was born. This small island somehow remained after the flood.

Cross the White River Bridge, go left at the Y and uphill to the house on the right, where the road turns sharp right. It is believed that Charles and Joel Waller lived here, both privates in Company C, 6th Vermont. Charles enlisted in October 1861 and died of sickness in May 1862. Joel served a year and came safely home.

Return downhill, and on reaching the Y, by the bridge, go straight uphill and quickly Kelly Road turns left. In the house on the knoll. Dr. Charles Smith lived after the war. He fought with the 14rh Vermont at Gettysburg.

Recross the White River to Route 107 and go left. Quickly on the right, two houses before the Congregational Church, is the home of James Thurber, who enlisted at eighteen in the 16th Vermont and fought at Gettysburg.

SOURCES
REDDICK, DON. *BUILDING A BRIDGE: STOCKBRIDGE, VERMONT*. GAYSVILLE, VT: STOCKBRIDGE-GAYSVILLE HISTORICAL SOCIETY, 2009.
RUTLAND HERALD, 1863–1864. VERMONT STATE LIBRARY.
STOCKBRIDGE TOWN RECORDS.
WITH THANKS TO BARBARA GREEN AND BARBARA VELTURO.

WEATHERS-FIELD

From Interstate 91 at exit 8, go west on Route 13, and in 1 mile, take Weathersfield Center Road. In 2.5 miles, the 1837 Weathersfield Meeting House is on the left, at the geographic center of town. The redbrick Weathersfield building faces the town Civil War monument and a grove of maple trees planted to honor Weathersfield's Civil War soldiers. During the war, town meetings took place in the meetinghouse basement. Several war meetings here encouraged enlistments.

A Weathersfield history said of the war years: "the town meetings were concerned largely with financing military bounties but the normal operation of Town government had to continue. The Town's operating budget was pared to essentials and the highway and school districts suffered from neglect. The cost of the Overseer of the Poor increased as the families of some soldiers found themselves in financial trouble due to the absence of their breadwinners. The financial strain of the Town nearly reached the breaking point. The prices of farm commodities, lumber, and manufactured goods were high but there was a shortage of manpower to produce them. Roads and bridges suffered from poor maintenance to a point where travel on the highways became a dangerous venture. As farms were abandoned and livestock reduced to the numbers that could be cared for, the tax burden increased at a time when the tax base decreased. The tax rate, which had remained at about twenty cents on the dollar of the grand list for many years, increased to thirty cents in 1864, plus an added forty cents to pay for the bounties and bonds. Due to the size of the town's debt, Weathersfield taxpayers would continue to pay nearly double their normal taxes for many years to come." In 1867, the town's long-term debt, due to the war, had been reduced by $4,000 but still stood at a daunting $17,801. Yet the town was determined to honor its soldiers, and at town meeting that year, voters appropriated $1,000 for a marble obelisk. Weathersfield people believed that by sending 136 men to war, they had achieved the highest percentage of men of any town in the North.

The monument was dedicated July 4, 1867, and the *Vermont Journal* said: "One oration was delivered by Colonel Wheelock Veazey of Rutland who commanded

the 16th Vermont Volunteers. The oration was filled with chaste and patriotic sentiments and afforded evidence that Col. Veazey is well qualified to fill important places in civil life."

In January 1863, the Weathersfield Center Soldiers' Aid Society was formed "for the purpose of furnishing hospital supplies for sick and wounded Vermont soldiers." Among many events it held was a festive gathering here on New Year's eve 1864 that raised $118.

Return north to Route 131 and go right. Pass under Interstate 91 and turn south on Route 5. In 4 miles, entering Weathersfield Bow, on the left is the red-brick Jarvis House, with historic marker. William Jarvis, once U.S. consul to Lisbon, brought large numbers of Merino sheep to Vermont. They thrived, and as more and more land was cleared for grazing, the state became more than 75 percent cleared. Thus, the very open Vermont landscape of the Civil War era came about.

After Jarvis died in 1859, his lawyer son Charles came home to manage family affairs here. At forty-one, he recruited a company from Weathersfield and surrounding towns, which became the 9th Vermont's Company D. When his men were issued poor food and clothing, Captain Jarvis used his own funds. His own pay went to charity because, he said, "Money earned in the cause of war should be used in the cause of the Prince of Peace." Jarvis and the 9th were soon stationed at Newport Barracks, North Carolina, and on December 1, 1863, he led a patrol into enemy territory. In a brief skirmish,

Jarvis was shot from his horse with bullet wounds in the abdomen and hand. He died an agonizing, lingering death.

The Weathersfield Bow Church, across from the Jarvis home, was packed for his lengthy funeral service, which included eulogies by officers and men of the 9th. At war's end, a mass funeral took place here for all the Weathersfield men who had died in the war.

The Bow Church, like the Center Church, had a Soldiers' Aid Society.

From Weathersfield Bow, go south 0.75 mile on Route 5 to where it turns right by a farm. Just beyond is a frame house from which Charles and Eben Haskell enlisted. Eben, a private in the 16th Vermont, came home safely from Gettysburg, Charles, a 9th Vermont lieutenant, served the war's last two years.

Return north through the Bow to Route 131, turn left, and again go under the interstate. In 0.75 mile, on the right, is a farmhouse with a small barn across the way. John Wright, in the 16th Vermont, at age twenty-three, was hit in the heel by shrapnel during the barrage that preceded Pickett's Charge. He returned home here but was never well, dying in 1895.

Continue west on Route 131, eventually going right on Lottery Lane. The large, old farmhouse, 0.3 mile on the left, was the home of Joseph Spafford, a 16th Vermont lieutenant, who fought at Gettysburg. His letters are preserved at the Vermont Historical Society and contain several nostalgic references to the village of Amsden. Return to Route 131, continue west, and soon pass through his beloved Amsden.

SOURCE

BUTTERFIELD, ERNEST L. *A RECORD OF THE INHABITANTS OF WEATHERSFIELD, 1760–1813.* WEATHERSFIELD, VT: PRIVATELY PRINTED, 1940.

HUNTER, EDITH YOUNG. *A HISTORY OF WEATHERSFIELD, VERMONT, FOR YOUNG PEOPLE.* WEATHERSFIELD, VT: HUNTER PRESS, 1989.

HURD, JOHN L. *WEATHERSFIELD CENTURY ONE.* MONTPELIER, VT: VERMONT HISTORICAL SOCIETY, 1905.

WITH THANKS TO EDITH HUNTER.

WESTON

Weston's Civil War monument, on the maple-shaded village green along Route 100, is surrounded by buildings that would have been familiar to the men who went to war in the 1860s. Listed on the monument are the names of seventeen men who died. At the top is that of George E. Meads, a private in the 1st U.S. Sharpshooters, who died of disease. His father gave the monument, which was dedicated on August 23, 1909. The Weston veterans, most of them members of the Sheridan GAR post, gathered for the dedication ceremony in the village school they used for a meeting hall, which still stands on the green's south side. The dedication included speeches, a picnic, and then a dinner at the Odd Fellows Hall. Also present were members of the local Women's Relief Corps chapter, founded November 10, 1883, the first organized in Vermont. The post also met at the school.

Go south along Route 100, and quickly come to the old village store on the left. Years after the war, a local woman remembered, "Jay Wilkinson lived down the street where the Country Store is now. He was a Civil War veteran and every day he would stomp up the street with his long cane, marching in military fashion, leading his cow. At night he'd march back." Wilkinson was a private in the 9th Vermont.

Just south of the store is the old Odd Fellows Hall, its fading symbol still visible, where the Civil War veterans gathered the night of the monument dedication for dinner.

Continue south and, on the right, the Old Parish Church towers above the street. November 18, 1861, a war meeting was held here, and the *Vermont Journal* reported that prayers were said and resolutions passed. One resolution stated that "the emancipation of the slaves of our land has become possible" and called on Congress "at its approaching session to abolish slavery as the only means of saving the Union."

Weston town meetings once took place in the church, and in July 1864, bounties of $500 were approved, though selectmen were authorized to pay as much as necessary beyond that to meet the town's quotas. According to the 1866 town report, Weston faced a war debt of $15,707.02.

From a population of about 700, Weston sent 91 men to war. A total of 13 Weston men served in the 16th Vermont's Company C, commanded by Captain Asa Foster. It is believed they gathered at the church before departing for Ludlow, where the company was formally organized. Foster was wounded in the attack on Pickett's Charge. Private Sylvanus Win-

ship, of Weston, had been killed at Gettysburg the previous day, apparently by artillery fire.

Weston's most treasured story from the Civil War deals with the Old Parish Church, which at the time was Methodist. According to a Weston history, titled *Waters of the Lonely Way*: "The Rev. Timothy Prescott Frost, the most noted Methodist preacher of his day, spent his boyhood in Weston . . . Not long before the outbreak of the war, a runaway slave was invited to the Frost home, and suffered a brief attack of sickness. The black man was put to bed in the choicest place on the premises, a parlor bedroom, where he was nursed by the Frosts until he recovered. Timothy, the young son, listened to several chapters in the life story of the slave. He (Timothy) went to the horse barn, knelt in an empty stall, and there before God registered the vow of a child that if American slavery should not be ended before he became a man, he would devote his life to the task." According to local people, the escaped slave grew up to become a preacher and once returned to preach in the Old Parish Church.

Across from the church, the first old house to its south, with a wide front porch, was the Hale family home. Almon Hale, 10th Vermont, was taken prisoner at Cold Harbor June 1, 1864, and died in Libby Prison. Private James Hale, also of the 10th, was killed at Cedar Creek.

Weston's Farrar-Mansur House and Old Mill Museum, on the green, has among its possessions a large thirty-one-star American flag made by Weston farm girl Nancy Burton. She raised the flag at her family's farm whenever word reached Weston of a Union victory. Drive north from the green 0.5 mile, and Burton Road turns right. The Burton farm was nearly 1 mile up it in now-wooded hills.

SOURCES

PANNES, ERNESTINE DUNAWAY. *WATERS OF THE LONELY WAY.* CANAAN, NH: PHOENIX PUBLISHING, 1979.

WESTON TOWN REPORT, 1866. FARRAR-MANSUR HOUSE AND OLD MILL MUSEUM.

WITH THANKS TO JEAN LINDMAN.

WEST WINDSOR

Mount Ascutney dominates West Windsor and many surrounding towns. In a tribute written to his friend, Major Richard Crandall (see Berlin), published in the July 1, 1864, *Vermont Watchman,* a man identified only as A. W. H. wrote: "Last August it was our lot to spend a night upon Mt. Ascutney. Our heads pillowed upon rock, our eyes fixed upon the sky, thick-set with glittering stars, we passed the hours, but not in sleep. He was telling me of his army life. Of that gallant charge made by Sedgwick's corps at Fredericksburg, he said, 'Oh, Mount Ascutney, to have lived a minute then, were worth a thousand years.' As he recounted the time when death had come very near to him, I could but feel that a kind Providence had abided him. Again, at the Wilderness, at Spotsylvania and at the North Anna he fought, but fell not." Crandall was killed at Cold Harbor on June 7, 1864.

West Windsor lies along Route 44, west of Windsor. Indeed, West Windsor was a part of Windsor until 1848. In the center of West Windsor's largest village, Brownsville, the Hartland Brownsville Road goes past the 1859 Brownsville Community Church. In July 1862, Pastor Lucius C. Dickinson left here to serve as chaplain of the 9th Vermont, until war's end.

In the frame house across the street Frederick Rice lived, one of forty-three men credited to West Windsor who served in Company A, 12th Vermont, and thus experienced the long march to Gettysburg. All survived, save for Privates Rosco Turner and James Mansfield, who both died of disease.

Continue on Hartland Brownsville Road to Brownsville Cemetery. This graveyard and others in the town contain an unusual number of 1864 and 1865 headstones. Mary Fenn, author of the Brownsville history published in 1977, knew her predecessor as town historian, Mildred Kittredge, who recalled many elderly West Windsor residents with memories stretching back close to the war. Fenn wrote: "Severe epidemics which took a heavy toll on the battlefields followed the boys home. In 1864, thirty-five West Windsor men, women and children died after being stricken with the dread diphtheria. The following year, there was a distressing number of new graves in the Sheddsville and Brownsville cemeteries. Twenty-three more townsfolk had succumbed to diphtheria and typhoid fever."

Past the cemetery the first redbrick house on the left was home to Wilbur Cady, who became a 4th Vermont private in September 1861 and died of sickness in the winter of 1863, near White Oak Church, Virginia.

In 0.5 mile, go right on Coon Club Road, and the Hammond family lived in the first house on the left. Four of farmer Daniel Hammond's sons were in the 12th Vermont—Stephen a sergeant, Jabez a corporal, and Ira and Ulysses privates. Jabez wrote home frequently, and his father answered. These quotes are from the father's letters to Jabez in November and early December 1862:

"My prayer is that you will have your health until the President shall unlock the doors, and Let you all out of prison . . . The black charger that chased the bear is in fair working order . . . the hogs doing well."

"Boys I have taken a good deal of comfort in reading your letters to myself and Neighbors . . . Hope you will be able to send us 4 or 5 a week . . . Ira your Black Horse looks first rate."

"The horses and cows are all in good comfortable quarters well watered and fed . . . the hens on their roosts with their roosters to protect and care for them. the guinea pigs are in the cellar the cats they go where they are amind to. Elwyn and Mark are in bed. Lovina is getting the potatoes for breakfast your mother is mending a shirt for Mark. Dan is using his old pen the same one he has had for three years the house is Warm as summer and I wish you were all here to enjoy the comforts that we enjoy. It gives me disagreeable feelings to think that thousands are standing and lying out of doors on this cold bleak night, with no shelter to protect them save the canopy of the stars."

All four Hammond lads returned safely home. Pass the Hammond house, and just up the hill, on the right, is the brick Hammond school, where the boys were pupils.

Return to the Hartland Brownsville Road, go right, and soon right again on Hammond Road. Follow it 1 mile, to a hilltop farm from which Seth Blanchard joined the 9th Vermont as a private in early January 1864. He died a month later, probably of disease.

Return to the Hartland Brownsville Road, return toward Brownsville, and in 0.3 mile, take Cemetery Road past the Sheddville Cemetery and turn left on Sheddsville Road. Note at the corner a marker for the first settlement of the town. The West Windsor town hall stood here during the Civil War. According to historian Fenn, "By December 16, 1863, West Windsor had voted a bounty of $500.00 to 'each volunteer who has enlisted or may enlist to fill our quota under the present call for troops.' There was also a vote authorizing selectmen to borrow money to pay bounties . . . At a special meeting on September 30, 1864, the Selectmen were authorized, not only to borrow money on town credit to pay the bounties, but in order to alleviate the situation, they were authorized to issue bonds, not to exceed $20,000, payable in ten years."

It was likely to the town hall here that two West Windsor men, Abel Prince, thirty-five, and Thomas Little, twenty-six, came in an attempt to enlist. But being black, they were denied. The two thus went to Boston and joined the "colored" 54th Massachusetts.

SOURCES

FENN, MARY. *PARISH AND TOWN: THE HISTORY OF WEST WINDSOR, VERMONT*. WOODSTOCK, VT: COUNTRYMAN PRESS, 1977.

HAMMOND FAMILY LETTERS. COURTESY OF SIDNEY HAMMOND, HARTLAND.

WEST WINDSOR TOWN RECORDS.

WITH THANKS TO MARY FENN.

....

WINDSOR

The following appeared in the *Rutland Herald* on July 7, 1863: "Windsor is one of the oldest towns in the State, having been settled as early as 1764. The location of the village so near the Connecticut River, with its broad meadows on the north, its venerable trees overarching, and sometimes darkening, the streets, its hilly surroundings with one respectable mountain to wit Ascutney, the quietude of its streets, the fort-like appearance of its wall-encircled State Prison, the busy clatter of the Rifle Factory, the dull, dusty snubbed look of the United States Court House with the Babel-like dissonance of echoes in its Court Room, the few tasty gardens and dwellings, the picturesque views, especially from in front of the Episcopal Parsonage, its grave yard with slabs almost ninety years old, the cordial courtesies of a portion of its citizens, the vicinity and cheer of the Levee at the Windsor House—all tend to leave in the memory of its recent visitors a cloud of pleasing fancies."

Entering Windsor from the north on Route 5, the Constitution House is on the right. In Elijah West's tavern, as it was then known, in early July, 1777, delegates from throughout the land that would become the state of Vermont met to adopt a constitution. As the convention's work proceeded, a British army under General John Burgoyne was moving south on Lake Champlain. On July 8, word reached Windsor that the key American positions at Fort Ticonderoga and Mount Independence had fallen. The alarmed delegates prepared to leave, but according to Ira Allen, a thunderstorm erupted out of the Connecticut Valley skies, preventing departures. So the delegates got back to work and approved the Vermont constitution, the first American constitution to outlaw slavery. Though it decreed only that males over twenty-one and females over eighteen were free of bondage, still it was a major step forward for human freedom in America.

From the Constitution House, continue south on Main Street into the village. The fifth house on the right past the Constitution House was the home of Judge William Evarts and was known locally as the White House because five presidents were guests here, including the wounded Civil War veteran Rutherford B. Hayes. Evarts, one of America's prominent lawyers of the Civil War era, successfully defended Abraham Lincoln's troubled successor in the White House, Andrew Johnson, in his impeachment trial. Evarts served Johnson as attorney general and was secretary of state in the Hayes administration.

Two houses beyond is the Stoughton home, now part of a retirement community. Attorney Edwin W. Stoughton was born in Springfield in 1818, and became a successful lawyer, specializing in patents. He served as ambassador to Russia in

1877. Stoughton was uncle to Brigadier General Edwin Stoughton, the ill-fated commander of the 2nd Vermont Brigade. After the general's capture by John Mosby, the uncle tried diligently, but unsuccessfully, using his political influence, to have his nephew reinstated as a commander in the Union armies. The young Stoughton sometimes visited his uncle's home, until his early death in 1866.

Contine south, and the brick-columned Windsor House, Windsor's prime hostelry during the Civil War era, is on the right. Across Main Street is a small park where the Constitution House stood in 1777. Turn right at the intersection on State Street, and soon on the left is the Windsor Public Library, a handsome Georgian Revival building designed by Henry Bacon, architect of the Lincoln Memorial.

Just past the library is the old state prison, built in 1809, now a retirement community. Much of the prison survives from 1977, when it closed. The cell blocks, where at the time of the Civil War inmates lived in solitary confinement, are now occupied by apartments. The *Rutland Herald* in 1863 said, "The State Prison contains seventy-nine convicts, about two-thirds of whom are French and Irish, and of this number six are females. The male convicts are occupied chiefly in the manufacture of scythes. Thirty dozen are made daily, the concern being run by Goodnow and Lamson, 53 Beekman Street, New York. The company furnishes all the machinery and some workmen and pays the State thirty-five cents per day for each man. The State has about a dozen as

police supplied with loaded muskets." The inmates made scythe handles, not blades.

Return to Main Street, turn right, and proceed to the American Precision Museum, on the right. Again, the *Rutland Herald* in January 1864: "The Rifle Factory, located on Mill Brook, containing a steam engine, with about 275 employees, having been employed for nearly two years on a contract to supply the United States with 50,000 rifles at $20 each, turning out now daily about 100 rifles . . . the stocks are made of black walnut, obtained chiefly from Pennsylvania, sometimes from Indiana."

Indeed, this three-story brick factory produced 50,000 rifles for the Union armies during the Civil War. Recent research has established that, operating out of this building, the firm of Lamson, Goodnow & Yale played a much larger role in supplying the Union forces. The North made more than 1.5 million rifle-muskets in about three years, along with tens of thousands of pistols and carbines. The majority were made using machinery designed or produced in Windsor. The firm Robbins, Kendall and Lawrence began manufacturing guns here in the 1840s, making rifles for British use in the Boer War. The building now houses a museum devoted to the machine tool industry. Included in the exhibits are Civil War weapons and the machines that made them at Windsor. In this plant were developed machines and processes that fundamentally changed manufacturing, helping to give birth to America's modern system of production.

Back north along Main Street stands

Old South Church where, in early July 1864, a funeral for Captain William Tracy was held. Tracy, of the 4th Vermont, was wounded at the Wilderness, then fatally at Weldon Railroad, six weeks later. A service with many Civil War veterans present took place here on May 30, 1883, when Windsor first observed Memorial Day. Soldier graves were decorated in the adjacent cemetery. Windsor sent 153 men to war and 22 perished.

SOURCES

Brown, Carrie. "Guns for Billie Yank: The Armory in Windsor Meets the Challenge of Civil War." *Vermont History,* Summer/Fall 2011.

Rutland Herald, 1863–1864. Vermont State Library.

With thanks to Judy Hayward, Ann Lawless, and Carrie Brown.

WOODSTOCK

Begin a Civil War visit to Woodstock at the Marsh-Billings-Rockefeller National Historical Park on Route 12, north of the village. The park offers a walking tour of Civil War Woodstock. Within the park is the brick mansion in which two important figures of the era lived. George Perkins Marsh was born here and during the war served as America's minister to Italy, working diligently to keep any European nations from entering the conflict on the Confederate side. During the war's deadliest year, 1864, Marsh published the book *Man and Nature,* the first major work documenting mankind's harmful effects on the planet. In 1869, Frederick Billings bought the Marsh

home, altered it to his Victorian tastes, and made it the centerpiece of a model farm, the Billings Farm. Here, Billings used advanced conservation practices, some certainly based on Marsh's writings. During the Civil War, Billings, who made a fortune as a lawyer in Gold Rush San Francisco, worked to make certain California remained in the Union. Early in the war, he visited England to procure arms for the Union cause, specifically for his friend Charles Freemont. Also, along with Frederick Law Olmstead, he was a founder of the Sanitary Commission, the Red Cross of the war.

Across Route 12 from the national park is the Billings Farm and Museum. The Windsor County fairgrounds once occupied the fields by the entrance. In the summer and fall of 1862, 250 recruits camped and drilled here, some of them sharpshooters in training. Others went to bolster the rosters of Vermont regiments. The men were housed in the fairgrounds buildings. The place was called Camp Dike.

Enter the village along Route 12, crossing Billings Bridge over the Ottauquechee River to Elm Street, lined with houses that predate the war. The yellow brick house on the right was the home of U.S. Senator Jacob Collamer, a Lincoln supporter, known in Washington as the Green Mountain Socrates. In 1860, Collamer was a member of the U.S. Senate committee that investigated John Brown's raid on Harper's Ferry. Collamer was seated in his garden, between the house and the Congregational Church, on a spring day in 1865, when his wife, Mary, told him of

Lincoln's assassination. His response: "What will become of the country?" Early in the war, Mary helped organize Woodstock women to work in support of the war effort. The *Vermont Standard* said in October 1861, "A large number of blankets and socks have been collected at the residence of Hon. Jacob Collamer. The success with which the ladies meet is highly gratifying."

Next door to the Collamer house, the Congregational Church was draped in black for a memorial service for Lincoln. It was a fitting site for that sad event, for in 1836 the congregation adopted a resolution stating that "we consider slavery . . . a violation of the law of God altogether and at variance with our Declaration of Independence and repugnant to the spirit of the Gospel." When the Woodstock Light Infantry company went to war in 1861 as Company B, 1st Vermont, the officers and men gathered in the church for a religious service. The Paul Revere bell, now in the south portico, rang in the belfry to celebrate Lee's surrender at Appomattox, then soon tolled for Abraham Lincoln. A funeral service was held here for Vermont's adjutant general Peter Washburn.

Continue on Elm Street and the Woodstock Historical Society, on the right, occupies the Dana House, which was the home of Charles and Charity Dana during the war. The Danas operated a store in the brick building next door. The Danas also collected items to be sent to the soldiers. Charity's brother, Charles Loomis, served in the west, an officer fighting under William Tecumseh Sherman. Charity received a letter from Charles here, just before the Battle of Shiloh. "At the last battle before Corinth" he wrote, "my stirrup was shot through with grape shot, making a relic which I am saving for Charlie."

In the house beside the Danas', Dana Whitney lived, a private in the 1st Vermont, the first Woodstock man to die in the war. He was shot near Newport News, Virginia, on June 22, 1861, his comrades said, by a Confederate "bushwhacker." Whitney and some fellow soldiers had left camp, apparently searching the countryside for some fresh local beef.

Gillingham's Store, a few doors down, was Hatch's Store in the 1860s, and Lieutenant Andrew Dyke, of Woodstock, operated a recruiting office on its second floor. The training ground at the fairgrounds bore his name.

The Woodstock village square looks much as it did in the 1860s. The Phoenix Block on the south side housed the offices of Vermont adjutant general Washburn, a Woodstock lawyer, who organized the Woodstock Light Infantry and made it the best militia company in the state. Washburn led it to war as part of the 1st Vermont, of which he was second in command. At Big Bethel, June 10, 1861, Lieutenant Colonel Washburn led half the 1st Vermont into combat. Returning home a hero, he was promptly elected state adjutant general. Washburn set up headquarters in rooms adjacent to his law office and for the rest of the war oversaw the administration of Vermont's war effort here. Assisted by clerks, he labored in offices on the upper two stories of the Phoenix

Block. Look to the pharmacy along Central Street and note the old door beside it, opening on a staircase leading to Washburn's offices.

Oral tradition identifies the large frame house at the corner of the square, once owned by abolitionist Titus Hutchinson, as an Underground Railroad stop. On the top floor of the building across the square, at the corner of Elm and Central streets, the local George Randall GAR Post met. Captain Randall, commander of Company G, 6th Vermont, in which many Woodstock men served, died at the Wilderness.

When the soldiers who trained at the fairgrounds left for war, they were given a send-off here in the square. A visitor to the town wrote, "My visit was on a beautiful autumn day . . . two companies of the stalwart sons of the Green Mountains formed in front of one of the village inns, and were bidding adieu to wives, mothers, sisters, relations, and friends . . . as the chorus sang, 'We are coming Father Abraham, three hundred thousand more,' which was sung from the balcony by the celebrated Barker family, echoed back from the mountains, the scene was deeply impressive." A restaurant is now in the stone building that was once the inn.

Walk east on Central Street to the triangular green known as Tribou Park. The monument, honoring the 289 men Woodstock sent to the war, was dedicated on Memorial Day 1909 with 1,500 people present. The *Vermont Standard* said, "The worthy old veterans were in exalted mood that day, and they gave three cheers and a tiger, which would have done credit to younger throats." Woodstock has two Civil War memorials, the other on South Street by the elementary school. That earlier memorial was not considered adequately impressive by the veterans.

Just east of Tribou Park is the Masonic Lodge, once the Christian church. The funeral of Private Leander Corbell, 6th Vermont, who died of sickness at Camp Griffin on January 5, 1862, was held here. Corbell's comrades contributed money so that his remains could be shipped home to his parents' house in the nearby village of Taftsville. Days later, the church's pastor, Moses Kidder, preached a sermon based on words from the book of John at a funeral for Private Asa Stowell. Stowell died of sickness on his way home from Florida, where he was serving in the 7th Vermont. From the brick house beside the church, George Mellish enlisted as a private in the 6th Vermont and served three years. His mother, Mary, wrote him faithfully and told him on March 5, 1865, "George, the Rebs are in a dreadful state. I do believe swift justice is their portion and the curse of slavery is the cause of all this just because his skin is darker, but the day star is arising for the black man." She also informed her son, "We have a new street where Mr. Ford lives it is Lincoln Street." Walk back toward the village square and soon pass Lincoln Street, going uphill on the left, named for the soon-to-be-martyred president.

Pass back through the square to the boat-shaped park. Local men who served under Captain Ora Paul in Company B, 12th Vermont, were welcomed home here with a celebration on July 15, 1863, less than two weeks after Gettysburg. Though the 12th did not fight at Gettysburg, Paul said, "What they were ordered to do, they have done. Where they were ordered to go, they have gone."

The lower floor of the Windsor County Courthouse was once the Woodstock town hall. Abolitionists Henry Ward Beecher and Wendell Phillips spoke here. A wide variety of wartime events here included war meetings to encourage enlistments and women's gatherings to make items for the soldiers. After the war, Thomas Seaver, who as colonel of the 3rd Vermont won a Medal of Honor for bravery in Upton's attack at Spotsylvania, presided here as a judge.

Two buildings behind the courthouse, on Court Street, is the Woodstock Light Infantry armory, now a dormitory for Woodstock Inn employees. For many nights after the raid on St. Albans in October 1864, militiamen patrolled the village.

From the park, take South Street, and soon, by the elementary school, is Wood-stock's first Civil War monument. Past the school the Vail recreational field is on the left. Look across the street to a brick house facing the near end of the field. The Mero family lived here. Four of Hezekiah and Harriett Mero's sons served in the 54th Massachusetts "colored" regiment. Andrew, Charles, Edward, and Sylvester may all have been in the Battle of Olustee, in Florida. In the house beside it, and just south of the Mero home, Austin Hazard was living soon after the war. Hazard, and his brother James, were also in the 54th; James recalled serving cannon during the bombardment of Fort Wagner, in

Charleston Harbor. It was there that the regiment, led by Colonel Robert Gould Shaw, made its doomed attack in 1863, the first heavy combat seen by a black regiment. Woodstock had one of Vermont's largest black populations in the 1860, perhaps as many as sixty people. Several local black men went south with the local company of the 1st Vermont Regiment when the war began. Not allowed to soldier in a white unit, they were servants to officers.

Return to the park and on its north side, the redbrick house by the covered bridge was once the Mower family home. A nephew, Joseph Mower, who grew up on a hill farm outside the village, often visited here. Mower rose to the rank of major general and commanded an army corps. A favorite of William Sherman, he led troops in the Vicksburg and Red River campaigns and in the March to the Sea.

Pass through the covered bridge, and the redbrick house at the southwest corner of River Street and Mountain Avenue was Peter Washburn's home. The adjutant general, who somewhat resembled Lincoln, in 1862 met with the president in Washington and heard him compliment the Vermont troops for their performance at the Battle of Lee's Mill. Washburn was elected governor in 1869, but died two months later. A private funeral service was held here on a stormy February day in 1870 that included the singing by a quartet of "Nearer My God to Thee." From here, Washburn's body was escorted to the Congregational Church by pall bearers, among them George Stannard, William Ripley, William Wells, and Frederick Billings.

Go east along River Street to the River Street Cemetery, where many Civil War–era figures are buried. Among the old stones are markers for seven members of the 54th Massachusetts Regiment. Also buried here are Senator Collamer, Private Whitney, and Frederick Billings. A Medal of Honor marker is by Thomas Seaver's stone. Washburn's grave, near the cemetery's center, is marked by a broken column beneath a massive spruce tree.

Go west on River Street, cross Mountain Avenue, and soon you are just above the Ottauquechee River. Looking across the river in this area, as a lad, Hiram Powers said that he saw a vision of a naked woman. Powers grew up to become a world-famous sculptor. His most famous work, *The Greek Slave*, depicted a naked woman in chains, which he said was inspired by his childhood vision. Though created as a protest against Turkey's domination of Greece, it also became a symbol of the antislavery movement. When the Powers family came to Woodstock in the 1700s, they had brought with them a young slave, Christopher Molbone. He lived in Woodstock until he enlisted to fight in the War of 1812.

Continue on River Street to the town recreation center, once a woolen mill owned by Solomon Woodward, which, for a time, made cloth for the War Department. Women workers employed here, seeking shorter hours, went on strike soon after the war ended.

Return to the park and go south on Route 106, to the village of South Woodstock. The village inn, where the road turns sharp left, is said to have once given refuge to fugitive slaves. Soon past the inn, Academy Circle is on the left. Turn here, and before you is Green Mountain Academy, also known as Perkins Academy, now a museum, where many future soldiers were educated. Among them was Thomas Seaver, whose army saddle is displayed here.

SOURCES

DANA, HENRY SWANN. *HISTORY OF WOODSTOCK, VERMONT*. CAMBRIDGE, MA: HOUGHTON MIFFLIN, 1889.

FULLER, JAMES. *MEN OF COLOR TO ARM*. LINCOLN: UNIVERSITY OF NEBRASKA PRESS, 2001.

VERMONT STANDARD, 1861–1865. WOODSTOCK HISTORICAL SOCIETY.

WOODSTOCK CIVIL WAR HISTORY FILES. MARSH-BILLINGS-ROCKEFELLER NATIONAL HISTORICAL PARK, WOODSTOCK.

WUNDER, RICHARD. *HIRAM POWERS: VERMONT SCULPTOR, 1805–1873*. NEWARK: UNIVERSITY OF DELAWARE PRESS, 1991.

WITH THANKS TO KATHY WENDLING, GORDON TUTTLE, JANET HOUGHTON, AND GEORGE GOODROW.

Acknowledgments

My thanks first go to the Woodstock Foundation, David Donath and Marian Koetsier and staff, for its sponsorship, untiring support, and generosity. I am deeply grateful for the generosity, and friendship, of Holly Hitchcock and the Donchian Foundation. For the help of dear friends Mary Stewart Baird, Peter Galbraith, Donald Miner, and Kenley Squire, I am most thankful. And to the Vermont Humanities Council, and Peter Gilbert, I say "thank you" for its generosity and assistance. And warm appreciation goes to the Vermont legislature, especially the Senate Institutions Committee, which has supported me on many occasions in efforts related to the Civil War history of Vermont. Also, a most important, and generous, Vermont foundation, which wishes to remain anonymous, is also profoundly thanked.

At the top of the list of sources is *Lest We Forget,* the Vermont Civil War Web site. Always this site was available as a starting point for a town, or as a source of information anywhere information seemed to be lacking. *Lest We Forget* was consulted for every town. To Tom Ledoux and all those who have labored long and hard to make it what it is, I am so grateful. And I thank the Vermont Historical Society and its knowledgeable and ever-helpful librarians, Paul Carnahan and Marjorie Strong. Always friendly Jeffrey Marshall, and his staff at the University of Vermont's Special Collections at the Bailey/Howe Library, was of service, as was the dedicated staff of the Vermont State Library, ever accommo-dating and expert. That library's holdings of Vermont newspapers were invaluable. Local libraries throughout the state were of great service, as were local historical societies. Town records were key sources, searched with the help of town officials throughout the state. The fine state history *Freedom and Unity* by Michael Sherman, Gene Sessions, and P. Jeffrey Potash was a faithful source of information. Key to my research was Abby Maria Hemenway's remarkable *Vermont Historical Gazetteer,* consulted for every town. G. G. Benedict's two volume *Vermont in the Civil War* was ever in use. Theodore Peck's *Revised Roster of Vermont in the Civil War,* published in 1892, is always essential to any Vermont Civil War research. Ralph Orson Sturtevant and Carmi Lathrop Marsh's wonderful *Pictorial and Biographical History of the 13th Regiment Vermont Volunteers, War of 1861–1865* was consulted each time reference is made to Vermont's most intriguing Civil War story, the nine-month history of the 13th Vermont that ended in glory at Gettysburg. For brevity's sake, *Lest We Forget,* Hemenway's *Gazetteer, Freedom and Unity,* Peck's *Roster,* and *History of the 13th Vermont* are listed only here as sources.

Also of great value was Ray Zerblis's *Friends of Freedom: The Vermont Underground Railroad Survey Report,* as was his counsel; most of my decisions on including fugitive slave sites came from Ray. *Men of Color to Arms!,* by James Fuller, was also key to dealing with sites that have an association with the history of blacks in

Vermont. James McPherson's wonderful *Battle Cry of Freedom* was frequently referenced. Also, my three books—*Full Duty: Vermonters in the Civil War; Nine Months to Gettysburg: Stannard's Vermonters and the Repulse of Pickett's Charge;* and *The Battered Stars: Vermont and One State's Civil War Ordeal During Grant's Overland Campaign*—were ever at hand. U.S. census data was also often referred to, as were *The War of the Rebellion Official Records.*

The H. F. Walling 1858 maps of Vermont were vital to my research, as were the 1869 F. W. Beers county atlases. Also referenced were James Whitelaw's Vermont maps, 1796–1824. My late dear friend Rebecca Munson was often consulted on genealogical matters. Jeanne Malachowski was my ever-helpful computer expert.

The names of many of the hundreds of people who helped me are at the ends of town descriptions. But it is an incomplete list. To those who might have been left out, know that I still deeply appreciate your assistance. The complete list would be too long to include, and impossible to compile. More than once, a local person's momentary guidance about a certain turn, or a little-known road, was key to a discovery. Many sites were found with the help of people who remembered information told to them by Vermonters no longer with us. Many people directed me to sites based on their recalled family histories. With these undocumented sites, I had to make a decision on authenticity. Many were rejected. All decisions were based on a personal knowledge base compiled during forty years of studying Vermont's Civil War history, and many years' experience as a newspaper reporter. I even appreciate the concern some Fairfield people showed me on a warm summer evening, in midproject. Having arrived early in that town to deliver a Civil War talk, I decided to search local cemeteries for Civil War gravestones. Seeing a woman by the Catholic Church, I inquired as to where those cemeteries might be. She asked which one I was looking for, and I said that it really didn't matter. Well, the Catholic cemetery was a mile down the road, she said, pointing in its direction. I thanked her and drove off. For some ten minutes I had been walking among the stones when a car screeched to a halt at the cemetery gate. A man came rushing toward me, waving his hands. What had I done, I wondered? Reaching me, the man, almost breathless, asked:

"Are you all right?"

"Yes, I'm looking for Civil War gravestones."

"Oh, thank God. The woman you spoke with thought you were going to kill yourself."

"Why on earth?"

"Because you were looking for a cemetery and didn't care which one."

Index

Names Index

419, 425, 436, 447, 476, 486
Douglass, Frederick, 18, 31, 38, 415
Douglass, Sarah Fisk, 319
Douglass, Stephen Arnold, 319
Dow, Amos, 299
Downer, Henry, 61
Drew, John, 108
Drew, Samuel, 120
Drew, Thomas, 120
Drury, James, 435
Drury, Joseph, 409, 435
Drury, Mary, 435
Dudley, Charles, 83, 84
Duhigg, David, 116
Duhigg, Dennis, 117
Duncan, George, 173
Dunn, Albert, 98
Dunn, Charles C., 98
Dunn, George E., 98
Dunn, Henry, 150, 151
Dunn, William, 98
Dunshee, Noble, 35
Dunton, Walter C., 328
Dunton, Warren, 80
Dutton, Benjamin, 467
Dutton, Ira, 249
Dutton, Laverne Breed, 344–45
Dutton, Louis, 39
Dutton, Solomon, 166
Dutton, T. T., 305
Dwinell, Harold, 376
Dwinell, Melvin, 376
Dyer, C. H., 71
Dyer, John, 439
Dyke, Andrew, 497

Early, Jubal, 26–27, 135
Eastman, Rev., 355
Eastman, Seth, 110, 388
Eastman, Willard, 42
Eaton, David, 44
Eaton, Eugene, 480
Eaton, Henry A., 50, 457, 480
Eaton, Solon, 67
Eckel, August, 96
Eddy, Daniel, 81
Eddy, David, 425
Eddy, Francis, 323
Eddy, Jackson, 222
Eddy, Mary Baker, 404

Eddy, Mercy, 360
Eddy, Oscar, 360
Edgerton, Benjamin, 400
Edson, O'Meara, 464
Edwards, Elisha, 411
Edwards, Jennie Morehouse, 165–66
Eggleston, Charles, 106
Eggleston, Harley, 106
Eggleston, Henry, 106
Eggleston, Joseph, 106
Eggleston, Myron, 106
Eggleston, William, 106
Eldredge, James, 374–75
Eldredge, Joseph, 400
Elkins, Orion, 310
Ellinwood, Eli, 237
Elliott, David, 306
Ellis, Asahel, 420
Ellis, Henry, 396–97
Ellis, John, 157
Ellis, Zenas, 329
Ellsworth, Charles, 193
Ellsworth, Horace, 161
Ellsworth, Josephus, 161
Elrick, Chauncey, 205
Emerson, George, 238
Emerson, Ralph Waldo, 353
Emery, George, 238
Emery, Mary Belle, 238
Estabrook, George, 418
Evans, Edward, 373, 374
Evans, Ira Hobart, 373, 374
Evans, Rev. J., 189
Evarts, William, 494
Everett, Edward, 48
Everleth, Henry, 420
Everts, Linus, 36

Fairbanks, Alfred, 458
Fairbanks, Charles, 457–58
Fairbanks, Erastus, 19, 127, 128–30, 353, 369, 388–89, 471
Fairbanks, Horace, 128–29
Fairbrother, Edson, 289
Fairchild, Benjamin, 162
Fairman, Edward, 440
Fairman, Mary, 440
Fales, Emma, 484–85
Farmham, James, 276
Farmham, Sena, 276
Farnham, Mary, 256

Farnham, Roswell, 75, 256, 262–63
Farnham, Willard, 312
Farnsworth, Orrin, 117
Farr, Eugene, 61
Farragut, David, 347
Farrand, Thaddeus, 238
Farrar, Elmira, 384
Farrar, Israel, 133
Farrar, Waldo, 384
Farrington, George, 237
Farrington, Henry, 237
Farwell, John, 265
Fassett, Gardner, 197
Fassett, Henry, 197
Faubus, Orval, 436
Fay, Arnold, 163
Fay, Luther, 484
Fenn, Mary, 492, 493
Fenton, James, 36
Ferriter, Luke, 416
Field, Martin, 428
Fifield, Orange, 266
Fillebrown, Henry, 462
Fisher, Harriet, 312–13
Fisher, Thomas, 303
Fisk, Edson, 227
Fisk, Edward, 392
Fisk, Ira, 227
Fisk, John, 227
Fisk, Julius, 227
Fisk, Pliny, 483–84
Fisk, Samuel, 227
Fisk, Wilbur, 29, 75, 146, 275, 387, 483–84
Flagg, Betsy, 163
Flagg, Elmer, 467
Flagg, George, 258
Flanders, George, 126
Flanders, Hannah, 266–67
Flanders, Janet, 271
Flanders, Royal, 266–67
Fletcher, Henry, 340
Fletcher, Ryland, 461, 462
Flint, Charles, 43
Flint, Henry, 303
Flint, James, 318
Flint, William, 44–45
Flood, Wooster, 200
Fogg, George, 307–8, 467
Follett, James, 439
Follett, Samuel, 439

Hall, Leonard, 92
Hall, Packer, 87
Halloway, George, 210
Hamilton, Eugene, 62
Hamilton, Joel, 330
Hamilton, William, 327
Hamlin, Hannibal, 165
Hammond, Daniel, 493
Hammond, Gilman, 263–64
Hammond, Ira, 493
Hammond, Jabez, 493
Hammond, Nathan, 264
Hancock, Cresmon, 407
Hancock, Winfield Scott, 148, 157, 163–64, 384
Hand, Harvey, 121
Hand, John, 121
Hanks, Nancy, 46
Hapgood, Charles, 85
Hapgood, Marshall, 85
Hard, Cyrus, 83
Harding, F. D., 305
Harlow, Henry, 268
Harmon, Argalus, 165
Harmon, William, 165
Harrington, Ephriam, 115
Harrington, George, 448
Harrington, Theophilus, 18, 324–25
Harris, Lucius, 132
Harris, Luther, 116–17, 132
Harrison, Benjamin, 57, 76, 78, 82, 98, 435
Hart, Gilbert, 359
Hartshorn, Elden, 187
Hartshorn, Margarette C., 375
Harvey, Eugene, 42
Harvey, George, 137
Harvey, Hiram, 179
Harvey, Walter, 104
Hasbrook, Jane, 385
Hasbrook, Josiah, 385
Haselton, D. W., 462
Haskell, Charles, 490
Haskell, Eben, 490
Haskell, Franklin, 275–76
Haskell, Franklin Aretas, 275–76
Hastings, Albert, 333–34
Hatch, Benjamin, 159
Hatch, Byron, 159
Hatch, Isaac, 59
Hatch, Lura, 159

Hatch, Truman, 159
Hathaway, William, 392
Hawkins, Floyd, 478
Hawkins, George, 478
Hawkins, Jewett, 360
Hawkins, Joseph, 360
Hawkins, Rush Christopher, 476
Hawkins, Zouaves, 476
Hawley, Rev., 217
Hayes, Rutherford B., 340, 494
Haynes, Aaron, 338
Haynes, Delet, 338
Hazard, Austin, 499
Hazen, Clarence, 228
Hazen, Jesse, 228
Hazen, Spellman, 228
Hazleton, Walter, 270
Heater, Solomon, 200
Heath, A. K., 265
Heath, Albert, 274
Heath, Amada, 274
Heath, Henry, 274
Heath, Nathan, 274
Heath, Viola, 404–5
Heath, William, 265
Hemenway, Abby Maria, 244; Belvidere, 233; Brighton, 177–78; East Haven, 181; Eden, 238; Fairfax, 198; Glover, 297; grave of, 470; Hubbardton, 330; Isle La Motte, 227; Jay, 304; Maidstone, 187; Marshfield, 382; Montgomery, 212; Randolph, 268; Salem, 296; Stowe, 247; Troy, 310; Vershire, 278; Victory, 189; West Fairlee, 280; Westfield, 311; Westmore, 313; Wolcott, 252
Hemenway, Amasa, 234
Henderson, George Washington, 160, 234–35, 294
Hennessey, Thomas, 345
Henry, Hugh, 464, 465
Henry, Warren M., 432
Henry, William (4th VT Regiment), 480
Henry, William (5th VT Regiment), 246
Henry, William Wirt, 148, 149, 402–3, 437

Herrick, Henry, 107, 127–131, 375
Herwig, Miriam, 268
Herwig, Wesley, 268
Hibbard, George, 89
Hibbard, Henry, 57
Hickok, James Butler "Wild Bill," 221, 228
Hickok, Polly Butler, 228
Hickok, William Alonzo, 228
Higbee, William Wallace, 38, 149–50
Higgins, William, 63
Higley, Erastus, 320
Hill, George Washington, 186
Hill, Seth, 244–45
Hilliard, Gilbert, 81
Hills, Zerah, 384
Hinds, Abel, Jr., 238
Hinds, Napoleon Bonaparte, 238
Hinkson, Calvin, 406–7
Hinkson, Edward, 406
Hinkson, Harriet, 406
Hinkson, Lyman, 406–7
Hinsdale, Mitchell, 166–67
Hitchcock, Elisha Pike, 346, 347
Hitchcock, Henry, 311
Hitchcock, Joseph, 192
Hitchcock, Robert, 63, 64
Hoadley, Edwin, 337, 338–39
Hoadley, William, 338
Hoag, Byron, 221, 224
Hoag, Huldah Case, 17–18, 52
Hoag, James Byron, 221, 224
Hoag, Joseph, 17–18, 52–53
Hodgdon, Carlos, 125
Hodgdon, Elizabeth Berry, 125
Hodgdon, Samuel, 125
Hodge, William, 274
Hoffman, Henry, 119
Hogaboom, Horatio, 195–96
Hogaboom, James, 210
Hogaboom, Orrin, 195–96
Hogaboom, W. R., 195–96
Holbrook, Calvin, 226
Holbrook, Frederick, 20, 21, 183–84, 389, 411–13, 416, 462
Holbrook, George, 226
Holbrook, Manlius, 185
Holbrook, Nathaniel, 226
Holbrook, Pardon, 439

Watts, Isaac, 122
Webb, Alexander, 78, 165
Webb, William Seward, 165
Webster, Daniel, 433, 436–37
Webster, Elergy, 287
Webster, Ellery, 454
Webster, Ephraim, 266
Webster, Joseph, 288
Weed, Anson, 167
Weitzel, Godfrey, 336
Welch, Elijah, 95–96
Welch, Hosea, II, 110
Welch, Rodman, 204
Welles, Gideon, 394, 471
Wellman, Marshall, 417
Wells, Charles W., 105–6
Wells, Frederic, 123
Wells, William, 23, 75, 77, 141, 146, 148, 149, 153, 283, 390, 403–4, 405
West, Elijah, 494
West, Ezekiel, 333
West, Francis, 119
West, Francis, Jr., 119
West, Levi, 119
Westcott, Hiram, 166–67
Westman, Orson, 236
Wetherell, Ephraim, 250
Wetherell, William, 250
Weymouth, William, 85
Wheat, Luke, 455
Wheeler, Chester, 310
Wheeler, Henry Orson, 230
Wheeler, John, 147
Wheeler, Marcus, 122
Wheeler, Orville G., 167–68, 223, 230
Wheelock, Edwin, 236, 237
Whipple, Thaddeus, 236
Whitcomb, Addison, 266
Whitcomb, Albert, 154
Whitcomb, Asa, 266
Whitcomb, Edward, 159
White, Henry, 460
White, Homer, 477–78
White, Marvin, 191–92, 196
White, Pliny, 293, 296
White, Robert, 102
Whitehill, Calvin, 124–25
Whitehill, Matthew, 307
Whitehill, Moses, 307
Whitehill, Peden, 125

Whitford, Orville, 33
Whitney, Almon, 243
Whitney, Alonzo, 260
Whitney, Dana, 497
Whitney, Orlando, 276
Whitney, Orloff, 193, 204, 205–6
Whitney, Phineas, 276
Whittier, Edwin, 46–47
Whittier, James, 46–47
Whittier, John Greenleaf, 245, 318
Whittier, Washington, 47
Wilbur, O. A., 376
Wilcox, J. J., 198
Wilcoxson, Mary, 206
Wilder, Henry, 166
Wilder, Orcas, 399
Wiley, Harvey, 462
Wilkins, M. N., 247–48
Wilkinson, Jay, 491
Willard, Frances, 107–8
Willard, Henry Augustus, 441–42
Willard, James, 431
Willard, Joseph, 441–42
Willard, Mary, 107–8
Willey, Henry, 233–34
Willey, John, 461
Williams, Cyrus, 352
Williams, Harrison, 357
Williams, James, 150, 357
Williams, Joel, 306
Williams, John, 327
Williams, Merritt, 191–92
Williams, Milo, 150
Willoughby, Guy, 150–51
Wilmarth, Honora, 116, 117
Wilmarth, Marshall, 116, 117
Wilson, James, 369–70, 401–2
Wilson, John, 417
Wilson, Rosalin, 401
Winch, Asa, 383
Winchester, Benjamin, 33
Winchester, Mary, 33
Winchester, Warren, 33
Winship, Sylvanus, 491
Winslow, Gordon, 171
Witherell, Philander, 250
Wolcott, Edgar, 152–53
Wood, George, 77
Wood, John, 438

Wood, Leman, 330
Wood, Thomas Waterman, 388
Woodbridge, Frederick E., 67
Woodbury, Eri, 296
Woodbury, Urban, 19, 75, 134, 144, 148, 167, 239, 241, 245, 389
Woodman, Jonathan, 138
Woods, Grace Pember, 361
Woodward, Guy, 197
Woodward, John, 63, 141, 235, 236, 301
Woodward, Jonathan, 128, 162, 303
Woodward, Jonathan H., 167–68
Woodward, Jonathan W., 167–68
Woodward, Solomon, 500
Wool, John, 147
Wright, Augustus, 90
Wright, Charles, 113–14
Wright, Chester, 386
Wright, D. M., 272
Wright, David, 123
Wright, Eber, 213
Wright, Henry, 123
Wright, Horatio, 398, 471
Wright, James, 123
Wright, John, 490
Wright, Riley E., 292
Wright, Spafford, 159
Wrinkle, Thomas, 444
Wrisley, Jacob, 404
Wyman, David, 96
Wyman, Freeman, 436
Wyman, Laura, 410, 411

Yale, John, 171
Yale, William, 171
Yattaw, Christopher, 66–67
Young, Ami, 351
Young, Bennett, 27–28, 214–15, 216
Young, Brigham, 444
Young, Homer, 115
Young, Joshua, 58–59, 145
Young, Josiah, 146
Young, Lewis, 63
Youngs, David, 361